NEW YORK REVIEW BOOKS
CLASSICS

NOTEBOOKS

VICTOR SERGE (1890–1947) was born Victor Lvovich Kibalchich to Russian anti-czarist exiles, impoverished intellectuals living "by chance" in Brussels. A precocious anarchist firebrand, young Victor was sentenced to five years in a French penitentiary in 1912. Expelled to Spain in 1917, he participated in an anarcho-syndicalist uprising before leaving to join the Revolution in Russia. Detained for more than a year in a French concentration camp, Serge arrived in St. Petersburg early in 1919 and joined the Bolsheviks, serving in the press services of the Communist International. An outspoken critic of Stalin, Serge was expelled from the Party and briefly arrested in 1928. Henceforth an "unperson," he completed three novels (*Men in Prison*, *Birth of Our Power*, and *Conquered City*) and a history (*Year One of the Russian Revolution*), all published in Paris. Arrested again in Russia and deported to Central Asia in 1933, he was allowed to leave the USSR in 1936 after international protests by militants and prominent writers like André Gide and Romain Rolland. Using his insider's knowledge, Serge published a stream of impassioned, documented exposés of Stalin's Moscow show trials and machinations in Spain, which went largely unheeded. Stateless, penniless, hounded by Stalinist agents, Serge lived in precarious exile in Brussels, Paris, Vichy France, and Mexico City, where he died in 1947. His classic *Memoirs of a Revolutionary* and his great last novels, *Unforgiving Years* and *The Case of Comrade Tulayev* (both available as NYRB Classics), were written "for the desk drawer" and published posthumously.

MITCHELL ABIDOR is a historian and translator of French, Spanish, Italian, Portuguese, and Esperanto. Among the books he has edited and translated are an anthology of Victor Serge's anarchist writings, *Anarchists Never Surrender*; Jean Jaurès's *Socialist History of the French Revolution*; and *May Made Me: An Oral History of the 1968 Uprising in France*. He was born in Brooklyn, New York, where he still lives.

RICHARD GREEMAN has translated and written the introductions for five of Serge's novels (including *Unforgiving Years* and *Conquered City*, both available as NYRB Classics). A veteran socialist and co-founder of the Praxis Center and Victor Serge Library in Moscow (www.praxiscenter.ru), Greeman is the author of the website the *Invisible International* (bit.ly/invisible-international).

NOTEBOOKS

1936–1947

VICTOR SERGE

Edited by
CLAUDIO ALBERTANI *and* **CLAUDE RIOUX**

Translated from the French by
MITCHELL ABIDOR *and* **RICHARD GREEMAN**

NEW YORK REVIEW BOOKS

New York

THIS IS A NEW YORK REVIEW BOOK
PUBLISHED BY THE NEW YORK REVIEW OF BOOKS
435 Hudson Street, New York, NY 10014
www.nyrb.com

*Cet ouvrage a bénéficié du soutien des Programmes d'aide à la publication de
l'Institut Français.*
This work, published as part of a program of aid for publication, received
support from the Institut Français. It also received support from the Mission
Culturelle et Universitaire Française aux Etats-Unis, a department of the
French Embassy in the United States.

Library of Congress Cataloging-in-Publication Data
Names: Serge, Victor, 1890–1947, author. | Albertani, Claudio, writer of
  introduction. | Rens, Jean-Guy, 1946– writer of introduction. | Abidor,
  Mitchell, translator. | Greeman, Richard, translator.
Title: Notebooks : 1936–1947 / by Victor Serge ; introduction by Claudio
  Albertani and Jean-Guy Rens ; translated by Mitchell Abidor and Richard
  Greeman.
Description: New York : New York Review Books, [2019] | Series: New York
  Review Books classics.
Identifiers: LCCN 2018029769 (print) | LCCN 2018054439 (ebook) | ISBN
  9781681372716 (epub) | ISBN 9781681372709 (alk. paper)
Subjects: LCSH: Serge, Victor, 1890–1947—Travel—Mexico. | Serge, Victor,
  1890–1947—Notebooks, sketchbooks, etc.
Classification: LCC PQ2637.E49 (ebook) | LCC PQ2637.E49 A2 2019 (print) |
  DDC 813/.54—dc23
LC record available at https://lccn.loc.gov/2018029769

ISBN 978-1-68137-270-9
Available as an electronic book; ISBN 978-1-68137-271-6

Printed in the United States of America on acid-free paper.
10 9 8 7 6 5 4 3 2 1

CONTENTS

INTRODUCTION

Memoirs of a Revolutionary, generally considered to be Victor Serge's masterpiece, is a work of ambiguous literary character, existing on the borderline between history and individual testimony. As a record of their author's itinerary, the memoirs cannot be taken entirely at face value. Serge's *Notebooks* are more intimate in character. They introduce us to the cultural and aesthetic universe of his everyday life, while forming the first stratum of his whole body of work, literary and historical, the foundation of a writing that strives throughout to establish direct contact with reality. Here the authenticity of the man, with all his passions and obsessions, emerges with clarity and in complete contrast to the accusations of duplicity that have been leveled against him.[1] Serge was an anarchist, a Bolshevik, and, finally, a Left Oppositionist. He was close to Trotskyism but never, properly speaking, a Trotskyist: Safeguarding individual freedom within the revolution remained too important to him. He walked a political razor's edge with his eyes wide open. It came at the price of his well-being and, on several occasions, his freedom. Serge's work as a writer remains credible because it was never in the service of an ideology or any kind of preestablished solution.

The *Notebooks* are the laboratory in which Serge elaborated the universe of an "I" in permanent relation with the "we" that surrounds it, furnishing a glimpse of the tragic stage of revolutions continually betrayed and reborn. Central to them are the contradictions between

---

1. See Jean-Luc Sahagian, *Victor Serge: l'homme double* (Montreuil: Libertalia, 2011), and Sandro Saggioro, "Gli ultimi anni di Victor Serge: 1940–1947," *Quaderni Pietro Tresso*, no. 57 (June 2006).

the fragility of the subject and the demands of collective action. If Serge speaks constantly of himself, it is not to air his personal difficulties but rather to make clear his perspective as a narrator, his place on the global chessboard. On page after page, the *Notebooks* demonstrate a stubborn fidelity, a total allegiance, and a passionate attachment to the revolutionary project. This places Serge in the company of George Orwell; it makes him the complete opposite of Arthur Koestler. "I hate the role of victim," Serge often said. "A necessity that resembles complicity often binds a victim to his torturer, the man on the scaffold to his executioner," he wrote in his novel *Unforgiving Years.* Far from bemoaning his fate or denigrating his persecutors (and God knows he had them), he sought on an ongoing basis to deepen the knowledge required to enrich socialist culture. In the *Notebooks*, for example, we see how seriously Serge studies Mesoamerican cultures, Mexican geology, even psychoanalysis.

The *Notebooks* begin in Marseille in 1940, in the immediate aftermath of the Nazi occupation of France. Serge has been taken in hand by Varian Fry's Emergency Rescue Committee. His first plan was to emigrate to the United States, but his anarchist and Bolshevik past constituted a major hindrance, and in spite of having the support of John Dewey, Max Eastman, and Sidney Hook, he was denied a visa. At this point, the Mexican option emerged, Mexico being one of the few countries still granting asylum to political refugees. Julián Gorkin, the leader of the Spanish Partido Obrero de Unificación Marxista (POUM, or Workers' Party of Marxist Unification), was in exile in Mexico where he sought to handle the administrative formalities necessary to gain entry for Serge and his family. In the United States, Dwight and Nancy Macdonald were in touch with Frank Tannenbaum, a former union activist and an adviser to the Mexican president Lázaro Cárdenas.

The route between Marseille and Mexico proved long and full of obstacles, however. Serge and his son, Vlady, embarked on the *Capitaine Paul-Lemerle* from Marseille on March 25, 1941, while Serge's wife Laurette Séjourné, who had failed to obtain a visa, stayed in France with Jeannine, his daughter from a previous marriage. Serge and Vlady arrived in Martinique, where they were held for a time in a Pétainist concentration camp. Taken in by the painter and POUM militant

Eugenio Granell, they eventually left for the Dominican Republic, thanks to a visa obtained by the Macdonalds. In Ciudad Trujillo they lived freely, but lacking a visa they could not leave the Dominican Republic. Finally, after an aborted break for Haiti, they caught a plane to Cuba, only to find themselves imprisoned under suspicion of being Soviet agents. The situation was eventually straightened out, and on September 3, 1941, five and a half months after their departure from Marseille and fifteen months after their flight from the Nazis in Paris, Serge and Vlady disembarked in Mérida in the Yucatán.

In Mexico City, Serge was greeted by the French revolutionary socialist Marceau Pivert, Gorkin and his fellow POUM militant Enrique Gironella, and the Catalan publisher Bartomeu Costa-Amic, all in all a representative sample of the exile community in Mexico at that time. Costa-Amic had just published a Spanish translation of Serge's *Portrait de Staline*, with a preface by Gorkin, and he was preparing to publish *Hitler Contra Stalin*, the book on the invasion of the USSR that Serge had written during the interminable wait in Ciudad Trujillo.

What were Serge's feelings on arriving in Mexico? In the first place, profound gratitude. "During World War I," he declared to the Peruvian poet Juan Luis Velázquez, "Switzerland granted asylum to internationalists. In our time, when internationalism has spread throughout the world, it fell to a country like Mexico, located between the Atlantic and the Pacific, to give asylum to revolutionaries.... Historical events do not occur by chance."[2] Then, used as he was to war-impoverished Europe, he was surprised by the lightheartedness of life, by the luxury cars imported from the United States, by the cafés overflowing far into the night. In the countless ads for the latest refrigerator and the fashionable nightclubs, he discerned an aggressive modernity.

Serge, however, had pressing concerns: he needed to find lodging and a job; Laurette and Jeannine must be brought over; above all, he needed to write, to bear witness for the comrades who continued to struggle against totalitarianism. Notwithstanding the Macdonalds' help, the business of extracting Laurette and Jeannine from Europe

2. Juan Luis Velázquez, "Marxista libertario ¿Nueva teoría revolucionaria? Hablando con Victor Serge," *Hoy*, no. 243 (October 18, 1941).

ran into countless bureaucratic obstacles, and it was not until March 1942 that they reached Mexico. Meanwhile, Serge changed apartments multiple times, and he would never succeed in finding a regular job in Mexico City. Between 1941 and 1943 he published a series of articles on the war in the review *Así*—these are summarized in the *Notebooks*—but the intrigues of Mexican Stalinists resulted in his losing that source of revenue. He also placed some articles in *El Hijo Pródigo*, a literary review with which Octavio Paz was involved, and in the Cuban review *Bohemia* and the Chilean *Babel*, and he was paid for a handful of articles that appeared in *Partisan Review, The New Leader,* and *Politics* (founded in 1944 by Dwight Macdonald). He wrote on cheap onionskin and wore his typewriter ribbons to shreds, and of course had neither the means nor the time to frequent cafés, where the exiles gathered. He had to economize on everything, even stamps.

Utter destitution did not, however, impede Serge's political vitality, as he continued to reflect on contemporary events and the new world that was being born. His Mexican exile was marked by the blossoming of the group Socialism and Freedom, which sought to reconstruct an internationalist worker's movement that, in the tradition of POUM, would transcend the divisions among anarchists, socialists, and communists. Socialism and Freedom brought together such independent leftist figures as Pivert, Gorkin, Gironella, Gustav Regler, the writer Jean Malaquais, and Leo Valiani, and produced two publications of high theoretical quality, *Análisis* and *Mundo*,[3] before disappearing, undermined by those internal quarrels that bedevil political groups in exile, and not only those. Nonetheless, the critical analyses that emerged from this short-lived group explored and debated most of the major issues, starting with the relationship between revolution and democracy, that would convulse the European socialist movement for the next fifty years.

"My situation and my oeuvre are unique," Serge explained to Granell, "in that I am a French writer of Russian origin and nationality, sustained

3. See Claudio Albertani, "Le groupe Socialismo y Libertad. L'exil antiautoritaire d'Europe au Mexique et la lutte contre le stalinisme (1940–1950)," *Agone*, no. 43 (2010): 241–61.

by two profoundly different cultures and two contradictory historical experiences."[4] In this profession of faith the key word is "writer." Serge was indeed a writer above all, and he found his true outlet in the form of literature—witness the many introspective passages in the *Notebooks*, as well as the countless articles, short stories, poems, and essays, almost all unpublished, that he wrote after leaving Marseille, to which must of course be added *The Life and Death of Leon Trotsky* and the *Memoirs*. Over the same period, he also wrote two novels: *Les Dernier temps* (*Last Days*), which recounts the moral and political disaster of France in the summer of 1940, and *Les Années sans pardon* (*Unforgiving Years*), a meditative story of vanquished revolutionaries set against the backdrop of Stalinism and World War II. At the same time, Serge finished his novel *L'Affaire Toulaev* (*The Case of Comrade Tulayev*), which dramatizes the psychology of communist leaders in the context of the Moscow Trials and the Spanish Revolution.

A notably important character in the *Notebooks* is Mexico. Serge recounts trips to Guadalajara, Ajijic, Cuernavaca, Oaxaca, Acapulco, Amecameca, and Erongarícuaro, and describes his ascent of Popocatépetl. In one of his short stories, Serge has a character respond to the powerful earthquake that shook Mexico City on February 22, 1943: "For my part," he says, "I'm used to human cataclysms. Leave me the hell alone, you geological cataclysms who can't bring yourselves to explode once and for all, who are down below, pervasive, like yet another lie!"[5] Serge was so intrigued by the quake that he took a trip to its epicenter in Michoacán in order to see the newly born volcano Parícutin. Two nearby villages, Parícutin and San Juan Parangaricutiro, had been evacuated, and Parícutin itself had been wiped off the map. Of San Juan Parangaricutiro, which was buried in lava, only the church belfry was left.

Serge's love of the lakes of Michoacán comes through in the *Notebooks*, while three entries on pre-Hispanic cultures, never published, recount visits to archaeological sites. That said, it is the human scene that attracts him most of all, and he pays particular attention to the

4. Interview in *La Nacion* (August 1941).
5. Victor Serge, *Le Tropique et le Nord* (Paris: Maspero, 1972), 8.

elderly and children. Serge was a portrait painter with a keen gaze, and caustic miniatures are scattered throughout the *Notebooks*. At Michoacán he encounters Dr. Atl (Gerardo Murillo), the great painter of volcanoes turned anti-Semite and Nazi sympathizer, and compares him to a character out of the Italian Renaissance. Under the influence of Vlady, Serge takes an interest in Mexican artists. There are portraits of Leonora Carrington, of María Izquierdo, and a harsh one of David Alfaro Siqueiros.

Serge passed his final years in great intellectual solitude. "I often feel like I'm being suffocated in my magnificent desert,"[6] he writes to Dwight Macdonald, in one of many letters that document his isolation. Nonetheless, he had the company of a small group of friends united by the struggle for a libertarian socialism. In the front rank was the Spartacist militant and theoretician of the Left Opposition, Otto Rühle, and his wife, Alice, a psychoanalyst, both of whom died in 1943. Also close to Serge was Fritz Fränkel, an Austrian doctor and psychoanalyst, who had organized the medical service of the International Brigades in Spain; he died in 1944. Another psychoanalyst, Herbert Lenhof, completed the circle. Among the Mexicans, Serge's best friend was Ramón Denegri, the former ambassador to the Spanish Republic and a stern critic of Soviet socialism.

Though the Mexican backdrop and political context remain in sight throughout the *Notebooks*, the deterioration of his relationship with Laurette goes unmentioned. The question of why Serge chose to stay in Mexico after the liberation of Paris is also unaddressed.

The *Notebooks* are largely free of complaint or recrimination, though not entirely. Serge laments: "To write only for the desk drawer, past age fifty, facing an unknown future, not to mention the hypothesis that the tyrannies will last longer than I have left to live, what would be the result?" In these final years he also suffered from a cardiac condition that brought out the twenty-one-year age difference between husband and wife. Their rift widened until Laurette grew irremediably

6. Serge to Dwight Macdonald, March 10, 1945, AHLS-Victor Serge Papers.

distant. She took up the study of Mesoamerican archaeology. She took on work to supplement Serge's pitiful earnings. On February 27, 1945, she attempted suicide, spending forty hours in a coma. "She's now safe," Serge wrote to Macdonald, "but none of the problems, psychological or material, is resolved." Laurette recovered in the "tropical countryside," and yet the couple emerged more damaged than ever from the ordeal. A year later Serge wrote to Laurette, who was away on a dig in Monte Albán: "If we had had a single day to ourselves, no telephone, no overwork, no irritations, a single day of relaxation and leisure together I would feel infinitely better about you, and better period."

In August 1944, Paris had been liberated. Germany capitulated in May 1945. Mexico was gradually emptied of its exiles, who returned to Europe, while Serge stayed on. From friends who had gone back, he feverishly requested firsthand reports: "My wife and I are waiting impatiently for your first letter, your impressions of Paris." Or: "Has *Esprit* come out again? Do you see Mounier? If you do—which I hope—send him my profound friendship and tell him that I would like to resume contact." Yet in November 1945, Serge proposed emigrating to the United States. Why choose a country forbidden to anyone connected to communism and whose language he didn't speak? The attempt was fruitless, in any case. In August 1946, Serge's friend Jef Rens, who was close to the Belgian minister of foreign affairs, Paul-Henri Spaak, raised the possibility of a Belgian visa. "I was very much touched by your letter and your suggestion—Belgium, which is a welcome one," Serge answered. "But before moving from here in one way or another I have to climb the slope, which is infinitely difficult. One doesn't suffer a blockade of over five years with impunity at this altitude and . . . in old age."

This is not the kind of attitude and dilatory response that we expect of Serge. His literary and intellectual raisons d'être were in Europe. Why then, a year after seeking to emigrate to the United States, did Serge refuse to return to Belgium, the antechamber to Paris, where his publishers, friends, and comrades were to be found? Four days prior to his death, in a letter to André Malraux, who as Charles de Gaulle's close ally was well placed to obtain a visa, Serge merely asked for advice on the publication of his books. Serge was getting ready to go back, as

Laurette's letters attest, but she was unwilling to under any circumstances. Attached to her archaeological studies, she appears to have kept him in Mexico. His interest in the United States may perhaps be explained by the close ties between US and Mexican archaeologists in the 1940s.

On Monday morning, November 17, 1947, Serge went to Vlady's house to give him a poem he had just written. Not finding his son at home, he walked to the Central Post Office. He then hailed a cab to go home. Somewhere along the way, he died.

About Serge's death, there has been much speculation. For a long time there were rumors that he had been assassinated: Vlady himself raised the possibility. Nevertheless, the correspondence and the *Notebooks* make it plain Serge was suffering from heart problems, and that his doctors had advised his departure from Mexico. "The damn cardiac viscera can put up with 2,000 meters less than they can the worst events," he'd written Rens.

Vlady would recount:

I found him on an operating table in the police station. A yellowish lamp illuminated the sinister room. The first thing I noticed were his shoes: they had holes in them. This shocked me, greatly, for he was careful about his dress, although his clothes were always of the cheapest. The following day, I was unable to draw his face, for they had put a plaster death-mask over it. I limited myself to drawing his hands, which were beautiful. A few days later, I received his poem: "Hands."[7]

In conclusion, let us listen to the testimony of Julián Gorkin, Serge's close friend:

A strip of cloth held his mouth closed, that mouth that all the tyrannies of the century had been unable to gag. One would have said he was a vagabond taken in by a charity. And in fact, had he not been an eternal vagabond of life and the idea? His face

7. Victor Serge, *A Blaze in a Desert*, translated and edited by James Brook (Oakland, CA: PM Press, 2017), 168.

still bore the imprint of a bitter irony, an expression of protest, the final protest of Victor Serge, of a man who, throughout his lifetime, had stood up against injustice....While filling out the burial papers, I answered the question of nationality with "stateless." Which he was. The funeral home director started shouting that he couldn't be buried if he had no nationality. How could he bury a stateless person? I asked Vlady, "If he could choose, what nationality would your father have chosen?" "Spanish," he said with certainty. The Russo-Belgian-French writer is buried in Mexico in the French cemetery with Spanish nationality.

—CLAUDIO ALBERTANI
and JEAN-GUY RENS
Mexico City and Montreal, 2012

A NOTE ON THE TEXT

The first publication of entries from Victor Serge's notebooks was in July 1949 in Jean-Paul Sartre's review, *Les Temps modernes,* which published several pages, notably on Ramón Mercader, Trotsky's assassin. In 1942 Éditions Julliard published a first version of the *Notebooks,* divided into two parts: "Old Notebooks," covering the years 1936–1938, and "New Notebooks," which covered 1944. The selections that had appeared in *Les Temps modernes* were omitted from this collection, while the correspondence with several of Serge's friends and comrades was added. This edition was the one used as the basis for the 1985 edition published by Actes Sud. In turn, this was the edition used by Mitchell Abidor in his translation of selections from the *Notebooks* for the Marxists Internet Archive.

In 2010 a major discovery was made at the Fundacion Orfila Séjourné in Amecameca, which held the archives of Laurette Séjourné. The founder of the archive, Esperanza Rascón, invited the Serge specialist Claudio Albertani to visit the archives, where Ivonne Chávez, a young historian and archivist, had identified nearly 1,500 pages of Serge's writings. Assembled in three large boxes, they included letters, notebooks, notes, photos, an unpublished short story dated 1918 titled "Journal of the Defeat," and notebooks from 1941, 1942, 1943, and 1946 of various kinds which, bound together with string, had not been touched in more than sixty years.

The blanks in the story were filled in through research by Claude Rioux and Jean-Guy Rens in the Victor Serge Papers, held at the Beinecke Rare Book and Manuscript Library at Yale University.

The work was published in France by Agone in 2012 and is thus the most complete version currently available.

NOTEBOOKS

1936–1940

ANDRÉ GIDE

Late November 1936, Paris—Battle of Madrid, Salengro's suicide, Jean Guéhenno (what a demagogue!) at *Vigilance*. Professor René Maublanc* at the same meeting worse than demagogic, clever with a hint of corruption. Feeling of hopeless muddle: it's a question of saving Spain. The rapporteur, Henri Bouché,* can't say that planes are being sent—and intellectuals who know they are being sent but that it can't be admitted blame Léon Blum for his inaction, etc. As I was leaving I exchanged a few words with Guéhenno on the trial of Zinoviev and Kamenev: he doesn't want to take a position and doesn't want to appear like he's not taking a position.

Magdeleine Paz* tells me that my open letter to André Gide made a big impression on her, but she thinks it was a mistake for me to publish it, as it looks like I'm putting him on the spot. I don't see anything wrong in this, I said. Great intellectuals are too fond of parading under the shelter of noble phrases. I hold Gide in too high esteem, I don't have the right to handle him with kid gloves; he must be able to understand this. "But that letter might block his trip to Russia!" "So?..." "Now he's in complete agreement with you, you have to see each other, but in secret: he doesn't want people to think you influenced him in the writing of his book." (It seems that A. G. is somewhat distrustful of me and also has a general fear of Trotskyism, which he only knows through Pierre Naville,* and his feelings towards P. N.—who irritates him—are mutual.)

Magdeleine Paz is setting up a confidential meeting between us. ("Try not to be followed.")

Rue Vaneau, an untidy apartment, full of autographed books and art objects floating in a kind of abandon. Everything has aged, the wall hangings and the rest, one lives there without really seeing what one has, attached to memories and ideas, of which things are no longer anything but tarnished signs. One lives there in a worn, detached state of living. On the mantelpiece, my pamphlet *The Sixteen Who Were Executed* was lying open, facedown, in the middle of being read. Soft, muffled footsteps—slippers—in the narrow corridor. Gide enters. A shape unencumbered with extra weight, brown and muffled as well with a kind of cape over the shoulders. Dark skinned, I think, flesh aged but smooth and well cared for, broad face, a wide mouth, deep-set eyes behind tortoiseshell glasses, a broad brow. A kind of languid sadness and, at times, a cheekiness at the corner of his mouth when it hangs half-open. When he expresses distaste he grimaces like a disgusted woman, very expressive and simian (when he speaks of Aragon and Ehrenburg*).

We embrace. He: "Well, I pictured you different, skinny, bonier, I don't know, emaciated. . . ."

His trip to Russia:

"I really hoped to do something to save your manuscripts. I wasn't able to do anything, either for you or about other things that mattered to me. I saw right away that there was nothing to be done . . ."

Tone and expression of a sadness without limits. From the moment he arrived, he discovered so much harshness and inhumanity that there was nothing to be done.

"The stupid cruelty of the antihomosexual legislation. I said that I'd talk to Stalin about it during the interview that was planned. Right then I had a feeling that the interview wasn't going to happen.

"Banquets, we were stuffed with food and speeches. In Georgia, in Leningrad. I couldn't eat another thing. There were times that I'd refuse everything after the hors d'oeuvres."

He spoke of a Georgian poet, a heavy drinker, a heavy eater, very patriotic, sly, who knew French well: Soviet and Montparnasse-style bohemian.

Bukharin tried to connect with me twice, in vain. "I'll see you in an hour."

"You'll see," Herbart* said to me, "he won't come back." Obviously. The new aristocracy. Having escaped the train and the interpreters he went off to see how the people live. Contrasts, poverty.

He shows me his manuscript, reads a letter from Jef Last.* "Last is very unhappy. He thinks and feels the same way as I, is viewed badly by the party, perhaps in danger."

We correct an expression I find too pessimistic, a "There never will be…." He tells about the pressure exerted on him to delay the publication of his notes on the USSR in the name of the salvation of the Spanish revolution. Militiamen sent him telegrams from the front. ("What can they know about what I write?") Tells me that the manuscript was given to Gallimard as a confidential document and was set by specially chosen typesetters in a secure print shop. "And you know what? Ehrenburg read it anyway, that swine." I answer that E. has long been a tool, a secret agent or someone in the complete confidence of secret agents. A. G. fears the reactions that will follow the publication of the book. Expects to be buried under insults. The author of *Corydon* senses that he is vulnerable to the vilest slanders. His courage, his great courage, is that of a timid man.

We talk about Pierre Naville, whom he finds harsh and curt, but whom he feels affection for. We speak of Léon Blum, whom he has just seen. He feels antipathy for Blum's sectarianism and prestige. I see him as disoriented, afraid of being isolated. I do my best to steer him toward relationships with socialists.

"In Leningrad a pleasant young naval officer came over to me and in a whisper spoke about you with great emotion."

Suddenly, as I was leaving, I don't remember with regard to what, his voice took on a something of the accent of a lower-class, slack-jawed Montmartre gangster, revealing the man who knows the dirty corners of Paris and the underside of life.

He's worried. As if he were afraid of himself. Ravaged. The disaster of communism. Spoke of the Moscow Trial. No illusions concerning that villainy and cruelty. I carry away the impression of an extremely scrupulous man, troubled to the depths of his soul, who wanted to serve a great cause and no longer knows how.

ANDRÉ GIDE—ARRESTS IN LENINGRAD (VERA, ESTHER)

Brussels, January 11, 1937, morning—I see him again at the Hotel Albert I near the Gare du Nord. "You see, I did come to see you..." There's something trusting in his tone, as if a fog that was between us has lifted since we spoke in Paris. His face has become hollowed, carved in relief. Ascetic, but accustomed to luxury. Ascetic in the depths of the soul and velvet on the flesh. A hesitant step, crisp gestures. He sniffs, a tic. One senses his firmness.

The last time I saw him he seemed anxious, full of scruples and doubts, feeling he has to cross a border; courageous enough to cross it, but barely. Lost. Tormented by the fear of harming the cause of Spain. And by the pain of losing the affection of the young, a warm and beneficent popularity that came to him late. But to keep it based on disillusion and lies? —No more.

I find him fortified, calm, ready to smile. Clearly changed: combative. The book is selling well. Hundreds of odious, slanderous, insulting press clippings arrive. He speaks of them with detachment.

We talk about Malraux, whose attitude worries him a bit. "M[alraux] is taking advantage of me. Scooping up the popularity I'm losing. Extraordinarily intelligent. Shrewd. He knows perfectly well that I'm right, but that doesn't bind him." About Jef Last, who's on the Madrid front: a great excuse.

He considers my contributing to the *NRF* [*Nouvelle revue Française*] completely impossible because of the *material* influence of Malraux and Jean-Richard Bloch.

My special issue of the *Crapouillot, From Lenin to Stalin*, is lying on the table. He thinks it's good, with a shift at the end that the reader can't follow. Wasn't I being partisan speaking about Stalin?

I answer that it was written, straight out, in two weeks and that I think it's objective.

Him: Your explanation of the Moscow Trial is the only one that's intelligible.

Him: They're calling me a Trotskyist. Why not?

His admiration for Leon Trotsky.

His coldness towards the French Trotskyists. Pierre Naville brought up by his family to have great ambitions. To be either Rubens or

Beethoven—or Lenin! He doesn't like this distorting ambition—but Naville is an upright individual.

Our long, disjointed conversation turns to the relationship between masters and disciples. I quote the words of Zarathustra-Nietzsche: "If you want to follow me, deny me."

Him: Buddha says: "If you encounter me, kill me."

Me: Don't repeat that too often. They'll do it. They won't miss...

Relaxing and laughing.

Discussed Spain, the POUM,[1] which is being slandered and which I defend. Munitions lacking on the Madrid front.

Discussed the death of Eugène Dabit,[2] who was so talented. Greatly affected by his trip to Russia.

Him: Workers that I know in Lille, angered by what was being said about my book, invited me to view poverty. We walked the alleys together, visited the home of an unemployed man. I said to them, "My friends, if only Russian workers had such apartments!"

He mentions Ehrenburg with disgust. I say: An informer.

Him: He came to ask me if I believed this and spoke for a half hour without my saying a single word... So he dropped the subject...

Again about Russia: the magnificent Russian youth—and the stifling atmosphere.

I say that I learned just two days ago of the arrest of my sister Vera Vladimirovna Frolova,* of my sister-in-law Esther Russakova,* and of one of my brothers-in-law, the musician Paul-Marcel or the sailor Paul. They are apolitical, used to living in fear. I think it's my writings, my open letters, that are provoking their persecution. Their arrest dates to September 6, the day after the executions of Zinoviev-Kamenev-Ivan Smirnov*; it's part of the wave of terror that's unfurling. I explain that having killed some they can no longer look the others in the eye or put up with their silence. The old guard of the party understands that it must disappear; it will disappear.

---

1. Partido Obrero de Unificación Marxista, Workers' Party of Marxist Unification, was the Spanish independent left-wing party Serge supported and which was wiped out by the Stalinists during the Spanish Civil War for its alleged Trotskyism.

2. The novelist Dabit died in the USSR while accompanying Gide on his trip there.

Concerning the impotence of intellectuals. Yet one can free oneself of moral complicity.

Pierre Herbart came in during our discussion. A handsome, elegant young man with a clear gaze. In Moscow he worked at *International Literature*, and his memories of it are of hypocrisy and suffocation.

In a short while I leave for Holland.

GEORGES LAMBERT—RUSSIAN PRISONS

January 27, 1937, Brussels—I have known G. Lambert since 1919. In 1920 we named him secretary of the French Communist Group of Petrograd, even though he'd only joined at the eleventh hour. He left the party during NEP. Married, hardworking, an ill-paid accountant at the petroleum syndicate, he lived in the same building as me on Jeliabova Street, though on the Volinsky *Pereoluk* side, in 1925–1930. Belgian; he traveled abroad; had dealings with a British consul; became suspect. Smuggled a little perfume. Closely watched, suspected of espionage. Certainly wasn't a spy: too weak and fearful. Living a reclusive, wary existence, he obviously couldn't provide any worthwhile information. Arrested in 1930; I couldn't do anything for him, living under threat myself. But as soon as I arrived in Brussels last April I brought his case to the attention of Foreign Affairs. Spaak wrote to Ambassador Le Tellier and G. L.'s liberation was easily obtained—which shows there was nothing serious against him.

He comes to thank me. We talk in my little office. Window looking out on a country landscape, the city in the distance. Liuba (Russakova*) delirious next room. G. L. is pallid, his features sharp and uneven, his wide, roving eyes a crazed blue. Emaciated, pitiful, he speaks with a joyous exaltation, loses his train of thought, rambles, clearly distorts whatever he is recounting, perhaps invents—but overall what he says must be true. (Thanks to his wife I kept abreast of his affair for two years.)

He spent merely seven years in prison. Returned to Brussels last October with fourteen francs, ill and not knowing where to go. Found a place in Antwerp.

After his arrest (Leningrad, 1930) he went seven months without shaving. "The torture of the beard," he says. (I know all about it.)

Thirteen months without being able to walk, read, or receive food from outside. On the eve of his arrest he was made to sign a request for Soviet naturalization (he'd asked for a passport in order to go abroad). This request was used to inform Belgian authorities who were interceding in his affair that he had become a Soviet citizen.

"Confess that you're a French espionage agent with the rank of colonel," etc. He was shown a deposition signed by a Latvian consul in Leningrad and another by Ramzin,* both of them implicating him. He doesn't know if these depositions were false or nonexistent. (Something odd: a Latvian consul made some strange depositions during the Kirov Affair in late 1934. Was he a GPU agent? He attempted to implicate Trotsky in the Nikolaev-Kirov Affair.)

G. L. is accused of having carried out missions on behalf of Zinoviev. They told him that Body,* Helfer,* and V.[ictor] S.[erge] have been in prison for some time. That Rubinstein (an old militant, vaguely of the Opposition, obese and insane) often saw him enter Zinoviev's office. He demands and obtains a confrontation, but it's another or a fake Rubinstein whom he doesn't know and who testifies against him—falsely.

They make him sign a statement that he denies having carried out missions for Zinoviev and others, in doing so accepting the eventual death penalty.

That very night he's awakened and brought to the office of the prison director (the Chpalernaya Prison) where he finds several members of the GPU. Threats. They finally show him the damning document: A "mandate" from the French Communist Group from 1920 to 1921 authorizing him to deal with the provisioning of the French Asylum. Finally they offer him: $15,000 plus $3,000 in indemnities for six months of relative deprivation of freedom. The money will be deposited abroad. He'll live in a hotel under house arrest. He'll be judged, will make a public confession in order to discredit those who are conspiring against the USSR. Will be sentenced to death and pardoned. They tell him his brother agrees to all this. He refuses to believe it, refuses: "I'm innocent."

They lead him to believe that he'll be executed but that they prefer to use him.

They send him down from the seventh floor and lock him up in the cellar.

They read him his death sentence.

"Perhaps they thought I was really strong; I was only hopeless, so hopeless that I had fallen into indifference and torpor. I was a human rag, half-dead"—but he instinctively understood that if he confessed he would most certainly be lost.

The guard in chief of the section (*natchalnik korpoussa*) comes in and says: "Congratulations!" Pardoned. Faints dead away.

Better treatment after this. Employed at 2 Gorokhovaya Street straightening out the library of the French professor Laronde—who had also gone through similar trials before being expelled. (His wife saw him at the time and told me that when walking down the street she could sometimes glimpse him at the window.)

They're talking about expelling him, they get a passport ready for him: if he agrees to serve.

Sent to the isolator[3] of Yaroslavl.

A regime of near total isolation, a good library, good food, no torture. Able to take walks in pairs after a certain amount of time. Extremely rare correspondence: prisoners held in secret are deprived of this and never see anyone. This was one of the best isolators, reserved for "personalities."

There G. L. met:

The Frenchman Léger, secret agent in Sofia at the time of the attack in the cathedral (1924), later claimed by the USSR—gone insane. Threw himself from the top of a staircase shouting, "I'll escape, I won't spare you," etc.

The Trotskyist Chekan, a man of great courage. He and his comrades demonstrated during the anniversary celebrations of the Revolution. As long as they didn't shout anything against Stalin they weren't attacked. The least allusion to S. led to beatings.

Kamenev's brother Rosenfeld, a painter, and his wife. They were implicated in a terrorism affair as a result of which the chief of the Kremlin guard, Peterson, and several of his men were shot in 1935. (Word of this secret trial of "the Kremlin guards" reached me and I mentioned it in *Russia Twenty Years After*. This affair is the source of the conspiracy psychosis that led to the Moscow Trial. Kamenev was

---

3. A pretrial detention center.

judged there along with his brother and sentenced to ten years' imprisonment, which certainly looks like a confession of his innocence.)

The Polish Communist Dombrowski—Representative? (This might not be the right name.)

A Pole, Turjanski.

A Turk, member of the Central Committee of the Turkish CP.

Members of the Central Committee of the Chinese CP.

The Left Social-Revolutionary Kamkov—imprisoned since 1918.

The former (recent) chairman of the Leningrad Soviet, Zinoviev's successor, Kondratiev.

Held also at Yaroslavl:

The old Menshevik economist Bazarov.*

Gvosdiev, member of the First Petrograd Soviet of 1917.

Vederevski, former member of Kerensky's cabinet.

During his travels G. L. saw lines of housewives waiting for potatoes near the train station in Minsk.

G. L. was expelled from Russia at the same time as the Austrian Schützbündler Hirlap, a veteran of the Viennese insurrection of 1934; the German philologist Professor Müller; another German, a Nazi spy; and others he wasn't able to identify.

In Yaroslavl it was believed that Tolmachev and Eismont had indeed been executed. An Eismont son may have been killed in Leningrad after the Kirov Affair.

G. L.'s wife and daughter are being held in Russia. He's taking steps so they can be allowed to join him. —He begs me never to mention his name.

LEOPOLD III

February 1, 1937—Dined with Louis Rougier[4] at the home of Dr. Walter Schraenen, who's a friend of the king. A severe, almost chilling house, an austere young scholar, his wife—the problems of cancer and those of the Moscow Trial . . . W. S. gives a portrait of the king:

4. After an official visit to the USSR in 1932, the philosopher Louis Rougier wrote a pamphlet titled *Can We Know the Truth About the USSR?*

Very religious, with a strong sense of duty. Scrupulous. In the face of parliamentary crisis twice threatened to form a government of technicians presided over by a general. The constitutional oath weighs on him—but he will respect it.

Weighed down by the feeling that he was the involuntary cause of the death of his wife, Queen Astrid. Has refused to remarry. Inflicts solitude on himself as a form of expiation.

Hardworking, he leads a sad life. Returns in the evening to Laeken, sees the children, dines tête-à-tête with the Queen Mother Elisabeth, who is delicate, pale, still beautiful. "A Wittlesbach," a transparent face with blue eyes, living in an almost silent madness. Sitting at the table, she appears to be waiting; sometimes she asks why the king—Albert I—is not coming. They answer, "But he can't come..." She replies, "Oh, that's true, I forgot..." She sometimes awakens during the night to play the violin...

Moscow: execution of Pyatakov,* Muralov,* Serebryakov,* Boguslavsky,* Drobnis,* and others (sixteen...). Radek and Sokolnikov,* pardoned—but for how long?

MURDER OF A PARTY GIRL

February 5, 1937—A café on the place de Brouckère. Conversation with a pretty tart who speaks an amusing "Bruxellois" patois... But what she says...

"I look carefully at the gentlemen. You have to make sure you've got them figured out....We're scared. A few days ago a 'party girl' was killed at the Hotel Moderne.... She was like me, brunette, thin, twenty-four years old. She left a little girl of four...

"A young blond man went upstairs with her. He had wine brought in. He must have been nice. Then they got undressed.

"He tied her hands with a stocking. Had she drunk too much? The only explanation is that she lost her head. —Men sometimes ask me: 'Let yourself be tied up, be my slave...' —'No,' I answer, 'but if you want I'll tie you up and you'll be the slave.' Isn't that more reasonable?"

(Sideward glance, an air of innocence.)

"The girl was naked. He strangled her on a chair with the other silk stocking. Before leaving he placed her on a stool and moved a wardrobe so that she wouldn't be seen right away when someone entered. He stole some small things." But, "he certainly wasn't a real thief..."

"The maid who found the corpse became sick—the shock, it's natural, right?

"We all chipped in for the child and the funeral. Can you imagine? We collected 9,000 francs....We had decided on a very simple funeral, decent, nothing more, to save money for the little girl. She's taken care of for a few years....That's swell, isn't it?"

FRITZ DAVID'S LIE

February 1937—Fritz David [-Krugliansky], executed after the first Moscow Trial, lied when he accused himself.

Information provided by a German émigré recently employed at the Soviet commercial mission in Paris. The F. D. Affair profoundly demoralized the German Communist personnel.

F. D.: subaltern figure, GPU agent, as such imposed as editor of the *Rote Fahne* of Berlin.[5] In Moscow he kept an eye on the personnel of the Comintern.

Attended all the sessions of the VIIth Congress of the Communist International, except, by chance, those at which Stalin spoke, because he'd neglected to obtain the special pass that was needed. The German personnel at the congress recall the incident, for they insisted in vain that F. D. be allowed to enter, while the special security guards remained inflexible.

However, at the trial F. D. confessed at a public hearing that he had attended this sitting in order to carry out an assassination attempt—and not having dared to, finding himself too far away, full of doubts, etc.

5. *Die Rote Fahne* (*The Red Flag*). Newspaper founded on November 9, 1918, by Rosa Luxemburg and Karl Liebknecht as the organ of the Spartacus League (Spartakusbund). On January 1, 1919, becomes organ of German Communist Party. Banned by the Nazis on February 28, 1933; appears illegally in Germany until 1934, then in exile up until the war.

THE WHITES AT KRONSTADT 1921

[Undated] The Whites sent Colonel Peredielov to Finland, with orders to organize food supplies to relieve insurgent Kronstadt, infiltrate himself into the fort, and propose his services as a former general staff officer. Peredielov was able to accomplish none of this; in his report upon his return, he admitted to this, tears in his eyes.

Kartashev* and old Tchaikovsky* were members of the committee that sent him.

ANDRÉ GIDE

May 8 and 18, 1937, Paris—Two conversations with A. G.: one of the themes, what can be hoped for Russia and socialism. His confidence in Russian youth is intuitive, but of a reasoned intuition. The reasoning behind mine is different. He finds the Popular Front impressive but less vigorous and healthy than it appears. (The race for jobs, for recommendations, etc.)

His entire oeuvre has fundamentally been that of a moralist engaged in a combat against oppressive conventional morality. Hence *The Immoralist*... His true teachers, Nietzsche and Dostoevsky. The physiological conflict (homosexuality) that all but outlawed him from society, and whose magnitude he became aware of at the time of the Oscar Wilde tragedy, rendered him fearful, exaggeratedly scrupulous, with a tendency to flee toward aestheticism (which provided him with much contentment and confirmed his feeling of superiority. The purism of his style was the ideal expression of an indisputable superiority—but it was disputed.... He was able to place himself in the forefront because he flattered the taste of the literati.). Pure language and delicate psychological problems treated with a reticent boldness and occasionally violent lightning bolts, like the idea of the "gratuitous act"—what more was needed to ensure success among an elite audience? But A. G.'s sincerity must have suffered precisely from the flattering approval of this unenergetic public. And the moral problem once posed, the social problem followed in its wake. The moral is the social. (A. G.'s unflagging interest in Zola, the writer from whom he is in appearance the most distant and whose public was the most different from his own.)

It was after the Russian Revolution that he committed his first great—and not in the least gratuitous—act of courage, dictated by his conscience and impulsed by the intellectual currents of the time: the justification of homosexuality in *Corydon*. The very scandal that resulted, and which he toughed out, was converted into a success. Nevertheless, he did not support the Russian Revolution as long as the latter was unpopular among the literati. It troubled him, and its cruelties upset his humanism. He only truly and publicly took its side around 1934, during a very bad period, well after the Soviet Thermidor.[6] But this lag is quite general in France; G. followed the current of the literary youth that embraced Marxism. At that moment there were in reality two schools of thought: Action Française, the doctrinaire rehashing of Maurras; and Marxism. (Consider the influence of Malraux on Gide. Malraux comes out with a mixture of Marxist—barely Marxist—revolutionism, aestheticism, and adventurism, which perfectly suited to the taste of the young, for whom the revolution is an attractive adventure because they feel boxed in by a senile society. The same tendencies in *La Révolution surréaliste*.) For emotional reasons they don't want to see that the face of the Russian Revolution has changed, they accept it as if it had remained faithful to itself. The CP's propaganda sustains these comfortable illusions and gives them material support: money, publication, invitations to Moscow, congresses... A rich revolution that exercises power distributes honors and advantages, easily seduces intellectuals by enabling them to be both revolutionary and conformist, quasi-heroic without running any danger, and loaded with benefits. In addition, the CP assures them of good publicity and places them in contact with a popular public. All of this must have seduced Gide to an extent and secretly troubled him. He closely followed Russian affairs (through Pierre Naville), but he was perhaps reluctant to surrender to the influence of that young man. The fear of being influenced is quite powerful in him: any influence is an attack on his individuality. He began to change at the Congress for the Defense of Culture in 1935, when it became obvious to him, a propos of "the Victor Serge Affair"

6. Reference to 9 Thermidor, date on the revolutionary calendar when Robespierre was overthrown and the term used by Trotsky to describe Stalin's rise to power.

—brutally thrown on the carpet by Salvemini,* Magdeleine Paz, Pou-laille,* and Plisnier[7] (and so elegantly evaded by André Breton)—that the congress was in perfect bad faith, completely manipulated by agents of the CP. He felt he had been duped, saw the moral ugliness in all of this. He requested an audience about my case with the ambassador of the USSR and left it full of doubts. The executions in Leningrad that followed the Kirov attack had already taken place and had more or less divided French intellectuals into two categories: those who accepted everything, like Aragon and J.-R. Bloch, and those who feebly preserved their consciences, like R. Rolland. A. G. gone beyond the age of moral reservations, but didn't want to take a categorical position before hav-ing seen things with his own eyes—without having gone to Russia.

Out of instinct he was rather against the Russian Opposition, tempted by the prestige of strength, of a transforming power, a power fundamentally—even if harshly—just and humane. I think he would have no hesitation in accepting Goethe's words: "Rather injustice than disorder" (Goethe, the exact opposite of Bakunin). In the sense that order constitutes a justice superior to secondary injustices—as well as a harmony. (There is also the other, purely conservative sense of this quote, but A. G. would not have accepted it. Goethe, I think, used it in both senses... Plenitude!)—The second great act of courage in his life was, upon his return from Russia, his open break with the official USSR. I know what this cost him. But he felt it was a question of his dignity, his very individuality. What was left for him of the gratuitous act became an act of courage: refusal to sacrifice his lucidity. This was painful because of the need to implicitly recognize that he had erred in adhering to communism; because of the friendships he had to break; because of the widespread sympathy he had to lose.

Gide had only ever known the "popularity" of literary circles and salons—a small thing... But there is a common side to him that he never expressed in his books. He loves the lower depths, the streets, the squares of Paris for a number of profound reasons, among which I see a need

7. Charles Plisnier, the Belgian novelist, called for Serge's release and was among those who greeted him upon his arrival in Brussels. Expelled from the Belgian Communist Party for Trotskyism, he joined the Parti Ouvrier Belge.

to commune with the crowd. The influence he suddenly obtained thanks to the CP, the ambiance of the public meetings, the friendship he encountered in working-class neighborhoods, the influence he acquired over young proletarian writers—at age sixty—were a bath of humanity for him. All of this coincided with the rise of the Popular Front, which was a rebirth of collective enthusiasm in France. (I had predicted it would appear at the moment when the country began to shrug off the apathy resulting from the loss of 1,700,000 men during the war; in other words, for the advent of the new generation twenty years after the battles, between 1934 and 1938. My elementary math turned out to be correct.)

What is admirable here is the vitality of the old intellectual, still ready to embrace renewal, able to make such a difficult break at this time of his life. That is his greatness.

THE DISAPPEARANCE OF ANDRÉS NIN

Late May 1937—I immediately understood that once Andrés* was arrested he was irretrievably lost (the psychosis of the Russians). Along with Colette Audry,* on that very day I begged Magdeleine Paz to take a plane to Barcelona to attempt to save him. She couldn't do so because of her work on *Le Populaire.*

But Magdeleine, Félicien Challaye,* Georges Pioch,* and the Limbour girl went in a delegation to the Spanish embassy. They were received by a friendly secretary who tried to reassure them, promised guarantees of justice, would transmit our committee's demands. When Magdeleine insisted on the dangers Nin was exposed to the secretary betrayed himself:

"Oh, him . . ."

Which means that it's probably too late for Nin.

"What do you mean?"

He sits back down, grows silent, evasive.

A few months ago in Brussels I had learned of a major plot being prepared to destroy the POUM; I had warned the Committee of the POUM, Gorkin,* and Nin. Everything happened according to the plan that I learned of by chance.

Defense Committee Meeting. Édouard Serre* of Air France tells us that he has taken it upon himself to speak to the Soviet ambassador about Nin, stressing that a crime committed against Nin would have serious consequences. "I've rendered the USSR enough services that they should hear me out. I was well received by the ambassador and he understood me perfectly. He's worried. He advised me to send a secret memo to Stalin, which he would deliver." We approved this.

Nin was kidnapped from a prison-villa near the Russian military aerodrome in Alcalá de Henares.

A Russian officer called Orlov* is probably in on this, and perhaps Antonov-Ovseyenko* as well.

KRIVITSKY

November 20, 1937—Arranged a meeting with Walter [Krivitsky*] at Colette Audry's apartment on Port-Royal Square. We meet in front of the door. Colette isn't home. We take a stroll through the dark streets, ending under the walls of the Santé Prison, on boulevard Arago. His remarks:

> There's a French family that loves me and that I love. When they learned of my "treason" they refused to believe it. When I told them my reasons their expressions changed and I saw that if they didn't throw me out immediately it was only because they wanted to keep a hold on me so they could act against me. They're admirably dedicated people.

> I had made an appointment to meet in a café with my agent, the man of that family. I saw that I was being watched and was afraid I'd be killed. He had already set it up. He truly loved me, like a teacher who taught him devotion and political consciousness.

> Your position as Oppositionists is morally correct but politically untenable. History has condemned you. I would read your articles and books with pleasure, and deplore the fact that you are lost.

> It's not customary to execute political leaders. Look at the Mensheviks, whom we could long since have liquidated. With officers it's another matter. (He thinks that General Wrangel

was liquidated.) And intelligence agents have no reprieve to
hope for. They'll get me.

I had decided to return to Moscow; I still don't know if it wouldn't
have been better. It's not death that frightens me, it's the wait,
it's the preliminaries, a useless and revolting torture. What I
feel most profoundly is regret for those good comrades, the
flower of the revolution, who were unjustly executed.

No, Stalin isn't mad. He has something grand in mind, and he
sometimes loses his head. It's terrible.

I will make no revelations. I'll do nothing that could harm the
USSR. There is nothing else but the cause of the USSR.

He noted that when he put his hand in his pocket to take out a
cigarette I watched him closely.

You distrust me, and it's only natural. Yet we'd be happy, you
and I, to die for the same cause.

Me: "Not exactly the same."

I speak of socialism. He answers that the road to socialism passes
through the might of the Soviet state.

I'm worn out. I could be killed on any street corner, and one day
I will be. All of this is unspeakably absurd.

Yagoda* was balanced. Yezhov* is unbalanced. Trilisser* was a
great Old Bolshevik, honest and perceptive.

PURGE IN RUSSIA

December 10, 1937—A witness recently arrived from Russia tells me
that Piatnitsky (Ossip Aaronovich), the incorruptible Old Bolshevik
who headed the Comintern's secret services (especially finances) has
disappeared. The head of the NKVD[8] himself has assumed leadership
of the service. It is officially admitted that the Comintern's secret
service is full of "enemy agents." Terror: "95 percent of the International's
former collaborators have disappeared...."

Disappeared: Béla Kun, Valetski,* Kostrzewa,* Ludwig Magyar*

8. Russian acronym for the People's Commissariat for Internal Affairs, the name of
the Soviet interior ministry from 1934.

("certainly executed") Hirsch Wolf,[9] Ernest Thaelmann's former secretary, Hugo Eberlein* (Albert). Kun, Eberlein, and Hirsch Wolf or Werner will probably be executed. There are other rumors that Kun died in prison after having been tortured.

Herman Sandomirsky* (anarchist, former director of the Balkan service at foreign affairs), deported to Yeniseysk, was surely executed, I'm told, before the Pyatakov trial.

Most of the German refugees are under arrest.

Kreps,* director of International Publishers, arrested in 1937, has disappeared. (It was he who greeted me one day in front of a globe and said with pride, "I have branch offices all over the world! I just opened one in the Philippines!")

Maurice Thorez is said to have been reprimanded in Moscow for having given the fight against Trotskyism an "academic form."

The leadership of the Comintern has passed to the executioner Yezhov. Expect action.

The German poet Ottwald*: Disappeared.

Piatnitsky—I met him a few times in Berlin and Moscow. Head of an old worker, moustache, Gothic nose, lively little black eyes. Ostentatiously simple, to the point of asceticism. Corruption and the economy were his obsessions. Inconvenient.

Hugo Eberlein, a Spartacist of the first hour, veteran of the German insurrections (and others, I imagine). Leader of the combat services of the German Communist Party, skillful, harsh, and cynical, the character of a good German officer. The face of an energetic cat, prominent cheekbones; small, metallic eyes.

REISS, KRIVITSKY, BASTEITCH—OTHERS

December 1937—For months I've been living in a stifling atmosphere of crime, full of darkness and revelations.

In July Henk Sneevliet* informed me that a secret agent of Stalin, based in Holland, from where he directed his services, had decided to quit secret work. Sneevliet had known him for a long time but hadn't

---

9. Serge's error: in fact it was Werner Hirsch.*

seen him in years. "Ludwig" [Ignace Reiss*] had been shattered by the executions of Kamenev and Zinoviev, by the atmosphere of terror in Moscow, by the decorations—the Order of Lenin—given secret service agents who had participated in the execution of the Old Bolsheviks. Ludwig warns us that the decision has been made to use terrorism against the Opposition abroad—against us. We decide to demand a public statement from him that would allow us to trust him and would place him under the protection of public opinion. Sedov* shares that opinion.

August 1. I give a talk at L'École Émancipée[10] in a room near the Bastille. I make public "Ludwig's warning" of the threat against us. (Also an article published under this title.)

August. Sneevliet negotiates a meeting with "Ludwig." Ludwig sends us his "Statement," which is strongly worded and vehement. The Committee for the Investigation of the Moscow Trial publishes it. Sneevliet coordinates with L., who is in hiding, a meeting which three of us will attend, Sneevliet, Sedov, and me. Sedov postpones the meeting.

September 1—Sneevliet makes an appointment to meet me at Café de la Rotonde on the boulevard Montparnasse. He arrives from Amsterdam for his meeting with Ludwig. There is no time to lose. L. is hiding in Switzerland, in great danger, and we have to make some decisions with him, in the first place in order to try to ensure his safety. If Sedov can't or won't come we'll go without him to Reims on the 5th. Sedov tells us he is indisposed. On the 5th we leave for Reims. Our rendezvous is set for the station snack bar at 10:00 a.m. A poorly chosen spot. The snack bar is small, deserted, poorly lit, has many doors and dark corners that lend themselves to dirty tricks. We wait for an hour, in vain. We roam the city. "This is strange," says Sneevliet, "Ludwig is always punctual." We drink champagne in a cabaret. A young blonde comes in with her date. S. tells me about the young people of his party killed in Spain, of the successive suicides of his two sons. The one who most recently committed suicide reproached him for failing to demonstrate enough active solidarity towards the anti-Nazi refugees being

---

10. Both a magazine and a movement, founded by French teachers in 1910. It was at the confluence of anarchosyndicalism, progressive pedagogy, and the counterculture, and its members campaigned for Serge's release from his Soviet imprisonment.

interned or turned away by the Dutch government. "But I don't have the means!" said Sneevliet. Despairingly. We speak of the errors of L. T. [Leon Trotsky], who's trying to establish the Fourth International without local parties worthy of the name. We conclude that it is harmful to play with the ideas either of a party or an International. —Second rendezvous with L. at the post office at 10:00 a.m. —We don't have the feeling we're being followed. The city is provincial, the nocturnal streets deserted.

On the 6th, no one at the post office. Worried. We go to see the bombed-out cathedral, which looks like it had been licked by enormous flames. At noon, waiting for our train at the station, I buy a newspaper and find a short report saying that a certain Eberhardt, a Czech, was found riddled with bullets on the Chamblandes road near Lausanne the day before yesterday, and that in his pocket was a train ticket to France. There's no doubt. Sneevliet leaves for Switzerland, I return to Paris, I inform the Committee of Inquiry, meeting in a café on place de l'Odéon. On the 13th we write an explicit press communiqué, giving the identity of Ignace Reiss. General silence in the press. Bergery,* at *La Flèche*,[11] promises me to publish it and does so. The silence is broken.

On September 15, in a small hotel near the Gare de l'Est Sneevliet brings me to see Elsa Reiss* and her child (ten years old). Elsa, her lips constantly trembling and her eyes welling with tears—gray-blue eyes, a full, oval face. By luck she[12] escaped the poisoned chocolates brought by Gertrude Schildbach.* The Sûreté considers her in danger and, as we begin to untangle the threads of the crime, over the telephone they recommend to S. that we change E. R.'s hotel, taking all possible precautions. A Polish comrade sent by Sedov arrives.

Elsa says that a secret agent went to see me in Brussels—they had something in mind. He spoke to Reiss and Krivitsky—both of whom knew me personally—with enthusiasm. The agent: Basteitch.*

Two or three days after my arrival in Brussels from Moscow, thus around June 20, I was in a café on the boulevard Anspach with Boris

11. A weekly published from 1934 to 1939 as the "Central Organ of the Common Front."
12. Son of Ignace Reiss and Elisabeth Poretsky (alias Elsa Reiss).

Pokhitonov.* We were sitting on the covered terrace. I observed a well-dressed gentleman with an intensely dark gaze who had sat down near us. I felt a certain unease and I mentioned it to Boris P. The gentleman came over to me and told me his name: Basteitch, whom I'd known in Vienna in 1923–25, a militant in the Balkan Federation—D. Vlakhov,* leader at the time of the assassination of Todor Panitsa.* At the time Basteitch was a revolutionary bohemian, one of the survivors of the Serbian organization that had carried out the attack in Sarajevo. At the same time that I met him I met Mustafa, of the same group but more influential, and Colonel Bojin Simić, a friend of Dragutin Dimitrijević,* executed at Salonika. There was also Koussovatz, a young Montenegrin. B. tells me that he lived in Geneva and that convinced me not to go to the appointment he had asked me for and which I'd agreed to... If someone like B. lives in Geneva, travels, and is well dressed, I said to myself, it's because he belongs to some political group which it's best to keep at a distance. I did well. (The idea of the GPU didn't occur to me...)

Early November. Someone, talking on the telephone to Gérard Rosenthal,* asks to meet us. Elsa thinks that it's Walter—a friend of Reiss who shares his feelings, an old secret agent himself. "You surely know him," she says to me. An appointment at Gérard's near the Gare Saint-Lazare. Gérard's law office is next to his father's clinic. Elsa, Sneevliet, Sedov, Gérard, me. A small man in a gray overcoat with a thin face—rumpled, edgy, and nervous, enters. I recognize Walter, met at a talk on French literature that I gave in 1927 at Leopold Averbakh's* in Moscow in the Kremlin, I think. He later came to see me with Brunn (Ilk)[13] and a third (Reiss) in Leningrad. All three of them were leaving on missions. We drank good wine and gaily founded the Society of Future Political Prisoners. Brunn Ilk had been my friend in Austria—our vacations on the banks of the Wörthersee, in Mariawörth beneath the Karawanken Mountains. He later headed the secret service in Yugoslavia—where he was imprisoned—in Hungary, and in France. He tells me that Bernard Lecache* was one of his agents. Was decorated with the Order of Lenin.

13. Serge presents Berthold Umansky (alias "Brunn") and his brother Mikhail (alias "Ilk"), childhood friends of Reiss become Soviet spies, as the same person.

Sympathized with the Opposition, had the courage to come see me in Leningrad after my expulsion from the party and my first imprisonment in 1928. On behalf of Trilisser, head of the secret service, had offered me the post of adviser to Chiang So Lin in Manchuria. I refused, saying that I didn't want to belong to a state organization called on to play what would probably be a calamitous role in the repression (1925–26). Elsa enlightens me about his end. Put in charge of negotiating with nationalist officers in Germany, he delegated Kippenberger,* one of the most dedicated German communists, to meet with General von Bredow.* In Moscow, after Zinoviev's execution, in charge of preparing the judicial investigation for Kippen's secret trial, declared him innocent and refused to pursue the case. Sent on leave to a rest home in the Caucasus and soon executed with his wife. Cases like this occur one after the other.

The discussion with Krivitsky is stormy. He admits that he knew of the preparations for Reiss's assassination and attempted in vain to warn R. during his stay in Paris. He couldn't talk on the telephone but he called the hotel nonstop and when R. answered "Hello" he hung up. R. had to have understood. At a café at the World's Fair he had participated in a meeting called by the special envoy from Moscow, where the execution was decided on. He avoided taking on a specific task. He claims to have saved Elsa, whose disappearance he was ordered to organize. He says to Sneevliet: "I have an agent in your party, but I don't remember his name. He saw you in such-and-such a month, went to your house, you saw him in your office..." S. explodes: "Bastard! Miserable wretch! You know all the names! I don't believe in memory lapses. The name!" K. gently shakes his head. "I don't know. There are too many names." He also says: "There are so many agents circling around you that I find it extraordinary to be safe among the five of you." His face is gray, wrinkled, calm; his profile puts me in mind of a fish. We decide to assist him, to attempt to legalize his situation in France. He doesn't want to make a public declaration.

"I'm not going over to the Opposition: I consider its politics utopian. Despite all its crimes the USSR remains the great power for progress. I won't betray it in any way. It's just that I no longer want to participate in crimes. I won't give any information to French authorities. I almost left for Moscow, knowing that I'd be executed. It was at the train station that I made the decision not to return, and an hour later I called you.

Those who carried it out:

Gertrude Schildbach, German communist, born in 1894.

Roland Abbiate,* alias François Rossi, from Monaco, 1899.

Étienne-Charles Martignat, French, 1900, "little fat man with his head sunk into his shoulders."

They probably fled to Mexico.

Renée Steiner,* subagent of Basteitch, rented the car and participated in the tailing. Swiss communist (1908). Schoolteacher.

Sergei Efron,* Russian émigré journalist; Semirenski, agent sent from Moscow; Pierre-Louis Ducomet,* photographer; "Michel," "Leo," "André," "Rossi" tailed him, etc. Pierre Schwartzenberg,* Russian émigré.

Gave the orders and organized the crime:

Spiegelglass,* Moscow's special envoy.

Grozovsky and his wife Grozovskaya, Lydia, functionary of the Soviet commercial mission in Paris. Bieletski, functionary of the same mission.

These functionaries, protected by diplomatic immunity, returned to Russia. Grozovskaya, freed on parole, disappeared.

The execution order had been submitted to Stalin and came from him.

Related facts. Knepigin, White Russian, kept a secret lodging house in the suburbs for agents on mission. Vadim Kondratiev* (White Russian) participated in the tailing.

Dmitri Semirenski kept a particular eye on Leon Sedov. He lived next door to him, 28 rue Lacretelle—Sedov at number 26. Ducomet, Sergei Efron, Schwartzenberg, Renée Steiner were assigned to Sedov.

"André" and "Michel"—not identified—were assigned to me. Acquainted with J. Prévost,* whom I frequently saw. (They organized his trip to Moscow and her affiliation with the Service, which she confessed to me.)

(Renée Steiner, Ducomet, Semirenski spent a certain amount of time in prison.)

Basteitch, Mustafa, and several others, later recalled to Russia, were expelled from the Yugoslavian Communist Party and disappeared. News of their expulsion was published.

AGABEKOV

February 20, 1938—In 1935 (I think) Agabekov* published a book[14] that is a truly extraordinary example of treason and betrayal. A high-level functionary of the NKVD secret service in the East, he ratted out all his agents and informers in Persia, Greece, Egypt, and Turkey. Professors, members of Parliament, ecclesiastics, postal employees...

(N. V.) knew him and drew me a detailed portrait.

Rather ugly, Oriental—Turkish—features, Agabekov appeared one day at the offices of *Poslednye novosti*,[15] bringing with him a prepared statement breaking from the USSR, which was published. Feared being killed at every street corner. The next day at five o'clock when he came to the editorial offices, two French inspectors were waiting for him to take him to Intelligence at the prefecture. He turned pale, begged someone to accompany him. Well received by M. Pasquier, he regained confidence. Observed that the curtains in the office reminded him of those in Trilisser's office in Moscow. Interrogated, he answered willingly, and what he said made their hair stand on end. The French naval attaché in Istanbul was his agent. All of the Egyptian diplomatic mail was read by his subordinates... etc. They promised him a document regularizing his situation while taking him, temporarily, to the Belgian border. He made the trip in a state of fear. This expulsion was made at the behest of F. P. B., probably a longtime secret agent, since the Kutepov* Affair. (I no longer remember who F. P. B. is.)

His motives: he'd fallen for an English girl in Istanbul who gave him English lessons. Had revealed his profession to her, taking an oath to renounce it. She followed him to Paris. They married in Brussels.

14. Agabekov actually published his *OGPU, the Russian Secret Terror*, in 1931 in New York.
15. White Russian newspaper published in Paris by the Cadet leader Miliukov from 1920 to 1940.

Remark: "I bought men the way they buy carpets."

At the Arts-et-Métiers intersection he suddenly asks the Russian journalist who is accompanying him: "How do you manage to live on a volcano without realizing it?"

Response: "This will go on for some time, you'll see."

Said he sympathized with the Opposition in 1923 until Zinoviev came to speak against Trotskyism to the personnel of the political police. A minority of 40 percent held firm, "but deep down, we were all sympathizers."

Head of the secret service for the Orient, lived in Istanbul as a merchant with an Iranian identity, well established, with a considerable bank account. Upon fleeing kept only 1,000 pounds sterling, which he considered due him. An attempt was made to kidnap him in Costanza, a man was killed, he had the GPU agents arrested.

In Romania he exploited the Siguranza by betraying secret services which he himself organized. Having made contact in Brussels with émigré Russians of the "Eurasian" group, ready to render services, he hired them for the USSR through the intermediary of a certain Dumbadze.* Sent one of them to Romania with detailed instructions. At the same time informed the Siguranza of the arrival of a secret agent. Informed Prague of his passage. Passed on copies of the reports he received. The "agent" escaped, but Agabekov was paid about 100,000 lei. Old Bourtsev,* having unraveled this plot, indignantly declared: "That adventurer fabricated an entire GPU!" Said cynically: "Why bother to put on kid gloves with the Siguranza?"

Lives comfortably in Brussels, adores his wife, speculates on the stock exchange.

PURGES IN MOSCOW

June 1938—We're at the Café de la Rotonde. He's an Italian with a massive and sad face who has just arrived from Russia; a Communist refugee living in Moscow, expelled from the Party and deported from the country. Doesn't belong to the Opposition. "All of the foreign refugees," he says, "were filtered by the NKVD. Many have disappeared, a certain number of Italians obtained authorization to leave without an authorization to return." He tells me of the terror, the night arrests, the disappearances that no one dares speak about, even among friends. He speaks softly and admits that, from fear, he hesitated before asking me for a meeting.

I note the disappearances he's aware of:

Weitz of Foreign Trade—Natalia Sats* of the children's theater, who is said to have been executed—Khalepski of Post and Telegraphs—Yakovlev, Agriculture, one of the leaders of the collectivization, member—I think—of the Politburo. —Sulimov,* president of the Council of People's Commissars of the RSFSR (this is old news to me, but he says most likely executed)—Bubnov*—Krylenko*—Akulov,* an honest man who had succeeded Yenukidze* (executed) at the secretariat of the VTSIK—Tal, ultraconformist historian of the Red Army—Rukhimov or Rukhimovitch—(several names have become undecipherable).

From the Commissariat of Foreign Trade (Rosengoltz,* executed after the third Moscow Trial): the Old Bolshevik Eliava, Kandelaki (who, being in Berlin, was charged by S. with secretly negotiating with Hitler), Frederiksohn, Vice People's Commissar Soudin.

The inventor of the great ANT planes, director of the institute of aviation research TSAGHI[16] Tupolev,[17] was executed along with his wife—Also executed was Wisner, Molotov's secretary.

Disappeared: Aytov, the family of Boudou Mdivani,* wife and two or three children (Mdivani must have been executed), Yevgeny Alexeivich Preobrazhensky,* very likely executed; his wife, Paulina Vinogradova, simulates insanity and the doctors are attempting to protect her in a clinic. One evening Preobrazhensky was dragged from his bed and taken somewhere in a car. He returned, recounted that he was sure he was going to his execution, was surprised when all they wanted was his signature on an anti-Trotskyist article written in advance ... "So much trouble just to sign a piece of crap that everyone knows is a piece of crap," he said.

16. TSAGHI: Central Institute of Aerohydrodynamics.
17. Contrary to what Serge wrote, though Tupolev was arrested in 1937, he wasn't executed and was released in 1944.

Nazarenus, former ambassador to Ankara (I met him in Leningrad at Yonov's* house) said to have died a suspicious death.

Otello Gaggi's* wife doesn't know what became of him in deportation. The NKVD refuses to answer her.

Luigi Calligaris,* deported for three years, was administratively condemned to five additional years of deportation. He was at Bukhta Nogaeva, from which he was kidnapped. Destination unknown.

The intellectuals of the liberal group Smena Viekh, who rallied in 1923–24, Duchêne, Kirdetsov,* Lukanov,* were deported to the region of Ineniseisk.

Disappeared: Uritsky,* Petrovsky,* commander of the "Proletarian Division."

The cellars of big railroad stations are full of prisoners. There are entire trains on the side rails, surrounded by barbed wire that are prison trains. Two hundred railroad cars full of prisoners at the October Station in Moscow. —Moscow is suffering a shortage of butter and meat, and rumors hint that it's because of food supplies being sent to Spain. —All forces are preparing for war.

ROSSI

July 1938—At the editorial office of *Le Populaire*[18] after the announcement of the trial of the POUM: Magdeleine Paz, Angelo Tasca* (Rossi). Heated discussion: neither willing nor able to do anything. M. P. full of good will, indignation, but feels weak. The editorial board isn't informed, is hostile to the extreme left, several influential editors don't want to get involved, even indirectly, in a fight against the Communists.

Rossi, agitated and discouraged, attacks me:

"We bet too heavily on moral strength. They can lie, kill, pile deceit on deceit and still be right against us in front of the working class. Look at that old bastard Cachin*: how many turpitudes and still he's applauded! After years of turpitudes their party is stronger than ours."

18. Newspaper of the French Socialist Party.

Me: Everything will be set right one day.

(What do I know?)

Rossi: Yes, and it's perhaps the two of us who will pay the price for the settling of accounts.

Conclusion: One crime more or less in Spain, what's the difference? Burn out. Don't disturb people from whom little can be gotten. Profound discouragement of R., a result of his experience at the Comintern.

Magdeleine Paz is going to ask writers for signatures. We'll try to insert a notice in *Le Populaire*.

The lives of a team of comrades are at stake.

ANTON CILIGA

July 19, 1938—Saw Ciliga* again, whom I had thought lost: the imprudence of going to Yugoslavia. He's back from Belgrade, saved by his Italian passport and his reputation as a writer. —Tall, gangly, pale, glasses, light brown hair, the air of a perpetual student beginning to grow old.

Portrait of Yugoslavia: Italian and German Nazi-fascists in power. The Slavophile elements—even the reactionaries—are pro-Soviet and Francophile. The Communists, influential and persecuted, organized demonstrations in support of Yvon Delbos.[19]

Arrested, A. C. demanded the right to communicate with a lawyer. The director of the Belgrade prison answered: "Consider yourself lucky that we didn't kick in your kidneys. Here Communists don't have lawyers."

They demanded he make false confessions related to "the Moscow Plot."

The Yugoslav Communists he knew in Russia and who are imprisoned in Yugoslavia revealed everything about the activities of the party and the Comintern. The authorities know everything. (Probably broken by torture.)

19. Chief of French diplomacy during the Popular Front from June 1936 to March 1938.

Something seen: in a corridor a man who'd suffered the bastinado, bathing his feet in a water bucket. Gendarmes helping him stand.

The prison director threatened A. C. with having his ribs broken and his kidneys smashed with truncheons. You die quickly after that and a moderate sentence of three years. "*I gatov tchelovietchik!*" (The bugger's done for!)

A. C.'s attitude:

"I'm a politician and not an informer.

"If you kill me, it'll make some noise. In any case, I'm Italian.

"I wouldn't tell you anything if you kept me sixty years instead of sixty days.

"If you put me on trial, I'll say that you tried to dictate false confessions to me." Freed.

He's working on theoretical problems, leaning toward an original form of libertarian syndicalism.

KLEMENT AFFAIR—KRIVITSKY

July 20, 1938—Rudolf Klement* (Adolphe) kidnapped from his home. Gérard Rosenthal writes me: "His meal was ready on the table; nothing was touched."

I meet with Walter (Krivitsky) at the Café Madrid on the boulevard Montmartre. He's nervous, gray, wrinkled, wary, looks worriedly at the people around us. Feels he's being tailed, takes fright at everything. I ask him about the Klement Affair. He doesn't see anything. "The GPU, for sure, but I don't see anything...."

W. K.: Are you sure that Klement hadn't always been part of "our service"? Since Trotsky persists in trying to organize an organization for which history provides no basis, then "we" are the ones—in reality—who should be organizing it...

He speaks of the secret service as if he were still a member of it: "We."

I answer that I knew Klement well enough in Brussels to be reasonably convinced of his probity. Sectarian and dedicated.

W. K. (mockingly): Reasonably! You're being naive. If he was truly influential then he must have been an agent, otherwise the job was poorly done.

"Well, then I think the job was poorly done."

He relaxes and tells me they're looking for him: "In the end they'll find me...." Laments his wife's nervousness.

"If they had only listened to me in 1923, today 'we' would have Goering and be the masters of Germany. We—the secret agents in Germany—met together after the failure of the insurrection. We didn't believe the tiny Nazi Party had any future: simplistic Marxism. I said: 'Anything is possible. In any case one of the leaders of the party has to belong to us.' I proposed putting in that position a man we could count on, a former officer, decorated and everything. An amazing man. He would quickly have become one of the top Nazi leaders ... he was assigned elsewhere."

Me: "But there are others in the Nazi party?"

W. K.: "Obviously, but not in the front ranks. Goering isn't one of ours.... My man would have occupied Goering's place; he was much stronger."

Demoralized, egocentric, full of petty professional deformations, terribly sad, W. K. believes only in the omnipotence of the secret service and is dominated by fear of assassination.

Returning to the subject of the Fourth International, W. K. tells me about the "Trust," that organization of White counterrevolutionary officers set up abroad and in Moscow in 1922–1923. The GPU executed everyone, including the organizer, his agent, "for having used methods of police provocation."

PROVOCATION AMONG THE WHITES

July 1938—I summarize several discussions with N. V., editor of *Poslednye novosti*, who knows the White-monarchist milieu quite well. (He himself is a liberal, a friend of Miliukov.) "The Whites were destroyed by *provocation* [double agents]" he says.

1922–1923: the affair of the "Trust"—an organization of former monarchist officers, set up overseas and with branches in Russia, particularly in Moscow (about two hundred people?). Organized by Agranov* and Yanichev (?). All of them executed, including Yanichev ("*provo-cateur*"). But Agranov later made a fine career persecuting the Opposition. Probably disappeared since, with Yagoda.

The terrorist organization of Larionov, Schulze (a young woman), and Opperput carried out several attacks in Moscow near the GPU (Kuznetsky), the other in Leningrad in the spring of 1927, at the party's club on the Moika.[20] Several of my friends were present: Abram Moissevich Feinstein, Menshevik pedagogue, who picked up the bomb and tried to throw it out the window, was riddled with shards. "My new suit looks like moths had devoured it," he later told me: Grigori Yakovlevich Yakovin* (Trotskyist) organized the rescue. Old Posern had hid himself under a table. Larionov took credit for the attack (monarchist militant, refugee in Paris). According to an official communiqué Opperput and Schulze were killed while attempting to cross the border. But in Orenburg Helena Vladimirovna Tchistosserdova, the wife of the deported Socialist-Revolutionary, told me long after the event of her idyll with Opperput, who in 1927 was in the cell next to hers at the Lubyanka Prison. He was young, handsome, thin, and in rags; she sometimes met him in the corridor and carried on a lyrical correspondence.

During the same period the old Russian monarchist leader Vasily Shulgin,* former editor of the *Kievlainin*, fighter in the White Army, one of the leaders of the emigration, a sincere man graced with great talent as a writer, was used by the secret service, which organized his trip to Russia, followed him step by step, and assisted him in preparing his book *Three Capitals*—on a whole favorable to the new Russia. Most of the people he visited in the USSR over the course of his clandestine visit were executed (the Affair of the Dietskoye Selo High School Students in Leningrad?). This was the end of attempts at counterrevolutionary organizing in Russia.

In 1924 Boris Savinkov* was also lured to Russia and arrested (but he suspected *provocation* and greeted it without surprise, his secretary—who had been arrested along with him—told me one day.

20. The Moika is a tributary of the Neva and runs through the center of Saint Petersburg.

In 1930 (?)[21] the hetman Annenkov* and General Denisov, refugees in China, turned themselves in to Moscow as prisoners—and were executed. Same backstage maneuvers.

Same backstage maneuvers in the Slastchev* Affair (Constantinople, 1920–1921).

The recent crime in Sofia: A bomb taken to the editorial offices of the newspaper edited by one of the Solonevich* brothers. The S. brothers had done time on the Solovietski Islands.[22] Escaped from Russia, they became extremely active monarchists. The bomb killed the secretary and Tamara Solonevich, the editor's wife. The investigation revealed that Tamara S. had been an agent provocateur for years. A student, sent to Russia, she met S. in Berlin; it's possible she was sent specifically to meet him. One assumes she was broken (Gestapo?) or cut herself off from the Service, or perished in an internal settling of accounts following the destruction of the cadres formed by Yagoda. (Spring 1938.)

General Skoblin* and his wife, the chanteuse Plevitskaya,* who participated in the kidnapping of General Miller*—secret agents. If Miller hadn't taken the precaution of leaving a note saying that he was going to a suspicious appointment organized by Skoblin, the latter would have succeeded him and the secret service would have been in charge of the White organization. (Skoblin disappeared, his wife was arrested in 1938). —Walter Krivitsky provided the two men who carried out this kidnapping in the heart of Paris. One of the two may have been a former Austrian officer turned Communist named Nebenführer who was decorated and then executed in Moscow. No witnesses. (Putting the pieces together.)

General Abramov* (Sofia), originally chosen to succeed Miller, refused. He had just learned that his son was an agent provocateur.

It's all but certain that Skoblin participated in the kidnapping of General Kutepov, Paris, 1926–1927. (During that period an agent from Leningrad bragged—being drunk—of having worked on that affair. Can't recall his name, he lived at the Astoria, First House of the Soviets.)

21. Actually, 1936.
22. Used by the Soviets as a concentration camp.

TWO ENCOUNTERS[23]

I only met Parijanine* twice in life, two unforgettable times. Year III
of the Russian Revolution (1920): I was living at the Hotel Astoria in
Leningrad, First House of the Soviets, two floors above Zinoviev.
Yevdokimov* and Bakayev* were my neighbors . . . Memory of a peaceful companion, straightaway you take me back among the shades of
great men, now shot! But such were our encounters, their only importance human; such are our times; and such are we, that in thinking of
you I see, I feel the nearness of the dead and the living; and that history
is carrying us away; history, which is made through all of us, inexorably, whatever our slight differences . . . We were well guarded and discreetly watched. The chief of the guard post telephoned to tell me that
a Frenchman with a letter from Guilbeaux* was asking to see me. A
few moments later I opened the door of my room to a misshapen being
who cast upon me the gentle gaze of a timid, mischievous man. He
appeared to be walking with difficulty, but this only looked to be the
case. I see him again advancing across the dark red carpet, holding out
a letter, explaining to me that he was returning to France—penniless,
of course—that Guilbeaux had led him to hope I might find work for
him at the French Section of the executive of the Third International . . .
And work was something I had plenty of! For Lenin, for Zinoviev, for
Trotsky, for the International, whose sole effective weapon around the
world was agitation, there were texts to be translated, revised, edited,
corrected, printed, distributed a hundred different ways, transported
across enemy Finland and Estonia or via Murmansk, the Arctic Ocean,
the tiny northern ports of Norway . . . I employed the most disparate
personnel, demanding of them nothing but the knowledge of languages
and a strict minimum of punctuality. Mme. de Pfehl, who in the past
had been received at the court (". . . and I can tell you, comrade, that
the Emperor was very good to me, for he was an excellent man who
loved the people . . .") routinely translated for me the messages of the
president of the Communist International to the world proletariat.

23. Serge's memorial article for his friend Maurice [Donzel] (1885–1938) appeared in
Les Humbles in 1938. Writer and translator (notably of works by Trotsky), he went
under the name *"Parijanine"* (Russian for "The Parisian").

M. Constantin P., former editor of the semiofficial *Saint Petersburg Gazette*, touched up the style, which at times resembled that of the Comtesse de Ségur, *née* Rostopchin. M. Bak,[24] ex-businessman, ex-journalist of a mine owner's association of the empire, a small, terribly pinched, and reticent gentleman with a hairless mask, agreed to translate theoretical articles, but not revolutionary appeals. "Forgive me, citizen," he would say, "but my conscience . . ." Naturally, I respected his conscience.

I had only the time to see faces, to chat, to dream, to understand men in haste. We didn't really hit it off, Parij and I. "Communist?" I immediately asked him. "No, not exactly. A sympathizer. . . ." And this sympathizer was leaving the country of the revolution in the middle of the Civil War, in the middle of the blockade, in the middle of the famine, in the middle of the terror? This didn't please me, but it was his business. In any case, he spoke perfect French, the French of an educated person, and knew Russian perfectly. It must have been in June: We were preparing the Second World Congress of the Communist International and I'd just received a massive manuscript from Trotsky. I entrusted half of it to Parij. I thought he flinched slightly when he saw the title of the book: *Terrorism and Communism*. Subtitle: *Anti-Kautsky*.

"Does that upset you?" I asked with a hint of irony. "No," he softly said, "not any more than does terror." I've remembered this phrase, or one like it, lit up by a firm and reserved gaze. We had to work quickly, very quickly. Trotsky had just dictated the book to his secretaries over the course of his perpetual travels, in the headquarters train that had taken him from one front to another over the past two years, across the devastated countryside prey to epidemics, to attacks by bands, to peasant uprisings, fought over by red, white, blue, and gold (Ukrainian), black, and green flags. The white nights stretched over the city a great, bright dusk of an infinite, poignant, and exhausting charm. We

---

24. This unidentified individual also appears in Serge's *Memoirs*: "Executed, a law-yer named Bak to whom I entrusted translations and who didn't hide his counter-revolutionary opinions from me."

passed more than one reader bent over the text of the *Anti-Kautsky*.[25]
I imagine Parij in his room in the International Hotel, beneath that
wan light, with his scruples of a grammarian, poet, and storyteller
putting the finishing touches to this text full of fierce power, to this
book of a victorious civil war. Since that time I think the International
Hotel has recovered its old name of the Hotel d'Angleterre. It's quite
possible that Parij occupied the same room where six years later a
completely different poet he loved, Sergei Yesenin, wrote his final verses
with a rusty pen dipped in a few drops of blood before hanging himself... In these same rooms I knew others of the departed: Raymond
Lefebvre, Lepetit, Vergeat, Sasha Toubin.[26] Dead men on top of
dead men.

For me, the memory of Parijanine is tied to that book, to that era.
The book was recently reissued under an incorrect title: *In Defense
of Terrorism*. In it Trotsky in no way defends what is currently understood as terrorism, but rather demonstrates the working class's absolute
need, in those revolutionary periods where it must either win or die,
to show itself strong and capable of using all the harshness of war...
In it he refutes Karl Kautsky's criticisms of Bolshevism in the name of
a democratic socialism that refused to accept any form of dictatorship,
even of the proletariat, even its own. In it he refutes Austro-Marxism,
the doctrine of the great Viennese socialists Karl Renner, Friedrich
Adler,* Max Adler, and Otto Bauer. At that time Kautsky was more
or less the ideologist of the Weimar Republic, the broadest democracy
there has ever been, though it was cemented with the blood of Liebknecht, Rosa Luxemburg, and the Spartacist workers. The Austrian
Marxists thought they were holding open the future by avoiding
taking power at the price of a difficult and dangerous battle. They
legislated for the working class with wisdom, prudence, and subtlety.
In Vienna they would construct the most beautiful working-class

25. Published in 1920.
26. The French delegates named here disappeared in the Atlantic Ocean while returning from the congress. In his *Memoirs* Serge concluded: "They disappeared in
the sea. It's possible they were swallowed up by a storm. It's possible a Finnish boat
met and shot them."

housing in the world, the wealthiest cooperatives, the best-designed swimming pools, the shiniest village halls ... Dead men piled on dead men. The Weimar Republic is dead, socialist Vienna is dead, Karl Kautsky has just died in exile in Amsterdam, Otto Bauer just died in exile in Paris, ravaged by the sentiment of defeat; the Third International has been shot by a thousand bullets in the back of the neck ... But it must be said that with all these deaths and defeats, the ideas contained in this 1920 book remain powerfully, prophetically alive (and several of the objections made to it by the Mensheviks, attached to the defense of worker's democracy within the revolution, take on a new force: this debate is in no way settled).

Once he completed the book, Parij took the train to Finland. I took the train to Moscow. I traveled with Angel Pestaña* of the CNT (died last year); in the dining car we met Frossard* and Marcel Cachin ... The Second Moscow Congress had established the twenty-one conditions for membership in the CI. It addressed an appeal to the anarchists. It discussed Lenin's theses on the colonial question, combated by Serrati* (dead men piled on dead men ...). Lenin, smiling and jovial, passed among us in the old, well-brushed jacket of his émigré days. Under the gilded wainscoting of one of the throne rooms of the Kremlin, Zinoviev, presiding over the session, shook his floppy mane. The throne had been relegated to the antechamber where the typists had installed their machines. A few steps from the throne and the Remingtons, a map, pinned over the wall hangings, held the attention of groups of commentators. Lenin, Radek, and Zinoviev stopped in front of it along with the foreigners, their eyes following the advance of tiny red flags that Tukhachevsky was driving toward Warsaw—in order to tear up the Versailles Treaty, create a soviet Poland, a socialist Germany tomorrow, and soon a United States of Europe. In our briefcases we all had Tukhachevksy's theses on the Red Army in service to the International. One evening a dispatch from Kharkov spread the rumor that Tukhachevsky, Rakovsky,* and Smilga* had entered Warsaw ...

I lost sight of Parijanine only to find him again through correspondence a few years later. We translated together *Against the Current*, Lenin and Zinoviev's wartime work.

I was living now in Berlin, now in Vienna. Crises were tearing the

International apart following the failed or defeated revolutions in Germany and Bulgaria. Lenin's succession being open, Zinoviev and Kamenev invented "Trotskyism" in order to refute it; and in their shadow there grew, still silent, the figure of Stalin, unknown not only to the masses, but also to the old cadres of the party and the International. Intrigue and conformism infiltrated the gears of the International. At the height of an obscure battle against Trotskyism Parij and I agreed, he in Paris, I in Vienna, to translate the admirable and heretical book Trotsky had just written about Lenin. We avoided signing this work, published by Hasfeld.* Parij was on the right side, I mean on the side of intelligence and historical good faith.

Years passed. Dark years, years growing darker and darker. The face of the Revolution, eaten away by incurable internal illnesses, was changing. It had become nothing but persecutions, ever-growing proscriptions, and the extirpation of heresy. People stopped thinking, stopped speaking; poets recited hexameters calling for the death penalty, today for engineers, tomorrow for economists, the day after for old socialists. The USSR became the largest prison in the world ... For me, this went on for ten years. In 1936, in Brussels, Wullens* brought me greetings from Parij. Things weren't going well for him, not in the least well ... He'd almost cashed in his chips, and there was something not very clear about his sudden illness. Was he beginning to be fed up with it all?

I would see him again after seventeen years, in 1937, in a small hotel in Ivry, one of those small hotels where frightened couples, frightening couples, émigrés, people without families, the unemployed whose lodging is paid for by town hall, beings abandoned by all, abandoned by themselves, live from week to week. Sleep merchant of the end of the night, banal and almost comfortable ... Parij opened his door to us: thickened, his eyelids heavy, a bit confused, since he received few visits. The wallpaper was the color of poverty, there were books on a minuscule table, manuscripts scattered on the bed, a bottle of cheap wine at the foot of the bed. He breathed defeat, disgust with life, and solitude. What is left to be done? And what's the use? When you're neither an arriviste, a clown, nor a hustler able to extract hundred- and thousand-franc notes from publishers financed by the real bastards;

when you've definitively taken seriously the ideas, landscapes, and faces worthy of being believed, worthy of being loved, there comes a time during periods of reaction when you ask yourself what's the use, what's the interest in continuing this game of life that's become dismal and a little sickening? Parij, getting by on his unemployment benefits, was still writing short stories and poems. Duhamel had just published a few of his poems in the *Mercure de France*. I believe that was his final satisfaction as what is called an *homme de lettres*... Along with Wullens, in that room where he passed his final days, we spoke of Moscow, of the Revolution, of the twenty years that were charged with more hope and suffering than any time in the past few centuries; of former camaraderie, of friendships that fell apart, of abandonments, of verbal pirouettes, of executions, and of our own friendship that had been formed across time, distance, mistrust, and misunderstandings, yet was dense and solid with its great weight of sadness (and there was certainly reason for this). It was pleasant, and even a little miraculous, to be together like this after so many years, so many shipwrecks, so much chicanery...We repeated this in the bistro over our meal, and there were moments when there shone in Parij's eyes a mischievous youthful glimmer. He made a few sarcastic remarks and spoke of projects, without believing in them of course. We were supposed to meet again but never did. He died in his unemployed man's bed, in the shadow of poverty-colored wallpaper; alone, tired of many things, but along with a few others, faithful to something essential.

BRANDLER (DZERZHINSKY, STALIN, SEMYONOV)

December 1938—We meet in the cafés on the boulevard Montparnasse. On his big head a small black beret with its brim turned up like a comical judge's bonnet. His torso is thick on short legs tilted to one side. He's deformed like a hunchback, though not a hunchback. Lots of mischief in his gaze, an ironic and familiar tone. He likes Laurette [Séjourné*]. "There are still beautiful women among us!" he says with satisfaction. "I thought that emigrations are fated to be cursed with not having any."

The policy of his group, the KPO,[27] is still reticent and prudent regarding the USSR. Brandler* seems not to have given up hope that the regime will set itself aright, or wants to treat it with kid gloves despite it all, or for demagogic reasons doesn't want to upset the masses who believe in it. But I'm fierce on this subject and he doesn't push the discussion. Bukharin's execution upset him, putting an end, perhaps, to his final illusions.

We prefer to speak of our memories. In Moscow, during the underground period, we used to meet at the Hotel Lux,[28] at Laurat's* or Duret's* with Engler* (Thalheimer* was present)... Laurat's wife was a police informer...

On Dzerzhinsky*: "I once had dinner in Kharkov with Dzerzhinsky and K. Radek. Dzerzhinsky said that during the Red Terror he sometimes resorted to a subterfuge that consisted in publishing news of executions that hadn't occurred. The effect was produced and lives were saved... Dz. said: 'We Chekists are part saint, part assassin.' Radek asked him abruptly, 'And you, what do you think you are? A saint or a bandit?' Dz. blanched, clenched his lips, got up from the table, and left."

On Stalin: "I had several cordial discussions with him concerning German Party matters. He was simple, at times jovial, friendly, full of common sense, of practical sense and peasant craftiness. Rather nice, inspiring confidence. A good-natured fellow who seemed to be well balanced. I can't understand these hecatombs... He must have lost his head."

Brandler thinks that in the Reiss Affair, as in the crimes in Barcelona, one can see the hand of Semyonov—that Socialist-Revolutionary terrorist who distinguished himself during the Civil War planning terrorist attacks against the Bolsheviks. He confessed everything at the 1922 trial of the Socialist-Revolutionaries and then went over to the service of the CP and was charged with special—very special— missions. "He must be a sadist, a terrorist by vocation, half crazy yet

27. Communist Party of Germany (opposition).
28. Moscow hotel where foreign communist delegations were lodged.

systematic." Easy to identify: a torn-off earlobe and a scar below it, the trace of a bullet. "He was in Spain. During interrogations comrades had noted a man with these scars, but sometimes on the left, sometimes on the right cheek, they said, and I'm not even sure which one it is."

(I'm told by N. [Boris Nikolaevski] that on December 6 or 7, 1937, a Soviet military attaché in Paris named Semenov or Semyonov requested the protection of the French authorities. He is thought to have acted after having learned from Barmine's* revelations of the disappearance of his friend Fechner. I don't know if it's the same Semyonov (I don't think so).)

MY BREAK WITH TROTSKY

1939—In late July 1936 Muste,* delegated by the bureau for the Fourth International that set up in the United States, came to see me in Brussels and on behalf of Leon Davidovich [Trotsky] proposed that I be co-opted into the bureau. Muste was an ex-minister, thin, austere, graying, with the look of a Puritan. (Later, shocked by the Moscow Trials, he left the movement and I'm told returned to his church.)

Around this time I was corresponding with Trotsky on the subject of the Spanish anarchists, who, according to Leon Sedov [Trotsky]* were "destined to stab the revolution in the back." I thought they'd play a pivotal role in the Civil War and advised Trotsky and the Fourth International to publish a declaration in sympathy with them, in which the Marxist-revolutionaries would commit to fighting for freedom. L. D. agreed with me, promised me it would be done, but nothing was done about it.

In January 1937 I participated in an international conference of the Fourth International in Amsterdam. The conference was held in Sneevliet's house in Overtoom, which had a comfortable meeting hall in the attic. The Trotskyists were already directing all their fire at the POUM. I took the floor to justify the POUM's participation in the Generalitat's government in Catalonia, based on the need to monitor and influence the government from within and to facilitate the arming of the masses. Along with Vereecken* and Sneevliet I proposed a motion of solidarity with the POUM, which concluded by urging the Spanish militants to maintain the unity of their party. Pierre Naville, Gérard Rosenthal, and Rudolf Klement spoke against this. It became obvious that while addressing diplomatic compliments to the POUM they were plotting to split it. Two Englishman who had come to Amsterdam told me that the movement for the Fourth International counted less than 100 members in England, and as in France, was divided into two rival organizations.

I returned from Amsterdam saddened and dismayed: the impression of a sectarian movement controlled by maneuvers from above, suffering from all the mental depravities we'd fought against in Russia: authoritarianism, factionalism, intrigues, maneuvers, narrow-mindedness, and intolerance. Sneevliet and his party had had enough, finding the atmosphere unbreathable. They were honest and ponderous Dutch proletarians, used to fraternal mores. Vereecken, who adored the Old Man, said to me, "I give you less than six months before you break with him. He doesn't put up with any objections."

Our disagreements grew increasingly numerous, but the Old Man's letters were affectionate—and I admired him beyond measure. When he wrote about the strikes of June 1936 that "the French revolution has begun" I responded: "Not at all. It's just the beginning of the French working class's recovery." I advised him not to constantly intervene as he was doing in the internal affairs of every single group, no matter how small, and to limit himself to grand intellectual labors. Finally, I wrote to him:

"An International can't be founded without parties.... No party can be founded based on such bad political morals and with a Russian ideological language no one understands." He responded: "You are an enemy who wants to be treated as a friend."

The "Bolshevik-Leninist" movement in France, composed of a few dozen militants and at most a few hundred sympathizers, employed an unintelligible jargon in its publications. It was divided into two minuscule "parties," the Internationalist Workers Party (Rous,* Naville, Rosenthal) and the International Communist Party (Molinier,* Frank*) who used most of their time and energy intriguing against each other and wrote entire books mutually denigrating each other. I bitterly reproached them for wasting their resources in this way while no propaganda was being done in support of our prisoners in Russia. I refused to have anything to do with their base squabbles, saying to Rous: "If I was a member of one of your two groups the atmosphere would lead me to immediately resign. You are sick sectarians." (During the Nazi occupation in 1940–1941, Rous attempted to form, along with Jaquier* of the PSOP,[29] a "revolutionary national party" adapted to Nazi taste, but he was arrested). These sordid squabbles, in which L. D. got involved, so poisoned the atmosphere that it rendered any serious investigation into the deaths of Leon Sedov and Klement impossible. At Sedov's funeral two groups showed up with different flags, ostentatiously avoiding any contact with each other.

From 1937 I completely cut myself off from this "movement" and wrote to Sneevliet: "This isn't a beginning, it's an end." But I abstained from any controversy and tried to render any services I could to the militants and to L. D. Ugly stories, like the Trotskyists' attempt to lay hands on funds belonging to the POUM, sickened me (a special commission, made up of Rosmer,* Lazarevich,* and Hasfeld straightened the affair out with great difficulty). The grand and noble movement for which we had given so many lives in Russia degenerated overseas into impotence and sectarianism. I continued to translate the Old Man's books, *The Revolution Betrayed*, *Stalin's Crimes*, *Their Morals and Ours*, and to defend him. In the public's eyes I remained the best known "Trotskyist" writer, while the "Bolshevik-Leninists" were doing their best to discredit me. For them I had become a "petit-bourgeois intellectual" whose "influence" and "dubious sympathy" was to be used. I was outraged by *Their Morals* for its assumption of possessing the truth, its intolerance and aggressiveness devoid of critical sense, though at the end of the essay there are some fine and moving pages. I said as much to some Trotskyists, who wrote about it to the Old Man, and this immediately earned me some sharp attacks. What was saddest about them was that they were always insulting and always based on incorrect information. It would have been so simple to say that we are in disagreement on this and that point, but the Old Man and his supporters had become completely incapable of speaking in such forthright language.

29. Parti Socialiste Ouvrier Paysan, independent left socialist party led by Marceau Pivert.

The terrifying atmosphere of persecution in which they—and I—lived inclined them to persecution mania and to the exercise of persecution.

TROTSKY'S ASSASSINATION (BASED ON AMERICAN NEWSPAPER ACCOUNTS)

Marseille, August 1940—On May 24, several automobiles brought a large group of armed men to Trotsky's residence; they succeeded in getting through the protective wall of the garden through a door that was opened to them and opened fire with machine guns at the window of the bedroom where Leon Davidovich was lying. The investigation established that twenty-one people had participated in this attack mounted by Mexican communists or by the Communist Party, but it was impossible to arrest the culprits.

In late July or early August Trotsky expressed the opinion to visiting journalists that a new attack against him would probably be committed when the offensive against Great Britain reached its culmination (the USSR at that point having to prepare itself to confront new risks and complications in Europe).

Serious precautions were taken. The garden was surrounded by high walls and watchtowers; it could only be entered through an armored gate.

On August 20 Frank Jackson,* a comrade who often visited Trotsky, "like a member of the family," arrived at 5:30. He met Leon Davidovich on the patio, not far from the kitchen, and asked if he could consult with him about some work he'd brought with him. Trotsky took him inside. Natalia Ivanovna*[30] was in the dining room that they had to pass through, and Jackson[31] asked her for a glass of water. N. I. offered him a glass of tea, which he refused. He and Leon Davidovich entered his study. Feeling completely confident, L. D. neglected to notify his secretaries—as procedure called for—that he was bringing someone into his study. A moment later sounds of a struggle and violent cries could be heard. Trotsky rushed out of his office, his face covered with

30. Trotsky's wife's first name and patronymic.
31. Note that this pseudonym of Trotsky's assassin was actually spelled "Jacson."

blood. His bodyguards threw themselves on Jackson, who had a pistol in his hand but, stupefied, didn't use it. They grabbed it from him and hit him in the face. Fighting back, he shouted: "They arrested my mother" (this could only be in Russia).

Trotsky, seated at his worktable and bent over a manuscript, had been struck from behind with a pickax whose point had smashed his skull and reached his brain. Nevertheless, he had the strength to fight his assassin, to call for help, to take several steps before falling, and to briefly speak. He said to his secretary, Joseph Hansen*: "Jackson fired on me from behind. I'm gravely wounded. I feel that this time it's the end." Hansen tried to reassure him by telling him that he saw only a superficial wound that couldn't be from a firearm, and that no one had heard a detonation. Trotsky replied, putting his hand over his heart: "No, this time I feel they've succeeded." He told Hansen in the ambulance that was taking him away: "Jackson is a fascist or an agent of the GPU." At the hospital, moments before losing consciousness, he called for Hansen, asked him if he had a notebook, and requested that he write down the following declaration:

"I am about to die from a blow delivered against me in my room by a political assassin. I resisted. He had entered my room to discuss some French statistics. He struck me. Please tell our friends that I am certain of the victory of the Fourth International. Forward!"

Natalia Ivanovna never left his side for an instant during the various procedures attempted by the doctors to save the wounded man's life.

Jackson, the assassin, was treated in a nearby room in the same hospital, under heightened surveillance. The police feared that his accomplices would kill him to prevent him from talking.

Over the course of his initial declarations he said that he struck Trotsky in an access of indignation at the moment when the latter "proposed that he go to the USSR to carry out acts of sabotage." This declaration constitutes one of the signatures on the crime, since in its flagrant absurdity it is in strict conformity with Stalin's directives.

The assassin first declared that his name was Frank Jackson, then that he was Belgian, son of a diplomat, born in Tehran (Iran) and named Van den Dreschd. He also declared that his name was Mornard. It is believed that none of these names is the real one and that, though he speaks French fluently, he is in reality Russian. He was active among the French and American Trotskyists. He was in France in 1936 when Trotsky's secretary Rudolf Klement, whose mutilated (headless) body was found in the Seine in Meulan, was kidnapped in Maisons-Alfort.

Jackson seems to have played an important role in the May 4 attack, after which he went to the United States. The gate had been opened to the attackers by one of Trotsky's guards, Robert Sheldon Harte*; Jackson, who was present, seems to have invited Sheldon Harte to open up. Sheldon Harte, who could have talked, was kidnapped and his body was found a month later under the floorboards of the kitchen on a farm twenty kilometers from there. American, of bourgeois origins, Sheldon Harte was the son of Jesse S. Harte of 2259 Fifth Avenue, New York.

Jackson was introduced to Trotsky's house by a young American woman of Russian origin, Sylvia Agelov,* whose sister Ruth was one of Trotsky's secretaries in 1937. Their father, Samuel Agelov, has a business in Brooklyn, New York. It seems that Sylvia Agelov, who was arrested, had nothing to do with the crime and acted in good faith. She viewed Jackson as a good comrade.

Several "left-wing" Mexican intellectuals, Stalinists and "friends of the USSR," are formally accused by Trotsky's entourage of having openly collaborated with the GPU in the preparation of the crime. James P. Cannon,* secretary of the Socialist Workers Party, openly accuses Stalin of ordering and having the crime carried out.

Mr. Hansen says: "Trotsky knew Jackson for more than six months as a militant familiar with the movement in France and the United States. Not for a single moment did we have the least reason to suspect he was an agent of the GPU."

1941

THE OLD HARBOR

Marseille, winter 1940–1941—Alleys gray during the day, darkened at night, bedecked with washing hung from windows in every direction. Narrow and slimy, stone exuding poverty, lovely old town houses turned lairs with cave-like entryways (sculpted portals on the rue de la Prison). Stench. Pizza places, Greek, Russian, Vietnamese, and Chinese restaurants. On the rue de la Bouterie gloomy bordellos, Black Cat, Magdeleine, Lucy, doors locked against the rush of sailors, notices in several languages. At the bottom of the alley the splendid light of the port, the spindly masts, the distant Notre-Dame de la Garde on the amberhued rock, the blue of the sky.

An Annamite or Chinese procession—funeral? festival?—passes through the rain under banners of cloth and colored paper. Trotting, thin and yellow faces of coolies, shrewd and sad.

One night, total darkness, wet streets, Algerians (Kabyles) in white turbans, khaki uniforms, wander the alleys in groups, seeking light and women, and finding nothing in the light but some sordid, stranded streetwalkers and in the dark a few worn-out, disheveled women, shimmering and pale, starving, who seem to smell of the dampness of the stones and the rot of the garbage. These great wandering devils with sunken eyes.

A harshly illuminated alley, dreadful food, fruits, nuts, crowds. Doors with bead curtains hanging. Swarming brats. Africans stagnating on the edge of the sidewalks.

A lively square, beautiful old houses, baths, the church below the hospital. We enter to see the Easter crèche, with all its tiny figures who work, saw wood, hammer at the forge, etc. For twenty sous the crèche figures start to move.

MARSEILLE

March 24, 1941—Hotel de Rome, the room a total mess. Around 9:00 taxi. Farewell to the streets: Canebière, Cours Saint-Louis, Poste Colbert. You go downstairs[1] and receive a letter from Labin.* The harbor, long wait in front of the fence. Simone Weil, in her loden cape, hunched, long hair, her eyes gray, intelligent, and a bit mad. Daniel Bénédite,* Paul Schmierer,* Consuelo de Saint-Exupéry,* bistro with the Bretons.

Shed 7, Pinède.[2] Enormous, filthy stable. Standing around, long wait, document controls, lines. Your presence, us, confident, sure of ourselves, unaware of the separation. Your courage.

Embarkation. You, Jean Gemähling,* Dina Vierny* on the dock, red flowers in their hands. How lovely, brave, gay you are. Final moments: us in the bows, standing under the wooden construction, your radiant and sad smile, Jean's sad air. Your little blue coat with its squared shoulders that made my heart leap when I lost hope waiting for you at Lilas and you came out of the metro. I gaze through a mist, I clench my teeth. Unforgettable. Saddened. We move away from the high hull of the *Florida*, which separates us.

Happy that Vlady*[3] is here, tall and solid; happy for him that he'll discover the world. I would like to stay. You.

Behind us people unwrap tinned foods and set to eating. A gentleman grooms a magnificent red cat in a basket (which in three days will throw itself into the sea).

Having left at 1:30, for a long while we watch Marseille fade into the distance, Notre-Dame de la Garde, the ferry, our memories. Evening gently gilded, thoughts of your solitude, I stifle the urge to collapse. "Be strong—be hard—I'll carry on—but really it's hard."

1. Serge is addressing his companion, Laurette Séjourné.
2. The Cape Pinède basin on the port of Marseille.
3. Vladimir Kibalchich, Serge's son.

SPAIN

March 25, 1941—We negotiate with the sailors for cabins; they rent theirs, 1,500 francs a head, space in a collective cabin. These seamen think only of exploiting the flood of refugees. Not a single gesture of solidarity towards a woman, an elderly person. "A bunch of bastards," Breton says. The head baker who traffics in bread and food is a former Communist candidate for the Chamber of Deputies. Among the passengers quite a few skilled intellectuals, a ninety-year-old Viennese urologist, a small, intelligent man (but when he falls asleep on his chaise longue, his mouth hanging open, he looks dead). A sharp mind, interested in everything.

7:00 a.m., mild sun, we leave the cloudy and snow-covered Pyrenees behind us. The green plain of Figueras: so many dead beneath that grass. Figueras of defeat, a gentle, peaceful landscape, green hills. Small Catalonian cities on the water's edge. The coast files by like a dream, real and unreal. High, verdant hills, castles on the summits. A large, square castle of red brick, flanked by a gray surrounding wall spreading down the slope, Castelldefels. A former POUM militiaman, nothing left but bone and nerve, with the hard face of a diseased miner (concentration camps in Germany, then front lines in Spain, prisons, and camps again in Spain and France), explains to me that this was the prison and the torture center of the International Brigades. Probably a Francoist prison now.

Waiting for Barcelona, landscapes flying past. Around 2:00, Barcelona. The four smokestacks of the electric plant visible first. The whole city gradually emerges under a light, bright mist, stretched across the length of the gulf. The gray towers of the Sagrada Familia; I remember them as phallic from close up, but from this distance they put one in mind of grieving hands raised in the air. The Christopher Columbus column can be seen clearly, the Customs Palace and the Gobernación near the port, the cathedral, the San Jaime tower. Montjuic in the foreground. The flat lines of the pink brick citadel; the rock, steep when viewed from the coast, appears to be composed of gentle slopes when viewed from the sea. Fog over the background of the city. I believe I can make out the Rambla de Flores, broad and gray, probably trees whose leaves have fallen. The Spaniards look on, tense. Thought of defeated men. Mental prayer. It's here that I must say farewell to Europe, while making the commitment to return. Not adieu, but au revoir. I attempt to write a poem, can't make it work. Too much feeling, too many thoughts; all deaths appear contemptible. Inspiration missing, I feel hard and lucid, confident as well, all of this clear, neither fever nor joy. (Perhaps a secret joy is needed to write a poem, even in the depths of suffering?)

As night falls we reach the mouth of the Ebro. Somewhere on the heights, in the sierra, a huge blaze—probably a forest fire. Calm sea, twilight despondency, absences. Thought of defeat.

March 26, 1941—Morning, the coast near Valencia. Steep, craggy coastline, mountains in the background. Little towns in the valleys and inlets. A rare fishing boat. No ships. No activity on the coast until this point, neither cars nor trains. In a precipitous valley hard against the sea a dreary factory hard at work. No men can be seen, and it's better that way. The tall, gray chimneys spit out their dense smoke in the solitude between the rocks, the sky, and the sea. Glorious solitudes, arid red rocks of Cape de la Nao.

Landscape of ruins, a vast enclosure, half-destroyed towers on the heights overlooking the sea. Below is a fishing village. Here stood Sagonte. Valencia, vast gray agglomeration.

Increasingly rare signs of life, bare rocks, sheer, dry slopes cut up into harsh ridges, mountains in the background. Desertlike Spain infinitely sad. This must make men hard.

(Yesterday, the gigantic rocks of Montserrat glowing red in the distance, in the heart of Catalonia.)

(Yesterday at 1:15, in front of Cape Nao, a citadel on the edge of the sea, a forgotten little town, feeling of oblivion, solitude all around. Ship alongside the little jetty. The cape is an upright spur of rocks with a flat profile jutting out into the sea. An enormous block surmounts it, massive as the back of a beast, and these gray rocks suddenly display orangish tones.)

We lean forwards, Vlady and I, over the bow slicing through the sea. The wind takes our breath away. To the right, mountains fall abruptly, peaks sharp as knives. The earth's motionless violence. We see the sun's rays penetrate the waters, perpendicular, pearly, and they seem to have a kind of shadow.

ALGERIA

March 27, 1941—Oran. Smooth sea, liquid silk. These Algerian coasts less savage, less harsh. In spots the sea as green as the Danube and the line ending the blue waters is visible a few hundred meters from the shore.

Oran: pile of modern buildings of no interest. Our civilization; mighty and impoverished. Heaps of people in heaps of masonry busying themselves with what? With holding on or with making money. The essential concern with the salvation of the soul (Christian Middle Ages) has been lost, the grandeur of the world and of life has not been discovered en masse. A barbaric castle drawn all in straight lines looks down on the port from a pyramid-shaped mountain. Gardens, dull suburbs spread out like an amphitheater. Small harbor. Kabyles and Arabs in rags slaving away; Frenchmen, uniformed and civilian, strolling by. Beautiful rags, beautiful heads, beautiful brown musculature, much savagery underneath. These men, driven to savagery by semi-slavery. Up close much violent ugliness.

Only the French go ashore, we are prisoners on board. Reflections on the absurdity of xenophobia in a people with a low birth rate, bled by two wars, which has more than a million of its people in various foreign countries, and at home dependent on foreign labor. A people of heterogeneous origins and which certainly owes the richness of its temperament, the varied aspects of its intelligence to this composite origin. Reactionary nationalism, the reflexive reaction of decrepitude.

The *Sidi-Mabrouk* is being loaded. Ant-men coming and going beneath their burdens. The *Gouverneur-Général Cambon* pulls out, assisted by two tugs.

André [Breton]'s impressions: Mediocre French provincial city. Crushing poverty of the Arabs. They hold out their hands, show you the six sous they have, look at you with severity... Dignified. We add two sous. On a street downtown twenty or so Arabs, among them veiled women in white, gathered around a garbage pail. The women beautiful behind their veils. A triangle-shaped cutout for the eyes. Many are streetwalkers. Little merchandise in the stores. They refuse to change French 500-franc bills.

Arabs come to unload the merchandise. Very expressive faces with a variety of deformities, but a few pure types, surprising in their nobility. Extreme hideousness, large mouths with crushed lips revealing yellow teeth, flat noses, husky and guttural voices. Miserable beings. Simian hands, long, spindly, flexible, and black, are excellent prehensile tools. The white man's hand has lost its strength: degenerated. The docker's gesture of two raised hands takes on extraordinary significance. But, what? —To think that the French live with these men almost without seeing them. Inhuman, this, and very dangerous.

A lovely sunset, the sky aflame above the castle, a gentle blaze. It is as impossible to write this as to remember it correctly or to see it well. One sees, one lives intensely, but not everything, for the poem changes from moment to moment and it is so immense that it can't all be taken in. Across from us, a rocky coast, all red. The water gray silk, pink, with hints of blue. Background light blue under the flame. An absolute sadness grows through this vision and it is the approach of night.

Night. The spears of the searchlights hunt the skies for a little silver fish that's said to be a plane, perhaps British. Someone is playing a harmonica in the dormitory. Beneath a weak bulb I read Leon Davidovich [Trotsky]. Some men are playing cards next door, swearing and spitting. Suddenly the memory: window on the Cours Saint-Louis; tea, the evening, and you came and sat at my knees, your eyes. What are you doing now? Heartbreaking awareness of being carried along by a wind. Yet available and confident. That dust in the wind smells strongly.

The Big Dipper at the zenith in the shape of a question mark. The Northern Lights shine softly.

Barcelona and all the dead, the poem won't come. It's there in my head, but it feels itself so stunted, it struggles so weakly to find itself that . . . Deliberated: despite everything the solutions of courage are the best. Feeling of captivity on this floating concentration camp, with its stinking hold. Absurdity of a motionless boat in the shelter of a harbor. To be outbound, launched onto the sea, justifies all.

March 29, 1941—Did I do the right thing in agreeing to this separation from Laurette and Jeannine*?[4] The distance grows with every turn of the propeller. Can we ever know what a separation is, what a separation will be? The comfort of thinking of Laurette's eyes when she was encouraging me to leave. Temptation of the petty, submissive life with its guaranteed warmth—which we believe to be guaranteed but isn't, or which evaporates. One drowns oneself in it. Forge ahead.

The coasts of Spanish Morocco are bare. Jagged contours, not completely arid. From afar the delicate vegetation gives the impression of moss on stones at our feet. Uninhabited, not desertlike. Elongated lines, delicate as African musculature. Coastal erosions with hints of richly colored sand sketch the forms of veiled women. We admire them along with André.

The long, supple, and craggy lines of the countryside put me in mind of slender blacks, full of the life force they aren't aware of, with smooth and scorched skin. Style of the land and man. Illusion? I gaze on the land, I consider this, and it seems to me that it's true.

March 30, 1941—Mist on the sea, gray seas in the evening, it could be the Baltic, which I've seen sunnier. The Rif coast. A country made for fighting with fierceness, with love, an elevated way of feeling oneself to be alive.

Melilla, city of no interest, on a bay. Franco set out from here. Further on, the bare heights of the coast are sprinkled with bushes and they have animallike shapes. Mountain with panther skin.

We are in a convoy of five ships. The one escorting the other four is a comical tub of the "wartime navy," a filthy trawler covered in rust and armed with a few small cannon. Long wait off the coast not far from Melilla. Signals. The war tub circles around us. Towards evening, in the rain, we pull out again in the opposite direction. It's said that difficulties have arisen in Gibraltar.

The night having fallen I contemplate the lights of the ships sailing parallel to us. Stars, my familiar sky already turned upside down. Taurus draws a perpendicular "V" below the zenith. The Pleiades clearly

4. Jeannine Kibalchich, Serge's daughter.

visible. They served as my guide on snowy nights when returning from Orenpossad.[5] I pointed them out to Laurette on the road to Air-Bel.[6] Saturn and Jupiter are visible above the crescent moon. These visages of the heavens are totally indefinable. I hope there will be a time when men will have a deeper, more consistently intimate relationship with them. I've not yet seen the nebulae, all I know is that they exist, and I can barely guess at that of Orion. Most men today live without seeing the universes above their heads and which they could see. The gentle sea, ever in movement and moving. One is so full of thoughts that they are no longer thoughts, but rather waves and winds of the spirit. It rains off and on. Neither sad nor fearful, tense, and of your presence.

We pass by small, bare granitic isles, the Chafarines, Spanish Morocco, where there is a lighthouse, and behind the lighthouse a cottage with an illuminated window.

NOMADS

March 31, 1941—The *Wirtschaftsemigranten* [economic refugees], on the lookout for the best places, have installed themselves between the central deck and the boiler Jews with money. They rent the cabins of the crew, stuff themselves, hang out with the staff, mingle only with each other, distrust everyone, play cards, read *Clochemerle*. We call this corner the Champs-Élysées and invade it in part because it is sheltered from the wind and the sun. They give us dirty looks. Shit.

The forward section is more densely populated but maintains a chic tone because of a group of filmmakers and well-dressed emigrants with cash who put on airs as if they were at a café on the Left Bank. (There are no banks anywhere.)

The upper deck, which is not really a deck but a kind of roof encumbered by lifeboats, is occupied by the Lams, the Bretons, and Vlady. Jacqueline sunbathes almost completely nude and scorns the universe which, by ignoring her, vexes her. Helene Lam takes care of Wilfredo, who is ill, the ganglia of his throat swollen; he's sad, stretched out on

5. Cossack city near Orenburg.
6. Villa Air-Bel was the residence rented by Varian Fry to house refugees.

a blanket with his head in his wife's lap. His eyes of an aged Sino-Negro child are full of animal desolation. But he's doing better. I sometimes climb up, and from there you can see the whole ship, the whole sea. It's Montparnasse.

At the stern of the ship, unplaned wooden tables under tarps, above the gangways that descend into the hold. Washbasins where René Schickele's daughter does her laundry while telling me about Walter Benjamin's suicide in Cerbère in October 1940 after a failed attempt to cross the border without a visa. Several friends had succeeded, he failed, and his nerves went. He sent his last manuscripts to Switzerland. On board ship we have a remarkable essay he wrote on Baudelaire. On one side, deck chairs, a kind of stable; on the other, horrible collective toilets of unpainted wood erected on the deck. Ropes, tools, brats, laundry, half-naked men at the rail shaving, ladies stretched out on their deck chairs in the sun, our German group of the IRA[7] studies English and discusses Marxism. The Stalinists, in small secret meetings around Kantorowicz* and his wife, both of them thin, with sharp profiles, wrinkled faces, and gazes both harsh and fleeting. Noisy and gay Spaniards. It's like Belleville.

In the bow, our German friends and their kids are going to set up a kindergarten, it'll be like a little corner of a square in Wedding that we will call Rosa Luxemburg Square.

The apolitical refugees are afraid of the politicals, whom they respect as dangerous people and scorn as people without money. The castoffs of Europe on a drifting wreck. Not much politeness, instead boorishness, battles over places at meals, battles over tables in the fresh air amid the congestion on the deck, where we eat. Every man for himself. André, always noble and impassive looking—though he finds all this horrific—repeats: "We're quite a bunch of bastards," and doesn't hide that he'd be much happier at Les Deux Magots. I rescued a touching old bourgeois couple from the crush of people. The man, with a round head and glasses, chubby and steeped in various forms of respect—for self and others—explains to me that he is an Austrian Catholic banker protected by the Vatican who emigrated to Brazil. "And you?" What

7. International Relief Association.

should I say to him? "I'm a friend of Mr. Trotsky's?" His eyes widen: "Ah!" But he'll continue to be polite and to ask me for advice, for he is traveling with two passports and wants to know which one he should use in this or that circumstance. Another couple just like them, but less chubby, showing signs of exhaustion, German shopkeepers, personal friends of Einstein ...

In the women's hold, children's games, shouts, chamber pots, the odors of a human herd. The men's hold in the evening, dimly lighted, has the appearance of a barracks in a concentration camp. We drag this atmosphere around with us, for it is part of our era. Two decks of plank beds. Women and their husbands isolate themselves behind a curtain of blankets. Men play cards and curse in Flemish. A young urbane Jew who knows all the world's brothels and casinos, from Shanghai to Moscow, and who says that he's "not interested in politics," takes a magnificent roulette wheel from his valise and starts up a game. Cautious, the emigrants only want to gamble matches and the game doesn't last long. I think of the swindlers with their marked cards who would visit the yurts of Samoyed hunters in the Russian north and Siberia at the end of the fur-selling season. The sharp little swindler on the raft of the shipwrecked. The Chinese cook with his smooth, thin face watches the ball roll between the red and the black. I say to André: "What if the Zaporog Cossacks were to write to the Grand Turk?"

"Rotten fish of Salonika ..."[8]

But who is the Grand Turk of today? There are too many—and André doesn't know which way to turn. He promenades his noble head through this crowd with an ironic and serious air. A young man sets to playing a beautiful, all-white harmonica. I go to bed with your shadow.

NEMOURS, ALGERIA

April 1, 1941—Will we get through Gibraltar? Rumors, hopes, fears. The sea and the sky give me confidence, and seeing everyone else so

8. Line from Apollinaire's poem "Response of the Zaporog Cossacks to the Sultan of Constantinople."

alarmed, I would be so ashamed to be alarmed plus I'm full of optimism.

The sea and the sky blend the blues and grays of liquid silk, but all realities are made of light. Boats in the distance on this calm, rippling sea that doesn't shimmer. Marquet accurately rendered this bottomless clarity in his painting of the Bay of Naples, which is in the Morozov Gallery in Moscow, I believe.

AT SEA, COASTLINE OF SPANISH MOROCCO

April 2, 1941—The coast is low and mountainous, gullied in all directions by the rains, in places well cultivated. Reddish rocks and green slopes, sandy banks to the sea, the backdrop rounded like the backs of beasts. The land is violet and blue in the morning mist. Around noon it's illuminated, even though the sky is cloudy, and it gathers together a mass of pink, rust, ochre, dark green, light green tones, somber touches of distant rocks, all of it full of life, almost carnal, sculpted by the waters. One can see that the earth is alive. It's astonishing that men haven't sufficiently realized this obvious fact and constructed a religion out of it.

André complains to the captain about the insufficient food. The well-to-do passengers, who are fed by the Chinese cook, disapprove. Indignation of the ship's crew (very well fed) who threaten certain passengers with imprisonment in Casablanca and announce they're going to close the storeroom and stop selling bread. These seamen are xenophobic, mercenary, boorish. No working-class spirit, not a sliver of human solidarity.

André's impressions of Nemours: an administrative stage set made out of papier-mâché. Banks three stories tall, overwhelming. No Arabs, or almost none. Squalid boredom, a corner of dead France in a killed Africa. Bistros of the suburbs of Nowheresville. All of this baking under a horrific sun. Officers, an air force colonel. Feeling of uninhabitability, uselessness, torrid tedium. Dirty postcards and five books in the window of the stationery-bookstore: *Monna Vanna*, *Ubu Chained*, and a *Treatise on Flagellation*. They must have taken Jarry for a specialist in perversions.

Two days ago, in the morning, while we were navigating in this area, a British warship pursuing a French convoy was fired on from the fortress and fired on it in return. Up there, in the fort on the edge of the green fields, a few men were killed: men who certainly had no idea of what was going on and who'll never again play belotte or make love with the *moukères* ... Consequently, this halt in our voyage.

April 3, 1941—Morning, eleventh day out, we pass the Straits of Gibraltar. The Rock silhouetted in light gray in the distance. The lovely land of Spain, white Algeciras in a green inlet. Silhouettes of English cruisers, an aircraft carrier. The Moroccan coast is wild, bristling with red rocks.

(In Nemours the red jacket of a young woman glimpsed in town. You. An unknown woman.)

Around 11:00 we pass Tangiers, a white, well-constructed city; opulent, buildings and villas on the edge of the sea, verdant hills. An airy spot, fertile fields. Great trading post of mercantile civilization, now collapsing. Comfortable.

Wind, sun, clouds; we're cold, we're burned. The Atlantic greets us with placid waves that cause the ship to rock so much that we can't walk or write. This rocking of the world brings on reveries. A reverie almost without an object, profound and poignant. Difficult to concentrate. I'm face to face with an immense "Why?"

At sea, opposite the *Rif*, a fishing boat with a strange black sail, a poor boat for hard work. Aboard, men in blue overalls. They wave at us and give us the clenched fist salute. We answer back. I don't like this salute, but I give it with immense joy.

Stormy sea, clouds, milky light over the Atlantic. The Moroccan coast fades away and becomes flat. One would think one was in the Bay of Bothnia in the off season.

How hard it is to think and remember in this tête-à-tête with the sea. (The discomfort has much to do with this, since on a comfortable boat one escapes this tête-à-tête.)

April 4–5, 1941—Early in the morning, Casablanca. Huge harbor, flat city, modern buildings. The formidable, unfinished *Jean Bart*, painted ochre yellow, resembles a bizarre feudal castle. Square tower, smokestack at a right angle, massive steel construction.

Blacks and Arabs, quite a few handsome subjects under their rags, wander along the docks, offering themselves to shop for us and rob us. Some steal shamelessly, others are honest. Perhaps the same ones, after all. They earn ten sous on a hundred sous of merchandise, but when given a fifty-franc bill they don't return, and the naive lady who trusted them with the bill is saddened by the thought of human wickedness, as if the black man wasn't right to hold on to the treasure that fell into his hands. Encounter with a young naval officer, braided, chic, 100 percent reactionary, polished as a prison gate. All the foreigners remain captive on board. "Gentlemen, we are at war." Him and us, to be sure.

The little we see of the city from the ship reveals it to be large, wealthy, modern. Constructed in thirty years. City of a plutocracy. Breton walked through the whole town: "Nonexistent," he says. "So bourgeois it makes you want to vomit."

Visits from friends: a young Italian socialist, a Freemason, a French socialist. Immediate warmth and mutual understanding—let's talk frankly, eh? and quickly...We speak of possible perspectives. They are waiting. People are spineless but are beginning to understand.

Received two telegrams and one letter from Laurette. I won't read the letter for a few hours in order to have the joy of waiting for that joy.

As we pull out, the city covered in light, laid out on flat and fertile lands, is gilded by the setting sun. Cruisers, submarines...Our exaltation. Finally, the real departure: a whole ocean to cross.

April 6, 1941—The letters received, those provisions for the journey. We are going along the Moroccan coast, low sand dunes. Edge of the desert. In the distance the white peaks, jagged and tormented, of the Atlas. And then the coastline rises, we follow the heights beyond which the Atlas floats, pure, inaccessible, tragically pure in the void.

The weather is lovely, the ship moves forward into the dazzle on a sea of wide, green waves. In fifteen hours only one small town on the coast, two or three church or mosque towers on the edge of the sea, amid the aridity, Mogador. A halo of sun envelops us. Africa is barren, blazing.

Toward evening, bluffs spotted with bushes like leopard skins.

Africa has both its own style of landscape and its own style of life. Above these hills the sky is of two superimposed tones, turquoise blue and translucent pink. The stars pierce through. Squatting on the coils of rope we listen to a Viennese militant talk about the underground movement in Austria under the dictatorship.

Conversation with Claude Lévi-Strauss, who draws me the portrait of the police chiefs of São Paolo, Brazil. "They are two madmen. One takes himself for a noble of old lineage and collects princely tableware, autographs of important people, or, lacking that, of their secretaries, as long as there is a coat of arms on the paper (a safe). The other has invented a classification of criminals based on types of animals: dog-men, cat-men, lizard-men, parrot-men! All of this with ultramodern laboratory material...." We concur that this may not be as mad as all that, at least on a plane other than that of criminology.

Calm sea. Germany and Italy declare war on Yugoslavia. The Yugoslavs declare they're going on the offensive.

April 7, 1941—The entire day we followed the coast of the Moroccan Sahara and the Rio d'Oro from a distance of eight hundred or a thousand meters. I find this name quite lovely: in these deserts it perfectly expresses the total sterility of gold and its luminous splendor. For hours, into the infinite distance, there's an unchanging landscape which I never grow tired of, which intoxicates me. Absolute solitude. One sees the world without beings. A sandy coast, steep then flat, assailed by white wavelets. Above, bare crests in the desert seem to form long, flat islands, their rims abruptly broken off by abrupt slopes. Nothing but the rust color of petrified sand with wrinkles and cracks. Not a bush, not a sign of life for hundreds of kilometers. No altitudes: these entablatures of sandy stones can't be more than a hundred meters high. Some of them resemble cones cut off above the base. All these lines of the universe are horizontal and nearly straight. The sea, spread out with barely a ripple, a liquid mirror beneath which pass broad, gentle movements. Tatters of elongated clouds fade into the desert sky, whose emptiness they disturb. The ship advances through a ceaseless glare. At dusk the Saharan dunes take on tones of pastel, gold, pink, light gray, mauve.

Nightfall. A few feeble lights on the coast: Cape Juby. Off the coast, motionless, a mysterious black vessel. Run aground? Ally? Enemy? Phantom? Orion's trapeze sways towards the mildness in the middle of the heavens, exactly as I saw it glimmer in the deep diamond-studded cold of certain nights in Central Asia.

April 8, 1941—Two kilometers away all day, the coasts of the Sahara. The flat desert, the naked earth anterior to the creation of life. Until now, in the face of these landscapes, I've felt that the earth is alive and that our life is nothing but a fragment of its life. Not here: this is the cosmic world, more foreign than the firmament to any life.

Fringed sea. Sun at the zenith; it's burning hot; in the shade it's cold. The ship has become a universe. The eyes grow tired of these emptied sights, it's as if one had been delivered up to the inhuman.

... On board: the cooks kill a steer and bleed it on the deck, in the middle of a circle of children, between the stinking men's and women's toilets (which are obviously no longer either gentlemen's or ladies'). A mother takes her little girl to see this. A sailor drinks the animal's hot blood and wipes his face with the back of his hand. "It makes you strong." He has a small head and a large mouth. His eyes are as dark as nail heads. The steer's hide remains on the deck, a strange sight: the skin, its head emptied of its contents, alongside a small heap of viscera of strange, dark colors. In the evening the gutted animal is hung among the stars in the moonlight.

Thought about the remains of men on battlefields and that prayers for the dead were a generous, exalting invention.

Bustle at mealtime. A gentleman strolls about more or less naked, fat, porcine, hairy, with flabby breasts tanned by the sun. He's only wearing the third of a pair of striped dress slacks, cut off above the knees. Around his neck a thin silver chain holding a medal of the Virgin hanging into his chest hairs. He's a Spanish or Austrian Catholic.

André waxes indignant: "Grotesque meat," he says. And he takes refuge on the uppermost deck to read *The Laws of Chance*.

In the evening, sudden case of the blues. Should I have left? Shouldn't I have tried to hold out at whatever cost? It's in Europe that life will begin again with unimaginable explosions. I write to Laurette. Difficulty, impossibility of *saying*.

The Nazis attack Yugoslavia, Marburg, Privalie, bomb Belgrade. I recall the Yugoslav border in Carinthia where I wandered with my backpack, spied on in the mountains by intelligent birds who, in order to observe me, flew past me with tiny wing beats and seemed to be asking: What are you doing among our thickets? At the summit of the Karawanken Mountains appeared green fields and villages, aerial cities that were perhaps happy. I wrote:

> Calmed by a smile
> of inaccessible glory
> the fierce firs' attack
> on the mountaintops
> is nothing but immobility
> Nothing more than life.

Motorized columns are now passing through these sites, rolling towards towns similar to our Russian towns...

April 9, 1941—At the latitude of Villa Cisneros[9] we head in the direction of America. Region of trade winds, foggy weather.

Encountered on board Doctor S., member of the Tunisian Grand Council. We talk of the war, and he takes me to his corner cabin obtained at great cost. "I promise you're going to see something marvelous!" He unveils a small painting, in fact quite lovely, a recumbent woman dressed in warm blues: it's a Manet, the portrait of the painter's wife, dated 1873, bought in Algiers secondhand for "five hundred francs, can you imagine!" Five hundred francs, five thousand, or five million, I don't give a damn, but to buy, to save a painting, to take joy in this, to save a moment of its soul at the moment when the great ship "Civilization" risks sinking straight to the bottom with all its Sistines and its Curie laboratories is good, Doctor, is splendid! We drink a glass of cognac—almost friends.

9. Former name of the Moroccan town of Dakhla.

Nothing but ocean. A Spanish fishing boat, bare, sails smoky gray...
For long instants it is difficult to tear oneself away from the absorbing,
even intoxicating, contemplation of the movement of the waves, movement
without a goal, movement for itself, the rhythm that is perhaps the
origin of everything. But this is nothing but the feeble outline of an
idea, and contemplation is stronger, for it doesn't contain an idea.
Simply the direct contact between a being and rhythm.

Seagulls at times settle on these waves and let themselves be carried
by them. The waters are heavy, massive, shimmering, and of an awesome
consistency. Mineral. They put me in mind of lava. André came over
to me and marvelously found the mot juste: "Isn't it unbelievable?"

The marvel of the ship that follows its course surrounded by uniform,
endless horizons. I came to realize that the ship officers hardly know
the stars; they don't give a damn. One of them said, "If only you knew
how sick of them you get." Strange feeling of the safeness of the ship,
this insignificant machinery that carries us across the eternal rhythms
and depths. Unreality of all that isn't the vast sea. Captivity. This could
easily become demoralizing.

With Lévi-Strauss and Dr. S. we discuss homelands (I have several
and feel that I am tearing myself away from all of them) and the goal
of the voyage. We're going "somewhere in the other hemisphere." L.-S.
says softly, "Nowhere." He doesn't expect to return. Return where?
And why? He has no attachments anywhere. I want to quote him a
poem I wrote: "The whole earth is man's tomb," but this wouldn't be
a response. We say that for our civilization the Atlantic is what the
Mediterranean was for antiquity, an inner sea, and that we shouldn't
talk about Europe but rather of Euramerica and Eurasia, notions that
are still beyond us because men have for too long lived rooted in their
birthplaces. The era of immense uprootings has arrived, as happened
in the past during the great migrations of peoples.

Urge to look at the portraits I have with me, but I resist it, as if I
were afraid to confront them. I'll look at them tomorrow, calmly, when
the urge is weaker... Thoughts of time's vast expanse, of what we are
in this vast expanse, we, floating on the crest of equally unimaginable
waves, ceaselessly making and unmaking themselves.

Bombardment of Kiel, docks ablaze, thirty thousand incendiary bombs.

April 10, 1941—In the middle of the ocean, somewhere off the coast of Cape Verde, our route to the Caribbean a nearly straight line. The hour changes almost every day at noon (a siren sounds) fifteen or twenty minutes earlier. The sea a deep blue, the dense blue of melted stone. Average depth of 4,500 meters. Orion dominates our sky. New stars appear above the horizon, Argo Navis.

Under the full moon a sumptuous path of sparkling, moving white light streams over the waves, leading nowhere but following us. Vlady compares the waves cleaved by the ship leaving a wide side-wash of white froth to marble in fusion.

I feel entirely on the fringes of my life. Hard to think and even read. The bustle of the deck irritating, deck chairs, chatter, shady deals with the Chinese cook, people gobbling conversations mysteriously picked up in a famished Marseille. A few travelers have cocktails made for them. The true end of the world will be the day there are no more cocktails.

In the (abominable) toilets a passenger in a cotton cap, gold-framed glasses, doll-like face, a good man, told me he was he was protected by the Jesuits and was expected in Brazil, an extremely ecclesiastical air, assures me that all is well in Yugoslavia. "You'll see in two or three days..." I stagger away because the rocking of the boat has gotten worse. Yes, all is well: dead bodies piled on dead bodies, blood on blood, and old rifles against tanks.

Lévi-Strauss, an ethnologist at the Musée de l'Homme, talks to me at length of the Indios of Brazil he lived among and who are intelligent, believers—Catholic and Protestant—dedicated, honest...In the process of disappearing. The crimes of the whites, voluntary and involuntary. In the past, in order to get rid of them, they hung up clothing of people who died in the hospitals of contagious diseases on trees in the forests. The Indios were extremely vulnerable to diseases transmitted by whites and blacks; epidemics lasted for years among them, reaching, moving to the Mato Grosso from São Paolo. The Brazilian Positivists tried to protect these races, but through simple contact with them the whites gave them exterminating diseases like the flu. In 1900 there were between twenty-five thousand and fifty thousand Indios in the state of São Paolo who today have vanished. Solution? Reservations, fencing them in, economic measures...When it comes to the brown man, the white man has become civilized: he no longer wants to exterminate him, but it is perhaps too late. Weakened races of diminutive stature and primitive culture. Lévi-Strauss hypothesizes about the natural fate that seems to weigh on all of South America. "Nothing but the hypotheses of an essayist, you know, these are such big subjects..." In summary, a continent inappropriate for the higher forms of life—up till now.

1. Diminished animal types (size, species). Disappearance of the horses brought over by the Europeans. No great herds of mammals in the wild state. No great predators. On the other hand, an opulent fauna of birds and insects.

2. Disappearance of the ancient civilizations, none of which managed to survive. The causes of the collapse and extinction of the Maya civilization are unknown. Large-scale epidemics? Conquests? Cortés stumbled upon a civilization in a state of crisis and his success was strictly due to this.

3. Contrast between North and South America as relates to the success of European settlement and modern civilization, which has until now only nibbled at the fringes of the southern continent and the Mexican high plateau.

I object that the Indian civilizations perhaps died of their barbarian organization and that one shouldn't divert social causes towards geographical hypotheses...Also that the Nahuas of Mexico, like the Incas of Peru, didn't die a natural death: they were purely and simply killed, the way people are being killed in Poland today. "Incorrigible Marxist," Lévi-Strauss says with a smile. "Who knows?"

April 11, 1941—A slightly humiliating physical malaise. Flushes of anxiety.

Full moon over the sea. Nothing.

Salonika taken by the Nazis. Panzers on the Vardar.[10] Belgrade ablaze, Zagreb taken. Retreat of the English in Cyrenaica.

Discussion of the working-class movement in the United States and the right to strike during the war.

April 12, 1941—Cloudy sky, oppressive weather, we advance in the thick heat as if towards a tropical inferno. Calm, gray sea.

First flying fish. They leap out of the waves and fly over them with a long wavy movement, zigzagging just like birds. Probably hunting or being hunted.

A tiny bird intrigues us. Against the light it looks black. Where does it come from? We're hundreds of kilometers from the nearest coast! It circles above the froth, sets itself down on the wave, keeping a good distance from the ship. The captain explains that this bird lives on the sea, is thought never to rest, and they say this is because it incarnates the soul of bad captains who perished at sea. It would be nice to believe it.

Depth: 6,000 meters.

EASTER

Sunday, April 13—Twenty-first day at sea. For the last five days we've been going across the ocean, without encountering the outline of a ship, towards an immobile horizon, as if our plowing the waves served no purpose. This could easily become overwhelming.

Warmth. Morning, heavy sulfurous gray clouds cover half the sky. Endless clouds, everything on the scale of the endless. Warm, light showers splash us. Evening, explosion of the setting sun, delirious mix of clouds and flames, we see dramatic cities and mountains burst forth between the zenith and the horizon, and our freighter stubbornly carries its cargo of scrap iron, merchandise, and men across a prodigious flow of unreal metals.

10. River that flows through Macedonia and Greece.

FESTIVAL OF NEPTUNE ON BOARD

Neptune in person has climbed onto the deck with a beard of rough hemp and a trident of silver cardboard, preceded by a kid shaking a bell. Demoniacal sailors and ship owners give chase to a passenger, whom they grab and drag to a canvas tub filled with seawater into which they gloriously throw him to loud laughter. The captain, dignified and serious, allows himself to be tossed in as well. The pumps splashing seawater all around the ship. Treasure hunt (packets of tobacco, sardine cans—all in all, Europe's real treasures). At nightfall, an improvised children's and adults' theater beneath the forward canvases. Mr. Marbourg's toast to the captain. Mr. Marbourg, a Jewish merchant, is a young, well built, bold rogue, with rather animal features, exuding overbearing, ultracunning baseness. A ravishing little Spanish girl of ten, looking like a princess in a Persian painting, recites: "Children, don't imitate Lucas..." Laughter and low singing. Marx Brothers sketch, Russian song: they're supposed to sing "Volga, Volga," but the four singers become confused, sing off key; the fifth takes them into the wings, shoots them, and then returns to the stage rubbing his hands, and sings solo... There was an idea behind this. A Pole plays the accordion with conviction, and suddenly all is beautiful.

Standing apart, in the darkness of the upper deck, I contemplate this spectacle. The ship ploughs the ocean into the night. Sky overcast, clouds that in places appear phosphorescent, but it's only an effect of the hidden moon. Warmth, space, the sound of the waves, slight rocking, the depths white and green like melted marble under the side lamps. I had a moment of intense solitude, a feeling not in the least painful, as if the sea and the future wouldn't allow me to truly suffer. It seemed to me that I was quietly calling you in the night, as if this weren't senseless. How wonderful it would be if you were here.

Brought up memories of Easter. My first Easter in Russia 1919, famine, danger, Red Terror, and the rest. I reached one of the summits of the life of this century. I see the agitator Voldin of the second section of Petrograd harangue the Party comrades in the main courtyard of our committee, the former palace of Grand Duke Cyril, near the Opera. The blue of the sky is pure, and gilded crosses float in it, above the toppled crescent. Gelfang, with his Gallic moustache, his eyes with dark rings below them, his face wrinkled with age and exhaustion, asks me if I have bullets for my revolver, for we're about to explore the rooftops of the neighboring apartment houses. Deserters and counter-revolutionaries are hiding there, it seems, and they have even brought up machine guns . . . Walks across the rooftops, the glimpses of the city, canals, bridges over the Moyka and the Fontanka, trees beginning to turn green, the deserted arteries seen from on high are all lovely in the early-morning hours. Dreary incidents in the houses, clicking of pistols around a bunch of chimneys, my fear of slipping on the tin slopes of the roofs.

> Christ is risen
> In truth, risen
> And on the earth, the lilacs

Orenburg, the church of Orenpossad (Vorstadt), the only one alive in the city. A warm night, that is to say a first gentle chill that seems to us to be warmth. The thaw has begun, but crusts of ice have formed on the puddles and several times I step in the freezing water. Women buttoned up in their miserable furs on their way to the church, sheltering small lighted candles in their cupped hands, spangling the street with stars. The entry to the church is blocked by medieval beggars chanting their lamentation in the name of Christ. A dense, suffocating, sweating crowd in the church, gilded miters and copes (so there are still some left?), and, kneeling, they kiss the image of the saint, one after the other, quickly, quickly. Persecution is vanquished.

Wednesday, April 16, 1941—Twenty-fourth day at sea. Five years ago today I left Russia, not suspecting that two months later I would infal-libly have been executed like almost all those I left behind me—good companions in struggle, of an astounding human quality.

What enormous inferno are we approaching? The very air fills with heat, a uniformly gray sea, overcast weather. Dissolvent calm, then slight nervous excitement. "The equatorial atmosphere," Lévi-Strauss says.

Once evening comes we feel better. We gather—the forty militants, escapees from various concentration camps sponsored by the IRA, which is paying for their voyage—in Montparnasse, that is, on the superstructure that encircles the upper part of the smokestack and supports the lifeboats. (Couples sometimes hide in these boats at night to make love.) The vents bother us. No guardrails, we see the lapping of the sea, no obstacle between it and us. The paleness of the tense faces stands out in the cool darkness, and one realizes that a vaporous and penetrating light reaches us from constellations rent by the clouds. I speak of another long voyage I once took, twenty days on the North Sea and the Baltic at the end of the other war, at the birth of revolutions, at the birth of our victory in Russia. Indeed, a voyage symmetrical to the one we are now on: we were climbing and we are descending history's slope. And we will climb again! I paint a portrait of Ilyich [Lenin], his simplicity, his basic, average-man personality, his lack of affectation and ambition, his disdain for effect; of Leon Trotsky, by contrast, sparkling with sarcasm and intellectual ardor, clearly superior to those around him in his splendor, his elegance, and his pride. I say that we are defeated only in the sense of fighters in a great army that has time on its side; that we mustn't let ourselves feel defeated but maintain victory in our souls; that we have an unforeseeable future in our hands, and that we have proved our capacity to face up to everything, to undergo everything, and to accomplish everything.

April 17, 1941—Five years ago today I left Russia, torn apart. Behind me captivity, the captives: my comrades. The simplest and firmest men I've ever known, living on ideas and devotion. All of them have perished since, shortly afterwards, because they were incapable of renouncing the truth.

Niegoreloye, a lovely name: the-village-that-didn't-burn, fire-resistant earth, last Russian soil. Our railroad car empty, we were the only travelers. The Soviet station, deserted and well kept, airy, buffet, flowers, murals—and no one there but the waitresses in white, the GPU uniforms, coats with green facing, officers in navy blue and white caps like naval officers, an elegance aimed at impressing foreigners. The closed faces of the uniforms. Faces bearing the complex seal of suspicion, authority, the usual fear; everyone is on their guard. Searches. My seriously ill patient[11] controlling her panic when she is taken, carrying Jeannine in her arms, for the body search. They searched for conspiracy even in my socks and shoe soles, innocent old soles. They take away a third of my papers and photos (all the rest were taken in Moscow). Our rags hurriedly stuffed into small, half-emptied valises as we rush to get on the train that's about to start moving. And the no-man's-land of the border begins, a steppe ravaged by old trenches, with a debris of barbed wire. From time to time guard posts. The train passes over this bare, gray earth under white clouds. The Petrograd front was like this in 1919.

Stolpe, a Polish station, cheerful, flowers, attractive little houses, newspaper kiosks where all the newspapers of Europe are sold. Friendly porters, a customs chief who asks me if we need any money...The *Vossische Zeitung*[12] is interesting, *Paris-Soir*[13] idiotic, full of stories about women, Madame de Pompadour, movie stars, a crime of passion...

Four days earlier Ramishvili, the Georgian Menshevik, had come to bid me farewell. His worn-out overcoat, his clean-shaven, sunken face. Eleventh year of prison and deportation.

"What would you like me to transmit to your comrades in Paris?"

"Nothing. They know..."

Fayna [Upstein],* her young Egyptian head with its black curls, apologized for not accompanying me to the train. "They'd be capable of locking me up for it!" (They'd just added two years to her deportation at the end of her sentence.) "In any case, Victor Lvovich, rest assured that I won't weaken." The athletic Vasily Mikhailovich [Chernyak], who loved to recite poetry about man's flight to the forest, ran his hands through his blond locks, wiped his teary eyes, and said: "It will take cosmic upheavals for us to again be free, and when that happens I think we'll be overtaken by events."

11. Serge is referring here to his wife, Liuba.
12. A mistake on the part of Serge. The liberal German daily was shut down by its publisher on March 31, 1934, in order to avoid its falling into the hands of the Nazis.
13. The most important French daily, it was founded by the former anarchist and socialist Eugène Merle in 1923 and was bought by the industrialist Jean Prouvost in 1930.

In the seventeenth century the Old Believers, rather than betray their faith, gathered in the forests of the north and were burned alive while singing psalms.

April 17, 1941—The wealthy Jewish "economic emigrants"—*Wirtschafts-emigranten*—cautiously pull dollars out of every corner of their clothing and baggage, have the captain's Chinese cook prepare them fine dishes and cocktails, sweep up the produce in the storeroom, set up kerosene stoves on the deck, cook, and play bridge. Their comical indignation when Breton and Flake, the woman doctor, complain to the captain the poor quality of the food: "You're going to spoil relations between the passengers and the authorities!" They look at us askance. In their eyes we are clearly a mob of troublemaking agitators and perhaps the cause of all evil.

Hot sea, barely shimmering, surface crossed by great swells. Oppressive weather. We advance in the calm, but it's a calm of cosmic ferment. The clouds compose symphonies of power and color.

Talks given these past days: A young German on prehistory. Discussion of Pavlov's experiments on conditioned reflexes and physiological psychology. A German doctor, tall, thin, his profile uneven and ravaged, who resembles a bush explorer newly emerged from the equatorial forest and stuffed with quinine—but he has only emerged from the Europe of concentration camps—explains Pavlov's experiments, repeating that it's been years since he's been able to keep up with scientific work.

Surrealist games explained by André Breton. Amazing success of questions and answers that we ask and answer separately, without prior agreement. Someone asked me, "What is historical materialism?" Without knowing the question, I answered, "A defeat we're transforming into a luminous victory."

Torrential rains. Spouts, jets of water ceaselessly descending from the sky, visible by the light of a lantern. It's an endless web, warp and woof endlessly crossing, suspended between the clouds and the sea. We are under a waterfall, a mild Niagara.

Night. We sleep on the captain's bridge; the Niagara begins to overflow our mattresses. A kid scoops the water with a shoe. An officer arrives: "Hey there! You're going to wake the captain!" Me: "Then let the captain come take a look at his passengers!" Silent disapproval of the right-thinking filmmakers and travelers. The captain doesn't show his face. It goes without saying that the drainpipes are blocked.

Sunday, April 20, 1941—Twenty-eighth day of navigation. Went out onto the deck at 7:00 a.m. The morning light is milky yet transparent. An enchantment you breathe in, that penetrates you through the eyes and every pore of your skin—and touches your soul. The brain vibrates with a joy of being for which there are no words. The muscles sing. Group in the bow, I approach it. We can see the island. A green isle, bathed in misty colors whose summits are like stones set in rings. It rests on the ocean; light seems to emanate from it.

The captain says:

"The pearl of the Antilles ... and the dishonor of France."

He explains:

"Business dealings, crooked deals, abandonment ... The sugar fields, the rum distilleries, etc."

The island stands out more clearly. We watch it rise over the ocean, it emerges from it, a marvel. For our eyes accustomed to Europe's measured landscapes and, even more, worn out by the gray masonry of cities, this is an exhilarating joy. Renewal of contact with the hot and violent earth, the earth that is part of a constellation, which the civilized forget. Vegetation streams down the slopes. In the distance the sugarcane fields are clear emerald patches (how poor this comparison is!). There's nothing but sun. The mountain stands out against the background, its conical peaks a purplish blue. Vegetation covers these heaps of rocks like powerful moss. Green life spurts from the rock on contact with the sky. Simple genesis. One could easily dream pantheistic dreams. What is the sun if not love?

Let's not wander too far, even in this widening wonder. Clouds of tiny flying fish, like dragonflies, swarm out of the pearly-blue sea. One can see them stretching their fins underwater getting ready to leap. A group of porpoises, either panicked or pleased by the opportunity provided them by the passage of this freighter, swims alongside the bow and frolics in the waves. They are more than a meter long, brown and blue, with slender, gracious heads—intelligent, I believe. They leap so high their entire body leaves the water.

MARTINIQUE

Ciudad Trujillo, May 25, 1941—Like Guadeloupe, this island is under the rule of an administration, and above all, a police, recently sent from France, with appointees named in Vichy but dictated by Paris; that is, 100 percent Nazified. The special commissioner of the service handling foreigners came here from the Occupied Zone. The two real authorities are the admiralty, led by superior officers of the Laval-Darlan tendency, hard-line and narrow-minded, and the secret service, most likely directed on the spot by German agents. This is the conviction of the inhabitants of the islands and this was my impression. Atmosphere of suspicion, snooping, informing, mistrust. The refugees who arrive here are carefully watched and in some cases must be considered to be in danger. Nasty tricks are possible.

The authorities live in a state of panic. Skillful pro-German, pro-Vichy propaganda had good results. The black population is neither Gaullist nor well disposed towards the Americans. It doesn't want any change, and fears it. The intellectuals are anti-Vichy and pro-English, but don't dare breathe a word of this. People are arrested and interned for the least word.

The American consul has no influence. He in no way facilitates the stay or the departure of refugees. A French officer warned us: "Above all, don't tell the consul that you are journalists or writers: the Americans don't want to take in any such. Think up other professions."

There is no organization on the island to which refugees can address themselves.

The admiralty may be asking Vichy to stop granting transit visas via Martinique. Because of the great number of refugees to be saved (several thousand) we must nevertheless try to keep this road open by pushing Vichy and the French representation in Washington in the opposite direction, by insisting to the French minister in Washington on the necessity of granting normal treatment to passengers in transit via the Antilles, without bullying or abuse (friendly approaches on the part of well-known Americans could be effective); perhaps by sending here an American citizen of firm character (for a brave man this would be the occasion to pass an interesting "vacation").

The French Admiralty will most likely not allow French ships to depart Martinique for New York for fear of seeing them seized. There are two possibilities here: obtain from the American government (or from New York authorities by appealing to M. La Guardia?) an assurance that the French ships carrying refugees will not be seized, or establish a regular transit via Ciudad Trujillo (come to an agreement on this with the Dominican government—personally address the head of state?). The latter could be a very good solution, for French ships offer scandalous travel conditions which could easily become dangerous (we traveled under such horrific conditions on the freighter *Capitaine Paul-Lemerle* that an epidemic was to be feared at any moment).

NOTE ON THE WORK OF THE AMERICAN RESCUE COMMITTEE

May 26, 1941. Ciudad Trujillo—The action of the committee continues feverishly, under truly difficult conditions. Around 150 directly threatened people have been able to leave France without exit visas, thanks to the help they received. Around 400 receive material assistance, many of them only able to survive thanks to this assistance. More than 500 are supported in various ways by packages sent to the concentration camps, occasional financial assistance, and various interventions. More than 1,500 files are kept up to date. Every case requires an investigation, which is always carried out in such a way as to select and sort. (Figures are approximate and cited from memory.) M. Fry* has formed a team of ten coworkers, several of whom have demonstrated devotion and courage and all of whom are threatened by the ill will of the authorities under German influence. The committee is watched over by the Gestapo and is regularly exposed to provocations or to repressive actions. Until now, thanks to its prestige, it has been respected, but it is certain that its situation has become particularly difficult since the resumption of the "collaboration" between Hitler and Darlan. Thus the immediate necessity of supporting it from America and, if possible, ensuring it more active protection by official American representatives.

Six German refugees, intellectuals of high quality, supported by the committee, committed suicide (before March 15). Among them, the playwright Walter Hasenclever* and the literary critic Walter Benjamin. When Rudolf Hilferding* and Breitscheid* were handed over to the Gestapo from the Free Zone, around February 12, their friend the Viennese lawyer Apfel died of a heart attack in M. Fry's office. On many occasions it had to intervene in the cases of individuals living under the direst threats. It is known that there are lists of individuals sought by the Gestapo. The situation of the Italian political refugees is also tragic. (Carlo Buozzi and Guido Miglioli* were handed over from Paris, perhaps Mme. Berneri [Caleffi]* as well.) Finally, the situation of the Spanish refugees has gotten so tragically worse that it is essential that it be immediately addressed.

We also know that secret organizations financed by Mr. de Lequerica[14] and by the Germans have been created to pursue, with the tacit support of certain authorities, illegal activity against individuals difficult to strike openly: Gaullists, foreign refugees, political figures, individuals hindering the activity of the Gestapo. Jacques Doriot's* Parti Populaire Français (PPF) furnished the personnel for these gangs. And so the personal safety of the members of the committee must be considered at risk.

The Stalinists, using Spanish refugees belonging to circles that actively collaborated with the Communist Party (Max Aub, Azcárate junior,* Corpus Barga,* Méndez Aspe,* Moix,* Ansio) seem to have carried out a laborious intrigue against the committee. They sought to provoke a split in the committee or the removal of Mr. Fry by obtaining influence over Miss P., who seems completely ignorant of the seamy underside of Spanish politics.

The activities pursued demand virtually unlimited workdays. Mr.

14. Franco's ambassador to France.

F. and several of his collaborators work night and day amid never-ending problems. They have acquired irreplaceable experience and knowledge of affairs. At this time it is impossible to assign an end point to the committee's activities, which are tied to events and upon which the safety and the very existence of several hundred refugees and the moral safeguarding of an even greater number directly depend. Alsatians and Frenchmen address themselves to the committee with ever-greater frequency. The creation of work companies in the Sahara will impose on it the obligation of investigation and assistance.

Through his devoted labors, complicated besides by money problems, Mr. F. has demonstrated a firmness, courage, and clear-sightedness that have given him a unique moral situation but have also made him the target of the dangerous hostility of the Gestapo and the Nazified authorities. Fortunately, an opposing current exists among the authorities.

Concentration camps. Imprisonment of tens of thousands of men, women, and children in often inhuman conditions. Ongoing epidemics and a high mortality rate after second year of privations. Need to intensify assistance and interventions. Pose the problem to the Red Cross. Push two independent but parallel actions: pressure on the Vichy government and a campaign addressed to public opinion.

If the situation in Europe worsens, foresee French emigration.

Consider the situation of the political refugees who can most likely not be received by the United States and who are even so among those most threatened by the Gestapo so as to obtain asylum for them in the countries of South or Central America: the cases of Brandler, Thalheimer, and Grylewicz.*

Obtain exit visas from the French government for Italian and Spanish refugees (for example, the case of Modigliani,* the case of Spaniards younger than fifty). Again, pressure on Vichy and campaign addressed to public opinion. In many cases, intervention by committees or prominent Americans with France's ambassador to Washington can be very useful.

Foresee worsening of the condition of French Jews in the Free Zone.

Scandal of the labor companies in Morocco and the Sahara, made up of foreign refugees.

REPORT ON THE PASSENGERS ABOARD THE *CAPITAINE PAUL-LEMERLE*

May 25, 1941—Embarked in Marseille on March 25, 35 people recommended and protected by the IRA: Kuno Brandel,* Hans Tittel,* Carl Heidenreich,* 3 Krizhaber, Alice Fried, H. Czeczwieczka, E. Bersch, K. Braeuning, 2 Oresch, 3 Osner, I. Reiter, H. Langerhans, M. Flake, 3 Barth, J. Weber, 2 Pfeffer, Capari, F. Bruhns, F. Caro, all in possession of danger visas or immigration visas for the United States; several visas have expired en route (Alice Fried). In addition, sent by the American Committee of Marseille: the André Breton family (3), the Jacoby family (2), the Wilfredo Lam* family (2), Kibalchich, Victor and his son.

In addition, about a hundred passengers, mainly Jewish businessmen (a few intellectuals) of bourgeois condition. (Several businessmen had danger visas.) Almost all for the United States. Voyage in unsanitary conditions with insufficient nourishment, makeshift toilets on the deck across from animal stable.

Upon arrival at Fort-de-France on April 20 most of the passengers were interned at the disused quarantine barrack at Pointe du Bout on a peninsula isolated from the city. Forty-five minutes on a launch to get to town. Officially "lodged" under the control of the military authority which delivered "leaves" to go to the city to see to administrative procedures. Guarded by black soldiers, excellent fellows, under the command of a (mixed-race) officer cadet. In town, closely guarded by Naval Security, Immigrant Services, the admiralty, agents of the "Secret." Conditions of internment: large huts with neither furniture nor bedding; straw mattresses to sleep on; no lighting; no fresh water; no medicine; tropical climate. Mineral water was sold for one franc a bottle and there was often none to be had. Upon arrival the authorities had seized all or almost all the passengers' money, according to the case, as a "security deposit" "to pay for your departure or repatriation." They demanded 10,000 francs security from stateless Russians for their eventual repatriation. This deposit also served to pay for lodging at the rate of 25 francs per day. Unspeakable and filthy food, more often than not tossed into the sea so that it was still necessary to pay 25 francs for corned beef[15] and sardines. We protested and refused to allow ourselves to be robbed this way, which resulted in conflicts and threats. Young Belgians were threatened with being "returned to France and handed over to the Germans." Others (myself) with being "deported to Morocco." Correspondence tightly censored, many letters disappeared.

The Transatlantic Company was repairing a steamer that hadn't sailed in some time, the *Duc d'Aumale,* in order to send it to C. Trujillo and New York with its passengers as well as those of the *Carimaré,* who arrived three weeks later and are interned in the mountains at the camp of Balata, which is said to be better (among them several nationals of the EMERSCUE). Departure set for May 17, tickets sold the 15 and 16. On May 17 the departure "postponed" because of international situation. Nevertheless, on the 18th all the internees from the quarantine station embarked aboard the *Duc d'Aumale,* where they found cabins and clean food. May 18 those who had obtained a Dominican visa (2 Jacoby, 3 Breton, 2 Lam, 2 Kibalchich) left for Ciudad Trujillo. The others, about a hundred people, including thirty five from the IRA, are interned aboard the *Duc d'Aumale.*

The words of Lieutenant Castaing of Naval Security: "We'll make those who have no more money work to pay for their lodging." "They pass under the control of the naval authorities." "The *Duc d'Aumale* will depart but won't go to New York"—"to an unknown destination." It's believed among the passengers in C. Trujillo that the *Duc d'Aumale* did, in fact, leave for "an unknown destination" with its passengers for the United States. According to a rumor, the admiralty is supposed to have requested authorization to disembark them in C. Trujillo or Haiti, but we don't have any precise information.

SITUATION OF SPANISH REFUGEES IN FRANCE
Early June 1941—At the end of 1940 accords were concluded between Vichy and Madrid that in effect placed *all* Spanish refugees at the discretion of the Francoist police. Since the beginning of January,

15. In English in the original.

Spanish and German agents have worked in French territory (the Free Zone) in concert with the French police. A special camp was reserved for certain categories of Spaniards in Saint-Tropez, where they could be easily locked up.

In March a special Franco-Spanish commission was formed in Vichy to implement the accords. It was made up of a first-class prefect, M. Jacquet, and two functionaries of the Ministry of the Interior in Madrid, Juan Nuñez and José Tejera. There were five local commissions: Marseille-Nice, Montpellier-Nîmes, Toulouse-Montauban, Perpignan, and Tarbes-Pau.

In the meanwhile Spanish police took part in interrogating political refugees administratively held in secrecy under various pretexts. They took part in searches, etc.

In the concentration camps in Argelès and Saint Cyprien, little-known Spanish refugees were kidnapped and taken to the border. We know of cases of men executed as soon as they arrived. Republicans transported in this way leapt from a moving train in the tunnel in Cerbère and were horribly mutilated (can't give the date, a not very recent event).

Late or mid-January Serrano Suñer[16] had a meeting in Paris with Laval. An agreement was signed at the Spanish embassy in Paris without Pétain having been consulted. This agreement established the collaboration of the Spanish and French political police, Spanish surveillance of French Gaullists in Lisbon, and large-scale activity in France by the Spanish police.

Thirty Spanish agents were sent to France. France designated special police superintendents to assist them. The Spanish government created a special fund. Since parallel action was being pursued with the Gestapo, the apparatus became extremely active.

Mid-February Darlan resumed and stepped up this form of collaboration with Spain and Germany. He concluded an accord related to the refugees with [Ambassador] Abetz.

During Serrano Suñer and Franco's visit to Montpellier the question of Spanish refugees finally received a "complete" solution: 1. The Spanish government accepted the principle of total repatriation; 2. The

16. Franco's brother-in-law and minister of foreign affairs in his first cabinet.

Vichy government consented to turning over to Spain all those accused by the government of common-law or political crimes. The agreement is secret, very flexible, and anticipates all cases. Commissions to apply the agreement are established. They act without consulting the local authorities. Transfer centers between the Occupied and Free Zones were created in Moulins (barracks 4 of the triage center of the Sûreté Nationale) and Saint-Martial-d'Artenset near Libourne. This center is two kilometers from the demarcation line and is headed by a Gestapo agent.

M. Rochas or Rochat was designated by Darlan to the central political commission established in Vichy to apply these various accords.

Finally, they are establishing an extralegal relationship with the party of Jacques Doriot, who received funds from M. de Lequerica and set up secret action (terrorist) groups, who held a conference in Marseille in January.

MAN AND RHYTHM

Ciudad Trujillo, June 10, 1941—A glow of pink watercolor shimmers between the heavy clouds and spreads over the small city. Everything turns pink and pale blue, the afterglow still luminous. I walk along the asphalt to the small, deserted harbor. Docks, yellow customs buildings, the water gray, the zone across the way brown, palm trees, huts. Old, crenellated walls, and a relic of the past, a portal. Coming through it, walking up to the city, a lone black man carrying on his head an entire stall, painted white and sporting a large number. With an agile step he passes through the crowd. He whistles while shaking a bell in his right hand. From his hands, from his lips, he is nothing but rhythm and sound. The whistling and the ringing are identical with him: this is the sound of the insect-man in this heat. Happiness of this man: because of the bell.

SMUG ASSASSINS

Saw the picture of one of Trotsky's assassins, the painter Siqueiros,* with his wife in a prison cell in Mexico City. The man and the woman, attractive, delighted, pose for the cameras, he with a casual gesture: "So what's the big deal?"—smiling. She with a steady gaze, smiling. Clearly satisfied with themselves.

"*TIBURONES*"[17]

People rarely swim in the sea. Every year the sharks devour some swimmer at the edge of the beach. Just looking at the warm, cloud-covered sea, at the very color of the heavy clouds, one senses that it is full of threats. A few months ago some panic-stricken cows escaped from the slaughterhouse at the water's edge and, either to cool themselves off or because they were being chased, threw themselves into the sea. They were immediately attacked by sharks and devoured after a terrible struggle. This in the heart of the city, between the dock and Avenida Washington.

Ciudad Trujillo, summer 1941—Mella Avenue. You climb, leaving on the right the former Franciscan convent, lovely with its pink stones, crenellated wall, tropical trees, decorative lanterns, deserted alleys. Heavy evening heat mixed with a tepid coolness. Editorial offices of *La Nación*,[18] a crowd standing in front of the blackboards, news from Russia: "*Les han rechazado, la linea Stalin....*"[19] Black faces.

The Apolo, movie house, Chinese café (perfectly clear), Chiang Kai-Shek, Trujillo, naked women with pink faces, decent and lascivious, Coca-Cola, blonde American woman in red, triumphant, but the Chinese are more human. A street opens out to the right, market, crowds, buildings (police), cafés, hairdressers, white clothing, explosions of electricity, heaps of bananas, of pineapples, of vegetables, the smell of fermenting fruit and garbage, a slightly putrid smell that goes well with this spot. There are dark side streets and others sensibly lighted, with little houses painted blue, green, or lilac, neat as a pin. There are plank houses that are little more than shacks, and this is

17. Sharks.
18. Dominican newspaper, edited by E. Granell (close to the POUM) who published an interview with Serge on the German invasion of the USSR.
19. "They repelled them, the Stalin line."

where the rent-girls live. The road: puddles, mud, ruts, garbage. Tall soldiers in wide felt hats stroll, blacks and Chinese wander or gather, animation around the hairdressers and the bars; small, noisy café, Dios y Trujillo,[20] back room with lanterns and billiards. Hookers everywhere, they make you think of those beautiful, pearly- or blue-winged flies you see swarming around rotting objects—or of flowers growing out of a swamp. Young girls, or well-built young women, skimpy dresses in dazzling colors, faces intense and sleepy. (Sleepy intensity, animal sensuality, vegetal vigor, life at its most basic. They're really nothing but sex organs adorned with a face and some fabrics.)

The vigorous Chinese woman with a flat face, big eyes, a long black chignon, a debauched look, a beautiful female, walks back and forth dressed in electric blue. The Malayan Girl (that's what I call them; they're products of unknown mixtures) is astonishingly slender in a short, striped dress, fine-featured triangular face, slanted eyes, lovely, sharp, smile; she clings caressingly to a black man who is taking her to the billiard room in Dios y Trujillo. She's nothing but a human stem of perfect loveliness. There are broad-faced Polynesian women, their skin the gold of peaches; black women with magnificent teeth; a few young white girls, lovely. This quarter of the city ferments on the spot, like Les Halles in Paris, but purer. Life is naked here, closer to the living earth, neither stones nor money have crushed it (the tropics are stronger than concrete and money, as I will see in Havana). Two contrasting tones: shadows and electric light; and there is flesh and fruit. Flesh and fruit, splendid and rotting and reborn in indigence at the level of animal contentment, prodigal of itself.

The blacks, boys and girls, grow tall like the palm trees; they are a head taller than the whites; long legs.

FESTIVALS

June 15, 1941—Corpus Christi, Feast of God. From a window, Plaza Colon, I watch the procession. A square plaza, beautiful palm trees, stone planters, metal benches, fountains, Columbus's statue. At the

20. The café bears the name of the national motto: God and Trujillo.

rear of the plaza, the cathedral built of old stones, severe and restful to the eye.

Almost no spectators. The different neighborhoods of the city parade by with small banners like this: two rosary strings of young girls and women strung out along the sidewalks, an empty space in the middle—a banner—groups of little girls dressed as angels in colored satin or silk, with tiny wings of paper or fabric attached to their shoulders, their hands joined (this must get tiring after a while). Priests looking very European, bald, bearded, in Templars' robes, direct the procession. Gentlemen with large rosaries around their necks. Crowds of young girls, bourgeois white people, well dressed, carry their banners with constipated seriousness: they look like they're on display. The women run the gamut from black to café au lait. Nuns bring up the rear behind the girls, old black women, stiff and touching, with colored ribbons around their necks. Women who've been servants for half a century. Two or three bands in gray or khaki uniforms. Brass instruments.

Firemen in red shirts and copper helmets, thin and gangly (most of them black or mixed blood).

The band. The little white wings should have been glued to *their* shoulders. (*Bomberos*).[21]

After them, marching separately, infantry from the nearby castle, Calle Colón. American-style, wide hats, khaki, well equipped, practical matériel, creaking drums.

June 16, 1941. Evening, 8:00–10:00—Same plaza, Feast of the Dominican Woman. Chairs, fans made of little flags, colored fountains. Small crowd. Standing around. Ladies at the podium reading speeches, loudspeakers, photographers. Straight out of René Clair.

WAVES—AWESOME SEA

June 16, 1941—A bad day, exhaustion, worries, obsessions. After nightfall, went to stare at the waves. (Constant subject of meditation: Have we reached the depths of defeat?)

21. Firemen.

A splendid sky, clear except at the horizon. Dominated by Scorpio, the yellow glimmering of Antares, which looks like the nacelle of a star-spangled parachute. Beneath it Sagittarius's cascades of stars lying horizontal. Behind me the Great Bear like a question mark turned upside down. Countless nameless stars. The two most beautiful ones of Centaurus, one bluish the other yellowish. The Southern Cross is inside the dark clouds on the horizon—there is no horizon, just impenetrable night filled with crushing hostility, the awesome sea.

Behind me there are pleasant homes with their illuminated lampshades; the tiny frames on the walls, the rocking chairs, the young girls in doorways. The cement ramp of the quay torn up in spots by a hurricane. The lanterns cast a gentle light on the rocks below. These are small-scale lunar landscapes, terribly jagged, ragged, bristly. Organically formed reefs devoured by the waves; this is what the entire coast is like, made up of minuscule fjords, inlets, indentations, rents. Shades of gray. From the open sea, impenetrable and oppressive, from the total darkness of the open sea, you don't see but rather feel the arrival of a swell; then you see it rising gray, a fringe of foam appears, expands, twenty meters out the wave is born, white, rolling ever faster towards the rocks, unleashing itself like an assault that makes the earth tremble with the muffled crash of a far-off cannonade. The foam dashes, swirls, returns, explodes here and there in a powerful spume, then falls again. A half hour of calm. This assault never lets up, the endless rhythm of the sea's day. I've already seen plenty of waves, so why am I struck by the powerful aggressiveness of these waves, by their wicked hissing, by the ceaselessness of their destructive surge? Because here I feel the destructive surge; this hot Caribbean Sea is not a gentle Mediterranean, it is different, dangerously mobile. Fearsome sea.

THE INTERNAL CLOUD

June 17, 1941—I shall not go mad, I am fated to remain implacably lucid, and I would even be intolerably so if I didn't still have an almost childishly tragic feeling of life. I have walked along the borderline of madness often enough to have become convinced of the impossibility, for me, of crossing it. And I am the author of that strength, having seen from too close up the indescribable defeat of the spirit and the unimaginable sufferings it brings in its train (Liuba). But I return to that borderline with an odd regularity, especially when you're not here. I would suddenly find myself there when you used to go way for an hour or when you were a little late coming home. I'd be angry with you for plunging me into that state of despair, you whom I love, you who are my salvation, for your mere presence drives away the darkness. I've been thinking of this for two days, struggling unsuccessfully, depressed and feverish. You know all this, you who are so sensible and honest, and I don't always succeed in pushing away from you the cloud that passes over your face and your being and makes you turn a bit nasty, separates you from me, overwhelms you with faults and unhealthy sorrows. "Cloud" is the right word for this, for it's like a heavy cloud that suddenly blocks the sun, and the color of the landscape changes, the joy of living is converted to sorrow, and one can see the despair in the movements of the tree branches. —Beloved, what clouds are passing over you at this moment?

THE CASTLE

All of this more or less dissipated just now when I was visiting the ruins of the headquarters and palace of Diego Columbus, the discoverer's son. You would have loved this site. I was talking with you the whole time I was there. I was pointing out to you what I was seeing, your name was on my lips. It is within the city itself, above the harbor, two steps from the city gates, on a prominence you arrive at through a small garden full of trees planted in groups in an odd and amusing fashion. The ruins are vast and rectangular, surrounded by walls and, on the river side, small observation posts and the rubble of a staircase leading nowhere. High walls of gray stone with large windows opening onto the sky, spindly pines, tropical foliage, the smokestack of the nearby *Presidente Trujillo* in the port. Seen from up close the stones come from what was the bottom of the sea and are eaten away by the rain. Through a bay window I was able to see, bright and clean, a disreputable neighborhood where young black men were sweeping the doorway of a dance hall. A bath of coolness, strange repose. Some bees have built their nest in a hole in the wall. People feed the pigeons, and their cooing fills the silence. I go out into the airy courtyard with its view of the harbor, the ship, the green savannah on the opposite bank. At the corners of the ruins, hard against the stone, cacti, which are trees, four meters high, are raising their erectile, hard, fleshy, armed branches to the sky. People carve their names into these branches: Inocencia, Rolt, Marguerite, Hipólito: a mass of names. Along the walls, at the base, a row of succulent plants with thick, knife-shaped leaves, green on one side, intense violet on the other. A sick old pigeon, having taken refuge in a corner of the stone, allows me to come close to him, since nothing mattered to him anymore. There are men like that. Another pigeon, black and pathetic, looked blind to me. They are fed copiously; they scurry over when the guard whistles. Some shrubs covered with violet flowers interested me to look at them closely. I saw this marvel: it is the leaves at the ends of the branches that are violet, magnificently so, and they encircle sparse, tiny yellow flowers the size and dimension of forget-me-nots. And so the too-discreet flowers are adorned with leaves. Small lizards ran across the walls inside the rooms.

The Château de Beaucaire suddenly comes to mind. What a lovely day that was, and how far away it is. I refuse to think about how far away it is, because you are near, you are coming, and I must, I want, to be able to feel you close in your absence, and all our memories must be present in this separation in order to enrich and find our strength. Our memories are us. You are every bit as real to me as everything I see, as everything I touch, I want to be yours at every moment. We are moving towards each other, united by our momentum and our communion. I am in you. You are in me.

NAKED HOSTILITY

June 20, 1941—Avenida Washington (Mexican consulate, pointless errand, visa not yet arrived . . .) Very long, curving slowly, some sections seem straight. On one side the sea, ravaged rocks, a balustrade. Paving-stone sidewalk, asphalt, vast gardens; on the other, the city. Sky and space.

Morning. Half the sky is covered with storm clouds, vast sheets of dark blue, threatening. Thunder grumbling in the distance; the air is charged. Vertical, torrid sun. Not a soul. The palm trees, planted in rows for perspective, are all chewed up, damaged, mutilated, their fan-like leaves yellowed. Some look like the hurricanes had ripped off nearly all their leaves.

Storm-colored sea. Not one boat. Low waves gather strength, rising slowly, break and dash themselves, foaming, against the astonishing rocks they reduce to jagged crags. Fjords, terrible landscapes. The grandiose in miniature, froth bursting and flowing back. —Grass yellowing.

All this is cruel—inhuman—beautiful, hostile to our forms of life. Neither ideas nor work, nor contemplation possible; no soul. The raw hostility of the tropics.

Late July 1941—Below my window, a little cemetery with a superabundance of white cement crosses. The whole dominated by the bourgeois bust of a matron turned towards the handsome trees of the Avenida Independencia. Last night, awakened by the storm, I saw the cemetery stretched out, beautiful, as if oblique, with all its crosses tilted under incessant lightning of a brilliant, motionless white, and the living spears of relentless rain. On an upright gray cross I can read: Porifiro Kepi.

Three Chinese, accompanied by children, often come to visit a fresh grave. They briefly meditate, talk amongst themselves with handsome, placid faces, and the children laugh. I'd like to know if they're carrying out a rite or if for them this visit is a duty. I don't know.

A poor woman has come back several days in a row. The grave that interests her is in the center, near the fence, just below my window. Perhaps thirty years old, already wrinkled, very thin, the body of a skinny little girl, a rather dark-skinned métisse with sharp features, lacking in grace. All in black with a small hat and drawn stockings, she looks like an insect. She comes under the beating sun carrying a small black purse and a black parasol. She brings flowers, a candle, tidies up around the grave, removes dead flowers, picks up a piece of paper, takes it away, sits a moment on another white, burning-hot grave, crosses her hands, waits. Once she lavished her diligent attentions on the being now buried there, and while he ate his meals, would sit off to the side, as she does now, not thinking that he would soon die. —Alone in the whiteness of all those crosses, under that horrible sun, I have seen her talking to the cross, her gestures discouraged: No really, I can't believe it, how is it possible? Then she would busy herself with the flowers. Then she lowered her head and gazed fixedly at the candle. And then a black gardener in rags and a sombrero came over and she gave him some instructions. Then once again her conversation with the cross, lips moving, head raised, she saw me, I was embarrassed.

This cemetery annoys me only because of its ugliness, its banality, the harsh halo of light over all those crosses. How simple and natural death is. How simple and natural, how beautiful is the love of the dead. How simple and terrible the solitude of the living who love the dead. I feel very comfortable among these neighbors. Only, I'd put in a few more trees and fewer identical stones. The rite reminds me of the cold view from the windows of Consuelo's studio. The dead are humbler; I like them better.

THE TOMB OF COYOACÁN
September 9, 1941[22]—Tall trees, wide deserted avenue, pure air, all is green, we arrive in the rain, Gorkin, Vlady, and me. The low house is surrounded by a wall painted gray topped by a turret (machine gun). We're received by two friendly young guys, a Mexican and an American, wearing cartridge belts and revolvers. We're led into a kind of ante-chamber, quite bare, books, filing cabinets, a typewriter. Natalia Ivanovna enters, petite, physically reduced to nothing, the body of a worn-out little girl; a tragic face, wrinkled, tense, ravaged, pale, and much aged. One can see that she used to be blonde and charming. Her hair no longer has any color, her step is hesitant. Active, straight, exhausted, a shadow, but there is something desperately determined about her. She listens to me with a pained tenseness, and it's painful for me to speak.

I can do so only in Russian, for it's Russian firmness that is required. Our differences, how the Old Man, whom we love, was unjust and unfair towards me in polemics (I don't say the word: imputing to me

22. Serge reached Mérida on September 4, 1941, and Mexico City the next day.

an article that I didn't write and which expresses ideas opposed to mine); that there is no Fourth International, no parties (don't play with the idea of party, with the idea of the International), that nothing can be built on sectarianism.

Nath. Iv: You disappointed him terribly after having filled him with enthusiasm. —The Fourth exists, you have to help in building it, look at our American section.

I propose an appeal to assist the Russian people, who are considered cannon fodder; an action in favor of the Oppositionists who have perhaps survived in the prisons. She nods, approves vaguely, reserved. Totally within the "line" of the sect; I sense that no collaboration will be possible. She stiffens.

An interior of great simplicity. The Old Man's office, a large table without drawers, notes on India, bloodstains. Plank bookshelves, bare walls. Map of Mexico. The laboratory, a work cell for a mind. It curiously resembles my own place, with far greater means: it's truly Russian and revolutionary, the style of several generations characterized by the stripping away of individualism, the search for objectivity. (Memories of my father's office.) A life-sized portrait of the Old Man. It looks exactly like him: the gray-green eyes, their firm, powerful gaze, the lips in the form of an eagle's beak. (Photos at G.'s house make a bad impression on me because of a new facial expression—from the final period of his life, coinciding with a certain lowering of the quality of his intellectual production and an increased irascibility—of self-satisfaction and scorn; an intense, terrible expression.)

We speak of Siqueiros's assassination attempt: about thirty bullets shot through the bedroom door. Several hundred all told. The window of the office looks out on the garden, cacti, and beautiful trees. Near the exit a cement plaque commemorating the assassination of Sheldon Harte, who was, with his look of a young disciple, a Stalinist. There were perhaps three traitors in that fortress: S. H., Sylvia, and Jackson. The Old Man sought his death: selection of his entourage based on political agreement.

In 1928 or 1929, on the eve of his arrest (exile to Alma-Ata) I took leave of him at the home of Beloborodov* (executed) at Sheremetyevskaya Pereulok, first or second floor, in a tiny room on the courtyard, an iron bed with copper balls, small table overflowing with maps. He was dictating the "Letter to Pierre." We spoke of the possibility of my crossing the Estonian border or my pretending to "capitulate" in order to escape. (Later Ndivani—executed—proposed that I flee via Manchuria, but I asked to bring Liuba and Vlady along; this wasn't possible.) House cordoned off, GPU motorcyclists downstairs.

The Old Man, his face yellowish, was suffering from liver problems and malaria. Pajamas with frayed sleeves. We embraced each other affectionately. Yakovin guarded the door, his vivacity, his ardor. Nikolai Karpov* participated in the discussion; I'd agreed to this but against my will (distrust). Karpov broke faith. Yakovin disappeared, prisons.

In that fortress in Coyoacán two armed young men are guarding shadows, a deserted intellectual laboratory, a devastated woman-child of sixty-five. Citadel of ghosts, haunted tomb, absolute distress. Around it rich vegetation, blue mountains, the great, radiant sky.

Letter from Krupskaya* to L. D. Fanny Yanovich* affirms that shortly before dying (in 1938, I think) Nadezhda Konstantinova Krupskaya wrote an affectionate letter to L. D. It was clear to F. Y. that L. D. was overcome by this letter, in which Krupskaya called on him to carry on the struggle. This was after the first Moscow Trials.[23]

DIEGO RIVERA

September 25, 1941—Met Diego Rivera. Going by his photos I expected a jolly, stocky giant. There entered a kind of clergyman, crystal glasses, broad, pale face, large, flabby fatigue-ridden body. I expected a robust intelligence with a gift for synthesis and revolutionary consciousness grounded in inspired common sense. He's an overgrown child (mental age: twelve), crafty, with a delirious imagination that applies itself to social affairs, goes from exaggeration to paradox, ceaselessly outlining complicated frescoes full of conspiracies, tales of vast corruption, international perspectives painted with a broad brush. He affirms that Trotsky's assassination cost millions and he knows who received them.

23. This final paragraph, written by hand, was added in November 1943.

That the Sinarquists[24] have seven hundred thousand organized men. That Stalin is secretly negotiating with Hitler. That forty million German-Americans will one day attack the West. Delirious and inconsistent. What must save him is his capacity for work, which, aided by great practical sense, organizes and sets aright an imagination in a constant state of eruption. From this his work derives a veritable bit of genius. I see in him the sole truly great painter of today (or yesterday), because he's returning painting to its true destination through large-scale murals, which speak to a people, which speak to and are an expression of the masses. I've never seen anything as beautiful as his frescoes. Alongside them, the stuff Picasso makes for art galleries catering to bourgeois collectors fed on intellectual refuse seems pale charlatanry! (A great personality to compare with him in Russia is Filonov.*) Impression he is reaching a dark turning point in his life, on the brink of physical old age. (Only fifty-six, has eye problems, etc.)

HILFERDING'S DEATH
October 10, 1941—Very much struck by the death of Hilferding. Spoke with the comrades about commemorating him. Response: No one among the Mexicans and Spaniards knows who he is. Subject for meditation: On the influence of a great scientific contribution on the level of international socialism!

Read a few pages on the modest heroism of Julián Besteiro* (also seventy years old) during the fall of Madrid (died in prison). An anarchist writes: "Men like these, we should follow them unto death." Besteiro had been a reformist, a moderate all his life; had begged everyone to avoid a civil war. Reminded me of the Belgian workers' cult for Vandervelde, "the Boss," even though he was a former minister and a signatory of the Versailles Treaty. Despite his policy of assimilation to the bourgeois order one could sense in him an absolute fidelity to the working class and socialism; I felt it as well. (Our conversation on the death of Kamenev; old Vandervelde, nearly deaf, his tiny eyes

24. Serge uses a form of the Spanish spelling of synarchism, a corporatist, anti-Semitic Mexican movement of the far right.

intelligent and sad, his voice trembling with emotion.) The socialism of these men is a bourgeoisified socialism, but it's the most elevated product of the consciousness of an era. They belong to an intelligent and generous bourgeoisie whose thought is guided by a scientific idealism. What they are unable to conceive of is the sentence hanging over a society of which they are the best, the most noble representatives, and the necessity in certain struggles for hardness, a destructive hardness, in practice inhuman and thus regressive (something that those energetic men belonging to less cultivated and organized peoples understand spontaneously: Bakunin, Durruti, the Russian revolutionary Marxists).

In accusing them of "treason" the Communists committed both a psychological error and a moral mistake. Reformism was a betrayal of the interests of socialism strictly from the perspective of the revolutionary class struggle, which could neither be the perspective of these men nor of the mass working class they so well represented. Enormous importance of the moral dimension in propaganda: the mistake of misjudging the adversary's true value. —Like Besteiro, Hilferding ended as a martyr.

If he was killed or led to kill himself it's because he refused any collaboration with Nazism. Moral strength and fidelity at seventy.[25]

TURNING POINT OF THE WAR

Sunday, October 12, 1941—Truly terrible, indeed intolerable to see things coming—uselessly. (In those moments when history goes against man the gift of clear-sightedness—a magnificent revolutionary dynamic when the struggle allows him to effectively manifest himself—becomes a torturous burden when he is reduced to impotence.) The disaster in Russia is unimaginable: destruction of entire populations. Don't visualize this.

Hitler is in the process of winning the war in Russia. Churchill is a continuation of Chamberlain: insular egoism, fear of initiative, fear of risk, fear of victory because of the certain revolutionary consequences,

25. Last paragraph added by hand.

inaction. He counted on the blood of the muzhik. If he occupied Spain during the Russian campaign everything would change on the Mediterranean front, the first totalitarian regime would fall, and Franco would drag Mussolini down after him. (But after? The terror of the English bourgeois.)

After Hitler's victory in Russia a probable new Russian revolution might improve the facts of the problem. Two hypotheses: A long war of attrition, the Nazis disposing of the resources of a continent and a quarter and probably, next year, of those of northeast Africa, thus an ineffective blockade, and their de facto victory. Or the entry of the United States in the spring of 1942 or 1943 with a massive expeditionary corps, millions of men. The Nazi empire would then collapse and the Americans could convince themselves they could establish an order in Europe in keeping with their wishes. Possible that this solution was envisaged during the Winston-Roosevelt talks, and this would explain English inaction during the war in Russia. At bottom they're happy that Nazism is destroying Stalinism while tiring itself a little.

ON THE ROAD TO PUEBLA

Saturday, October 25, 1941—Relieved of my worries about you, I took a long trip with some friends—a Frenchified American couple, a Frenchman—to Puebla, about a hundred kilometers through the mountains. Overcast weather, the countryside looks like nothing in Europe, except on a high plateau the gentle rolling woods like those in the Harz, or a road through a pine forest in the mountains which could well be in Russia. These resemblances recall the unity of the world; they touch me. Explosion of magueys[26] along the road: magnificently decorative bushes formed of bouquets of broad and tall hard leaves, like enormous vegetal daggers... To the right Popcatepetl, blue-violet, covered with low clouds at three thousand meters. Green plains, exquisite churches here and there in the greenery, as in Russia—and they sometimes even share a similar baroque style. (Grandeur and universality of that commercial society of the seventeenth century of which the Jesuits

26. A plant from which is made mescal, tequila, and pulque.

were, to a certain extent, the soul. Relationship between the flexibility of their casuistic and capitalism's liberation of man—liberation of some men through money.)

The road twists through the mountain at a height of three thousand meters, we enter clouds that are nothing but light fog. Rio Frío, a town straight out of a Western movie, not at all picturesque, commercial, one wide street, cafés, fried food. The little town of San Martín Texmelucan, extraordinarily charming. Baroque church, cupolas, pyramid-roofed bell towers, carved doors, an open work belfry, like those in Provence, all of it coated in a gentle pinkish gray, so that the stone resembles flesh. A charming interior, stoups a meter wide, a life-sized wooden Christ, realistic and suffering terribly, lying in the entry, a rather tall altar, entirely gilded. —Colorful little plaza with a big, pink church combining various styles. I immediately thought: How you'd love all this, how wonderful it would be to spend a day in this village with you, to admire so many things together! The pale pink cartouches on the facade of the first church are in the style of Indian embroideries. Above the gutters Indian masks, refined by contact with European art, retain the power of their expressions, sad and tragic. A large section of the facade of the other church, on the plaza, is decorated with arabesques in imitation of Arabic art (Arab influence in the earthenware, the flat, brightly painted facades). Little girls selling fruits, three mules slowly dragging a cart in which a family is traveling...Coffin sellers on the streets...A little Indian with a big hat looks at me because I have my binoculars in my hand; I hold them out to him: *Mira!* He refuses with a smile, and when I look at him through the binoculars he hides. Not intimidated, not hostile, smiling and uncommunicative. Passive resistance, Vlady observes.

Huejotzingo, broad plaza with trees five to eight meters in circumference, magnificent churches, their variety grows monotonous for a mind caressed by these elegant and ornate forms, with their patina, colored pink, gray, yellow, and gold; these cupolas, these bell towers, these evocative walls. Market, crowds of Indians, poor but not wretched, almost nothing European about them. Beauty of these types, silence of this crowd, odor of charcoal, of fermenting fruits. Braided objects, colors. Conversation with the French shopkeeper: they have no needs, we have nothing to offer them. —This is their defense. —Slow movement, activity without cries or tumult. Abundance of fruits, peppers, greens. —A rather well maintained little town.

Cholula with its 365 churches scattered around a plain of magnificent gardens, and all around it a circle of blue mountains. The highest church, the Santuario de los Remedios, is built on a high hill overlooking the city; that is, on top of several superimposed Indian pyramids overgrown with vegetation. We visit the underground passages of one of the pyramids that, after fifty-two years, was being covered over with a new building. Frescoes in red and black, enormous death's heads with staring eyes; they are simultaneously death and life, red outlined in black, stylized, thirty to forty centimeters wide. A triangular flattened nose, striking round eyes, the teeth a rictus. In an underground area sacrificial stones, near which the skeleton of a young girl was found. Our guide, a not-in-the-least-bit-stupid young Indian, explained that the victim placed her left foot here, the right foot there, her legs spread, her throat was slit, at which point the heart was ripped out, for which there was a hollow space behind the sacrificer's platform. Our French fellow traveler chuckled over this "paving stone." Above, in the open, a tomb with the bones of a couple, the man killed, the woman buried alive along with him, all of this too perfectly restored. More touching than the bones is the small shell necklace that has come undone and the household items. The pyramid dates from the eighteenth century.

We climb the paths up the slopes and arrive at the paved terrace of the church, luminous under the sun, inundated with sun, three yew trees planted there from which one sees the scattered churches, the circle of mountains, an enormous church surrounded by high, dark, crenellated walls, the Capilla Real?—like a fortress. On the other side, rectangular gardens overflowing with trees and magnificent flowers and the wide terraces of the *manicomio*, the insane asylum. With my binoculars I can see a madman standing in the courtyard talking to himself and gesticulating as if he were washing his face. The guide explains that "they are treated very well. They have radios and movies…" A boy offers us a white kid for two pesos. Another sells Vlady a small sculpted head for two centavos.

Puebla, the plaza surrounded on three sides with arcades, shops. Gentle rain in the heat. Green plaza, superb palm trees, beautiful parasitic plants, oily, with bouquets of pale green leaves clinging to the base of the trunks. Amazing cacti, some with white spikes laid out in the shape of a star; others round, bursting forcefully from the earth. Subject for thought: these plants, their appearance, their unity with their world. Tall, vast pink cathedral. Twilight. As we stroll, newspapers: the taking of Kharkov...

Return during the night, rain in the mountains. Spears of rain seem to explode in front of the car, in the feeble light of the headlamps, we are bounding towards a star of rain—irritated, flagging, violent. The pines stand out, pale green, opaque and light, born of the night. One day, my darling, all this charm will be here and you will be next to me, I'll place my hand in your lap, I'll touch your shoulder. Less worried, more peaceful, I can better bear waiting for you, I feel less regretful about living without you.

Centuries-long stagnation of this beautiful Indian race, taking refuge in a minimal existence, a vegetative existence. Is it about to die or to be reborn? The indecision can last a long time. The formidable American machinery works perfidiously behind the scenes at destroying it. In any case, it's obvious that it has within it an enormous charge of life, but one very different from ours. Feeling of incommunicability.

STALINISTS

October 1941—Insidious battle with the Stalinists. A review (*Hoy*) had offered me the possibility of becoming a regular contributor; I learn that the Stalinists have invested in it, the editors would like to shake off their yoke but they can't, and my collaboration seems to be impossible. That same day Editions CIMA, which would like to publish a translation of *Midnight in the Century* told me the same thing: they have Stalinist money and their sponsor is opposed ... Finally, the review *Bandera Roja*,[27] in the October issue, no. 10, published a long

---

27. Journal of the Mexican Communist Party.

article by Comorera* (GPU, very influential) entitled, "The Trotskyists, Hitler's Agents," which begins with these words: "The CP of the USSR, brilliantly led by its secretary general, Comrade Stalin ... has annihilated the Trotskys and Bukharins...."

And then there's this passage: "It was believed that Trotsky's death put an end to Trotskyism. When the dog dies the rabies dies with him, as the old saying goes. But the bigger dog, Hitler, is still alive ... and Trotskyism continues its labor of treason...."

The article is mainly directed at Gorkin and me and asks how I was able to leave France when the real antifascists were turned over to Franco, etc. It denounces "Doriot, Déat, Pivert,* Paul Faure, Spinasse,* Araquistáin*" as Trotskyists. It's a hysterical and ridiculous, but also criminal, hodgepodge, and it's essential to note in it the admission of Stalin's assassination of Trotsky.

The same issue of that review contains a long article, a portrait of Álvarez del Vayo,* member of the editorial board of *The Nation*! You see that I was right to tell you that *The Nation* was Stalinizing itself with its new board.

JUÁREZ'S TOMB—RUE HAXO

November 2, 1941—The Day of the Dead. On the street they sold little skeletons, white or golden, skillfully made; death's heads made of sugar with green or red eyes and names written in sparkling colors across the forehead; buns in the shape of skulls or bones. Evocation of death in sugar and charms ... Went to visit the small cemetery and church of San Fernando right nearby. A courtyard closed on all sides, the pinkish-gray stones of the church, slabs with names from the 1860s on the wall, as if coffins were buried there, and probably this was once the case. Abandonment. A small office, typewriter, etc. under the vaults where in the corners stand old coffins removed from graves, emptied of the remains calcified by the earth and time. The tombs in the garden are overwhelming and lacking in style. Strange need to suffocate the dead beneath such heavy and pitifully proud stones. Juárez's tomb, with no inscription, massive and simple, colonnade and beautiful monument of white marble, weeping women bent over the long, virile body. An arm perfectly expresses immobility, the end of strength. The head is noble and true, amazingly simple, one sees the fallen man, a powerful and serious man. Juárez has many profound similarities with Lenin: I find that the Lenin of Mexican independence is fully revealed by this marble statue. I was alone. Thought about how over the course of our lives there are successes, and as I contemplated Juárez recalled one of our successes, our visit to the Wall of the Hostages on the rue Haxo.[28] Do you remember that gray afternoon? We were *good* together, intimately so, neither exalted nor jubilant, and Paris was gray, the Pré[29] was gray. We went out shortly before twilight, walking the dull streets on the heights of Belleville, which always put me in mind of the barricades of the Commune. Rue Haxo, the small new church of white stone with brick walls and well-tended gardens, a passing cassock. A young and almost merry priest showed us the spot where the hostages fell. We entered an inquisitor's office where another priest, emaciated and curious, asked us if we knew anyone who had recollections of the event. You, his gaze fell on you. He thought we were father and daughter, doubtless with a slight suspicion. This bare office, papers and crucifix, severity, dryness, intelligence, sharp and cold. We so carnal together and so different from this corner of the world and completely on the other side. We returned via the Avenue Gambetta. I certainly kissed and caressed you when we got home, as we spoke of that world of organized faith that was closed to us, perhaps emptied of real faith.

Juárez, Lenin, Mexico, let this not be a mere descriptive phrase: man carved out of a single block; life, thought, and action all one; powerfully rooted in the soil, his own, his race; educated and intelligent, not an "intellectual" or a scholar at his desk nor a manipulator of ideas for the pleasure of it: knowledge in the service of life. A very practical idealist. Humane, capable of being harshly utilitarian (executing Maximilian). Not a philosopher, a surgeon operating on a nation.

28. Spot where the Paris Commune executed its most important hostages during its final days, including the archbishop of Paris.
29. Pré Saint-Gervais, where Serge lived upon his arrival in France in 1937.

GABRIEL MORÓN

November 7–8, 1941—Anniversary of the Russian Revolution. Memories of our anniversary celebrations in deportation, of Soviet demonstrations, the brawls of 1927...We've reached the depths of defeat. Meeting at the Ibero-Mexican Center, talk by Gabriel Morón, a good lad who was governor of Almería and head of the security forces in Madrid during the revolution (until the Nin affair). Left socialist, talks like a radical,[30] is ignorant of the abc of the class struggle; the revolution of 1848 or even of 1844, below the level of a Soviet schoolboy of thirteen... "Instead of a Nonintervention Committee the democracies should have formed an Intervention Committee!" Childish words. No theoretical intelligence, a childish and confused consciousness... No common language with better-trained minds, discussion almost impossible. Total intellectual poverty.

With Gustav Regler,* Feuchtwanger,* and a few other Germans and Austrians we then move to a discussion of the nature of the Nazi economy. These are men of an infinitely superior quality. Excellent sounding of the depths of the problem. Left there and went into the coolness of the night feeling my spirit refreshed. Solitude. If you were waiting for me at home I'd be happy to be alive. I am almost so because I remember and I know that someday you will be waiting for me.

Gloomy anniversary of October. Leningrad and Moscow besieged, Rostov lost, Crimea invaded. How distant I am, despite myself, from the Russian nightmare. And for the first time I try to imagine it as in some way abstract. Otherwise it would be intolerable.

THE SOLITUDE OF THE OLD MAN

November 1941—He had truly no one around him. Devoted and narrow-minded bodyguards. Natalia Ivanovna at the end of her wits since Liova's death;[31] worn out, irritable (not with him). No other intelligence. And completely cut off from Europe and especially Russia, which he loved more than anything else in the world, Russia-Revolution.

30. In the sense of the French left-liberals, the Radical Party.
31. Their son, Leon Sedov.

At bottom, I understand him. Natalia Ivanovna told Vlady that I was the last person to bring him fresh news from Russia, in 1936! Terrible solitude, no one to talk to. What constituted the strength and the grandeur of the Russian revolutionaries was that they constituted an environment. Lenin and T., with around them Bukharin, Zinoviev, Lunacharsky,* Smirnov, Bubnov, these fifty men of the first rank, those two or three hundred militants of the second rank, of the highest quality, formed a cultivated milieu, educated, trained in the Marxist method, animated by a revolutionary passion, profoundly honest—a nearly unique success in history. Their intelligence and characters mutually fortified each other and were multiplied by their contacts. (I insist that intelligence is a social as much as a bio-psychological fact, though the psychological is social by definition: either Beethoven in a village in the Auvergne among the deaf, Einstein among illiterates, Trotsky in Coyoacán during a time of international reaction.) Juan Luís Velásquez* brings him a poem, "Soledad de Soledades," and the Old Man spends days reading it, has it translated for him word for word . . . Solitude, one of the factors in his hardening. Terrible to be so strong, so great, and so alone. (The struggle for some of us.) Terrible and diminishing.

Surrounded by traitors, Sheldon Harte, clearly Siqueiros's accomplice and the Old Man didn't want to admit it. From party spirit, it is said. I think it was more from human feeling, a kind of repression of this abject disappointment. The young disciple, so alert, so pleasant, was nothing but an agent of the GPU. Informed of this, the Old Man closed his eyes to it, had S. H.'s name engraved on a stone in the garden in Coyoacán, and in so doing threw off the investigation, playing the assassin's game. Sylvia, Jackson's wife, probably semiaccomplice (knew Siqueiros's address; living with Jackson for two years, never wondered where the money came from; her attitude after the crime according to Fernandez; was supposed to leave by plane with J. the day of the crime). Natalia still refuses to admit Sylvia's betrayal, the same human respect, repression. J., after the first attempt, contributed to paying the cost of building fortifications for the house . . . The Old Man drove around in J's car. J. participated in the shipping of the Old Man's documents to New York! Yet completely lacking in any intellectual quality, nothing in his past of any worth. Sectarianism—choice of men based on political sectarianism—and solitude are the heart of the drama.

November 19, 1941—I've learned from a reliable source that various people (one of them must have passed through Cuba or have lived there, probably South American, journalist or writer, with a revolutionary past) have come to Mexico City to lay the groundwork for Jackson's escape. The prison director, dead set against the Trotskyists, is supposed to have been bought off or won over or both. —I'm also told that J. could escape but prefers to play for time. In certain Stalinist milieux this affair is spoken of without anyone contesting that this was a Stalinist undertaking.

J. in his cell, books, magazines, constructs model airplanes, regrets nothing, lives well. (D. N. recently saw him.) —What's the source of the money that is paying for his defense and assuring J.'s well-being? His defender, Medellín Ostos,* a well-known lawyer, "not Stalinist," (but whom I'm told has long since been won over) pleaded "professional secrecy" in refusing to answer that question, which Natalia Ivanovna had asked him in an open letter.

BELLAS ARTES LECTURE

November 15–16, 1941—Wednesday the 12th I gave a talk at the Palace of Fine Arts: Europe 1941. Small room, more or less full; spoke in French translated by Julián. A small Communist shock troop arrived to prevent the meeting and tried to seize the podium, but a few determined friends held out against them. The brawl lasted an hour and ended with the arrival of the police. Julián chaired the meeting magnificently, having taken off his glasses as a precaution: he catapulted the attackers from the podium . . . I was then able to speak in a friendly atmosphere, freely and about everything. I've learned that a second Stalinist troop was in the hall ready to "bash my face in" and win the battle. But it didn't intervene because the orders were to avoid bloody incidents (obviously, at this moment[32]) and because the attitude of Vlady and two or three comrades standing back not far from me looked

32. Added by Serge in the margin: "preparation for Jackson's escape."

too resolute. They did well not to attack us. We scored a success, the first of its kind.

SPANISH ANARCHISTS
November 17, 1941—Attended talks on the Spanish revolution at the Ibero-Mexican Center. Small, pleasant rooms, fifty attentive people. Cardona Rosell,* respected CNT economist, on the collectivizations. A short little man, slightly potbellied, well dressed, an oblong head with a prominent skull; glasses, well spoken, sententious, pencil in the air, visibly listening to himself, very provincial schoolmaster. A good technical report, but this anarchist is nothing but a kind of trade unionist who has forgotten all his anarchism, if he ever knew anything about it. The industrial collectivizations derived from "the moral imperative to continue production" (never spoke the words "class struggle"); the government, "distracted" by the war, the government, which included CNT ministers, "didn't legalize the movement, and then in 1938 decided to turn the enterprises over to the owners who asked for them. The problem of power not posed. —Munis and Gorkin pose it very well and Gorkin spoke of the nineteen thousand antifascists imprisoned under the Republic, whose government included anarchist ministers. An anarchist, young, lean, boney, something dried out and bitter in his face, explains that the CGT didn't run aground—*no ha fracasado*— because it decided not to make the revolution in order not to resort to terror, not to adopt totalitarian measure, out of humanity. (Abdication and march to defeat out of humanity, "We were faithful to the humane!") Says that in Russia they always persecuted the anarchists (here I am embarrassed, for it's true, but this has none of the significance he sees in it, since it was harmless until the Stalinist Thermidor). —Surprised that Gorkin declared himself to be a libertarian Marxist —Cardona Rosell replies at length, not taking into account the responses to what he'd said, ignores the problem of power, the relationship between economy and politics, but insists on explaining why the CNT wanted to found a trade-union bank (instead of imposing the nationalization of the banks; so that one day the state could seize the funds assembled by the unions!). Speaks of the superiority of the Spanish over the Russian

proletariat, "who had just left serfdom behind." Crass ignorance and smugness. Total ignorance of the doctrine of Bakunin, Kropotkin, Reclus, and Malatesta concerning the state, the need for violent revolution, and the destruction of the state. Degenerate anarchism. Based on these replies, the only conclusion to be drawn from this discussion would be the uselessness of any discussion in such an atmosphere of mental debility. Crushing feeling of the intellectual deficiency of the working class, of the degeneration of the working-class movement in our era of revolutions. Perhaps its grandeur was tied to that of capital? Working-class consciousness, born of class antagonism under prosperous capitalism, was powered by defectors from the bourgeoisie (an opulent class is capable of forming such defectors, animated by a disinterested idealism; that disinterested idealism is the product of powerful classes certain of their future) and declined when the overflow of the spiritual force of the bourgeoisie ceased to nourish it. This coincides with the shriveling of bourgeois thought, which in this time of danger can no longer offer itself the luxuries of generosity and the scientific spirit. Since the Russian Revolution the world has not produced either a Marx or a Kropotkin—socially impossible. The capitalist system is cracking open, experiencing earthquakes, following a period of degeneration in the workers' movement. Everything must be begun again from the very beginning, the essential task is to maintain an element of clear consciousness and of our historico-scientific acquisitions.

Leaving the meeting Vlady says to me: "What a nightmare."
Nightmare of the intellectual poverty of revolutionaries.

OROZCO, JUSTICE

November 18, 1941—Met A. R., unhinged, unhappy, ill, who tells me that your Cuban transit visas have been confirmed, also confirmed that they were sent, and that René's visa is assured.[33] A ship arrives in Vera Cruz tomorrow, another is leaving Lisbon, a third will leave Casa in December… Is it possible, is it real that you are finally going to come? I am strangely unable to imagine what I most desire; I'm like I

33. René Valentini, Laurette's son, who had been with his grandmother in Italy.

was during the last hours of my imprisonment, when I couldn't believe in freedom yet I was telling myself that if I didn't know I was going to be free in a few hours there would nothing left to do but kill myself. A black spot, at moments a great worry, your exit visa.

We went to town,[34] into the Palace of Justice to see Orozco's frescoes. A blocky gray building lacking in character. On the inside: staircases, low vaults, courtyards, arches, all of this rising into the gray of the stones beneath crushing ceilings; it's fine. Quipped: the Cellar of Justice. A bold idea to place those powerful frescoes there, it brings it to life, it causes a breath of justice to pass through the low, geometrical cave. Passionate drawing in two colors, flaming scarlet and gray. A plaster figure of Justice, drunk or downcast, blind, with a broken scale, standing above a mob of men with death's heads masks swarming among the paperwork and the crumbling stones in the middle of a hideous tumult. A huge red lightning bolt, a gigantic flame falls obliquely on all this, another Justice-Revolution puts an enormous torch to the files. Another panel, the same splendid lightning, the same swarming of repulsive monsters busy at base tasks, the same Justice-Revolution pursuing them with a sword—symbolic figures of Quetzalcóatl,[35] a flag used so that the red is a flame, enormous half-alive skull merged with the soil. Admirably placed above the grand staircase a panel depicting the red flag of the Mexican revolution mutilated and insulted. And way down at the bottom of the stairs, through the open door, as if on a movie screen, the movement on the streets can be seen.

An art fecundated, even in its architecture, by great mass movements. Direct link between this art and the peasant wars, Zapata, Morelos.[36] The breath of the revolution prevails over its betrayals and disappointments. Art, at times, is a form of vengeance.

November 28, 1941—Arkady Maslov* died suddenly on a Havana street on the twentieth. He had just received his American visa, something quite astonishing. (Arkady Chereminski lived at the Hotel San Carlos.)

34. Guadalajara.
35. The plumed serpent, main deity of the Mesoamerican pantheon.
36. The operational base of Zapata's army.

An inquest was opened and a GPU poisoning is considered quite possible. A stroke as well: he was around fifty-five, corpulent, probably an overeater, tropical climate—Normal death has become abnormal, indeed almost unbelievable for some men...With Ruth Fischer* he had led the German CP after Brandler—1923. Regular practitioners of dirty tricks, "amoral" tacticians: I always avoided him for that reason. Broad intelligence, good economist, tremendous revolutionary romanticism under an unromantic appearance; capacity for intrigue and work behind the scenes, European erudition, tireless dynamism. During the First World War a German secret agent. The case was judged by the International Control Commission of the Communist International; he was acquitted against the vote of Clara Zetkin.* In Germany under Weimar enjoyed a strange tolerance (leader of a party though a foreigner). In 1923 arrested at Luna Park as a pickpocket (provocation so as to take him to the police station? warning? blackmail?). Attempted to establish a far left under a democratic banner. Joined the Fourth, but a break with Trotsky ensued. —His adversaries in the old party, Brandler and Thalheimer, have just arrived in Havana.

Maslov is said to have fallen, struck down by a stroke, in the redlight district, perhaps after leaving a girl's place. (Shachtman,* come from New York, carried out the inquest.) Natural death...Wretchedness of an old man in that electric, carnal, semitropical Havana. To have such a broad vision of the world, to live for the revolution, to write those excellent articles on economy, and to go off, driven by loneliness and need, to those streets lined with gaping dressing gowns and eyes like proffered vaginas....

SPANISH REPUBLICANS

November 28, 1941—Ibero-Mexican Center, Elfidio Alonso,* Republican deputy from the Canaries, advocates the "return to the Republic of Figueras"! with Negrin and what's left of the Cortés. Julián Gorkin replies to him: "A conservative who wants to conserve what no longer exists." Munis advocates a landing by refugees who would leave the Baleares with arms provided by England, and he defends a united front with the Communists (tactic of the Fourth). All of this is idiotic: a small, useless massacre that will kill off the last fighters, a united front with a dissolving fascist-leaning party that's headed towards its definitive crisis. —Obvious that the republicans looking forward toward returning to Spain on British trucks and returning to the old constitution. Childishness of this political thinking, total nullity.

Gorkin alone has fully structured political ideas and poses the whole problem like a revolutionary and warns that Spain will be no one's colony.

A slip of the tongue by Elfidio, which I note, almost provoked a serious incident. He spoke of the excesses of the revolutionary "mob," then explained that the word is not as pejorative as it appears.

GPU

December 3, 1941—My informant tells me that Stalin's agent ("The Cuban"—an intellectual with a revolutionary past come to Cuba bearing $17,000 and instructions from a personal envoy of Stalin, a Russian who arrived in Cuba a few months ago) considers the project of Jackson's escape to have failed, given the measures taken at the prison. He repeats that everything was ready. The Cuban is preparing to depart (Havana? New York?) to report on the failure.

The friends of Ruth Fischer and Maslov consider Maslov's death to be a well-executed crime, stress his perfect health the day before, are angered to hear me talk about a stroke due, for example, to the climate. Say that he felt he was being spied upon by the GPU, was extremely active. Say that the American authorities will stifle the affair the same way they stifled Krivitsky's assassination and the Siqueiros Affair.

They advise me to be prudent. Nice of them!

December 4, 1941—A few days ago Natalia Ivanovna received an offer from a Mexican policeman to kill Jackson for 50,000 pesos. She thinks that the GPU cooked up this intrigue: kill Jackson and accuse the Trotskyists. (If J. had escaped, wouldn't the Trotskyists have been accused of kidnapping him?) She communicated the evidence to the Mexican authorities, who authorized communicating to the press. I think the American press will hush up the story.

The American Magazine refused to publish a reply by John Dewey*
to the disgraceful article by the former American ambassador to Moscow, Davies (December issue). (I also wrote a letter to the editor.)

The blackmailing gendarme disappeared during the investigation.

December 5, 1941—As opposed to the renegades from the bourgeoisie
who gave the working class all of socialism's great thinkers, we should
make note of the parvenus issued from the proletariat, the saddler
Ebert, the worker Noske, the bricklayer and then schoolteacher Mussolini, the professional revolutionary ("accountant") Stalin, the unemployed painter Hitler.

In the social crisis that is coming to a head in Europe, the ruined
and disappointed middle classes could give socialism a new intelligentsia. But because of their ignorance they would have to reinvent or
relearn the great ideas. On the other hand, many technicians have been
won over to a version of collectivism (plan, etc.), along with a large part
of the young people of good will: their unconscious socialism.

What is coming: the revolutions of dark consciousness. The revolution is far more in things than in people's consciousness, which has
not yet become aware of the changes that have already occurred in
things. A command economy is, but few men see this, know what it
is, that it is a necessity. Lack of imagination: in general people don't
see either what is needed or what is possible.

SPANIARDS—IBERO-MEXICAN CENTER
December 5, 1941—What was striking in this discussion was its childishness and ideological inertia. People not even capable of thinking.
Defining thinking as an activity, contact with reality, "adaptation to
experience." None of this.

No one listens to a person who differs, attempts to understand him
or respond to him. They just repeat themselves. Infantile self-satisfaction.

The old party ideas with their closed systems, which once satisfied
the needs of certain social milieu, are now nothing but inertia, consequently an obstacle to experience and thought. The effect of simple
self-interest: the representative remains attached to the (republican)

idea of the Cortés. The socialism that receives assistance from its group in the party tradition that no longer exists. Petty interests created and intellectual inertia. Old ideologies, a heavy ballast.

Condition for life: clear the path, cast aside the old formulas and ghosts. Let the dead bury their dead.

THAT BOLSHEVISM WAS A PRODIGIOUS HUMAN SUCCESS

December 5, 1941—A period of about sixty years had forged revolutionary intelligentsia (its leadership composed for the most part of intellectuals of bourgeois origin but resting on a much larger number of worker militants; consider also the rural origin of the workers, their social health—little effected by the corruption-wear of the big cities—and the provincial origin of the intellectuals, same quality; religious antecedents of both. Social function of religion in old Russia as well as its spiritual importance. Entanglement reaction-religion) constituting a success that for the moment is unique in modern world. Its general traits: capacity for conviction, unity thought-action, personality, not individualism, social consciousness, energy, capacity for sacrifices and desire for victory. Superiority of the Bolsheviks: the weapon of Marxism, intellectual training superior to the old idealisms. Nevertheless, the Bolsheviks are in no essential way different from the Narodniki, the Mensheviks, the anarchists, the maximalists, and others. Common environment that demonstrates the freshness of spirit and the vigor of the Russian people at that moment in history; era of social progress, growth and optimism of the bourgeoisie, world war. An astounding historic success, comparable to the birth of a man of genius (social birth).

December 6, 1941—With Julián went to the Apolo. Lower depths of Mexico City. Enormous square plaza, at the far side of it this low building, lit-up sign. A dark plaza with a bad reputation, sinister. Fishy men who offer you photos of naked women, others mumble who knows what propositions.

The room is a kind of shed, filthy and cold. Dances and a succession of a dozen poor girls, either naked or who undress as they sing couplets.

Crude lighting, forlorn and garish backdrop. A few beautiful Polynesian girls (of Indian and Chinese blood) with round shoulders, their shapes soft and blurred, their faces flat beneath their black hair. There's nothing more disagreeable to look at than the vulgar and blatant eroticism of some European women, one skinny, one half-old, both look Jewish. The suffering of a girl with a poor figure who feels ugly and clumsy and crosses the stage twice to the sound of insults. Her forced smile, her visible panic, they call her a fat frog. Spaniards perform a revolting play. Wretchedness of all these beings who perhaps don't know it; they don't seem to be ashamed of it. But what would be worse: that they be aware of the job they are doing or that—after all!—they be happy with themselves. The reality is probably mixed. A crowd of kids stamping their feet, males in heat and shabby old gents in glasses. Some who came alone, sad. They come to this the same way animals go to warm themselves in the sun. Wretchedness of sex, wretchedness of life: like grass and the wildflowers attached to the cracks in the stone on the edge of the path. The almost ferocious grandeur of this wretched manifestation of the power of life (even in the powerlessness of the person). Sinister mugs. A door held together with wooden planks looks like a Constructivist decoration. Resemblance with Russian hovels.

WAR IN THE PACIFIC—PROBLEM OF THE RENEWAL OF IDEAS

Sunday, December 7, 1941—Signifies that in reality there the only solutions left are international ones. Need for total reorganization.

Infinitely probable victory of the Americans, but they'll be rudely disappointed, expecting a quick and relatively easy victory. Have no idea of the energy of a very different race, terribly energetic, very poor, not at all bourgeoisified, and backed into a desperate situation. If the Japanese succeed in notably reducing the American Navy through partial successes, defeating them will be a long and difficult process.

In working at this the United States will also work at unleashing social revolution throughout the Far East, as in Europe. The worldwide crisis of 1918–1921, expanded and deeper, will return, along with the extraordinary progress of mass consciousness and the almost complete disappearance of ideological frameworks and movements. The positive side of this: to what extent have the ideas of yesterday, given the force of inertia of those who hold them, become obstacles to a creative empiricism and the appearance of new ideas (to the renewal of socialism)?

FACES OF MEXICO CITY

December 9, 1941—Churches. Old reddish stone that puts one in mind of Indian land—the red clay of tropical countries—and of Indian flesh. Stone and brick. High walls with no ornamentation, bare and sad, eaten away by the sadness of time; above them a low cupola sometimes decorated with faded ceramics. A doorway richly ornamented with lifelike sculptures, a baroque tower from which the bells have often been removed, the crucifix almost always removed, all of it looking like a ruin, impression of dismantling. Wild plants grow in the corners, at the top of the decapitated tower. Something desolate about all this, and tragic, a volcanic wind has passed over these churches and they match perfectly the old Indian woman with her immobile, near-black face, squatting in the entryway in her black serape.

Prostitutes. The Calle del Órgano, a long uneven line in a commercial neighborhood, edged by bare, cracked walls and wretched little houses, mostly one story. Taverns with glass doors and broken panes. Doors onto the sidewalk of workshops (carpentry), tiny stores where in the shadows one sees an ancient Indian woman, hooked nose and white hair, serving the girls biscuits, black peppers, and Coca-Cola. The girls live on the edge of the sidewalk, their beds behind the door. They squat in the doorway, sew, knit, or smoke. Mixed race, few delicate types, most of them young, many of them well-built young girls, with heavy, peasant faces. Their type puts me in mind of the broad, flat faces of Oceania, with pug noses, thick lips, thick hair, a vegetal force.

At a window two seventeen- or eighteen-year-old girls, the youngest with fine features, golden skin, sharp nose, well-defined oval face, tiny elongated black eyes—charming, but with a hard and already degraded expression. She's standing, wearing a short dress of Indian pink, and picking the lice from the heavy, gray head of a sleeping old woman. She smiles, and with her head gestures an invitation, her hands never once stopping their movements. The other girl, leaning on the window near the fence, is pretty but vulgar. The bed is behind them.

The street is strangely bare, low walls under a white sky. All along the wall girls squatting on bricks. There are heavy and lethargic ones and young, resigned ones. They smoke.

Universality of male and female desolation in the big city from which there is no possible escape. This *calle* is like the street that climbs from the boulevard de la Chapelle to Sacré-Coeur Basilica; to the alleys of yesteryear near Khitrov Rynok in Moscow; to sections of the Ligovka or the Pushkinskaya in Leningrad ...

DEATHS

Arthur Holitscher* died in Switzerland a while ago. His noble square head, heavy, crowned with a white crew cut, his solid traits, his air of a great, sybaritic humanist, poetic and sad. Our encounters in Leningrad-Moscow where he came, very understanding, in 1920–1921: he saw the problems clearly. Then in Berlin in 1923–1924, his comfortable, well-lit little home near the Olivaer Platz. Yellow wood furniture—one would almost say gilded—lawns, trees, people, houses, a pleasant modern Brueghel-like atmosphere. His wife, much younger than he, a noble head as well, blonde, a high brow, burning with life—I saw only her portrait, which he showed me with a bitter smile—had just left him. I thought: the man was too selfish, perhaps the woman too, they lack grandeur, an intimacy they were truly seeking, thought they had—and the fierce beast within them, despite everything, unconquered, needy despite their culture and intelligence, defeated the couple. It was perhaps good for the wife ... His books on the shelves, travels, America, Russia, China, Palestine, he loved discovery, an intelligence more comprehensive than creative: his essay on Baudelaire, whom he loved above all others ... A globe with all of his travels marked on it in various colors ... To have covered the world, to have worked so hard, to have thought so much only to arrive at the desert—he said to me with a wave of his hand. He saw that the European crisis would reach Central Europe, and this was weighing him down. Came to see me in Lichterflede, we spent a pleasant evening with Vuyovich,* Heinz Neumann,* a Hungarian, good revolutionary, talking revolution, we spoke of the assassination attempt on Von Seekt being prepared; I said it would fail (two old Spartacist workers were supposed to fire on Von Seekt during his morning walk in the Tiergarten; Germans and of a certain age, I thought they'd waver at the last minute, and I was right, they twice saw him walk past, didn't dare ... October or November 1923). Met H. for the last time in Moscow in 1928 at an international writers' conference, he was with the German Communist writers who were in on their way to becoming obedient Stalinists, while I had just refused to shake Vaillant-Couturier's* hand. We embraced; he embarrassed by his friendship with an Oppositionist, we promised to meet: we never saw each other again. He had had the courage to understand the revolution but lacked the courage to understand and condemn the counterrevolution within the revolution. Deep down, he certainly understood, but to break again with a milieu, the only one in which he could find any support, a certain resonance for his final labors? His end must have been a bitter one.

I learn that his end truly was bitter. He was losing his sight, he was all alone and had lost his corner in life, his books, maps, souvenirs, and Berlin. A refugee in Switzerland, imbued with the ideas that had sustained him, both Epicurean and Stoic, he asked Dr. F. B. for the means to a peaceful end, and F. B. gave it to him.[37] But H. wavered at the last minute without wanting to admit it to himself and only took a portion of the dose. It made him seriously ill and diminished, and he feigned anger with F. B. for having given in to him and for "having cheated him" in his final escape attempt.[38]

December 12, 1941—Charles Rappoport,* seventy? older? died in a hospital in Cahors. Saw him the last times on the café terraces, Paris, La Source, Le Dôme, in the front row, alone, so he could look at the figures of passing women through the thick lenses of his glasses, which allowed him only blurred images. Abandoned, he rejoiced in a handshake,

---

37. This is probably Dr. Fritz Brupbacher (1874–1945), anarchist and doctor to the poor, briefly a member of the Swiss Communist Party, and close to *Révolution prolétarienne*.
38. Last paragraph added by hand in blue ink.

quickly snuck in an anecdote, spoke of people of the century gone by, of Jaurès, of Lenin. The end of his life: people pointed him out, no one took any interest in him, people passed him by, too old and always the anecdotes...The air of a worn-out old faun or a short, fat Socrates; seated like a sad toad, still trying to see; a final eagerness to live, hardly ever succeeding anymore...The boulevard passed.

In 1922 in Berlin at the home of Dr. Goldenberg, on Kurfürstendamm, sagacious and salacious, told me that he took silk stockings to Moscow to seduce the typists of the Comintern and the little prostitutes of the Tverskaia. "There won't be a revolution in Russia for the same reason that there won't be a counterrevolution in Russia: hunger." Saw him again in Moscow, a well-dressed Socrates, large overcoat and broad-brimmed fedora, in the entrance to the Marx-Engels Institute (Riazanov*), we only exchanged a cold greeting because I was in the Opposition and he lived on the small manna of *Izvestia*.[39] Selling himself to the revolution—even Thermidorian—must have seemed preferable to him to selling himself piece by tiny piece to the Parisian papers. There was something visibly lacking in him, and his appearance cried of it: a bit of nobility. The personality of a little Lithuanian Jew humiliated from birth, from even before birth, and sly; quickly perceived that he was smarter than the others, humor and sarcasm (vengeance). A foundational training in the Russian revolutionary ambiance, then that of French socialism, congresses, cafés, eloquence, idealistic petty bourgeoisie accustomed to living well, fine wines, brothels, dirty jokes, playing with ideas; remained Marxist in all this, refused to adapt himself beyond a certain point and that made him a personality, with another adaptation: the guest of "advanced" duchesses...The character of a good, average, Russian revolutionary drowned in the socialism of Parisian congresses and cafés. At bottom, there was something invincible and tenacious about him, like Trotsky and Yeltsin,* whom a different environment made great. Adapted himself to communism, but too clear sighted to be at ease in it, too intelligent for the times; degraded himself in order to scrape by with *Izvestia*, swallowed his

39. *Izvestia* (meaning "dispatch" or "the news") was the daily newspaper of record in Russia from 1916 to 1991.

bitterness when Riazanov died, continued on until the third Moscow Trial, but Bukharin's execution was the last straw. With the third trial, at more than sixty years old, he resigned from the Party. Better late than never, but I hesitated for some time after to shake his hand. Symbolic, those pitiful final days. Our final conversation at the Dôme. Rappoport asked me to form a jury of honor for T., the GPU agent gunned down on the rue Denfert-Rochereau by other agents because he betrayed them, I don't know for whom . . . T. had sought us out, but since he didn't provide an acceptable explanation for his differences with the GPU and I was well informed, we let him drop. Rappoport insisted without having understood anything. Pitiful.

By contrast, old Boris Mikhailovich Yeltsin, frail and ill, in an old, ragged little overcoat, at the back of a yard covered with snow and frozen sewer water, little wooden houses of wood, low and wretched— Yeltsin waving a final goodbye to Vlady and me (we were leaving, he remained in deportation "his true place"). His large head, his still-black mane brushed back, goatee and monocle, he looked unconquerable. I said to him: "Like Trotsky, you're a satanic Jew"—because of his inexhaustible internal source of energy, prophetic idealism, and moral energy. —Rappoport, the same race, but submerged in the social decomposition of the Third Republic.

WAR IN THE PACIFIC
December 19, 1941—Conversation with Vlady. Hong Kong fell in a few days, Singapore is threatened. The British fleet in Singapore went out without planes! The two largest ships destroyed. Pearl Harbor is out of action, the Japanese Navy came within a hundred miles of the coast and launched its bombers . . . Neither American intelligence nor its patrols knew or foresaw anything. The Philippines probably lost, insufficient forces for any prolonged resistance (ten thousand Americans, seventy thousand Filipinos). Possibility for the Japanese to seize the Dutch East Indies and even land in Australia and so win the war—at the beginning. American aviation won't be ready for six months to a year to send for example squadrons of any strength to Vladivostok. Long war to be expected.

Lack of foresight and preparation of the Americans. How could the president have sent a note that was equivalent to an ultimatum without putting the fleet and the air force on alert? They were truly convinced that the Japanese wouldn't dare!

Contributing factors to this incompetence: conservatism, inability to reflect on reality, lack of revolutionary imagination.

At bottom: a decline of the intellectual energy and dynamism of the bourgeoisie, which senses confusedly that this crisis is leading it to an end. Various forms of repression[40] enter into this, they no longer want to confront reality clearly, they wait until they are surprised by events and forced to act.

CUAUTLA—MOUNTAINS

December 22, 1941—I write these notes in light of the cable announcing that your trip is confirmed for early January. Would this be the end of the great anxiety? I think of your joy and don't know how to measure mine.

Went to Cuautla yesterday, car. Unity of the world. I recognize everywhere the landscapes of another continent. The Popo[41] puts me in mind of the Kazbek; the reddish glow over on the plains at the foot of the mountains of the valleys of Georgia. As we were leaving there were moments when the road was like Orly's road near the forest of Fontainebleau. But tall, upright cacti suddenly appear, from which the peasants make hedgerows. Others spread their large, oval, spiky leaves of a pure green in all directions. There are explosions of magueys, bouquets of gigantic grass. Why do they seem so beautiful to me? It's because they harmoniously, victoriously display vegetal energy; powerful, but not immoderate, on a human scale and in a way intelligible, since they are like a prodigious grass—while the cacti are disconcerting, strange. The plains are covered in a white mist which is not fog: one would say an opaque brightness. Above it, as if in a Japanese print,

40. Note that Serge uses the word *refoulement*, the word for "repression" in the Freudian sense.
41. Common diminutive for Mount Popocatépetl.

appear the profiles of Ixtaccíhuatl and Popocatépetl, two snow-covered mountains beyond several hills profiled in hints of gray, blue, and violet. Ixta means "the reclining woman," and it's astonishing: it really does have the shape of a woman with high breasts, her hair loose, covered in white. This shape can be made out from several sides; when we take the road in the other direction we'll see the woman's face sculpted in crude, perpendicular slopes, a face of ravaged force. This should be even more magnificent than on the road out, for it will appear in the softness of the evening, above the verdant plains and reclining on a bed of horizontal clouds above the darkened mountain. One can see the shape of the extended arm. Popocatépetl is a pointed cone, symmetrical, with a lateral pike. It has a pure outline, simple, grandiose, its slopes of a sparkling white or broken up with dark rocks. There is a gap between the two neighboring summits; they tower over the road, the countryside, summits of the earth.

Zapata was killed near Cuautla. Busy little town in which I see no originality. Nearly tropical, we descended into a region of triumphant plants. There are the high leaves of banyans, banana trees; one bathes in heat and sunlight, lizards scurrying on the trunk of every tree, palm trees rising tall, explosions of red and violet flowers appearing among the trees, we admire the large bindweeds of a savage blue, plants whose leaves are forty centimeters wide bear flaming red lilies on their two-meter-long stems. The enormous, turgescent, pale-gray trunks of the silk-cotton trees. What is lacking in these exhilarating forms of life? Intelligence. It isn't born of the planet and the sun—it is the fruit of a fierce and prodigious effort across time.

I'm observing a beautiful orange cat. He toys with a lizard the way he'd toy with a mouse, allowing it to flee, hiding under a wad of crumpled paper, patiently watching as the lizard, playing dead, starts breathing again and feeling reassured. He snatches it carefully between his beautiful little white teeth to carry it to a convenient spot where he can play with it. He ultimately devours it slowly, swallowing it whole.

I made a movement, the cat grumbled, with a mistrustful look in his black-slitted yellow pupils. Does this creature in dark black glasses want to take his lizard—to eat it, obviously? The first signs of intelligence, carnivorous intelligence.

On our return at nightfall a magnificent moment when we stop at the crowded town square of Amecameca (in Aztec: "many wells"). Bright blue facade of a school with ogival windows. Next to it the large openwork triple portal of the church, white, with grass growing in the brickwork on high. Lofty facade and church belfry in pink—and above it, the Reclining Woman in her snows, face to a sky that has turned even more intensely blue as night begins. In the sky only one star shines, white. Went through the gated portal alone: when you turn around you have behind you the activity of the plaza, on the other side illuminated arches, a corner of the marketplace bathed in electricity. Here a darkened garden is in front of the church, tall crosses tilting to the right over old graves. Silence, star, mountain, spaces, three small bells high up in the pink-hued stone hold your gaze. I'd like to return here with you at this same time of day so I can, at a moment like this, feel your shoulder close and see this corner of the world reflected in your eyes. (All along the road the sturdy plants and the new flowers made me think of the happiness you'll feel discovering them ...)

Perhaps the ultimate function of intelligence: to contemplate, that is, feel the world becoming conscious of itself (Élisée Reclus).[42] Surpassing carnivorous intelligence.

RICH JEWS

Lunched at the pension of Zhenia Orlansky in Cuautla, like Le Vadoue,[43] in the middle of Mexico. Plenty of grub, the irritating white skin of plump young women, colorful slacks and blouses, the faces of smug and well-groomed beasts. The men the same, except with glasses. The noises—they never stop stuffing their faces. I share your horror of feeding troughs; you'd flee this place and I'm restraining the same impulse. Chubby, stupid children: a twelve-year-old girl has the face

---

42. Reclus wrote in his book *The Earth and Its Inhabitants*, "Man is nature becoming conscious of itself."

43. Serge is referring to the pension opened in the 1930s by the painter Ismak Kogan and his companion Frieda Mandelstam in the village of Le Vadoue. It served as a refuge for Jewish families until the couple was arrested in 1941.

of a thirty-year-old woman, sure of herself and sullen. The faces express nothing but practical egotism, reflect nothing but bourgeois pettiness. Petty-bourgeois businessmen, they live only for profit so they can eat *en famille*. I know them well. If you were to ask them to give a fifth of their fortune to save poor Jews they'd look at you like a dangerous madman. The best give 100 pesos twice a year. Rodents.

They are of the opinion that it is necessary to burn the cities of Russia in order to fight Hitler. That Stalin is a great war leader ... That Germany must be destroyed. That nothing should be said at this time that might hurt Stalin. That wealthy America will rule over Europe. They are afraid of revolutions.

While we spend this sunny day here and these people their day feeding their faces, war in the snows of Russia, Europe rationed, bombed, desperate, new butcheries in the Far East. Commercial intelligence (rodents) still has a long way to go to attain a collective sensibility (breadth of vision, imagination) and a sense of history (from which the sense of duty and the abandonment of individualism like an old worn-out skin): the road to the realization of man.

FRENCH PRISONER IN GERMANY

December 26, 1941—Good meeting at Dr. Fränkel's* with recently arrived comrades. Report by N. on French prisoners in a camp in Germany. 120,000, of whom 100,000 work outside the camp. Food: 200 gr. of black bread (sawdust) and two bowls of powdered fish soup daily. Famine. Living on parcels. Discipline bearable, Bavarians not really nasty. And yet: dogs trained to attack the khaki uniform and unleashed on prisoners who cook rotten potatoes in old tin cans or who step off the plank sidewalk onto the road.

Mentality: animalistic-primitive. At the beginning they all hoped for a Nazi victory so that it would all be over and they could go home. Annoyed by England's resistance ... Followed by a growing hatred felt by all of them (more intensely by the Yugoslavs and the Poles) for the German (not the Nazi, the German), a biologically reflexive violence. Growing interest in the causes of the defeat, immense military experience endlessly discussed, few political generalizations, overwhelming idea of the basic superiority of the Nazis. No ideologies or propaganda. Majority working in war industries or agriculture, noncoms who refuse forced to work at breaking rocks. Humiliation of the noncoms of the Mobile Guard, chief warrant officers in rags, pushing wheelbarrows alongside Spanish "clients" they recently stood guard over in the French camps. (Laughter.)

We come to the conclusion that in France there is a large mass of totally backward people, below the level of any even minimally structured ideas or social conscience; a nearly animal level of existence. (This was a revelation for many of the militants mobilized during the Phony War: a predominance of men who didn't wash, dreamed only of drunken binges, spoke of women only in ignoble terms.) Consider whether this is a backward state or a state of bourgeois degeneration? A comparison with the average Russian peasant forces one to lean towards backward due to social degeneration.

REACTIONARY WAR

December 28, 1941—The social-psychological causes of France's defeat (fear of a victory over the reactionary order benefiting a necessarily social revolution) are unmistakably at work among the Allies.

The anti-Nazi emigrations stabbed in the back by the State Department in Washington. An agreement is said to have been reached between Churchill and Litvinov in Washington (today's papers) on concerted action and future status of Europe (!), the USSR committing itself (!) not to implant communism in defeated Germany...Good lord!

Parades and diplomatic demonstrations of Allied governments exiled in London (the Poles magnificent: generals and colonels in full uniform being blessed by archbishops, propaganda photos!). What does this have to do with the guerrillas in Polesia,[44] the acts of popular resistance, the terrorism of the patriots, etc.? An abyss is being dug between these rulers of yesterday heading phantom governments and the people they

---

44. Throughout the war Jewish partisans maintained an active resistance against the German troops in Polesia (the region today divided among Poland, Ukraine, and Belarus).

now claim to represent and will claim to govern tomorrow. Real Europe against official and reactionary Europe. Elements of future civil wars.

Press of the last few days: King Carol [II of Romania] joins the "Free Romania" movement of the United States and hopes to recover his throne after the victory of the democracies...!

A Spanish Republican government is being formed in Mexico City: Martínez Barrio,* Albornoz* (Justice), Prieto* (ambassador to Washington), Negrín* (ambassador to London)... Nothing learned, nothing forgotten, those responsible for the shipwreck are disguising themselves as lifesavers.

IN THE WAR'S WINGS

Late December 1941—Obscure points concerning the Nazi retreat in the USSR that winter and typhus don't completely explain: Why didn't they take Leningrad (calculating on the fleet capitulation?) and Sebastopol (same calculation)? Why are they abandoning the Leningrad–Moscow railroad, Orel, and renouncing Rostov and the oil road? Three weeks ago it was said in Washington (newspapers) that the halting of the German offensive against Moscow could be the result of secret negotiations with Stalin and Soviet neutrality in Vladivostok. (This neutrality can also be explained by their legitimate lack of confidence in the United States and its allies until the completion of their preparations.) Is there a Soviet-British collaboration for defense of the Caucasus? Could the Nazis have abandoned Rostov on the condition that the British don't enter the Caucasus? A game of dupes with multiple losers.

The Wavell offensive in Cyrenaica, February 1941, is thought to have been halted to mollify Mussolini, whose fall London fears. Can the September (23), 1941 failure in Dakar[45] be explained by the disapproval of the United States?

These past few days (December 26), Gaullist forces under Admiral Muselier occupied Saint Pierre et Miquelon; Washington disavows

---

45. Error by Serge. The attack on Dakar by British and anti-Vichy French forces took place the previous year, on September 22–25, 1940, before the United States entered the war.

this and calls for the reestablishment of the Vichy status quo... Mid-December agreement reached between Admiral Robert-Vichy and Washington on status quo Martinique. United States handles Vichy-French empire gingerly as future advance post of the American economy in Eurafrica. Above all, fear of revolution and social changes. Christmas messages Churchill-Roosevelt and pope almost alike and totally hollow. Not a living word in Europe.

REVOLUTIONARY PERSPECTIVES

Late December 1941—Japan's infinitely probable defeat brings in its train a Japanese revolution of a necessarily social character awakening of the masses in China. Long war brings with it impoverishment of the United States, worsening of social problems, prerevolutionary situation in the United States between the revolutions in Europe and Asia.

A federated Europe, with a state-directed economy, centered on German, British, and (secondarily) French industry and Russian, will in any case be a fearsome competitor for the United States on the Asian markets... Immense markets unable to pay, from which the necessity for a new system of exchange. Devaluation or depreciation or partial elimination of gold. (Resistance to this by the United States, monopolist of gold.)

American monopoly capital will probably attempt a creeping colonization of Europe, with armed interventions against social movements. Europe uncolonizable and ungovernable by foreigners. Defend *Europe's right to self-determination, its right to socialism.*

In Europe, the dangers of a revolution of dark consciousness. Contradictory impulses: need for a directed, federated economy equally safeguarding the interests of all peoples and anti-German national reactions, sometimes furious (Yugoslavs, Greeks, Poles, French). Socialist dictatorships to overcome these reactions?

If American industry boycotted a socialist Europe in revolution, it would open a crisis at home, strikes, unemployment. A tilt toward military intervention rather than boycott would collide with the revolutionary spirit of the American masses, who will no longer want to fight far from home, this time not against Nazism but against socialism.

1942

FIFTY-ONE YEARS—BALANCE SHEET OF AN EFFORT TO THINK CLEARLY

January 1942—Meditation: To what extent have I seen clearly? Lifeline. Revolutionary passion inculcated by Russian milieu, childhood, adolescence, rational spirit, will for objectivity coming from my father, his positivism inclined towards simplifications, his "Robespierre-ism," admiration of Spencer. Russian atmosphere in 1905 Belgium. Childish desire to show off in the first months of my anarchist activity, horror of stagnation, romantic need to fight. Soon afterwards: awareness of the impossibility of living in this world. City-with-no-possible-escape. Paris. The One against all. Anarchist-Individualist period; ignorance (read nothing of Marx, repugnance for bourgeoisified socialism, with its political scheming and jostling for position). By age twenty, had overcome the desire to *appear*; will to *be*, hence disdain for appearances.

Prison, awaiting the Russian Revolution, which would be worth living and dying for. Sordid and hopeless to live for oneself.

1917, Spain, crisis. War and the self-centered egotism of everyone. Desire to go under fire at the front. "Life is not so grand a thing that it would be a misfortune to lose it or a crime to take it"[1] (the depths of despair of our anarchist individualism). Preparations for the Barcelona insurrection July–August 1917, along with Anna[2] am the only one in our foreign anarchist milieu to rally to the movement. Influence of

---

1. A line Serge used in *Birth of Our Power*.
2. Perhaps Anna Estorgues, better known as Rirette Maîtrejean, Serge's companion and briefly wife during his anarchist years.

Seguí,* empty chatter of Borobio (*Solidaridad Obrera*³). My judgment on this movement quite right: "birth of our power," doomed for the present, incompetence, recklessness, good, strong instincts, no brain. Depart: Russia, revolution, there it's serious, great.

Interned at Précigné, I maintain that the Russian Revolution cannot but lead to the peasants seizing the land and the workers taking over production. I write to Pierre Chardon* (published in *La Mêlée*, 1918) that in this way a great step will be taken, after which abject combats will recommence on a renewed social terrain. Right.

Activities in support of Bolshevism at the camp.

Russia, early 1919. With Nikolaenko* on the train from Beloostrov, surrounded by snow, we analyze an article by Zinoviev, in the *Sievernaya Kommuna* I think, on the monopoly of power (one-party government). Dangerous, this. Nevertheless, joined the CP as an anarchist because it was the sole force carrying out the revolution. Right. Indignant at the persecution of dissidents, anarchists, and Mensheviks, encounters with Gorky and Martov,* fight against that persecution. I was right.* Likewise consider the belief that War Communism is the realization of socialism to be insane (discussion with Vassilieva,* Yonov, Mazin*). I see it as a historical expedient which must be reconsidered and replaced by a more flexible and humane system.

1919, strong will to live, will not be killed stupidly, precautions against typhus, effort to develop a rational courage, void of Don Quixotism. Right. Extremely worn down by the Terror, whose necessity I accept. Concept of double duty, defend the revolution, combat its flaws from within. I write to Rirette [Maîtrejean*] that I am determined not to "make a career in the revolution" (1920).

1920–1921, Kronstadt, we (with Body, Helfer) determined not to fight against a starving people. Indignant at Zinoviev's lie about General Kozlovsky. Sympathy for the Workers' Opposition, but afraid that its faculty for disintegration is much greater than its capacity for organization and reformation. Do not join. Attempts at mediation with

3. Anarcho-syndicalist paper founded in 1907

the anarchists (Goldman,* Berkman,* Perkus*[4]) between Kronstadt and the party. Right.

1921–1922, supporter of NEP, though a latecomer. Discussions with F. de los Rios (at the Lux) and the mediocre and venomous G. Leval,* I explain there was another solution, "communism of associations," a call for the (controlled) free initiative of the unions, cooperatives, and various associations of intellectuals. Still think it would have been the right road. Discussions on the Cheka, likely to strangle the Revolution (partially published by Leval in *Le Libertaire* in Paris, which was perfidious). Discussion on this subject with Vaillant-Couturier, Morizet,* Souvarine,* Julien,* Vuyovich. Right.

1923, Berlin, I write to Souvarine (executive of the Comintern) that the November 7 insurrection [in Germany] will fail for it doesn't co-incide with mass movement. Neumann's preparation, assassination attempt on von Seekt (military dictator), I predicted its failure, psychological reasons. (Bureaucratization and corruption of the party, discussions with Pierre Pascal,* conference of the three Internationals, Genoa Conference, we saw a dark future, anticipation of Thermidor, 1922).

1923–1925, Vienna, influence of Lukács, who was a magnificent dialectician. Theoretical understanding of Marxism. Discussion with Joffe* about the Comintern's adventurism in the Balkans—in agreement. Clandestinely join the Opposition in 1923, Trotsky, Preobrazhensky. Conflict with Béla Kun over manipulation, of French CP, "in violation of the statutes," recalled to Russia.

1926, Russia, immediate awareness of the malaise of the NEP. 1927, Opposition struggles, Chinese revolution. I write to Marcel Fourrier* that our situation is that of Marx in 1848, defeated in advance, but we have to fight. Olga Petrovna Bosch and Kotziubinsky*: after hesitating I join the active group in case a *coup de force* is attempted. Consider it a good thing that it wasn't attempted.

4. In his *Memoirs* Serge describes this Russian anarchist deported from the United States as "the young secretary of the Union of Russian Workers of the United States."

1927 or 1928, turned down Brunn (Ilk, executed), come to offer me on Trilliser's behalf post of adviser to Chang-So-Lin. Reason: it seems to me the Cheka, which directs the work of secret agents overseas, will be called on to play a disastrous role in the upcoming struggles within the revolution. I was terribly right.

At that time I decided, given the growing reaction, to dedicate myself to history and literature, novels, to work at defending and ripening my ideas. Duty of a witness, conclusion that intellectual activity remained the only one possible. In the face of the degeneration of the Comintern, horrified by the amount of wasted labor.

1928, meeting of the Opposition circle at the Ozet in Leningrad, Nevsky, I spoke openly and clearly of the degeneration of the Comintern. (No one yet dared admit this, Trotsky persisted in a formal fidelity and deep loyalty to an organization that it was already high time to think of replacing. To a certain extent this was possible. Souvarine also saw things clearly and said what needed to be said at the time.) In 1927, at the Opposition's center in Leningrad at Karpov's home, I'd declared that the Chinese revolution was in crisis. I maintain that my articles in *Clarté* on "The Class Struggle in the Chinese Revolution" are my best work, clear-sighted in all their predictions from one month to the next. (Nearly cost me my life, Preobrazhensky's warning.)

1928, Russakov* affair, Kreps's warning that they may very well cook up a diversionary espionage affair against me, Solovki[5] or executed; I answer him by announcing the publication of *Year One* [*of the Russian Revolution*].

Silent disagreement with Trotsky during the trial of the "industrial party,"[6] Menshevik center, Chekists mostly agree with the thesis of the prosecution and even see in it a confirmation of most of their positions! I see through the whole fraud and the basic reasons behind it. (Conversations with Polevoi,* devastated, who *knows* the fraud: episode of the Menshevik Sokolovsky whom he knows and whose enormous lie is clear to him. The *Opposition Bulletin* saddens us.)

---

5. Solovki: first Soviet prison camp (1921) on Solovetsky islands in White Sea.
6. Falsified 1930 trial in which the economist Nikolai Kondratiev* was the principal defendant.

1929–1931, captivity-deportation.[7]

1933–1936. Immediately suspected Sobolevicius's* treason, 1932, understood the catastrophic arrest of Ivan Smirnov, suicide of Zina Lvovna Bronstein* in Berlin.

In deportation Mikhail Alexandrovich Chabion*[8] informs me of the founding of the Fourth International, proposes forming a committee—probably a provocateur. Refused. Don't see with what elements a new International can be founded.

1936, Belgium. Correspond with Leon Trotsky. Obtain from him that we will demand release of all socialist and anarchist political prisoners persecuted in Russia—that we will demand freedom for Soviet parties (which he then did in *The Revolution Betrayed*), that we will adopt a fraternal attitude towards the Spanish anarchists. (He promised to publish a text addressed to them, but didn't.) Disagreement with T. over the premature founding of the Fourth, poor internal methods, policy towards the POUM, historical questions: Cheka, Kronstadt-NEP, Bolshevism's intolerance; in general, his intolerance and his sectarianism.

June 1936, disagreement with T., who sees in the strikes "the beginning of the French Revolution." In agreement with Monatte,* nothing but the awakening of the working class—with a certain revolutionary inflation. August–September 1936 deciphered the original enigma of the Moscow Trial. (T., interned in Norway, reduced to silence, proposes that I continue his book.) Conference of the Fourth, Amsterdam, polite split with the "majority" over unity with the POUM. Same period, my warnings to the POUM about the assassinations being prepared against it; proposals on the question of the regime: bourgeois democracy in its form with socialist content, imitating the Republic of the Far East founded by the Bolsheviks in 1920.

1937–1939, parallel labors, Spanish revolution, counter–Moscow Trial and assassinations, discussion with Trotsky, literary works.

7. Lapse on Serge's part. From 1929 through 1932 he lived and wrote, under heavy surveillance, in Leningrad. His "captivity and deportation" dated from 1933 to 1936, as is clear from next entry.

8. History professor arrested in 1938.

1939–1940, the war. The impotence of the socialist movement leaves me in a certain confusion. Laurette is often right against me in our discussions, even though her way of thinking is too linear. Impossible in my eyes not to care about the defense of the democracies, even when they openly betray themselves, like the Third French Republic. Period of groping. Everything becomes clear on the roads of defeat, new revolutionary perspectives open for all of Europe. Sudden feeling of seeing things clearly. To Pitaud,* during the period of the armistice (Souillac): "There will be a socialist-leaning and national revolution."

(Since 1936, Spanish revolution has posed the question: A planned economy, of necessity, but directed by whom and for whom? *From Lenin to Stalin*.)

Before the Moscow Pact, maintained that the USSR wouldn't join the England-France bloc. After the pact, maintained that it concealed an extremely bitter struggle: "Stalin is winning the battle of the Baltic." Discussions with Modigliani, Marseille, 1941, on the USSR and the occupation of Bulgaria. Atlantic, April 1941, discussion with Rémy, Breton, Lévi-Strauss on the Russo-Japanese pact and the invasion of Yugoslavia. I see in this the first manifestations of the Russo-German war.

Up till now the general ideas of the book I wrote in Ciudad Trujillo[9] at the beginning of the Russian campaign have been confirmed on every point, even in the strategic details.

SPANISH ANARCHISTS

January 2, 1942—Newspapers. Attack on a cashier at the Cervecería Modelo, connects with Spanish anarchist Sánchez,* found lying naked in a wretched lodging where he lived with two women, fired on the police and killed himself. Nearly classic anarchist newspaper cliché. One of Sánchez Añon's women, María Murillo, had given herself *Armonía del Vivir Pensando* ... Among those arrested, a former member of the National Committee of the CNT, Marcos Alcón* (innocent).

9. *Hitler Contra Stalin.*

This attack will probably serve to justify the creation of a concentration camp. Psychology of the irresponsible revolutionary, romanticism, resentment, individualist violence.

Julián tells the story that a detainee (a priest, I believe) who was being driven on a road in Catalonia offered his guards 200 pesos. The car breaks down. The prisoner inspects the motor along with his guards. One of the latter: "I don't know how it happened, I shot him in the head and I was happy, really happy!"—about what?—"I don't know, about that." (Early in the revolution.)

J. has a very healthy judgment of "mass terrorism," which spontaneously increases crimes, useless executions, and makes enemies for the movement. It quickly becomes a counterrevolutionary factor. We were with Péret,* and I go off on Calas,* a young bourgeois dilettante who had just told the revolutionaries of the Paris cafés: "Be sadistic!" (setting the house on fire). Nothing could be more antisocialist. On the contrary, revolutionaries have the duty to introduce consciousness into mass violence and to fight against the unhealthy currents (sadism).

SURREALISM

January 2, 1942—Socially conditioned to an appalling degree. A totally failed escape (or rebellion). (Great escapes-rebellions that were successful: Russian nihilism of the years 1860–1880, Marxism, anarchism; intellectual discoveries fecundated by mass fermentation. Role of numbers, that is of the social environment. Escape is only possible if within the society there develops an oppositional milieu that is broad and vital enough.)

Definition: poetry and painting based on psychological automatisms in order to free the faculties of expression from reason, from all constraints, and to allow them to attain or reveal a deeper, truer, more original reality than the one organized by reason.

Two elements in this: a revolt against the bastardized reason (good sense, common sense, bourgeois sense, abdication of intellectual effort, conformism) of a decadent epoch; post–World War I France, bled dry but enriched, its bourgeoisie triumphant but exhausted. In this sense the movement can be considered revolutionary in the immediate, because it leads to taking position against the ruling order of things (Henri Michaux: *Je contre* [I Against], very strong.)

But beyond the bastardized reason of the moment its criticism is aimed at intellect per se ("in itself" an improper term, the intellectual is always socially conditioned), more precisely, at the rational intelligence that built science and philosophy and took flight with the experimental method (Bacon, Descartes) during the Industrial Revolution, thus from 1760. Objective vision of the world, irreligious; forming of an enlightened consciousness that feels its power, a prodigious revolutionary lever, because man has finally discovered himself, individualism overcome. Rigidity, harshness, natural limits of enlightened thought at each moment in history. From this flows its retreats, its interest in obscure ideas, discovery of the subconscious, intuition, religion, etc.; these fertile retreats supported by reactionary social tendencies that exploit tradition and the religious spirit—psychological inertia. Revolutionary aspects of the Bergsonian dialectic and its general reactionary tendency. The fact remains that consciousness is essentially enlightened, and perhaps all the richer for being better nourished—with mastery of the deepest elements of life, which are unclear and plunge deep, far beyond consciousness.

The Surrealists' negative attitude towards the rigorous scientific spirit (it can only be rigorous: objectivity incompatible with complacency), their lack of scientific culture (ignorance of Marxism, superficial Freudianism, André Breton unaware of Pavlov, study of astrology—A. B. and Pierre Mabille*—without any knowledge of astronomy, interest in magic without any knowledge of sociology, ethnology, and the history of religions) bespeak a weakness, a retreat before serious effort, the attraction of the facile effect, pleasure in intellectual effervescence; hence an inner captivity… Effervescent intellectual bohemia, relatively rich compared with sclerotic academic thought— weak and inconsistent compared with revolutionary thought. Hence the attraction of cheap objects; the facile exploitation of the bizarre, of madness, of paradox (rich, to be sure, and revelatory, but which require more real attention and objective knowledge).

Movement superficially revolutionary and profoundly reactionary.

Enriching in literature and painting (this should be considered separately: crisis of the plastic arts in the decadence of bourgeois civilization) through its novel parallels, boldness, appeal to methods destructive of convention, explorations into the unknown, and break (far too local) with mental inertia.

Overwhelming downside: given the impossibility, by the use these second-rate methods and within this bohemian milieu, of a genuine break: descent into facile sexualism, into affectation, even charlatanism, and a revolutionism that is nothing but scandal-seeking (snobbery). None of this precludes the sincerity of men who belong to a society where sincerity is superficial. "Automatic writing" and its tricks: the writer duping himself. Often consists in presenting drafts as completed works; carelessness, self-satisfaction, creative impotence. A. B.'s method of writing: hard work armed with dictionaries in order to seek out rare words or unexpected associations; an extremely rational effort that strives to give the impression of automatism and which attains only the esoteric.

Literary effects, Jacqueline telling me: "You wrote, 'The singer sang...' The correct word isn't poetic. But if I had written: 'The singer slept...'" From Gongorism to the flattest ornamental literature the goal of refinement is this: adorn reality, disdain the direct expression of reality. Was it Voltaire who said: "Don't say 'the moon;' say 'the star of the night.'"

Low quality of the Surrealist rebellion: 1. Strictly literary, never reached outside the reviews and the cafés of Paris; 2. Searched for shocking effects—scandal, publicity—not the useful, liberating revolutionary effect; 3. Aimed only at a select, often wealthy, public (painting sold well), *NRF*[10]; 4. Indigence of its internal positions: more will to show contempt—in order to aggrandize oneself—than to understand and appreciate; stylization in order to maintain an identity despite a certain incoherence.

A propos of the Surrealist survey: "Is suicide a solution?" I was right in saying in *Literature and Revolution* (1930) that proletarians and revolutionaries think of conquering the world, of fighting, and not of

10. *Nouvelle revue française*. Prestigious literary review founded in 1909.

the solution of suicide, which is that of young, maladjusted, or desperate bourgeois or petit bourgeois. (Something that's completely different, the suicide of a revolutionary, which can be a solution; there's nothing in common between Jacques Rigaut[11]—*Lord Patchogue*—and A. A. Joffe, Maria Joffe,* Evgenia Bosch,* Paul and Laura Lafargue—it's the way a life was lived that defines the value of the period placed at its end.)

I said in Marseille: "An interesting discovery in the world of art, made under the worst conditions in the cafés of Paris in the atmosphere of decay in the aftermath of the First World War."

ANDRÉ BRETON

André. Completely stylized. A personality that is nothing but a pose, deliberately fabricated and put on like makeup. Lacking a real personality. Always performing, the world is a stage for him. But if the actor is nothing but his role, there is no longer an actor, there's nothing but a fictional, false person. It's not surreality that's achieved, but unreality, inconsistency.

None of his ideas holds up under a critique that is the least bit thorough and takes things seriously. As coherent as a well-constructed arabesque. Bits and pieces of Marxism, astrology, Freudianism, Sade, and the *NRF* picked up at the flea market of hackneyed ideas. Taken as a whole it's nothing but a purely literary idea (the word "literature" to be understood not in the sense of the direct, imperatively sincere expression of life given it by Dostoevsky or Lawrence, but in its *NRF*–Deux Magots sense: something adulterated, a game, a form of commerce, provocative). "Automatic writing" through use of dictionaries: fakery, false automatism, less revelation and spontaneity than in the plain writing that doesn't call itself automatic. Method employed due to lack of spontaneity or the ability to work founded in self-confidence. (But since there is no self, nothing but a role.) The automatism—in this case real—of his reactions in discussions and in life due to a pose adopted once and for all and

11. Writer and opium addict, close to the Surrealists, who committed suicide in 1929 at age thirty-one. Served as the inspiration for the main character in Drieu La Rochelle's *Le Feu follet*.

which can't be modified without risking losing all (all = the apparent personality; style with no depth, style for style's sake; reality demands that style be a living form, the necessary form of a substance, and not a gratuitous arabesque suspended over the void). Drama of a failed personality. Culpability of the literary bohemia of Paris; too many petty mechanisms (vanity, desire for authority and fame, women, money) to attempt a true escape, one that was, after all, possible when the man was young. He now feels it's too late. Certain that he has understood all this insofar as he hasn't repressed his awareness of it. All he has left is to carry on in his role, hence a certain bitterness, an underlying sourness.

Could have been great if he'd been able to break with the petty side of himself instead of cultivating-stylizing it. Simplified himself, removed a lot of Parisian appearances in order to become a real person—a writer. Dominated by appearances and working hard at avoiding admitting this and even fooling himself about himself. Yet again a role: inner life is part of the act. Remarkable representative of decadence.

Is there not something profoundly unfair in this objective judgment (which I want to be objective)? A. B.'s perfect dignity should not be underestimated, nor his strength of character (and at times courage), which even his internal stylization bears witness to; his truly poetic impulses; his lively, uneven intelligence that proceeds more by whimsical outbursts and probings than by prolonged effort, deeper at times than it is broad; more egoistical—that is, more preoccupied with his own importance than with obtaining real understanding. The stuff of a strong and great personality, but spoiled by Paris, by between-the-wars Paris, living off the literature of which Verlaine said, "The rest is literature."

Up to a certain point objective judgments are necessarily unjust. 1. Because they can never be completely objective (impersonal); 2. Because they don't consider the person from within, identifying with him like a novelist or poet, and hence are ignorant of the essential elements, which are only made accessible to intuition by sympathy. (In this sense sympathy and love perhaps achieve a different objectivity, one of a nonscientific order, since it is not subject to precise verifications but is more elevated, deeper, more alive. The entire difference between the truth of the work of art and that of nonfiction.)

January 3, 1942—Conversation with Dr. F. and others (Oettinghaus*)
on Willi Münzenberg's* end. Babette, his widow, a very fine, intelligent,
strong, and gracious woman, has no precise information. The facts: held
for a while at Buffalo Stadium, he seemed to be demoralized (F. ran
into him there). During the period of the armistice, interned at the
camp of Chambarron, which he left (escaped from?) with Harting and
five (young) Communists. Harting, formerly a right Social-Democrat
and union functionary, has since become a Nazi agent. A woman wrote
that she was alarmed to see Willi leave with people who posed such a
danger to him (reported in Marseille by Reine). June. —In September
a decomposed body that had hanged itself or been hanged was found
in Saint-Marcellin, in the Lyon region, with W. M.'s papers in a room
that had long been locked. Superficial investigation by the mayor, M.
Dorly, mention in *Le Petit dauphinois* (didn't find it in the issues of
September 20–23 I'd been told to look at). Gibarty, who was his
longtime secretary, doesn't rule out suicide—panic at the approach of
German patrols—but considers it very improbable (character, past).
Given his dynamism and energy, and that he had money, the means
with which to cross the Atlantic, a legend came to be created among
the émigrés in Marseille: that he had arranged a substitution of bodies—that's how improbable suicide seemed. Silence in the press. Here
they tell me that suicide is probable: demoralized, panic fear of the
Germans, an "animal fear" often observed in him to "a disconcerting
degree."

Obviously this is connected to his total demoralization. Admirable
beginnings as an internationalist militant during the First World War,
Socialist Youth Organization, he then became one of the Comintern's
most important businessmen, the official corrupter of Western intellectuals and handler of funds (aid for famine-stricken Russia, Soviet
films, Hoym Verlag, anti-imperialist congresses, Congress for the
Defense of Culture). Protected by Zinoviev, refused to report to Moscow at the time of the trials. Said to have spoken angrily of these trials
in private. Would certainly never have returned from Moscow. Didn't
break with them, was expelled for lack of discipline but remained the
manager of certain businesses, maintained contact and it seems remained
an agent of the Comintern. On the eve of the war attempted to set up

a pro-Stalin German popular front. During war collaborated with Deuxième Bureau (intelligence) at Radio Liberté. Corrupted and corrupting revolutionary, when he made his inner break with Stalinism was unable to find any bedrock on which to stand—it was too late—no idealism, empty, clinging, probably with sincerity, to the idea of a democratic Germany worth fighting for that would open the gates to a socialist revolution; saw everything gone to hell with France's collapse, now thought only of himself, for his management of money and comfortable life must have turned him into something of a hedonist.

Total collapse, suicide an obviously possibility. Secret execution by a GPU hit squad as well.

Psychologically, his case analogous to Krivitsky's, about which the same doubts remain, with a greater possibility of a well-organized assassination.

Forty-five, forty-eight years old?

TINA MODOTTI

January 7, 1942—The day before yesterday, in the afternoon, Tina Modotti* died in a taxi on the way to the hospital: extremely suspicious "heart attack." Tina Modotti was the wife of one of the bosses of the GPU here, Sormenti, an Italian, who made several trips to Moscow, and owns a bookstore here under the name of Carlos Contreras.[12] We know that for some time she's been in disagreement with the GPU, which she had long worked for, and that she feared for her life.

On January 10, 1929, her boyfriend, a Cuban Communist militant, Antonio Mella,* was assassinated at her side on a Mexico City street. Valente Quintana,* the chief of police, found among Tina M.'s papers a detailed itinerary of the routes she and Mella were going to take the evening of the crime. Indicted, influential figures in high places intervened on her behalf, she was freed and left for Moscow. She had worked with Sormenti in Albacete, Spain (International Brigades, [André] Marty).

12. Sormenti and Contreras were the pseudonyms of the Italian Comintern agent Vittorio Vidali.*

From unequivocal eyewitness testimony—that of Sandalio Junco*
(leader of a union in Cuba, the Authentic Revolutionary Party[13]),
related by J. L. Velásquez—we know that at the time of his assassination Mella had announced to the CC of the Cuban Party his support
for the Opposition. The crime was attributed to Machado's[14] agents,
and it's possible there was dual responsibility for it.

To be placed alongside the mysterious deaths of Max Hoelz* (USSR,
1930, accidentally drowned, murdered, according to Elsa Reiss) and
Hans Beimler* at the University City on the Madrid front.[15]

Supplemented May 6, 1942—Sandalio Junco, member of the Authentic Revolutionary Party of Cuba, was killed in a brawl on May 4 or 5
while participating in a demonstration in commemoration of the death
of Guiteras* in Cuba. Julián had mentioned his name in relation to
Mella's death in an article published in *Así*.[16] The Auténticos, influential among the workers, form the Opposition, while the CP supports
President Batista, since he is in power. S. J. must have been liquidated
during a counterdemonstration.

THE RUSSIAN MYSTERY

January 15, 1942—The winter goes a long way toward explaining the
German retreat in Russia; that and typhus. Not everything: how to
explain that the Nazis weren't able to take Sebastopol in Crimea, almost
undefendable on the land side, where the winter is mild, as in Germany
itself? Hypothesis: Nazis winded—close to defeat. Not very probable
at this time, premature (even though they're winded, they're not that
winded).

Or a tacit or explicit pact with Stalin: We won't advance any further
and you won't attack Japan (Vladivostok, key position for bombing

13. Founded in 1923, a nationalist, corporatist, socialist party, which certain
Trotskyists joined.
14. The Cuban dictator at the time, overthrown in 1933.
15. The last phrase added by hand in the margin.
16. Weekly magazine that for a time published antitotalitarian exiles like Serge,
Gorkin, and Luis Araquistáin.

Japan's industrial centers). Matsuoka concluded the USSR-Japan Non-aggression Pact in Moscow in April on the way home from Berlin. At that time Hitler was already preparing the invasion of Russia for *June*. The German declaration of war against the United States synchronized with the Japanese attack demonstrates that Germany and Japan were solidly linked to each other. Matsuoka didn't trick Berlin and wasn't tricked by them: a well-staged ambush.

The 13th, in Kuybyshev, the Lozovsky* declaration concerning normal relations with Japan and renewal of the fishing treaties.

Mystery of the defense of Leningrad, surrounded, besieged, June the siege half lifted. Reasons: 1. Impossibility of resupplying the city; 2. Intention to seize the fleet, desire to create an atmosphere of competition.[17]

Mexico City, January 18, 1942—Dear friends:[18] I must inform you about the fight we are obliged to carry on. Three days ago I sent you some typical clippings from Stalinist newspapers, but things have become even worse. I'll sum them up:

The campaign unleashed October 1 with Joan Comorera's article in the Spanish Communist Party's review *Nuestra Bandera*.

Early this month, a plenum of the Central Committee of the Mexican CP denounced us as the "shock troops of the fifth column, etc."

Same attacks at meetings.

January 13, seven deputies maneuvered by Communist deputy Carlos Zapata Vela* sent a statement to the government denouncing Marceau Pivert, Julián Gorkin, and me.[19]

The same day, they sent their denunciation to Washington.

The 15th, the wide-circulation daily *Excélsior*, reactionary and partial to the American blacklist, published an article by its Washington

17. Last paragraph added by hand.
18. This letter to Dwight and Nancy Macdonald* was transcribed by Serge in the notebooks.
19. Their expulsion, as well as that of Munis and Regler, was demanded due to their services for the fascist cause. Zapata Vela was not a Communist deputy, however, but rather from the Party of the Mexican Revolution, later the Institutional Revolutionary Party.

correspondent saying that the American press is looking into the affair and that it will be discussed at the conference in Rio de Janeiro! The "John Willes" who signed this article, datelined Washington, and who probably isn't John Willes, is definitely a GPU agent; I mean a journalist in the pay of the GPU. I've been reading his articles for some time with amazement. He entirely fabricated imaginary and—extremely clumsy—accusations against us, for none of his lies hold water. *Excélsior* is publishing our response.

We respond with accusations in the weekly magazine *Así*, to which Julián and I contribute. Two of our three articles were sabotaged at the printer and are incomprehensible.

In the meanwhile, we receive confidential warnings (there are quite a few people sickened by Stalinist methods but who don't dare break with the CP because they're living on assistance or work they give them...). I was told last night that my assassination has been commanded and set for soon. The words of a well-known Communist were quoted: "I wouldn't give a penny for V. S.'s skin."

The violence and the systematic character of these attacks prove that they're ordered by the GPU and probably on the orders of Moscow itself. We think they are the result of the failure of Jackson's prepared escape since it's known that we were responsible for the failure of this escape, ordered by Stalin himself and for which an agent was sent from Moscow to Havana. They definitely have a goal. What is it? The precedent of Trotsky gives us an idea. The Stalinists reckon on the American public being favorable to them and that they have to take advantage of the winter victories to attempt what they probably couldn't attempt with impunity in the spring. These are the facts and the way they're generally interpreted here.

Our defense. We ought to sue Comorera and a few others for slander, defamation of character, and incitement to murder. (Comorera played an important role in Nin's assassination; he has since been to Moscow; he was or is Moscow's representative in Latin America.) But due to lack of funds we haven't yet done anything.

We are addressing a complaint to the government and distributing it this week to deputies and the press.

We are responding in the few newspapers open to us, and not by defending ourselves (for what?) but by denouncing, behind the slander, the preparations for our assassination.

Julián and I live in the same house, in a neighborhood that's deserted in the evening, and the glass and light wood doors of our lodgings are worthless. Living together across the street (in order to keep an eye on us) are between seven and ten Stalinists, one of whom is dangerous, known for having proved himself in Spain. We've decided to move out together when our wives arrive.

Generally speaking we are optimistic. If they were to do away with one of us, the other two would continue the struggle with a terrible advantage. Doing away with all three of us, on the other hand, presents some technical difficulties and would cause an enormous scandal whose consequences are difficult to foresee.

I think that the things most to be feared are: 1. A mysterious "heart attack," but it's relatively easy to protect oneself against this; 2. A villainous denunciation supported by false documents—but this could in no way have serious or lasting effects; 3. An attack on the street by "angry young people" (the press campaign looks to be preparing this), but it poses the same problems as an assassination.

There is no question but that these campaigns will handicap us in terms of work and means of existence.

We receive many expressions of support, but they are all Platonic. The Stalinists' superiority comes from the enormous amount of money they have. Two to three hundred recently arrived refugees, a certain number of whom have long been disgusted, depend on them for their existence. Finally, everyone says you can do many things with money here, as in all of Latin America.

Nevertheless, the moral and political advantage is all on our side. Please give this information to our common friends. Yours sincerely,

MAGRIÑA
January 21, 1942—Perhaps deciphered by chance the ugly enigma of Antonio Mella's assassination here in 1929. Two weeks ago I questioned L. O. about the "Cuban" of the GPU in charge of organizing Jackson's escape. He told me that this summer he participated in a Communist

meeting where a Cuban who matched this description took the floor. With some difficulty recalled the name: Magriña. I just met G. T., who told me: "The other day I passed Mella's assassin on the street.... My father, a magistrate, investigated the affair. Funny, but the Communists said that this 'killer in Machado's pay' had himself been killed in Cuba.... The fact that he's here and that they're circulating this rumor to a certain extent confirms the GPU version of the crime....

"'What's his name?' —'Magriña.'"

The descriptions match: Magriña, forty to forty-eight years old, handsome, well built, tall, elegant—"the kind women like." Early February—L. O. learned that Magriña recently died of tuberculosis (?) in Mexico. Magriña's second death?[20]

Mexico City, January 23, 1942—Dear friends,[21] In a recent letter I informed you of the literally criminal campaign unleashed against me and my friends by the GPU. It hasn't ended, naturally. Here is the continuation:

The seven Stalinist-leaning deputies (one or two of them total Stalinists) who form the shock troops demand our internment as 1. "Trotskyists";—2. And consequently, members of the fifth column. Francisco Zamora,* a Mexican journalist who enjoys a certain credit, a courageous man of the left, defends us, saying that we are socialists like many others and deplores the intervention of deputies in campaigns led by the GPU. The deputies immediately accused the (moderate) daily *El Universal*, which Zamora writes for, as a supporter of the fifth column and protested against Zamora's attacks, which are said to be "an insult to the legislative power!" This morning *El Universal* appeared without a response by Z. and *without his daily column*. The GPU gang has thus made some progress.

The office of the president of the republic has replied that it transmitted our complaint-protest to the relevant services for investigation. We addressed an open letter to these seven deputies, which only one paper briefly summarized. In general everyone's mind is made up.

20. Last paragraph added by hand.
21. Letter to Dwight and Nancy Macdonald transcribed in Serge's notebooks.

The small Communist-leaning papers that are sprouting up like mushrooms after a rain attack me in a hysterical fashion, though without coming up with anything serious.

We receive all kinds of friendly warnings. I've been told of the presence of a GPU killer, a Cuban, mixed up in some very dark adventures (precise information to be verified). We're told that they're cooking up a machination against us, that they seek to introduce a provocateur among us whom they will seem to sacrifice when he announces that he is a Gestapo agent ... This seems to me to be difficult, for the circle of our sympathizers is a narrow one. I am more afraid of the fabrication of false documents, which can be used to prove anything—momentarily.

Send all, or most of your letters certified mail; I'm certain that various letters, principally those from my wife, have been stolen (excellent material for the fabrication of falsifications); this morning I received an airmail letter from France dated December 5 and not postmarked in Mexico! Censorship don't bother us, but it's all but certain that the GPU has introduced agents into the postal censor's office and that it has its own apparatus for intercepting and using letters. (Even back in France and Belgium I was convinced of this.)

Question of refugees: about two hundred Stalinists arrived on the latest boats, Spaniards, Germans, etc. On the other hand, I've learned that they've managed to place men in the consular and visa services who, again invoking the fifth column, systematically close the doors to anti-Stalinists or sabotage the issuing and sending of visas. (The letter delayed a month and a half that arrived this morning spoke precisely of this.)

COYOACÁN

January 30, 1942—With Julián, visited Natalia Ivanovna. This fortress-home, with its rather beautiful garden, its powerful cacti the Old Man enjoyed collecting, its big chicken and rabbit cages where he fed the animals, its cement plaque with a hammer and sickle on it standing in the middle of a small lawn, its small plaque dedicated to Sheldon Harte near a gate, and Natalia, a living shadow, accompanied by a tall young American with a revolver at his hip—"the tomb of Coyoacán" is all I ever call it in my mind. The sadness of the void felt there is extraordinary: it's on the abandoned books, in the freezing, bare kitchen, in the (closed) office-laboratory of the Old Man, it's within Natalia.

The plaque dedicated to Sheldon Harte is an insult. There are nine chances out of ten that he was an agent provocateur. The hammer and sickle pain me inside this tomb: for me it is no longer the glorious symbol of the revolution, but the insignia of an inhuman fraud. Nevertheless, I understand why the Old Man was attached to it, and one day this emblem will perhaps recover its purity. I have my doubts. New departures require new symbols and words, as well as a profoundly new content. It's only through renewal that we move forward. But I'll never make this poor, tiny woman dressed in gray wool understand this, she whose face is ravaged by suffering. She seems always to be about to burst into sobs, but even the sobs have been extinguished, and this is how she lives—a shadow. She has a kind gaze; one senses she is loyal and noble.

Difficult discussion on the defamation campaign we're the object of and the GPU's preparations against us. N. I. reproaches us for not agreeing to join with Munis, the official Trotskyist. "You reject him. He's young, unknown, and consequently more easily assassinated. You demonstrate that your disagreements with us are greater than with the GPU. . . ." We'd have too much to say in answer to this and it's obvious that, faithful to the memory of the Old Man even unto error, answering would serve only to hurt her. More obvious still that our disagreement is a question, not of ideas, but of mentality. In the hardening of his final years the Old Man pushed the defects of the Bolshevik mentality—the Bolshevism of the decadent period—to their extreme, comparable to the psychological traits Stalinism was able to turn into a strength (and which flow from the totalitarian spirit). She is incapable of understanding that one can only *move forward through renewal*, freely and to a certain extent contradictorily. When I tell her that the future will show who it was that carried on the Old Man's work for socialism, we or the sectarian groupings of the Fourth International whose incompetence is obvious, she lowers her head, making a bitter sign of denial. I realize that I'm hurting her and change the subject.

We say that we can't collaborate closely with the comrades of the Fourth International as long as they don't change their language and methods. In the latest issue of their newspaper, *19 de Julio*, they still call Nin and the comrades of the POUM "traitors" to the Spanish revolution. —N. I.: But the Spanish revolution was objectively betrayed. Subjectively we know that Nin and the others were honest revolutionaries. Me: That's precisely it: objectively and subjectively, the very argument Stalinism used against the Old Man, Krestinsky's* dilemma at the Moscow Trial! A completely false reasoning, since it ignores psychological and moral motives, which are also real facts, inseparable from material facts and every bit as objective. —I also say that it's impossible for us to work in solidarity 1. With good comrades who've been stabbing us in the back for years while we're fighting the same fight as them, but with greater influence; 2. With an anonymous "Executive Committee of the Fourth International" made up of unknowns who publish dumbfounding manifestoes. I quote a document that at one and the same time calls for the abolition of the GPU and for ultra-summary (*sic*) tribunals and the immediate execution of the worst bureaucrats. I say that my friends and I in the Opposition in Russia had reached the conclusion that the forthcoming revolution must immediately establish real guarantees of justice, moderate its power for vengeance, and abolish the death penalty, which has been so badly abused in the USSR that the revalorization of human life has become an essential question for socialism. —N. I. sadly shakes her head. She endlessly takes up the same reproaches and arguments...We part on friendly terms but without reaching a conclusion. We'd passed a sad twilight hour talking with the impotent shade of the Old Man.

On the death penalty: Riazanov maintained the *correct* position throughout the debate on the revolution (his interventions at the central council of the Congress of Soviets). *Remember Riazanov's contribution.*[22]

GPU

February 7, 1942—Discussion with Denegri.* An influential Communist—whom he asks my permission not to name—spoke to him

---

22. Last paragraph added by hand.

about me so he could communicate this warning: this Communist says he admires me greatly though he doesn't know me personally. (He is hostile towards Julián—he might be a Spaniard.) He sends word that there has recently been talk of our physical suppression ("attacks on Serge and his friends") and that the preparations are already in place. That the bookstore in the Iturbide passage is closely watched[23] and might be the spot chosen by the *pistoleros*. I answered that we had noticed obvious surveillance and some fishy-looking characters. Denegri adds: "It's a directive from Moscow and it's based on the opinion that your group has taken up Leon Trotsky's activity and in reality is carrying it out on an even more dangerous basis."

He also says that we must leave the neighborhood of Ejido, heavily populated by Communists. Sormenti lives there, Xavier Guerrero* as well (same house!). The addresses these people live in are said to be 32 (S. and G.?), 18, 14. Says that the Mexican police one day discovered Haikis, who was Moscow's ambassador to Spain during the Civil War, at Sormenti's house, come to Mexico under the name of Jacomet, probably to lay the groundwork for Trotsky's assassination. Disappeared immediately afterwards. D. is convinced that Tina Modotti was "suppressed."

February 8, 1942—Following yesterday's warning, we received reports from various sources that there are currently discussions going on in the cafés of Mexico City concerning the assassinations being prepared against us. A certain psychosis created by the Spanish and Trotsky affairs plays a large role in this. But it is also a fact that just among the German émigrés who arrived on the last ship there are at least thirty people who worked for the GPU, mainly in Spain. A difference of opinion was reported to us between two Spanish Communists and two foreigners, probably Germans. The Spaniards are against the attacks. They say that Nin's disappearance did the Party immense harm and that now is not the time. They add that if Gorkin was killed Maurín* would survive and would one day ask questions. The two Germans reply that Serge, Gorkin, Pivert, and Regler are obstacles,

23. The bookstore belonged to the publisher Bartomeu Costa-Amic.

and that these days obstacles must be suppressed, even if there is a price to pay...This discussion occurred openly, in a group, at the Café Madrid, frequented by Comorera and his friends. It is reported to us that Comorera is saying the same types of things.

(The two foreigners who argued in this way were: Heriberto Hirsch, of the CP and probably the GPU, residing at the Hotel Canada, and Boris Strauss, "Russian," "psychiatrist," who was a member of the International Brigades in Spain as a doctor. Along with them, Enrique Guttman is brought to our attention.)[24]

February 18, 1942—Calumny is tightening the bonds of friendship with Regler; I even think that long-term work with him will be possible. His virile, tortured head of someone very high strung. Much wear and a kind of candor mixed with delicacy. When he is feeling well his face is not at all wrinkled, very much an old-time German romantic (happily, the breed is not extinct). What he's going through is hard for him, and even more so for his wife, Marie-Louise [Vogeler],* with whom he lives in perfect harmony, even as far as their expressions. Tells me he was unable to work for two weeks beneath the flood of grotesque and delirious slanders, that he couldn't even imagine this himself, that it made him a nervous wreck. Men who were his closest friends, like Erwin Kisch,* deliberately lie in order to sully his reputation ... Me: This atmosphere allows you to understand from the inside the psychological mechanism of the Moscow Trials. This is a new development in spiritual decomposition, based on faith and corruption. They know they're lying, but think they're not totally lying because it's by virtue of a higher interest.

Regler is weakened as a result of his wound. He sometimes seems to be floating in his old suits, but his gaze still has a blue awareness of concern, the gaze of a man ready to suffer and eager to get to the heart of things.

Seriously wounded in Madrid, he received a blood transfusion (kidneys, etc.; saved by an admirable Spanish surgeon who was executed by the Francoists). When he regained consciousness he was anxious:

24. Last paragraph added in blue ink.

What blood? From whom? —From a Catalan. The idea of having Catalan blood in his veins overwhelmed him. He wanted to know the donor, shows a picture of them together: a vigorous lad with his face drowned in a beard and a prominent brow. "I played some records for him and was pleased when he said he didn't like Wagner but liked Mozart." "I forgot to ask him his profession, but as he was leaving he told me on his own: bullfighter." We spoke of the influence of blood transfusions, perhaps very profound. (I think also of the influence of love for women.)

This reminds me of the story Vauthier[25] told me in Pontarlier in 1939. A seriously wounded German being treated at the hospital. They tell him he's going to get a blood transfusion. He asks, "From whom? A Frenchman?" "Yes." He says he'd rather die. And what did they do? "Very well," said the doctors, "let him croak."

February 19, 1942—Saw Lionello Venturi* again, Hotel de la Reforma. I hadn't seen him since the day Jacques Mesnil* took me to his house on avenue Henri-Martin in Paris, in that vast apartment full of boxes and files on art, with its old oak furniture and its lackeys in livery. Carlo Rosselli* was there with his wife, that's where we got to know each other. Venturi looks rejuvenated. A magnificent sexagenarian, tall, corpulent with an impressive head, a high dome, bald, something Lenin-like about his brow, kind, attentive blue eyes, a pointy, stiff white chin beard, healthy coloring. Extremely patrician. —Regler, Paul Chevalier,* Marie-Louise Vogeler Regler, a Dutchwoman.

We speak of the war, which, in the end, will be won, "monstrously, stupidly won." I say that the Allies have not yet addressed a single energetic word to Germany capable of awakening the German people the way Wilson awakened them in 1918. —Venturi cites the Atlantic Charter, but it assumes unilateral disarmament, which eliminates any guarantee of economic equality. V. adds that he sees no other solution than the United States of Europe, about which we are in agreement, but he formulates a concept of it that is quite correct: "United States

---

25. The Vauthier family took care of Serge's daughter Jeannine in Pontarlier until she was able to join her father with Laurette Séjourné.

of the regions of Europe, for if it's simply a matter of uniting the old states we'll have accomplished nothing." —Me: "Economic and national regions."

His son—met in Marseille at the American Committee, arrested in Spain, handed over to Italy—was deported to the south of France, free, allowed to go to a neighboring village. Studies, writes good letters, sends photos. We recall that Francesco Ghezzi* has completely vanished in the USSR. Venturi and Mesnil did all they could, but in vain.

February 25, 1942—Somewhere near Veracruz in a spot that recalls the Vézère Valley. Emerald basin. Big green and black torpedo boats. Fourth day that I have been waiting for you in Veracruz, with Sara, and the latest worries don't succeed in troubling my joy. The Cook Agency had announced the arrival of the *Nyassa* for Sunday the 22nd. Leaving Saturday night I learned at the last moment that at the Gobernación[26] it's thought that the ship will be here Sunday morning or Saturday night. On Monday they lead us to hope it'll arrive that evening or Tuesday morning. Tuesday evening—nothing, and it's not even known if it left Cuba. To sum up: an epidemic on board (typhus), disinfection in Havana, the passengers in Triscornia.[27] Another rumor: it went to Norfolk in the United States, the passengers disembarked there, a phone call said to have been received, won't be here for another week … We contemplate returning to Mexico City. We call Paca:[28] the Cook Agency insists to him that the *Nyassa* is expected the morning of the 25th (today). This morning: a functionary of the Oficina de Migración says that the *Nyassa* will arrive Friday or Saturday. —At times the idea of the epidemic on board torments me. How many storms you traverse accompanied by our Jeannine with a smile on your face, my love. It seems to me that they must shun you, like darkness, the light.

February 27–28, 1942—Veracruz, waiting for you. Newspapers: Stefan Zweig took poison at age sixty along with his wife in Brazil, Petropolis,

26. Ministry of the Interior.
27. Quarantine camp outside Havana.
28. Nickname of Frances Toor.*

"worn down by emigration." Last book: *Brazil, Land of the Future*. Sincere, I think. Faith in the future and lassitude. I understand and approve his act. I love you, I'm waiting for you, and you'll help keep a fierce desire to work and fight. That's far better, no matter the times. Ever onward is the best solution, *as long as* it's available.

The days of this extraordinary wait grow longer, as if fate wanted me to develop a taste for it. I feel strong and ethereal. A letter from Germaine Pivert[29] mentions your name, you're here, the letter is from Norfolk, Virginia.

Driven by Babette [Thüring*] we visited Boca del Río by car, a fishing hamlet with palm trees, a restaurant (El Mago). Waves' foam, dunes, thought of you, of Dieppe ... Ballet of fireflies at twilight. In the distance a boat, all lit up, entered the harbor. Briefly thought it was the *Nyassa*, rushed by car to the quay... It was a sorry little coastal tub.

Climbed to Puente Nacional in the high vegetation. Turquoise pool, flowers, large buttercups at the summit, gray, leafless trees. There are white flowers like this as well. The purple and red flowers stream over the almost dark leaves. How you'd love all this, would bathe in this sun, these flowers, our calm, and our wealth!

Exhausting trip to Medellín, a big, sleepy town under a beating sun deep in the brush. Dusty, bumpy road, where with difficulty you can go fifteen or twenty an hour through a tropical steppe. The car crosses an amazing little bridge made of dilapidated planks (space in the middle). On both sides steep slopes, you descend and climb in a cloud of dust at your own peril. An amiable Indian matron with a wide, flat, toothless face makes us pay fifty centavos for this exploration. Medellín: the plaza with its tall, beautiful pines, stone benches (garish white paint), a strange little church with a pitiful tower and belfry, like a humble Russian church. In the entry we find an office of the Churches of Latin America, Eucharistic congress, with pictures of Roosevelt, Churchill, Ávila Camacho*—the pope in the middle—Hitler, Mussolini, Franco. Caption: "May God inspire the rulers!" No one going by, we see hardly any people, everything is asleep in the sun, a great silence emanates from the vegetation. Impoverished interiors, the doors

29. Marceau Pivert's wife.

sometimes ajar, as if abandoned. Two groceries across from each other at the corner. One is called La Lucha, the other El Baluarte.[30]

Young red bulls with widely flared horns are harnessed to a cart, and large tapered blue birds (jays?) fly between their legs, cleanse them of flies. Beautiful scene of a river in the brush beneath trees of an absolutely fantastic vigor. Enormous trunks, interlacing of powerful rising branches, each curve is swollen with power. Giant leaves. A breathtaking slender butterfly with black wings marked with red spots resembling eyes and a straight, yellowish-gold stroke in front. No roads in this part of the country, from Veracruz it's only possible to go in two or three directions. It takes days to reach Córdoba in the neighboring mountains.

From the edge of the sea one can see the white cone of the peak of Orizaba, same outline as Popo. But it rises in the distance above exploding palm trees.

March 2, 1942—Yesterday, Sunday, Boca del Río, beautiful beach, palm trees. Evening, the wind picks up. Is this the final day of my wait? This morning, 8:30, ran to the dock: violent wind, difficult to walk. Packets of froth, blinding mist. Through my binoculars I try to examine a large trawler that has entered the port. Disappointed. A passing sailor says to me, "The other ship's coming in," and gestures toward the port. Through the gusts of spume I glimpse, behind Wenner-Green's[31] yacht with its three SSS (the Southern Cross), the outline of the *Nyassa*, tall and gray.

The *Nyassa* passes close to the dock in order to face the wind. In the stern a few people. Not you. Marceau is also fighting the wind in order to see. We question each other. No one? The *Nyassa* seems empty.

Ran onto the old dock with its waterlogged planks; terrible wind, people, handkerchiefs. Irritating to not be able to see the faces on board. Marceau is finally able to recognize his family, I seek you in vain, alarmed. There's talk of epidemics on board. —Suddenly, glimpsed, all alone at the front of the ship, your silhouette, amazingly the same as always: orange sweater, your hair. Exactly like our first meetings

30. The Struggle and the Bastion.
31. Swedish millionaire, inventor of the home vacuum cleaner.

near the Eiffel Tower. Motionless, you don't wave, you look sad—alone. When you finally respond to my signs, I think I see you smile.

All of this is amazingly simple. Passed the day wandering around the city in the wind, returning hourly to the quay. Difficult to realize the immense joy. It's so simply beyond me and renews me. You haven't changed. Will you still be mine? I feel a bit of fear. A bit. Almost certain that our love has deepened, been sealed with a confidence, a will, and a tenderness touching on the absolute.

Saddened not to see Jeannine, but you immediately understood my appeal and showed her to me. Secretly saddened at the thought of René. Evening, went to see the *Nyassa* at anchor in the basin, completely illuminated. Thought of the long voyage, the risks, the miracle of your arrival. Love you.

STEFAN ZWEIG'S SUICIDE

April 4, 1942—Stefan Zweig committed suicide in Rio in the last days of March. I was in Veracruz, waiting for the *Nyassa*, about whose fate the darkest rumors were circulating, which I didn't take seriously (it nonetheless seemed unimaginable to me that Laurette was arriving). I read about it in a newspaper. Sixty years old, with his wife, thirty years younger...Barbiturates. A magazine photo shows them lying asleep next to each other. On the bedside table a glass, a bottle of mineral water, a box of matches, the final small objects of life, useful, of no interest, like those we cease to even see. He in a short-sleeved shirt, tie, closely shaved. I think of the final toilet, accomplished with small satisfaction without the least interest in living. Small moustache trimmed at the edge of the lips, regular face of a handsome, high-strung man, the mouth is hideously open so as to snatch at the air, expression of calm sleep, the hands are joined (he's lying on his back). The woman has placed her head on his shoulder and, in a tender impulse, her hands on his. The woman's hand is admirably delicate and strong (strength is needed for an end like this one).

His final book had just come out: *Brazil, Land of the Future*. I'm certain he was sincere. Not the same future, a land, a man, a couple. His final message said that he could no longer live this way, in this collapse of a culture and a world, in reality like the stranger he must have felt himself to be in the Americas...Poorly thought out, better felt. Zweig was never a fighter, nothing but a great, refined artistic intellectual—and at bottom weak, weak in his habitual comfort, in his understanding of culture as a definitive acquisition of unique value, in being accustomed to literary success and a comfortable way of life. I recall his house, that of an infinitely privileged patrician on one of the hills of Salzburg, in one of the most beautiful, the sweetest and most romantic to contemplate, the most civilized scenes in the world, a landscape humanized in its least details (1924, we missed each other, I also missed Latzko,* who also lived in Salzburg, but in poverty). I understood many things about the man by admiring his house: he felt he was being read in the name of Art. At the time he writing novels with good psychological insight into feelings, a facile success, but quality nonetheless. All of this lacking profound vigor, a surface humanism lacking intellectual depth, based on a superficial vision of the tragedy of the today's world. A turning away from the face of the tragedy: Let me live with my noble ideas, the psychologist and poet has the right to this charming house on the side of the peaceful hills, the right to music, the right to a privileged existence, for his nobility enriches the world.

The hurricane uprooted and crushed this intelligentsia; it could only find a new meaning for its life by understanding the hurricane and throwing itself into it with all its soul. True for a social category; impossible for most of those who constitute it. His end seems logical and courageous. Nothing more natural than the dignified refusal to live in conditions you can't accept. The uprooting, the emptiness, old age as well with its diminution of vital capacities, doubt at being able to live in order to attain to moments that are worth the trouble, the fear of physical diminution. Above all, the suffocation of an intelligence that has lost its nourishing environment, the exchanges that made it vibrate. Under the harsh sun of Rio, this must be particularly sharp, intolerable.

Heard some stupid commentaries about this end: he had a valid American passport (what a pity that this passport was lost!), sufficient royalties, an easy life, what more did he need? (This is the reasoning of the asphyxiated who are so asphyxiated that they don't even realize their asphyxiation.) (I recall old prisoners granted some privileged little task who marched their rounds in the courtyard with a happy look on their faces.) He's also reproached for having taken his much younger wife with him—as if the absoluteness of love were absurd and worthy of condemnation. This death is greeted with indifference by the comrades—there are too many of them. Imagination, human feeling, intelligence have all sunk lower.

Other suicides of German intellectuals: Toller in New York a few years ago; Walter Hasenclever (*Marriages Are Made in Heaven*, which I saw in Leningrad), Walter Benjamin (a remarkable essay on Baudelaire)—about W. B., René Schickele's daughter told me that having failed in an attempt to cross the border, Pyrenees, while some mutual friends had succeeded, he lost hope and killed himself in a small hotel.

PAUL MARION, JACQUES BENOIST-MÉCHIN, OTTO STRASSER

April 18, 1942—Jacques Le Roy-Ladurie has just been named minister of agriculture in the Laval cabinet (with those two perfect scoundrels Paul Marion* and Benoist-Méchin*). Met him after the publication of one of my books. Was president of an association of agriculturalists of France, offices at the corner of Avenue de l'Opéra. Of old Norman stock, big landowner, mayor of a big city, lord of the manor. Tall, clean cut, elegant without ostentation, a long oval face, gray, meditative eyes, a high, domed brow, a remarkably cultivated man, loving his race, his Norman region, possessing a thorough knowledge of its history, the land, business related to the land—tormented by ideas, healthy, foreseeing the onrushing social catastrophes, scorning the bourgeoisie he was a member of, not knowing what to hold on to. Requested an interview in order to speak openly. "I was one of those who made February 6.[32] This can't go on, everything is totally rotten. I see that I mistook a movement lacking either intelligence or energy for the beginning of the revolution. We need a revolution, and we're headed towards it full speed ahead, and that's what I want to talk to you about. How should

---

32. February 6, 1934, the date of fascist riots in Paris that nearly brought down the government.

it be made? What should it be?" He wanted to meet revolutionaries with whom he could agree. Eagerly questioned me about the Russian Revolution, the totalitarian systems. "We're going to have to collaborate when events are unleashed...." Not in the least hostile to socialism—on the contrary, but absolutely no faith in the Socialist Party, parliamentarians, Blum. We had long, friendly conversations and got along very well. The theme was always the need for a revolution. I see in him a pedigreed bourgeois, one of those who understands that capitalism is done for, is enamored of the economic and the technical, nourishes the perhaps unconscious ambition to become the organizer of a new regime. He spoke to me of Laval, his neighbor in Normandy, with humor and an unmistakable contempt: "A shrewd actor, biding his time.... Do you know what he said to me the other day? 'Aren't I a real revolutionary? I had nothing, was the son of a peasants, and now here I am, a rich man,'" with extensive landholdings...(He loves the land.) "Aren't I making a revolution?" Le Roy told us this with a slightly sarcastic laugh. I said: "A joker." He answered: "More than that, despite it all, he's very impressive. The great *parvenu*...." We wandered in the area of the Gare Montparnasse one evening.

He told me a story about the exportation of apple pulp (after making cider) to Belgium, from there the pulp was then sent to Germany for war production. "I went to tell the ministry of agriculture about this, and I was really 'well received': they all but told me to let businessmen run their businesses!" We once had dinner at Pitaud's, in a little apartment near the Porte de Saint-Ouen, with Otto Strasser,* short, slightly puffy head, sparkling, metallic eyes in the banal face of a German noncom or traveling salesman, smug, referring to himself a "great revolutionary" (Le Roy's amused look), optimistically commenting on the Norway affair,[33] for he saw in it the first step of a suicide, ending by telling us in the car that he was going to rest up while he could, for in six months he could very well be part of the government of a different Germany. Strasser got out of the car near the Gare Saint-Lazare, Le Roy said, "Ooof! Yet I still can't forget that he was one of the creators of Nazism."

33. Probably the invasion of Norway in April 1940.

These four, Laval, Marion, Benoist-Méchin, Le Roy, in the collaborationist government at this unstable moment, when the poor dismasted ship is carrying its crew where no one wants to go, to a destination no one knows, seem to me to form a symbolic team.

Paul Marion, very "average Frenchman," intellectual with the gift of gab, well spoken, generally skeptical, strolled around Moscow (1927–1928) for the political bureau of the party, collecting anecdotes concerning poverty, cooking up with the GPU some dirty story against another lowlife, the lawyer Guiboud-Ribaud[34] sent by the Friends of the USSR (who understood and went along with it), and explained to me that the Trotskyists were madmen because they were being crushed; that he remained in the CP "with no illusions" because, when all was said and done, it was the only force...The mug of an athlete with no personality; mediocre and full of self-assurance; no idealism or scruples.

Benoist-Méchin asked for a meeting through Picard, a bookseller on boulevard Saint-Germain, and we went for coffee in the back room of the Capoulade. (Students playing cards.) A bureaucrat-intellectual in glasses, shifty eyes, carefully chosen words. Interested in the Ukraine, the story of Makhno,* in order to write something about it. Something just didn't sound right. I knew he was a musician, had just published a three-volume history of the German Army (1938) and written a commentary on *Mein Kampf* for the illustrated magazines. Long trips to Germany. Spy, I told myself, but for whom? After our talk I concluded: Deuxième Bureau in liaison with the German General Staff—but I didn't think he was a double agent. After an hour I saw things more clearly. He was seeking information on the Ukraine for a German campaign there, doubtless belonging to the coterie in the Deuxième Bureau pushing in that direction. The conversation became more focused, I told him that events were going to take a different direction. Which? That of least effort, I said, that is, the partitioning of Poland between Germany and the USSR—and he looked to be struck, even disconcerted by this idea.

The team: the parvenu Laval, parliamentarian of the last days of

---

34. Member of the SFIO (Section Française de l'Internationale Ouvrière), the socialist party, he wrote a book favorable to the Soviets, *Whither Russia?* (1928).

parliamentarism, man of Money and the State, like a greedy, wily peasant driven by the times into an enormous adventure from which there is no turning back; the ex–intelligence agent, double or turned double, young and clever; the political arriviste, totally banal, who failed to carve a journalistic or parliamentary career out of the Third Republic, having arrived too late, and whose passage through decadent Bolshevism provided him with economic notions and revolutionary cynicism; the young, energetic, and idealistic bourgeois who wants to understand the great upheaval and serve it, but without any doctrinal views, attached to his Normandy, bound by financial relations, conservative in the middle of the storm, torn by sincere revolutionary tendencies, a traditionalist nature, respect for strength, and admiration for crimes that succeed thanks to their skillful execution. Adventurers of a transitional phase, very different from each other, but corresponding to various categories.

(Guillaume Tarde, Charles Peignot, Reichenbach—the latter a Jew, which changes everything—were of the same type as Le Roy.)

Le Roy Ladurie didn't enter the government,[35] but Hubert Lagardelle* (CGT, 1906, friend of Sorel) did. For a long time had been adviser to Mussolini; ideologist of corporatism.[36]

OTTO AND ALICE RÜHLE

April 19, 1942—They live in Coyoacán, Colonia Acacias, in a subdivision that forms a garden city. A modest gray, square house surrounded by a small garden. Vigorous cacti, nopals, *órganos*[37] ring it, sufficiently spaced out that they don't form a hedgerow. In little squares of rocky earth other cacti, small gray balls with long, almost white thorns. Some in bloom: they have tiny red flowers jutting out in a circle around the plant.

The house's interior is light, well organized, furnished in the German style, with average taste and an intelligent and meticulous concern

---

35. Error by Serge. Le Roy Ladurie did become a minister but stayed only six months and then joined the Resistance.
36. Final paragraph added by hand.
37. Variety of cactus whose branches grow vertically, resembling organ pipes.

for modest comfort. The bookshelves are planks laid on bricks. *Goethes Werke*, of course. Heine, quality. The *Chronique des Pasquier* by Duhamel, who is a friend.[38] Rühle,* corpulent, in well-worn white flannels, his head the color of light brick, the skull smooth, the face harsh and fleshy (lips) but fine featured, his blue-gray eyes sharp and cold, a pouting expression, powerful jaws, a brow of stone. One feels him to be so substantial as to be tough, tenacious, a man who'll never drop anything once he's sunk his teeth into it.

German to an extraordinary degree. He'll tell me over the course of our discussion that the Germans are the only people in Europe accustomed to serious thought—and what a contrast with the barbarism, the standardized cretinism of the Americans! "But look at what Nazism has reduced them to!" (Laurette, one evening when we're out together, points out to me the perfect cut of his clothes; the gray-green, vaguely *feldgrau* color of his slightly velvety raincoat, whose cloth resembles loden; the small, dark-green hat that is missing only the Bavarian feather; the brown check suit; the brown polka dot tie. Alice [Rühle*], in a green suit, looks like a stroller on the Potsdamer Platz even in Mexico.)

At bottom, he's very bitter, indeed in pain. His strong round red head of a good bulldog (at times his inflexible glance is as hard as his bones; there's something of a ram about him); suffers from continual tics that deform his mouth, and when they occur he passes his hand over his face. Sixty-eight years old, I think of the tragedy of the end of such a life in our times. Grew up and was formed at a time of great hopes, and there's nothing now that justifies such hopes or even allows one to keep them alive, if not a desperate tenacity. He says: "Freedom was a need for us, an essential value. The younger generation no longer knows what that is: the lost need of a bygone era."

We talk about the United States: "They're totalitarians without knowing it. Millions of people read the *Reader's Digest*, that revolting crap, intellectual nourishment of the lowest order. It kills the intelligence. Same newspapers, same radios everywhere, same soaps, same

38. Serge met Duhamel in 1927. Duhamel was an active participant in the campaign to free Serge from his Soviet prison.

cities. It all ends up by producing standardized men who carry the totalitarianism of weak, emasculated beings in their veins. Anyone who tries to escape has no choice but to go mad, that's how worthless he feels. The United States is closer than any country in the world to a totalitarianism of ants." I answer that the social contradictions are giving rise to minorities awakened by a feeling and spirit of opposition; that this overheated and standardized civilization is composed of a few great centers, fortunately surrounded by backward, uncultivated regions in contact with the prairies and the forests; where people often own only one book, and that's the Bible. I tell him that these human reserves that haven't been molded by the press and the big cities, however disappointing they may be at present, have maintained a health that is unintelligent but intact. He shakes his head no, grimacing indignantly. I add that mechanical progress knocks the rough edges off large numbers of people and constitutes the basis for a new education of characters and minds. He becomes enraged and castigates my use of the word: "Progress? I'm not a progressive. Fascism, too, with its technical concentration, is a form of progress, of great progress—but I'm a socialist, you hear? A socialist!"

His idea is that totalitarianism will impose itself by the very fact of industrial civilization and crush man for a long time to come. Socialism is essentially humanism.

He sees in the Soviet and Nazi regimes nothing but the apogee of capitalism, characterized by the exploitation of labor. The Russian Revolution was able only to complete the necessary work of a bourgeois revolution. He doesn't want to admit that collective forms of property constitute an enormous change. "They're even worse, since they disarm the individual." I feel his stubbornness, I see the emotional basis of his ideas so clearly that I break off the argument by changing the subject. We speak of the Opposition in the USSR.

He paints "Merry Christmas," "Happy New Year"[39] etc. cards in a Mexican genre: a little cactus Christmas tree, a carousel, a woman selling oranges, a market scene, "Made in Mexico, trademarked..."[40]

39. In English in the original.
40. In English in the original.

Childlike and meticulously well done. "This small business isn't doing very well at the moment," Alice tells me. She, forty-eight years old, thin, lively eyes, sharp profile, determined, sells knickknacks in town, teaches when she can, runs the household, takes care of her aged child, succeeds in maintaining a material dignity, and never stops thinking.

ALICE RÜHLE ON TROTSKY

April 19, 1942—His extraordinary innocence on occasion. "Since I sometimes write poetry, I'd shown him some poems. His secretary came to see me: the Old Man would like to see you. He loves the things you sent him to read. Leon Davidovich in fact had said to me: 'You're a real poet. This is truly, truly beautiful. Could you possibly write an anthem for the Fourth International?'"

One day some Mexican workers brought him a *calavera*,[41] a death's head made of sugar, painted red and shiny green, that resembled Stalin... His irritation. (I can't recall who told me this story.)

Alice Rühle talks about Natalia Ivanovna, whom she thinks looks better now than when the Old Man was alive. "She was totally inhibited by the Old Man's powerful personality. Quiet, self-effacing, never intervening in anything.... She's much livelier today." This is perhaps true, but A. R.'s peculiar insight places a different accent on things and it requires a very acute way of viewing matters to notice any relaxation after inhibition in N. I., who so fully incarnates distress that she gives the feeling of life's uselessness.

Early May 1942—Total confusion: On May 1 Indalecio Prieto gave a long speech at the Ibero-Mexican Center. The positive part: a vague corporatism, nothing more... Julián exclaims: "They're corpses!" and he's right. He explains that Prieto is adding to the disappointments of his life as a skeptical reformist, bon vivant, and pessimist that of not having known what to do with the treasure he had at his disposal. Not even created a newspaper, not even supported a movement. Thanks to

41. Literally a "death's head" but also the word for ironic poems written for the Day of the Dead and for skull-shaped candy.

the victories of the Russian winter, Negrín is regaining influence. At the Junta de Auxilio a los Republicanos Españoles[42] one of the four leaders has openly declared himself to be pro-Negrín. Martínez Barrio, dreaming of the presidency of a government-in-exile that the Allies will end up authorizing once Franco inspires in them more distrust and fright than the most moderate Republicans, is handling the Communists with kid gloves. They influence the Republicans and the Lamodda faction of the Socialist Party and would very much like to have a president of the Republic in their pocket with a new Negrín government. The Cortés of Figueras, its sixty deputies hanging on to the last of the Republic's funds, will participate in the maneuver. But Prieto's speech gave rise to a nearly generalized indignation among the socialists and unionists. Prieto answers: "I don't give a damn."

A few days later, Jules Romain's talk at the Bellas Artes: "Mission or Abdication of France?" The French genius, Voltaire, etc., the speaker cites no living authors and ends by calling for a League of Nations with a powerful army to maintain order in Europe. The fear of thought, the inability to see, the fear of commitment, the incurable petit bourgeois mediocrity, corpse-like.

Met a young Czech who explained to me that the forty Czechs in Mexico City, reactionary on a whole, are divided into several "liberation movement" tendencies. "You understand, almost all of them have money and they all came to Mexico a long time ago as a result of things like fraudulent bankruptcies because Mexico had no extradition treaty with Europe...." Free Romania must be the same story. On the 8th or the 9th, in a church in the Madero, service and speeches in support of Free Romania, with King Carol and Mme. Lupescu. Carol (whom I met last winter in a salon; he has the withered, sharp-featured, and pale face of a worried swindler or gangster) talk of Romanian democracy! Professor Cordero Amador* goes even further. He's an orator of the wordy style, a fat fool with a fat coffee-colored ball of a head, bulging eyes, and a potato for a nose. He speaks in front of anarchists, in front of Gaullists, anywhere you can have your picture taken at the podium. A pesky hornet, totally unintelligent. I read in *The Nation* (April 11)

42. Aid committee for Spanish refugees.

that the US State Department has recognized the Free Hungary organization led by Tibor Eckhardt, former leader of the "Awakened
Hungarians," Nazified and anti-Semitic...

Recently, in a speech he gave in London, de Gaulle alluded weight-
ily to negotiations that are supposed to have taken place between Vichy
and the Allies (United States); it is said to have been a question of the
Allies' total recognition of Vichy, de Gaulle's movement then doomed
to extinction. (The Admiral Muselier Affair in Saint-Pierre-et-Miquelon,
Cordell Hull's protest, etc.; Muselier's subsequent "arrest" in London;
the denial of this arrest, the press agencies reporting that Muselier is
republican while the Gaullists are reactionary—but whose interest is
it in to say this?) De Gaulle adds that Free France should be able to
count on its allies and that France is headed towards a great revolution,
make no mistake about it! Under the Cross of Lorraine?

Stalin vows to have no interest in Germany's postvictory internal
regime. He reassures Eden, Hopkins, whomever you'd like: no revolution! The word "revolution" no longer figures in the Soviet press, and
it's never heard in speeches, obviously. Two things are evident: that
Stalin is taking his allies for a ride, seeing much further than they do,
and that he is afraid of a revolution that would escape his control. He'll
thus do everything possible to control it and is beginning by conning
his bourgeois partners. Sikorski, in the meanwhile, gave a revolutionary speech on the new democracy! I have a definition for all this: a
game of dupes with multiple losers, for they'll all lose their stripes and
probably their heads.

And American public opinion, according to *Fortune*, appropriate
title of the magazine for wealthy and barely literate businessmen, serious (May): 82.3 percent think that the United States should dictate
the peace ("*should be the chief designer of the peace*"); the vast majority
think that the future organization of the world should "safeguard
private initiative" (which no longer exists anywhere, but which is the
faded mask of capitalism) and is opposed to "any collectivism"—all of
this as clear as it is idiotic. In the April 11 issue of *The Nation* a professor Borgese, G. A.[43] calls for the sending of an American expeditionary

---

43. Giuseppe Borgese, Italian antifascist writer refugee in the US.

corps to Siberia—since there are no ships for invading the European continent and they're afraid to touch the Iberian Peninsula! He advises the great northern route, the junction with the Chinese Army through Siberia, and "*as a final goal Burma, Thailand, and Singapore.*"[44] He has no idea of what Siberia, the USSR, Stalinism, the Arctic, or Central Asia are, yet it's published with the headline: "AEF to Siberia," a recipe for winning the war.[45]

May 6, 1942—With Gustav Regler at his home in Coyoacán, the excellent oxtail pot-au-feu that he's proud of having prepared, Marie-Louise, Walter Z., Herbert Lenhoff.* Memories of the atmosphere in Barcelona end of the Civil War. A reception at the consulate general of the USSR, wines, gaiety, the entrance of the general they'd brought down from the upper floor, everyone standing to greet him; he, cordial: But sit, comrades. —Another general, N., recalled to the USSR, gay, his wife showing friends the Spanish souvenirs they were taking with them, the picture postcards of Toledo, shawls, clothing, everything of the simplest taste. "Afterwards Koltsov* (Mikhail, from *Pravda*) told me when I ran into him, 'You know, N. was arrested as soon as he landed in Odessa....' Everyone at that party knew what awaited him. He alone had no idea...." We speak of Koltsov, who also perished shortly afterwards. Much journalistic talent, capable of being not too superficial, used to doing dirty jobs, degraded by Ehrenburg's regime, became flabby and cynical, declaring that after having seen the Bukharin trial he "renounced trying to understand anything," thus using "Russian mystery," according to Regler, as a clever alibi.

About Hemingway, recently arrived in Mexico City. Regler speaks of him with affection. "That big beast, for he's enormous, a bit drunk, without which he would never have been quite so honest, pressed me against a wall near Tampico, saying: 'You're right, but don't do anything stupid. All these bastards, from Stalin to Guttman should be killed, but you have either to join the Party or remain in it in order to get a shot at killing them.' Distraught, sees only one real force with money,

44. In English in the original.
45. The rest of this entry is missing.

organization, and masses: the CP. Disappointed by American and English democracy, sickened by the France he loved, breathing best on the boulevards of Paris. The democracies led by old incompetents who, on top of that, are reactionary." Through these twists and turns he arrives at a kind of fascist mentality…"Red fascism."

GUSTAV REGLER: THE FELDMAN CASE

May 6, 1942—Gustav Regler: careful and at times heavy discussion about Fr. Feldman, whom we visited together last Sunday. Feldman, Hungarian, Jewish, high-ranking functionary of the CP in Budapest starting in 1929–1930, carried out various missions in Spain, major in the International Brigades, functionary in the Russian apparatus in Barcelona, thus a GPU agent. Intelligent, wily, "he only told me 80 percent of the truth about himself; why does he remain silent about the rest?" We weigh all sides of the question. Is it possible that in a circle of fifteen friends the GPU has no one? From the Russian point of view this seems inconceivable. "A Krivitsky," I say, "would have found such a hypothesis mad." I also say that we should and must welcome those who come over to us from Stalinism, and that they won't be unimportant men, but rather those loaded with heavy responsibilities. Every case must be judged individually. About Feldman: his means of existence are known—more or less (lives well, villa, car). Certain as well that he left the Stalinist apparatus before the end of the Spanish war, sought refuge in France, from whence the GPU had him expelled, then in Belgium. That he had Walter Z., whom he didn't know personally, freed from a CP prison, that he speaks out with indignation about the crimes…Did he come over to us out of a need for activity and contact? This would be natural. Did he "quit the service?" and did he then, perhaps his hand forced, join it again? This is the point that needs to be cleared up. His wife suffers greatly, is worried and tormented. Neurosis—or a situation she knows about and which we don't. "The atmosphere in their house is like a Strindberg play"—that airy, fresh house under the beautiful clouds and the tall trees where we passed so pleasant an afternoon without my being aware of anything. We decide to maintain a fraternal attitude while keeping our eyes open, and even to postpone the necessary discussions with F. about these matters...

The San Angel road, the wonder of stars through the high branches, the intense black of the night.

PROBLEM OF FREEDOM

May 6, 1942—The *problem of freedom* must be completely rethought. Recent concepts eroded: bourgeois "freedom," anchored in private property, commodity production, competition, the alienation of man (Marx), inaugurated in Europe by English and French revolutionaries. Anarchist thought has a direct connection with this. Anarchism is the great idealism. Engels's concept: freedom defined by the domination of nature, practical activity, (dialectical) consciousness, the end of man's exploitation by man. Bergson and his solution to the enigma of determinism: through movement and continuous creation. (Determinism, the philosophy of the apogee of mechanization.) Not necessarily push the inquiry as far as the problem of the constitution of matter: the indetermination of corpuscular movements within gases. The problem of freedom is essentially human and social and requires a real solution, powerful, in the course of struggle, for the struggle. We feel it confusedly, impossible to give it up, the complete failure of authoritarian ideas in this regard.

Erich Fromm's book, *Escape from Freedom*, rich and insufficient. It is from an obsolete, disfigured, indeed extinct freedom that man in capitalist society in crisis has a tendency to flee *when he sees no chance of winning if he defends himself.* Analytical section convincing, positive section barely sketched, proceeding from a facile, traditional dilemma.

I see two foundations for a new theory of freedom:

1. Collectivized production requires a free worker, thus freedom (criticism, control, initiative, invention, in short, collaboration with the productive apparatus), "like an organism living on oxygen." This is proved by experience, observed in Russia. Without this freedom for the producer, huge overhead costs,

unconscious and sometimes conscious sabotage; the machinery functions only thanks to a state of siege.

2. Is intellectual production subject to different rules? Being also a form of production, it requires the same oxygen. (Stagnation of literature under totalitarian regimes, vertical fall of Soviet literature in 1927–1930.) Study the psychological mechanism of thought control and the resistance it gives rise to: need for escape, spirit of opposition, self-censorship,[46] hidden thoughts. Consider the advantages of thought control as a Weapon (thus practical) in a given combat at a moment in life when the higher forms of thought become superfluous in practice (for he who, engaged in the combat, thinks only of survival: thought control manifests a return to the basic conditions of the struggle for life). thought control exists as a function of the war of classes and of powers; at bottom, it's the death of thought (the suffocation). Its psychological and social consequences disastrous, but they only make themselves felt over time by reason of the immediate superior efficacy of highly centralized organizations. From all of this we can deduce a concept of intellectual freedom that is neither abstract nor idealist, rooted in the needs of society.

(Note that societies throughout history have always leaned toward thought control for immediate efficacy in action and maintaining privileges: this is what kills religions and sustains churches. The clerical function can be reduced to the maintaining of a spiritual conformism that succeeded in stifling the spiritual. For centuries clericalism and bigotry against the spirit and religion as a caricature of itself have ended in failure. What role did thought control—theocracy—play in the end of ancient civilizations?)

Mexico City, May 7, 1942—Dear friends,[47] although the Stalinist campaign against us has stopped, at least in the press, the atmosphere is

---

46. Again in the Freudian sense.
47. Letter to Dwight and Nancy Macdonald inserted by Serge in his notebook.

still bad. From several sides, and particularly from a reliable source, we're assured that "they're preparing something." I already wrote to you of the concentration of forces here: a far-flung apparatus, large number of personnel, GPU in particular. I told you that on two consecutive occasions "stones" were thrown at the windows of a friend's house where we take tea Friday evening at the hour we're usually there. By chance, we weren't...We later went to look at the holes in those windows and we all thought they looked like bullet holes. This happened at the house of a doctor friend, a humanist and psychiatrist who never in his life saw the effects of a bullet and who, what is more, is a big, old, wonderfully admirable child. *Fake* policemen have shown up in several places asking for Julián's address (we've obtained information confirming that they're fake and that the authorities have his address). One night, about 2:00 a.m., we—Julián and I—received an insistent phone call from a so-called American, just arrived from New York, who wanted to see us immediately in a night bar on some urgent matter, but who was unable to give us the name of a reference and who thought we were in Coyoacán. I'll skip lesser indications that we're being watched as well, as well as the frequent discussions in Spanish and German communist circles about our killing, its political advantages and disadvantages.

Obviously, nothing will be done without a direct and categorical order from Moscow, but a hypothesis must be envisaged. We have no certain knowledge of what's going on in the USSR, where the situation is certainly more serious and difficult than is generally thought. On the eve of a political and strategic crisis the GPU could decide that it must urgently rid itself of its enemies and that the best moment to do this has arrived, since the military prestige of the USSR is high at this moment and they can count on the indulgence or silence of the democratic countries. Who knows if they'll still be able to do so in three months?

REARGUARD BATTLES

May 12, 1942—According to Erich Fromm (*Escape from Freedom*) attachment-incorporation into something greater than oneself responds to a great need: escape from abandonment, from intolerable isolation.

Same idea in Freud: *Es, Ich, Übermensch*. This applies perfectly to the psychology of the Russian revolutionary party. Depending on the era and the men this attachment can result in the fulfillment or the abandonment of the self. In both cases it overcomes individualism, but with either the plus or the minus sign. For example: Zinoviev's and Kamenev's attitude in October 1917 on the eve of the insurrection, which they considered a mistake; activity and faithfulness to the party. In 1923, Trotsky's capitulation, disavowing Eastman* after having provided him the text of Lenin's will: *"Right or wrong, my party."*[48] Trotsky is at the border between degrading capitulation and exalting fidelity because the party is at the limit where degeneration begins (what's unfortunate is that it can't be seen clearly and that doubt must weigh in favor of the optimistic hypothesis). In 1936–1938 the forced confessions of the Moscow Trials, abdication of consciences in the face of a party that has lost its soul.

Spoke about all this with Lenhoff a propos of the rearguard combat of revolutionaries. I say that we must be hostile to sacrifice, especially to the psychology of sacrifice with its aspiration to suffering, which sweeps away problems, lightens responsibilities, and aggrandizes us while leaving the initiative to the enemy. Elements of suicide and slave morality, Christianity of the vanquished—in no way that of Christ, whose sacrifice was completely different, a sacrifice victoriously consented to. Be harshly realistic, determined to hold on and win, but also know how to accept rearguard battles, lost in advance, with the sangfroid of officers carrying out a costly but useful operation. For we are totally committed and it is above all the future that counts for us, constantly moving forward. No total responsibility, no absolute decision without that. A rearguard battle in order to save the greater part of our forces and ideas responds to precise historical necessities that we cannot evade. It's a local and momentary defeat that saves something essential and leaves us feeling a satisfaction thanks to which we escape the demoralization of defeat. The main thing is not to feel ourselves defeated.

In 1923 in Berlin all of us, even the expert militants of the German party I frequented, knew that we'd be defeated if the insurrection took

48. In English in the original.

place on November 7: we were nevertheless determined to fight, and to have done otherwise would have been treason. In 1927 at the *Glavkonzeskom* I said to Trotsky that we—the Opposition—will be defeated but that we had to fight or the revolution would flicker out without a final blaze, without awakening consciences, without a cry of alarm. The events in China didn't allow for the delaying of combat, which would have been desirable. Trotsky answered that we had to take our chances when the moment came, and he made a broad gesture with his arm: "The rest doesn't depend on us. One loses his head, like Liebknecht, the other becomes Lenin" (verbatim). Today, we are both the extreme rear guard and the infinitely extreme vanguard in the forefront of events.

[...][49] opinions corresponding to obsolete, totally condemned interests...What's strange all the same is that so great a cataclysm, and one whose causes and nature is on a whole so clear, has not awakened at least some courageous intellects. It's true that they'd be quickly reduced to silence, but the little they might have succeeded in saying could perhaps produce the effect of an unforgettable lightning bolt in a stormy sky. This war is being carried on with the barest minimum of strictly utilitarian intelligence, strictly limited to immediate functions. Beyond this, on all sides, the refusal to understand. There is less of this refusal among the Nazi-fascists, for they require a certain understanding of the mortal danger they are facing in order to spur on their energy. A fearsome politics of desperadoes: it succeeds in dominating the flabby bourgeois spirit still thirsty for blindness.

The tragic advantage of all this will be the preservation for future explosions of immense repressed, virgin forces which, once they emerge, will prove to be vastly superior to the shambles of this dying world, despite the enormous proportion of confused and hesitant understanding they contain.

SPANISH REFUGEES

May 16, 1942—Eight hundred Spanish refugees have arrived on the *Nyassa*. On the train from Vera Cruz, announced for 8:00 a.m. but

49. A page is missing here that cannot be found.

which arrived at noon, a cheerful and silent crowd of several thousand refugees applaud, and that hail of applause is more touching than any demonstration. On the platform hugs, emotional outbursts, people seeking each other, people finding each other as the improbable comes true. I see an old bareheaded man with a sad, yellow, wrinkled face who shouts from the middle of the crowd, his hands raised, and I recognize him as a magistrate of the High Court of the Republic I recently met. Men I don't know but who think they recognize me shake my hand warmly. Had it not been for the crimes of "our" Stalinist totalitarianism this could have been one of those moments of communion and collective joy produced by great mass movements; but every one of these thousands of people knows or senses that anyone in this crowd may be a treacherous and dangerous adversary or a compromising or threatened militant whom it would be better to stay away from. People evade my gaze and, cutting through the crowd in search of Olga Nin,* I never lose sight of the possibility that here as elsewhere I could very well be victim of an attack. A hidden fratricidal struggle is present everywhere among us. Met Don Álvaro, Mecca, Arago, de Miguel. The *Nyassa* witnessed a naval combat between an Allied convoy and a Nazi submarine, which attempted to use the Portuguese vessel as a screen.

Very few comrades among those arriving. Mostly republicans and right socialists (Prieto). They are the ones who control the funds and the organizing of aid. Even in defeat the class struggle continues, and the high functionaries, magistrates, senior officers, and politicians are saving themselves, leaving the revolutionaries behind. France just turned Cipriano Mera* over to Franco; the American press didn't make a peep. An anarchist bricklayer who became a true military chief and one of the most authentic heroes of the defense of Madrid has no publicity value. I've even been told that this emigration of moderates has met serious objections from Washington, that Prieto had had to make several trips there in order to receive its reluctant authorization, and that Washington wanted to authorize only the emigration of women and children to (Latin!) America; that is, of noncombatants least threatened with reprisals. I reply that this reactionary stupidity (which diminishes the social value of the emigration, risks wasting forces that will be precious tomorrow, and increases resentment) will probably have a positive side: it tempers men by freeing them of their illusions and leaves the energetic elements in Europe, where despite it all they have a chance of survival.

Seeing these thousands of refugees, thought that each one of them—man, woman, or child—has several replicas among the two million dead of the Civil War.

HENK SNEEVLIET
May 17, 1942—Opening an American newspaper I read that on April 15 Sneevliet and eight of his comrades of the Dutch Revolutionary Socialist Party were sentenced to death by a Nazi military tribunal and executed. Our Spanish friends, accustomed to such news, greet this with little emotion; they don't seem to realize that we have lost one of the best and surest of men ... He must have been a few years older than I, maybe fifty-five. We met in 1921 at the Third Congress in Moscow, without really getting to know each other. In Amsterdam I told him that in Moscow I'd caught a glimpse of a certain Maehring, delegate of the Revolutionary Party of the Dutch Indies—"But that was me!" Deported during the war to the Dutch Indies, he had dedicated himself to founding a native party (the Sarekat Islam?); became popular, infatuated with the people and the land. He spoke of the place with love. "What beauty, what purity of line, what intelligent gentleness in the women! And the freshness of their skin!" At a museum in The Hague we stopped in front of the Malaysian gold plate from a royal treasure that had been brought over and he grimaced with rage: "Look at all that our bandits pillaged from them!" He told of the taking of a palace, the massacre. It was in 1936, some of the comrades of his youth where still jailed for life on an island penal colony, he hadn't forgotten them, doing what he could to write to them, taking steps and issuing protests in their favor.

Before a bourgeois edifice in The Hague he pointed to the line of people waiting at the door. "Look at these imbeciles, will you! They're waiting to see the presents offered Princess Juliana ... And we're supposed to be one of the most civilized peoples in the world!" At his home at Oovertom 452, I think, we held a conference of the Fourth International, with which we were both in the process of reluctantly breaking. After the meetings, in his sober office, he read to me, translating, poems by Henriette Roland Holst* on the great period of the Russian Revolution, on Lenin and Trotsky. He asserted that Roland Holst was one of the great poets of the time, with the dual handicap of writing in the language of a small country and being a passionate revolutionary. He was probably right. We organized wonderful meetings, especially in Rotterdam, where I would show up with him at a union office on the edge of a canal, guarded by old pipe-smoking sailors who looked to be the calmest, most reasonable, most faithful men in the world. Loads of bicycles at the doors, the black water, the gentle, slightly misty sky, the gray-faced houses, peaceful as well. We spoke of the reasonable possibility of a victory for the Spanish revolution, as well as its dangers, in front of two hundred concentrated, serious, attentive faces.

Whenever he came to Paris to see me at the Pré-Saint-Gervais he brought me the offering of our Amsterdam friends, a half head of cheese, a dozen cigars... I see him in the evening on the boulevard Montparnasse, suddenly emerging among the passersby: long overcoat, a soft hat of dark green material pulled down over his aging, wrinkled face with its expression of stubbornness and energetic, sad concentration; gold-framed glasses. He saw quite clearly the coming of war and the inevitable crushing of Holland; spoke of the fascist tendencies of the Dutch bourgeoisie as well. "It's only afterwards that socialism will have a future...." Like me, he loved and admired Leon Trotsky, but for us, mixed with these feelings, were an irritation, a growing revulsion against his authoritarian mania. "The Old Man wants to rule over us without understanding anything about our situation. He's encouraging three or four narrow-minded fanatics from Rotterdam who type up theses aimed at splitting the party. It's pitiful and idiotic...." We were agreed in thinking that a new International can't be founded without first having two or three real parties or groups in two or three important countries, and that nothing can be established on just one head with a "Bolshevism-Leninism" increasingly unintelligible to the people of the West.

In September 1937 we took the train together to Reims for the rendezvous with "Ludwig," Ignace Reiss—assassinated in Chamblandes with his train ticket in his pocket...We waited for Reiss in the station buffet—deserted—and then the next day at the post office, in vain—and we had evil forebodings. We roamed the city, followed by the GPU without our realizing it, even though there was little activity. Being alone in this way gave us a feeling of intimacy. As we drank amazingly good and cheap champagne in a small establishment where the tables were shaped like barrels and where, in the night, aside from us there was only a couple of young lovers—the young woman with platinum hair and the look of a tourist—we felt close to each other. He spoke to me of the suicide of his two sons and of the death of two of the four young people of his party on the Spanish front...His second son had thrown himself into a canal after arguments with him on the subject of the aid to be given German refugees. The party, too poor and throwing all its efforts into Spain, couldn't provide sufficient assistance to the refugees. The son admonished the father for living comfortably while the German comrades were dying..."What more could I do?" The next day, in the cathedral square, we raised our heads to look at the faces on the sculptures ravaged by the explosions and fires of 1915. The contours of the stone had been rounded, as if sculpted by waves of fire. At noon, on the station platform, we read in *L'Humanité* of the murder of an unidentified man near Lausanne and we immediately understood. Sneevliet left for Geneva. He returned with Elsa Reiss while the Dutch Communist press asked what mysterious role he and I had played in the crime at Chamblandes, where "a Gestapo agent" had lost his life! Together with Leon Sedov we met Walter Krivitsky at Gérard Rosenthal's. Sneevliet growled with ill-contained rage: "That bastard! He's come over to our side so as not to be executed! He participated in the assassination of Reiss, his best friend!" It was true. Walter, in whom I saw nothing of the smiling young Walter I'd come across in the past in Moscow at Averbakh's home and at my place (the evening that Brunn and I and somebody else, no doubt Reiss, three young secret agents about to go on a mission, founded the "Society of Future Convicts" over a good Caucasian wine). Walter was small, thin, wrinkled, with an angular face, nervous, gray complexioned, enigmatic, and tense. He repeated that he didn't feel capable of joining an op-position to the USSR whose international function was still revolu-tionary. He told of the meeting held with the leaders of the GPU in a café at the World's Fair (Spiegelglass, Moscow's envoy) where the ex-ecution of Reiss—who was in Paris at the time—was decided on in his presence. He had warned him by ringing up the phone in his hotel room several times without talking to him, since the telephone was under surveillance. He was ordered to liquidate the widow before re-turning to Moscow. He had agreed to return, certain of being executed, but at the last moment, at the train station, he'd changed his mind. Sneevliet exploded in a rage when Walter told him that there was an informer in his party in Amsterdam and that he had gone to see him on such and such a date—but W. didn't know the name of the informer and S. wasn't able to recall the visitor...The scene between them was painful.

During the invasion of Belgium he was stuck in Antwerp, wrote asking me to get him a French visa—but there was no one left to talk to. I imagine him going to his execution with his customary calm, the same scowling face of a good and thoughtful bulldog.

JEANNINE

May 20, 1942—The director of the Franco-Spanish school, after having consulted his council, refused to admit my Jeannine because of the revolutionary influence she might introduce into the school (seven years old!), and he spoke of Bolshevism. For fear also of "criticism" that might be directed at the school. This pedagogue is a perfect reaction-ary beast. Little Theissen, son of German émigrés, had been admitted with a provisional exemption from tuition. The kids of paying parents, who are of the worst class of landowners, looked askance at the poor little boy. Punches, Theissen expelled, everything back in order.

Claude told Jeannine the story of Jesus crucified between two thieves. Calle Madero Jeannine stops in front of a display window, notices three crucifixes. "So the one in the middle is Jesus and the other two are the bandits?"

GORKIN'S TALK ON SPAIN

May 22, 1942—At Fritz Fränkel's, talk by Julián on the POUM. Present were several combatants from the International Brigades with Regler, who told us that he'd just learned the truth about the May 1937 events in Barcelona. He'd only known the legend, forged by the CP, of a "Trotskyist" plot. "I see that it was impossible for those of us in the trenches to know many essential things about public life."

Julián gives an excellent idea of the feeling of the beginning of a revolution and the difficult situation of a minority party that represents more consciousness than strength. It was the most consciously revolutionary party, armed with solid knowledge of Marxist doctrine. Its founders had split with the Communist Party in 1929 (the Catalano-Balearic Federation,[50] later the Worker-Peasant Bloc). Decisive role of the personality of Maurín, the Leader. (One perceives the weaknesses of a party controlled by a Leader.) Long hesitation about breaking with the Comintern, "thanks to that revolutionary opportunism we were able to maintain contact with the masses and truly form a party—the masses wouldn't accept any opposition to the Comintern."

(This magnificent instinctive fidelity to the symbolic organization of the first victorious socialist revolution became a regressive factor when the Russian Revolution began to be corrupted. "Revolutionary opportunism" consisted in blinding oneself and others by abdicating the right to criticism and free Marxist thought to the bureaucratized leadership of the Comintern. It perhaps allowed for the creation of a party, a minority one, but it prevented the Spanish militants from joining in the combat for the reform of the Comintern and the Soviet Union while this reform was still possible in 1923–1926. The Italians, Rossi, Ercoli,[51] and Gramsci had the same attitude; the Germans Brandler and Thalheimer, as well, and thus all of them allowed the crushing of the Opposition of 1923 and 1927. The error, in a great international organization, of subordinating the largest, the most general interests to immediate local interests.) (On Maurín: role of long imprisonments

50. More properly: the Communist Federation of Catalonia and the Baleares.
51. Rossi was the pseudonym of Angelo Tasca, Ercoli that of Palmiro Togliatti.

in his life, which isolated him at moments as decisive as that of 1923; complex influence of his brother-in-law Souvarine, jealous of the Russians, inwardly hostile towards them, inclined to look after the interests of the moment, on the spot, and what is more completely pessimistic about Russia and the revolutionary movement.) Julián finds this policy to be correct and stresses Maurín's value (in my opinion this value was the result of his having had the good fortune to be formed during the good period of the Russian Revolution, in direct contact with the Bolsheviks). The party felt the loss of Maurín, who disappeared during a trip during the critical days of July 1936.[52]

In 1934 the Catalano-Balearic Federation took the initiative in the forming of the Workers' Alliances that were behind the insurrection of October 1934. The principle of workers' alliances in opposition to that of Popular Fronts with the bourgeoisie, rejected until the last minute by the anarchists and Communists, who rallied to it on the eve of the insurrection. Such alliances might have formed a majority in parliament and taken over the reins of the Republic.

1936. The party enters the Popular Front in order to avoid handing the electoral majority over to the right as a result of an electoral mechanism that eliminated minorities and favored the blocs, a law passed in order to ensure power for the republicans and the socialists. The anarchists and syndicalists vote in order to free the thirty thousand prisoners of the 1934 insurrection.

"We had no program, no brain, no program" when events took us by surprise in September 1936. The Generalitat of Catalonia refused arms to the POUM on the evening of the 18th, even though it was known that the military uprising was about to occur. A former comrade obtained eighteen rifles which were to prove decisive in the street battles the next day. A group of comrades supported the assault guards who were retreating before the soldiers and the situation was saved. The POUM had just issued a call for a general strike (Nin thought it would fail . . .) and provided the first small shock troop, whose interven-

52. Incarcerated by the Francoists and thought dead, Maurín was freed in December 1946, along with Cipriano Mera, the anarchist military leader.

tion was crucial in the early moments. The following day the CGT and its masses took the initiative in all areas. "A few men and a few rifles at the critical moment can play a role of incalculable importance." In fact, had Barcelona fallen by surprise Madrid and Valencia probably would have immediately fallen as well.

"The next day we saw that our program was completely out of date. We were worried about rents while the workers were taking things in their own hands.... The spontaneous initiative of the masses was way far ahead of the party...."

The party's entire development occurred through a series of crises provoked by 1. The Russian question; 2. The Catalan question. Party influential in Catalonia alone. Formed by fusion with the Trotskyists, Andrade,* Nin.

Spontaneous initiative everywhere: Five comrades seized control of the water service. Gironella* formed a POUM cavalry with four hundred horses—where did he find them? He also formed an orchestra that made a big impression. "The first revolutionary funerals were for our people, killed at the front...." The first tank was a POUM tank; it couldn't go far but it was stationed in front of a party office where it worked wonders. The first ambulance on the front. The anarchists were frightened by the organizational ability of a party they considered insignificant and took for communist. This woke them up. "Our division, in several columns, had seven to eight thousand men. The party had the same number."

In 1931, during the first phase of the Spanish revolution, Joaquín Maurín thought it had to go through a bourgeois-democratic phase, while the Comintern issued the slogan of the Communist seizure of power, though they were in fact powerless. Dual aspect of the question: the bourgeois democratic revolution—1848—is no longer possible: its objectives can be obtained only by the socialist masses and must be surpassed by broad nationalization measures implying a planned economy. (The experiment of conservative bourgeois democracy had been thoroughly exhausted in Spain.) Nevertheless, J. M. was right because there was no working-class organization capable of seizing power or even of understanding the problem. A dangerous period of political education and transition was thus necessary…To a large extent this state of affairs was the result of the accumulated errors of Bolshevism dating back to its early days, in 1918. By refusing all socialist and anarchist tendencies the right to existence, by establishing the monopoly of power, the one-party state, and directed thought, it had dug a pit between the Communists and the socialists and anarchists that was deepened during the struggles within the Comintern. The persecution of dissidents in the USSR caused a moral split in the working class. When the monarchy collapsed not a single working-class group wanted any part of an authority that would have led to a Russian-style dictatorship; that is, towards prison for all except the Communists. Bourgeois democracy seemed infinitely more agreeable.

DISCUSSION WITH OLGA NIN ON ANDRÉS'S DISAPPEARANCE

May 23, 1942—She is convinced that he wasn't murdered in Spain, but sent to the USSR. The investigating magistrate's secretary came to see her after Nin's kidnapping and showed her three photos: two unknown men and me, the latter found on Nin (the two others might have been Franco agents in order to lump us together). He was polite, even sympathetic, and told her, "I assure you that you have no right to call us criminals. Your husband is alive, but he's far away and we can't do a thing." A long time after, at the Paris police prefecture, a high functionary said to her: "You're not a widow. We have solid reasons to believe that Nin was sent to Moscow." This information came from French counterespionage. She said that Álvarez del Vayo (foreign minister at the time) definitely knew the truth of the affair, concerning which, he said of her: "Poor woman, she'll suffer for a long time to come."

Connect this with two memories. Two days after Nin's arrest we sent a delegation to the Spanish embassy in Paris (Magdeleine Paz, Georges Pioch, and perhaps Félicien Challaye). Received by a secretary who assured them that the accused members of the POUM would benefit from all the guarantees of justice and were in no particular danger. Pioch posed the question of Nin: we wanted to know where he was. "Oh, as for Nin," the secretary said with a hopeless gesture, "I can't promise you anything." He quickly realized his misstep and said only one more thing, "I don't know anything about it ..."

A short time later we met with delegates from the International Labour Party[53] and militants from various countries to prepare the defense of the POUM. Édouard Serre, who was the head of Air France and rendered great service to the Spanish Republicans and to Soviet aviators, told us that he'd taken it upon himself to attempt an extraordinary *démarche* to save Nin. He had gone to see the Soviet ambassador in Paris, Vladimir Potemkin, and had spoken to him of the gravity of the affair. The ambassador thanked him for his intervention and asked for a written note, which he promised to give to Stalin ...

A VISIT TO OTTO RÜHLE

May 28, 1942—Otto Rühle shows us around his "*castillo chiflado*," the crazy castle, the coo-coo castle, a tiny house in a cactus garden. His office is on the second floor. Maps of Mexico City, books, a cot. Simple and sumptuous moonlight enters through the window. Portrait of a young him (photograph, reproduction of a painting), with his hard Bismarckian head haranguing a factory crowd. It perfectly expresses the determined and relentless energy for which intelligence—rigorously methodical—is essentially a weapon which is within him, which is him ... He rests on a cot made of a carefully conceived large crate with removable lids, painted yellow, and which contains his manuscripts, conscientiously tied up in packets. In the smallest detail the hand of an artisan in love with his craft, a hand inseparable from the thinking brain, a brain that has in no way diminished. With a childlike pride he undoes a packet containing three folders filled with pages recopied and filed. It's a summary of Marx's works based on the texts themselves, in Spanish. "I spent five years working on it...." He lovingly shows us his books: big, finely bound tomes, a *History of the Revolutionary Movement in Europe* from the peasant wars until the Russian Revolution in three volumes. A beautiful *Illustrated History of Working-Class Customs*, notebooks on pedagogy, works on sexuality. "This is all that's

53. Actually the Independent Labour Party.

left to me of forty books, many of which were burned in Germany."
Note of regret in his voice when he speaks of the twelve thousand
volumes of his library lost in Germany. He shows me Spanish, English,
French (the Karl Marx) translations; I can feel that he loves his work,
his oeuvre, that at age sixty-eight he feels the same pleasure as a thirty-
year-old when he feels the weight of his first book in his hand.

This strength, this health, this vitality are good. I think that I too
love my books and papers, that this has often given me strength, and
that, thinking about them, I approved of myself. This is the natural
attachment of the artisan for the work of his hands, into which he has
put the best of himself and not just for himself; in which, on the other
hand, he finds justification of himself, a justification one always needs.

Laurette is filled with wonder by two lions, a lion and a lioness of
braided straw, Mexican handicraft. They have wild manes, a miniature
terrifying expression. The anonymous artist who made them probably
never saw a lion except in pictures, but he knows what ferocity is, the
innocence of animal ferocity, the childlike beauty of the terrifying
expression. Otto shows us drawings he made in india ink to sell to
gringo tourists (five pesos for a midsized drawing on good paper, signed
Simonova). Intelligently stylized, the essential indicated with a single
strong line or brushstroke, work of excellent quality. His entire personality is summed up in this: his love of reality, his gift for observation,
a tendency toward generalization (implying the tendency toward abstraction), the choice of omitting secondary details while noting the
characteristic one. He learned to draw past age sixty as an émigré. Each
page is finished, perfectly clean, covered with transparent paper. German correctness in the smallest detail.

The conversation. On the capacity of the German people, the only
one that could totally reproduce Russian totalitarianism: this is the
great danger. Revolutions don't repeat themselves. We've persisted in
thinking in terms of the Russian Revolution in a world where the
Russian Revolution can't be repeated. He considers Lenin a Jacobin
adapted to his time and place.

As the hour grew late, fatigue accentuates the tics in his bony and
fleshy face. Fatigue turns his ideas aggressive, he speaks of the indis-

pensable destruction of this class culture in its entirety, this culture of oppression and corruption with its Shakespeare and Goethe—into the fire, all of it! There's no further need of it, there'll no longer be a need for it. I answer mildly just so as not to give my approval to a paradox born of irritation while avoiding increasing his irritation. He knows full well the value of this heritage and that Goethe, if he were to have only one reader, would still be essential (aside from past accomplishments).

Alice having referred to their "petit bourgeois" comfort, makes with a jovial gesture of mock anger: "I take that sin on myself!" Alice says she feels on edge; she senses the approach of an earthquake "as far as Peru." The next day, the 29th, there was an earthquake in northern Ecuador, province of Esmeralda.

PIERRE SEMARD EXECUTED

Late May 1942—Pierre Semard,* executed in Paris April 15. We met several times in Berlin in 1922 (our discussions at the Vaterland Café on the Potsdamer Platz, vast as a railroad terminal, with its orchestra of thundering brasses). In those days he was a tall, streetwise Parisian working stiff who was beginning to discover revolutionary ideas. Secretary of the railway workers union, working-class accent, cigarette butt at the corner of his mouth. Athletically built, a slightly simian face, not ugly. Naturally, the Party was going through a crisis. Frossard, still secretary, assured me of his attachment to the Comintern, symbol and organization of the Russian Revolution: "I'll never leave the International, you'll see. There are guys who say I want to have a political career? Me, I don't give a damn. Only the working class and socialism count for me." Semard, with whom I discussed the attitude of Frossard, who was on the point of leaving, judged him with good sense: "Deep down he's a politician," and in his mouth the word implied disapproval. He reproached the Russians their lack of understanding of the mentality of the French worker. With him I also met Richetta,* his shock of red hair, his working-class accent. Rather sad, for he was tormented by his misunderstandings with the Russians, and he had maintained a certain libertarian sensibility.

Semard went along with the whole evolution of the Comintern, probably grumbling to himself, but keeping discipline. Caught in the gears (union functionary then secretary general of the Party), forced to sanction and then supervise shameful maneuvers, increasingly "committed" and with a strong sentiment of fidelity. Around 1926–1927, probably as a result of divergences within the Political Bureau regarding some change in party line, the rumor was spread that he had had dealings with the Tour Pointue.[54] This was certainly a slander, but since there were police informers among the Party leadership he might have had connections with one of them. He was dismissed from the leadership but kept his functions.

The Nazis are in the process of destroying the cadres of the French CP who, under orders, were caught in an ambush at the time of the Moscow Pact (Péri, Sampaix,* already executed, Gitton* gone over to Doriot and assassinated). Being the only communist party that remained legal, PCF didn't suffer the purges that physically eliminated an entire generation of leaders formed by Zinoviev in other countries (England excepted), a generation that more or less knew the heroic period and witnessed the advent of Stalinism. Stalin is keeping in reserve Thorez,* Duclos* (wily politician, vice president of the Chamber of Deputies, GPU), Marty* (unhinged, living in fear but who can serve as a symbol: the Black Sea Revolt, prison, Spain . . .) and is allowing the Nazis to rid him of the rest. As a bonus, this creates martyrs. The calculation is obvious, for it would have been simple to warn them in time and order them to go into hiding.

In Paris, the Communists published Semard's last letter to his family, which is perhaps apocryphal: "I'm going to be executed in a few minutes. . . . I'll show the executioners that Communists know how to die like patriots and revolutionaries. . . ." His "final thoughts are on the final victory over fascism, the Red Army, and Stalin. . . ." He asks the railway workers not to "collaborate" with the Nazis. He died courageously, signing a final article for *L'Humanité*, having no other language at his disposal . . .

54. The seat of the Paris police prefecture.

GPU

June 14, 1942—We're informed that four GPU agents, known as operational, probably Russian, arrived in Mexico City recently (within the last week or two). Their presence is supposedly known by Lombardo Toledano.* Coming from the United States—perhaps to "take care" of us: it is suggested we take precautions. Also possible they've come to take care of Jackson, the trial supposedly entering a decisive phase on July 10. Finally, it's also possible they're here to instruct Mexican subagents.

June 11, unexpected arrival of several Soviet superior officers (General Ilya Sarayez) and, the 12th or 13th, of a Mr. Bruce Wickers, "American" and "charged with a mission by the Soviet government" ("friend of Roosevelt," according to word on the street). It's possible that the four agents prepared these visits.

MEXICO CITY NIGHTS

July 5, 1942—Plaza Garibaldi, sinister and gay, the gaiety of a green-eyed sugar *calavera*.

On a corner, a vast canvas construction, crudely illuminated, where about a hundred people are playing a kind of bingo. The figure is announced (*diablo, pavo, águila, sol*), you put down the seeds, and once the page is filled you win. A blonde woman with a fleshy face, noncoms with little moustaches, sombreros, city hoodlums, people. Faces like old-time Texans. Outside, at the threshold of a doorway through which a bed can be glimpsed, two women are chatting.

Low one-story houses, closed, with flowers and dwarf palms at the door. A bar with a flaming sign, full of mechanical music. The darkness all around and the alleys down which shady couples disappear. A *policía* passes, casting here and there the beam of his flashlight. The useless deployment of this feeble beam makes us laugh.

Beautiful trees, palms in the center of the plaza.

On the opposite side *mariachis* are playing without an audience. The sign of the near-empty Salón Tanapa.[55] Hairless dogs. A half-mad

55. The Salón Tanapa, founded in the 1920s and whose neon sign still lights up the Plaza Garibaldi.

woman, drunk, dances to the sound of the strings. Men in serapes drinking soft drinks; decorative. Lemonade stands, indigent. People squatting on their heels, sleeping in a heap with their dogs on a dark corner. Further along, the Guadalajara *café de noche*, the creaking music of the *mariachis*, pitiful dance hall girls (a few pretty young girls of sixteen), the atmosphere of a gambling den. The spectacle-wearing official and the little dance hall girl in her flaming red blouse.

People passing: a little man with glasses, thin and square shouldered with a mummified head, wearing a raincoat and felt hat: the little murderer of prostitutes; alongside, a limber step, round shoulders, a man wearing a short leopard-skin jacket and wide-brimmed fedora, his holster sticking out from his hip. He walks tilted slightly forward as if he was headed for some encounter, ready to fight.

Calle Aquiles Serdán, crowded, much prostitution, girls under twenty. A block of old houses in the process of demolition, the peculiar effect of a bombardment. A girl, seventeen, the light coloring of a European, but she's made up so she has a copper-red complexion and dyes her hair a fiery brown. Wearing a red jacket.

"*CAMIONES*"

July 10, 1942—The drivers and conductors of local buses—those horrible yellow-and-coffee-colored tin cans on wheels that carry compacted human cargo—decorate their vehicles . . . I have seen little Nazi flags on them—before Mexico's entry into the war. Technicolor photos of boxers, soccer stars, and swimmers ring the driver's seat of a Roma-Mérida–Chapultepec bus I often take downtown. On the windshield a little red airplane. Above the gears he placed the most beautiful of the ornaments, the one that clearly means the most to him: a small death's head—a woman—brunette, probably of wax, with a beautiful rictus, encircled by some kind of big flower of white mousseline, like a voluminous bridal gown . . .

Another bus: half-naked women cut out from American illustrated magazines. The large-breasted blonde and brunette. On the back of the driver's seat a blonde spreads her offered thighs.

PRECOLUMBIAN SCULPTURE

July 10, 1942—(Museum). At first sight, a distant but striking kinship with Egyptian figures (statues) and groups. Similar kinship with the tree structure of Maya symbols in particular, with Hindu-Malaysian art (Khmer); kinship with Chinese art: certain animals put one in mind of dragons. These are distant kinships, their originality is powerful. (Maya priests recall Assyrian profiles.)

Aztec sculpture is hieratic.

Symbols of the earth divinity. Figure of a peasant woman with braided hair: the productive and fertile earth.

An overloaded, massive symbol of the devouring earth. The least detail is considered, it is thought in stone, a cruel and naturalistic vision of nature (no mysticism). The whole is a jumble of ordered forms inspired by tropical vegetation. Two strong profiles of snakes join at the top, forming the two monstrous eyes of a human head. Men's hearts and hands devoured. Interlacing snakes.

Art was a form of communication with the living earth. The symbols made of stone are sculpted on the bottom, on the side that's placed down and that touches the ground as it speaks to it.

Some works of a very strong and stylized realism. The unforgettable death's head, carnal and emptied of life.

A flat human figure with hands joined in sorrow over the belly bears an expression of mortal distress, without a cry, completely mute.

The enormous phallus, whose foreskin, or what is left of it, is jagged.

The Adorer, tiny human figure, sixty centimeters, in gray stone, with a crude, powerfully carved face, with thick lips, massive but upraised features with blank eyes (colored stone in the past). The adoration is in the petrified movement of that head.

Circular votive stone, called the Aztec calendar. Face of the sun god (hanging tongue, fire). Four rectangular cartouches containing symbols of previous suns.

Cosmogony. Four successive suns, four life cycles wiped out by cataclysms. The fifth sun shone at the time of the conquest and a cataclysm was expected. These suns are also related to the elements: earth, water, air, and fire.

Barbaric and intelligent materialism, exaltation of life, enormous capacity for labor, observation, and thought; hieratization.

WAR IN RUSSIA
July 10, 1942—Russian front pierced between Kursk and Kharkov. In a week Stalingrad, Riazan-Moscow, and Rostov directly threatened, the black earth and the harvests lost. Collapse of the front. Probability that the USSR will be hors de combat in the fall, cut off from the Caucasus.

Three weeks ago I had a long talk with Max Diamant.* His theses: that the USSR is infinitely stronger than is thought; that Stalin will retain the prestige of the victory; but that Stalinism will adapt and lose some of its violence. Conclusion: accommodate oneself to this outlook, follow the twists and turns of the Stalinists. —A few days ago Julián reproached me for underestimating the strength and vitality of Stalinism.

I responded to M. D. that we know absolutely nothing about what's going on in the USSR; that according to the little we know and my long experience, the internal situation must be indescribably tragic; that defeat was probable and that it was a question of learning to what extent it could be limited (the Nazis don't seem to me to be capable of reaching Trans-Caucasia and seriously threatening the Urals this year); that Stalin will remain the organizer of defeat and that in this or some other way his regime will probably go under.

STREETS OF MEXICO CITY
July 12, 1942—Calle Licenciado Primo de Verdad opening onto Moneda. The church with its short, slender tower leaning backwards. The sober facade of old bricks red as dried blood leans backward all in one piece. Little ornamentation, serious and sad.

Mata Hari school *de bailar*,[56] balconies and couples gently twirling above the trams. Downstairs, *cantina*.

56. Dance.

Streets of Mexico City.

Hospital de muñecas y santos.[57]

Pulquería El Amor Libre.

Carnecería[58] La Esperanza.

Farmacia del Indio Triste (Moneda).

Pulquería El Purgatorio.

Carnecería La Flor de las Américas

Carnecería El Imperio Azteca.

Carnecería Lucifero del Alba.

On a main street workers carrying naked display dummies. Their stiff, pink women's bodies, with their fashion magazine heads, above the movement of the street and the broad, dark-skinned faces of their carriers.

RÜHLE

August 5, 1942—Me: Otto, why don't you write your memoirs?

Him: It's impossible for me to write for the American public, whose needs and education are profoundly foreign to me. In any case, I won't write my memoirs for anyone. My experience is too discouraging and all I would do is spread discouragement. As for me, I'm not discouraged, on the contrary, I still have faith in the future, but others would be. I can't ask them to have my strength and my faith.

We're in general agreement on the major subjects. That this war is the end of capitalism, that the world will be overturned from top to bottom, that it's the end of colonial domination, the end, or the beginning of the end, of gold . . . Taking his coffee he twists his wide mouth and poses his gray gaze on me: "What if we wrote a second *Communist Manifesto*? We won't call it 'communist' of course, the word having been sullied. . . . We have to provide a new explanation of everything, and this has become possible, since we can see the broad lines of the earthquakes in progress. . . ."

57. Doll and saint hospital.
58. Butcher shop.

DEATH OF RIAZANOV

August 10, 1942—An old Soviet official on a trip abroad reveals the death of Riazanov, somewhere in deportation in the north two years ago! (Published in New York.) He vanished in 1931 at age sixty-one. He finished out his life with nine years of captivity and misery. What became of his female partner, slightly younger, who was a true partner in his labors, his thought? I was in Moscow when the drama occurred: accused during the trial of the "Mensheviks" (Groman,* Sher, Rubin,* Ginzburg,* Sukhanov,* Ikov) of having hidden in the safe of the Marx-Engels Institute documents dealing with the negotiations with the Second International concerning a "Franco-Polish military intervention in the USSR." Stupid and ludicrous. Rubin, a talented economist and his protégé, compromised him out of cowardice: made the "required confessions." Long, fruitless searches at the Institute, violent scene between Riazanov and Stalin, who'd ordered it. Riazanov, corpulent, with his noble mane and white beard, thundered freely at the Institute and thundered in front of Stalin. "Where are the documents?" "Unless you bring them yourselves you'll never find them!" Stalin pretended to believe the accusation (or believed in something like it: capable of that).

The trial of the "Mensheviks" was a put-up job, all of them fake Mensheviks, of course, long since on the margins of the party, with which they had only loose contact, except for Ikov. In an intercepted message Ikov had just denounced the provocation and imposture of the Ramzin trial. They broke him by arresting his only son, and he made the confessions that were ordered. Bazarov violently refused to do so and was sent to a concentration camp for ten years. Braunstein, envoy of the Menshevik Central Committee, was already in an isolator and refused to talk. At a conference of economists Groman had despairingly denounced the catastrophic situation created by frenzied industrialization and collectivization; altercation with Milyutin.* Groman felt himself condemned for having posed the question of responsibility. Sukhanov brought together in a kind of political salon intellectuals who had spoken among themselves against the imminent economic catastrophe and tested the waters about the possibility of the forming of a new Soviet government with Vasily Blyukher* (whom Vera Figner was to sound out).

The confessions were turned by the GPU into veritable staged performances. The accused, broken by the threat of death and appeals to their Soviet patriotism in the face of the danger of war. Later, at the isolator of Verkhne-Uralsk, Sukhanov revealed these performances, demanded that the promises made to him by the security forces be kept, engaged in lengthy hunger strikes, and disappeared (1933–1934?). I thought that the political goals of the trial of the "Mensheviks" were: Accusing of sabotage in the service of foreigners the great socialist technicians who, in the committees, had denounced the terrible sabotage organized by the police bureaucracy and who, in the case of a crisis in the regime, formed a team ready to step in and direct the economy; of responding (like the Ramzin trial) to Bessedovski's revelations[59] about the diversionary work in Poland (led by Unszlicht*—disappeared—and Ambassador Voikov*—assassinated by a White in Warsaw: several terrorist attacks, the explosion at the citadel of Warsaw, the espionage affair of the officers Baginsky and Vetchorkevitch): We're not the ones preparing the war, it's you! Basic psychology of agitation.

Whatever the case, while they were preparing the trial Riazanov, informed, knew that they counted on exploiting the false confessions of one of his collaborators at the Institute, a neurotic named Sher. Face to face with high functionaries, Riazanov protested vehemently against these methods of deception and agitation built on fabricated plots. This was the cause of his disappearance. (I learned what went on behind the scenes of this affair from Julie K.,[60] Polina Vinogradskaya,* who worked with Riazanov, Polevoi, connected to one of the accused, Sokolovski—sabotage of the textile industry—who told me with tears in his eyes as he read the account of the trial: "He's mad, he's confessing even to the unbelievable!") Riazanov had just been fêted as one of the great Marxist scholars when he was "liquidated."

I saw him for the first time in 1921 or 1922 at the Grand Theater

59. Soviet diplomat Gregory Bessedovski had defected in 1929 and published a book in France, *Yes, I Accuse! In Service to the Soviets* (1930).
60. Possibly Julia Kolberg, Serge's distant Georgian cousin on his mother's side whose family had known Stalin from prerevolutionary days in Tiflis and was to some extent protected by him.

during formal session of the Moscow Soviet. Trotsky spoke—as always, magnificently, but I didn't like him very much at that time; he seemed to me to incarnate authoritarianism and overweening historical pride that I called "posing before history." Riazanov, already in opposition, couldn't speak in public, the Central Committee having forbidden this, after some of his discreetly devastating comments. During the session he suddenly appeared in a loge near the stage, wearing a white jacket and looking a bit like a graying Zola, his chest square. Hailed by all the young students, who waved at him. After the official speakers came a clamor: "Riazanov to the speaker's platform!" Which is probably what he wanted, and it was the Moscow Committee that invited him to speak ... His manner was to contrast Marxist humanism with Bolshevik harshness and authoritarianism, but without seeming to, basing himself on the texts. Often sarcastic, in the style of Marx. (Among the remarks he made at a congress or in the Central Committee: "I'm not one of those Old Bolsheviks whom Lenin for twenty years called old imbeciles....") I loved him because in the fights at the Central Executive of the Soviets he fought tirelessly against the death penalty—and within the leadership he called for limits on the terror and the functions of the Cheka.

In 1922 met him by chance in Berlin. He had aged a great deal, his hair gone white, but he had taken on a slightly Olympian air. He had come to find archival documents of Marx's. We briefly spoke in an Untergrundbahn[61] station. Afterwards in Moscow I barely got more than a glimpse of him.

The first Marx Museum he created, in a small town house from which the Porcelain Museum had been driven to make room, was deserted every time I visited. Fifty thousand communists in Moscow and not a single visitor! Marx's notebooks from when he studied Russian at age fifty. Letters to Jenny Marx and Engels about his poverty: a child sick and no money to pay for a doctor. The Marx-Engels Institute expanded and was installed on Maly Znamensky Pereoulok in the former residence of a wealthy family, the building vast, one story,

61. Berlin subway.

and surrounded by a large garden. Riazanov had a house built with an ideal study in the corner where the garden met the street. We said that he alone among the old revolutionaries had fully realized his life's dream and completed his labors by building this comfortable shell for himself. "Now he'll no longer pose any opposition." And he didn't, but he maintained an independent attitude and remained outspoken; he protected and hired at the Institute all the heretics, from Mensheviks to Trotskyists, gave work to Souvarine in Paris and Pierre Pascal in Moscow, corresponded with Kautsky, received Vandervelde. We said of him that he was a great liberal in the heart of Bolshevism, the first of two, the other being Kamenev, and they resembled each other: the same massive heads, both wearing glasses and with the same light eyes of self-confident intellectuals, the same graying beards, short and thick, the same manes, the same dignified bearing, the same simplicity.

I last had news of him in 1933. In a city on the Volga a deported comrade—like him—met him in a cooperative full of poor people buying rationed items. Grown old, weakened, his clothing tattered, he was still grumbling... He was allowed to scrape by in a dilapidated library. His works, though, had been pulped.

For the Marxist intelligentsia Riazanov's disappearance was a kind of symbolic decapitation. It provoked only a muffled ripple—no reaction. Pokrovsky* was underhandedly hunted down. Deborin,* his back to the wall, one day left a letter on his table saying he had lived for Marxism his entire life and that, ceaselessly denounced as an enemy, he no longer understood anything and no longer wanted to live. He threw himself from a bridge over the ice, was picked up in a pitiful state and put in a sanitarium.

Spoke of all this with Rühle in his garden. Among the nopals, the cactus, the flowers pollinated by black hummingbirds.

COYOACÁN

August 15, 1942—Natalia—in the garden, amid the cacti, while the two bodyguard-secretaries are picking nuts from the tree for Laurette

—bursts into tears in the middle of the conversation and breaks off: "To think that a week later we would have unmasked the assassin, the crime wouldn't have been possible.... Leon Davidovich suspected something. During his previous visit Jackson had briefly entered the study. L. D. said to me afterwards, 'An odd young man, he's muddleheaded, he entered with his hat on and sat on the table.... Hmm...'" (This was the rehearsal for the crime, since J. committed it in exactly this way, seated on the table in order to strike him with a downward motion, L. D. bent over a manuscript. So he had been given instructions.) "Knowing that L. D. was thinking about this, I didn't push him...."

I say that I don't forgive Rosmer, usually so circumspect, for having introduced J. into L. D.'s household. "Not at all. J. asked to be received. We consulted Marguerite Rosmer,* who answered: 'His thinking is completely disorganized. He says he's a member of the majority of the American group but doesn't understand a thing about it. You'd just be wasting your time with him.'" Natalia tells me how J. patiently laid siege in order to be admitted. He helped the Rosmers by giving them lifts in his car. When, after the first attack, the police impounded L. D.'s car, Natalia one day allowed herself to be driven to the station along with the Rosmers in J.'s car, and that's how she met him. She later invited Sylvia for tea and Sylvia came with Jackson. "I couldn't slam the door in his face...." As she speaks, tears run down her pitiful, gray face, lined with deep wrinkles.

"I remember as if it were yesterday the end of the Central Committee meeting (in 1927) when the split became deadly. We were waiting for L. D. to return. Pyatakov came in first: he was pale, emaciated, undone; you remember his long face with its high forehead, his scraggly goatee. He asked for something to drink, gulped down two or three glasses of water one after the other, and at last said: 'I saw a lot of things at the front, but nothing ever got to me like this....' L. D. came in, tired, tense, he, too, pale. Pyatakov turned to him: 'Why did you have to say that? You know he'll never forgive you for it, nor your children, nor your children's children.' 'I had to,' L. D. said, and he explained that he had called Stalin the 'gravedigger of the Revolution.' Stalin, furious, walked out, slamming the door violently. —And today the Nazis are in the Caucasus, and L. D. is dead for having been right, for having foreseen everything!"

Laurette points out to me Natalia's stifled little laugh, almost a sob. It's a moan combined with a pitiful sad face whose eyes give off a mild blue glimmer—of kindness.

August 24, 1942—Visited Natalia Ivanovna, embarrassed for having promised Gorkin the translation of L. D.'s final book (*Stalin*); now Munis is asking to do it, and even though he doesn't know how to write he's a member of the party. N. I., worried, asks if Julián will be offended.

While we were talking I tried to analyze the tragically sad expression of her pitiful face and I realize that a kind of humane modesty has prevented me from looking at her closely until now. One can still make out the former regularity of her features, her hair in long, wavy locks on both sides of her face are still light brown—mixed with gray—and they must once have been nearly blond once; her forehead is broad and her features are pronounced, her face small... Her skin looks somewhat puffy and wrinkled now, her eyes have become smaller, her eyelashes have fallen out and her eyebrows nearly: her eyes seem to have been devoured by tears. Her gray-blue pupils have a direct and benevolent gaze, but one feels that everything weighs on her, that like a wounded animal she would prefer to isolate herself in a dark corner, roll herself into a ball, and wait for it all to end.

I spoke of Marc Chagall, who is here working for the Ballets Russes. N. I.: "I saw an exhibition of his work a long time ago in Moscow. I recall a couple in green caftans, the woman in a pink scarf, flying across a sunny sky.... It was funny and I said to myself that this painting should be rejected (*otritsat*), but there was so much charm in the color and the sky and the movement...."

Moved by my book *Midnight in the Century*: "You're the first to have captured the psychology of moral capitulation.... Is Kostrov a real or an imaginary character?" I answer that he was inspired by Mikhail Alexandrovich Chabion.

August 24, 1942—Otto Rühle stops by, he's looking for a subject for a talk at the Jewish circle. Talk about the war? Impossible. About socialism? It's a vital problem for us, but not for these people. Future prospectives? In the short term they are bleak, and we'll have to pass through hell in order to get to the other side . . . We finally settle on "the social aspects of the war." He rapidly lays out his ideas about its causes. The decline of the rate of profit through the increasing proportion of constant capital, leads capitalism to its end—and to war, an attempt to escape into the impossible. War enormously increases costly investments in unproductive or destructive production. This war is an immense revolution which capitalism as such cannot survive; it ends the profit system, it will impose production for consumption. The war will be long and ugly, for both mentalities confronting each other are doomed. However, the capitalists still imbued with liberalism, neither able nor willing to understand the march of history, place themselves in a position of inferiority in relation to adversaries who, having come from the lower classes, were not handicapped by capitalist traditions and interests and have gladly—and often intelligently—surrendered to historical necessity and are thus better armed by a more modern, productive apparatus. They too are at an impasse, but their impasse is much vaster, and they have immense advantages in strategy and even social strategy.

VERA FIGNER

October 30, 1942—I can't no longer recall the approximate date of Vera Figner's death[62] in Perm or Viatka, probably "evacuated" and placed under discreet surveillance. Ninety years old. I met her in 1928–1929 (seventy-four, seventy-five years old) when she asked me to translate her memoirs into French. The public of their publisher, the *NRF*, bought only a few hundred copies of the first volume, so dense and so rich: her childhood in the Russian forests, her family and the epic tale of the Narodnaya Volia [The People's Will]. The second volume, including nearly twenty years in the penal colony, scientific work pursued in the

62. Figner, born in 1852, died June 15, 1942.

Shlisselburg prison, the resistance, revolution, the Azef* affair, never saw the light of day in French. This lack of curiosity, this provincialism of a great literature horrified me. (Also the fact that there weren't two thousand readers on the left for such books.) Vera Figner was a tiny old woman, frail and upright, her features drawn tight by wrinkles that still recalled the sober and regular beauty of her youth. Extremely alert, interested in everything, with an uncompromising character sustained by a profound moral pride. She remained the intrepid member of the executive committee of the Narodnaya Volia. One could feel that she was ruled by an absolute rectitude, tempered by resistance struggles to the bitter end, stiffened by a will whose underpinning was the dignity of being. Which provoked many conflicts. Among the survivors of czarist prisons, she maintained vis-à-vis the Bolshevik government an outspokenness which was occasionally merciless. At the beginning of collectivization she agreed to come out of political retirement and attempt to facilitate a change in the Soviet government, and she took it upon herself to ask Vasily Blyukher to accept a post in a Council of People's Commissars that would have brought together Right Communists and a few important intellectuals and which would have given the USSR a more humane government and made peace with the peasant masses. These conversations ended with the trial of the so-called Union of Mensheviks (Groman, Sukhanov, gone forever...), Bazarov's deportation, the trial of technicians... No one dared touch V. F.

Even though our relations were affectionate I had conflicts with her that were occasionally amusing. In a footnote to a text by V. F. I'd written that Sophie Perovskaya was Jeliabov's wife.[63] V. F. was angered by this indiscretion—known to all historians—and asked me to remove this note, "since they had never informed anyone of their relationship, which in any case was no one's business." Thus she made a sharp discrimination between private and political life, private life having only a subordinate importance.

When I was leaving the GPU's internal prison in Moscow in 1933

63. These two Narodnik leaders, organizers of the 1881 assassination of Czar Alexander II, were executed.

to be deported to Orenburg I received from V. F. little letters of encouragement, if not of congratulation. She wrote, as she did in her youth, on small sheets of lined paper in a tiny, delicate, well-drawn handwriting, the letters rather straight and slightly trembly.

The end of her life, after the Moscow Trials, must have been frightfully bitter, and she must have borne this stoically, as one more sacrifice imposed by history... The period of the dictatorship of the proletariat followed by that of the bureaucracy were for her times of ordeals and protests. In reality, she was an authentic Jacobin, in love with the "people," a liberal, attached to the notion of freedom.

Around 1932, I think it was, she stoically bore up under the terrible blow of the death of Mikhail Petrovich Sazhin (Ross),[64] seven years her senior and her companion, an indomitable and solid old man still vibrating with a passion for anarchism. Sazhin had known Bakunin, fought in Paris during the Commune, was later sent to a Russian penal colony... Ghezzi invited him to speak at a commemoration of the Paris Commune at a big factory in Moscow in 1927 (?). Leaning on his cane, he gave a speech about the real people's revolution, about freedom and federation. The Communists on the platform didn't know what to do, the chairman tried to cut Sazhin off by pointing out to him that his time was up, but the old man, loudly banging the floor with his cane, answered furiously: "You'll let me finish! I'm talking about freedom!" Anyone else would have been locked up that very day. But what could be done with the last Bakuninist?

In Leningrad I sometimes passed in front of an old house on Voznesensky Prospekt, now Mayorova Prospekt, not far from an old baroque church painted a faded yellow. The one-story house, with a small balcony looking out on the placid, sad landscape of the Moika, formerly painted yellow and now soiled, was the one where Vera Figner and Nikolai Kibalchich* made the bombs that would tear Alexander II to pieces on March 1, 1881; the house where Vera Figner, with the terrorists at their posts, waited for news...

64. M. P. Sazhin (aka Armand Ross) (1835–1932), originally in exile in the United States and Europe, had been arrested in 1876 and deported to Siberia, where he met Vera Figner.

GPU

November 1, 1942—Hannes Meyer,* or Mayer, an important architect, many buildings in the USSR, medium height, corpulent, about fifty-five years old, beautiful Germanic head with sharp features, gray-blond hair, always bareheaded. Connected with Sormenti-Contreras. Said to be one of the GPU's right-hand men here. According to the German émigrés who know him, is supposed to have participated in the preparations for the two attacks on L. T. Lives on Calzada Villalongín, modest apartment.

Other German agents: Bodo Uhse,* gone over to the Communists from the secret military organizations, Black Reichswehr, etc.; Lambert (Zimmerman); Radványi* (*Tiempo*[65]), husband of Anna Seghers; Gertrude Duby,* who worked in New York for a long time.

DEATH OF VICTOR MARGUERITTE

November 1, 1942—Victor Margueritte just died (March) in France at age sixty-six. I don't know if he still lived in his quaint little apartment on the boulevard de Courcelles, where I visited him in Paris shortly before France's collapse. Become blind, he had a nobility of appearance—the look of an old, emaciated nineteenth-century French officer—and character. His intelligence was still lively and insatiable. We had long talks about the Moscow Trials, about the strange moral weakness of French intellectuals, about the war, which he romantically hated (being the son of a general who in 1870 commanded the charge of the cuirassiers at Reischoffen). Author of bestselling *romans de moeurs* like *Prostituées, La Garçonne*, in the past he exploited with a banal talent his knowledge of Paris, the public's taste for scandal, and a certain left-wing moralism. When old age, mourning, poverty, and blindness descended on him he revealed a simple and lucid stoicism that wasn't lacking in grandeur. His evolution over the past few years was exemplary of the confusion of many. In the first days of the war he signed, along with Déat, Jean Giono, the philosopher Alain, and the anarchist Lecoin, a tract calling for "peace at any price," motivated by nothing but "horror of war." Pursued by the courts, most of the

65. Mexican magazine inspired by *Time* magazine.

signatories, first of all Déat, repudiated their signatures (Alain and Lecoin stood firm; I don't know what Giono did). It was a sad affair, one in which Margueritte demonstrated courage. "Nothing," he told me, "can justify war; nothing could be worse." His ideas were an anarchist-tinged pacifism and in reality were nothing but an emotional reaction. He doubtless witnessed the debacle with great sorrow, and probably with no great surprise, having spent most of his life denouncing the corruption of the Third Republic since the Commune. When the former socialist minister Spinasse, along with some former collaborators of the recently imprisoned Léon Blum, founded *L'Effort*, "organ of national reconstruction," to support the policies of the marshal and the idea of collaboration with the victor, I was saddened to see an article in this paper by Victor Margueritte, wrongheadedly calling for reconciliation with Germany…

(Plisnier drove me to his home in a clinic on the avenue de Tervuren in Brussels in 1936. Already nearly blind, he lived in a chair. Beautiful bony white head, still virile, with a long moustache. Truly something luminous about him. Alongside him his companion, about forty years old, long brown eyes, heavily made up, bulky Algerian jewelry, seemed to be infinitely devoted to him, but we found her irritating, though I can't explain why. She would soon die.)

His line of thought: weak with a generous and superficial generosity, profoundly inconsistent—incapable of rigor and effort—lack of a solid foundation—proceeding from a hedonistic individual and social vitality that was only skin deep; that of a frivolous society that felt no need to truly think—very much a petit bourgeois of the Third Republic.

DAY OF THE DEAD
November 11, 1942—During the Day of the Dead festivities that followed L. T.'s assassination *calaveras* resembling L. T. were sold on the streets as well as little cardboard coffins containing a dead Trotsky made of sugar.

Jeannine's repugnance when she sees children eating *calaveras*. Already European, her slightly horrified protests. They didn't last: she quickly learned that despite it all, they taste good.

THEFT IN NEW YORK

November 14, 1942—Chapter VI of my novel,[66] being read by the Maison de France publishing house in New York, was lost. It was the chapter that was bound to be stolen, the one on the confessions. It's probably in a desk drawer in the Kremlin. I speak to Natalia about this and tells me about the case of a comrade Brown (or Braun) from Los Angeles who was working on a biography of the Old Man. A Japanese domestic, in whom he had complete faith and who'd worked in the house for twelve years, left, taking with him the manuscripts.

Natalia. Went to see her with Señora Hidalgo y Plaza,* wife of the ambassador of Chile (a socialist), who's returning home. As we were leaving a beautiful sunset over the garden, the sky of pure gold in the branches. N. surreptitiously takes my hands: "Look at the beauty there is on the earth," and she turns away, her face ravaged by tears. A moment later she joins us in the garden to offer roses to Señora Hidalgo.

A WAR WON

November 15, 1942—Rommel in flight in El Alamein...A great war has been won by the Allies, lost by the Nazis—a great war that didn't take place...I expected it, I'm convinced it was part of the plan of the Hitlerite general staff, for such an adventure could open immense horizons to it: taking Baku, taking Alexandria, Cairo. Seize control of the oil, cut off Suez, hold the most modern capitals of the Muslim world, appeal to this world and announce its "liberation," begin the dismemberment of the USSR with Central Asia, and influence even the Muslims of India. Besides this, the Nazis have established a good surveillance and propaganda post in Afghanistan—and the Americans have just discovered Afghanistan, they're sending a diplomatic mission there (late by an entire historical epoch). This vast undertaking failed in the face of the enraged—magnificent—tenacity of a few Red troops who defended Grozny in defeat, despite defeat, their backs against the mountain, and before British tenacity at the Egyptian border. Receiving blows has taught the English how to deliver them.

66. *The Case of Comrade Tulayev.*

(There's also the wearing down of the victors; clear failure of their aviation.)

Which doesn't change the fact that a few weeks ago the situation was truly worrisome. I wrote a carefully argued article about this that I proposed to an American agency, without sending them the article. A young man in glasses answered that he didn't have the authority to buy articles without consulting New York and so on...I met with William Henry Chamberlin,* who was extremely evasive. He couldn't place an article himself and advised me to write to...but thought that because of my position on the nationality question in the USSR there's little chance the article would be published...In the meanwhile Washington had thought about these matters, since Wendell Willkie flew to the Middle East and returned with a not-very-encouraging view of things.

DEATH OF EDO FIMMEN

December 14, 1942—Edo Fimmen* just died in Cuernavaca (sixty-seven years old). A diminished man, he'd been awaiting his death for the past year, sometimes half-paralyzed, cared for by his wife, Alida de Jager,* an intelligent idealist, enormously agreeable. I hadn't wanted to see him in that state, but also held a grudge against him for his occasional lack of courage. Met him in Vienna and Berlin in 1923–1925. Leader of the Amsterdam Trade Union International; he was on its left and corresponded secretly with Zinoviev, Lozovsky, Nin—and me. At the international trade union congress in Vienna he was supposed to speak and categorically take a stand, but on the preceding days Martens and his other colleagues showed him photos and copies of his secret correspondence, deposited at Münzenberg's house in Berlin and seized. He fell silent. "They've got me in their grip," he said with a violent bitterness, and his anger exploded against the imbeciles who'd allowed his papers to be seized...He was tall, fair haired, a thick moustache, firm gestures; completely at home in the International Transport Federation—the head of an old sailor with a concrete mind, hot blooded and extremely practical. He never clarified, probably held back by his material situation, attached to his confederation and unable either to go over to the Communists, whom he scorned and detested, or to the impoverished, hunted Opposition . . .

December 16, 1942—Conversation with Keppler,* former democratic minister in the Otto Braun cabinet in Prussia.

Keppler: What do you think about the war?

Me: Still very long. I don't believe that Germany will collapse quickly. Possible, but more probably a long and horrible defensive war. Also possible, great changes in Germany and a revolutionary war by the successors to today's Nazism. Not impossible that the Nazis, at the end of their strength, attempt a revolution.

K: Yes, for the German people it's a question of survival. The end of the war could be hastened if a policy of continental reorganization was adopted, giving the German people reasons to have confidence. But they don't want this—or are incapable of it. Besides, think of the governments in exile, capable of playing the most catastrophic role: retrograde, nationalist, determined to oppose the reorganization of Europe.

Me: They're more and more in over their heads, and soon will be completely so. It will become impossible to listen to them. The people will have their say.

K: I don't believe in a European revolution. After all, the Thirty Years' War ended without a revolution. The masses will be exhausted and apathetic. The working class isn't rising from its decay or its disappointments. Disorders, yes, but no great outbursts, no creative faculties, no great ideology, no faith, no great men. And in such an atmosphere the necessity of a state-controlled economy will bring back other totalitarian institutions.

Me: Totalitarianisms themselves can differ in nature, in the way they treat man, as well as in institutions. Note that this war is less deadly than the preceding one and that the losses are more widely spread across the population than in the previous one. In 1914–1918 Europe lost six million energetic young men and opened an era of revolutions. Only in Russia are the losses in men serious, and there they above all touch the peasantry and the cadres of the totalitarian regime.

K: In Russia Germany has suffered terrible losses too, and they'll grow even worse . . . But from the economic point of view Germany will have an enormous advantage, even in defeat: the state-controlled economy is in place and the old forms of capitalism have been liquidated. But in the Western countries they'll continue to fight to return to an intolerable capitalism.

Me: An economic and social reorganization of Europe will impose itself and the masses will push for it. This is what I call the European revolution, with just reprisals against the totalitarian leaders.

K: I fear fatigue, degradation, famine, the discouragement of the masses. The reactionary elements in the victorious countries will have a free hand and they're capable of coming up with no solution—except perhaps fascism with a new name, partly despite themselves.

He has a Prussian face, bony and muscular, the left side scarred by student rapiers. His eyes are dark and murky, his complexion ruddy.

CONVERSATION WITH LENHOFF ON THE OUTLOOK FOR THE FUTURE

December 26, 1942—Me: The last six months have clarified things for me. Positions have already become clearly defined. Hostility of the United States towards the Spanish Republicans and de Gaulle; advances to Franco, allowing him to see that his regime, modified by a Catholic monarchy, could carry on after an Allied victory. Darlan episode.[67] How many Darlans are contemplating their future moves! The day of their defeat two-thirds of German generals will suddenly reveal themselves to have always been "democrats." Silence everywhere concerning Stalinist totalitarianism and universal complacency in the press toward the dangerous myth of Stalin's victories . . . Churchill curses only Mussolini, not the fascist gangs. They're getting ready to play the card of a reactionary reorganization of Europe with all the leftover rejects of the

---

67. Vichyist admiral who went over to the Allies in November 1942. Assassinated in December of that year in Algiers.

defeat of Nazi-fascism. In all of this an immense conservative incapacity, based on a fear of social change and the shriveled selfishness of declining classes. Lack of imagination and generosity, blindness.

L: But still with more class consciousness and even ability than socialism and the working class have.

Me: Agreed. We are perhaps the last of the Mohicans. We have no idea what the European masses are thinking. My confidence is based on the mechanisms of history. No one wanted this world war, for which they all laid the groundwork despite themselves. This shows to what extent today's humanity, dragged along by the functioning of an enormously perfected industrial machine, is incapable of consciously mastering its destiny. Think of the infinitesimal percentage of men graced with idealism and critical, that is, scientific, thought, even in the highly civilized nations. The spontaneity of events is shaking up the masses and productive forces and leading us to needed transformations that no one dares clearly conceive. This is how the great revolutions of the past occurred.

The discussion turns toward the perspectives for the German revolution.

L: The German proletariat is exhausted and for the most part has been replaced by captive foreign workers. In 1918 it was intact. The Nazis will maintain their fanaticized SS army until the final moment. You know that German aviation has been placed under party control, which is a civil war measure. For the German people to be able to rise up the Allies must destroy this final Nazi redoubt inside Germany, that is, occupy the territory. And thus they will paralyze the German people in their turn.

Me: Possibly, but all this is complex and full of unpredictable elements. There will remain a compact nucleus of German proletarians educated by this experience and who'll have learned that nothing is gained by resigning yourself, by not making the needed revolutions. Germany is now paying for its passivity in 1919, 1923, and 1932. The foreign workers held captive in Germany are getting to know the German worker and to distinguish between him and Nazism. This lays the groundwork for solidarity. The young Hitlerite generations are being devoured by the war. The young people of 1942–1943 no longer have Nazi blind faith and enthusiasm. It marches *todeswärts*[68] because it can't do otherwise. Hitler will perhaps have the Marie-Louises[69] of his 1814, but it's not with them that he could win a campaign against Germany itself. I think that the totalitarian compression must be followed by a violent decompression that will immediately change the face of Europe and that no foreign intervention could control. Europe in revolutionary decomposition will be governable by no one, it will have to find its own way for itself. It's the survivors of the paratroopers and the *Panzerdivisionen* who will settle accounts with the Nazi leadership. It should also be noted that Social Democracy no longer exists. The SD was a party of moderate revolution in appearance and of bourgeois stability in reality. It fulfilled a dual function in 1918: symbolically satisfying the masses and cheating history, while in reality bogging down the movement. There is no longer anyone there to fulfill this function. Shortsighted, bourgeois moderation has no more leaders than socialism does. The future German Darlans will only serve for a moment, and perhaps usefully, for that moment of transition is needed to give the popular movements the time to gain awareness and form cadres. We'll need a European "Kerenskyism" that will not exclude the Kornilovs. (The latter, incidentally, must have rendered great service to the Russian Revolution.)

L: Don't lose sight of Stalinism. The German Stalinists are certainly active and long lived. It's true that they're cut off from Moscow and will probably receive many surprises when they regain contact with it. I think that at the end of the war and with Russia terribly weakened, Stalin is fully capable of total capitulation before Allied capitalism and of collaborating with it against the European revolution.

Me: I have no doubts about that. I think he's even capable of negotiating with Hitler before that and to turn his coat several times. But if the internal and continental situation appears to him favorable for the revolutionary gamble I think that, being despite it all a sincere old Bolshevik, he would prefer to play the revolutionary card. With the

68. Towards death.
69. Young conscripts of the final days of Napoleon's empire, named after the emperor's wife.

Allies, he'll only use trickery. He'll prefer this card because it might be the safest one and is more in keeping with his mentality. But I say all of this based on my impression of the extraordinary vitality Russian totalitarianism has demonstrated. Modern totalitarian states represent entirely new historical phenomena, and we have no idea of their capacity for resistance. We know nothing of what goes on inside their organisms. Elementary logic leads us to believe that in all likelihood all the totalitarian states will succumb together, and the Stalinist one is certainly weaker than the Nazi.

L: Not from the point of view of economic structure. It exploits a formidable revolutionary capital.

Me: Yes, but that tradition, that formidable revolutionary capital will also have its demands, which will coincide with material demands, those of the peasant masses, for example, from whom the war demands that everything be taken without their being paid in merchandise of equivalent value. That can't go on indefinitely. Great distances combined with weakened communications surrender the economy to local powers and relieve the population of bureaucratic pressure. The fighting men will also have their own demands. The young generals of the Red Army will not allow themselves to be executed by surprise like the Tukhachevskys, grown old in devotion and submission to the Party. Without a smashing victory, which nothing allows us to count on, followed by a political change—of which it is perhaps capable but of which it is horribly afraid—Stalin remains the man responsible for collectivization, the massacre of the country's cadres, and the invasion that reached the Volga and the Caucasus. And he's sixty-three years old.

L: Then how do you explain the magnificent Russian resistance?

Me: It's the resistance of a young, energetic people that felt it was constructing a new world, for which it was ready to accept everything. And don't forget that in 1812 the Russian people's resistance to the invasion was magnificent as well; that in 1856 under a decrepit regime, the Russian resistance in the Crimea was astounding. And finally, that the armies of Nikolai II, under an unpopular regime in decomposition (which only the initiated knew) in a prerevolutionary era (which only the revolutionaries knew) fought even better for three whole years— since they occupied enemy territory, entered Prussia and Galicia, took millions of prisoners, defended Russia better against invasion, and were still in Asian Turkey in 1917.

L: France resisted to the full.

Me: Unquestionably, but it was the Russians' initiative at Tannenberg that allowed the victory on the Marne. Russia saved France before Verdun saved Russia from a more thorough invasion. These are great historical details of enormous weight. The political conditions of the Russian people's existence—and they in large measure command its material condition—seem to me to be such that one must foresee a profound political revolution made by the young generation, tempered in the fire of war. The changes in line that Stalinism will have to carry out in order to avoid this are of such breadth that they risk unleashing events instead of controlling them. Suffering is so great that even terror runs the risk of losing its value. In addition, the Soviet press gives the impression of a sclerosis of its apparatus for which no remedy can be seen. I wonder if the only viable, flexible apparatus is not that of the war, and it dominates the masses only through the necessities of war.

TROTSKYISM

End of 1942—The rifts within Russian communism have had various repercussions in the workers' movement. While the official Communist parties were becoming penetrated with totalitarian mentality, international oppositions were forming. The most energetic of them gathered around the last great survivor of the Bolshevism of the heroic era, Leon Trotsky, exiled successively to Istanbul, Oslo, and Mexico City.

Foretelling clearly the approaching world war and the social movements to which it will give birth, profoundly attached to the doctrine of Bolshevism, Trotsky proclaimed the need for a new revolutionary Marxist International as early as 1934. His error was in believing that one can deliberately call forth a revolutionary movement at a time of defeat for the European working class. An authoritarian mentality, even though he was the leader of the democratic tendency of the Russian CP, a schematic mentality despite his vast socialist culture, in a word, a voluntarist, in 1936 Trotsky rallied a handful of American,

French, Dutch, and other militants and proclaimed the founding of the Fourth International. It's not known if a real founding congress was held. The small groups and parties of the Fourth International immediately split over this very question, and the Fourth I., without having obtained real influence anywhere, went from expulsions to splits, all the while pitilessly—and basely—persecuted by Stalinist communism, which systematically resorted to slander and assassination against its militants. (Erwin Wolf* and Moulin in Spain, Rudolf Klement in France, Ignace Reiss in Switzerland, and Trotsky himself perished in Mexico, assassinated by Stalin's secret police.)

Established at a time when socialist internationalism was disintegrating everywhere, amidst the confusion of vanquished ideas and movements, employing a "Bolshevik-Leninist" language from the Russian past in countries where this theoretical language is necessarily unintelligible, endlessly invoking a tradition falsified by powerful Russian totalitarianism, the Fourth International was only able to form tiny groups here and there, which nowhere played an appreciable role. It had only one head, that of Trotsky, who provided it with its entire intellectual baggage. It insisted on mechanically applying to the Second World War the analyses and propaganda slogans formulated during the war of 1914–1918. Its organizational and polemical methods, the very language of its militants, showed it was marked with the defects of decadent Bolshevism; that is, the totalitarian mentality.

In the USSR itself, where the government applies the term "Trotskyism" to all oppositions in order to justify their annihilation, the Fourth International appears to have found no echo. The Left Opposition, to which Trotsky belonged, was completely exterminated by the service revolver. Its few survivors, if there are any, will, like all of Soviet youth, have to reconnect with the tradition of socialist thought by taking into account extraordinary experiences that call for a free and severe critique of Bolshevism, a new language, and new ideas.

The Fourth International has a few groups in the United States and feeble nuclei around the world. Its doctrine remains that of the Bolshevism of 1917–1927, seriously deformed by persecution and impoverished from lack of manpower: sclerotic and outdated. The Fourth

International can be only be viewed as a sect whose possibilities for development are extremely limited.

As for the work of Trotsky himself, fighter, historian, and thinker, it belongs to socialist culture.

1943

January 1–3, 1943—Taxco by car with Martínez. More than two hundred kilometers by road, towards the Pacific, across a vast landscape of mountains under a hot sun. This volcanic earth, violently convulsed, constantly opens onto new horizons of sharp-edged ridges against mild, lustrous skies. The rocks here shattered in all directions in the era of geological revolutions. Aridity, little cultivation, the impression of a land without people, given over to plants armed with prickly thorns, splendid magueys with enormous, drooping, vase-shaped leaves, *órganos* rising straight up to a height of five meters or more, terrifying perpendicular cactus bushes of so intense a green that they seem almost black. There are areas of stony desert with silver tones. Near Taxco a semicircular hole in a wall of mountain cuts the horizon.

The town is laid out in tiers on steep slopes with small, horizontal plazas that astound one. Twisting alleys paved with sharp gravel; climbing or descending them requires feats of acrobatics. Dilapidation and good hotels for gringos, silver- and goldsmith shops—the mines are nearby—owned by foreigners, of course. Above the meager and crowded market there rises from the noble baroque church a tall pink tower with dark tones, a richly ornamented portal, its stones full of movement. Shaded plaza, kiosk, benches, *muchachas* and *muchachos*. At the entrance to the plaza, at the foot of the church and a chic hotel, a steep slope leads to the most pleasant prison in the world. "Please, come in," they tell us. The office–guard post looks out onto the alley. The back of the room is composed of a sculpted wood grillwork giving onto a crisp whiteness. There, with their sombreros and their cigarettes, the prisoners promenade with nobility. A magnificent young man, draped in an immaculate white serape offers us through the fence a beautifully colored basket of braided straw that he has just completed ... Haggling, cigarettes ... We wonder if this isn't a prison for tourists.

During the evening on the plaza we enter a horrid little theater made of planks and faded canvas, the show costing ten centavos for a quarter of an hour, *la tanda*.[1] Women lacking in beauty, young or on the decline, and ambiguous men rattle off couplets full of lewd allusions. Dressed in showy finery, the handsome man of the troupe wears a Russian blouse of turquoise silk. He's frightening, the handsome man, with a flat, fat face with twisted features and the smile of a pederastic dandy. The leading lady is a tall and skinny woman with a large black mouth planted with gold, with uneven features and coal-black eyes in blue orbits. We learn that she's a man, despite the décolletage and the feminine voice. Taxco is a main center of homosexuality. The room is filled with all kinds of people, with women and children, and everyone laughs contentedly. Neither popular art nor folklore, it's big-city trash making its debut. So much human baseness and degradation in such lovely sites!

The town is out of the early Middle Ages. Peasant women's figures à la Breughel. Steep slope: over a *pulquería* a coffin merchant leaves his door wide open on a crudely lit interior, where reigns a beautiful white coffin lined with pink cushions, ready to receive a young Catholic girl. Another merchant displays—stacks up, rather—children's coffins.

Martínez, who's been doing business in the country for twenty years, talks about the good old Mexico, where the Indios were such nice people. "Look at those two kids who didn't make a move to save the pig I was about to crush. They were waiting with joy to watch the blood flow and calculating what they could get me to pay!"

Hotel Sierra Madre, Talleres de la Delicias (silversmith).

Baths of Tehixtla, a river beneath beautiful banks of a tropical Marne, little wood plank bridges suspended on cables, better hold on to the steel wire that runs above it. The water is roiling, the foliage forms a brushland. In a dance hall a strange mixed-race girl with fine

1. Tanda: each section of a show, played in series.

features, half-Flemish, half-India, which results in her having slanted blue eyes, sharp cheekbones, a lovely European chin, brown hair, and the figure of a Belgian village girl.

On the main road taken by the buses a drunken Indio has fallen asleep—in complete solitude. The buses take a small detour around him.

The way back: Hours of radiant road towards the Ixta and the Popo white with snow and gilded by the sun, a peaceful, boundless landscape where the peaks sparkle like the Fujiyama of postcards. Battle of a powerful elongated cloud that has bumped against the Popo and in order to embrace it has assumed the shape of an angel melting into that of a monster.

Festival in Jojutla,[2] piles of American knickknacks—this production is killing Indian art. Wooden horses, etc. We enter the hut of the snake charmer, a lazy young Indio seated among inert snakes of all sizes, some the dark gray of lava. He handles them, warms up their heads with his lips. This spectacle disgusts Laurette and Zina but charms Jeannine, who asks me if the snakes are dangerous and shivers with pleasure.

Street singers sing the lament of compulsory military service—patriotic—after the one for the end of the *hacendados*,[3] which seems to be full of irony.

The next day a bus crowded with poor people went up in flames, taking with it its human cargo, because an imbecile of a driver filled it up with gas by the light of a match. The second accident of this type in the region in a week ... A good business, coffins—and death is such a natural thing!

In the dust of the evening the streets of Jojutla are pink and blue. The crowd is quiet, not noisy.

Broad-brimmed black sombrero decorated with silver, black shirt, knife at his waist, tight pants molding his svelte legs, a Byronian Don Juan posed at the street corner in the middle of the crowd, magnificent, motionless; he astonishes us with the perfect beauty of his sculpted ivory face.

2. Village in the south of the state of Morelos.
3. Large landowners.

VLADY'S FRESCO

January 1943—Great joy at having visited the Molino de Bezares with Don Ramón,[4] three kilometers up the Toluca road. Uncluttered landscape, magueys, a barren site. The former windmill is now a restaurant. The owner, a friendly little Spanish woman, tells us that Diego Rivera began but never completed a large fresco in the barn. This is the one that Vlady and Iván Denegri worked at with so much enthusiasm during the winter of 1942–1943. At that time the Molino, since sold, was owned by ex-president Ortiz Rubio.[5] Mme. D. speaks to me of her worries. She was afraid that the two young men, who frequently walked the thirteen kilometers on foot at night, would be killed or attacked. Letters with threats and denunciations rained down on her. They were accused of preparing an attack against the nearby powder works. They were denounced as communists creating a propaganda fresco. Ortiz Rubio was threatened. The latter was upset because his son had just killed the governor of Mexico City, Zárate Albarrán, in a bar.[6] A committee of experts from the museum came to see the fresco and one of them (Orozco) wrote that it was a remarkably interesting work. Campaign mounted by the CP and fueled by artistic jealousy. Diego Rivera came to see it but did nothing to defend the young men. Ex-president Calles also came and was very unhappy about the figure of a soldier with a brutish head (painted by Iván) that "insulted the army." There was talk of destroying everything, and it probably wasn't done as a result of negligence.

I understand Diego's indifference before the half-completed fresco. He must not be happy to see young men, scarcely fed and totally unpaid, using poor-quality material, make something so clearly superior to what he's doing at present. I feel real joy at seeing that Vlady is already a fully developed artist, filled with things seen and reflected upon that he's able to exteriorize. Two-thirds of the work is his: around fifteen

---

4. Ramón Denegri, whose son Iván painted, along with Vlady, the fresco in question here.

5. President of Mexico from 1930 to 1932. Plutarco Elías Calles, who is mentioned later in this paragraph, was president from 1924 to 1928.

6. The governor of Mexico City was seriously wounded on March 5, 1942, and died three days later.

meters in length by three in height, the entire upper part of the wall. It's forcefully drawn, the colors rich and varied, the vision chaotic and rich, with an internal unity. From left to right: a tank rolls across green grass, moved from inside by a naked man with bright red flesh and no face. Lower down a young, brown-haired dreamer, hair tousled, wearing a blue work jacket, looks to be walking down to the butterflies and flowers of the field that he doesn't see: self portrait of Vlady, excellent (but he made the face asymmetrical with an absent and concentrated expression). Below, the colors shade to brown, a corner of Montparnasse lit by a candle, a young man reading a tract, another plucks the guitar, a painting by Picasso (line drawing of a naked woman, leaning back, her breasts upright), another painting serving as a window looking out on the tall houses of Paris and the Eiffel Tower in a seminocturnal sky. The Parisian atmosphere is rendered in the glimmer of a guttering, gloomy fire. Very good, life-sized portrait of Gironella. Movement of French and Russian crowds, towards the top Jouhaux* speaking, soldiers and sailors coming from the east, the people of Russia, lumpy shapes and poverty; real, lifelike people of the Revolution with rifles and cigarettes. Towards the middle a statue of a naked woman that's no more than a block of flesh, squatting and seen head-on. A female artist with yellow hair, a pug nose, and slanted eyes in the face of a joyful death's head raises her leg—it's a cancan. A man in a boater for whom nothing exists apart from raised legs one can see for twenty francs. Down below this an old intellectual, who could also be an old artisan, seated, the his posture tired and discouraged, seems to have lost all his illusions and to be asking, Why live? The figures from the Russian and Chinese revolutions march and interweave. The background, more developed, the colors richer and better contrasted, is quite beautiful. Above a niche Lenin, reduced to a skull and an arm, calls the Asians to the west (reminiscence of Alexander Blok's "The Scythians"[7]). Wounded soldiers, one Chinese, hold each other up; a magnificent group of Asian cavalrymen, the horse's heads are powerful, the slant-eyed men simple and lively. Below, blocks of stone and overturned safes; gray of steel or rocks

7. Poem in which the Revolution offers peace to the West; if not, Russia will unleash its Asiatic hordes.

in the darkness upon which, in white outline, is the larger-than-life form of a young suicide, naked, distorted, his hair tousled, still holding the revolver. From his limbo he raises his head towards the men, horses, and plains of the terrestrial surface ... (Vlady showed me some sketches of this suicide during the winter of 1941, at precisely the period when I was thinking of killing myself and I wrote "The Suicide of Dr. C.") Small, luminous panels at the top, beneath the beams: a reddish European field with haystacks, an Indian drawing... Above the crowds, at the very top, a massive Stalin with a low forehead seen in profile, a heavy rope around his neck ... This is the detail that caused a storm of protest and killed the fresco.

The section done by Iván D. is less strong and rich. But there's the tiny-headed military brute, his legs spread, standing firmly, his body girded in leather. And under a streetlight, a girl in green, who has the sad air of a Parisian street corner.

Standing in front these visions, a lovely Parisian Surrealist who draws analytic snow crystals in white on black paper explains to me that she doesn't accept the fresco as a type of art, because the artist is a slave to the space he must fill, and this is something she can't accept, as if there wasn't space on a canvas or a piece of paper, as if one painted to fill and not to exhale the visions with which one is overflowing and for which there is never enough room (when they exist).

July 25, 1943—Passing through De Bezares with the Ménils* and the Malaquais* and find nothing but whitewashed walls.[8]

"TROTSKYISTS" AND REVOLUTIONARY MENTALITY
January 8, 1943—Julián Gorkin's talk (mid-December) on Trotsky's assassination earns me a hysterically bitter letter from Natalia. I'd sent her affectionate wishes for the New Year, telling her that we're all living in a kind of void, but that we belong to the future and the future needs her. She sees these expressions as a sign of demoralization, the desire to flee present responsibilities, etc. Once again we have here her

8. Last paragraph added by hand.

perverted logic of political interpretations, and it reminds me in a sad way of how the Stalinist press criticized L.T. and all of us, when we posed questions about the economic development of the USSR, for a supposed "lack of faith." I responded affectionately, but with a firm clarity. I fear an idiotic split. All of this evil is a result of the fact that several "Trotskyists" went to that meeting as if to a political battle, angry, bitter, and violent, brought up foolish incidents, and finally accused G. of "slandering an assassinated Trotskyist," because, basing himself on the dossier, Gorkin laid out a mass of evidence that leads one to believe that Sheldon Harte was himself a GPU agent. There is at least as much evidence for this as against it. And the Sylvia Agelov case sadly is just as obscure. These sectarians reported to Natalia in their manner, and that manner is not essentially different, in its tortuous way of reasoning and interpretation, from the indictments of a Vyshinsky. At the meeting I had protested vigorously and defended G., clumsily, insufficiently prepared, but in good faith.

The fact remains that poor, great L.T., carried along by that same mentality of Bolshevism in its decadence, broke—sometimes with an unspeakable violence of expression and, in my case, a frivolity approaching disloyalty (by imputing to me an article I didn't write and which expressed ideas opposite to my own)—with men who understood him, loved him, and stubbornly followed roads parallel to his own: Ante Ciliga (the sole authentic representative abroad of the Opposition in Soviet prisons), Henk Sneevliet, Vereecken, Max Shachtman, myself (the only representative abroad of the 1923 Opposition and Soviet deportation), while at the same time he admitted amicably into his home a wretch without a past or ideas, and possessing an abundance of suspect money, who entered Coyoacán via the intimate life of an inexplicably stupid—or complicit—little female militant.

The real drama in all this is the perversion of a revolutionary mentality that was extraordinarily elevated, luminous, and powerful, and with which L.T. himself was long suffused to an admirable degree. Which was the source of his grandeur and his historic role. The great generation of Russian revolutionaries was the fruit, unique in history, of fifty years of struggle and selection at a time of rising civilization. The main role in the Russian Revolution was played by an intelligentsia characterized by its lack of individualism, its moral sense, its sense of individual life integrated into the course of history, and its objective thought. (The Bolsheviks were superior to other Russian revolutionaries only because Marxism and the spirit of organization provided them with a particularly effective and resistant spiritual armature; they were more *complete* than the others. And among them L. T., the least sectarian, the most artistic, the freest spirit, the least deformed by the narrowness of party life, was easily the greatest.)

It's necessary to study how this mentality became perverted with the exhaustion of men, the disappearance of the old generation, the inflation of the revolutionary movement, the birth of the totalitarian regime, and the spiritual decline of the capitalist world that had produced the scientific spirit and socialist idealism.

About Sheldon Harte, the young Trotskyist or GPU agent assassinated at the Desierto de los Leones. American from an extremely wealthy family. The government of the United States, which demanded indemnification from Mexico for Americans killed during the revolution, didn't even request an inquest. The assassins were known and arrested. They were the painter Siqueiros and the Arenal* brothers.[9] Siqueiros fled Mexico and appears to have been hired by a Mexican consular office in Chile, where he continued to paint frescoes. The Arenal brothers may be at liberty. The affair was hushed up in broad daylight.

EUROPE'S SILENCE

January 11, 1943—Dwight Macdonald writes me from New York that my novel *La terre commençait à trembler* [The Earth Began to Tremble][10] and my memoirs interest American publishers, but even more, they frighten them. They're afraid of the subjects dealt with, all those social dramas of old Europe, afraid of ideas and intelligence, afraid of the public's reaction (which might be partisan and awaken sentiments that

9. In reality a brother and sister.
10. Published posthumously as *L'Affaire Toulaèv* [The Case of Comrade Tulayev].

would better be left sleeping in time of war—or even worse, indifferent), and afraid of the atmosphere of thought control. They're left to their own devices, those poor publishers thirsty for money, caught between governmental orchestration of printed matter and the demands of a rather unsophisticated public who must be seduced without being awakened. All of that plus the utilitarianism of wartime results in a degradation, a general flattening, that is basically similar, though to a lesser degree, to that of state-controlled literature in totalitarian countries.

Note the effect of Europe's silence. It's been years since the great intellectual laboratories of Europe, which led the world, which boldly provided new spiritual nourishment very year—often detestable, but *new*!—last produced ideas, books, men, and fashions. Moscow was the first to go dark, under the boots of Thermidor: Dostoevsky, Tolstoy, and Gorky have become as impossible as Pilnyak, Meyerhold, and Eisenstein. Then Germany went dark and finally France. It's been five years since Moscow, Rome, Berlin, Paris, Vienna, or Madrid have given us a single book, a single new name. And most of the great names of the past have been suppressed. A general decline in culture, the effects of which the United States and Latin America must feel strongly.

The émigré intellectuals are cripples and, to whatever small extent they demonstrate revolutionary energy, are nearly outcasts, almost totally boycotted. I know this from experience.

CARLO TRESCA

January 12, 1943—Just as I was going to start my talk (self-criticism of the Russian Revolution) at the German socialist group, Léo entered and interrupted to inform us of Carlo Tresca's* assassination in New York. Tresca was leaving a restaurant in the heart of the city: busy street, machine gun, car, the act of professional *killers*.[11] Great idealist, Tresca, wealthy, very much a bon vivant, Italian trade union leader, influential antifascist and imperiled anti-Stalinist. Thanks to him the

11. In English in the original.

Mazzini League[12] has escaped Stalinist influence. Had participated in the Dewey Commission[13] that absolved Trotsky. From that time received many threatening letters from Communists, for a long time didn't go out without a revolver.

PICASSO, ART, REVOLUTION

January 18, 1943—Discussion with Laurette about the ideas of Paalen,[14] with whom she spent the afternoon: art as a factor in revolution; that is, in the transformation of man. Moral transformation of man is needed, a Picasso as great as a Trotsky; profound revolutionary impact of artistic creation...

Picasso? The man is not great. Followed profitable trends while cunningly closing his eyes to those struggles incompatible with successful business. The way he avoided me at the Deux Magots when I found Dora Maar (or Mare) at André Breton's table: he was connected to the Communists and the Negrín government, which had given him some lucrative commissions. Had no interest in hearing what was going on in Russia and Spain, feared being seen with me. Dora's embarrassment in this regard. A great artist in the era of the decadence of painting reduced to living off the snobbery of the rich. Remained in Paris during the occupation, sold well and much—it is said—to the Germans and was tolerated. In any case, didn't cover himself in glory.

I don't think that a small man can accomplish a great revolutionary oeuvre. Its very definition implies a social, thus moral, value and a courageous attitude. Revolution *in painting*? It's possible. First, recognize what painting is in a given period, what it expresses, for whom, what human needs it responds to. The builders of cathedrals worked for the peoples whose spiritual (and social) lives they expressed. Mi-

12. The Mazzini Society was an antifascist organization founded in New York in 1939.

13. The international commission established to examine the charges against Trotsky, established in 1937. Serge testified before a branch of the commission in Paris concerning the GPU's methods.

14. Wolfgang Paalen (1905–1959), exiled surrealist who founded the magazine *DYN* in 1942.

chelangelo painting the frescoes of the Sistine Chapel expressed, in the civilized society of Italy, the aspiration for a new humanism—contradictory and violent, but freed of the terrors of hell. Rivera and Orozco painted on the public squares for the Mexican people. To them they cried out: "Look at yourselves in the mirror of our frescoes. Look at how great you are!" It's possible they were barely understood, but some did understand them. No great work is immediately understood by the masses. It must first be accepted, must create and teach its language. Picasso paints for a strictly bourgeois "elite" of decadent collectors. Within these limits, recognize that he is prodigiously interesting.

During revolutionary eras all problems are posed in terms of life and death. There is no longer any artistic creation in totalitarian Europe— and almost none elsewhere, where the war effort absorbs all energies while provoking a general stupefying effect in all domains of spiritual life, except in that of industrial technique. Obvious that art will be saved by the European revolution, if it triumphs. Spiritual life requires as preliminary conditions well-being, freedom, and intellectual flourishing. Once these conditions are established it modifies them by aggrandizing man. To invert these givens is to obscure our vision of reality.

CARLO TRESCA (CONTINUATION)

January 20, 1943—They have arrested "an Italian petty criminal, a recidivist," who provided the car used in the crime, but he remains absolutely silent.[15] A fascist or a communist crime? If it's a communist crime, the Americans say, it will be hushed up the same way the Krivitsky affair was hushed up, the same way the Siqueiros affair was hushed up in Mexico, the same way the Jackson affair was hushed up. A Mexican journalist with whom I discussed all this told me that the trial of Trotsky's assassin is becoming absolutely impossible. Think about it: at the very moment we're sending an ambassador to the USSR, at the very moment when we're awaiting an ambassador from Stalin! But, I

15. It was Carmine Galante, a New York mafioso who was arrested but released in December 1944. Though it's all but certain Galante and Vito Genovese killed Tresca, no one served time nor are the reasons for the killing known.

ask him, what's left of the dignity of the democracies if a totalitarian government can force them to modify the actions of their institutions in order to cover assassinations and ensure the killers impunity in American republics?

RADEK, RAKOVKSY, PRISONS

January 20, 1943—An issue of the New York Menshevik newspaper that I just received (*The Socialist Courier*, 1–2, January 5, NY, the organ of Abramovich*—naturally!) contains some horrifying news. From reliable sources: Rakovsky, dead in prison; Radek, killed with a pistol shot in prison by one of his guards shortly after his sentencing, the assassin arrested and disappeared. A special prison constructed in Yakutia, from which no one has yet emerged and from which correspondence is prohibited, held until summer 1941 many well-known Bolsheviks of the Old Guard, among them Bubnov, Rudzutaks,* and Eikhe.* In 1939–1940 all the widows of well-known executed Bolsheviks remaining at liberty were arrested and interned in a concentration camp fifty kilometers from Moscow. In 1940 this camp held around thirty thousand women and children. At the beginning of the invasion there are said to have been many executions in Soviet prisons about which nothing specific is known.

STALINISM AND DEMOCRACY

January 20, 1943—Dwight [Macdonald] writes me from New York that American publishers are frightened of my books. Brentano is rejecting the novel and also refusing to provide me with the usual notes proposing revisions or giving a reason for the rejection. The Maison de France simply responded: "Impossible at this moment." Duell, Sloane, and Pearce said the same thing about my memoirs. James Henle (Vanguard Press) allows it to be understood that there is "a kind of law" prohibiting the criticism of Stalinism at this time … Dwight comments: "There's nothing here but cowardice on the part of these sheep."

Don Ramón tells me of his encounters with American and Mexican capitalists, conservatives turned fervent admirers of Stalin. Observe the tendency of simple men, reactionaries in particular, to admire warlords. In the confusion of the era the reactionaries felt comforted at having a Führer to follow (the profound human need to obey the father). Now that open admiration for Hitler is forbidden in the countries at war, they are hanging on to Stalin with all their craving for the abdication of personality and the acceptance of violence.

Conversation with V., a journalist, who recently saw Lombardo Toledano. Toledano spoke to him of the clerical threat. The Church, sensing the approach of the European revolution, is thinking of strengthening itself in Latin America, where it can still dominate...There is supposed to have been a conference of the leaders of the churches of America in the United States to lead the conquest of power. Synarchism,[16] which is fearsome here, is not just a Mexican phenomenon; analogous movements are said to exist all over Latin America (this is probably true). Toledano is calling for a union of the left against this threat. The journalist is very impressed. Where can we go without a union of the left?

I prudently respond that the CP is a totalitarian party led by agents of a foreign power: it's not a party of the left. Where would an amorphous movement of the left go in a country with neither a socialist party nor a liberal milieu nor an intellectual movement of the left when a totalitarian party equipped with paid cadres, disposing of unlimited funds, supported by a distant but powerful state, led by secret agents starts manipulating it? You would unfailingly end up with the same moral and material disasters as the Spanish Republic.

V. has been very much struck by the Spanish experience, doesn't know what to say to me, but repeats: "The threat is great and Russia remains a shining star for the people."

I hear this at the very moment when I learn of Radek's assassination in prison, Rakovsky's death in prison, the existence of a mysterious

16. Violent political movement of the semifascist Mexican Catholic right totally opposed to the populist and secularist policies of the revolutionary governments that ruled Mexico from 1929.

secret prison for Old Bolsheviks in Yakutia, the internment in 1939–1940 of thirty thousand wives and children of executed Communists in a special concentration camp not far from Moscow—one of the most unimaginable of earthly hells...I don't speak of any of that. What would be the use?

BREAKS

January 22, 1943—The year begins for me with two breaks, one distressful, the other quite simply aggrieving. The saddest thing to see in this—besides the usual absurdity based on unintelligence—is the base, socially explicable feeling one might hope to see surmounted in people whom one would profoundly like to hold in higher esteem.

André Breton criticizes my lack of understanding of Surrealist art and my sequestrating of Brauner's* paintings because—neither he nor his friends having done anything to save B. for a year—Laurette refused to send him any paintings for an exhibition which he was more interested in than in B.'s fate. He had struggled to restrain his criticism for some time. One can see the man's vanity is wounded by the involuntary competition—imagined by him, the banal field of competition being the only one he knows how to place himself on—of a mind different from and often more rigorous than his. (The right attitude would be to revel in differences when they are of equal merit and, in any case, to recognize in another person the right to be different from ourselves, even if he is wrong or demonstrates lack of comprehension: and yet, who's to take the first step?) But the worst thing is that if I were a publisher with funds André would treat me in a friendly manner, as he does X. and Z.—pure cretins as he says himself. So here we see him falling into ordinary baseness, he who has such a grand allure at times that one is tempted to demand more real personality of him.

A different kind of break with Natalia since Julián's talk on L. T.'s assassination. The gossip of narrow-minded malevolent sectarians is sufficient evidence for her, and she forgets that she and I are perhaps the only two survivors of twenty years of struggles within the Russian Revolution—which we survived by a miracle. She forgets my ten years of resistance to being crushed, my struggles on behalf of L. T.; in summary, a whole body of written works, in point of fact unique. She forgets all this because on the one hand there is the sect and on the other the universe, and the sect is right against the universe, and the sect considers those closest to it to be the most hateful. Distant religions that are far apart and totally different can be indulgent towards each other, but sects of the same religion must hate each other: family hatreds, competition for the possession of the same truth.

Demyan Bedny* once said about proletarian literature: "Three snot-nosed little writers who belong to us are dearer to me than three great writers who don't." The negation of grandeur and the abandonment of the human to the sect. The roots are perhaps deep: the tribal spirit.

This too—alas—in common between the two breaks: that I exist too strongly and that I am at present completely isolated, materially defeated, with no money, no platform, no party, no support. Instinct leads to striking the weak, and when one is dealing with a strong person, whose existence alone affirms something but who is disarmed socially, all those with the competitive spirit feel the itch to beat them black and blue.

(With Natalia all of this is certainly unconscious. She's someone pure, crushed by her suffering and devoted to the sect because the sect, for her, is the shade of the Old Man. As a result, base sentiments take back their power over her. The Old Man, during his final years of hardening in his in solitude and pride—last defense—was a sectarian.)

PERSONALITY

January 24, 1943—Don't seek to "be personal": that's the last way to become it. A lady says to me: "I think this genre of art is worth nothing, etc. I think that. . . ." I want to say to her: "It's a fine thing that you think, Madame, but it would be more important to think correctly. It's not your ideas—if we admit they are ideas—that have any value because of you, but you who should have value because of your ideas. There is a truth in all things that is in no way personal, which expresses necessities independent of ourselves, and this is what must be gotten at; to understand in order to then pronounce. The petty prejudices of this one or that one have nothing to do with this impersonal truth-reality."

Superficial thought, which is nothing but appearance, simulacrum, conversational games, or a way of filling the void within oneself by admiring oneself in a cheap intellectual mirror and by enjoying oneself as a nonconformist by adopting little ready-made systems. It invents its own little conformism and arrives at nothing but a society game of no interest. Internal inertia lands on its feet garbed in a few unexpected rags. Real victory over this inertia (conformism) is the fruit of disinterested rigor, impersonal in its knowledge of reality, its search for the truth. Then, taking strong stands responding to needs that dominate us, we must reject, condemn, and combat. This is the affirmation of a real personality.

CARLO TRESCA (CONTINUED)

January 30, 1943—According to the *New York Times* the investigation is leaning towards the GPU. Conversation with Leo Valiani [Paul Chevalier].

L: It's a warning from the Stalinists to the entire democratic left. At a time when the USSR is growing weak and civil war is in the works in Europe, the CPs are going to receive marching orders to eliminate bothersome individuals.

Me: Then why didn't they kill me?

L: You're categorized a "Trotskyist" in the eyes of public opinion, so the signature on the crime would be too clear, while Tresca's assassination can remain obscure. What's more, they know that no form of intimidation will work with the two of us: it's democrats they mean to intimidate, "men of the left . . ."

The January 22 issue of *Tiempo* published an incredibly cynical article about Tresca, which amounts to a moral signature of the crime (the editors were inspired by Radványi and various Communists). *Tiempo* accuses Carlo Tresca of having collaborated with the fascist leader in the United States, Pope,* who converted to democracy the day the United States entered the war. I have an issue of *Nazione Uniti* dated January 1, the organ of the Mazzini League, the group Tresca was a member of, which violently attacks this Pope, who is favored by the State Department... *Tiempo* writes that while Tresca's body was lying on the ground "an unknown man went over to one of the reporters and asked, 'Is that Tresca?' 'Yes.' The unknown man said, 'What a pity, But he's deserved it for a long time.' The assassinated anarchist had no other epitaph."

On the other hand, *Time* (January 24) writes that C. T. had "powerful enemies among the Communists and ex-fascists whom he fought bitterly." The *New York Times* indicated that the investigation is leaning toward Communist circles. Someone wrote to me: "A well-executed crime. The fascists had no obvious reason to commit it. There remains the other hypothesis, impossible to speak about in a letter."

November 1943—S. S. thinks that Tresca was killed by ex-fascists converted to American democracy who remained very influential. Margaret Tresca,[17] whom I just saw, thinks otherwise. Investigation halted for reasons of "high politics."[18]

THE WAR

January 13, 1943—Stalin was invited to the Roosevelt-Churchill conference in Casablanca only out of politesse: he didn't send anyone. 1. Reciprocal distrust;—2. Weakening of the USSR, famine and military exhaustion;—3. The USSR is still at peace with Japan. Stalin *is not tied* by the formula of "unconditional surrender" of Germany, Italy, and Japan. Russia is fighting its own war: there is no alliance, but rather coincidence.

In French Africa Giraud against democracy and the forty-hour week, anti-Semitic legislation "attenuated" (!!!), lots of antifascists in

---

17. Margaret Tresca visited Regler in late 1943. She suspected Vittorio Vidali (alias Contreras/Sormenti) of being behind the assassination.
18. This final paragraph added by hand in the margin.

prison. Marcel Peyrouton succeeding Yves Châtel.[19] Entente with de Gaulle on the "French Republic" impossible. In short, under American occupation a Vichy-fascist regime, strangling of the republic!

I hear it said: "The real fight against fascism in Europe will begin after the war...."

The American are creating a situation like that at the beginning of the Civil War in Spain: a fascist-leaning army from Africa against the republic on the continent. In their fear of popular movements and their horror of revolutions they manage only to foment European civil war in broad daylight.

THE WAR IN RUSSIA

January 31, 1943—The seizure of Maikop—oil!—by the Russians is a significant success, far greater than mere victories in the papers. How to explain that Russia is able to undertake such offensives without fuel, with transport in an unimaginable state, and horrific poverty in the rear?

People's war against the invader-devastator. Surprising vigor of the totalitarian apparatus. Disdain for suffering and sacrifices (as at the time of industrialization).

On the Nazi side: prelude to collapse? Not likely at this moment. Idiotic strategy of prestige. Use of Italians and Romanians on the Russian front, who surrendered en masse. Enormous underestimation of the enemy and the Russian winter.

I'm quoted this line from a letter from Switzerland: "Our relatives (in Germany) are drinking the good wine of 1917."

The success of the submarine war and resistance in Tunisia demonstrate that Nazi power is not yet all that low.

The Russians are wearing themselves out in the winter war; they'll practically be at the enemy's mercy in the spring (in June), as they are

---

19. Though liberated, French Africa, under General Giraud, remained subject to Vichy's discriminatory measures. The Vichyist Peyrouton replaced the Vichyist Châtel as governor general of Algeria.

doubtless well aware; behind the energy of the winter offensive is this: we'll have nothing left to lose in the spring.

THE NAZI DISASTER AT STALINGRAD

February 5, 1943—How to explain it? Unlikely that Nazi power is on the eve of collapse.

1. Underestimation of Russian energy.
2. Enormous difficulty for the Germans to bear up under winter war in Russia, and, in contrast, astounding Russian energy, popular and totalitarian, to fight this war.
3. General error in strategy, insufficient forces of poor quality left on the Russian front on the premise that the Russians couldn't attack in force: Italians and Romanians who surrendered en masse.
4. Crisis of transport and fuel of the Nazi army. This crisis made retreat, defensive movements, and the reinforcement of the army in Russia impossible. Aggravated by the winter, which requires protecting the men against the cold as they are being transported (impossibility of using open or poorly covered trucks; only the Russians can allow themselves this).

On the other hand, probable that the Russians have expended much of their materiel and men in the frightfully costly winter war, knowing that once the spring arrives, without the advantage of the cold, they won't bear up under the shock.

Forecast: in the spring—June?—absolute necessity for the Nazis to attack in the direction of the oil, Maikop and Grozny, without reaching Baku; Baku virtually saved by the Russian victory at Stalingrad. Perhaps they'll attack in the direction of Moscow in order to disorganize the rail and industrial centralization of the Soviet state.

Or else, necessity for the Nazis to retreat further and go over to the defensive, preparing Germany for a lengthy siege. Beginning of the end.

Not a single Russian went to Casablanca, Roosevelt-Churchill discussions; invited out of politesse, at peace with Japan, carrying out a separate war, aren't bound by the formula of Nazi capitulation.

In order to propose a separate peace to a USSR that's exhausted but invincible because of its vastness and the energy of a people defending its very life, Germany needs a victory that brings prestige and weakens the enemy.

JEANNINE

February 6, 1943—Jeannine questions me about the stars, about how the earth was made, where man comes from: From monkeys? Then where do monkeys come from? And fish?

"You know, Papa, I think about that all the time, the stars, the earth, the animals.... And also about the bicycle you have to buy me."

She sees a portrait of Julián in an illustrated magazine: "Why did they print this, Papa? Are they going to put him in prison?"

She coughs at night and comes to me: In a sleepy and doleful voice, gently but insistently: "Stay with me a little while, Papa." She puts her little arm around my neck. Slight tone of reproach: "You're always looking after Laurette."

ASÍ, JACKSON

February 9, 1943—It appears my break with the magazine *Así* has been consummated. Last week *Así* published an article by a certain Karl Ritter, a small-time Stalinist agent, denigrating Trotsky on the eve of the trial. This week the rectifications I sent them weren't published, or my article ("The Axis Weakens"), but there's a portrait of Jackson on the front page and an interview with him, in which the reporter compares him to Charlotte Corday—a paid secret police agent, still paid today, compared to the believer Charlotte Corday, who sacrificed her life! Jackson puts on airs in front of the camera, a prosperous look, a well-tailored suit, visibly bucked up by those backing him and speaking the language of the Communist Party, quoting Anna Seghers and explaining his "disappointment" with Trotskyism by talking about

James Burnham*! Every sentence sounds like a back-office fabrication, but it's presented in a way that will impress the ignorant; that is, everyone. And since nothing else will be published ... In short, the CP-GPU has completed its infiltration of the Mexican press. No one who presents the facts, no defense of the truth will find a home anywhere. A situation worse than that in France during the Popular Front, since there at least there were avant-garde publications and groups and a free organ like *La Flèche*.

In losing my collaboration with *Así* I lose my only source of income here. I lost it defending the Old Man while his sectarians are obstinately shooting me in the back—as always.

NEWS FROM MOSCOW

February 18, 1943—Someone passed on to me, in confidence, some remarks made by a Spanish officer, Communist, recently arrived from Moscow—and quite happy to be here.

In Moscow: horrific poverty, nothing to eat, people feeding on thin cabbage soup; large numbers of homeless in the bitter cold; foreigners, even Communists, isolated and being watched, many concentrated at the Hotel Metropole; tremendous general discontent: "The Trotskyists are everywhere and no longer have any hesitation about criticizing.... A strong presence in the army."

About the Comintern: the Spanish CP led by La Pasionaria.[20] A certain number of Spanish refugees in Moscow have disappeared. The Russians "think that the two countries they will be able to dominate are Spain and Mexico.... A strong effort will be made in this direction. They're already gathering their collaborators.... The tactic of the Mexican CP will become even more flexible and will consist in rendering itself more agreeable to all, but with an internal discipline more rigid than that of the past, utilizing *all possible methods* against their enemies among the CNT, the socialists, and the 'Trotskyists,' whom they'll attempt to isolate in the eyes of public opinion."

These last words are said to me as a warning.

20. Dolores Ibárruri (1895–1989), Basque Spanish Communist and civil war leader.

THE EARTH TREMBLES[21]

February 22, 1943—For me, it all began with a dream, strange because of the intensity of the memory it left in me (I usually forget my dreams) and by the need I felt to speak of it to Laurette and Fritz Fränkel. Thursday, I think, I dreamt that I was in a wooded park on the edge of an asphalted avenue on which passed, on which had just passed, a parade (I no longer see the parade, but I have the impression of white clothing). A hot and sunny day, Mexican. Across from me, on the other side of the road, standing out against a background of foliage, there was a beautiful, twisted tree with long branches and above it a building under construction taller than it was wide, with large bay windows hanging open; a large crowd, the people like ants; the building was of gray cement. I was suddenly struck with vertigo, accompanied by slight nausea; I sought to hold myself up but I saw the tree across the way floating with a wavy movement and I understood that this was an earthquake. The tall building then slowly broke in two and the upper half began to collapse. The ant people within began to scurry around madly... I thought of Laurette and Jeannine and returned home: nothing had happened to them.

Saturday evening the maid, Esperanza, told me that, while in the garden with Jeannine, she'd felt an earthquake, "*un temblor*"—the trees shook—around 6:00. Many people observed this. Working at home I'd noticed nothing. Yesterday, Sunday morning, Avenida Insurgentes, I saw a tall gray house, brand new, the rear of it split in two as if it were made of cardboard. Firemen were picking through the rubble and a Green Cross ambulance was standing by. It had collapsed during the night after the shock (a young Catalan woman killed, her husband and children seriously injured, calle de Coahuila 221). The house was exactly the same gray as the one in my dream, the lopped-off floors gaped exactly like the building in my vision. I saw an iron bed still standing in a yellow bedroom.

A half hour later, on the tram with Fritz Fränkel, we spoke of earthquakes and I told him what I'd seen and what I'd dreamed. F. F. told me the dream must have had symbolic meaning. I answered that

---

21. Much of this entry would be used by Serge in his short story "The Earthquake."

that was quite possible and that in my writings I had several times used the word "earthquake" to describe great events. That in my last novel there was a character who was a seismologist. I didn't even think at the time of the actual title of that novel: *La terre commençait à trembler*... And it may be rather bizarre, but I repressed precisely that. I added that I have a boundless love for contemplating the starry sky, that for me it's both a need and a pleasure, and that I never look at it without expecting a cosmic event or catastrophe, as if a star were suddenly going to expand and explode—as if an enormous star were going to arise and fill the night with fire—my feeling that this would be natural, that the serenity, the calm of the sky and the immobility of the constellations aren't natural, or in any case not definitive. F. F. made no comments. (I observe that I've almost never spoken of this to anyone, I think I only ever said it to Laurette, and that in passing.)

In the afternoon, after the meeting at the Ibero-Mexican Center I read with interest that a small volcano has just started to erupt in Parangaricutiro, Michoacán; the population of several pueblos is being evacuated.

Shortly after three o'clock, in the middle of the night, I awoke feeling the bed shake. The shaking grew stronger and sort of stabilized, rather strong. Laurette woke up saying "Jeannine, Jeannine," but she wasn't frightened. I wasn't afraid either, but felt a slight nausea, and worried about the dangers (Is the house built solidly enough?) and wondered, as the shaking continued and grew, if this wasn't going to turn into a cataclysm. We heard the people on the upper floors moving around, gripped with fear, and neighbors coming down the stairs. I decided that it was better to go outside, mainly to feel ourselves in the open air, and stood up. There was no electricity. Laurette, who'd also gotten up, said: "But it's over." It was over. I opened the balcony window and there were people in pajamas on the street looking joyful. I cursed the fact that this should be the night when we would have no matches. A short while later the electricity returned and then went out again, and Jeannine was frightened. According to the newspapers there was another shock, weaker and shorter, that we didn't feel. The first had lasted about six minutes, so strong that the seismometers broke. I thought of the stupidity of the danger of being knocked out by ceiling beams and had a hard time going back to sleep. We brought Jeannine next us, and Laurette and Jeannine quickly fell back to sleep—I think.

This gives rise to an extraordinary animal panic, mixed with an enormous sense of powerlessness in the depths of one's being: one feels the earth floating on something and the vague idea of mountains breaking.

Went to see Fritz Fränkel this morning. He tells me that yesterday evening, with Otto Rühle and Alice, they spoke of *temblores*. I say: "So it was something that was in the air. There was a lot of conversation about it." Indeed. He tells me about the amusing panic of the dogs, who ran around the house as if they were mad, and then:

"You now, I have an interesting client, a charming young woman incapable of harming a fly, who complains of being obsessed with killing." (I know her by sight: a small blonde with sharp features, blue eyes, an anemic complexion, a large mouth and lovely curls; half flapper, half elegant, a tiny, friendly Viennese woman). "She'd just told me that she was expecting an earthquake and had even gotten her clothing and bags ready so that everything would be in place. That she was not in the least afraid, but when she heard the fire trucks and the ambulances she felt satisfaction knowing there were victims...."

I said, "We need these small cosmic experiences to round out our social experiences."

And I realize that I'm not really joking but that I really think this. Everything hangs together, that's what I feel, like the people of the Middle Ages who, amid social chaos, fed on the Apocalypse and lived in expectation of the year 1000.

People say that the earthquake was punishment for the murder of a priest in the neighborhood of La Merced that occurred just a few days before. That in Parangaricutiro (San Juan) while dividing a field, a cross had been removed from the hill where the crater opened.

The village priest refused to leave his church, which contains a miraculous Christ. An old man of 107, on the other hand, left on foot. The photo reveals his gaunt and energetic face.

Within a few days the volcano had a crater several hundred meters deep and a plume of smoke higher still.

The beginning: a tiny Indio working in his field saw the earth gently rise "as if it was breathing" and, escaping through tiny crevasses, smoke and licks of flame. He fled, terrified, to the village, where no one wanted to believe him.

Quake during a corrida. The spectator was on the *azotea*.[22] From up there he saw the entire arena rock like a basin filled with men. The bull staggered. Fear of falling from the *azotea* into the basin.

Workers building a skyscraper. They hold for dear life onto the metal girders fifteen stories up, which oscillate gently back and forth.

I'm told that according to the geologists Mexico is threatened with a geological catastrophe. It seems that the earthy massifs are bound to collapse and the Pacific could very well reach the region of Cuernavaca.

MEMOIRS

February 28, 1943—Jeannine's birthday. Completed the memoirs, whose French edition I'll probably call *Memories of Vanished Worlds*...[23] What is left of the worlds I knew and struggled in? Of France before the First World War, of the war, of the victory, of Spain, where the revolutionary yeast was fermenting so powerfully? Of Europe of the "birth of our power"; of Russia of the great, epic years? Of the Europe of boundless hope, of Germany and Austria at indecisive turning points, of Russia reaching Thermidor, of the West of the Popular Fronts? Nothing of these worlds will be reborn; we are headed, full steam ahead, *toward the new*, through disasters towards unforeseeable rebirths or towards long twilights that will, at times, look like rebirths ... And how many deaths behind me along these roads! Three or four generations of comrades ...

The book is done, and here I face an impasse. Is it publishable? It's dense and a difficult read, for I wanted it to be a precise and well thought-out testimony, not an emotional tale of the adventure of the Self, which would be necessary for a best-seller. But that's not what's wrong with it: it accuses the Stalinist regime pitilessly, objectively; it

22. Rooftop terrace.
23. Published posthumously in 1951 by Éditions du Seuil, which gave it the title *Memoirs of a Revolutionary*.

accuses even more than does my novel,[24] considered unpublishable "at this time" in New York by virtue of what a publisher called an "unwritten law" that prohibits criticism of Russian despotism, "*our ally.*"[25] And so, the richer, the more intense, the more irrefutable, and the better it puts its finger on the wound the world is suffering from, the less chance it has of being published. This will probably change, and perhaps soon, but how to live while counting on this "soon" that could last an epoch, when each quarter has its weight of rent and daily bread?

There are times when I have the crushing sensation of an impasse closed off at both ends. It's no longer an impasse but a vast prison yard. No way of placing an article in an American magazine (the same reasons, and my name inspires fear), two big, unpublishable books crying out the truth, no possibility of work here. I tell myself I have to fight by adapting, writing in halftones, steering clear of problems where the least *mot juste* is like salt in a wound; that even given these conditions there is a way to pose the human question, but there are moments when I feel discouraged . . . The way things are going will my mere signature handicap my writings, even if I succeed—which will be difficult—at putting in them only a murmur of what should be shouted?

If I were younger—with more muscular force—I would wait and do whatever job to earn my bread. But all that's left me is a brain, which no one needs right now and which many would prefer perforated with a definitive little bullet.

February 1943—Cuernavaca, lovely pink churches, feudal, wealthy residences, cafés, terraces. Diego's [murals] repeat those of the presidential palace in Mexico City. From the terrace of the palace of the Cortés, the horizon. Chic boutiques. Nothing intermediary between the poverty of the Indio and the opulence of the few.

Alida de Jager, face peaceful beneath white hair, the gaze and speech of an old, enthusiastic militant thinking ceaselessly of her return to a Europe in revolution . . . "Will Lord Halifax provide us with a bombardier to return home?" I don't think so, I say.

24. *The Case of Comrade Tulayev.*
25. In English in the original.

The pools of Cautla are full of Jewish families who picnic endlessly, stuff themselves, sunbathe, exude successful business, and clearly couldn't care less about the Jews of Europe. Which of these face-stuffers would give half his fortune to save a few of them?

Chalco, the poplars, the canals, men working at dusk loading vegetable trucks headed for Mexico City. Solitudes. Same situation in Xochimilco, but big dance halls with garish red and yellow electric bulbs, where a crowd of dancers twirls amid the smell of fried foods and the din of American music machines. Later, along the road, the beneficent night.

Indios. A pueblo a hundred kilometers from Mexico City. The people have vaguely heard about the war. "The war in Spain, *verdad*?" we explain that it's the war against the Nazis who...Commentary: "Esos maleantes Judíos-fascistas!"[26]

HITLER

March 3, 1943—Discussion with Lenhoff and Fritz Fränkel about "the Hitler problem." I wrote that "Hitler doesn't exist," that he's the "loud-speaker with an hysteria coefficient" of a *brain trust*[27] of big technical experts... Lenhoff maintains that it's impossible to play such a historic role—after having followed so difficult a path—without having great intelligence. I answer that the historical success of a personality depends on completely different factors and that in certain eras men who are clearly mediocre but who answer (by their very mediocrity) a social need can have dizzying careers. That anyway, Hitler's career seems to have been meteoric through the catastrophes of an ending society.

Returned to this subject with F. F. I say that nothing in Hitler's writings, speeches, or acts bears the mark of great intelligence. On the contrary, many of his assertions pose a challenge to intelligence. The nineteenth century defined a form of intelligence, rational and disinterested, one of whose characteristics was the scientific spirit (the chain goes from Aristotle to Spinoza, Marx, Lenin, Trotsky, embracing

26. "Those villainous Jewish-fascists!"
27. In English in the original.

men of thought and men of action to varying degrees: Napoleon partakes of this; Hitler, passionate, profoundly irrational, not lacking in imagination but not in the least creative, does not). F. F. answers that we ought to expand our notion of intelligence and to include in it qualities of intuition, powerful feelings, will, and judgment not strictly rational.

We agree in concluding that the nature, the forms, the "style" of intelligence (and of genius) vary with the era and that rational intelligence, which in our eyes is the summit, is not the only valid one. A Hitler certainly has a striking superiority over most men, men more rational, more intelligent, more cultivated, better educated than he, one that is very difficult to define which derives from faith in himself, will, fanaticism, an ability to dominate, and magnetism.

Another case: I recently read an article on the founder of a religious sect in India whose influence still extends to millions of disciples. He died relatively young twenty years ago after having taught a moral theology based on Hinduism, Christianity, and Islam. He was certainly a man with an extraordinary force of soul, powerful persuasive ability, and personal magnetism. From the scientific point of view his doctrine obviously doesn't stand up to criticism. Europe, between the end of the Roman Empire and the end of the Middle Ages, produced great men of this quality. The fact that modern India still produces them shows the time lag between its civilization and that of Europe.

Hitler a product of the European crisis.

EHRLICH AND ALTER

March 4, 1943—Stunned by the revelation—newspapers—of the execution in Russia of Victor Alter* and Henryk Ehrlich.* Communicated by the survivor Litvinov, himself living under a suspended sentence, to William Green of the American Federation of Labor, one of many interventions since late 1941 ... Recently a message signed by American labor leaders, Albert Einstein, Fr. Kingdon,* and Reinhold Niebuhr, addressed to Molotov, again requested the liberation of E. and A. These grand old socialist Jews were sacrificed at the very moment Hitler is exterminating the Jewish people of Poland. They took their first steps on the road to death when the GPU arrested them at the time of the

dismemberment of Poland. A crime heavy with meaning: 1. It's a declaration of war on international socialism (bolder than the Moscow
Trials, which were an affair among Russians and Bolsheviks). Communism will obviously attempt to find support among the unprincipled
and uninformed semireactionaries and liberals; 2. It's a slap in the face
to the Polish government and the indication of a strong-arm policy
towards Poland; 3. It illuminates with a singular and sinister light the
silence of the Soviet government about the massacre of the Jews of
occupied Russia; 4. It indicates a new outbreak of the policy of assassination and terror (what is the fate in the USSR of those Polish and
Jewish socialists friends of E. and A. who are *unknowns*?—its similarities with the assassination of Tresca).

No money to send a telegram—or a series of letters. No Mexican
newspaper willing to publish the truth, or event run a short. Not a
single Spanish comrade able to translate two pages quickly! I'm enraged
by our total powerlessness.

Litvinov's communiqué naturally accuses the victims of "treason,"
of "espionage," and calls them "enemies of the people": the style of the
Moscow Trials. The papers publish this at a moment when the prestige
of the winter victories is beginning to be tarnished.[28]

WAR, OUTLOOK
March 5, 1943—Stalin isn't associating himself with the Roosevelt-
Churchill decision of "unconditional surrender" and asserts he wants
only to liberate the territory of the USSR, territory extended by conquests at the time of the friendship pact with Hitler. Evidence of a
determination to annex the Baltic countries, to crush Poland and even
Finland even in the depths of the invasion. And so the conflict is
henceforth open between the USSR and the other Allied Nations. The
possibility of a separate peace between Russia and Germany also remains
open.

A Germany changing its facade, proclaiming itself "democratic"
and legalizing the CP, governed by generals and technicians, could

28. Last paragraph added by hand.

negotiate with the USSR on the basis of economic collaboration for the reconstructing and partitioning of Eastern Europe. Stalin would thus once again save his regime, and the "new" German regime would pose quite an embarrassing question for the Allies or would continue resisting them, bolstered by an appeal for the defense of "popular democracy."

REACTION TO THE EXECUTIONS OF EHRLICH AND ALTER

March 9, 1943—Fritz Fränkel saw some rich Jews, a certain Elias and his wife, who admit they understand nothing about "politics," albeit thoroughly Stalinized. Fritz, speaking to them about the assassinations of Ehrlich and Alter, the husband, embarrassed despite it all, said to his wife: "Yes, I haven't told you about this yet." And he added: "But they were Trotskyists!" in a tone that signified that it went without saying and that one can, one must, kill Trotskyists. Radványi has already brought together a few wealthy Jews to talk to them about the crime and to give them this explanation. They're full of admiration for him.

ON FRANCE'S DEFEAT

March 15, 1943—At Fritz Fränkel's house a talk by Jean Malaquais, his impressions of the war. Germans and Alsatians, he saw the best and the worst mixed together. Didn't see any killing of prisoners who couldn't keep up with the march, as Gurland recounted, but saw them given cotton wadding, tincture of iodine, and alcohol. Described the kindness of the Alsatians, their extraordinary efforts to help. The unimaginable stupidity of the wartime army's daily routine, the pointless duties tasks and orders, the total infantilism of the officers, the filth and the turpitude of the men, who talked only about wine and fornication, never washed, degraded themselves at any opportunity. Péret interrupts: "It was like that during the First World War! I swept the courtyard of the barracks in the middle of a heavy wind." Jean Malaquais, having said that the proletariat didn't exist, a brief debate begins between Marceau and me. Marceau Pivert says that since 1914 great progress has been made in consciousness, that the working class didn't want to fight for imperialism. M. P. takes his customary leap into the pure theory of a bygone era.

I respond: the Trotskyists were revolutionary defeatists, which, given their insignificant numbers, had no importance. The PSOPists[29] were revolutionary pacifists, half the PS was pacifist (Paul Faure), the Communists, numerous and influential, were circumstantial pacifists, given the Hitler-Stalin pact and that the popular masses on the whole felt that two wars in one man's lifetime was too much, they didn't want a repeat performance, and they felt that the low birth rate in France didn't allow for a new bloodbath. Half the PS, with Blum, supported the virile attitude of resistance, but it was discredited by the failure of the Popular Front and Blum's policy of nonintervention in Spain. The majority of the bourgeoisie had fascist leanings of various kinds and didn't want to fight "for Poland" or "for Danzig" against forces that stood for order. The working class "didn't exist politically"; had no politics of its own; no leaders: Thorez, a deserter; Duclos (GPU), refugee in Moscow; Blum, honest but discredited; no one in the front ranks and not a single living word. Result of these cold showers: the defeat of Spain, the Moscow Trials, the incompetence of the socialists, the deceitful maneuverings and treason of the Communists.

M. P. reminds us of the factory occupations...

The decomposition of the Third Republic rendered it undefendable, but one can see today that a certain verbal maximalism based on the most elementary ideas contributed to this. It discredited bourgeois democracy without being willing to admit that since the birth of fascism there was a new situation that imposed the defense of even bourgeois democracy as a position to fall back on, wait, and from which an attack could later be launched. Revolutionary thought stumbled about among old formulas while the danger grew.

Walter Oettinghaus, with the warm voice of the orator at great assemblies, says that Communist propaganda was *the* great demoralizing factor. He's right, but profound causes predominate over that one: the weakening of an entire people by bourgeois comfort.

---

29. Serge's interlocutor, Marceau Pivert, had been the leader of the PSOP (Workers and Peasants Socialist Party), a 1938 left split from the SP.

I DREAMT THIS LAST NIGHT

March 16, 1943—We, Laurette and I and some people I no longer see, were in a tall building in a city at war. Seen from our windows were tall, gray constructions in the Parisian style, but made of concrete and glass, modern. On the deserted street someone was looking up at the daytime sky while raising his right arm and index finger and pointing at something up there. Leaning over the balcony I raised my head and saw in the sky a short bar of incandescent white light surrounded by a light halo of pink fire that grew as if it was descending on the city just above our heads. It was falling quickly, and it was a blinding, fabulous hot light. I saw it appear, the sharp beam of a spotlight—in the middle of the day—cutting off the upper parts of the houses across the street. I thought it was a new weapon, fearsome, destructive. I shouted: "Close the windows!" and started to close mine, which had a kind of bolt. The bolt, under my fingers, was shining with the light of a bright blue fire. Laurette was walking in her usual fashion, her back well arched, towards the back of the vast apartment to warn or attempt to save someone, perhaps Jeannine. I wanted to hold her back or join her—frustrated— I thought of taking her in my arms—to die together, since this was likely. No fear at all. The regret that this vision would be extinguished in me. At this point I entered a half-waking state, for the doorbell of the apartment was ringing, but I continued to see. The enormous light entered the room and everything that was on the wall, a painting, a large mirror, began to gently undulate, turned yellow, fell apart. I also saw that the light passed through the walls. I sensed it was destroying everything, that it pierced everything, and I woke up thinking that it would probably devour only part of the city... The doorbell in fact was ringing.

THE EARTH TREMBLES

March 18, 1943—During the night, in the half-dream state that preceded sleep, I suddenly feel a slight trembling of the earth shake the bed, the stones of the house, everything. It continued, it was insidious, as if the earth were shivering. That night, doubting myself, awoke Laurette. "Of course," she said, "it's quite clear." It stopped and then started up again for some time. Earth laboring, fire fermenting below. I listen the way one listens to the beating of a heart.

> At night when you're afraid
> Don't listen to your heart beating,
> It's a strange sorrow.
>   (Paul-Jean Toulet)

But I don't feel that sorrow. Perhaps deep down a physical disquiet. What dominates is curiosity, emotion, the satisfaction of contact with cosmic reality—the contact I so eagerly seek in the contemplation of the stars.

KUYBYSHEV PRISON

March 20, 1943—Alter and Ehrlich were probably executed at Kuybyshev. They passed through the GPU building where I myself slept one night, June 6 or 7, 1933. Perhaps, they pondered the danger that suddenly overwhelmed them in same the basement cells I had known ... Arriving on the Volga, accompanied by an elegant and pretentious brute from the GPU and a small escort party, I woke up in the night to the song of nightingales. The train was running through some woods along the Volga, I think. I gazed out at the night through the window: it was extraordinarily cool, full of sounds, somber and vast ... The elegant brute in glasses, the frames cut at right angles in keeping with the latest optical fashion, had me taken at 6:00 a.m. from the station in Samara to the GPU by a little soldier from that town, who marched behind me in the middle of the street, his rifle lowered. The streets were deserted and rosy, filled with a cool, gentle light. I glimpsed the Volga, fringed with old yellow buildings in the commercial style of the last century. The river was cluttered with motionless tugs, barges, and wooden rafts; the sky was turning blue on the opposite shore. Samara was a provincial city, its houses for the most part low, painted in bright colors, and not too dilapidated. There was nothing imposing about the GPU. The officer excused himself for not being able to give me a good cell, since there were—of course—too many people. I asked to be alone, and he had me taken to a kind of cellar, full of straw, where, in fact, I remained alone with the darkness and this litter for human animals. Called to the shower I encountered a big, bearded character, horribly thin, who introduced himself: Bocharov, Ovan Yegorich, secretary of a cell in Stalingrad, Right Opposition. Dark and laughing, a twinkle in his eye, a gentle voice, his speech measured. We would become good friends, for he too was going to Orenburg. We were taken together to a large cell on the ground floor, furnished with raised boards for sleeping, in which another Communist was being held, Mtveyev, a worker from Perm, thirty-five years old, who had spoken out on the question of salaries—accused of Trotskyism—and whom I educated about Trotskyism . . . We were happy to have been only deported, happy to meet and to speak freely: we were overflowing with joy and friendship.

Bocharov had spent six horrible months in prison in Stalingrad, in a narrow cell holding fifty lice-ridden, sick, starving men. This for having raised objections to a directive from Ptukha, a member of the Central Committee, about collectivization: "Applying it will lead to famine." The famine came there as it did everywhere (and Bocharov's father died during it); subsequently, Ptukha himself perished.[30]

MEMORIES OF JEF RENS

About a month before the invasion of Belgium Jef Rens,* at the time the chief of staff for Spaak, minister of foreign affairs, passed through Paris and we had a long talk in the back room of a café on the place de la République. I asked him if Belgium would be invaded. "Almost certainly, but not right away. . . ." He added that the Albert Canal was unbreachable; that the general staff hoped to successfully defend the border until the arrival of the Allies; that the Meuse formed a formidable second line; that the entire country was a fortification. He told me that for months Spaak and the king had tried in vain to get Holland to understand the danger and consider a common defense. "The Dutch hope to be spared even if Belgium is strangled. . . ."

30. Serge is in error here. Articles by this member of the Institute of Demography continued to appear into the 1960s.

We also spoke of Ehrlich and Alter, whom he already (spring 1940) thought lost, probably executed. Spaak had taken steps in their favor and written to Moscow without receiving a response. The ambassador Rubinin went to foreign affairs to talk about a copper deal that was in trouble. Belgium sold copper to the USSR, which then passed it along to the Nazis. Informed of this, the Belgian government had decided to put a stop to it. Rubinin insisted that the contract be implemented. "We won't speak like minister and ambassador, Comrade Spaak, but like socialist militants...." Rens said. "This allowed them to raise their voices as much as they wanted, but Rubinin got nothing. As he was leaving he briefly stopped at the door to say, "About your letter concerning Ehrlich and Alter, Comrade Molotov feels there's nothing he can do...." It came out as if he was saying, "No copper? Well, too bad for Ehrlich and Alter." Spaak had the impression that all hope was lost.

EHRLICH AND ALTER MEETING[31]

April 2, 1943—Yesterday evening we had a tumultuous gathering that closed with a real moral victory over some dangerous hooligans. I passed a dicey quarter hour with Jacob Abrams*—an old friend of Debs* who edits the left-wing Jewish daily—caught in a small office with no way out and with no weapons while the Stalinists sacked the club and a few blood-smeared comrades fought against them. We were lucky not to be torn to pieces. Gorkin and Gironella were seriously wounded but aren't in danger. We were commemorating Ehrlich and Alter!

Laurette, who arrived in the middle of the brawl, made some interesting observations: one of the attackers said the "Jew Gorkin" was up there. Others on the street repeated that it was a "German" meeting. The CP had recruited and organized a veritable *mob*[32] with quite a few young roughnecks and some drunken thugs. Not a comma of this is

---

31. Letter to Dwight and Nancy Macdonald copied by Serge and inserted in his notebooks.
32. In English in the original.

an exaggeration. Vlady was brave and full of sangfroid. The police arrived in time to prevent anyone from being killed.

BLOODY COMMUNIST AGGRESSION IN MEXICO CITY

April 2, 1943—Yesterday evening the Spanish refugees' Ibero-American Cultural Center organized an invitation-only evening to commemorate the deaths of Carlo Tresca, Victor Alter, and Henryk Ehrlich. Maldonado (CNT), Jacob Abrams (Jewish socialists) Julián Gorkin, Paul Chevalier, and Victor Serge were to speak for the socialist refugees of Europe. The Ibero-Mexican Center is located on one of the busiest hubs of the city. As early as eight o'clock, a gang of about two hundred Communists began attacking the building, hunting for the speakers in order to beat them up. They completely wrecked the club, much of the bar, and the billiard room: it was a veritable pogrom. The attackers even tore up the books in the library and the watercolors on the walls. Armed with clubs and broken furniture, as well as with knives and revolvers (a few shots were fired at the windows), they formed a shock troop, obviously recruited off the streets, probably paid, led by a few Party militants who were shouting: "They're Germans! Enemies of Mexico!" They met determined resistance, and the arrival of the police prevented them from spilling more blood. Julián Gorkin received quite a serious head wound; Enrique Gironella, formerly a professor in Barcelona, later editor of *La Batalla*, received a serious head wound, probably hit with an iron bar. One of the attackers was admitted to the hospital and there were about thirty wounded on all sides. While this was occurring, "Communist militants" called the newspapers to tell them that workers had just prevented a fascist meeting from being held that had begun with shouts of "Long Live Hitler! Long Live Franco! Long Live Mussolini!" This version was repeated to the police by all the arrested attackers, who numbered twenty-three. Thirteen of them, accused of assault, attempted murder, and breaking of furniture, were sent to prison. Among them a professor at the teacher's college, member of the CP. After the police intervention the meeting—attended by around three hundred members of the Jewish colony, the European socialist emigration, and sympathizing Mexican circles—was able to open and adjourn in perfect calm. All the announced speakers spoke, as well as *Licenciado* Madero, grandson of [former president] Francisco Madero, to render homage to the memory of Carlo Tresca, Victor Alter, and Henryk Ehrlich and to join in the protests raised against these crimes by the labor and socialist organization of the United States. The homage to Carlo Tresca didn't allow for any precise accusation, but the cases of Ehrlich and Alter provoked the angriest of protests against the totalitarianism that murdered them as well as a great number of defenders of the freedom of opinion. Nevertheless, all the speakers stressed their admiration for the Red Army and the Russian people, who are being stabbed in the back by the crimes of despotism.

The attitude of the Mexican authorities was perfectly correct. This morning the Communists made a great effort to influence the press but without any noticeable results, the attack being obvious and clearly criminal. Their daily paper *El Popular* gave, in fifteen lines, a totally dishonest version (underline the word "totally") that attempted to minimize the seriousness of the pogrom. The deliberate organization of an attempt at collective murder must also be underlined. It should be recalled that three weeks ago a Communist team led by Leo Katz and Zimmerman (Lambert) had violently broken up a commemoration for Alter and Ehrlich at the Jewish Center of Mexico City. That first time the attackers had started the brawl by shouting: "Death to the Nazi spies!"

April 3, 1943—Situation: rent not paid, 25 piastres in my pocket; Laurette doesn't know if she'll be paid this week (60 pesos). For lack of money, I couldn't send a telegram to New York about the attack of the day before yesterday. No weapon; and I'm advised to change address, to always be accompanied, to take taxis in the evening. It is believed that the Mexican Stalinists, worked up, could very well attempt to "liquidate" me. Impossible to publish a single line in the United States; two big books lying stalled there and here as well. I don't even know if the final chapters of my memoirs have reached Dwight. Impossible to publish anything here: the Stalinists are blocking me at *Así*. My mere name inspires fear. I even wonder if I succeeded in writing a novel about love and stars whether it would be published . . .

Stalinist penetration is so great here that they have agents in every newspaper, even those of the right. No one is interested in anything, people live on clichés without ever wondering what they might once have meant. In the United States neither publishers, magazine editors, nor the wider public understand anything about the problems I discuss, which are those of the end and the birth of a world. Bourgeois publishers are afraid of revolutionary ideas, even if they're expressed with extreme moderation (though it's true that the mere facts cry out). Left-wing publishers are all Stalinized. The socialist émigrés don't like me: for them I'm a "Trotskyist" (it's a handy word) and at bottom, most of them fear intellectual competition. There and here, the Trotskyists denigrate and detest me because they detest heresy. Completely stuck.

April 4, 1943—Concerning the bloody Communist assault on the Ehrlich and Alter meeting, here is some additional information.

The armed assault on the Ibero-Mexican Cultural Center where the meeting was being held was organized by the leaders of the Spanish and Mexican PCs: Mije, Comorera, Encinas, and Contreras (Sormenti). About a hundred men took part, two-thirds of whom were recruited among the Indio lower classes. The orders were to strike hard. The attackers were looking for Julián Gorkin and Victor Serge, whom they didn't know by sight, and they asked several times that they be pointed out. Once he was picked out, Gorkin was struck in the head and wounded. An attacker also threw himself on him with a pistol, but was knocked over. The object of the attack was to commit an anonymous murder, with some poor Indio devils armed with nail-studded boards set up as the culprits.

Professor Gironella, wounded while defending the entrance, was taken to a clinic: a skull fracture is feared. Twelve Communists were charged and arrested.

While the attack was going on—an hour before the beginning of the Ehrlich-Alter meeting—Communists called the newspapers saying their militants had stopped a "fascist-fifth-columnist" rally. All the attackers were instructed to say that they were just passing by on the street when they heard cries of "Long Live Hitler! Long Live Franco!" They all recited this lesson to the police. *El Popular*, a daily run by the

Communists, had the impudence to print this version and to announce a campaign of union meetings aimed at obtaining the expulsion of "agents of the fifth column" and the Gestapo. No Communist or Communist-leaning paper mentioned the names of Ehrlich and Alter.

On a whole, the Mexican press provided a satisfactory account of this attack and the meeting that followed, which was held in a calm and dignified atmosphere.

ASSASSINATION OF CASTILLO

April 4, 1943—The Communist attack took place Thursday April 1. On Friday, April 2, a Spanish socialist, known to be antitotalitarian, that is, anti-Stalinist and connected to the Italian socialist group and the Mazzini League, the printer Fernando Castillo Ramírez, thirty-six years old, was assassinated in broad daylight in the heart of the city on Calle Puebla as he was leaving his home. A car was waiting on the street. Someone came up behind him and tapped him on the shoulder. Castillo turned around and a witness heard someone say, "That's him." A second assailant shot him at point-blank range. He was shot again as he lay on the ground. *El Popular* (Sunday, April 4) asserts that "this regrettable crime seems to have been due to a tragic error!"

We don't know if this crime should be connected to the Communist attack on the Ibero-Mexican Center, but we know that Castillo's only enemies were among the Stalinist printers, that rumors are circulating among Spanish socialist émigrés about the preparation of attacks, and that there is constant talk of the "liquidation" of one person or another by the Communists.

ANNA SEGHERS

April 4, 1943—In March 1941 I observed on the *Capitaine Paul-Lemerle* a woman who looked to be fleeing the other passengers and isolating herself alone with the ocean. She spent hours alone on a deck chair, exposed to the wind or the light tropical rain, sometimes getting up to walk around a miserable spot on the deck deserted by those sheltering themselves from the wind or rain. Poorly dressed, her hair unkempt under a carelessly tied gray kerchief, she would talk to herself, her gaze mad, her face tormented by distortions I recognized only too well. She looked like Liuba during her times of illness, during her big crises of neurosis or semidementia. She would sometimes take a thick school notebook from her clothing and write with her pencil, moving her lips all the while. I watched her with sympathy, the distress in her face attracted me, and I thought that I alone vaguely understood what she was feeling.

Her family took good care of her, but by willingly leaving her alone. The family was tragic as well: a tall young girl of twelve or thirteen, a tall boy about fifteen, both gangly with the look of wild children, nervous and miserable. The husband, a broad-shouldered individual of medium height with a graying brush cut and a preoccupied, fleeting gaze behind his glasses—a pitiful intellectual of the vigorous and woolly rodent type. I was told it was Anna Seghers—writer: *The Revolt of the Fishermen*, a quite good German proletarian novel—married to Radványi, a Hungarian Communist, all-purpose Stalinist agent, GPU collaborator, murky lecturer on the Marxist dialectic, etc.

At the camp of Pointe de Bout in Martinique Anna Seghers seemed so infected with some kind of neurosis or onset of madness that, running into Radványi, I offered to help him take care of her. He answered that he knew she was very sick and that he would ensure she got rest in Mexico City. We spoke of this calmly, forgetting, it seemed, the rest. I was deeply moved.

In early 1942, in Mexico City, Anna Seghers signed, along with E. E. Kisch, Lombardo Toledano, and a few other Stalinist intellectuals, a letter to *The Nation* in support of the accusation of "Fifth-Column Gestapo, etc." launched against Gorkin, Pivert, and me by Mexican deputies in the pay of the CP. Six months later some American *fellow travelers*[33] and critics who were regulars at Litvinov's receptions, turned Anna Seghers's melodramatic novel about the Gestapo into a best-seller.[34] I was told: She's a poor woman; her husband is a twisted, small-minded agent. He makes her do everything the Politburo desires.

33. In English in the original.
34. *The Seventh Cross*, which was also made into a film starring Spencer Tracy.

Yesterday, on the bus, Calle Bucarelli, I saw a woman of about fifty get on, her hair almost completely white and pulled tight against her temples, with a full, relaxed, sharp-featured face, and worried blue-gray eyes... Elegantly dressed in a light orange coat and accompanied by a tall young girl. She sits next to me and I recognize her... I look her right in the face and softly say:

"Anna Seghers?" "Yes" "How can you not be ashamed to participate in such infamous slander campaigns? You signed a letter against me accusing me of.... You know full well that you're lying—and in how dreadful a fashion!"

A slight trembling passes across her face, her gaze turns dark gray: "Monsieur, I don't speak French, I don't know you...." "*Wenn so, Ich spreche deutsch*.... Ich bin VS...." She turns to me with an almost friendly half-smile; I sense a kind of sympathy: "Oh, it's you! You've changed so much!" "What matters isn't that we change, it's that truth and falsehood exist. It's that the conscience exists. I speak to you with no animosity, I know you're an acceptable writer, that your books are sincere and that you have a conscience.... But do you have any idea of what you're doing? Yesterday the people who dictate your slanders tried to beat or kill us. Aren't there papers it makes you blush to sign?"

I see her anguish; it looks like she's going to break down in tears—which would be good. But she clenches her lips and stands up. To her daughter: "Come, darling." And standing in front of me, her self-assurance regained, she leans towards me: "I never blush at combating men who attack the USSR."

April 6, 1943—We receive a number of confidential reports on the attack against the Ehrlich-Alter meeting of April 1. Contreras (Sormenti) appears to have been one of its main organizers. Among the attackers were four *pistoleros* charged with liquidating the speakers during the brawl. One of them is thought to have been seriously wounded. Lombardo Toledano just wrote to *Licenciado* Madero condemning him for "covering for" the Trotskyists. Leon Trotsky is clearly behind all this. An official of the Gobernación said on the morning of the 1st: "Tonight will be the end of Trotskyism in Mexico City." This functionary's name is Davalos or Avalos (could it be the director of tourism?).

Precise rumors: Communists are going around saying that if one of their wounded dies they'll "liquidate" all the "Trotskyists"; that if the organ of the movement Socialism and Liberty[35] appears they'll destroy the printing press; that if that organ is sold on the street they'll beat up the vendors.

The twelve attackers arrested red-handed and recognized by Gironella and Gorkin, who were wounded, as well as by other witnesses, were set free yesterday due to "lack of proof."

An official at the Ministry of the Interior, named Sandoval, was one of the organizers of the attack.[36]

CONCENTRATION CAMPS

April 8, 1943—Zita Seldtke on the concentration camp of Rieucros (Lozère). Around four hundred women. Many foreign prostitutes, exploited and brutalized by the inspectors (who go so far as to beat them). Scornful Stalinist women, living among themselves, disciplined, reprimanding anyone who allows herself to talk with a socialist. Many Germans, Austrians, and others interned without cause, without their files containing a morsel of evidence; arbitrariness of the prefects. Zita herself, freed, remained there six months without having been told about it. There were only two people freed: a highly esteemed courtesan and a certain Try (Goldstein), Russian, English by marriage, her husband killed in Spain, GPU agent, mixed up in the Reiss affair.

The camp was near the woods: no surveillance, but escape punished with six months to three years of prison. On hot days the woods were full of naked women. A man on the road: excitement. Disappointment: "It's not a man, it's an inspector!"

Not far from Mende, a little old provincial town, full of interesting

---

35. A political and cultural group consisting largely of antitotalitarian exiles, among them Serge, Pivert, Gorkin, Paul Chevalier, and Gustav Regler. Founded in Mexico City, in 1942 it published two journals: *Análisis* (1942) and *Mundo* (1943–1945).
36. Last sentence added by hand.

old stones and good people, a majority on the left; it was invaded by husbands.

Seldtke spoke of the days she spent interned on the ship *Massilia* in Marseille. Two thousand people picked up in a raid by order of Vichy. They even rounded up foreign workers on the docks. It took Seldtke four days to reach the end of a corridor filled with desperate men in order to pass a note to a mobile guard; he had her exit visa, etc., and she was immediately freed. "Why didn't you say so sooner?"

He tells the story of Adamov,* that Russian poet-tramp, with his tragic ravaged face of the mortally ill and his wild eyes, took three days to assemble a pencil, a sheet of paper, and an envelope in order to get out a letter and reach the door, doing so at the price of endless waits and shoving. A mobile guard took the letter and ripped it up in his face. He cried.

They passed through the small, torrid camps of Morocco. Neither water nor shade, a vertical sun. They'd drag their straw mattresses into the edge of shade marked off by the line of the roof and would shift along with the movement of the sun. At night the jackals prowled among the mattresses, eating ordure and those who died of exhaustion or shipboard accidents.

Old Herman Dunker, professor in the Marxist schools of Germany, expelled from the Party, nearly blind, abandoned and boycotted by the Communists. His cadaverous appearance and the flies sitting on his eyelids when he lay down.

STALIN'S MISSION

April 13, 1943—We go out to the movies with Jean and Galy Malaquais. Night nearly stifling. Malaquais told me he's started a novel on the "desertion of the revolutionaries." I wanted to answer him that he's not enough of a revolutionary himself to deal with such a subject, which in any case is a false one. That with his propensity for describing man in the darkest colors he risks writing a very bad book, inventing desertions and problems that can't be found in the real world.

I say: We had many deaths but few deserters. The ones who left after the struggles were brought in by the tide and were never revolutionaries.

M: And Zinoviev and Radek and the others?

Me: They remained faithful until the final hour to a revolution and party in the process of destruction. They covered themselves in mud and allowed themselves to be executed in order to serve despite it all. What they lacked was a clear political vision of the drama they were participating in. The courage to pitilessly see things clearly. The courage of a mother admitting to herself: "I gave birth to a monster." They can be reproached for an error in judgment—a capital one—nothing more.

M: And Stalin, you think, wasn't a traitor? To have massacred Lenin's party, made the Russian Revolution what it's become, is that not treason?

Me: In polemical terms, perhaps . . . But I don't like polemical terms that do violence to the truth. In my blocked novel[37] I think I presented an accurate psychological portrait of Stalin. He didn't break faith, he changed, and history marched on: he bears the heavy burden of a mediocre and powerful personality. He believes in his mission: he sees himself as the savior of a revolution threatened by ideologues, the idealistic and the unrealistic (recall Napoleon's contempt for the ideologues). He fought them as he could, with his inferiority complex, his jealousies, his terror of men superior to him and whom he couldn't understand. He cast them from his savior's path by the only methods he had at his disposal: terror and lies, the methods of a limited intelligence governed by suspicion and placed at the service of an immense vitality.

He made himself and circumstances made him the leader, the symbolic figure of a vast new formation of parvenus of the revolution; headstrong, tough, unscrupulous, clutching on to power, living in fear and panic and claiming to embody the victorious revolution. In reality, they incarnated a new phenomenon that socialist theory never predicted: the totalitarian economic state, one of too weak a culture to allow

37. *The Case of Comrade Tulayev*, whose manuscript was blocked in New York and London despite support by Dwight Macdonald and later George Orwell.

individual freedom, and thus fated for state-directed thought. Directed thought means at one and the same time absolute confidence in oneself, material confidence, and fear of oneself, awareness of one's own weakness. This totalitarian system, Stalin built it, served it, and doesn't betray it, and so it is the only one with which we can identify him.

PRESENT-DAY MARXISM AND REVOLUTION

April 14, 1943—Otto Rühle: The Marxism of the nineteenth century was the quintessence of bourgeois idealism. Marx's revolutionary cleverness was to demonstrate socialism's necessity, not by morality, philosophy, or sentiment, but by the very science that constituted the grandeur of the bourgeoisie. The dialectic goes beyond and transcends logic, but it remains bourgeois. Through their ideas—faith in progress, juridical notions, humanism—the great socialists were great men of the bourgeois world. Lenin and Trotsky seem to me to be the last bourgeois revolutionaries. In this sense Lenin's "proletarian Jacobinism" is revelatory. This is why, when the capitalist world truly entered its final stage, they weren't up to the challenge. They understood socialist revolution in terms of yesterday's history.

Me: This is especially true of Trotsky, Lenin having died before he could be overtaken. Trotsky and the Russians in general didn't understand the totalitarian economic state that was being born before their eyes. Our opposition was infantile and blind in relation to this event; we thought in terms of an ideal democracy (of bourgeois birth) while what was needed were entirely new terms, which haven't yet been found.

O. R.: From this came the error of T., who didn't want to see, couldn't see, that a new social system was being created and maintained, and who maintained that the Soviet state remained a "degenerate," "sick," "bureaucratized," "Bonapartist" worker's state. How can you talk of degeneration when the productive apparatus continues to develop at great speed? When a new virile and powerful category (class) is being formed? It was the old socialism that was obsolete, with its traditional oppositions of capitalism or collectivism, working class or bourgeoisie. Throughout the world capitalism is as obsolete as is the Russian

Revolution. . . . I'd love to live long enough to see what will happen next. Anyway, if they don't kill me I feel like I could live another hundred years.

Me: Look at what's happened in ten years, from 1933 to 1943! The next ten years will see the outlines of a completely different world.

O. R.: *Blitzgeschichte*! (Lightning history!) Yes. Marxism must be completely rethought. The very idea of revolution must be completely renewed.

He also says that Hitler, when he sees all is lost, will have two possibilities: a war of destruction in Europe—let us all perish under the ruins: gas, bacteria, etc.—or social revolution: complete nationalization, the dispossession and extermination of the capitalists in order to place the Allies before the fait accompli of a revolution that would be impossible to reverse and would rally millions of workers to him. All the issues of the great political game will be confused.

AXENTIEV DEAD

April 16, 1943—Axentiev has died in the United States . . . I recall an evening in the winter of 1909–1910 in Paris: the meeting room of the Learned Societies, Axentiev at the podium speaking about modern philosophy. He was astonishingly handsome, tall, well built, an open face with sharp features, his long light-brown beard, his eyes blue, his gaze infinitely friendly and intelligent. What is more, a speaker totally devoid of demagogy, natural and noble in the simplest sense of the words: one could feel that a strong soul was speaking. Quoting Lessing, gesturing with his hand as if to grasp something invisible. He said: "It's not so much grasping the truth that's important, but rather maintaining a constant striving towards the truth."

He was at the time member of the Central Committee of the Socialist-Revolutionary Party (S-R), a party surrounded with a halo of pure sacrifice and defiance to tyranny thanks to the terrorism of people like Savinkov, Sazonov,* and Kaliaev.* Eleven or twelve years later in Russia, the newspapers of our heroic period often cited his name, calling him a counterrevolutionary—and in fact during the Civil War, along with Chernov* he had attempted to form a "democratic government" against us on the Volga. His adventure ended with the Directorate of Omsk, when Kolchak had the S-R directors arrested and deported to China. The idealism of the great liberals served only the reaction, which killed them or mocked them.

But Axentiev never broke faith. He remained a liberal revolutionary, a humanist full of political illusions, totally unable to grasp the harsh, concrete realities in struggle, but always carried beyond and without by an inner drive.

BOURTSEV

April 17, 1943—Vladimir Lvovich Bourtsev has died as well in Paris a few months ago, of poverty and old age (ninety years old). The Nazis had offered him the possibility of collaborating and improving his situation. Liberal and patriotic, tough on himself, he refused. I met him two or three times in Paris in early 1910 (or late 1909). It was in the aftermath of the Azef affair,[38] during which he had demonstrated amazing moral courage and an extraordinary investigative spirit. He'd also just unmasked Zhuchenko and a few other agents provocateurs. I was in my romantic anarchist phase and was involved in the Reichman affair. It seemed to me that provocation mania demoralized revolutionary circles and that it had to be opposed. Reichman was a young Romanian intellectual with a flabby, handsome face of false nobility and intellect, framed by long, wavy hair; an aesthete, egocentric, certainly cowardly, with refined literary tastes. In Romania he had taken part—a pitiful part—in an attack on Brătianu,[39] who had been shot at by a railway worker. Reichman was waiting for the railway worker in a getaway car. Either the terrorist ran in the wrong direction while trying to escape or Reichman himself fled from cowardice, but the terrorist couldn't find the car and was captured. Brătianu survived.

38. Yevno Azef was the leader of the terrorist branch of the Russian Socialist-Revolutionary Party, organizing assassinations, while at the same time working for the Russian secret police, the Okhrana.
39. Liberal politician Ion Brătianu, several times prime minister of Romania between 1909 and 1927.

R. was accused of betrayal after he was arrested and freed. A "court of honor" was formed to judge, composed of notables from the League for Human Rights. I was convinced he wasn't an agent provocateur, but simply an intellectual poseur and coward. Jaurès's *L'Humanité* published a long, accusatory interview by Jean Longuet* with Bourtsev. This was the usual socialist way of proceeding with anarchists: accuse them of provocation. I went to Bourtsev's home with a comrade, Hugo, son of a banker it was said, a calm, handsome young man whose surname I didn't know, and we were immediately received. Bourtsev disavowed the interview. He had a poor opinion of Reichman, but no proof and had expressed only a generally unfavorable opinion. "Well then," we said, "issue a retraction." He refused. We then told him that a car was waiting at the door and that we'd take him forcibly if necessary to the editorial offices of *L'Humanité* to confront him with Longuet… He softened and promised to issue a retraction, which he did that very day. (But we had to go down to *L'Huma*, twenty guys determined to wreck their furniture to make sure that the retraction got published, Longuet having started by saying the interview was inaccurate, "But that's journalism, you see!") Bourtsev asked me to come back and when I did he amicably asked me about my father. At that time he was a graying intellectual, with glasses and a pointed gray goatee, a rounded forehead, a particularly sharp gaze, very kindly in his manners, indulgent towards men, and very hard in his revolutionary defense work. I see him dressed in gray, his eyes—it seems to me—gray as well, tapping on the table with a nervous, delicate, wrinkled hand. He lived modestly in a small, well set up apartment with windows open onto a wide, airy boulevard.

He was nothing but a liberal, foreign to socialism, which he didn't understand, supporter of an English-style monarchy or a French-style republic; all in all, a republican of 1848. He defined himself: "a liberal with bombs"—a resolute partisan of terrorism.

Bolshevism terrified him and led him to a delirious form of anti-Semitism that constituted the violent eclipse of an intelligence. In Smolny I read his atrocious articles from Paris about Lenin and Trotsky: his style was like an imitation of Drumont* or of Léon Daudet.*

In 1937 in Paris an honestly constructed play called *Azef* was being performed in the banquet room of the *Journal* on the rue de Richelieu.

I went there in order to see once more some of the faces and to breathe in some of the atmosphere of the Russian emigration of yesteryear. On the stage Azef, seen from behind, was speaking with the imperial chief of police. The public waited for him to turn around to see his massive and repulsive face—authentic. (The agent provocateur had a heavy, fleshy, and repugnant face that contrasted with the noble ones of Axentiev, Chernov, Gots,* and Gershuni* and the anonymous but solid and normal face of Savinkov.) There then appeared Trepov,[40] preparing to report to the czar and who would be killed in a few minutes by Sazonov's bomb (Sazonov-Savinkov-Azef). This was recent history and a few men and women in the theater were revisiting their own past. To a certain extent I was with them, on the same plane ... In the front row of the orchestra I recognized Bourtsev, completely white, the paleness of old age, but with the same sharp gaze, on the whole hardly changed.

AMERICAN PERSPECTIVES

April 20, 1943—Discussion with two American intellectuals. They accept that traditional capitalism is finished, but think that the wealth and power of American capitalism are such that a wide margin for maneuver remains open to it. What's likely is that the United States will see the establishment of a command economy directed by and for capital; that it won't seek to dominate Europe given the difficulty of the task and the isolationism of the masses ("The soldiers are isolationists; they say that Hitler has won; they want to go home...."); that their natural domain will be South America ... A period of American occupation of Central Europe is to be predicted and it's being seriously and even intelligently prepared.

I have many objections to these opinions: the end of gold as an economic power; South America's weakness as a market; the impossibility of isolationism in the future; the decisive seriousness of the European problem. But I'm struck by the fact that the idea of an exploitative collectivism, of a capitalist—and hence fascist—type, is what

40. Imperial police chief of Moscow and governor general of Saint Petersburg; one of the organizers of the suppression of the Russian Revolution of 1905.

presents itself as a historical probability to advanced and enlightened minds.

The problem of Europe: a Europe unified by socialism or by a continental semisocialist regime would be a competitor for the United States—and a base for revolution—as fearsome as a Europe unified by fascism (unless the United States transforms itself in a socialist direction). On the other hand, maintaining a divided Europe of a half-totalitarian, half-old-liberal type seems an impossible task.

TECHNOCRACY
April 21, 1943—I've come to think that just as in 1848 Marx was correct in foreseeing the inevitable worldwide development of capitalism, we must now foresee the inevitable phase of command economies that will rapidly lead to technocratic regions (James Burnham is right on this point).

It's been objected that this would result in monstrous Stalinist-style regimes. Perhaps in backwards countries with a low living standard and consequently prey to profound social upheavals. But in Russia itself, if, instead of a regime run by a political party of declassé and parvenu revolutionaries justifying their dictatorship through their sense of historic mission, we'd had one of technocrats who boasted of their competence and public service, the consequence would, I think, have been a more enlightened, rational, and human government. In a way, the Communist bureaucracy was the complete opposite of a technocracy, and for that matter it was just when it came time to transform Communism into Stalinist totalitarianism that they saw fit to do away with all the technicians in the terror (1929–1932).

TROTSKY'S PAPERS
April 24, 1943—The Old Man, always fearful of an attack or of fire, worried about the fate of his archives, which contain unique documentation of the Russian Revolution and totally refute the Moscow Trials. Several times he was offered to part with them under advantageous conditions and he refused, for he also wanted to have them close at

hand. In late May 1940, in the aftermath of Alfaro Siqueiros's attack, it was only by chance that the papers escaped destruction: the incendiary device left in the house by the attackers failed to detonate. The Old Man knew that this aggression signified a categorical order from Stalin, with a strict timetable for its carrying out and the granting of unlimited funds. "We're living under a suspended sentence," he told Natalia. In order to at least save his archives he agreed to sell them to Harvard University, but under less attractive conditions than had been previously proposed. No one thought to stipulate in the contract that the documents should remain accessible to reliable individuals. Photostats weren't made, since that would have been too expensive. There were two whole rooms of papers (what was mad was to not even make photostats of a few hundred essential pieces, correspondence with Lenin, etc., but a certain panic reigned in Coyoacán). The archives left for Harvard. For a time Jean van Heijenoort* was authorized to consult them as a friend and collaborator of L. T. That authorization was then refused him. Recently Boris Nicolaevsky* wrote Natalia that he was beginning a history of the Opposition and requested her authorization to consult the archives. Natalia recommended him to Harvard—which has just replied with a refusal! The archives have thus fallen into the hands of hostile individuals who are sequestrating them. All kinds of disappearances are now possible, and even brazen falsifications.

While we were talking about this, someone said: "If Litvinov paid them a hefty sum, do you think he could buy them and remove some documents? —The scandal would be hushed." Besides, what has become of the very notion of scandal?

Natalia just told A. that former ambassador Davies* is said to be unhappy about the Warner Brothers film based on his book *Mission to Moscow* and was contemplating at the very least making serious modifications to it. The White House is supposed to have advised him to resign himself to it: "Let's grant Stalinist propaganda that satisfaction!" (There was a scene showing L. T. and Ribbentrop in private conversation; Warner Brothers cut it out in the face of the protest of intellectuals...)

...One rainy evening in November 1936 I was in the garden city of Lilas at Rosmer's house. Gérard Rosenthal and other comrades came during the night to pick up bundles of papers: a portion of Trotsky's archives that had been left in France. Taking the most careful precautions, they took them to the Institute of Social History at the home of Boris Nikolaevski, 7 rue Michelet, behind the Luxembourg. A few days later I saw that the service entrance to the Institute had been cut through by an electronic blowtorch: during the night around eighty kilos of papers belonging to Trotsky had been removed—nothing else had been touched. They'd gone directly to the filing cabinets holding them. B. N. employed only one secretary, in whom he had absolute confidence, (Menshevik turned Trotskyist) Lialia Ginsberg, I think. He suspected a young man who occasionally worked at the Institute. The policeman sent to carry out the investigation laughingly declared to Leon Sedov that he was a "specialist in Trotskyism." Sedov, feeling he was being trailed on the streets, had two suspects arrested: a White Russian and an Italian, who were released due to lack of a charge. The investigation came to nothing, naturally. It was most probably by monitoring Leon Sedov's correspondence with his father that they knew of the transporting of the archives. The majority of it eluded them, the GPU having acted too hastily: had they waited a few days they'd have taken it all. I think the remaining papers were sent to Amsterdam, to Dr. Posthumus's* Institute of Social History...The Gestapo must have showed some interest in it . . .

BERGSON

April 25, 1943—Brief discussion with Jean Malaquais about Bergson, whom he considers "the philosopher of bourgeois reaction." The various fascisms having made much of intuition, the irrational, etc. I respond that his reasoning is linear, containing an element of truth, but terribly schematic and inadequate.

Bergson, employing a nimble dialectic, fundamentally rational and intelligent, arrived at a time when science had reached new frontiers. The materialism and the mechanical determinism of the preceding epoch were about to quit the scene; energetics, atomic physics, and psychology no longer being compatible with "natural laws" understood as being every bit as stable as the economic laws of capitalism at its apogee. Bergson provided a renewed vision of the problem of determinism-freedom by demonstrating that the formal antinomy is resolved by a common creative dynamism. His discovery of the role of intuition coincided with that of psychologists (Freud), who explored the unconscious and the preconscious. It's not a matter of knowing if this or that discovery might furnish weapons to reactionary political movements, but if they are true. It's certain that enemies will turn every conquest into a weapon of social combat.

The "Bolshevik" (decadent Bolshevik) theory according to which there is no science or truth that is not determined by class is in contradiction with humanity's spiritual development, even though it is glaringly obvious that those sciences whose gains have an obvious socially revolutionary impact are handicapped or terribly deformed by class interests. The function of intelligence remains to anticipate and to seek. In true intellectuals this function overcomes class mentality and social interest, sometimes consciously, sometimes unconsciously. In addition, the pressure of the lower classes plays a stimulating, fertile role in the intellectual researches of the upper classes. In itself, knowledge tends towards objectivity, especially in the case of the modern sciences, beginning with the end of the eighteenth century. Culture is the work of the wealthy classes, made in their image and to serve them. It includes civilized behavior, morality, religion in its developed forms, art, and even language.

THE CLOUDING OF CONSCIOUSNESS

April 26, 1943—That enlightened consciousness in its rational forms— the scientific spirit, the search for truth, the critical spirit—is a difficult and recent historical acquisition made by a small number of civilized people. The stages of its formation after theological times: Renaissance, Reformation, the bourgeois spirit, Encyclopedism, the French Revolution, the Industrial Revolution and the advent of the sciences, Positivism, the idea of progress tied to the optimism of the triumphant bourgeoisie. —The simplistic schematism and rigidity of the sciences in the nineteenth century, their practical success. —Theories rendered obsolete by the complexity of problems while society entered a crisis of growth and transformation. Causality questioned. What remains is the scientific spirit, the method. Naturally a tendency to question it and to diminish it for reasons of social reaction and decline of intelligence during a chaotic era. In order to minimize it, they even cite the instability of scientific notions themselves.

Little by little, at the beginning of this century, the scientific spirit imposed itself to such a point that it won over the masses in countries with highly developed civilizations and strongly colored all of intellectual life. The civilized person's mentality based on the notion of the proven, on correct reasoning, on precise information, on the law. Ability to distinguish at the first glance what has been satisfactorily proved from what hasn't. Humiliating embarrassment at employing a poor argument. Concern for intellectual quality transformed into a concern for dignity. During eras of social breakdown this mentality takes on profoundly revolutionary aspects.

What I call social breakdowns embraces different and vast phenomena. Living conditions have immensely changed; painful and dangerous dissonance between institutions, accepted ideas, and new facts and needs; wars, economic and moral crises, revolutions; helplessness of the individual in confused situations, his insecurity, yesterday's beliefs discredited, the groping, experimental new conceptions (the old ideological superstructures collapse, the new are not yet formed, we are living among shaky and ruined buildings); the mass production of books, newspapers, and standardized ideas spreads beyond the circles accustomed to written ideas and reaches masses who had until then been sheltered from such intellectual shocks; scientific vulgarization and the critical spirit itself, by adapting to uneducated publics, lower their standards to such a point that they end up denying themselves. Example: the stupidity of a certain antireligious propaganda, the heavy-handedness of materialist propaganda, the childish mechanisms of vulgar determinism

And in the social battles that began at the end of World War I, the unleashing of emotions. Proletarian passion versus humanism in the Russian Revolution, the elements of a new faith in revolutionary agitation and Marxist dogmatism. The preventive counterrevolutions in Italy and Germany, molded by the school of the victorious revolution and imitating it in the organization of the one-party state, the establishment of thought control, the creation—at once conscious and unconscious—of social myths. The cult of the dead Lenin, the cult of the Leader: at bottom a psychological reaction, the return to primitive mentalities. (That despotisms are based on the primitive mentality.) The deliberate irrationality of Nazism (blood, race, *Lebensraum*, the Leader-Father).

The intellectuals, upholders of decomposing bourgeois culture—disorientated—reveal a penchant for abandoning the scientific spirit, which is rigorous and tends to impose the taking of risky, sometimes impossible, positions (the courage of the historian in totalitarian countries). Resignation of the intelligence, which allows itself to be molded by emotions and the armed big interests; tendency for the state to turn intelligence into its servant (so that it not be its mortal enemy).

The ability to distinguish between the proven, plausible, valid, hypothetical, honest, or falsified assertions is lost; the feeling for valid proof and correct reasoning (dangerous methods which give rise in the oppressed thinker to a feeling of the intolerable) is lost. Henceforth the Leader is always right; conviction proves guilt; lies are good if they serve a cause that should be served; the notion of impersonal truth fades away; a certain impudence takes on the appearance of power: by shouting loud enough, by ensuring large press runs, one can easily make a useful thesis prevail, even if it is a hundred times false in itself. Assassination becomes the supreme argument and proves through suppression that the man was wrong. The quantity of printed matter, the vigor of the repression, the delirium of the orchestration provide empirical proof through their success. The underlying idea is that force is the sole practical truth. An era of clouded consciousness.

In reality, the latter is by definition weak and ill and it knows or feels this. It is betrayed by its excessive lying, despite its efforts not to recognize falsehood. A false Trotskyism is invented in order to refute it, given the impossibility of engaging in discussion with the real Trotskyism—or any other rational discussion. That two times two is five is proved by capital punishment. A moment arrives when the enormity of the forged or false allegation gives it an appearance so imposing that the average man is afraid to doubt it.

It should also be noted that there are of course few minds of a certain quality, few men possessing certain precise knowledge or a certain form of courage, and as a result physical repression is effective for a considerable length of time. By executing the three hundred scientists who truly understand Einstein's relativity or the three hundred authentic psychoanalysts and burning their books one certainly obtains a momentary stabilization of thought at a lower level. In much the same way religion can only be truly destroyed through the destruction of the believer.

At the same moment, production, war and tyranny, and technical scientific research are developed, pushed to even higher levels. And since they require a true scientific spirit, intelligence finds a refuge and an opening. Oppression also mass-produces tortured minds. That overall, clouded consciousness is both waning and, despite itself, being reborn.

MUSEO NACIONAL

April 29, 1943—National Museum, hall of codices. Two pre-Cortés codices reveal the existence of books, drawing of a high quality, acceptable technique and density of content. Rich colors of one of the manuscripts. The Spanish influence adds little to the post-Cortés codices and produces nearly comical results: genealogical tree of Moctezuma with Austrian coats of arms and the tree ... a nopal! Breviary drawn and painted in watercolors by *misioneros*: the prayers are represented by human figurines with elements from Mexican and Christian calendars, all of it childlike and penguinesque (thought of Saint Colomban, who, according to Anatole France, evangelized the penguins).

Stonework of absolute perfection. The sculpture at times recalls the Egyptian and sometimes the Chinese manner, but always distantly. Delicate gold work. Religious mask of stone from Chichen Itza decorated with green tiles. Maya art is the richest, combining an accomplished realism with an unquestionably ancient hieratic stylization, filled with meaning and of a great intensity of expression. Three elements dominate the style: stone, the stylized vegetal, and man, particularly the male profile. Miniature Totonac[41] terra-cotta funerary masks, most

41. A pre-Columbian society located in the center-west of Mexico, in the contemporary states of Puebla and Vera Cruz.

likely votive portraits of the dead, individualized, some with a striking expression of suffering, others with the smile characteristic of the dead.

Unique pieces, silver plate, gold, sculpted stone are placed in display windows that could be opened with the wave of a thumb. It's true that a guard is keeping an eye on the visitor and a small poster forbids him from "talking with them about personal matters!" Pottery and collections of a variety of objects are piled almost helter-skelter in neglected galleries. Neither inscriptions nor explanatory labels; no attempt at scientific presentation. The relics of Indian civilization are given nothing but a shelter in the midst of disorder, negligence, and poverty. This archaeology, unique in the world, representing a precious human treasure, in truth seems to interest no one—except perhaps looters, for much has been stolen, much has been smuggled, and a large number of important works have left for the United States or are hidden in private collections.

Through the window one can see the activity on the Calle de la Moneda. A military tailor has put a wonderful slogan on his sign: "*Mexico, sobre todo*." On the second floor of a house a clothing workshop: the boss and his ninny of a son daydream at the window while women work in the room behind them.

One leaves there having been dazzled by direct contact with a vanished human world that was magnificent, full of creative gifts and capacity for work; and with something like a neglected cemetery, overwhelmed by an unpoetic decay...

The *yugos*, sculpted stone yokes, form a large horseshoe, sometimes with a finely worked interior (one contains a portrait in profile; another with the head of a powerful nocturnal bird of prey on its rear section), were used by the Totonacs as frames to support the dead person's head.

FALSIFIED VALUES
April 29, 1943—This is a time of falsified—that is, betrayed—values. Anyone even slightly well informed has the sensation of breathing lies of such low quality that they don't even contain the involuntary homage to truth proper to useful and, in a way, decent, lies, which only aim at misleading moderately. Back in Russia, propaganda-publicity

blasting from the press, loudspeakers, movies, etc. literally slapped us in the face. Illuminated transparencies on trams rolling down darkened winter streets proclaimed "The press for the masses!" precisely at a time when it had become practically impossible to buy a newspaper. The empty co-ops were full of posters about "Feeding the people: the prime task and the prime concern"; "Soviet humanism" was proclaimed by turning the country an enormous concentration camp and shooting people without letup. Gorky—a Gorky emptied of himself, dried out, reactionary and tormented by vague remorse—was apotheosized by celebrating the struggles of his youth, his boldness in marching against the current and confronting oppression—at the very moment when anyone who showed any hint of imitating this example perished. I met a young working-class Communist woman who had been sent to prison as a Trotskyist for having exclaimed at the tribune: "Everything we read on the propaganda transparencies is in complete contradiction with reality.... I wonder if I haven't gone mad!"

In Mexico I note that this totalitarian falsification has spread around the globe to a far more serious extent than may first appear. It is basically impossible to publish any news, any article, any book that is simply truthful. It is only interests that speak—the interests that pay. All the values that are praised are tainted. On July 14 I saw a pro-French demonstration in front of the presidential palace. I went over to it. On a truck surrounded by flags (orchestra, filmmakers, green uniforms of the CTM[42]) a speaker spoke of the French Revolution, Liberty and Equality etc.—and he was an acrobat of a congressman, ready to carry out the lowest tricks, one of the ones who stupidly slandered us on behalf of the GPU. The democrats are pro-Stalinist, that is, pro-totalitarian; the Communists are, in fact, anticommunist... Counterfeit money circulates so freely that it has eliminated the real. The reading of American newspapers gives the same impression, with the reservation that there remain important islands of resistance and thinking minorities that are not completely reduced to impotence.

---

42. Confederación de Trabajadores de México, official union organization led at the time (and until 1997!) by Fidel Velázquez, who succeeded Vicente Lombardo Toledano.

Under capitalism, everything being a commodity—truth, information, thought, knowledge, like the rest—we are subject to the laws of the marketplace in the realm of spiritual production, and this has meant the domination of large-scale producers at the service of large-scale consumption; the proliferation of degraded products and fakes. But still in the free market worthwhile intellectual products also found a buyer and ended up fulfilling a need... In today's world, divided between totalitarian command economies and a capitalism of trusts drifting towards some unknown future, naked force has been substituted for mercantilism and its relative freedom: naked force knows only how to suffocate. In the nontotalitarian countries there is a strong tendency to imitate the customs of the totalitarians or to fall under their influence, on the right from spirit of reaction, on the left from stupid idealization.

USSR-POLAND

Late April 1943—The breaking of diplomatic relations between the USSR and Poland demonstrates the latent conflict between the Allies and Stalin. Stalin's game on two chessboards:

In the event of a separate peace with Hitler—or with H.'s more or less camouflaged successors—Poland would pay the price for the agreement; continuation of the partitioning of the country, the establishment of a diminished Polish state sacrificed to the two powers.

In the event of the collapse-defeat of Germany, the formation of a Polish satellite to the USSR, called on to serve as the base for the Stalinist conquest of Germany from within (CP and pseudodemocratic government whose essential gears will be in the hands of the Stalinists).

Impossibility for the Stalinists to stop at the Vistula during the future chaotization of Europe. The bureaucratic command economy has a natural tendency to expand in order to survive. If Russian totalitarianism were to survive, the existence in its vicinity of democratic regimes—socialist leaning or not—would be impossible.

The key question is that of the German regime. Even after a crushing and bloody defeat, Germany, in the heart of the continent, with a compact population and concentrated industry—that could only be destroyed momentarily—remains stronger than the peoples around it, who were more weakened by war and oppression, are less homogeneous, less equipped with industries and technical knowledge. Even in defeat Germany maintains European hegemony. It becomes the essential country for the reconstruction and reorganization of the continent. In this sense it also decides the fate of Russia, whose prosperity it can ensure and against whom it could constitute a renewed threat. The Allies have a vital interest in facilitating a regime similar to theirs in Germany. The totalitarian USSR has a vital interest in provoking the establishment in Germany of a regime similar to its own. Irreducible conflict.

The sole reasonable solution that can be seen today, that of a socialist or socialist-leaning united states of Europe, is incompatible with Stalinist totalitarianism and even more so with the conservative mentality of the Americans and the British, called upon to evolve towards a revolutionary solution.

LEGEND OF TÍO GORGONO

May 1, 1943—At the Piverts', Díaz de León tells the story of "mi tío Gorgono"[43]—his actual uncle—a character still famous in Aguascalientes. At seventeen he murdered an aunt, frequented a famous cabaret where the young people of the city demonstrated their worth by shooting out the lights with pistols so they could have knife fights in the dark. ("Your guts annoy me, Señor!") (Episode of a man who in a fit of bravura slit open his belly and chewed on his own entrails . . .) Gorgono later killed a woman by hitting her on the head with a rock and tossed her body in an *arroyo*. Sentenced to death, his lawyer saw no other way of avoiding execution than to advise him to kill someone in prison in order be tried a second time—to gain time. In the Aguascalientes prison Gorgono was a shoemaker and the object of general respect; with an awl, he murdered a prisoner who had been impolite to him. Sentenced again, probably under another governor, remained

43. In Serge's novel *Unforgiving Years* the character Don Saturnino plays dominoes with Don Gorgono.

in prison a long time. He was freed by the revolution. He returned to his home with a long, flowing beard, saw that he no longer had any relatives—"and remembered that he was the one who'd killed them." Put a stick of dynamite in his mouth and lit it...Gorgono's children are still introduced in Aguascalientes with admiration. Díaz de León wrote a puppet show based on this life, which the public judged immoral and earned him the resentment of his hometown.

In the old days the prison of Aguascalientes had neither gates nor guards. The prisoner was taken to it by gendarmes. The head of the prison would come out to meet him and would violently trace with his knife a line in the sand at the entryway while proffering fantastic imprecations—and the prisoner was honor-bound not to cross that line.

Díaz de León also recounts a legend of Mexico City: on a Calle Juan Manuel that is today a section of Venustiano Carranza Avenue there lived a wealthy señor who would go out at night and ask passersby for the time. Once told he would exclaim: "How lucky you are to know the time of your death!" and would kill him. "Finally his own guardian angels hanged him...."

USSR—"DEMOCRACY"?

May 2, 1943—I'm told that in American (capitalist) circles it is expected that at the end of the war the USSR will once again become a semi-capitalist republic....To be understood in conjunction with a certain pro-Stalinist propaganda in the United States. Such promises must have been discreetly made to naive and crafty individuals like J. E. Davies.[44] What's amazing is that people fall for this! That the Russian autocracy in its current form can't last is obvious; that it will seek to last by donning a new costume is probable, if history allows it the leisure. But it would be foolish to say that camouflage or camouflaged

44. Joseph E. Davies, US ambassador to the Kremlin (1936–1939), famous for his uncritical attitude toward Stalin's Moscow frame-up trials. In Davies's 1941 book *Mission to Moscow*, he depicted the USSR as moving toward democracy and justified Stalin's invasion of Finland. In May 1943 Roosevelt sent him to Moscow on a special wartime mission to arrange a private meeting with Stalin.

adaptations could resolve the problems of the rights of the masses and the relations between Russia and Central Europe. Likewise, the only thing that is completely impossible is the return to the capitalism of yesterday and the day before in countries which have set out on the road to collectivism and the command economy.

Nevertheless, one must consider a hypothesis that Stalin might be considering. The reconstruction of the USSR can only take place with the assistance of German industry—if Germany itself hasn't been totally devastated—or American industry (capitalistic planned economy), which would offer the possibility of the restoration of certain forms of capitalism in Russia through concessions, debt, and control of the Russian economy.

MEXICO—THE PLAN

May 5, 1943—Conversation with D., a Mexican, remarkably intelligent and well informed about the issues. I tell him that I have observed indications of an imminent economic and social crisis: rise in prices in a country of semicolonial poverty; appearance of the paper peso, which will replace the metal peso and raise prices even higher; scarcity of products imported from the United States; speculation; hoarding; plus, with the peso in reality pegged to the dollar, and the latter setting out on a skillfully managed but spectacular inflation—what is to be predicted? I tell him that in this period a weak state with a complex, seminatural economy of at least ten million Indios; capitalist in the cities; ruled by trusts at a higher level; and finally, subordinated to the trust-ruled and -directed economy of the United States—that is, the greatest power in the world—that such a state can neither administer nor defend its interests without knowing itself and beginning to put its own economy in order. That without an attempt at planning it can't reasonably either escape from or deal with a crisis; that in an era of inevitable worldwide planning it must sooner or later be considered here, and that the later it comes, the greater the difficulties it will confront... The establishment of a planning commission would be in the vital interests of the country. It goes without saying that this commission must begin its labors by exercising extreme discretion in order to avoid being either foiled or quickly conquered by private interests. D., extremely interested, agrees with me.

According to the newspapers the market value of the peso has fallen forty-nine centavos in just a few months.[45]

RESISTANCE CAPABILITIES OF TOTALITARIAN SYSTEMS

May 6, 1943—They are new systems, of extraordinary power, which unite the revolutionary innovations of the plan and collective management with the old methods of appealing to primitive instincts, despotism, and thought control. We know from the Russian example that they can resist famine, near-total unpopularity (Stalin had the peasants, the workers, the technicians, and the thinking elements of the party against him, yet he held out with the support only of the bureaucracy and the repressive apparatus); from the Nazi example that they can prepare and make war with heretofore unknown vigor while emerging from poverty and social disorder; by the Italian example that they can resist when an entire country no longer wants either to resist or support... *We don't know how a totalitarian state dies.* None of the observers who know Russia would have said in 1941 that the Stalinist regime would survive an invasion comparable only to that of Genghis Khan. It was possible to accept the ultimate invincibility of Russia, served by its vastness and populated with 180 million energetic people, but it seemed that defeat condemned the regime. Stalin himself must have been surprised by the vitality of his regime, whose high functionaries predicted its fall at the time of the Battle of Moscow in December 1941. (The French Empire in 1870, the Third Republic in 1940 succumbed with far fewer defeats; the German and Austro-Hungarian empires succumbed through exhaustion in 1918, before invasion; the Russian empire perished under less destitution than that suffered today by the Russian people.) Totalitarian regimes are sensitive to attrition, and it is inconceivable that they not succumb once a certain degree of attrition has been reached. But their capacity for resistance to attrition and

45. The final paragraph added by hand.

their ability to attract and concentrate the energy of the masses are something new. Two years after the invasion and the loss of its richest lands, the USSR continues to resist magnificently.

Is it probable that there will be lesser resistance on the part of Nazi Germany? The general tendency is to believe that after a large-scale military defeat, the Third Reich will collapse like the kaiser's Germany under the violent attack of Foch and English tanks. Isn't this believing in a historical myth? Shouldn't a resistance to invasion by the Third Reich comparable to that of the Russians at Stalingrad be viewed as every bit as probable? We don't know if totalitarian regimes are capable of transforming themselves in the middle of a fight—of renewing themselves. (This is difficult to conceive. In the long run their structural rigidity is probably their greatest weakness; a sclerosis of power.)

One is also generally inclined to say that revolutionary ferment will occur with the first great defeats. I don't think so. No revolutionary ferment can effectively manifest itself as long as the totalitarian machine hasn't begun to break down. The conviction of defending the very life of the nation brought about the unity of the USSR and ensured, in part, the continued existence of the Stalinist regime. Nazi Germany appeals to the same conviction, and the threat of a more severe Versailles suspended over it is all it needs to psychologically strengthen resistance to the bitter end.

ROUGH DRAFTS OF A FUTURE EUROPE

May 6, 1943—Conversation with M., a well-read—relatively—prominent merchant... He's pessimistic: it took six months to push the Nazis out of Tunis, where they took over in just a few days... Is it possible they'll be pushed out of Europe? "Instead, I foresee a negotiated peace" he says and quotes me from the book by Culbertson[46]—the bridge player—on the future organization of the world, a little book that's selling like hotcakes, praised by Max Eastman, Dorothy Thompson, and others. A map sketches a Germano-Scandinavian federation with Germany and Austria and reaching as far as Finland. There's

---

46. *The World Federation Plan* by Ely Culbertson, published in 1942.

MAY 1943 · 271

another federation of Central Europe and the Balkans which would
be, and this is obvious, without being written, the satellite of the Germanic federation ... Strange and rather childish ... It should be noted
that all the projects being outlined in conventional circles are the result
of a certain childishness. The conformist thinking of today cannot be
realistic.

MODERN PAINTING

May 10, 1943—Cubism, Surrealism, German Expressionism (Oskar
Kokoschka, his portraits), Russian Suprematism, etc.—what has become
of the human form? Analysis decomposes it, the search for abstract
symbols tends to reduce it to an algebraic sign. This painting thus
proceeds from scientific intellectualism: reduction of reality to an
ultimate mental equation. (The idealist illusion of the very concept of
the equation embracing living and creative reality!) Equations are valid
for constructing machines: in spite of himself, the painter's eye is
dominated by the vision of the world of a builder of machines.

On the contrary, the Greeks—as well as the artists of all primitive
civilizations before religious hieratism imposed symbolic conventions
on them—proceeded from love for the human form. Later, landscape
artists would proceed from love for the earth: Van Gogh's tree is viewed
by an eye charged with emotion, which looks on it as if it were a human
face. This love for the human form, for the real man revealed through
the portrait, for the human earth which has disappeared in the modern
schools, has been an incredible loss. Since this idea struck me I can see
more clearly why I am so hostile to them before even thinking of understanding them. The living form has no need to be reflected upon to
be grasped: we participate in it. If a cerebral effort is required to enter
into contact with a work it is because that work has become literary-
metaphysical, become a construct of the spirit (the spirit of an era) and
is thus detached from direct contact with life. It conveys a mentality
particular to men of these times, speaking of trees and men in the
special language of a culture that allowed man and the tree to be crushed.

The merit of certain Surrealists (Brauner, occasionally Ernst, above
all de Chirico) is to have rediscovered man in inner nightmare, which

they make visible. De Chirico's power: in him this nightmare almost directly reflects external reality (his synthetic landscapes of the bare, modern, deserted, inhuman city…). The love of man has become the love of man's nightmare. The importance thus assumed by the nightmare is a sign of the times.

Duchamp, his grids, *The Bride and Her Seven Bachelors*.[47] No longer either drawing or painting nor plastic vision. An abstract projection of lines inspired by the design of machines and diagrams. In a sense Duchamp reaches a summit: in order to achieve simplification these constructions project themselves into the void. Gratuitous machine design reduced to the absurd. (At bottom, submission to the machine with a love-hate of it.) Observe that his grid constructions are an intelligent variation on prison bars.

MEXICAN ECONOMIC CRISIS?

May 11, 1943—The paper peso makes its appearance and the beautiful peso coin disappears—obviously. Prices rising and merchandise disappearing. In a few weeks the cost of living is double what it was a year ago. Causes: exports to the United States, the lack of transport (given the exports), speculation, the absence of planning. Sugar has become rare and goes from forty centavos the kilo to eighty, and we're in a cane-producing country! The entire American border must have been surrendered to the gringo black market … No meat in this cattle country.

To be foreseen: big economic and political problems in the remote regions of the country, dearth of agricultural goods (lack of low cost industrial products), and a vertiginous drop in the value of money due to a scarcity of commodities … Met a businessman who has traveled a great deal. We speak of the difficulties ahead. He's smiling and takes on the knowing air of a professional: "Opinions vary," he says. "On the contrary, businessmen and financiers think that we are headed for an era of prosperity, passing through minor, momentary difficulties.…" These people, I say, are exporters. They grow wealthy in paper dollars

---

47. The actual title is *The Bride Stripped Bare by Her Bachelors, Even*.

and even gold, but not being able to purchase machinery in the United States they won't even be able to invest their capital in new industries, whose creation will cost time and impose a harsh period of trials ...

ENERGY, HUMAN ENDURANCE

May 18, 1943—Discussion with Fritz Fränkel and Herbert Lenhoff about moral energy. They think the Germans are quite exhausted, which could hasten the end. F. F. says that "the German feels himself destined to serve under good conditions," to "serve without suffering," we add. I answer that our idea of morale and of energy was until now too bourgeois. Formed in another half century, that of comfort, of softening, of playing the odds with fate, of man accustomed to well-being, progress, and the rational. Conventional wisdom is going out of fashion; it was valid only for a time. On the eve of the October 1917 insurrection the Bolshevik C[entral] C[ommittee] studied the situation. Local militants told of the apathy and indifference of the discouraged masses. Lenin answered that they were discouraged because they had no useful tasks to perform and lacked a precise outlook. It's certain that the October revolt took place amid an indifferent mass (in the capital) and was the work of an active minority, observed with sympathy by these masses. During the Civil War years we constantly felt the apathy of the masses, who nevertheless remained a prodigious reservoir of energy. John Scott* recounts having seen the young Russians mobilized in August 1939. A spectacle of apathy, misery, and resignation that he describes as lethargic. These same masses fought furiously and are still fighting under even more wretched conditions. When Scott uses the word "lethargy" he reveals his American inability to decipher the Russian mind-set. The Russian man has learned much; he thinks, he has an acute and intelligent sense of reality, he is profoundly active. But he scorns and fears useless agitation, ineffective action, gesticulation, vain words ... Despotisms have rendered him circumspect and taught him the value of silence and economy of movement. He's hungry, he's barefoot, but he doesn't get angry or protest: this would be vain and risky. He becomes taciturn, and the American who views him through the windshield of his car is surprised by such "Slavic resignation." But should this Russian man glimpse a real possibility to wangle or fight, then a colossal energy, premeditated and resourceful, is awakened in him.

We speak of the misery of Europe: undernourishment, discouragement, nervous depression ... Fritz Fränkel says that depression, in the individual as in the masses, follows great nervous tensions. I respond that our former idea of human endurance is false, bourgeoisified. The human being is made so as to survive in a world of harsh struggles, and not in a padded society. His natural condition is that of an animal delivered over to unforgiving, chaotic nature (Nietzsche explained this well). The depressed man regains his energy after a few nights of sleep; the masses regain theirs in a few months or a few years. Unconscious self-repression serves to make peoples and classes forget the atrocity of war in the same way that mothers completely repress the sufferings of childbirth. Examples: after the Russian Revolution the years of depression—the desire to live in the best possible way, by enjoying oneself—facilitated the Soviet Thermidor. But a new, colossal energy revealed itself during the struggles for collectivization, the famine and industrialization. A new, brief period of calm in 1933–1936, at which point the massacres of the revolutionary generation and the war arrived.

BLAISE CENDRARS

Blaise Cendrars, met at the Grasset offices, a thick Scottish wool scarf around his neck and a beret. The ruddiness of a wine drinker; a heavy, Gothic face, quite vulgar. Sad, speaking in a raspy voice, a Paris accent, a voice empty of hope. "This damn filthy war." Speaks of young pilots who go off to be massacred at age eighteen because thanks to their vigor they resist the blood spurts to the brain during high-speed aerial maneuvers that cause blackouts in men of twenty-five. "All the blood rushes to the head with the violence of a hurricane." He says that "our aviation is working away, but we're not yet there. . . ." I sense he is very bitter, almost desperate. I'm told he lives alone, spending time with mediocre journalists, *Paris-Soir*, etc., tired of everything, expecting nothing of men, "a real bunch of bastards," a "fucked civilization. . . ."

Two minor masterpieces in his oeuvre, on the war: *I Killed, I Bled*. Lovely poems as well. No grand impulses, a realistic and imaginative love of adventure—a narrow-minded love. No ideas. "Ideas, the ideal," he'd say, "nothing but bloody seesaws."

THE EXTERMINATOR RATS

May 20, 1943—In Leningrad, in the destruction during the Civil War, the rats multiplied fantastically, particularly in the areas around the warehouses, on the banks of the Neva, and at the port. They were a scourge. At the time when they went to drink from the river the sound of their teeming swarm spooked the horses, who didn't dare go any further... In order to combat them a Chinese man invented a species of exterminator rat. He locked up a hundred rats two by two in cages and left them without food, so that one of the two would end up devouring the other, dead or alive. He locked up the fifty survivors two by two, and so on until all that were left were three or four fearsome beasts accustomed to devouring their like. Apparently these exterminators worked wonders among the apartments.

MEXICO CITY—SNAKES

May 20, 1943—Conversation at the dinner table about snakes, a lovely subject. Laurette was excited to learn that in hot regions snakes are kept as house pets. It's usually a large snake, more than two meters long, with a large head, a moustache, and cat eyes. It eats small rodents and begs crumbs from the table. It's said it sucks the milk from young mothers. The story of the traveler who found one in his bed: Ah, the people said, it's the *chata*![48]

Eva T. recounts that a few months ago, in the state of Vera Cruz, three young people traveling in the *selva* reached a region where there are stones hollowed out and pierced by water. One of them sat on a rock and collapsed, dead. The second, while trying to help him, sat on

---

48. Affectionate nickname given to women.

the same rock, which was clean, and also fell over. The third went to get help, and it was discovered that the rock contained a nest of minuscule red snakes, hardly bigger than earthworms, extremely quick and poisonous, the *coralillos*. Eva recounted another story that's told in Vera Cruz. In a prison there was a cell in which men were mysteriously dying. A man decided to solve the mystery and entered it, determined not to sleep ... He saw an enormous scorpion come out from between the stones. Eva said that sitting on the peristyle of a hacienda she saw a magnificent snake approaching that made a rattling sound as it advanced. Its head was strong and colorful ... She admired it, but the people around her were afraid for her, for it was a *cascabel*, a rattlesnake.

END OF THE COMINTERN

May 22, 1943—Don Ramón Denegri, much moved, comes over at 3:00 to tell me the big news published in the noontime newspapers: Stalin has announced the dissolution of the Comintern! Afterwards, discussion, etc. "The whole town is talking about it." The text of the Executive Committee's decision is ambiguous: it doesn't call for the dissolution of the parties or that of the movement, but only that of the International, in reality long since dead and reduced to a government bureau. The Presidium will "dedicate itself to the struggle against fascism" and so can maintain a semi-existence. Many things will obviously follow. The parties will be brutally shaken up or transformed, a secret apparatus will be maintained, but this symbolic gesture, which I explain mainly by Stalin's need to refuse the Allies some more substantial satisfaction (a change in attitude towards Japan?) constitutes a solemn disavowal of our murdered ideals and an open abandonment of its militants.

In Russia he has completed the liquidation of the heroic ideology of the past at the very moment when great peoples—bled dry, ruined, and engaged in a mortal combat—need more than ever to rediscover their faith in themselves and their confidence in the future. Official abandonment of socialist internationalism at the moment when history has placed on its agenda the international reorganization of the entire European continent along socialist lines. Since Stalin can renounce neither his own collectivist regime nor expand it towards Western Europe at the first opportunity, it also serves as an enormous recantation. He doubtless thinks that the Soviet Army and state are henceforth the sole real combatant elements and that he'll be forgiven all his recantations, just as he has been largely forgiven all his crimes, so long as he succeeds in holding out and acting, either by ruse or by force.

I lived this tragic story from its beginning to its final period.... What anger and what despair it would have given rise to eight or ten years ago if anyone had made this mad prediction: that one day the KKI[49] itself, on the orders of the leader, would cause the Comintern to self-destruct! Now, for the younger generation of Russians, this has no importance: it has too many wounds to heal, dead to confront. For the thinking minority it is a clarification that will ferment in many consciences.

THE END OF THE TOTALITARIAN STATES?

May 29, 1943—We know how totalitarian states victoriously resist crises of all kinds and how they combat them; we don't know how they succumb. Until now experience has demonstrated that they have a capacity for work, combat, and endurance greatly superior to those of the other states of modern times. (In certain essential aspects their mechanisms put me in mind of ancient agricultural empires, the Chinese and Egyptian, which had a millennial social stability. These empires were based on a rationalization of agriculture, a vast bureaucratic apparatus, and on thought controlled by the theocracy.) Totalitarian states push the limits of human endurance far beyond what bourgeois psychology thinks possible. By simplifying the structure of society, by liquidating the former superstructures and laying bare the essential economic and political gears, they subject men to the rigor of a law that, like natural law, is both overwhelming and obvious. In external and internal conflicts, action being total, the boats are instantly burned, no retreat is possible, and every fight becomes a fight to the death.

49. Russian acronym for the Executive Committee of the Communist International.

Totalitarianism suppresses all middle-of-the-road solutions, compromises, and tolerance, probably because it is still too weak, new, and threatened to impose itself otherwise, for it seems it would gain by admitting some compromises with the individual, the group, and even with the outside. As I wrote in 1933 in my testament-letter to Magdeleine Paz,[50] one of totalitarianism's resources is that of counting only with big numbers. It then crushes the individual with impunity and, more often, drags him along, because dealing in big numbers carries with it a self-evident justification, even when it is inhuman and cynical.

W. Graebner, an American journalist, has published data on the great suffering. It has reached the levels of the great famine of 1932–1934, with the war added on. It is worse than the Volga famine of 1922 due to the great scope and general suffering of the war; it surpasses, by the organization of the collective effort amid poverty and the organization of the famine itself, the black years of 1919–1921. People held out under all these circumstances, and they are still holding out. Always on the brink of catastrophe, of course, just as a living being brushes against mortal danger with every movement. Russian psychology has little to do with this. The decisive factors are: 1. The moral capital of a revolution, which provides new reasons for living; 2. The mechanism of totalitarianism; 3. The mortal peril and hardship itself, which stretches energy to the extreme.

Fear that the end of Nazi totalitarianism will be drawn out and heroic, with an endurance comparable to that of the Russian Revolution. Europe will come out of the war devastated, as it did after the Thirty Years' War, leveled, forced to start anew from zero, with populations accustomed to organization amid privation and combat (collectivism), thirsty for freedom, and instinctively leaning towards equality.

OTTO RÜHLE

June 9, 1943—Met Otto Rühle on the wide and sunny Avenida 20 de Noviembre. He in a light-gray suit, white straw hat, bow tie, pink faced,

50. Large excerpts from this open letter, smuggled out of Russia the eve of Serge's arrest, are included in his *Memoirs of a Revolutionary*, pp. 326–28.

JUNE 1943 · 279

blue eyed, happy to be feeling better, childishly content with this old man's vigor. "Alice is in that shop over there...." Alice is trying to sell silver chains. O. R. assembles them and they earn between fifty centavos and one peso on each chain sold. O. R.: "I've begun a book, and it's been years since I had the desire to write one." What's the subject? "*Die Weltrevolution*,[51] the time has come...." This is something we agree on. Alice comes out of the *regalo*[52] shop and explains: "Because I'm well dressed they take me for a foreign customer and they're all smiles. When I offer my wares their expression changes.... I've been to seven stores and haven't sold a thing."

At their home in the evening with Laurette. We browse through his books, *The History of Revolutions*, *The History of Proletarian Mores*. I see a portrait of the young Cromwell. "A strong man," I say to O. R.: "No, not at all, I assure you. In his final moments he was still wondering if a sinner could lose divine grace, and he was trembling...." I don't answer that this isn't incompatible with passion and power, quite the contrary. I say: "Another case that interests me psychologically is that of Robespierre, so mediocre yet so strong and so hesitant during Thermidor." O. R. laughingly explains that he wrote a book about Robespierre and that Alice, while burning manuscripts of books already published, burned it by mistake.

The newspapers announce the invasion of the European continent. If it were ready, they wouldn't announce it. We both think that this is far from being the case—most likely not this year. The Russians are thus being sacrificed. Months of preparation are required just to attempt something serious in the Mediterranean. O. R. proudly shows us images of his heartbeats: the rhythm is perfect. Alice explains that the aorta is inflamed but that this is normal at sixty-eight...

THE ALTERNATIVE IN THE USSR—LEON TROTSKY
June 12, 1943—Conversation with Jean Malaquais about Leon Trotsky. I say that the alternatives for the Russian Revolution were between the

51. The World Revolution.
52. Gift.

bureaucracy—government by Party opportunists—and the establishment of an extremely restricted Soviet democracy of skilled technicians and administrators. In short, an enlightened collectivist totalitarianism with a strong technocratic tendency. We didn't realize this—no one did—but a few intelligent technicians, like the humanist-engineer, thought of it. (Bogdanov* as well.) The object of the trial of the technicians was to parry this "danger," well understood by Stalin, who feared the bourgeois spirit of the engineers and feared even more the infringement of expertise over political power.

With his abilities L. T. could have made himself the leader of such a regime, which would have been a kind of enlightened absolutism. We'd have been spared Stalinism's bloodbaths and the destruction of the cadres they cost us. In the world of yesterday this regime would have been clearly progressive. Jean Malaquais: "Don't you think L. T. was mistaken not to have been willing to go down this road?" That road could be taken only by a coup d'état, and we never stopped thinking about Thermidor and the Eighteenth Brumaire. L. T.'s grandeur was to live out a socialist idea that proposed to break with the burdensome tradition of bourgeois revolutions. His revolutionary conception was more linear as well, his fidelity to the party was absolute. He was the incarnation of the Marxism of 1905–1920. In order to safeguard the purity of ideas for the future he preferred to remain a symbol and perish.

MEN AT WAR

June 12, 1943—It's commonly thought that war and social chaos bring in their train man's return to the savage state and the predominance of antisocial instincts. The decline in general culture is indisputable. "The price of a human life has sunk to zero," Jean Malaquais tells me—and this is certainly the case for bombed cities. The concern for labor and combat efficiency obliges the war technicians to be forever thinking of how to best manage their men and materiel. But I'm thinking rather of other human factors in war. For the soldier war is living from day to day, and daily life, even on the battlefield, constantly imposes solidarity on him. We don't know in what proportions inhumanity and solidarity are wastefully expended in the very heart of the butchery. In general, you don't see the enemy you're firing at, and can barely make out the houses of the city you're destroying. This facilitates the somber task. It happens that a pilot in the middle of his work risks his life to support a comrade he sees in danger; that the frontline infantryman risks his life to rescue a wounded man. I recall, near Ligogvo in 1919, the fraternal fury of a sailor who gesticulated and cursed because a clumsy infantryman had exposed himself to bullets that were whizzing by... He identified with him, and exposed himself in order to make him duck. I tend to believe that from the psychological point of view more humane sentiments than inhumane ones are displayed on battlefields, and that in this way, through the very negation of the respect for human life, a new consciousness pierces through, one more active, more effective, more generous in its capacity for sacrifice and support.

SUPERMAN

June 18, 1943—Film in Technicolor: Superman, athlete in tights with an *S* on his chest (the dullest imaginable vision of the Superman), in daily life he is a nice young man in tortoiseshell glasses (a nearsighted Superman, that's not bad at all) who works for an average American newspaper in an average American city. The plot: a ridiculous and fanatical scientist puts the planet in peril through his experiments with gravitational pull. Superman controls electricity by flexing his biceps, flies to the stars and blows them to pieces with a head butt. Then he gets back into his sport coat, his felt hat, and kisses the secretary... Mixture of great imagination and unspeakable stupidity. S is the average and myopic American. Quite a fall from Nietzsche's *Übermensch*, who, even though he didn't catapult meteors into space, prefigured many things.

THE DEATH OF OTTO AND ALICE RÜHLE

June 24, 1943—Otto had suddenly taken to bed, heart attack. I telephoned to come see him. He asked me to wait till tomorrow. I had no great desire to see him laid up. I felt that, so solid, so proud of being solid as an old oak, he would find it painful to be seen old and weak and that he'd bristle at any solicitude. I overcame this feeling and two days later, on a sad afternoon before a rainfall, I rang their doorbell unannounced. I arrived before dusk in the middle of a downpour. An Indio was sheltered in the entrance. There was a faint light in the fourth-floor windows. No one answered at first when I rang the doorbell and I hesitated before ringing again. I understood that they wanted to be alone, alone with their struggle, and perhaps no human face could do anything for them anymore. I didn't want to call them on the phone. The downpour continued and night fell. Across the street, the yellow wall of Shirley Courts and the lowered iron curtain of the workshop where Jackson obtained the pickax to assassinate Trotsky. Solitude. A taxi suddenly broke the solitude and a young girl in a red cape got out and ran to seek shelter under the awning over the door. Delicate face, childlike and intelligent, wide brown eyes. Her red cape was a stunning sight in the desolation of the storm and the first fading of twilight. I thought that she was perhaps waiting for Alice to go upstairs with her and that her sparkling eyes would speak to Otto, whose hard face, with a bitter and worried expression, I saw collapsed into his pillow. But another car came from the opposite direction and the red cape ran to it—vanished. I rang in vain and then slowly walked away, hunched over and with a heavy step, down the Calle del Rhin under the rain . . . I was calm and deeply sad, but feeling a kind of secret contentment at not having seen Otto fighting against the unknown, I who could do nothing for him, he who, despite his intelligence and his will, could no longer do anything for himself. Without our knowing it, this was actually our last encounter.

L. said: "He might die in a few days, and he might also overcome this attack and live for years." I hadn't repeated this statement to Laurette. Superstitious feeling that the name of a dead man shouldn't be spoken when death could be so close.

A few days previously I met Alice in town. We'd walked along the Avenue of the 16th of September, in the sun and the crowd. "I began a little book," she told me. "I have to write it. I'm at a critical turning point in life, I think a lot about life conceived as a dream. My theme is that humanity is in a kind of half-waking dream and is approaching a true awakening...."

"But Alice," I said. "There are no readers or publishers for such visions. Try to summarize your ideas in an article that could be published by *Cuadernos Americanos*."[53] She saw I was right, since the practical spirit always won the day with her. Our discussion veered off to the subject of the differences in age in a couple. She'd just said, "The only goal in my life is Otto. I'm happy he feels better and has gotten back to work." I was perhaps wrong to speak of age differences and their seriousness, but Alice's remarks had alarmed me and I thought that it was possible to talk to her about almost anything. (I was right in this.) I said: "What is tragic about a couple with a wide age difference is that it must be reasonably accepted that one will go well before the other.... This is a terrible problem with no solution." Alice replied sharply: "No, we don't have any problem with this. Otto has always been younger than me, more dynamic, he's never thought about this. He sees his whole life before him, and he's so right." I had touched on a sore spot and we spoke of other things.

Another encounter with Alice, a week earlier, at the Quetzal bookstore. "Will you please come with me to a really disgusting café on Bolívar? Diamond sellers gather there and I'm going to try to sell a ring—this one, which is a souvenir of the past. I no longer need such souvenirs, I need money...." She explained to me that recently she had had the ring appraised and that in the course of one of these appraisals a stone had been replaced by a fake gem. Some too-elegant men in the café looked over the remaining gems and one of them gave her some good advice: "Don't sell it now. In three months your ring will double in value." I too advised her to borrow money in order to save time. "Let's get out of here," she said. "All they talk about is money." Between their cocoas all they did was talk about money in a confidential tone. "Where can 300 pesos be found, Alice, in this city full of millions?" "Yes, where," she said with a smile. We drew up (useless) plans.

At our house. I had told her a strange dream. She sketched an

53. Bimonthly literary review founded in 1941 by Spanish exiles. It appeared until 1984.

analysis of it, and then: "I too just had a strange dream. I was in Prague. We were taking a taxi, four of us, and we were riding around the city. There was my sister, who killed herself, another relative who also killed herself, someone else, and me. . . ."

Another time at our house. Sitting in front of the lamp, Alice has just read a poem of mine, "Suicide of Dr. C.," written in 1934 in Orenburg, which I'd forgotten and suddenly reconstructed in Mexico City while walking in the rain in 1941. Alice said: "For me, suicide is the most natural of things. There are many instances when I don't understand why people go on living."

As Claire Gr. tells it: "Alice called me at around 2:00. Drs. Becker and Fränkel had arrived an hour earlier and Otto was feeling better. Alice asked me to come over, since she wanted to go out for a minute; there was nothing to eat in the house and she wanted to pick up a few things. I came an hour later, Alice opened the door, calm and attractive, with the shadow of a welcoming smile on her lips. She softly said to me: 'I think it's all over, he's dead. Would you like to see him?' She'd already covered his face. I suggested calling a doctor. 'Yes, please. Go ahead,' she said, simply. There were letters on a table (dated Sunday, four days previously). I called from a neighboring grocery, the phone in the apartment being out of order (A. had cut it.) As I was leaving the store I saw Alice standing on the sidewalk then collapsing. The idea didn't occur to me that she'd thrown herself out of the window. As she fell she'd probably had the strength to right herself before completely collapsing. . . ."

"She'd had the idea of throwing herself out the window," Dr. Fränkel said. "I'd heard her say, 'If N. comes I'll jump from the balcony.'"

We interpreted her final decision in this way: Everything had long since been settled. The farewell letters written a few days ago. Alice had barbiturates and cyanide. As long as she was alone with Otto, who she sensed was dying, lucid and aware, she was calm. She was seized with panic at the idea that friends would come, that they'd affectionately embrace her, that she she'd have to see faces, do and say things. To see no one, not waste a minute, act quickly, quickly so that it would be nothing but a splintering crash—and the end.

She had a skull fracture, a fracture of the spinal column, the bones of one arm completely smashed, the other arm torn, and the pelvis smashed. They gave her a blood transfusion and she survived for an hour at the Red Cross, lucid all the while. She was interrogated, for social suspicion never loses its rights, and she repeated that she didn't want to survive Otto and that she was happy to die. Shots of morphine eased her suffering.

Black coffins with a kind of window at head height. It's at the Alcazar on the Calle de Tacuba, where Trotsky's body was laid out. Vast offices downstairs, a kind of administration of death, typewriters. They both have the same waxy green color. Otto's firm visage has collapsed, aged. He's an old man—which he never was—with a sloping forehead, eyes sunk into their sockets, his mouth closed and bitter. Death's expression on his face is one of desolation, bitterness, of a struggle that ended in defeat. He said three days ago: "But what's wrong with me? I have absolutely no intention of dying. I want to see the end of the war—and the outbreak of the revolution."

The asymmetry of Alice's face had been corrected. She often had one eyebrow noticeably higher than the other. Her forehead bulged from a wound. She's smiling. Her expression is one of calm, of contentment, with something tragically luminous about it.

The crematory oven of the Panteón Civil de la Dolores is a dismal gray building. As we offer our final farewells over the two coffins covered in red, the crackling of the fire, which sounds like burning wood, can be heard . . . Smoke escapes. The remains are pushed out of the coffins into the oven, with a low door of black metal. Workers fuss about with no particular haste to keep the fire going. Otto's body is put into the oven first. Alice waits, smiling, in her black box. Claire and Laurette are crying on a bench. Alice's India servant, who hasn't left the bodies for over thirty hours, stands sobbing, draped in a kind of brown wool habit. People are leaving. It seems there isn't any gas to burn Alice. Was there enough? Not enough? The workers argue with a supervisor. This will take some time yet: the human corpse burns poorly in this primitive oven. We leave. Alice remains alone in her coffin, waiting for the fire. "It pains me to leave her there, it's as if we were abandoning her," Laurette says to me. I gaze indifferently at the stones, the concrete, the monuments on the bourgeois tombs, which are rich and vain and in the worst bad taste—the ultimate vanity, in fact. Above that of the poet Amado Nervo* a kind of metallic catafalque has been built . . . It would be so humane to renounce all these accoutrements, these accoutrements of pride, stone, and cash, and bury the dead beneath beautiful trees and well-mowed grass.

July 6, 1943—At the Rühles'. Alice's coat and felt hat hanging near the door. Nothing has changed. The box with tiny silver chains that she tried to sell, the cardboard [. . .]⁵⁴ that we recently gave them, two bottles of cognac on the table, this familiar interior and us, intruders in the void. With F. B., Fritz Fränkel, E. K., we are preparing an inventory of the manuscripts. F. B. envisions publishing them later, in Europe or elsewhere. An American publisher just told him that "Marxism is of no interest right now." I say: "Either we publish or we perish."

Where can the work of a life of ideas be safely stored? There are only a handful of us in this city who understand its value. It would be impossible to entrust them to a library: the rats would devour them if the Stalinists didn't set fire to them. We speak of what was left in Europe, in Dresden: books, documents, manuscripts . . . "If the Nazis haven't destroyed everything," F. B. says, "and if Dresden hasn't been destroyed."

The telephone rings while we're working. The cord attached to the earpiece is cut. Who is calling by mistake—or unaware? *"Gespenstlich"* (ghostly), says Fritz.

E. K. was there for Alice's final moments at the Red Cross. She didn't suffer very much and died peacefully—all in all. Upon seeing her arrive Alice "apologized for causing this bother." Alice said that she wanted to die. "It's fine like this," and twice murmured: "Otto."

In her final letter, written the previous Sunday, "foreseeing the worst," Alice listed about fifteen people whom she thanked for their friendship. Only fifteen at the end of a life. She wrote: "My life was beautiful and rich, though my personality didn't allow me to get all I could out of it. It was quite long as well. . . . I hope that you'll see the better times we thought of, the socialist times. . . ."

Spoke of the serious disagreements between the B's and the Rühles.

54. Illegible.

When Alice met Otto she was twenty-eight and Otto's daughter was twenty. Otto lost his sexual potency just a few months ago, at sixty-eight, and this had affected him a great deal.

Upon learning of the catastrophe Mme. B.'s first remark to Claire Gr. was: I'm sure that Alice poisoned Otto and then killed herself. Mme. B. opposed the incineration of the two sets of remains together and even insisted on separating the ashes!

Formally disinherited by Alice, the stepson tells us that he asks only that he be allowed to keep the manuscripts and that he has no interest in the material inheritance. But on the day of the liquidation he came with a list of objects he is requesting as souvenirs: the watches, the two typewriters, the pens, and even an eiderdown comforter, the only bedding item of any value. But he didn't take the old man's glasses: they've been allocated to me.

RÜHLE—COWARDICE OF THE INTELLECTUALS

July 23, 1943—Discussion with Larrea* at *Cuadernos Americanos*. A Spanish intellectual of high quality, concerned with questions of philosophy and mysticism, with a rationalist turn of mind. Thinks that European culture is coming to an end through man's profound exhaustion and that it must "become American." I dispute his opinions. It is undeniable that the Western European is sick after a long century of flourishing and decaying capitalism. Has man been affected in his depths? I'm inclined to think not. Larrea says that civilizations grow worn out and wear themselves out.

Long face, gray eyes, aquiline nose, the expression of a nervous and tense personality.

I went there—as an experiment and out of duty—to propose an essay article on the Rühles, their ideas and activity. If it was only up to him he would immediately accept it, but he fears the effect my name will have. When I add that along with John Dewey, Otto Rühle proclaimed Trotsky's innocence and that this can't be ignored, Larrea says; "I wonder if our car could carry so much weight.... What matters most to me is that the cultural work continue" Me: "But what difference does cultural work make if it excludes civic courage, the courage to defend freedom and to speak of courageous people?" (I naturally soften my words.) He lets it be understood that if I dealt with other subjects, with literature or archaeology, for example (!!!) my name would pass, but that mentioning Trotsky in an article signed by me is truly frightening…"People are already saying that we're Trotskyists" (!!!) Me: That's precisely why, invited by León Felipe to collaborate more than a year ago I didn't propose anything to you. I would feel myself to be guilty of cowardice if I kept quiet about the things I needed to deal with, being the only one capable of doing so, even if I were to write about neutral subjects, even those that tempt me. Obviously the conversation goes nowhere. Larrea will speak with the editor and give me his answer in a week. Let us put the cowardice of intellectuals to the test one more time… They are constructed to degrade themselves under every form of tyranny as long as they're allowed to make a living and write criticism about Góngora or Maurois. What's strange is that in actual situations they are far more cowardly than it is reasonable to be. This is because the roots of their cowardice are deep: the fear, at bottom, of taking a firm stand and seeing clearly, because seeing clearly forces you to make a commitment. "Culture" allows them to escape into a fog of ideas and words, a sustaining fog, an alibi… Poor culture. Also bound by their material situation, vanity, money…

Early August—Larrea's response: "Dear friend.…The political situation not yet having been clarified (?!)…" His approaches to the editorial board have naturally failed. Their culture is one of alibis and nothing else. Filling the void, filling life while risking nothing. Nothing, not even simply shocking a few mediocre individuals; not taking the slightest real risk, assuming an attitude the tiniest bit true, that is, morally courageous.[55]

ZAPATA, CUERNAVACA, TEPOZTLÁN

July 23, 1943—Cuernavaca, with the de Ménils and the Malaquais. At the Palacio de Cortés (*ayuntamiento*) the clothing worn by Zapata the

---

55. The final paragraph added by hand.

day he was assassinated. Under glass. Enormous white straw sombrero, unornamented. Soldier's leggings, green cavalry pants of gray-green material. Big black spurs. Crafted leather holster. Long-barreled revolver. Brown cotton *cincuenta-centavo* socks; they're quite moving. The jacket is not there, too much blood flowed into it.

Beautiful road winding through switchbacks towards this landscape that, having seen it from the heights of Cuernavaca, I'd nicknamed "Franciscan" because it put me in mind of those delicate denticulated mountains that the Italian primitives painted in the background of a portrait or a view of a city. The road climbs and one can see an impressive rocky fortress looming, carved by erosion, wind, and rain into terraces, overlapping planes, towers and dungeons. Fantastic and feudal. Tepoztlán is in the valley at the foot of that fortress on which stands a little Indian sanctuary of days gone by. Uncluttered peaceful town, plaza, little market, meats. The big church fronted by a vast garden courtyard of noble abandon. A service taking place in the church. The nave, very vast and tall, well proportioned, gray, almost bare. The altar is simple. The organist, an old man in a white jacket, is playing a small organ and playing it well. Women are singing and singing well. The priest is assisted by boys in colored vests...

Dialogue between Jean and a fifteen-year-old boy with velvety eyes: "Do you believe in miracles? —Si, Señor. —If someone gave you a *tostón* or a peso or two pesos would that be a miracle? —No, Señor. —Do you know how to read? —A little. —Would you like to learn how to read well? —I would. —Why? —Because that would be good, I could read beautiful things. —Perhaps that's a miracle? —No, a miracle is something completely different and much greater."

He hadn't done anything for us and when Galy offered him a fifty-centavo coin he refused it: "Why?" They had to insist and to tell him to share it with a silent little friend before he agreed to take it with great dignity. "He's very nice," says J. de M. "The only way he could have answered you better would be by throwing a goat turd in your face."

Upon returning to the city I catch a glimpse of a newspaper headline in a restaurant: MUSSOLINI EXPELLED FROM POWER. We've been waiting for this day for more than twenty years. In 1931 I wrote (in *Literature and Revolution*): "We're not afraid to break with obligatory optimism, for we proceed from a confidence in the future that, even in the darkest hours, breaks all the bonds of pessimism. The Communists in Mussolini's prisons are the magnificent incarnation of the heroism of the proletariat and its faith in the future. The Gramscis and the Terracinis* know they are almost nothing at this time, that they could be assassinated tomorrow, that they will perhaps never see the light of day, but they understand history's inexorable laws, they know how parades end...."

ECONOMY AND PSYCHOLOGY

July 24, 1943—Conversation with Jean de Ménil on Mussolini's fall. From now on in our complex world economic determinism will, in politics, sometimes give way before psychological determinism. Power being concentrated, the choice of roads and methods depends on one man or on several, and consequently on their intellects. It is Stalin's character that gave Russian totalitarianism its monstrously bloody forms: an enlightened tyrant, one more intelligent, would at the very least have avoided the Moscow Trials.

Mussolini's fall was the direct consequence of an error he could have avoided committing. If, in June 1940, he hadn't stabbed defeated France in the back he would have kept Italian forces intact, America was pandering to him, and he would have had a chance to survive the world war, even while rendering services to the Third Reich, for which Italy was the weak point. It was his pride as an empire builder that led him down this fatal slope.

The same applies to Hitler. By attacking the USSR he committed suicide. Without the exhausting war in Russia he would have an army of several million men, not in the least demoralized, ready for a prolonged defensive resistance and capable of repelling any attempted invasion. He would draw on Russia for the economic resources he lost through the war. Soviet power, albeit a threat in the long term, left the present forces of the Reich intact at their highest point. But Hitler surrendered to his contempt for the Slavs, his contempt for Marxism, and his lack of understanding of socialism. He will die of them.

Note how the wind changes. I have heard thoughtful men—

revolutionaries—compare Hitler to Napoleon. People are beginning to see in him the great adventurer; that is, the man of a great historic adventure, inferior to his era and to his task.

SANTIAGO TIANGUISTENCO

Sunday, July 25, 1943—On the way to find Santiago Tianguistenco, where a fiesta has been announced. Meet up with Laurette in front of the church of S. T. Toluca road. We stop at Molino de Bezares and I say to de Ménil: "Come see my son's fresco, it's really beautiful...." "Restaurant Tippedi...." We climb the little stairs and there we are, in the stone-walled barn, in front of walls covered over with whitewash. The fresco has been killed. We find nothing say to each other.

... After Toluca it takes us more than two hours to travel forty kilometers via a narrow road hedged by corn fields on which we bump along, avoid nearly invisible obstacles, pass over dried out mountain streams, get stuck in rocky mud ... The site is limitless, the air on the heights fresh and healthy beneath the sun. Altitude 2,600 meters or more. The main street of a village, narrow, steeply sloped, is like the rocky bottom of a swift, twisting stream.

Finally, Santiago Tianguistenco. No activity. The square plaza, its kiosk, its squares, its cement benches like every plaza of that sort. The baroque church, tall and rather beautiful, preceded by a square courtyard behind white walls. A sermon is being preached in the church.

Twenty Indios in dirty white shirts and work pants kneel with their musical instruments and begin blowing them. They play well, with fervor, they are simple and fierce. The procession arrives, you can see two or three gentlemen in business suits carrying candles. A small, dark-red canopy, three priests beneath it, mestizos wearing glasses, ecclesiastical faces. They lead the cortege and the musicians successively to the four little altars decorated with faded silk and flowers. The crowd, women, children, Indios, many barefoot, humble and touching, kneel four times. A pounding sun. In the bell tower young men are exerting themselves swinging back and forth an enormous old bronze bell and ringing others. At the top of the tower, but outside it on a cornice, a young worker is leaning, posed like a Michelangelo. Suddenly rockets explode and shoot upwards, forming tiny clouds in the illuminated sky, like flowers of smoke at the tip of a white branch that trembles, vibrates, and fades. Bells and explosions, brass instruments and din. A Catherine Wheel spins with the loud noise of a fusillade, and the music and song are encircled by smoke.

The de Ménils knelt. Brief discussion with Jean and Galy, who see in all this nothing but clericalism and poverty, etc. Yet there is much more to it, the ardent faith of the poor, a faith whose roots plunge far beyond anticlericalism and clericalism. I say that these men would fight fanatically for Cristo Rey without asking for even one more tortilla. And these are the very people who expropriated the lands of the convents.

… In the countryside another tiny baroque church, mossy, very beautiful, surrounded by a rectangular enclosure of fresh grass and old trees. While young men are sweeping up noisily, women in black headscarves are softly singing the mass to themselves. Humility. Indios tell me that the town, almost invisible beneath the foliage, has more than two thousand inhabitants, three hundred of whom have jobs…

Pulquería Las Horas Felices…

The same day Laurette explored this region in a *camión*.

"They're amazing rolling boxes, the first buses of creation, never cleaned or patched up since they first started pitching and tossing along the road. Where there's room for twenty people a hundred manage to pile in, one on top of the other with total resignation, suffocating while the smothered children cry and chickens die in their baskets. The ticket taker is an eel-man who circulates around this human magma, treading on people seated on the floor. The roof of the bus is as overloaded as the interior. I saw feet covered with a layer of protective filth, as calloused as animal feet, hanging in front of the window. A child of fourteen months, as frail as a six-month-old, slept in my arms. Fleas, sweat, unspeakable poverty, illness, resignation, the Middle Ages. A watery-eyed old man nevertheless spoke, apropos of a shoving match that led to nothing, of 'defending right and justice.' When we came to the dried-out streambeds through which the unbelievable bus jounced, constantly seeming as if it was about to tip over, the women spoke of the fearsome '*barranca*,' of *autos* '*volada*,'[56] made the sign of the cross and prayed. Then they thanked God for having escaped without injury. Obviously it's dangerous. We're running alongside ravines and precipices, and in the event of an accident it would be impossible for anyone to pull free while the jalopy would immediately burst into flames.... The fare: one peso (from Toluca to Tianguistenco; this is six to eight times more expensive than the comfortable trip from Mexico City to Toluca.)"

Laurette's adventure in Tianguistenco (the *cacique*, fear, the inn under surveillance, the young men ready to be killed in her defense ...)

TEOTIHUACAN

July 27, 1943—Road along the high plateau running amid fertile fields (corn). This could well be Central Europe. All around, horizons of gray or blue-tinted mountains above which rise piles of clouds often pierced by a violent sun.

Seen from afar the pyramids of Teotihuacan look like tall termite hills flattened at the top, looming over the low vegetation. We approach them without feeling any special emotion. A small glass-roofed museum of red brick in the latest bad taste clashes with the site. One emerges at the foot of the Pyramid of the Sun and it is transformed into a vision that words can't express. The words "grandiose," "overwhelming," "inhuman" come pitifully to mind. They don't say anything, they are the words of Europeans, and we are before a concept of the world, an architecture that sprang from a human soul different from ours, formed, like ours, by the millennia, but by other millennia. The mountain is strictly geometrical, and so carefully thought out, built by the hands by workers (who had no domestic animals, no form of transport except the human backbone, but who nonetheless clearly had a highly ingenious system of ropes and pulleys), built of volcanic stone. Statistics: height, 60 m; sides, length 224 m, surface of the base, 50,143 m, approximate volume, 1,300,000 m. Except for this last dimension, these figures in no way account for the vision. The modest height seems

56. Fearsome ravines and cars blowing up.

overwhelming and inhuman because of the massive slopes and linear stairways, which trace a pattern on the stone like an embroidery in a single color. Man is nothing but an insect on these steps.

I was struck with vertigo before reaching the first of the five or six successive terraces. I split off from our group and wandered around the buildings at the lower levels. Cyclopean architecture. The mounds one walks over conceal other ruins. Some walls have kept a bit of their red coloring. Here and there the floor is made of slabs of an ancient black-ish cement. The entire pyramid must have once been covered in cement and painted, most likely in red. Back then, it flamed at sunset and sunrise, blazed at noon, stone, fire, noble lines, dominant thought as naked severity. In that world man must not have counted for much, either for himself or for society. What is symbolized is the absolute domination of man by the rigor of the universe and of the vision. Theocracy.

On the plain, between the ruins, grow nopals reaching a height of two meters. Tangled, opulent, bristling with and torn by thorns, they defend their powerful vegetal flesh against the void, a prisoner of their strength. This perfect plant, of a combative energy, is flawless: it has set its own limits for good and all. Refusing to be devoured, it is cruel. Armored with thorns, it is sure of itself and powerful on arid soil and in volcanic rock. That is all. Between this plant and the vanished so-ciety there is a striking inner community.

Between the nopals, I catch a glimpse of the Pyramid of the Moon, covered in greenery. It's a regularly shaped hill and it transforms the landscape. The vegetation strips it of its inhumanly human quality.

Throughout our visit an enormous fragment of a dazzling rainbow remains planted on the horizon like a wide scimitar of weightless fire whose gold, orange, and violet are intense.

TEOTIHUACAN—THE "*CIUDADELA*"

The overall setting is that of a vast sacred city laid out in straight lines.

The temple of Quetzalcoatl, nicknamed the *ciudadela*,[57] recalls a

57. Citadel.

Vauban fortification or evokes a Roman camp. Enormous square enclosure with low terraces which, viewed from the plain, look to be at ground level but in reality are rather elevated. The interior was capable of holding a hundred thousand people. The same sensation again on the staircases made of tuff. Seen head-on they look to be smooth, but when you're on them you're between two waves of stone and the steps can barely be made out.

Part of the temple itself has been restored, badly it seems (Paul Rivet*). Whatever the case, the view is extraordinary, that of a world we cannot know. You pass under a steep slope of massive stone, down a narrow road cut at a right angle and emerge facing a gray-and-rust-colored wall, overwhelming, bristling with enormous heads of hieratic snakes and ornaments that are neither geometrical nor living, of supple and harsh lines, tiled surfaces, marked with four circles resembling eyes. These circles, like the enormous eyes of snakes, might have contained crystals. Here and there traces of reddish coloring. I think of the poverty of our imagination and the richness of the imagination of men. This architecture of such simple means is inconceivable for us: the Cyclopean slope, the straight or angular cutoff, the terrace, the smooth and dizzying staircase, the hieratic snake, the symbol with its snake teeth and four eyes (if they are eyes), which is perhaps nothing but a hieroglyphic.[58] Nothing could be less compatible with these works than the Gothic cathedral, all columns and upward thrust, expressing at one and the same time mysticism, individualism, and the community. Whoever conceives and understands the latter can neither conceive nor understand the former.

I have the impression that I'm contemplating one of the most intense things that can be seen in this world: that of being in direct contact with a humanity completely different from our own, which we can perhaps touch only through the very depths of life: the enormous material effort of labor and the abstract sovereignty of geometry. I also have the impression of seeing almost nothing of what I glimpse. You would have to wander alone here under an incandescent sun, in the starry night, in the bewitching moonlight. One would perhaps then

58. Though the Mayas, Aztecs, Totonacs, and Olmecs did use pictograms, "hieroglyphs" is not the proper word for them.

obtain a feeble notion of the contemplation imprisoned in these stones: terror, elevation, magic, will.

FRESCOES IN CHOLULA

July 30, 1943—Tunnels excavated inside the Great Pyramid of Cholula, below the cathedral.[59] Well-preserved frescoes run along a buried facade, topped by massive painted cornices. They uniformly depict death's heads, four or five times larger than life, with enormous eyes and powerful teeth—or a bird's head that looks like a death's head. Red, black, yellow, and blue green, the features done in black. When the colors were fresh, the pyramid, ringed by these intense masks blazing in the sunlight, must have imposed a symbolism horrifying in its monotony and harshness.

Beneath the terrace of the church we (Dominique and Jean de Ménil) suddenly see Popo in bluish mauve, with its point of brilliantly shining snow encircled by shifting clouds. Thus the gods showed themselves.

Cholula is supposed to have been the cradle of the civilizations of Monte Albán, Teotihuacan, and Tenochtitlan. The most ancient pyramid is said to date from the first century after Jesus Christ.

AMECAMECA

July 30, 1943—Overcast weather. As we began the climb to the church of Señor de Monte Sagrado, which sits atop an isolated mountain above the small town, we see a group of a dozen pilgrims in front of the higher stations of the cross, several women, some young men, a corpulent gentleman with a European face, a vigorous forty-year-old face, thick brown eyebrows, a small, trimmed beard, deep-set brown eyes. Shabbily

---

59. The Great Pyramid of Cholula, larger than the pyramids of Egypt, was covered with vegetation at the time of the conquest. It was mistaken for a mountain and a cathedral was built on its flat summit. In the 1930s archaeologists dug five miles of tunnels through it, revealing inner chambers dating from earlier overbuilt pyramids. On the horizon looms the majestic pyramid of Popocatepelt's snowcapped volcano.

dressed in a canvas jacket girded by a monk's rope, he is climbing the hill on his knees, stopping in front of each station along the road, indicated by an earthenware plaque bearing a text. It is he who loudly intones the prayers that the others—who are also climbing on their knees, sometimes standing up to rest, which he never does—take up in chorus. These voices, in a slow rhythm, quiver and rise in the solitude.

As we pass the group we see that an old Indian woman of at least seventy, stubbornly walking on her knees, is at the head. She raises her eyes to us, which seem to me full of wrath. We are perhaps foreign to them, and insulting—men without faith. But they told Jean de Ménil that they were praying for us and for peace and, upon learning that he is French, for France. Jean de M. rejoins us, touched, and I tell him: "I'm happy you gave them an impression that we aren't boors." Malaquais complains of the delay and condemns religious superstition, etc.

Before reaching the upper terrace, the fetish tree, an old tree with a bumpy trunk and spread-out roots, the object of a cult. A number of meaningful offerings are suspended from it: sandals, braids, locks of hair, linens, children's clothing... Someone says that it's "a disgusting sight." Rivet explains that the two cults, that of the tree and that of the church, complement and complete each other, and that the church was probably built on this summit because the mountain was holy. In any case, it is exactly what a holy mountain should be: it dominates an endless landscape and seems to rise up over a world. And in clear weather, it confronts the two masses of snow, rock, and light of Ixtaccíhuatl and Popocatépetl, the reclining woman and the virile spur,[60] which takes on rose tones of fire and flesh at dusk.

The nearly dead olive tree at the top surrounded by a fence with this inscription—in writing imitating an ancient manuscript—written in blue on earthenware: *"Bajo este olivo Fray Martín de Valencia de coro con los aves loaba al Señor."*[61]

---

60. The outline of Ixtaccíhuatl resembles that of a woman reclining (the volcano is also called the Sleeping Woman) while the conical shape of Popocatépetl recalls the male sex organ.

61. "Beneath this olive tree Brother Martín de Valencia, in chorus with the birds, praised the Lord."

Below, under the light rain, Rivet explains to me the origins of American man, the three prehistoric migrations: the Asians via the Bering Strait; the Polynesians and other Asians via the islands of Oceania; the Australians-Melanesians via the Antarctic. American ethnologists contest this theory. They want American man to have had only Nordic-Asian origins.[62]

OAXACA—SANTO DOMINGO

July 31, 1943—Oaxaca. Otto Rühle and Alice returned from there with an impression of poverty, sorrow, and boredom. It was their last trip. I can understand that Otto already carried within him the discouragement of his final days. His eyes no longer saw things with the love of life that reveals them and gives them life. He was defeated (doubtless as much by bitterness as by a sudden involution of the organism).

My impressions are completely different from his. Small Spanish town, clean and beautiful, beneath a sun that beats down like a cudgel. Laurette says that the sun weighs on your entire body like a physical object. Beautiful tall trees, raised kiosk, arcades, cafés with outdoor terraces, shops on the *zócalo*.[63] (I find a cloth merchant there, a Polish Jew with whom I speak Russian and who answers showing no sign of surprise.) The churches are massive and austere, built of large rectangular stones, yellow gold or pale green colored, with scant ornamentation. They make you think of fortresses, but with sumptuous sculpted gates. We visit Santo Domingo.[64] The interior porch has a low ceiling with a magnificently sculpted high vault (sculpted white wood). A genealogical tree bears saints, life-sized human figures that are intensely alive. The ceiling of the level above this porch is also sculpted, and light penetrates in gilded profusion, producing the image of two superimposed works. Nave, apse, and choir, all the high vaults are painted and sculpted, with a richness that does not overwhelm you despite the lavishness of the gold and colors, of the lines and circles. It is a continuous blaze,

62. The last sentence added by hand.
63. Central square.
64. The convent of Santo Domingo de Guzmán.

JULY 1943 · 299

geometrical and alive, where bad taste is swallowed up in the overall effect. The highest of the vaults, above the transept, is dizzying, with a blue sky painted at its highest point. Churrigueresque,[65] the organized delirium of the baroque, of a baroque overheated by the Mexican sun. This land produced riches and exaltation, it gave a sense of power that had much to atone for—and which admired itself. It's also certain that the colonizers found remarkably intelligent laborers among the Indios, who were immediately able to adapt to the needs of European art.

THE VOLTAIRE

At the trading post of M. B., French ex-consul who resigned so as not to serve Vichy, we have the impression of an opulent colonial emporium. Textile shop, a large patio full of plants and little aviaries where red and green birds go all aflutter when we approach them and fly from one end of their big cages to the other, then return to examine you with their tiny shining eyes, which are ringed by colored circles... Stocks of brightly painted pottery manufactured for sale to Americans. The master's living quarters are full of Dufayel furniture,[66] but contain an extraordinary Indian work that Rivet immediately requests for the Musée de l'Homme...It's made of wine-red terra-cotta (about fifty centimeters in height), a human mask, small, encircled with ritual ornaments analogous to those we will see around the figurine on tomb 104 in Monte Albán. A high and wide tiara with plumes and jewels, widely fanned out, sits atop the mask. The work is delicate, the material seems to have grown out in all directions, like a plant. What's most striking is the human mask, which is lifelike and lively, with a smile of irony, or even of mischief. "But it's Voltaire," I say, "the *Zapoteco* Voltaire!" and this is the name we give the work. The almond-shaped eyes shift their gaze when you change the angle at which you're standing, the pupil being represented by a detail elevated by the hollowness of the eye.

Another work, of perfect simplicity of synthesis: a round stone, well

65. Spanish baroque style widespread in New Spain, characterized by abundant ornamentation.
66. Large furniture store in Paris.

polished, presents on one of its sides the clear and faint sketch of a human face, life-size. Its lines and surfaces are so faint that you need to shade your eyes to see them clearly. And this face is neither masculine nor feminine; it's gentle, severe and simple, algebraic.

M. B. sells antiques to Americans. A thriving business.

The marketplace is a universe. I rediscover all the faces of Central Asia there, and it surely contains all the faces of Asia, but the flesh is more fiercely dark, almost completely lacking in yellow tones. I am forever struck by the unity of primitive peoples. This is both obvious and mysterious, since no direct link can be found between this civilization and those of Asia and Africa. People acquainted with the markets of Morocco say that they give the same impression. It must be admitted that the human foundation is a common one, as the various types demonstrate, and that the primitive economy succeeds in creating common forms of life. Women here have a fondness for white blouses decorated with red or green embroidery. The market women, squatting in front of their merchandise, are breastfeeding their children. An overabundance of fruits, peppers, cold cuts (blood sausages), diced up and cooked pigs and lambs, all of this greasy, red, giving off a heavy odor of animal grub. A square bazaar rimmed with arcades, a pump in the middle, exactly like Russian bazaars, a courtyard of potters and basket weavers. Small objects of ground and carved lava. A variety of whistles and tiny bells with a lovely tinkle. A young Kalmyk girl wears a wreath of white onions on her head ... The Indian pharmacies with their dried plants, shells, goat and lamb bones (which are rubbed together to ease rheumatic pains). An old witch with abundant white hair floating down to her shoulders, with gray-black eyes veined in red and an exquisitely regular, aquiline profile offers us her remedies and, with great dignity, allows herself to be photographed by Jean de Ménil, whose embarrassed maneuvers she pretends not to notice. Sun, sun, faces, faces of the unknown—yet so close—man.

MONTE ALBÁN—THE TREASURE

July 31, 1943—Little museum of Oaxaca, said to be the former gendarmerie building, white patio. In one corner, a policeman has put down his rifle and is busy braiding something with brightly colored wool. The treasure room is well fitted out, display cases with electric lights, indirect lighting from the ceiling. One is dazzled by this unique wealth. Each object represents an incalculable amount of labor executed with the most basic of tools by men who attained the summit of their craft, masters of their materials and animated by the breath of great art. A perfectly formed cup of rock crystal was probably worn down by sand and water. The most delicate golden jewels were molded using the lost wax process imported from Peru. Pendants with tiny, elongated bells, a sacramental ornament representing a vigorous and elegant human head topped with diadems and tall feathers in a square fan, above a kind of breastplate overloaded with hieroglyphics. All of this barely ten centimeters square. Hollow amber wheels of rock crystal or gold served as earrings. All the circles are perfect. Necklaces of coral, of shells with carnal tints. Skull decorated with turquoise mosaics (one sees the origin of today's *calaveras*). Antiquity: the Zapotec sanctuaries of Monte Albán go back to the third century after Jesus Christ, the Mixtec conquest to the eleventh?

While an excessively seedy little man, with the features of a rat, red eyes, and a stammer, shows us the jewels kept under wraps, which he takes from a cookie box filled with cotton, the guard in light-gray uniform never takes his eyes off our hands. He has a large, almost black, head, thin lips, eyes elongated but not slanted, the head of a Mexican idol, impassive and benevolent, and he occasionally, slightly creasing his eyelids, makes a feeble attempt at a smile. "*Estoy siempre listo*,"[67] he says, showing his beautiful teeth. The museum guards fuss around us as well: one can see they love their work and riches.

They show us a Zapotec (Mixtec) codex that hasn't yet been studied. It's a large white cloth, perhaps two square meters, covered in black drawings with a small amount of blue, dating from the conquest; probably the story of a family or a tribe with paths indicating their migrations. Spanish horsemen are drawn on one of the edges. During the revolution this codex, duly folded, served as a saddle blanket for a partisan: horse sweat imprinted the shape of the saddle on the cloth.

67. "I'm always ready."

Tomb 107, when it was opened, was full of mephitic air, so poisoned that it extinguished fire. It had to be aired out before it could be entered. In it were found disassembled jewelry, blackened and shining, mixed in with earth and debris. There was so much that an archaeologist's two little daughters, as they separated them out, said: "I'll just pick out the gold and you the jewels and shells...." (told to Laurette by M.).

What emotion do these objects give rise to? There is astonishment before the work done by unknown hands for unknown eyes; men so distant from us and to whom we suddenly feel so close that we can communicate with them, since they had the same slightly magical feeling for ornamentation and the expression through ornament of a vision of the world and man's nobility. The vertigo of the centuries and the surprise at finding ourselves there—of being present. For me, the feeling of human community across tombs and unknowable history. I think of the Heleno-Scythian antiquities of the Hermitage and the mediations they plunged me into. They resemble these by the fineness of their gold work, as well as by their naturalism and stylization. There the motif of the reindeer of the polar regions joined with the perfect outlines of Greek dancing women, birds, eagles with unfurled wings, the ancestors of heraldic eagles.

OAXACA, MONTE ALBÁN

August 1, 1943—Limitless circle of nearly barren mountains; below, the crops growing in the valley, the churches and the town of Oaxaca. We climb arid slopes and the circle expands, the blue, gray, and green planes are stacked one on top of the other. Suddenly, Monte Albán, unforgettable fortress of mountains that are temples covered in earth and meager vegetation, and the sober, clear pyramids, their air of incomprehensible fortresses, their staircases, their profile of gilded stone at right angles. It is immense: from the top of one pyramid you can see another twenty, some uncovered and reconstructed, others barely emerging from the earth, and you realize that under all the nearby elevations are probably edifices still to be excavated. The holy city must have been the size of a large modern city. Zapotec civilization, later ruled by the Mixtecs. Probably dates to the first years of the Christian era, with origins far more distant still. Style analogous to that of Teotihuacan, but richer, more varied, less cyclopean. Bas reliefs showing human forms, probably gods, bent, with realistic profiles and big heads; hieroglyphic elements. The ruins of houses with water pipes. The ball game,[68] completely restored on the side of a hill from which the entire countryside can be seen, is a stone ditch into which you descend via long, rectangular, steep steps. The massive ball of raw (?) rubber, would bounce off the steeply inclined walls, the players would receive it on the kidneys and, with a movement of the hips, try to knock it into one of the square niches in the corners (?).

Close encounter with a tiny green lizard who flees at my approach and then turns around and gazes at me for a long time. A little further on, a block of stones of a luminous gray, almost white, sculpted, evokes an upright sign with a large head, idol or image. And solitude.

Tombs. They were probably painted in bright blues, greens, or reds that are still fresh, solid profiles of warriors or priests, of a design similar to that of the Nahuatl codex. Above the entrance the figure of a plumed divinity decorated with massive necklaces, like the Zapotec Voltaire, but with a more banal expression, alert, showing its tongue (terra cotta). Tomb 107, where the treasure was found: remains of a fresco, the carved stone slab that closed it up.

OAXACA-MITLA

August 1, 1943—Flat country, the valley, the crops bright green although poor, the earth cracks beneath the heat of the sun. There haven't been any big rains in two years. The entry into the little town is astonishing. Alleys open out lined on both sides with tall, bright green *órganos* that form fences and reach a height of two or three meters. The car advances between these spiked hedges, into an emerald-green vegetal world. A

68. *Juego de pelota, pok-ta-tok* (for the Mayas) or *tlachtli* (for the Aztecs). Ritual game widespread in Mesoamerica.

plaza, enormous trees, set apart, with abundant, spindly foliage. Tiny marketplace. Beribboned Zapotec women in black dresses, some very young and carrying their babies, rush over to us to offer us fake figurines, shawls, and fabrics. They too could well be from Africa, tanned, copper skinned, with broad faces and rather beautiful teeth.

The ruins are those of a city of palaces rather than of temples, very different from the pyramids, but conceived with the same geometry of square courtyards and steep stairways—like the *ciudadela* of Teotihuacan. Low structures, about four meters high, decorated with symmetrical panels, all of whose motifs are borrowed from the Greek with great wealth of imagination. We see rounded forms, derived from the Greeks, only in an underground passage, a vast rectangular courtyard with a low altar in the middle. Small rooms, also decorated inside, traces of red on the stone. The rooms are long and narrow and were probably divided into bedrooms giving onto the terraces. Massive square entryways, enormous monolithic lintels.

The colonial church was constructed over the palaces themselves, with materials borrowed, in part, from them. Its wall merges on the right with that of the Zapotec buildings. In the latter we see fragments of deep red frescoes covered with hieroglyphics along the edge of the vanished roofs (the style of the codices). The guards are Indios who have spent their lives here, obliging and smiling. A handsome man in a sombrero, a loose short-sleeved short, white with red stripes, white pants, sandals, a bushy moustache, weather-beaten skin, and big sunken eyes under the strong arch of the eyebrows. The other, with the museum cap, has a delicate face taut with long wrinkles, so coppery it looks black. He teaches us a few words of Zapoteco—it's a musical language with singsong, hissing intonations, which makes me think of Russian.

From the plaza a small pyramid can be seen on top of which they built a low chapel, doors open, candlelight in the shadows within. Rivet explains that in order to superimpose one belief on another the church was built on top of the temple—and the two religions united in one dual sanctuary, one killing the other, though not completely. Farther away, on the mountain, the cyclopean wall of an ancient fortress.

CITIES IN THE SKY

Return at nightfall. Suddenly, the clouds and the sun project landscapes, veritable mirages onto the sky into which we are descending. A blue seacoast, a large port with golden basins, islands floating on lustrous waters somewhere to the north, in Alaska or Siberia...The colossal form of a kneeling devil rises from leaden clouds, staring attentively at something. From below mauve and white lightning flashes intermittently illuminate it amidst a chaos of aerial mountains. And then the form imperceptibly turns and flips and becomes a human profile, gigantic, with distorted lips. Fritz would say that we're using the sky as a psychological test. I think of how primitive man saw the gods in this way and established contact with inaccessible worlds. Laurette, the most imaginative of us, was the first to discover these visions and, as soon as she spoke of them they become obvious and real.

TLACOLULA

The end of the market day at Tlacolula, pottery, fabrics, buses filled with departing people (boxes for piling human beings into). The church with its large, grassy courtyard in front of it. Small church to the side, splendid, like an old reliquary, its interior of finely worked silver, patinated, dusty. We walk through the half light and the jewelry. A small caravel is suspended from the vault, offered as an ex-voto by sailors who escaped danger thanks to the Virgin of Tlacolula...

TULE

As night falls we arrive at Tule, which I like to pronounce Thule—he was a king... *Plazoleta*,[69] white church decorated with garish blue paintings, probably very effective. What's amazing here are the trees. The oldest is a cathedral of spindly foliage beneath which is an old trunk made of a hundred trunks gathered into one, broad as a good-sized building, with endless mysteries, hollows, nooks, profiles suddenly

69. Small square. The word *plazuela* is more often used.

appearing, monsters, arches, lairs. How many men holding each other's hands would it take to encircle it? Thirty? Fifty? This tree is said to be two thousand years old. (Sabino, conifer...) It is imposing, wrinkled, hollowed, like an ancestor of the world.

LAND OF CACTI

August 2, 1943—Heading north out of Oaxaca Laurette and I, sitting on the step of the rear platform of the car (the last car), the landscape whizzing by. The train rocks and bumps along the narrow way that snakes along between sheer, occasionally overhanging cliffs and a ravine, at the bottom of which a little stream rushes over white stones. The site is as magnificent and wild as those of the northern Caucasus. On all sides sharp peaks whose gentle slopes are covered with low shrubs, for the rocks bear very little soil. Hours pass without our seeing an Indian hut or a plot of farmland. Sterility. Rocks and dull green, low bushes. A froth of fog hangs around the summits. The lost stations with two or three habitations are called Etla, Magdalena, Santiago Suchilquitongo, Telixtlahuaca, Ardilla, Las Sedas, Escondida.

And then the countryside changes, the rock is lighter, gray or yellowish, the stream swells into a magnificent *arroyo* filled with a mass of fallen rocks; there are fewer shrubs but cactus begins to dominate the world and soon reigns virtually alone. The masses of *órganos* explode and rule. They are enormous chandeliers with countless branches held aloft by a solitary or by multiple trunks and reach, I think, four or five meters in height with a volume on the same scale. Some are a deep green, others a green-gray-silver impregnated with light. The highest branches are perfectly straight. The entire tree bristles with countless thorns. When the rounded hills appear at a distance from the train they're striped from summit to base with thin perpendicular lines, which are simple "fence-post" *órganos*. Almoloyas, Organal, Temillín. Just before Temillín the rails passes through a narrow defile, between cracked reddish rocks whose stratifications are so distorted they form the letter "S." And in this world of red rocks, under a sky streaming light and blazing heat, the *órgano* lives alone, at the height of its power. This landscape is probably unique. The aloes reappear only further north, when the cacti loses lose their vigor and become increasingly rare.

Small coal mines, we pass through stations cluttered with sacks. Mules wait for their loads. Slowness, immobility, sun. The *arroyo* becomes a low, at times rather wide river running over a rocky bottom. White wading birds land on the water. Very few birds; the great heat causes them to take shelter.

Arid lands. The first town is Tehuacán, more than halfway between Oaxaca and Puebla (366 km).

COMMUNIST ATTACK IN MEXICO CITY

August 4, 1943—One might have hoped that the formal dissolution of the Comintern and the arrival in Mexico City of Soviet ambassador Umansky* would, at least for a time, put an end to Communist attacks on antitotalitarian socialist refugees. But this isn't the case. *El Popular* recently published unambiguous death threats against me. The president of the Society of Friends of the USSR, José Mancisidor* attacked us in *Todo* magazine, once again denouncing my friends Julián Gorkin, Marceau Pivert as well as me—along with Leon Blum!—as the "leaders of Goebbels's Fifth Column."[70] Finally, last Sunday (August 1), during a private meeting of Catalan socialists at the Orfeo Catalan, that is, at the club of the Catalan republicans, a group of Spanish Communists burst in and attacked the attendees. The journalist Jordi Arquer,* author of a work on the Catalan phenomenon, which was just published here, received a serious head wound; professor Enrique Gironella, editor of *Mundo*, who had been seriously wounded (skull fracture) at the Communist attack on the Ehrlich and Alter meeting of April 1, was wounded in the arms and legs; Doctor Tusso, former director of the Barcelona hospital, former deputy mayor of Barcelona, known for his generous social activity, was struck. Once the raid was carried out, the Communists fled before the police could be called. These attacks recall nothing as much as the exploits of the Italian

---

70. The article was published in the April 24, 1943, issue of *Todo*. Serge wrote a lengthy reply, dated May 5, which was not published.

Fascists against the houses of the people at the time of Mussolini's march to power.

SURREALISM'S ADAPTATION

August 6, 1943—In 1926–1928 they were shouting "Down with France!" and wondering if suicide was a solution—and it was one for Jacques Rigaut and René Crevel. They published *La Révolution Surréaliste*, delegated Aragon to the Kharkov Congress,[71] called Barbusse "an old pain in the ass," adopted Marxism, defended exhibitionism, etc. In 1936 Breton was a Trotskyist. In 1937, upon his return from Mexico, he lectured on L. T. at the Fourth International and belonged to our Committee of Inquiry on the Moscow Trials. In 1941, at Air-Bel, the mere mention of the words "officer," "admiral," "priest," or "religion" sent him into a sputtering rage, and he pulled a face when, during the English bombardment of Marseille, Laurette and I went out at night to watch the points of white flame explode in the distance, near the port… And now I read in *VVV*,[72] *Almanach 1943*, his "Speech to the Students of Yale," lavishly written, by the way. He speaks of combating Hitler, Mussolini, and the mikado, without the least allusion to totalitarianism in general and Stalinism in particular. The word "revolution," which Wells and so many liberals currently throw about, figures nowhere in this essay, nor the names of Marx or Trotsky. For the initiated he demonstrates his fidelity by a line on the dialectic of Heraclitus and Hegel, grandfathers not likely to be compromising. Compared to André Breton, Dorothy Thompson looks like a daring revolutionary. This could be entitled "A Moderate Discourse for Right-Minded Students," and this discourse comes after preposterous praise for some lackluster men of letters capable of doing moderate favors and who are designated "great initiates."… Nevertheless, the *Almanach*, especially its illustrations, still has an irritating and interesting originality, perhaps still alive. The banal middle-aged mellowing of A. B.?

71. The International Conference of Proletarian and Revolutionary Writers.
72. *VVV*, Surrealist review published in New York from 1942 to 1944 and edited by Breton, with the collaboration of Marcel Duchamp and Benjamin Péret.

I also meet Pierre Mabille. He's completely round: his head and his face, with big round eyes, a fleshy and round mouth, corpulent, round on round, flabby and beefy, a bestial thickness—one senses the heavy eater who loves himself above all else and takes delight in himself as a gastronome. Comfortably dressed, intelligent, talks to everyone with detachment and skepticism, friendly and charming, gets along with everyone, mixing together in his ironic conversation—with occasional flashes of conviction—voodoo, astrology, medicine, Gaullism, Marxism, ex-Surrealism, and so on and so forth. Harsh in his judgments of people, but only of those who are of no use to him. A Trotskyist, he recently dined with Ambassador Umansky and Simone Téry,* and suddenly he's the favored physician of the wives of the big French businessmen here. He offers himself the pleasure of committing himself—in his own eyes and those of a few friends—all the while committing to nothing in reality and even demonstrating consummate skill in profitable maneuvers.

Their revolt was nothing but a revolt of literary cafés. The system serves as their justification. Their worldview is nothing but a spiritual game that serves to aggrandize them before the internal mirror in which they admire themselves in private. Theirs is a mutual admiration society that leads to many pinpricks. What part did the love of publicity play in André Breton's admiration-friendship for Trotsky? At the very same time Breton was writing (*Minotaure*[73]) a flatly servile paean of praise to a Mexican minister, General Almazán.

Yet there was, there is, something profound, alive, a kind of painful and daring revelation in Surrealism. It's just that the Surrealists are rather small compared with their discovery.

MIL CUMBRES[74]

August 19, 1943—With Jean Malaquais and Galy, Chita de la C. and Paule Mathieu, the Morelia-Pátzcuaro road. Meal in the shade of a

---

73. Surrealist review published between 1933 and 1939. Breton and Mabille were on the editorial board.
74. Literally, "A Thousand Summits."

wood on the way to Morelia. We drive through alternating rains and sunshine. Mil Cumbres, at some 240 kilometers from Morelia at an altitude of around 2,600 meters, is an immense site that reveals itself to us beneath clouds, blue rains, sun peeking through, vistas of luminous sky, and fog floating on numberless peaks—there might well be a thousand. It's the earth's outer bark that we see, wrinkled, pleated, with its green points that look like pyramids and form a continuous line of slightly pointed heights, ravines, and slopes always covered in green lichens, which, when we approach, are the beautiful foliage of temperate climates with bursts of nopal and cactus. What bourgeois imbecile titled a book *Nothing but the Earth*?[75] The sight of great terrestrial space is as intoxicating as a strong wine, one that would procure a winged lucidity, an exaltation simply oscillating between the desire to sing and the desire to leap from the crest of these heights, as if all one had to do was unfurl one's wings. This landscape stretches out along the road for a good hour's drive. Solitude, not a house in sight.

PÁTZCUARO

August 20, 1943—The Posada de Don Vasco in Pátzcuaro, an expensive hotel for American tourists in the old Spanish style, recently built, spacious patios, an incredible Victorian salon with armchairs upholstered in flowered fabric. Old women gloomily converse there, looking like powdered frogs. Their conversation has only two ranges: gastric self-centeredness and malicious gossip. Their sole purpose in life was to procreate, and that's probably enough.

The hotel is expensive; they charge as much as ten pesos per bed. Clean and tasteless food in a large dining hall where groups of gringos display their athletic or puritanical boredom. Few expressive faces. The Mexican waitresses wear long, clean skirts that hang down to the floor, like Gypsies.

In the evening we play a game of questions and answers, with some success.

75. *Rien que la terre*, by Paul Morand, published in 1926.

"What is the lake of Pátzcauro?" (Me)

"It's the arrival of a long-awaited ship on a desert isle." (Gordon [Onslow Ford*])

"What is magic?" (Me)

"The flower that awakens a revelation in you." (G.)

"What is morality?" (G.)

"The darkest night with only one star." (Me)

"What is happiness?" (G.)

"It's the simplicity of the dream." (M.)

"What is poverty?" (M.)

"Above all, bestiality." (Jacqueline Onslow Ford)

"What is Rimbaud?" (M.)

"The unavowed End." (J.)

"What is shame?" (J.)

"Obscurity." (M.)

"What is destruction?" (M.)

"Strength with an internal weakness." (J.)

What is drunkenness?" (J.)

"An extinct volcano." (M.)

In the morning, the great lake is stretched out like a gentle mirror of the sky. In the distance to the right, above hills still blue, rises an immobile column of dense clouds, somewhat more compact and greyer than the clouds, dense and stagnant at the base, wider and wider as it climbs, like an enormous bouquet of vapors rising high into the sky: this is the smoke of Paricutín.[76]

Prodigious starry night over the lake. It seems incomparable to me, more scintillating and richer than the most beautiful nights I have experienced, even those of Orenburg, with their blue constellations spread wide over the steppes, their phosphorescence muted by the snow; more light streaming than at Pointe-de-Bout in Martinique, where I could see the Polar Star and the Southern Cross at the same time, while on both sides of a tongue of land feeblish waves caressed the sand with low song. Such a profusion of stars that I try in vain to situate just one.

76. One of the youngest volcanos in the world, "born" February 20, 1943 (see entry dated February 22, 1943).

Those of the first magnitude disappear in this astral tide. The lake is a deep black. On the near horizon, covered with clouds, lightning flashes out with such regularity that we wonder if there isn't a lighthouse on the other side of the lake. It is only the breath of the storms that surround us.

PÁTZCUARO—O'GORMAN

August 20, 1943—A small town, old province of Spain, plaza with old trees, arcades, pink and blue frescoes. Gates of carved wood close off the patios behind the street entrance. A street curves around a steep hill, with wide awnings in front of low houses; the green grass of the pavement. On the corner a fountain for the washerwomen with a fresco showing a saint dressed as a horseman bringing down a dragon.

The movie house bears the name of a Tarasco *emperador*...[77] Next door, a church has been converted into a spacious library, with worktables well laid out and lighted. The apse, tall and wide, is completely covered by a fresco by Juan O'Gorman* representing a vision of the conquest of pre-Cortés Mexico, inspired by syntheses of Rivera, but airier, constructed with more vivid colors, where the blue sumptuously stands out. It's perfectly drawn, rich with symbols, lively, powerful. I think of O'Gorman, that tall, thin lad with his tattered clothes, his long face tattered as well, who speaks with a kind of doubt in his gaze, a lack of assurance, knows all too well his limits, seems only with great difficulty to surmount a serious inferiority complex, scrupulously ponders the problems of Marxism, seldom dares to express an opinion... The other day I asked him for an article for *Mundo*. "Completely out of the question," he said. "Why?" "I don't know how to write. I know how to paint a fresco, to construct a house, to teach math, but I'm incapable of writing." This pleased me. The houses he builds have extremely narrow staircases straight out of medieval prisons, tiny kitchens and bathrooms like those on poor boats, exterior staircases uselessly suspended over the void, narrow bedrooms in a row, like corridors, and (in his house) without doors. The strictly rationalist and utilitarian

77. "Tarascos" was the name the Spaniards gave the Indians of Michoacán.

architect feels a fear of space that dominates his calculations and which he poorly compensates for by vistas of the void. He lives with a tall American woman with nearly red hair and strained features, stretched by the harshness of life ... Standing before his fresco I am happy to see him capable of a work so strongly constructed, so conscientious.

Teatro del Emperador Caltzontzin. The city guards the memory of Don Vasco de Quiroga, bishop and governor appointed by Charles V, protector of the Indios, builder of churches. Pátzcuaro, in Tarasco: place of delights.

August 21, 1943—Erongarícuaro, eighteen kilometers from Pátzcuaro via a road that goes through several villages along the lakeshore: nopals, maize, a church, generally pink. Gordon and Jacqueline Onslow Ford live in El Molino, a large house hard against the hill on the edge of the lake. Gordon thinks that there used to be Tarasco constructions on this spot, and he shows me a loaf of cut earth full of household debris, fragments of vases, animal bones. From the house's terrace the lake is slate-colored, vast, with bright reeds lining the bank below and gentle hills, pearly, green on the other side. It could very well be a lake in Italy, and I'm gripped by a memory of the Wörthersee, which has the same enchanted contours. I arrived there the day of the execution of the three in Sofia,[78] I spent a privileged moment there with Liuba and Vlady. Brunn and Léna joined us and we spoke at length about the crisis of the revolution, of the replacing of the old cadres, of the firmness that had to be maintained. At the time Brunn was a secret agent in Yugoslavia and told me not to cross that border under any circumstances. An article I had published in *Clarté* on the Sarajevo affair of 1914 (documented by Mustafa, Basteitch, and Colonel Bojin Simić) had led Belgrade to make the decision to have me killed without any fuss if I were to take a walk over the Karawanken Mountains.... They attracted me because from their peaks one could see a land of dreams, verdant plains and little villages with white cottages about which it was easy to fabricate illusions, illusions that might contain a

78. Probably Chablin, Yankov, and Minkov after the attack on April 16, 1925, at the Cathedral of the Seven Saints.

sliver of reality. In any case, the view from up there must have been splendid.

Here I find anew a vision of the Wörthersee, and this absorbs me, makes me smile in the void without any real sadness. Never have I more clearly felt that life must pass, our lives, while the world and the great life remain, are renewed, continued, one and many, with brother lakes in Carinthia and the Michoacán, and men every bit as different, every bit as much brothers and peers on these banks and under these skies. William Fett questions me about the war in Russia and the Stalinist system; Jacqueline talks to me about the Fourth International and the near future... I respond to them at length. They live imprisoned in their concerns about art and philosophy. Jacqueline, thin, an elongated, wrinkled face, with beautiful worried eyes, with abundant graying black hair falling to her shoulders, is writing an essay on a high, slanted desk of white wood onto which the typewriter is jammed. It's in a large, cool room, empty despite its bed and the few books and paintings. Gordon paints, crosses the lake on a pirogue, admires the beautiful Indian women bathing, does brickwork, whitewashes the walls, picks up ancient stones, and constantly returns to his thought-out visions, treated like theories by his intelligence, with an engineer's penchant for straight lines, perfect ellipses, the proportions of symbols laid out like the structures of ships. His investigations tend to explain the world in accordance with a strict comprehension that even organizes intuitions. His essential need is to understand. He reminds me of Balmont's axiom: "The entire universe must be justified for it to be possible to live in it." A believer's nature, of the Puritan race, descendant of those who found all truth in the Bible, from Genesis to the New Testament. He needs a Genesis and he seeks to elaborate it in his paintings. The mathematics and mechanical design he studied at a naval academy in England hinder him and inflict on him a decorative rigor and stiffness that are strong but abstract and metallic. I don't know if his undertaking is possible with so much intellectual discipline in abstract cosmic investigation. There's nothing abstract about the knowable universe; the best theories explain only a glimmer of it, striking but desiccating. I think Gordon needs more unthinking enthusiasm, a wild enthusiasm, purely visionary, in order to arrive by intuition at the vision he seeks, synthesizing it through the unconscious. Enthusiasm means everything to him, and yet he is paralyzed by the rigor of his thought. One feels he is disciplined in all regards, smiling affably but without kindness, sociable and solitary. The personality of a lumberjack or a vigorous sailor, muscles that want to leap, loins made for the games of the centaurs, and a brick-tinted face, round, artless, with tiny brown eyes, like those seen in engravings from Old England. Among his paintings one, a partial success, particularly struck me. It is perhaps called *Mexico*, and whatever the case is a kind of hieroglyphic that clearly signifies Mexico. Panel of a meter and a half by a little less. Perfect curves stand out from the blue of the sky and the water, somber though transparent, and the greens of dense vegetation, and the shape of the eagle and the lines of snakes, but all of this is nothing but living geometry, entanglement of the sky, water, mountains, and light in the selva, nocturnal light, primordial beings. It gives the impression of parts of the night sky, of a sky that is truly unique, that of this country, and which is loaded down with all these symbols. It's harsh and grand. I also noted, on another canvas that's been started and on which man is to figure, or rather the concept of man reduced to some animal graced with a developed brain, I noted the success of a star *en pointillé* of yellow lights, geometrical but real, intense. Lines and some kind of pillars, straight as steel girders, seem to me to diminish this construction that seeks to express life.

Gordon greeted us looking like a savage, his cheeks bewhiskered, his fisherman's pants rolled up over his calves, a stained shirt, an amusing pajama top worn over it, and a sombrero: a boy-tramp from a happy port that doesn't exist. The Victorian style of his childhood makes a sudden comical appearance in a bedroom set up like a living room thanks to solemn armchairs around a simple round table, thanks to a bizarre divan that could well be a venerable piece of family furniture but, thank God, is nothing but bric-a-brac. All of this floats in an uninhabitable void, and a violent painting shines within it, both dead and distinct, like a destructive challenge, all of hieroglyphic lines and surfaces (hieroglyphics of Einstein's time that a solitary intelligence elaborates for itself and that perhaps no one else will ever decipher).

Paule is struck by this ambiance of a charterhouse without renunciation, of concentrated labor in the magnificent desert, of solitude during an infernal war. She says to me: "They're admirable, but what egotism!" "Perhaps," I say, "that of total self-sacrifice," and I think: "Of a self-sacrifice perhaps misplaced, perhaps wasted...." But if a strong work comes out of it, as is possible, neither the self-sacrifice nor the egocentrism will have been wasted.

Thought that for Laurette—as for me—this would be the ideal place for relaxation and meditation. The light from the lake dominates everything.

Gordon presents William Fett to us, a tall young man in glasses, with an anemic look despite his bony build, sandals, corduroy pants, sombrero, and a timid, thoughtful gray gaze. W. F. lives in a house in the village, rented for seven or eight pesos a month. We enter two rooms, the walls decorated with watercolors, one frugally furnished with modern furniture and with books on the classics of painting: El Greco, Botticelli, Cézanne, Van Gogh... In the United States "Fett received a first prize for painting and he was done for, good only to make posters.... Fortunately he saved himself, he discovered Mexico and art that thinks." A landscape of volcanic mountains done eighteen months ago is dull. Fett didn't succeed in expressing through the blackening sky the grandeur and the taciturn sadness of extinct volcanoes. Freed of academic realism the same way we take off an old city suit to go into the forest, he now paints, at a rate of one or two a day, enormous watercolors in velvety, striking colors that are internal landscapes. They often resemble (as Jean Malaquais remarked) viscera displayed in a fantastic anatomic preparation, and the fact is that the motif of larvae in the entrails of the earth, animals with the outline of scorpions, brown, barbed with curved paws, often appears in his compositions. W. F. has a visceral vision of the earth, but he sometimes outlines a noble mountain with animal contours, a blue torrent running with the impetuosity of a bounding beast. These are nothing but trial runs intoxicatingly reproduced by use of simple tools, nothing but a box of watercolors. One can see a man seeking himself, an adolescent artist: a temperament, sap, but there's nothing organized about his soul, an organic and passionate vision that thought has not enlightened, that lived experience hasn't fortified.

PARICUTÍN

August 22, 1943—Leaving Uruapan the car turns off into a deeply rutted road under low branches. We're advancing at ten kilometers an hour. Drive through a pitiful village of ramshackle huts, little black pigs playing in the puddles, an absurd refreshment stall with a Coca-Cola sign; poverty and isolation. The ashes begin to dye the earth gray-black, ash invades the landscape, the route becomes increasingly bumpy with unpredictable sudden curves that constantly put the brakes and springs to a breakneck test. For a long time we drive through a sinister wood where the soil is of dark ash. Daylight ending. In this half death of the earth, beneath the dull, distressed foliage, at the side of the road into which tires and footsteps sink, there suddenly appears a ridiculously frightening grave. The upright board of a cross remains. Alongside it a kind of scarecrow, tilted backwards and made of the ragged clothing of the murdered man, has the air of a drunken ghost staggering through the ash under the desolate branches.

The volcano suddenly appears in the distance, bizarrely close, at the edge of a clearing. The massive column of grayish smoke climbs and spreads, colossal, towards the heavens. One can see opaque masses of gas, ash, vapor, smoke passing ponderously over each other. They have the shape of inflated entrails, in labor, they don't break up but rise, rise and rhythmically embrace in bursts of thick red fire. From here, the steady breathing of these explosions is audible.

Entering San Juan Prangaricutiro offers an "apocalyptic" spectacle, Paule's expression, simple and true. Night having fallen, we come onto a vast square under an enormous plume of smoke that spreads out from the volcano and at its zenith appears to cover the entire countryside, threatening to bury us in hot ash and asphyxiating smoke whenever it moves on. Vast, bare plaza where the rain is denser because of the black earth. A few grocery stores blaze with electricity in the solitude. Around them outdoor Indian kitchens before which intensely black human forms bustle about, broad-brimmed hats and serapes over rounded shoulders. The church's facade is high, severe, its towers rise toward the smoke. A large stone cross stands against a background of stars in a fragment of calm night. In the center of the square the noise of the crowd, the stomping of horses, all of it muffled, low, in the darkness on the ashy ground. The heads of small, pitiful horses with large, expressionless eyes surround us, mixed with heads of Indios with root-lined hands shoving pieces of rope in our faces. We are momentarily submerged by this crowd of horse rumps, saddles, human faces, horse's heads, and harnesses. Alcoholic breaths blow in our faces; a drunken Indio, gaping mouth and blurry eyes, harasses me like a maniac: he points a black rope resembling a snake at my chin and demands a peso—to climb the volcano on horseback. Horsemen of whom we can see nothing but teeth under their hats, rise and float in the darkness above the crowd glued to us. I suddenly glimpse, at the end of a long street with low houses, completely swallowed up in the darkness, the striking red flame of the volcano. The blazing clouds burst out of the crater, darken, dim, and then burst out again in a rhythm of respiration.

... Alone, guided by a sixteen-year-old villager, Sebastián López, a handsome, attentive boy of thoughtful speech, I take the strange path up to the crater. López swings a miner's lamp that makes a small circle of faint light on the absolutely dark earth around us. We talk about the war, and he asks me which countries are fighting against which others, and who will win? He doesn't ask why and seems not to know that Mexico is also at war. Yet he's a serious young man, quite pleasant. We advance climbing and descending, our feet sinking into the soft ash in the middle of an ink-black night. I guess that we are passing through a completely dead ghost forest on the side of a hill. Cosmic sighs and muffled detonations come closer. At bends in the road we can see the perfectly drawn curved line of the crater, above which climb prodigious purple flames, carrying away the black clouds. March to a cosmic furnace in total night.

On a hill across from the crater, at a few hundred meters, the *campamento*, a few wood huts where beer, coffee, and food are prepared over coal stoves. A few tourists and horses, all of it ghostly and somberly real. At the heart of darkness the dazzling eruption, a sort of fireworks display—monstrous, monotonous, terrifyingly powerful.

The light from a window shines six hundred meters ahead of us in the solitude, apparently right at the foot of the crater under the terrible volcanic plume. It's the home of Dr. Atl,* and we head there. Through the window I glimpse the group of friends with a lively little old man with a short gray beard, laughing and gesticulating. We have a moment of joy at finding each other and meeting, as if this were the edge of the world in one of the last shacks still standing after a flood of lava.

DR. ATL

Dr. Atl ("water" in Aztec) is Spanish: Murillo.[79] He resembles Blanqui in his final days. Delicate, fine features, trimmed beard, alert expression, determined, good humored, but beneath it there's something relentless, perhaps disoriented: imperious reason having primacy over all the rest—or a solid sliver of madness. The cords in the lining of his old, rumpled suit show through in back. His nails are horny, hard, and black, his hands delicate and virile: there's something of a faun about him. His lodging contains only one thing of value: a powerful oil lamp. He sleeps on a *petate*[80] without undressing, washes only occasionally, eats Indian food prepared at the *campamento*, drinks deplorable coffee that a child brings him, which he joyfully offers us and which remains one of the best coffees I've ever tasted in my life. A large painting he's just begun is on the easel. Drawing materials are all over the place. Atl shows us his studies of the volcano, extremely conscientious, not the least hint of impressionism, perfectly realistic, and for this reason they give the impression of direct contact. His intention is to prepare documentation for his study. "I intend to paint ten large canvases, the different aspects of the volcano...." (He is sixty-eight years old.)

I had great prejudice against him because of a deliriously anti-Semitic book he wrote that is still sold in fascist bookstores. He was one of the remarkable early figures of the Mexican Revolution, one of the founders of the union movement, organizer of the Case del Pueblo of Mexico City and the red battalions that in 1915 ensured Venustiano Carranza's victory over Victoriano Huerta, and thus the promulgation of a constitution that, even before the Russian Revolution, in 1917

79. Dr. Atl (Gerardo Murillo) was in fact Mexican, although he studied in Europe.
80. From the Nahuatl *petatl*, a woven rug that serves as a bed.

promulgated amazingly revolutionary labor legislation. Next a political adventurist, an archaeologist and geologist, he carried out digs and made discoveries, discovering the ancient pyramid of Cuicuilco,[81] created museums, embezzled funds, linked up with the reactionaries, passed for a fascist, fell into an anti-Semitic delirium, all of this with nonchalance, force, passion, confusion, and disordered intelligence. For him life was nothing but an adventure, in the grandest and most banal sense of the word. He will say to me, as we walk through the ashes of a devastated landscape: "The worst thing in the world is order. Once you allow yourself to impose order within, you're lost. It was disorder that saved me. Nothing is more beautiful than disorder."

Dialogue in the warmly lit shack in the heart of the violent night, to the sound of explosions:

Me: I've known your name since the heroic times of the Casa del Pueblo. You were a revolutionary.

Atl: Yes. That's so far away now. When we think of the past it's hard to know if we should laugh or cry....

Me: You have to continue.

Atl: Continue from mistake to mistake, sure. I continue by studying volcanoes. This one is my son.

Me: From now on, no more chance for error.

For years he fled cities and retired to the greatest possible heights on extinct volcanoes. For a long time he lived in a hut in the middle of the snows of Popo, painting and meditating (if he knows how to meditate—I rather think that he abandons himself to his reveries and passionate contemplations). Fallen ill, taken to the hospital, he escaped as soon as he began to recover in order to return to his hut at the edge of the snows. His paintings are luminous, deserted, no living being is ever seen in them, nothing but the harsh mountain with its lines of terrestrial energy.

I feel myself forgiving him for something unforgivable, anti-Semitism: he has no choice but to hate men, at least in the abstract, for

81. Located in the Pedregal de San Angel, to the south of Mexico City; this discovery should rightly be attributed to Manuel Gamio.

he is all benevolence and doesn't want to know that among his guests this night there's a Jew, Jean Malaquais. He needs to believe he is hating, hating deliriously in a disordered way, thinking he has unmasked the universal conspiracy—and it's not his fault if he loses his way in this abominable childishness that others, good technicians, have used methodically to carry out the murder of a people. He himself is so close in personality and vitality to the great Jews! Moreover, he speaks to me of Trotsky with sympathy; perhaps this delirium belongs among his past errors. I don't ask him: it no longer matters.

He speaks French like a Parisian. "I studied at the École des Hautes Études of the Sorbonne. But I developed my true philosophy on the boulevard de la Villette and the boulevard de la Chapelle...." "Me too," I say. "That's where I began mine...." And I see he's like a Parisian bum.

We are all squatting outside on a mat facing a crater that breathes, sings, and exhales subterranean fire. It's cold out. The purple flames are rising without letup and falling in a rain of incandescent stones that we can see streaming to the bottom of the crater, hundreds of meters off. When the volcano catches its breath, its outline dulls, then blackens. We follow the rising of the meteors and their fall. Some of them reach as far as the green stars and float among them for a long moment. The Milky Way falls on the volcano so that it seems to have two infinite extensions: the dark, heavy, threatening extension of its clouds and the aerial, glacial, softly luminous one of the Milky Way. In contrast with the terrestrial blaze, the stars are a shimmering steel blue tending towards green. We hear the hissing descent of the lava to our right. And we see red slides flaming down the crevices of the hills.

Atl says he's lucky, amazingly lucky. He's been waiting years for a volcano to awaken, and his wish has been fulfilled. "I love this one like a son!"

Warmed by tequila, asleep lined up alongside each other on the cabin floor to the sound of the cannonades. Fiery red glimmerings pierced the poorly joined planks facing me. I could see white lightening flashes, some in the shape of a cross, shining in the volcano's plume. The stones falling from 1,500 meters struck the ground hard, the sliding lava gave off a faint, nasty hiss. I awoke several times wondering if we weren't going to be crushed under the burning stones that seemed to be seeking us out. I remembered the bombing at Nevers and regretted that Laurette wasn't here to experience as well this bizarre tranquility in the midst of danger and the charm of an inexpressible contemplation.

About 6:00 a.m. discovery of a unique landscape. Its only colors are yellowish ash, pale sky, heavy smoke, graceful vapors, total annihilation of the vegetable world, and while the light grows it becomes darker beneath our feet, more arid. The flames from the crater are pink or, at times, blood-red, but the opaque whiteness of the surging clouds cloaks them. To the right a cliff of rusty-red, flesh-toned rocks: these are the basalt rocks Paricutín has given birth to, bursting from its core. Further down, beneath the mound we are standing on, white crevices, lips of stone, crack open along the dark mountain that forms the base of the volcano and exude vaporous fumaroles rising slowly into the air. As far as the eye can see the heights are completely ash colored, around us a spindly forest is dead. The skeletons of the trees are yellowish, not a single leaf. But no: I can see two or three green buds on a charred tree.

Indio horsemen are heading towards us across the ashy crests. They're bringing up the horses for the return trip.

San Juan Parangaricutiro was a large village spread out among its cultivated fields on a plateau in a verdant countryside; a rich village all in all with a beautiful church. The entire countryside as far as the eye can see is nothing but ash. All the gardens, all the cornfields have died. A few houses are still inhabited along the wide, dead streets. A few stubborn magueys pierce the crust of ash.

The nave of the church, high and wide, rather poor. A group of the faithful is praying there. They're standing facing the choir. The church is full of a furtive sound, gently rhythmic. The barefoot faithful backing slowly out of the interior toward the exit, executing a kind of dance step. The shapes of men in serapes and women carrying babies rolled in shawls on their breast hop, perfectly upright, take a cadenced half step forward, a small step back... It's long, it's a magical dance in the Christian church. An old woman enters and walks to the altar on her knees.... They're tan people, thin and wretched, with tense faces, and sunken, serious eyes. They dance past us without deigning to see us.

An Indio sweeps the church square covered with ashes. The immense overhanging cloud of Paricutín covers up half the noon sky.

August 23, 1943—Jiquilpan, town on the plain, birthplace of President Lázaro Cárdenas,* who has showered it with favors: small modern barracks, monument to the fatherland on a high mound (an eagle that's not too bad seen from a distance), well-being and cleanliness. A church has been transformed into a library, simple and gracious little pink baroque facade. The interior, well lighted, pleasantly furnished (very few books) dominated on all sides by Orozco frescoes. Those on the sides are vigorously drawn in black and white: a frenetic melee of larger-than-life horses, an execution scene, the peasant rebel falling under the bullets of the firing squad, an elementary crowd stampeding, bodies and members leaning forward, heads reduced to enormous mouths. It could be called *The Clamor*, for it shows clamor without the glow of the spirit—nothing but the rise of oppression and poverty that killed minds or prevented them from being born. The fresco in the back is in color, a powerful and neglected retake of the one in the Palace of Justice of Mexico City. —Orozco, drawing at times perfect or passionately careless, powerful, facile symbolism redeemed by obvious sincerity. The revolution forged characters, its storms were in the nerves, the hands, the eyes of the artist.

At the back of the library three glass cases full of riches. Not far from here vast ruins were discovered buried beneath the earth that, whenever an American institute deigns to take in interest in them, will give birth to an archaeological city. Probably the remains of a Tarascan city. Bone necklaces are decorated with gray shell inlays in checkerboard form. Bones are carved in the shape of stylized animals, a bit like bears. I've seen nothing like them until now. Two large vases, broken but reconstructed, where not a single piece is missing, are painted with well-preserved frescoes, an entire codex to be deciphered.

At Tzintzuntzan ("the murmuring bird" in Tarasco!),[82] a spacious

82. Actually "the hummingbird's place" in Purepecha.

church where they display a fake Titian that in no way resembles a real one. Scaling up a path of rocks and brush. At the top a partially cleared pyramid, magnificently situated as always above the gentle bend of the lake. It must have been tall, one surmises that all the nearby mounds cover buildings. A particularity of this pyramid is that a portion of it was circular with high steps, perhaps these steps served as the base for a smooth surface? The stones at the base are carefully carved. Some bear signs, a double spiral. Abandonment, a boat guarded by dogs, we're greeted by inoffensive barking.

VIRGIN OF ZAPOPAN[83]

August 24, 1943—Peaceful boredom of nocturnal Guadalajara. Paule wants to dance, she drags us to spacious deserted nightclubs, stupidly illuminated by colored neon, sometimes somber, sometimes harsh. The walls of one of them is splashed with a painting of a snowy fairground scene. It's stiflingly hot. A carriage with a slowly trotting horse takes us to the hotel a half century late, but it only lasts an hour.

The procession of the Miraculous Virgin of Zapopan, transported to Tlaquepaque.[84] This Virgin protects against lightning: seeing the crowd dragging and surrounding her, I have no doubt she performs many other miracles. Several groups of dancers precede her down the street. They're hallucinatory and probably hallucinating. Dressed in Indian costumes whose traditions must date back to pre-Cortés times; plumed and masked heads, devil and animal masks, they slowly advance in pulsating groups, the bodies bent, turning in place with each step and hopping without bending their knees. They wave whips and rattles filled with hard seeds that make a tiny dry sound, like the gnashing of countless teeth. Many wear long tunics of red or blue velvet decorated with braids. Among them there are also workers in overalls and un-masked faces, serious and motionless as masks. A group is preceded by a sprightly lad in a tawny leather vest and work pants, wearing a mask

83. Virgin of Hope.
84. Zapopan and Tlaquepaque, both officially municipalities, have been incorpo-rated into the metropolis of Guadalajara, Mexico's second city.

of hard wood with a big nose and a cruel mouth. He brandishes a small whip and twirls it over his head, it looks like he's leading the dance … The Virgin's image is in a beautiful gray car covered with flowers, hauled with rope by men whose expression I can only define as energy, a dark energy, concentrated within itself, harsh, gloomy, burning, ready to transform itself into the desire to kill—only to fade away. A tide of women in black shawls holding children and old women hobbling on their canes accompanies the float to the chant of a litany. I was almost knocked down by this flood, there was so much violent haste in its advance.

All that Jean Malaquais can find to quote concerning this sight is Marx's "religion is the opium of the masses …" A great remark with a certain profundity, but ridiculous here applied vulgarly like a master key. Such phrases don't open eyes but rather close them. This people needs opium to live; mystical opium is a tonic for its primitive, impoverished, and powerful inner life. And what other remedy do they have against a reality from which there's no escape? What is more, its faith is not external, is not only socially given. It rises from the most profound human depths. Here Catholic rite mixes with Indian paganism, touches on the magical, and awakens the tribal man of the past millennia. Rather than repeat a nostrum emptied of meaning by political agitation, I prefer to turn to Jung: "The spirits [of the primitives] are the manifestation of unconscious complexes." And Freud: "… a large part of the mythological concept of the world, which profoundly penetrates the most modern religions, is nothing more than psychology of the external world." (*The Psychopathology of Everyday Life*, ch. XII)

SURREALIST SOIRÉE AT PIERRE MABILLE'S

August 31, 1943—Pierre Mabille, his jacket off, more than corpulent, his head fat and round, his eyes with a hint of gray green also fat and round; he licks his fingers while savoring a delicious boeuf bourguignon. Michette, corpulent, wearing slacks, eyes of the same color, a pinched and regular face with tiny, hard features. Leonora Carrington,* who has been told she looks like Charles I in Van Dyck's portrait, and it's true but in feminine form, sentimental, hard, and mad. She has a beautiful elongated face with a square forehead, pale and symmetrical. Her nose slightly turned up at the tip; dark, intensely fiery eyes, full of self-assurance and anxiety—clearly schizophrenic. Slim, a head of thick dark hair. She creates madwoman's drawings in gouache with bits of landscape floating over islands, women's clothing suspended in the air or the void, flayed animals, hands scattered here and there, nightmare or dream silhouettes outlined with a fine brush amid vegetal greens and delicate yellows and greens. All of this covered with lengthy minuscule texts in which I read only that the universe is the result of the couplings of nothingness. Besides, one of the drawings is hanging upside down on the wall, and it's been agreed that it should be flipped around every two weeks. Superstitious, she fears prophecies. It was predicted that she would lose three parts of her being, and she just had a tooth pulled. She says she also cut her fingernails and toenails, and to round off the three things she chews the fingernails of one hand. We spoke of the conscious and the unconscious, which for her are essential and must be brought to the surface if we are to escape the mysterious and live fully, even though she says this is "extremely dangerous." With me she is friendly and mistrustful: "I feel you are so different." "Certainly," I say, but, answering a question, I reassure her that I will never feel the least hostility towards her. "Is that from contempt or indifference?" "Neither" I reply. But I find it difficult to explain to these black eyes what it is. Her husband Renato Leduc, a journalist, a tall, graying Mexican. Benjamin Péret, pale, pink and gray, the head of an eighteenth-century Voltairean abbot and a Gothic profile. Remedios Varo,* almost a skeleton, a Gothic face as well, but completely asymmetrical. Esteban Francés,* with his air of a good-looking Mediterranean boy who smilingly admires himself and is confident of his success with women and his way of talking: amiable, insignificant, and velvety. Finally the Wolfes,* pleasantly average, and me.

Pierre Mabille leads the games. The game of Prophecy about the end of the war, the future of Surrealism ... Last night Seligmann* and others gave the dates and even the precise hour of the armistice, etc. Seligmann is supposed to have foretold the date and the hour of Germany's entry into the war against Russia, erring by only a few days on the date but getting the time exactly right, eighteen months before the event... I respond: An armistice, if there is one and not several, between 1944 and 1945; climax of the European revolution in 1948. We then find ourselves together in Paris in disappointing though exciting circumstances. In two years Surrealism will be a fruitful holdover... Also played at questions and answers with some striking successes: Pierre Mabille: "What is friendship?" Victor Serge: "A violent but, at bottom, reasonable mystification." Miriam Wolfe: "Who will bring us fire?" V. S.: "Comrade Prometheus." P. M. "How can we go from darkness to light?" Renato Leduc: "By the service staircase." Wolfe: "On tiptoe." V. S.: "Why had the little boat never sailed?"[85] (This question was found to be terribly frivolous by Michette and P. M.; one must concentrate)— Wolfe: "Because it was afraid of the waves."

Even if we take into account answers with multiple or vague and twisted meanings that could apply anywhere, there are too many striking correspondences for the game not to reveal some subconscious communication. Leonora had posed a twisted question about "How to make love when?" Her husband, Renato, who is no longer young, answered, "By turning back the clock."

The answers concerning the future of Surrealism are revealing. Three stars: Breton, Péret, Mabille. A center will be established in Mexico that will radiate throughout the world... Surrealism will transform itself. It will play a role in the European revolution... The pride of a coterie that takes itself very seriously and doubts its accomplishments is laid bare here. Much childishness; the narrow, even egocentric culture of a circle essentially concerned with filling up the emptiness of life with self-admiration; an unhealthy pleasure in lingering endlessly on the edge of mystery, sexuality, madness. In short, the atmosphere of a Parisian literary café, interesting, limited, decayed.

LARREA, SELIGMANN

September 11, 1943—Sounding the depths of obscurantism: Juan Larrea's book *Rendición de Espíritu*, Giving Up the Ghost, To Die, I'd translate it as *Capitulation of the Spirit*—two thick volumes to demonstrate that

85. Line from a children's song.

the history of the world gravitates around Jerusalem, Rome, and Santiago de Compostela; that the Spanish Civil War was its crucial crisis; that after this spiritual death of Europe the very shape of the Iberian quadrilateral, situated at the center of the planet (photo of a globe)— as long as one is willing to view the planet that way—as well as its orientation indicate that the spirit will be reborn in America. Prophesies from *Revelations*, the number 444, which is found between 1492 and 1936, Saint James's death in the year 44 of our era, the 44 degrees of longitude between Jerusalem and the Finisterre, where Santiago de Compostela is located, Christ's 33 years multiplied by Santiago's 44 ... In Russia during the Revolution intellectual products of this kind proliferated in mystical circles, and it was the Apocalypse, that great book of historical delirium, that was made use of, though 666 was the preferred number. What's astounding is that Juan Larrea takes himself seriously as a prophet, the revealer of a universal truth, with the practical sense to publish his own work. "The defeat precisely locates the navel of the world...." What is puerile is that Larrea hasn't even thought of other historical tragedies, of the civil wars lost in different ways, of how easy it is to draw poetical axes on maps. A Russian mystic would ask, Why not Jerusalem, Byzantium, and Moscow pointing towards the Pole, supreme purity, symbolic whiteness, etc.? Chronology and arithmetic lend themselves to this.

In *VVV* (Surrealism, NY) Kurt Seligmann writes a commentary on Paracelsus's sixteenth-century prophecies. Necromancy or prophetic clairvoyance ... Pierre Mabille in an article in *Cuadernos Americanos* justifies prophecy by determinism and vice versa ... Visited the Seligmann exhibition, about twenty canvases, beautiful colors, bright and occasionally radiant or transparent. Neither reality nor dream nor even nightmare, but the fabricated vision closest to the visual nightmare, besides gratuitous. Thought of Tolstoy's words about Andreyev's* terrors: "He makes them terrifying, terrifying, but they don't scare you." They are mechanical-cadaverous ghosts made of rags, of fragments of skeletons and skeletons of machines churning in the void, to be bought by essayists who will then write about "the delirious vision in modern art, etc.," an interesting subject for an expensive journal on glossy paper. Seligmann must be an extremely sensible man, who skillfully exploits this vein and certainly feels no fear in front of the quadrangular, white, and gaping maw of his refrigerator.

This obscurantism, partially manipulative but sincere in its abdication of forthright thought engaged with reality, places itself *on the left* ... Intellectual decomposition of the left under the shock of defeat ... The circle is closing now; the libertarian, rational, revolutionary tendency touches the fanaticism on the opposite side, which is belief, violence, the irrational, trance, eyes closed. The snake is biting its tail.

The next gallery in the Palacio de Bellas Artes is occupied by an exhibit of María Izquierdo,* whose drawing has made progress. I admire with relief the beautiful, extremely stylized heads of Indian women with intense eyes. The flesh and the spirituality of the gazes are moving.

FAKIR

September 22, 1943—Swiss or German, his name was Harry von Wickede and he claimed to have studied Hindu science. He had been a fakir in a circus and once even burned his mouth while swallowing fire ... What's certain is that he wanted to escape poverty at any price. What sensational trick could he try? He imagined having himself crucified under controlled conditions, with doctors who assured him that pierced by aseptic golden nails his hands and feet were in no particular danger. An impresario smelled a profitable affair and provided the capital, some $1,500 or $2,000, I think, for the publicity. They rented the former Carta Blanca Café,[86] covered the facade with posters showing laughing death's heads and a handsome young man in a whimsical oriental costume and a white turban nailed to a wooden apparatus. Ads explained that this "experiment in resistance to pain" implied no sacrilegious allusions to the more serious crucifixion of Our Lord Jesus Christ. Msgr. Martínez, archbishop of Mexico City, deemed this all proper. For the price for a peso paid at the ticket booth facing onto the street, the public could see the fakir with both feet and one hand nailed with golden nails to a complicated contraption equipped with ingenious hookups for the satisfaction of his needs. Costumed, kept going by

86. Actually, La Blanca Café.

injections, assisted by a doctor who frequently listened to his heart, surrounded by nurses, he smoked as he calculated the receipts and envisioned finally leaving his worries behind. The impresario proposed a tour of the provinces, and maybe even overseas! The deal of a lifetime! He had announced eighty days on his cross that wasn't, and he remained there for 488 hours, 45 minutes (more than twenty days) before the eyes of the doctor and his funder, until the exhaustion of his heart and his muscular strength, taking in 70,000 pesos, around $14,000, probably more than half of it for himself. He asked Don Maximino [Ávila Camacho*],[87] who had come to see him, for Mexican citizenship... A brute of an American doctor, while touching the nails to ensure they were well planted in his feet, caused him to howl with pain. The newly wealthy fakir was able to make future plans. He was taken to the Gillow Hotel in such perfect condition, according to the doctor as reported in the newspapers, that he declared he was "ready to start again next week." At the hotel he was seized with cardiac pain, fell suddenly into his death throes, implored: "I'm dying! Save me, save me!" and died despite the injections... The physician of the enterprise said his death was due to natural causes, "totally independent of the experiment in fakirism." The autopsy revealed an embolism. In the meanwhile, the poor devil's funds disappeared.

I didn't go to see him. I found the spectacle more degrading than the sight of young girls waiting beneath the dark porches of San Juan de Letrán for taciturn passersby, which at is least justified by human animality.

He excited a good deal of erotic and sadistic interest. Women went to see him and made amorous proposals. One said to him: "With me you'd have no need to earn your living this way...." I'm told that there was a young woman who went to see him as often as twice a day. "Think about it: I saw him wasting away twice a day." Some old Indias took pity on him and prayed for him. He suffered enormously the final days of the exhibition; he was frightened and irritated and muttered curses. The impresario likely prolonged the torture. Of the 120,000 pesos taken in, only 8,000 were left to the state as heir. The rest was frittered

87. Mexican general and politician; governor of the state of Puebla.

away on the costs of publicity, installation, etc. The pretty and cadaverous Mme. Pivert speaks to me of the fakir with excited eyes.[88]

DOCTORS, DEATH

October 2, 1943—A few friends at our house with Fritz Fränkel and Paul Rivet. We talk psychoanalysis, war in Russia, the formation of collective myths... Herbert Lenhoff has to get up early in the morning and apologizes for having to leave; two patients died at his clinic today, two or three others will die. They're cancer patients at the end of their rope whom Revesi, a great doctor but a disordered mind, admits in order to test a new treatment, perhaps a great discovery, which acts on the metabolism. In any case he provides relief and prolongs resistance somewhat. "Bad days," H. L. says. Revesi suffers with each death; he's high strung. "The patient is a matter of indifference to me because I'm indifferent to death. But what interests me is the struggle against the invisible enemy. In medicine there are cases where everything adds up like in arithmetic. In the case of cancer we are fighting hidden forces, groping in the dark. We parry their blow at one point and they strike another. This is what makes the struggle interesting. Naturally, there is also duty: prolonging resistance out of consideration for the dying person's next of kin." I answer that I think that this isn't a good state of mind for the physician. He should take an interest in his patient as a human being who must be defended with a kind of love, Christianly, I would say. H. L. agrees that perhaps I'm right. "Fighting the way you do, could you be optimistic?" "It would suffice to be conscientious; but Revesi, with whom I spoke precisely about this just yesterday evening, answered: 'We must profess an optimism of action.' In this sense the doctor, in serious cases, has something of the mentality of the revolutionary."

WAR IN RUSSIA

October 3, 1943—All summer the Wehrmacht has beaten a retreat in the face of an exhausted and malnourished Red Army, supported by

88. Perhaps—likely—Germaine Boulleau, wife of Marceau Pivert.

a starving rear with weak lines of communication. It's not impossible that the explanation for this is a secret or tacit accord between the two belligerents. Why wouldn't totalitarians negotiate while they're fighting each other? The practice of not doing such a thing dates to the times of chivalry and is reinforced by the parliamentary control of democracies. The realistic cast of mind calls for negotiations while on the offensive. It's also possible that a grand political maneuver is in the works after the shortening of German lines. Hitler no longer had any interest in occupying destroyed territories from which he can't profit at present while inflicting on his troops the torture of winter in the heart of Russia, with long and execrable lines of communication. The hypothesis of the Nazi regime's internal disintegration also can't excluded. (Remember that we don't know how totalitarian states die.) The Stalinist system is certainly much more impoverished, more damaged, materially weaker. But it has the moral advantages of the defense of its territory, the memory of the Revolution, of collectivism, of a victorious resistance. The advantage as well of climate and geography.

Hitler lost the war on Russia in two stages, failing in the attack against Moscow in 1941 and then in his attempt to cut off Russia from the Caucasus. He erred concerning the solidity of the regime and the spirit of the Russian people. He aimed at the dismemberment of the USSR and a materially profitable rapid victory ("Victories are hungry," I wrote in July 1941). Stalin lost the war in a different way, by opening territories to invasion and destruction that are so vast and so rich that Russia hadn't suffered a similar disaster since the Mongol invasion. But then he held out, held out magnificently. Today two series of problems are posed to him for the salvation of a regime crushed under frightful responsibilities: 1. How to regain popularity by giving the country a feeling of security? —2. How to reconstruct?

Totalitarian collectivism is economically incompatible with different neighbors. If Stalin doesn't dominate the countries on his border—and Germany is henceforth a neighboring country for Russia—he has neither security nor assured reconstruction, and he will need to isolate himself behind a continuous Wall of China as well as to arm himself. If new democracies emerge in the center of Europe, their influence on Russia, shaken by the monstrous shocks of the war, will be an agent for disintegration of the totalitarian regime. All the more so in that the economic and spiritual reconstruction of these democracies could be much more rapid than that of Russia. No illusions: Stalin's salvation lies in the domination of Central Europe.

Who will help him reconstruct? The Americans are far away. They will have to participate in the reconstruction of all of Europe and continue the war against Japan for perhaps years after the fall of Nazism. What is more, they will favor the regimes most suitable to them. Nothing could be more natural. They probably won't participate in the reconstruction of the USSR without posing conditions.

On the other hand, industrial Germany is near. Russian Marxists have always considered its economy complementary to the Soviet agricultural economy. German industry will be greatly damaged, but not destroyed. In eighteen months of work Germany could very well reconstruct new factories more modern than the old. It will accomplish real prodigies with a planned economy. Thus for Stalin: get his hands on this economy of tomorrow. This can't be done without a conflict with the Anglo-Saxon powers, today or tomorrow. In reality, this conflict has begun, it's simply a matter of camouflaging it, attenuating it, of avoiding any sharp and brutal forms by buying time. To this end, the adoption of the following schema: no "Bolshevization" of Germany (but is it still a question in Russia itself of the Bolshevism of Lenin and Trotsky?); maintaining the facade of a ˝capitalist democracy," "parliamentary," capable of according some satisfaction to Anglo-American capitalism and fooling international democratic opinion; establishment planning there, with the cooperation of the current leaders of the German economy; having ministers who are in their pocket holding the levers of command; controlling censorship, the security forces, the army, and all the secret services through trusted agents, Communists or "Free Germany" people—in a word, taking control of the apparatus of a pseudodemocratic state, as the Stalinists succeeded in doing in Spain after the elimination of Largo Caballero.* Recall in this regard the experience of the Republic of the Far East founded in 1920 by the Bolshevik CC in order to give substantial satisfaction to Japan and to avoid a massive Japanese intervention between Baikal and Vladivostok. It was a parliamentary republic, with semicapitalism, a legal opposition, a certain freedom of the press, etc., and Japan recognized it. The democratic republic lasted only two years, totally governed in any case by Moscow. As soon as the international situation allowed it, it was Sovietized (1922).

OUTSKIRTS OF MEXICO CITY

November 6, 1943—The southeast of the city along the extension of San Juan de Letrán becomes a vast city with wide avenues and mostly low houses over which the clouds stretch out like the sad hanging laundry of the poor into the dusk. Market stalls block certain *calles*. Shops, boutiques, wretched *consultorios* of doctors and dentists, shady hotels with broken windows, cantinas where through the open-work doors one glimpses noisy groups of poor devils in big hats. Everything bespeaks clutter, filth, dilapidation, a swarming and strolling crowd, affliction in the middle of abundance, making do, odd jobs, sordid foods (entire windows filled with tripe of a beautiful copper red exhale a fatty stench sweet to hungry nostrils). It puts one in mind of the area near Saint-Ouen, the flea market, but more airy, more colorful, more spacious. Loads of children, the jostling of young men playing on the crowded sidewalks and streets with a gentle violence.

It was there that I saw the Indio carry his cross. He advanced through the crowd with the dancing step of his bare feet, bent beneath a heavy cross that may well have been two meters high and one and half meters wide, a mortuary cross made of wood and covered with flowers. These formed a double design, white and near-black, probably purple flowers. In the shadows the white flowers looked phosphorescent. The bearer was trotting along, disappearing beneath his burden. Men in white shirts and soft little hats accompanied him, speaking animatedly. This, I thought, was how from century to century they carried the burden of revolutions—and how they now carry a foreign world, with its buildings, its banks, and its hierarchies.

Aquiles Serdán, calle de Cuba, a strange crossroads whose aspect I've already seen change several times. The old streets were lined with small shops and restaurants. At around 9:00 the girls set up shop in the doorways. Whole blocks have been demolished, little by little the bombed-out landscape is disappearing under the work of the cleanup crews; modern houses will be born. The square survives, pitiful and animated, crowed with young streetwalkers, some taciturn, some gay. The ugly ones are taciturn and station themselves, all alone, off to the side, keeping an eye out for drunks. The young ones, dressed in colorful shawls, chew Chiclets or smoke as they gossip. A dance hall glows red, a bookseller has set himself up next to a vast storefront haunted by men in glasses. Across from the bookseller the Varsovia Agency offers, under a shining neon light, a sumptuous car for newlyweds, upholstered in white satin and lace, like a marital bed. It's touching, ridiculous, and almost indecent.

Discreetly illuminated shops of coffin sellers mingle with the cafés. Here they have a bourgeois air. Elsewhere I've seen sordid ones, three walls painted gray, children's coffins on shelves, and an indolent half-breed slumped over the table, his felt hat falling over his eyes. Buses, trams, cars, the din of the street. Policemen joke with the girls or drink in the bars.

SUSPICIOUS ACCIDENTS

November 14, 1943—Conversation with someone worried about the three suspicious accidents that have occurred over the past few months in Mexico City in Communist and Russian circles. 1. On the evening of April 1, Anna Seghers, crossing La Reforma in the rain, was hit by a car, fractured skull. Her husband, László Radványi (GPU, an old-timer, from the period before the Great Purge), speaks of an organized accident and shuts up. Anna Seghers is unstable, idealistic, tormented, half-mad. Probable crises of conscience. Very nearsighted, an accident is extremely plausible. 2. Kamaranski,[89] Russian-Jewish chemist, Communist, connected to Lombardo Toledano, fell near the Zócalo[90] between a tram and its wagon. Killed on the spot. Stories were published that he controlled $2,000,000 in capital. Accident quite plausible, easy to

---

89. Komarovski [*sic*]: devoted and in-the-know Communist, henchman of the secret service, was crushed to death by a tram on the way to a reception for the Soviet Jewish delegation. [Note by Serge]
90. Central square of Mexico City,

provoke. A chemist and wealthy, he might have rendered delicate services. (September, I think.) 3. Two weeks ago M. and Mme. Muir,[91] White Russians, wealthy, took shelter under an awning in the evening near Buenavista. Rain. M. M. turned around, didn't see his wife, "calmly" returned home, received a phone call informing him that, run over by a car or a motorcycle, Mme. was found dead fifteen meters away... In the morning *Excélsior* spoke of the strange accident, but the afternoon and evening papers made no mention of it. Strange attitude of the husband, who seems to have been afraid to realize what happened. Accident hardly credible. The Whites who entered the secret service were recruited at the time of Yagoda and Yezhov, thus compromised and compromising, suspect in the eyes of the GPU and capable of understanding too many things. In any case: murky.

JACKSON, GPU

November 17, 1943—Otto Schüssler,* who was Leon Trotsky's secretary and knew Jackson, tells me of his recent confrontation with him. The assassin is primarily concerned with refuting the accusation of belonging to the GPU. (Obviously, only since there's been an embassy of the USSR in Mexico City!) He said to O. S.: "You're 'slandering' me. How can you prove I'm a GPU agent?"

O. S.: That's my conviction, supported by the following:

- You came to Mexico City with a Canadian passport that had belonged to a (killed) combatant of the International Brigades.
- For years you had at your disposal—and in prison still have— considerable funds of unknown provenance.
- The letter in which you justified your crime before having committed it is written in the style characteristic of the GPU and its content is similar to the fake letter of Rudolf Klement, assassinated in France by the GPU.

91. Murov. The accident occurred as they were returning from a meeting of the club Friends of the USSR... In both cases it's possible the itineraries of the victims could be known or predicted. [Serge's note]

- I think you participated in the kidnap-murder of Klement. You were in France at the time and told me you'd spent time on the Pyrenees. Klement's letters were mailed from Perpignan. At the pretrial investigation you lied about the K. affair saying you had no idea who he was. It was impossible for a "Trotskyist" living in France not to know him.
- Trotsky's assassination itself followed the Moscow Trials.

Jackson, calm, rested, well fed, well dressed, wore in his boutonniere the insignia of Victory in the Mexican colors.

PRIETO

December 3, 1943—Conversation with Indalecio Prieto. Nuevo León Avenue, a small town house, well lighted, furnished in simple and sure taste, ordinary but very comfortable, denoting a man who without any particular effort surrounds himself with comfort. Lawn in front of the dining room. Comfortable study full of finely bound books that are rarely touched; a study for agreeable conversation, not for work (in the normal sense of the word). Prieto is enormous without being obese, his corpulence thick and supplely muscular, and a vigorous complexion which would seem flabby were it not for his nimbleness and the impression of confident strength that emanates from him. His massive head with its wide, flat shaved skull, pink and bluish, rests on an amazing double chin that swells to ten centimeters. His features are thick but well defined; almost no eyebrows, blond or rusty. Straight nose, pink mouth, big and soft, the blue-gray eyes disappear beneath fleshy eyelids. Slippers, gray smoking jacket, open-collared shirt, he looks like he's wearing a dressing gown, crosses his legs high up. A strange human animal full of agile vitality. He probably works without notes or papers, dictating, speaking, reading as little as possible, with an excellent memory, a mind ever alert. He's molded of an intelligent material that doesn't concern itself with intelligence as a reality distinct from others.

On the Junta de Liberación that has just been established: "We need a starting point, a period of provisional constitutionalism.... Then the

Spanish people will go wherever it wishes.... We don't intend to dictate anything to them. The AMGOT[92] is preparing Spanish-language personnel. An invasion of the continent through Spain is possible. We're reversing the argument according to which the Allies have no one to talk to in the Republican emigration.... The Communists remain outside: I don't want them and the PS doesn't want them. They did too much damage to the socialist cause and to the Republic. And now they're spreading it around that the USSR will have hegemony over Europe. We will not accept any tutelage."

Me: The Stalinists aim for hegemony over industrial Central Europe, which in reality would be hegemony over the European continent. But the Anglo-Americans and the peoples concerned will never agree to this without a bitter struggle. Much bluff in all this: it's not because Stalin is strong; on the contrary, it's because he's on the brink of defeat and his country is exhausted that he's applying the tactic of the diplomatic offensive and is seeking salvation in solutions that are extremely difficult and even those whose success is totally improbable. He's at an impasse.

I. P. on the social forces in Spain: The Socialist Party is by far the most influential. The Lams succeeded in splitting it, but they are nearly powerless. The Basques are holding back: they didn't vote for the constitution of 1931 and they're carrying out the policies of the Vatican.

He estimates that the Spanish emigration numbers about fifteen thousand in Mexico, ten to twelve thousand in Africa, including the crews of the fleet, three thousand in Tunis, four thousand in Uruguay and Argentina, and a few hundred in England and the United States.

The conversation wanders. I. P. tells me that in a report on the activity of N. B. (Communist), which Eduardo Villaseñor* had a copy of, he quotes this statement of N. B.'s: "There are two men who must disappear, Trotsky and Prieto...." "When Trotsky was killed I communicated this document to various friends."

92. Allied Military Government for the Occupied Territories.

SBERT

December 4, 1943—A vast and messy, though sunny, fourth- or fifth-floor apartment on Avenida Amsterdam. Antoni Maria Sbert, of the Esquerra Catalana, former adviser at the Interior Ministry of the Generalitat. He crossed the Pyrenees with Companys* among the last combatants. Thin, emaciated, black-framed glasses, narrow face, a very sick man. "My party represents the Catalan radical petite bourgeoisie and bourgeoisie. We're prepared to agree to whatever revolutionary reforms Spain may want. We want true freedom for nationalities in a united Spain. The ideal would be an Iberian federation including Castile, Catalonia, the Basque country, Galicia, and Portugal.... The Basques are Catholic and conservative, but they approved our entry into the Junta de Liberación, traditionally we represent them. Collaboration impossible with the Communists, who have been disloyal in many circumstances. After a mysterious phone call, their ministers would change their position from one hour to the next. Negrin? If he wants to respect constitutional forms he has only to resign and we'll accept his resignation. It might also be a matter of the legal continuation of the Defense Junta of Madrid, which was the last de facto and de jure government of central Spain...."

Like Prieto he dreams of a federation of Latin countries, France, Italy, Spain.

"I've learned much from Marxism, but I fear ideocracy.... By feeling and philosophy I am a Christian, without being either a Catholic or a believer." He has an alert gaze, feverish even, benevolent; one feels that for this man ideas are living things.

MARTÍNEZ BARRIO

December 6, 1943—Second visit to Diego Martínez Barrio, Calle Ana-huac 21a. A modest bourgeois house. Immediately to the right of the entrance the study: books, old-style Spanish furniture, neither luxury nor artistic taste: simplicity, souvenirs. Photos under glass, group pictures from the time of the Republic. One shows the president of the Republic in a top hat, Don Diego with his minister of war in formal uniform, both of them in a landau on the street. Another photo, this one strange. The presidential tribune in the style of the pre–World War I French Republic, the calm official personages, Don Diego. In the foreground cuirassiers in a scrum of horses and smoke; in the background the street. "A bomb had just been thrown, to be sure, more of a firecracker...." The government wasn't disturbed by such minor events. I find Don Diego at his desk, cutting the text of a speech by Prieto out of the newspapers. He pastes the clippings onto blank pages. There are also photos to be filed. Thickset, fiftyish, slightly gray, square face, straight nose, thin lips, pale, even greenish complexion. Simple and good humored. He began as a bricklayer and then opened his own print shop.

"I represent the most moderate party. We want the starting point to be constitutional, but there is no social transformation to which we are opposed. My feeling is that large-scale rural and industrial property will disappear.... Franco several times missed the boat with the monarchists. The only true monarchists in Spain are the Carlists of Navarre,[93] but Don Jaime is dead, his successor, an octogenarian pretender, is dead, and all that remains of that line is the Hapsburgs, the brothers of Empress Zita. The son of Alfonso XIII, Don Juan, has no supporters and absolutely no popularity.... And would provide a solution for no one.

"We created the junta so that we could no longer be attacked for our lack of unity. Spain will be whatever it wants to be: neither the emigration, which is small, nor any external power can dictate to it.... No regime can be imposed on it, it will come about on its own.

"The Basques, whose leadership was for the most part educated by the Company of Jesus, demand total self-determination.... We don't want the Balkanization of Spain; we won't oppose constitutional reform and a federative republic.

"The Mediterranean was a melting pot of civilizations. Latin Europe has an undeniable spiritual impact and enormous influence over Central and South America. This is the line of our future.

"What's likely is that Spain will be dragged in during the final phase

93. The Carlist movement, traditionalist and royalist, antiliberal and antirevolutionary, called for the installation of the Bourbons on the Spanish throne.

of the war. Hitler can't abandon this position without a fight. Franco is nothing but his creature.... The Spanish temperament is completely refractory to totalitarianism. Do you know the story of the priest who told a little Spanish boy that God created the earth in six days. '*Y porque*?' the child answered. We are the country of *porque*."

I ask him if it's not imprudent on his part to have the windows of his study facing the street, on the ground floor, protected only by flowerpots..."Bah, I'm a fatalist. And anyway, when the time comes we take precautions." A gray-haired woman in an apron is moving around in the apartment, probably his wife. The constitutional president of the Cortès and the Republic in exile is paid 600 pesos per month and earns perhaps as much contributing to *La Crítica*[94] of Buenos Aires.

VIRGEN DE GUADALUPE

December 11–12, 1943—From midnight to 3:00 a.m. at the Basilica de Santa María de Guadalupe with Laurette. The great churches are built at the foot of the hill of Tepeyac (at the summit, Capilla del Cerrito, the cemetery). The *capilla* is probably sitting on the site of the temple of Tonantzin, goddess of the earth and corn, "little Indian mother," venerated by the Aztecs. Archbishop Zumárraga, at the time of the conquest, had this temple destroyed, but almost immediately it had to be replaced. On December 9, 1531, the Indio Juan Diego, walking over the holy mountain of which only ruins remained, saw the Brown Virgin appear before him on the road to the chapel of Tlatelolco. Surrounded by celestial music and light, the Virgin spoke to him, ordering him to "tell the bishop that she desired the construction of a church on the site of the temple of Tonantzin in order to protect her Indio people." Juan had three visions. In order to convince him, the Virgin made roses grow out of the rocks (and it is there that the Capilla del Cerrito was built). All of this recalls the discovery of the Gospel of Saint Mormon. Why doubt the sincerity of the visionary Juan Diego? How can we not understand the good intentions of the priests who

94. Sensationalist daily with wide circulation.

educated him, encouraged him, and believed themselves the instruments of Providence by contriving the proof of his visions? There must have been hesitation and struggles within the clergy, for the construction of the great churches only began in the early seventeenth century, and the Brown Virgin of Guadalupe was only declared patron and protector of New Spain in 1754. The pope obviously ceded to wise practical considerations in admitting the Indian reincarnation of the White Virgin. It's interesting to note that the clergy of New Spain had undertaken the construction of the sanctuary a half century before the Holy Father's enlightened decision.

When we arrived La Villa[95] was holding a fiesta. It's a small, populous town lying at the foot of the holy mountain. Abundance of shops and cantinas; a large colorful marketplace. A dense crowd is gathered here in an enormous kermesse. Around it there are even harshly illuminated attractions: ferris wheel, swings, shooting galleries, a whole carny. The sanctuary plaza and the spacious *zócalo* with its beautiful trees are occupied by crowds camping and moving about. Everywhere one stumbles over whole families piled up sleeping under serapes. Walking is difficult near the lighted shacks piled with things to eat: you run into lots of tiny kitchens set up on iron charcoal stoves. The crowd is so thick in front of the sanctuary that we aren't able to get close to the fence that blocks access to the wide-open doors. The church is tall, opulent, simple, in red and white stone, a kind of Spanish Saint Sulpice, that is, in brighter and more ornate colors, yet as a whole mediocre, crudely illuminated by spotlights. Above the large portal of the fence the Union de Albañiles[96] has erected a violently multicolored painted image—*La Virgen Morena*[97]—made of painted canvas and flowers. People are nested under the bells in the two towers and others have climbed to the top of the high fence (five meters?). People drink, eat, get drunk, processions of drunks bump into each other, couples wander, many beautiful girls, many silent and nearly taciturn pilgrims

95. The neighborhood in which the basilica of Santa Maria de Guadalupe is located.
96. Bricklayers' Union.
97. The Brown Virgin.

come from the countryside, the decorative silhouettes of poor people, sombreros and serapes—and the women, the children sleeping on the ground at the feet of those who watch over them. The young people of the city are turbulent and the people from the countryside well behaved, serious. For the former this is a fair, for the latter a great night of faith and passion. For many the two are united into a single whole, as has always been the case.

We climb the steeply inclined alleys or staircases that lead to Tepeyac. At moments the lighting is crude like the stage set of an old opera representing some nocturnal site in a small Italian or Spanish town; then the moonlight shines down, the darkness becomes soft, enchanted. The crowd climbs, calm, colorful. In the *capilla* the ambiance becomes suddenly, simply, extraordinarily intense. There is a perfect harmony among the (grandiose) site, the sky, and the people. A wide stairway, bordered by a half-destroyed stone ramp, gives access to the square of the *capilla*, no bigger than a cathedral portal, a flat, sober facade (baroque). The door is closed. On the square, among stones knocked down by destruction or reconstruction, two large groups have gathered, one in front of the closed door of the chapel, the other against the left-hand wall, in a roomy corner. Families are sleeping in a pile, pitiful banners, the national flag next to the religious banner of the pueblo. The group by the door is in prayer. Squatting men and women sing in chorus, to the enervated sound of the rasping guitars. The voices are tired, raspy, gently frenetic. I observe a man of about fifty, gray haired, with an energetic face, a white man, perhaps a schoolteacher with the goatee of a rural intellectual who, his hands in a trance, makes the loudest of the guitars twang. Old Indian women with somber faces of brown earth lined with deep wrinkles can't take their eyes off him as they sing. They're celebrating a mass. The songs cease, the handbells are rung, the chorus takes up the orison in a murmur, all the foreheads turn and bow before the door of the chapel, some leaning against it. There is a feeling of all-encompassing fervor. When they tire, the neighboring group begins its song to the sound of guitars held by young men standing, some in suits, in their Sunday finery, others in white village shirts. One of them has opulent black hair, a wild mane. Incident: in the front row of the spectators a drunk, held up by his son, bows his head and staggers, respectful but appalling. (At first I had thought he was ill.) They evict him without any commotion. "Señor, this is a temple. Please go." They push him off, open the way for him, his boys dragging him without protest. The guttural and discordant song rises with passion, monotonously:

a-a-a-a-a la Virgen de la nación.

I can also make out the words "Cristo Rey" and "deliver us from evil." They're endlessly repeated to a trancelike rhythm. The children are asleep at our feet, rolled up in brown blankets between the large scattered stones. Unfurled on the walls are the colorful rags of the banners; before us the reddish facade of the chapel. When you raise your head you can see the high sky, incredibly simple and beautiful: the piles of white clouds against a murky blue background are luminous. And at the zenith, just above our heads, the magnificent full moon. (The full moon at the zenith was certainly connected to the cult of Tonantzin, the mother.) When you turn your head slightly you can see, beyond the stone ramp, the immense horizon, but, in the foreground, below the rock of Tepeyac, the domes of the sanctuary and the great Capilla del Pocito, covered in colored tiles from Puebla: they turn it gold. An electric blue cross burns above the sanctuary. Between the trees of the plaza below the bright fires and the tumult of the kermesse, the human swarm. But it is here that the prayers of the pilgrims come from afar reach their height.

Halfway up, on the ruined staircases, looking out on this illuminated nighttime landscape, on the limitless city with its golden yellow light, a more humble group has stopped by a bend in the road on a *plazoleta*. Still more banners, families sleeping in piles, the group of litany singers who ceaselessly, humbly, repeat the same words to the same tune:

> *A la una y a las dos*
> *A las tres y a las cuatro*
> *A las cinco y a las seis*
> *Dieron gracias por el alma ...*[98]

---

98. "At 1:00 and at 2:00 (etc.) they gave thanks for their souls."

In the crowd down below young people are getting worked up by a guitar and Indian instruments. They want to dance clumsily. Across the pediment of the church shining out in blue neon is a Latin motto. The muchachas think it is in English. They don't know that Latin exists.

In three hours of strolling through this crowd I did not observe a single unpleasant incident.

TLANEPANTLA

December 12, 1943—Tlanepantla, large pueblo on the plains, not far from Tenayuca, the Pyramid of the Sun, whose squat shape and central staircase rising deep pink above the foliage we see as we pass. The architect Fabela and General Hector López,* ex-governor of Guerrero, drive us to the presbytery, where we are expected for lunch. A large dilapidated church, which, it seems, was the first in the country, a neglected traditional patio. The curate is an old man of seventy-seven, quite imposing, copper colored, with an aquiline profile, and a white, unkempt beard. His caped cassock is worn out and stained, but he is quite striking, a strong feeling of dignity and importance. He's the doyen of the curates of Mexico, more than fifty years of service following four years of novitiate. Visited Spain and Italy, which he crossed from one end to the other, took an interest in the study of folklore and of a large swath of Mexico. He knows much but clearly had only the most rudimentary education.

His apartments, large whitewashed rooms laid out in a row, are full of a bric-a-brac where the best is cheek by jowl with the worst. Banal, seedy religious knickknacks, life-sized old saints honestly sculpted in the sixteenth or seventeenth centuries from a single tree trunk and conscientiously painted and gilded, thrift shop paintings, well done portraits, an old Italian post-Renaissance profile of a man attributed to Veronese (the priest asserts that it is a Veronese, given to him by a fishermen who'd stolen it in Russia). A lava vase forty centimeters high by forty around, of a bizarrely deformed roundness that makes it look limp. Discovered nine meters underground, it dates from an era when potters left their work to dry in the sun ... Beautiful masks of admirably polished stone, the splendid profile of a sparrow hawk in black stone, large archaic stone masks, drawn in horizontal lines of carved jade, a collection of Aztec seals that bring to mind the seals of Chinese antiquity, whose (generally) square shape and sober hieroglyphic design they share; a rather large *mujer bonita*[99] with her legs spread, realistic and primitive (fifteen centimeters high: the figurine is seated), a number of objects uncovered during excavations, and a few fakes. A beautiful terra-cotta Tláloc.[100] Above these imaginatively classified collections (there is a box of small heads from the archaic period with this note: Melanesian type) is a lovely, brand-new carved wood frame, made of perhaps a thousand pieces put together one inside the other. A large marquetry escritoire that supposedly cost seventeen years of labor... On a chair alongside it, a notebook: *Valsas de Chopin*. In the corner a tiny woman's bed, slippers beneath it, a blue pillow. This little museum of bric-a-brac is full of clean beds: a half-dozen servants, housekeepers, female cousins, orphan girls live with the priest. The largest room is decorated with skillful cloth reproductions of feather garments from the period of Moctezuma. There is also a lovely shiny black mantilla with trimmings that belonged to Empress Carlota[101] and large capes that belonged to Hidalgo and Morelos. (Possible.)

The old priest says that morality has declined since the revolution; that people ate better in the past on less money, that there was less poverty. All of this is probably true, but in reality it comes down to saying that the introduction of money into a country with a largely patriarchal economy intensifies the exploitation of labor.

General Héctor López tells us about the etiquette of the old-time marriage proposal. Three letters were required, the first signed "You know who," the second signed with initials, and the third formal with a complete signature, at which point the parents deliberated... "Young man, I used to write these letters for six centavos a piece," which represented a pound of meat. This was during the time of Don Porfirio [Díaz]. We had a long lunch in a sad-looking dining room, under spiderwebs, in the half light and the cramped space. There are six of

99. Beautiful Woman.
100. God of rain and fertility.
101. Charlotte (1840–1927), wife of Emperor Maximilian.

us guests, and there's a young black half-breed, typical sacristy rat, with a portfolio of sketches of characters and costumes under his arm (poorly done schoolboy drawings that he shows to Laurette at great length), a gaunt, respectful character pickled in piety, with a large black moustache, glasses, a Tartuffian smile; a fiftyish priest in civilian attire with a reserved and prudent blue-gray gaze (he's a folklorist); a handsome young Basque refugee priest, a corpulent and cultivated young man, well fed, with the air of a practical, well-behaved bon vivant. He speaks to me about the independence of Euskadi, of total independence, cutting all ties with Spain! He knows Marr's Japhetic theory.[102]

The old priest thinks that France is prey to communism. We part making serious vows of friendship while Indios come to tell him that they're waiting for him for a baptism. He says there are no nonbelievers in the area, and I'm inclined to believe he's right. Except, he adds, for a few hotheads who say, "Thank God I'm an atheist." If this devout old man, one of those who constitute the force of the church, has not had a successful career in the ecclesiastical hierarchy, General Héctor López explains to me, it's because he has always been of the people, close to the people, and so in conflict with the archbishoprics.

Leaving the presbytery we come upon a rather pleasant little circus. Good acrobats, a naive audience that takes pleasure in everything.

THE INTERNATIONAL?

December 16, 1943—Second discussion about the International. The first, a few days ago, at the Commission for International Relations of the independent socialist groups, this one at the Ibero-Mexican Center, "Socialism and Freedom." A small turnout, neither the Spanish anarchists nor socialists came. Marceau Pivert deplorably, confusedly served as rapporteur, with documents from the International Labour Party[103] that he read out loud for an hour and a half, never attempting

---

102. The "linguistic theory of Japhet" postulates a common origin for the Caucasian languages. The Georgian historian Nicolas Marr (1864–1934) called himself a "Marxist linguist."

103. Again, should be the Independent Labour Party

to make its essential points clear. Everyone agrees that there's no question of reconstituting the International before there are mass movements in a liberated Europe. Nevertheless, two tendencies stand out: mine, and I'm nearly certain that I'm alone, and that of the others, more emotional than reflective. I say that it would be a suicidal mistake for the socialist left to isolate itself from the masses; that it's necessary to meet the masses where they are, as they are, masses who tomorrow will be objectively revolutionary and subjectively moderate. The line I propose is that of the march toward a single Socialist International, rallying all the socialists of the world, with freedom for tendencies and the formation within it of an intransigent left. Unity, solidarity, liberty (this excludes the totalitarians, that is, the assassins, and the calumniators, but I feel I must stress this). Most of the comrades would clearly prefer a tendentious International; that is, a sect where they could feel at home in order to play at conferences, at the leaderism of minorities, etc. This from attachment to the tradition of half-dead parties, from illusions (the hope of rallying large numbers—Julián Gorkin likes to repeat that we've seen small groups of refugees become great political forces), from ignorance of social psychology and faith in the seductive correct doctrine, and from a profound doctrinal and moral hardening. What sclerosis of the spirit in these militants! Rather discouraging. Most would be charmed to have a tiny party of thirty thousand men in Spain or France that would believe itself pure and that would be powerless.

GERMAN PROSPECTS
December 18, 1943—Conversations with Herbert Lenhoff on the prospects for Germany. H. L. believes that the disintegration of Nazism has begun, that the effect of the bombings of Berlin is one of the major factors, along with the feeling that the war can't be won and the memory of the defeat of 1918. He thinks that late April, the end of winter, could be the opening of a period of sudden changes. The Reich's inability to carry out reprisals in the air war seems to him to be revelatory.

Me: It's certain that Nazi aviation has been greatly weakened, but it's not inconceivable that it's being held back as the ultimate weapon. The enormous power of the totalitarian state, the sole modern mechanism of oppression to have realized an inhuman perfection, leads me to believe that Nazi resistance will be lengthy. I imagine that in the destroyed and starved-out cities the handful of armed and determined men (since they know they'll be cut to pieces if they lose) who represent the totalitarian state will continue to mislead the disarmed and desperate survivors for a good long time.

Herbert Lenhoff: Four hundred thousand SS Nazis maintain order in the rear. They are the ones who are the first to arrive in bombed-out places to finish off the severely wounded in the rubble and to repress movements of revolt, and even of recrimination . . . But I think they'll be overwhelmed.

"In the long term, no doubt."

H. L. lays out a possible variant for the end of the war: the disintegration of the Russian front, the SS executed by frontline troops responding to the appeal of a German army formed in Russia of prisoners duly furnished with an ideology and duly led. He can't imagine soldiers of the Wehrmacht opening fire on Germans back from Stalingrad and preceded by encouraging tracts. The civil war would begin at the front. Through the breach one hundred thousand Germans allied to—in reality instruments of—the Russians would pass . . . It's only then that the British and the Americans would invade in order to counterbalance the Russian influence in Germany with a minimum of losses.

I find this idea quite interesting. It's unlikely that Stalin hasn't thought of it. It remains to be seen if the state of general misery and deterioration of the country allows him to equip a large enough German force, and this in secret. In any case, it can already be seen that the seed of the Third World War is germinating in this one.

GREAT MEN? HITLER, STALIN
December 18, 1943—The discussion with Lenhoff drifts to the theme of great men. I note that Hitler's twilight strips the Führer of his Napoleonic halo. This halo, I saw it born on the roads of France at the

time of the defeat. In my conversations here with Fritz Fränkel and
Herbert Lenhoff I became aware that they are inclined to find exceptional qualities in Hitler, ones that, in history, make a great man. I
think that my thesis, laid out in my book on the war in Russia,[104] is at
bottom the most correct, though too schematic: Adolf Hitler is the
coefficient of hysteria—and of hysterically visionary will—of a *brain
trust*[105] of German neoimperialism. I accept that this coefficient took
itself seriously and, having reached the heights of power, grabbed the
brain trust by the scruff of the neck and made it march. But then begin
the catastrophes that, far from aggrandizing Hitler, put him back in
his place. Napoleon was a truly great man, by which I mean that seen
up close he demonstrated an energy, an intelligence, a capacity for
work, for initiative, for the domination of circumstances as exceptional
as the gifts of a Beethoven. His great mistakes (the Russian campaign)
were those of a great man. He was never stronger than in defeat, when
the course of history necessarily turned against him: the French campaign in 1814, the Hundred Days, Waterloo. The *Mémorial* [*de Sainte-
Hélène*] is a dense and rich book, the work of a modern spirit. He was
essentially rational. Try to read a speech of Hitler's! His great mistakes
are those of a visionary: anti-Bolshevism, anti-Semitism. We are no
longer living in a time of visionaries, even if European civilization is
suffering an eclipse.

Stalin has to a far greater extent the stuff of an authentically great
man (it being understood that there are great men with vastly different
qualities). He is mediocre and bloodthirsty, but he is a product of a
great socialist, that is, progressive, revolution, while A. H. is born of
the decomposition of German and European capitalism, of a surge of
savage energy in a society playing its final card for salvation. (Note that
in any case German capitalism is lost.) A. H. became great with the
support of the black Reichswehr, reactionary governments, and big

104. *Hitler Contra Stalin*, written in the wake of the German invasion of the USSR,
was published in Mexico in 1941 by Bartomeu Costa-Amic, translated by Eric
Adroher (Enrique Gironella), with an introduction by Julián Gorkin. As a result,
the publishing house, Quetzal, was ruined, thanks to maneuvers by the Russian
embassy and local Communists.
105. In English in the original.

capital. He received power without a struggle and has remained in power with the support of foreign finance along with that of British and probably American conservatives. He has benefited from the complicity of international reaction; he has vanquished only the weak, the democracies undermined by the spirit of reaction. In the face of the strong—England, the USSR—his machine has found itself blocked, even with the advantage of a controlled, concentrated, planned economy.

Stalin had to carry on an infinitely tougher personal struggle, with (in the beginning) little chance of imposing himself. At the time of Lenin's death he was of little importance and had to deal with Trotsky and many others who were immeasurably superior to him. He was carried along by the social forces of Thermidor, without realizing it at first, but he still had to know how to channel and use them. 1. Through ruse, dark tenacity, maneuvers, and corruption he conquered the party apparatus; 2. During the collectivization campaign he was within a hairsbreadth of destruction, with the entire country and almost the whole old party against him. He was able to put an end to this peasant war, at first horribly lost, without suffering a final defeat and holding on to power; 3. In doing so, he was able to construct the most totalitarian state that has ever existed on the foundation of a socialist ideology, half totalitarian in its soul (absolute Marxism) and half democratic, liberating in its aspirations; 4. With the bloody *coup de force* of the purges and the Moscow Trials he achieved total victory over the old Party; that is, over the Revolution itself. The victory of Thermidor was complete, since it ended in the physical annihilation of all his adversaries. But in the wake of the "legal" murder of Zinoviev-Kamenev-Smirnov Stalin's situation was infernal and filled with mortal peril; none of the survivors of the old Party could forgive him. He held out cleverly; 5. He began by catastrophically losing the war against Hitler, but with tenacity, good sense, skill, and courage carried out the recovery of Moscow and Stalingrad; 6. Now, in an internal situation almost certainly hopeless he is playing an extremely skillful game of poker in the field of international politics which is only adventuristic, and likely catastrophic because of the weakness of the Stalinist regime; but it's the sole courageously rational game. Through all this, he has demonstrated a sober (Marxist) realism, perseverance, boldness, in short, the qualities of an average man with a rather special formation, but very strong, and it is precisely this man who, in history, is called (de facto) a great man.

H. L., who agrees with me, adds that Stalin was served by geography—the immense spaces of Russian Eurasia—and by the moral capital of the revolution: powerful active sympathy around the world, the confusion in the USSR itself between the social revolution and Thermidor.

In the Stalin-Trotsky duel Trotsky was (fatally) ill served by his superiority. He possessed all of Stalin's qualities with, in addition, a more elevated modern intelligence; the nature of a great humanist; imagination; inflexible moral rectitude; and a great, imperious idealism. It was the fight of the honest pugilist who is suddenly stabbed in the back; that of a great man ahead of his time who never tires of appealing to men's higher capacities, rational intelligence, and disinterested idealism . . . On the other hand, Stalin's extraordinary skill, one would be tempted to say his dark genius, was to mobilize, use, and then subdue the human tendency towards inertia and regression. The struggle of 1927–1928 unfurled between a revolutionary minority who wanted a dynamic revolution and the large majority who wanted rest . . . It should be observed that all his life Trotsky sought to innovate, to persevere in innovating, even by forcing events, while Stalin all his life stuck to using the oldest psychological forces: the cult of Lenin, the sanctification of the mummy, nationalism, the hierarchization of society, the cult of the Leader-Father, the return to old Great Russian patriotism (Alexander Nevsky, Peter the Great, Souvorov, Kutuzov . . .) during the war.

ART AND CHAOS—CAVES OF CACAHUAMILPA
December 26, 1943—On the Taxco road, ninety-eight kilometers past Cuernavaca, a fork turns off toward the north, an excellent road that runs through a tropical landscape, banana trees, isolated coconut trees, sugarcane fields. The coconut trees, elevating their star-shaped tufts atop tall, thin trunks that rise above the neighboring foliage move me because they are connected to memories of discovery and the sea, the discovery of hot lands, the shimmering landscapes of Martinique, the

burning blue sea and those tall, noble palm trees, powerfully holding high their explosion of leaves. The cane fields are the intense and fresh green of young wheat, but taller and topped with flowers spiked with feathers of a silvery, ashy, nuanced mauve, heavy and svelte and lush. Rich villages with beautiful old Spanish houses doze among the rivers under a green and golden peace.

Cacahuamilpa, in Aztec "the Cocoa Fields," is a truly wretched hamlet of gray huts and rags hanging on a rocky slope above a little stream hemmed in by gray cliffs, a landscape similar the Lozère, but narrower. The beautiful road, built for tourism by Mexican Petroleum, leads only to the caves, the population survives solely on a few jobs in the caves and the sale of Coca-Cola and cooked chicken to tourists. The Indias solicit visitors a hundred meters away, trying to sell them refreshments. A poverty from which there is no escape on this nearly sterile land, barely conquered from the rocks.

Visiting the caves requires a walk of at least two hours. They were the bed of a subterranean river that today passes somewhere underneath. A Nahua *teocalli*[106] was found there, as were skeletons believed to be Zapatistas or their prisoners. In one of the rooms furthest from the entrance, a petrified human skeleton. How did that man, a fugitive, torture victim, treasure hunter, boldest of the bold, make it so far in, with the trembling light of a lamp and a dog? How many centuries ago? Petrifaction takes a long time. A mound of stones was erected and a cross was erected on it, hung with electric lights—a monument to the unknown explorer. The caves have only been partially studied; it's not even known where they lead.

The sight from the entry is appealing and appalling. They are lifeless cathedrals, gray, black, born in the shadows, made for the shadows, which appear immense with their high vaults and fantastically carved walls. Stalactites, stalagmites, fountains, sculpted blocks are piled up, stretch out, opening onto plazas and sumptuous passageways. But if anything in human architecture vaguely resembles the impression produced by this subterranean architecture it is the most immense Gothic cathedral, where one feels one's smallness amid the grandeur,

106. Mesoamerican pyramid topped by a temple.

reverence, and even fear (assuming one is not a stranger to the mystical sensibility). But there are many differences between human art and the involuntary work of nature. Art is proportional to us on several levels, first of all that of comprehension. It is orderly, it constitutes a victory over chaos, over the elemental (this is even true of the art of the insane, which is the residue of a chaos unconsciously ordered in a different way by the defeat of the rational and the victory of the subconscious). I'm tempted to conclude that a great work of art is always an elevated and complete victory of the conscious (and by "complete" I mean that in this success the conscious embraces a world of things that practical reason—which shouldn't be confused with it—normally excludes: a victory of the unmutilated consciousness, on the contrary, by the exaltation of being, and this might be one of the meanings of the Freudian term "sublimation"). In front of these subterranean cathedrals, these temples of Angkor, these elemental deliriums of waters hollowing the stone that forms the rock, one feels despair more than exaltation, because it is the achievement of a kind of death. Life is everywhere denied, as if it were completely useless. The immense rooms follow one after another, with formidable monuments, snow-slides that shine brightly (thanks to a well-placed electric bulb), thrones, phallic columns, heaps of monsters. Our naive animism runs freely and one sees that animism, too, is a conquest of chaos. These rooms have been given names, and "rooms" is already a name that humanizes. There is the room of the two thrones, of the dead, of the organ, of the palms. We laugh when the guide shows us the eagle devouring the snake, the bust of Cárdenas, Lenin's profile, the fish, the bear, but as in clouds, one could find the entire human universe here. Rocks as large as humans impress me because their undersides are gray and black and sculpted like cerebral matter. Neither moss nor lichen, nor the shadow of the smallest form of life. Water oozes and drips everywhere. The air is heavy, warm, unhealthy, the air of a strange tomb, colossal and empty, where no remains of life would ever have been enclosed. A few skeletons count for little in this vast space. Immediate contact with the inanimate world.

We all have a sentiment of the grandiose, but a joyless one, oppressive. Jeannine says: "It's beautiful, but I don't like it." One cannot love what is completely inanimate. I think Laurette feels this way too. With

Michael Fraenkel* I find a colossal and monstrous profile of Stalin. We had the same thought at the same time, but we had just been talking about Stalin. Relief at seeing daylight at the end of the path on the way back: a pink and gently bluish light that forms a vault of its own. Upon seeing it we smile and breathe easier. When it bathes us at the foot of the staircase Michael Fraenkel and I look at each other contentedly and laugh. Our faces look green and our hearts are a little tired.

FIESTA IN TETECALA

December 26, 1943—On the way home we catch a glimpse of the fiesta in Tetecala. Several stage sets have been erected high over the small church square, each representing a simplified room. Near-life-sized characters made of colored paper are hung on one of them; I guess they're going to be set on fire. We go along roads that seem to be streambeds, boxed in between the fields, towards the game of *toros*. A plain with vast rudimentary enclosures, a wide spectators' platform (crowded), behind which a band blows dutifully into its brasses. In the vast enclosure a large number of peasant horsemen—who aren't wealthy—in bright-colored shirts and broad-brimmed hats. Their animals beautifully harnessed. Lassos. A young man is mounted on a vigorous little gray *toro*; as a saddle the young man holds on to a rope (passed under the belly of the beast). They excite the *toro* with colored capes, attack him with a barbed stick; they expose themselves to his fury, he charges, delivers furious blows with his horns, and the glory is to be grazed by them. When the beast is truly furious a horseman throws his lasso at him, catches him by the foot, flips him over…The *toro* struggles in the crowd of men and horses…The surrounding landscape is limitless. Plains, cultivated fields, mountains on the horizon, horsemen, everything is bathed in the blue of the softest and most softly alive evening.

THE IDEA OF REVOLUTION

December 28, 1943—I feel a certain astonishment tinged with discouragement upon seeing what a linear and mechanically traditional understanding the best comrades of our emigration have of revolution. Yet they saw the Spanish revolution! They must remember the Russian Revolution! Deep down in them there still exists the schema of a struggle between two principal classes, one necessarily wresting power from the other, then establishing socialism and marching towards an assured future. The excellent schema of the *Communist Manifesto* of 1848, which provided a satisfactory ideology up till the First World War and, as a result of particular historical circumstances, in Russia (though this must be examined more closely). Today an enormous effort is required to bring socialist thought up to date. Among the survivors, the lack of general culture, the lack of cadres, and a deep attachment to a facile tradition impede this effort, and this could one day be extremely serious. One can see the germ of their future defeats in the spiritual inertia of the old revolutionary minorities. If they do not better comprehend our era they are headed only to failure or defeats, the consequences of whose repercussions may reach far beyond them.

Proceed from the following general observations: That the social transformation of the capitalist world has begun and is even far advanced. That the era of revolution began with the First World War and the advent of the first state-directed and planned economy in Russia. That the defeats of the European working class were due more to the diminution of proletarian strength resulting from the technical revolution and the enormous increase in production (with the decrease of labor employed) than to the masses' subjective incapacity (lack of understanding of economic changes, moderate character of the masses), this factor being called upon in the future to play a new, powerful role. That the schematization of two essential classes is largely outmoded due to the enormous influence accumulated by functionaries in collectivities, by administrators and technicians. Henceforth the very technique of production requires the collectivization-directing-planning of the economy. That the Russian Revolution and its Thermidor bring out the complexity of the revolutionary problem. The revolution is not comparable to a smooth-flowing current: it carries along, uses, mobilizes counterrevolutionary currents; by its very essence it is a contradictory process (in their turn and despite themselves the modern counter-revolutions—fascism—have swept along, mobilized, and used the revolutionary currents of history and accomplished a certain transformative task which it will not be possible to profoundly reverse). That if we must expect powerful awakenings of the European masses it must also be admitted that their profound moderation, their immediate practical sense, opposed to combative idealism, and their traditional ideologies will remain important political-psychological factors. And finally, that explosions of revolutionary energy are followed very quickly by psychological reactions that are manifested by indifference, lassitude, and reactionary tendencies. In Germany the revolutionary effervescence began in November 1918 and didn't last beyond early 1919. In Russia the revolutionary explosion began in March 1917 and was extinguished by late 1918 (from then on, revolution organized by the party; that is, by the governing and authoritarian minority). In Spain the popular explosion, magnificent in July 1936, flamed desperately for the last time during the events in Barcelona in May 1937.

THE UNWRITTEN CLAUSE OF THE ARMISTICE

December 29, 1943—Reread, while writing my novel of the defeat,[107] various documents about the end of the battle of France. Jean Montigny's pamphlet (*The Truth about a Dramatic Month*) is perfectly clear. In it, Laval appears as the stage manager, the veritable mouthpiece of a formidable personage who remains in the wings. It is he who calls on President Lebrun not to leave continental France; he threatens, he considers criminal any intention to continue the fight with the forces of the empire, what can be saved of the fleet, or England. More than anything, he fears this decision; he seems prepared to resort to a *coup de force* against the three presidents (Lebrun, Herriot, Jeanneney[108]). It is he who announces to the silent ministers the reform of the Constitution "as something that goes without saying, which everyone knew about, accepted, and approved. He wasn't specific and no one asked him to specify anything" (Montigny). This occurred in Bordeaux. In

107. *Last Days*, written in 1943–1945 and published in Montreal in 1946.
108. Respectively, the president of the republic, the Chamber of Deputies, and the Senate.

Souillac, on the road, in a small café on the town square where fleeing refugees were still passing through, just as the request for an armistice was being published, I ran into two Belgian magistrates who knew that a change in regime had already been decided upon in principle at Hitler's demand. A few days later, but before anything was printed about the convocation of the National Assembly, a socialist from Agen, returning from Bordeaux where he had just seen the socialist ministers Février and Rivière, told me that regime change was the unwritten clause of the armistice. Hitler would never consider negotiating with a republican parliament. The "unwritten clause" served to break the parliamentary resistance.

It seems certain to me that Pétain was put in power upon clear instructions from Hitler, and this would explain his proud phrase: "I make France a gift of my person in order to ease her suffering" (message of June 15–16). For some time Laval had had ties with Mussolini, perhaps through Hubert Lagardelle, who was in Italy. He was convinced of the imminent defeat of England and he must have received promises from Mussolini for an authoritarian France destined to become a satellite of the Axis.

The hesitations of Reynaud, Mandel, Campinchi, and Daladier about sailing to northern Africa, their idea of going to London, P. Reynaud's stupefying allusion to a French government that would, if need be, be based "in our American possessions" (June 15) are explained by the conspiracies of the French right. The military and civil authorities of Algeria and Morocco, infiltrated and controlled by Laval's rightists, didn't want a French government in Africa: they arrested Mandel in Casablanca and refused General Gort and Duff Cooper an interview with him.[109]

We knew full well before the war that the reactionary organizations, the Cagoulards and the rest, so strong in the army, had enormous influence in Morocco. I recall having discussed with Maurice* and Magde-

---

109. In late June 1940 Duff Cooper (British minister of information) and General Gort went to Morocco to explore the possibility of continuing resistance in North Africa. The authorities in the protectorate prevented any contact with the French ministers, notably with former interior minister Georges Mandel.

leine Paz information sent by socialists from Morocco. They said that "military cliques" dreamed of "repeating Franco's operation in France."

YAROSLAVSKY

Late December 1943—In early 1933 I was in a cell in Moscow's internal prison with Nesterov, Rykov's former chief of cabinet, who has since been executed without trial. I remember that we one day jokingly wondered, "Is it this year or next that Yaroslavsky and Stetsky* will stroll around this same cell?" Stetsky, who at the time was Stalinism's official ideologist, has vanished into total darkness; Yemelyan Yaroslavsky, Old Bolshevik, died of natural causes in Russia in December 1943 at age sixty-five. He had had an admirable career of revolutionary struggles, prison, deportation to Siberia, escape, organizer of the workers' Red Guard in October 1917 . . . He later became the Party historian, a conformist and right-thinking historian, but at a time when there was still a certain concern for the truth. As soon as he was accused of "Trotskyism," his *History* was removed from the libraries. An unscrupulous bureaucrat, Yaroslavsky became the official insulter, persecutor, and corrupter of the imprisoned oppositions. In the early days no one did more than he to fill the prisons and the icy hamlets of the polar circle with courageous men.

Nevertheless, cast from power, the Thermidorian Central Committee charged him with the leadership of the antireligious movement, that is, the Society of Atheists, and its publication, *Bezboynik*, "The Godless." On this new terrain Yaroslavsky became one of the incarnations of the intellectual mediocrity and degraded morality of the regime. Attached as he was to the old party he must nevertheless have suffered terribly from the falsity of the Moscow Trials and the extermination of his generation of militants. But he kept quiet, served to the bitter end, and approved all the crimes. The Hitlerite invasion forced the government to seek reconciliation with the believers, and Yaroslavsky saw his antireligious publications and his organizations that persecuted the faithful suppressed. This was probably his final disillusionment.

1944

ACQUIRING THE SENSE OF HISTORY

January 5, 1944—Men need a sense of history comparable to the sense of direction of migratory birds. A metaphor more amusing than valid: it is an element of consciousness, quite distant from instinct, that we have been in process of acquiring since the Encyclopedists. In the past great ministers had it, and it is what made them great: great Jesuits, a Bossuet (more eloquently than intelligently), a Vico. With Hegel and Marx historical vision suddenly acquired a kind of plenitude. In Marx it is coupled with a will to dynamic, objective, and passionate action, and one might ask if the enormous spiritual magnetism of Marx's work can't to a large extent be explained by this revelation of the *historical sense*. (It is certain that the concept—the myth, in Sorelian terms—of the "historical mission of the proletariat" was the living flame of Marxism and that it was this flame that rose so high with the Russian Revolution.) Compare in this regard Marx's fertile power with the healthy and sometimes vigorous mediocrity of historians of the French Revolution like Thiers, Guizot, and Louis Blanc, who made what were, all in all, the same discoveries as Marx in the realm of historical methodology, but without passion, without dynamism in action; in a word, as men of the library for whom history is a scholarly autopsy and not the study of a living continuity.

The historical sense is the consciousness of participating in the collective destiny, in man's constant becoming. It implies knowledge, tradition, choice, and thus, conviction. It commands an obligation, for from the moment we know that we understand, that we have discerned the possible directions, we must live (act) according to that awareness. Among civilized man's acquired senses, the historical sense lags far behind several others, for example, the sense of hygiene, whose spread over the last half century has been extraordinary. This is because the historical sense enters into conflict with dominant interests. For the same reason history remains an enormously imprecise science. The wars and revolutions begun in 1914 will give, indeed, are giving a probably colossal impetus to this form of lucid consciousness, despite—or even because of—the partial and momentary obscuring they provoke. 1. A remarkable historical sense tends to crystallize in a few educated men, a few men who are thus exceedingly dangerous. 2. A vague, diffuse, tendentious, and groping historical sense gradually and broadly penetrates the spirit of the growing masses. The spirit of reaction, the narrow interests and cultural ties among the masses, mental inertia, fear of reality—all these exercise a countervailing effect, while thought control seeks to coordinate these regressive tendencies. (In the long run, however, such thought control will be shown to have been doomed from the start, since it proceeds from a consciousness of history, which, if enlightened, must condemn it, and if benighted, will only lead it into the abyss.)

Examples (to be expanded on): the great clear-sightedness of a few Marxists before and during the First World War; the blindness of statesmen, of the intellectuals and *tutti quanti* during the period Versailles–Russian Revolution–capitalist restoration in Europe. The doctrinaire blindness of Russian Marxists as totalitarianism grew. In both cases a subjective (emotional) factor played perhaps the decisive role and that factor was fear: the fear of seeing the dangers, of becoming aware of the inevitable. Conflict between instinct and knowledge. Ferrero[1] was right to stress the immense importance of fear during troubled periods of history, but I feel that he only viewed the problem superficially. Incommensurable role of fear in the Soviet Thermidor. The Moscow Trials were dramas cooked up by a visionary and courageous fear in the same way a man prey to panic turns around and furiously confronts a danger amplified by his imagination.

Psychologically, the conflict is between fear (primordial anxiety) and consciousness.

1. The historian and essayist Guglielmo Ferrero (1871–1942) was especially known for his works on Roman decadence.

Trotsky was a characteristic example of a man who, in order to live, strove to integrate himself into history and whose intelligence never ceased subordinating itself to the sense of history. He says this clearly in the final pages of *My Life*. That at the end this doctrine and this voluntarism confounded his thought at a moment when real—historical —lucidity perhaps ceased to be possible, with neither analyses nor syntheses being doable in the rush of events, changes nothing in the case. He carried on the fight with weapons that had become insufficient. It must be noted that he was brave; that is, he had overcome fear in himself.

The foreboding of a historic catastrophe prevailed in France from the moment it was understood that the Spanish revolution was defeated. From that point on this foreboding was profound, and people sang, "All is well, Madame Marquise. . . ." It was worthy of a Cagliostro. The Phony War was the war of a people (of a regime) that no longer had faith in itself. At Vichy, reaction and pacifism threw themselves headfirst and eyes shut into the onrushing catastrophe, clinging to all their delusions in order to avoid seeing the extent of the disaster and avoid imagining what struggles *imposed themselves*. Yet it was *visible*, obvious that these struggles would impose themselves and that a policy of shutting their eyes wouldn't spare a single drop of blood. Failure of the historical sense: fear.

LONG-LASTING REACTION?

January 6, 1944—The Americans I meet (an old socialist journalist and his wife, a young woman who's a socialist functionary, a narrow-minded professor) believe that the United States is headed for "twenty years of reaction," that is, if it doesn't head towards its own form of fascism (planned economy, conservative regime, harsh exploitation of labor). This is a general feeling that bespeaks a dimmed sense of history in the making as well as a lack of courage and an inability to pose problems in clear terms. At bottom they are prepared to accept this fate rather than look clearly at the effort required to make for oneself another possible fate. And so, they prefer to not see the alternate possibility. A major factor in intellectual myopia: difficult to escape the influence of the immediate and, while breathing the air of an industrial jail, to imagine the air breathed in the mountains. Penchant for bowing before concrete, immediate facts and refusal (fear) of questioning them so as to theorize them and perceive their contradictory dynamisms.

Same nearly general attitude before Stalin, who appears at the apex of his victories—built on unimaginable ruins in the middle of an unspeakable disaster. The display of totalitarian Russian force crushes and obliterates judgment. People can't imagine that behind and beneath it there is an incommensurable weakness and that the very source of Stalin's energy is his acute awareness that every week he survives mortal peril. (This is a form of conscious energy forgotten by the prosperous bourgeoisie during a century of security.)

THE EARTH SHOOK

January 10, 1944—The earth shook with great force twice today between 3:00 and 4:00. The whole house swayed. First I saw the shutters shaking as if in a strong wind, then the bookcase teetering, then the electric bulb dancing in the air. Laurette, in the kitchen, didn't want to go downstairs. We rushed out onto the street where the children were kneeling, perfectly calm. The trees, the telegraph cables, the line of the roofs gently swayed. Twenty minutes later, I was writing when the table slid away beneath me, the entire room seemed carried away by a gentle rolling movement. It was like a powerful attack of vertigo. No fear, but an underlying feeling of physical anxiety, followed by a feeling of depression. Often at night I think I feel a kind of subtle quaking coming through the floor and the bed (and perhaps it's true). Similarly, in Paris, we thought we heard far-off warning sirens, or during the bombing at Nevers I listened at length to the mosquito hum of the planes coming back through the night sky. Difficult to distinguish between apperception and nervous expectation. The latter implies the onset of hallucination. The waking state, of expectation, is to a certain extent a creative state.

I am forever expecting some kind of cosmic event, as if the immobility of the sky, the normal return of the constellations to their places, weren't really natural. I do not have the feeling of cosmic stability. I don't know where I got this from.

A few days later—San Juan, Argentina, in the Andes, was destroyed by an earthquake. The newspapers don't give the exact date. Between three thousand and four thousand deaths in a small city of some thirty thousand inhabitants.

DZERZHINSKY

January 12, 1944—In conversation brought up memories of Dzerzhinsky. I didn't know him personally, only saw him briefly. I recall his sharp, ashen profile, his thin goatee, his strong brow beneath his small uniform cap (he was carelessly dressed in a soldier's uniform). The hard, exhausted face of a man under tension, an authentic inquisitor, that is to say a man of faith, disinterested, thoughtful, pitiless out of duty, perhaps from a kind of goodness. He was a romantic who loved the Romantic poets and could passionately recite long passages (recounted by Radek). A studious man lacking in ambition, educated in the penal colonies. Radek said he was capable of crushing all opposition—all the heresies, crimes against Marxist unity—within the Party, which he idolized, without worrying about the means. But on the same score, he would have been capable of standing up against Thermidor, incapable of allowing any bending of the truth in the investigations and verdicts. He often revised Cheka decisions, always in the direction of utilitarian justice.

A counterrevolutionary officer, member of a military league in 1918, was arrested and sure of being executed. He wrote to Felix Edmundovich saying, in substance, "You have no need either of my death or even my captivity. It's enough that I be *hors de combat*. I offer you my word of honor that I won't fight you in any way for three years...." Dzerzhinsky accepted his word and freed the officer. (His name is mentioned several times in the *Red Book of the Cheka*.) Arrested again by chance by a provincial Cheka, this officer was nevertheless executed a short time later as a hostage.

In 1918–1919 the Association of Former Revolutionary Prisoners was still meeting, Bolsheviks and anti-Bolsheviks who had worn the same chains holding no-holds-barred debates. D. came to a meeting at which members of the Central Committee of the outlawed Socialist-

Revolutionaries, who were then engaged in a civil war against us in the Volga region, participated. Cheka agents were guarding the exits in order to arrest the Socialist-Revolutionaries as they left. At the end of the meeting Dzerzhinsky proposed to Vedeniapin, I think, that he take them in his car so that they not be treacherously caught in this trap. They accepted, and D. dropped them off—free—on a square white with snow.

Above all he feared the "rot" and the corruption of the Extraordinary Commissions.

January 15, 1944—Short, affectionate letter from Natalia in response to my New Year's wishes. It was bitter to think that, sole survivors of the Russian Revolution here and perhaps in the world, we were so completely separated by sectarianism. And this was not the humane spirit of the real Bolsheviks. Great joy in these few lines in a trembling hand in the same blue ink as the Old Man's, in the lines that stumble like Natalia's steps in her garden that is a tomb. I think with sorrow that the book just published by Marceau Pivert, Julián Gorkin, and me,[2] with weak pages by J. G. on Bolshevism and Trotskyism, which he is incapable of understanding, will be bitter for Natalia and that she will perhaps not be aware of my solitude in these collaborations. There is no one left who knows what the Russian Revolution was in reality, what the Bolsheviks were, and people judge without knowing, with bitterness, with simpleminded rigidity.

GUSTAV REGLER

Break consummated with Gustav Regler, who has moral and intellectual value and idealism. What is it that finally rendered this long, slow, unspoken, lame break complete? He is neurotic, a poetic nature, a Rilkean. He had fallen under the personal influence of Rilke, an authentic intellectual of the family of Western European men of letters.

---

2. *Problemas del Socialismo en Nuestro Tiempo*, published in Mexico City in 1944. Serge's contribution was "War of Social Transformation," never translated. Gorkin in his text called Bolshevism "a specifically Russian deviation of socialism."

Capable of grand gestures and even more of beautiful written attitudes, incapable of long waits, captivity, of resignation to the unpopularity, material worries, and isolation that revolutionaries know how to bear up under—*must* know how to bear up under. These men of letters require a minimum of public approval, of contact with wealthy, cultivated society (of agreeable patronage in a word), of external success, to acquire a certain consistency in their own eyes. They have to be carried along by the current, they are more social figures—performers—than they are personalities. They exist only through a sounding board. Regler severed himself from us as soon as he saw we were (socially) weak and likely defeated for a long time to come. He sought out wealthy and sympathetic Americans... He was angry at the shabby émigré community for having adopted that attitude towards it. Then there was the drama of Marie-Louise's illness. There wasn't a day to waste in attempting to save M.-L., and we told him so kindly but firmly. His attitude was that of a big, neurotic child. He was afraid to look the disease in the face and allowed himself to be advised by homeopaths and became aggressive towards those who disapproved of his actions, even those who said nothing, like me... Now that M.-L. seems to be truly lost he will never again dare look in the eye those former friends who saw clearly and spoke courageously. His guilt feelings have turned into hostility towards us, and with time could turn him into an enemy. Spoke of all this with Fritz Fränkel and Herbert Lenhoff, who know him better than I and feel affection for him; they see things the same way.

PAUL RIVET

January 17, 1944—I was convinced that the Stalinist influences that prevail here at *Free France* would not allow Paul Rivet to continue our friendly, even affectionate, relations. I didn't go to his talks in order to avoid compromising him by shaking his hand in public! He had told me that Simone Téry and Umansky overwhelm him with politeness. Starting in November we quite naturally stopped seeing each other. For the New Year he sent me a few words in which he expressed the opinion that the Russians would be in Berlin before the Allies. "Who cares where deliverance comes from?" I answered him that Stalinist hegemony over Europe wouldn't be a deliverance but a new nightmare (not adding that this would also be the beginning of the Third World War). He recently paid a visit to J. M., seizing the occasion to tell him—knowing full well that it would be reported back to me—that despite everything socialism has triumphed in Russia, and Europe must take that road ... He also told him that he just had a chair in French literature given to a Lady Assine, a Turk become French and Stalinist. Enough is enough, and we'll no longer see each other. "With the greatest of my affection" he wrote me on the fourth. And he's a rather a great man: a real, honest old scholar from the better days of the Third Republic ... A pity. For the thousandth time this poses the strange problem I can't resolve: Why so much poltroonery among the intellectuals and why such a sudden and base collapse of scientific conscience? They have an insurmountable fear of swimming against the current: they always have to be carried by the tide, "on the right side of things," not too far from official honors and money. Paul Rivet doesn't have a personal fortune, he is materially dependent, but doesn't he have sufficient personal authority to assert himself without servility or renouncing thought? He could, with a bit more guts. But it's guts he's lacking, accustomed as he is to parliamentary mores and the politesse of salons, in which one smilingly rubs elbows with one's worst enemies. He doesn't know that the totalitarians only accept this game in order to take advantage of it, and he doesn't want to know ...

... Shorter, his movements crisper, he resembles André Gide. Same high, rounded forehead, same flat and beautiful temples, same aquiline nose, fine and strong, almost the same strongly carved mouth with a controlled sensuality, same pince-nez over a more open gaze. Simple, cordial with all who come to see him, affectionate with the museum guards, the Zapotec guides of Oaxaca, nothing distant about his bearing (contrary to Gide, in whom one readily observes a kind of aristocratic egoism mixed with timidity, with a desire to flee people). A sense of humor, constant irony, a jovial manner of telling stories. His stories about the generals are those of an old antimilitarist, and quite good. Besides, a conscientious scholar whose contributions are real, even though his style is poor. Loves archaeology, ethnography, and his Musée de l'Homme in Paris with all his soul. Patriotic like Jaurès, a socialist in the same vein, without Marxism and with liberal opportunism, and within him a grain of old Jacobinism. About seventy years old, a lively mind, agile limbs, I felt real pleasure seeing him climb the slopes of the ruins of Monte Albán under the Mexican sun.

He demonstrated great courage during the occupation of Paris, remaining at his post at the Musée de l'Homme, participating with Chiappe in the organization of a worthy resistance at the municipal council, and then of underground resistance with young collaborators, two of whom were executed. "You'll see," he told us. "I have all the Parisian newspapers in my collection." He spoke so often of this as something that he had at hand that I thought the collection was here. "No, not at all, it's under the big Easter Island statue at the museum . . . You'll see it when we return."

January 18, 1944—Victor Basch* and his wife were assassinated on a road not far from Lyon, probably by the collaborationists. V. B. was of the same generation as Rivet. I had the same argument with him, but openly, harshly. The "Dreyfusard revolution," that amazing movement of the masses and the elite that turned bourgeois France upside down on the question of the innocence (of one single man) and the truth made Victor Basch, who was one of its artisans, one of the éminences grises of the republican Republic. That moral and political grandeur was enough for him. In 1937, president of the League of the Rights of Man, supporter of the Franco-Soviet pact, but also a French humanist of old stock, he didn't know what role to play in the central committee of the league, where the minority (Magdeleine Paz, Félicien Challaye, Gaston Bergery...) was demanding an investigation of the Moscow Trials while the majority, worked on by Communist sympathizers, shied away. In the past the league had intervened on my behalf; during the Russian Revolution it had condemned Bolshevik terrorism, and now it preferred to remain silent in the face of the Thermidorian terror of a more or less allied power. Finally, Victor Basch invited me to meet with him. He lived near the Luxembourg, in a typically gray and quiet Parisian building, an old-fashioned apartment furnished at the end of the last century, full of gifts, (yellowed) photos, and paintings covered by time with a kind of opacity. He inhabited the past. He must have been between sixty and sixty-five, rather small and thin, the close-shaven face of an actor or a judge, a gray complexion, a deep, warm voice. He wore a kind of floppy necktie in old-radical style. For hours we amicably discussed the legality of the Moscow Trials and the methods of the GPU. He was well informed and vacillating but barricaded himself behind impartiality. "You understand, Serge, I want to hear both sides of the story." "Yes, the executed and the executioners." I was friendly, even respectful (and the fact is that this veteran of a radical Republic already dead by that time inspired a certain sympathy in me, despite his clear desire to shirk) but I argued forcefully; that is, with no possible reply. In the end he assured me that I had made an enormous impression on him, that the league should organize an inquiry with both sides represented, and that he would invite me to testify, along with Charles Rappoport . . . The inquiry never took place.

During the fall of France Victor Basch's son committed suicide.

January 19, 1944—Same chapter of the *bankruptcy of the liberal intellectuals*, who had been great in the previous century . . . An American author, Howard Selsam,* writes in *Socialism and Ethics*—a dual subject about which he clearly understands nothing—that human activity "has been heading towards freedom with the slave revolts of ancient Rome, the Cromwellian revolution, the American, French, and Russian revolutions, John Brown's raid on Harpers Ferry, the great strikes of the modern workers' movement, and the trials and executions of saboteurs and spies by the Soviets."

An example of total intellectual dishonesty. What is an intellectual worth without probity of the intelligence? He's nothing but a counterfeiter. If he thinks he's on the left (in France, the case in the past of Malraux, Guéhenno, Jean-Richard Bloch, and the scientists Perrin, Langevin, Wallon) too bad for the left, for they are no longer anything but demoralizers.

For the past two centuries the whole effort of clear thinkers has tended towards the establishing, the conquest, of a certain notion of precision in the assessment of facts, of truth demonstrable and demonstrated by impersonal methods of investigation; that is, as objective as possible. The morality of intelligence is inseparable from the simple exercise of the intelligence, in the sense of scientific thought. The distortion of verifiable facts, the refusal to recognize them out of admiration for the powers of the day, out of inclination to follow the great currents of opinion molded by the powers of the day, constitutes a total bankruptcy.

It should be noted that Selsam shows himself to be as dishonest and ignorant concerning the English Revolution as he is concerning the Russian Revolution. The English Revolution is only Cromwellian in the primers of bourgeois education. An Augustin Thierry—not to mention socialist historians—took into account the popular aspirations manifested in England at the time and quite correctly stressed that Cromwell was in reality the strangler of the spirit of freedom that never ceased struggling against him for a day. He was the Stalin of the British revolution. In this sense Selsam is at least logical in his dishonesty.

January 22, 1944—Met Paul Rivet at the Malaquais's with Audel (or Hodel) of the Jouvet troupe and the de Ménils.

He seemed to be sinking into himself, diminished, depressed, unrecognizable. The cheerful old man who so spryly climbed the paths of Monte Albán seems to be no more. The bureaus full of careerists, the bitterness and sudden discouragement of aging have dealt him a blow in just a few months. Of his trip to Algeria he remarked to Marceau Pivert: "To die there or elsewhere...." Contrast with his vigorous language when we saw each other for the first time at the National Liberation Committee: "I fully intend to return and participate in the settling of accounts, and I assure you I'll be merciless. When you see my museum...." etc. He always spoke of his museum like a thing immediately at hand. Added to his depression was a visible malaise in regard to Jean Malaquais and me. Vis-à-vis J. M. this was expressed in a scornful response, tossed off in a mocking tone: "How do you intend to get to Algeria? By swimming?" I barely unclenched my teeth. Decided to write him an affectionate letter, though speaking clearly of the underhanded or overbearing pressures the Stalinists certainly exerted on him to prevent him from continuing his good relations with us, which certainly did him as much good as they did us. There is also the question of the principle of antitotalitarian socialism and the conflicts geminating on the subject of Stalinist hegemony over Central Europe.

Jean de Ménil quoted something said by a New York financier involved in French affairs:

"We foresee a command economy constituted in three zones: a nationalized zone, the banks, transport, etc.; a controlled zone of large capitalist industries subject to the plan; and a zone left to private initiative, small-scale industry, medium and small business, etc."

All in all what Lenin would have wanted in early 1918, before the Civil War forced the Bolsheviks to proceed to the nationalizations advocated until then only by the left Communists (Bukharin, Pyatakov, Radek).

The same financier adds:

"This is reasonable but seems to me quite utopian. Either controlled industry will escape control or it will attempt to control the rest. I can't help but think that nationalization will be imposed to a far greater extent than is foreseen."

January 23, 1944—Beautiful corrida with Luis Procuna. We were in the top gallery, which is called the roof, the *azotea*. The colossal basin of the arena contained a huge crowd. Behind us, at a height of eight stories, a view of the spacious, sunny horizon, the expanse of the city, radiant banks of mist above the outline of the mountains. At our feet the arena, turned momentarily a sad gray by a cloud veiling the sun. At those moments the game of the man and the beast turned dreary and its banally tragic absurdity suddenly looked as if written on a faded page. The sun reappeared, everything changed, and the bloody game regained its meaning. Observed the tiny hand movements of the torero at the *toro*, which he speaks to, which he tries to lead and psychically dominate. The knowledge of the *toro*, the meticulous and intuitive observation of his personality, the secret contact that's established between the killer and the beast must play a capital role in the mastery of a good matador. The excitement, the whistling, the *viva*s and *olé*s of the crowd establish another stormy magnetism between him and the multitude of spectators. (It is from the point of view of these psychological influences and communications that the combat should be studied.) Luis Procuna (gold and yellow suit) was magnificent. The *toro* hit him, lifted him up, tossed him over his neck, seriously wounding his thigh. Agility of the man in falling correctly, in not losing his self-control for a second. The crowd shuddered, the matador calmly righted himself and continued the bullfight. He must be so tense that he doesn't feel the pain. He knew the beast and toyed with him. After he killed him the *olé*s granted him the *toro*'s ear and he circled the arena twice in a sweat, brandishing his trophy, saluting. He was hopping, moving the wounded leg as little as possible. I knew it was the final contest of his contract. Had he failed to finish, he says, people would have felt for him but would have considered him defeated, so he would have had little chance of obtaining a new contract for this season. He fought in order to impose himself on the enterprise.

Jeannine was sitting next to me, very attentive but not in the least nervous, taking things concretely. At times I was a nervous wreck and turned away. The sentiment of the price of human life, the horror, become instinctive, of blood pointlessly spilled and of cruelty. None of these notions yet being stabilized in the child, she would simply get used to these games as to any other reality.

Reflection of a female friend (Dominique): "It's not the ear that should be the trophy, but the testicles, the organs of virility...."

The ear is obviously a substitute. The idea of the castration of the vanquished occurred on its own to this young woman, a believer with an upright soul and not in the least knowledgeable about Freudianism.

GPU, TASS, ETC.

January 25, 1944—Discussion with Marceau and Julián about the plots against us since the opening of the Soviet embassy here. Mexican functionaries gave Julián warnings that appear to be serious and even proposed to take protective measures on his behalf. For the moment the fire seems to be concentrated on Julián Gorkin, probably because he's considered the most bothersome on the subject of Spain and because the signature on an attack on me would be clear to all. The two "journalists" from the TASS agency, Potemkin and Lachevich or Darchevich (?) have sent long, expensive telegrams to Moscow principally mentioning J. G. as being tied to the synarchists, disposing of funds, leading a widespread clandestine network, and what is more, expelled from various countries and condemned in Spain for high treason as an agent of Hitler. These dispatches upset the censor, who obtained information and realized that this is a campaign like the ones aimed at Trotsky before his assassination. Probable objective: if these dispatches are published in the USSR, that of preparing public opinion for a crime that would also be a scandal; if they aren't published, the same preparation in leadership circles. Aside from this, it is perhaps also a clever way of attracting the attention of all the secret services, the various censors, and counterespionage agencies before releasing forgeries. In any case, this is being done on orders from Moscow with a precise objective.

To be connected to this is the campaign sketched out in *El Universal Gráfico*, which recently published an article saying that with Natalia Trotsky we are founding a new International and that we are the organizers of railway workers' strikes! (The Communists themselves play an important role in these strikes.) Gregorio López y Fuentes published our denial.

Jesús Hernández,* former Communist minister of public education in Spain, and who is probably nothing more than a gangster, arrived from Moscow with Anton, the same Anton who led the campaign against the POUM during the Civil War. They stopped at the Hotel Hipodromo, from which Jesús Hernández vanished without even regularizing his papers. He's said to be at the Soviet embassy. People are wondering whether he will be put in charge of secret work or leave with a new identity for Algeria or Spain (via Portugal, the normal route). It is believed that he is in disgrace and that the dangerous missions confided to him are a way of getting rid of him.

Added—On Thursday, February 3, the TASS agency sent a telegram to Moscow about us containing these words dictated by M.: "Moscow is surprised that the governments of London and Washington have not yet obtained from the Mexican government decisive measures against these enemies of the United Nations, etc." It's about filling the files of all the censors in the world.

CLAUDEL PERFORMED BY JOUVET

February 1, 1944—The auditorium of Bellas Artes, vast, opulent, red velvet and copper, packed. Its style is aimed at the comfortable luxuriousness of a time of newly wealthy merchants, but the curves of an architecture already dominated by concrete and metal predominate. It's very expensive and only well-dressed people can be seen. The French public of Mexico City consists solely of businessmen whose businesses have rapidly prospered in the tropics under a semicolonial regime and of their entourage. The mercantile hothouse produces beautiful young girls in moderate numbers, chic young men with empty faces, and fat parents, a mere glimpse of whom lets you imagine their apartments, the armchairs and knickknacks, the painting in the dining room. Few Mexicans, the presidential box is empty. Strange that they have so little curiosity about real theater. Jouvet in his dressing room. Backstage is spacious, the dressing rooms set up like offices . . . Louis Jouvet receives us in a brown dressing gown while removing his makeup. He has a Gothic head, a vigorous though long neck that seems scrawny, large pupils in round pop eyes the blue of polished stones, a rather hooked nose. A sort of distraction in his expression—a man who lives on tension and relaxation over a continuous internal vibration become monastic. He has something of the visionary, the fanatic (fanatical artisan of his art), of the deceiver about him—and he's certainly crafty. I asked one of his female collaborators and she responded evasively, laughingly: "Visionary to be sure, but also a real operator." Stubborn, hardworking, obsessive, proud. He looks dulled down after his efforts on the stage: we're the tiresome intermission intruders. Onstage he is grave, he admires himself and admires every word he pronounces in a confident voice—in a regal voice that, of course, monarchs aren't capable of. He pontificates on stage, and it's gripping.

The emotion of hearing a crowd speak French, of seeing young French faces. But this crowd is too conspicuously rich. In a box near us the former king Carol, his sharp-featured face of an elegant, worn-out rodent. Mme. Lepescu, next to him, in a fur coat, is a model of vulgarity, without the least bit of intelligence, vice, aggressiveness, or anything at all: banal, well into her forties, heavily made up, her hair dyed, her profile heavy, her eyes bovine. Next to these insignificant beings a someone, the Court Minister Urdărianu, athletic and square shouldered, a long head, dark, tanned, bags under his sunken, hidden eyes. The man of the casinos, the bizarre witness in the affairs of false checks and suspicious deaths; the witness who will never say anything he doesn't mean to, but who can be counted on for any low blow. (I'd met them at the home of Ed. V. upon arriving in Mexico City and seen them from up close and already had this impression.) Around them bankers, diplomats, society types. Claudel's Christian verses fall like flattering rain on these men content with themselves and with the degraded, stupidly anti-Christian, antihuman world they are making. They feel themselves ennobled, imagining that they understand something about these verses, but in reality they consume this tragic poem as if it were a well-made mayonnaise.

Painful to think that this great Christian, Claudel, passed most of his life—all of his social life—in diplomacy, surrounded by worldly hypocrisies and taking pleasure in them. In contrast, what happiness and courage in Nietzsche's solitude! Man *alienated* from himself (Marx): he puts the best of himself in his work, and the rest, well, the rest is "nothing but literature," lived out, miserably bourgeois.

What a mockery that this Christian clamor, which resonates so strongly, posing every problem with such humble and elevated grandeur, should be cast before this wealthy public that, all in all, is blissful, iniquitous, and stupid; before these two-bit diplomats; this thieving, fascist, murderous, anti-Semitic, dissolute businessman-king. The mockery seems total: the negation of all the values affirmed in creative suffering and thought. Image of this society ending in the negation of itself. This *social* vision that imposes itself on me in order to separate me from this world (how "Christian" I feel!) is incomplete. In each of them can be found society and man himself, man in the face of love, death, and fate, with his load of bestiality and spirituality. It is right, it is good, it is necessary that this cry be thrown out to all, beyond the social, from the very depths of the social in order to touch the eternal and profound man beneath the thick, contemptible envelope of the financier, the socialite, and *tutti quanti*. Some, however few they may be, will be touched: art is justified, it hasn't completely sold itself: it has maintained its incorruptible essence.

DREAM: EARTHQUAKE

February 4, 1944—Noted this intense dream last night: I was with Jean de Ménil in a room colored mahogany or deep, red velvet. Dominique and a child had just gone to the bathroom or into another room. The earth began to shake, the entire building—it was a kind of skyscraper—swayed back and forth in slow, wide arcs, further and further. I felt great curiosity and looked out the window, which was narrow and high. An immense, magnificent urban landscape was laid out before me: a bend in the Seine, seen from on high, silvered by the moonlight, the little bridges standing out in a delicate black outline over the metallic water. In the right foreground the Tower of the Dog at the Kremlin, massive, the color of faded brick bathed in shadow; lower down the square roof of a tottering tall cement building with lighted windows, swaying. I didn't see the shaking of the city, our building seemed to be the only one swaying. I went to another window, I don't remember what I saw there. I thought that we had to go downstairs, I hurriedly called Jean and Dominique, annoyed that D. was so slow in leaving the bathroom or the other room. Then the idea occurred to me that it would be pointless to go downstairs, that we wouldn't have the time. I returned from the landing to the main room. Suddenly, the whole building began to tilt to one side, falling. I said to Jean, who was calm: "We're going to be crushed," but I still had hope, and then, when I understood there was nothing to hope for, I said: "We're going to be killed, unless this is a bad dream, a flight into neurosis." I put both my hands on my face and woke up; that is, the dream continued but I now thought with relief that I was awake.

Here there is a break, then I find myself alone on the street, at night, a kind of Avenida Juárez (I have the feeling that it's Avenida Juárez, but it's wider, with a vaguely Parisian atmosphere). I'm worried about

Laurette and Jeannine, I want to get home quickly, I tell myself that the house on the Calle Hermosillo is solid and must have resisted the quake. I enter a small tobacconist's shop on the corner, I ask for Virginias and while the shop owner looks for them the earthquake starts up again. The shop owner continues to serve me and, encumbered with a package, with difficulty I gather together thirty-five centavos and a torn *planilla*[3] that I don't want to lose. At the same time I think that it's idiotic to worry about pennies, a *planilla*, and cigarettes when the earth is shaking. I leave, the ground is still moving in swells, kids are chasing each other on the asphalt, they're about bump into me, I get angry. The asphalt is wet, it has rained, there are neon signs, I raise my head towards a small hotel whose softly illuminated windows are covered by cream-colored curtains; it's somewhere on the Champs-Élysées.

(I'd spent the evening with Jean and Dominique de Ménil at a concert at Bellas Artes where the hall was dark red, monumental. In bed I often have the sensation of a light, prolonged earthquake. The words "flight into neurosis" relate to Freud's theory about religion, which I have often thought of recently—but the intervention of psychoanalysis into the dream itself is strange. Paris, Moscow, and Mexico City mixed together form for me nothing but a completely natural internal site.)

I'd just heard a symphony concert. A powerful concerto by Grieg and Stravinsky's *Firebird* Suite had carried me into the depths of a formless but intense reverie, almost without ideas and images. During the day I'd worked on a description of the concentration camp of La Saulte (novel) without succeeding in fixing the image of Lieutenant Cyprien.[4]

I was rather depressed, sad, for private reasons and because of an overall view of history that often torments me. I'd spoken of it to D. in the restaurant and to Audel and realized it did me good to talk about it. To be clarified.

3. Bus ticket.
4. References to a locale and a character in Serge's novel *Last Days*.

SCIENTIFIC SOCIALISM AND PSYCHOLOGY

February 17, 1944—"Scientific" socialism, that is, with sincere scientific aspirations, indeed nourished by contemporary advances in knowledge, and adroit enough to find support in the enormously effective myth which science was becoming, thanks to the dual advent of modern industrial technology (scientific, in effect) and an infinitely expanded vision of man and history—the scientific socialism of Marx-Engels-Lenin-Trotsky-Bukharin was, in fact, the furthest advanced point of the nineteenth century's active knowledge. Impossible to separate knowledge from activity, knowledge is action, domination of nature and even human nature, utilitarian dynamism even in its most disinterested aspects, those furthest from practical activity. In this sense Nietzsche's proposition that *what is true is what serves life* is profoundly correct: the search for truth is a combat for life; the truth which is never settled once and for all, being forever in the process of becoming, is a conquest ceaselessly recommenced through a more useful, more stimulating approximation to an ideal truth that is perhaps inaccessible. Scientific socialism was born around a half century before modern psychology. It is natural that social-economic questions were posed before those of the knowledge of man's depths. The capitalist century was that of the primacy of the economy. Previously theology concerned itself with man's depths, but its solutions and point of view fell into obsolescence. (It should be noted that Sigmund Freud, Alfred Adler, and others felt the need to react against "soulless psychology" and gave the word "soul" a precise meaning.) The great Marxists, principally the Russians, absorbed in combat and intoxicated by practical success, ceased to follow the current of the developing sciences. Lenin's philosophical book, *Empirio-Criticism*, is the weakest of his works. Among Marxist works, Engels's *Anti-Dühring* is the one that is the most dated, and I seriously doubt whether anything can be learned from Plekhanov's monism. The vulgar application of the thesis according to which "Marxism isn't a philosophy but a method of transforming the world" was often an intellectual defeat. In reality, Marxism remained a philosophy while losing from sight the fact that the world can't be transformed without a constant renewal of its philosophy, without a permanent updating of the most general ideas in keeping with growing scientific gains.

The result of neglecting this updating, of the (at times legitimate) mistrust of psychology by socialists, of the attempts (not entirely unsound) at explaining psychological thought using the methods of historical materialism, has been that socialism has allowed itself to be outstripped by science and that the new sciences, no longer fecundated by the influence of idealistic socialism, have all the more strongly felt the influence of reactionary currents. During the Russian Revolution these phenomena produced a veritable intellectual catastrophe that greatly facilitated the advent of totalitarianism. The excuse of the great Russians was that they didn't have time; that they had only had ten years to work and almost always under the threat of death.

The theory of ideological superstructures essential to historical materialism, based, in the final analysis, on the economic structure of societies, cannot survive without a major updating. Corollary: the understanding of the role of the individual in history can no longer content itself with the Marxist vision of the last century. If it is true that Napoleon was a product of the bourgeois revolution, this general truth is so general that it obliterates the entire problem of Napoleon's personality. I think of the well-intentioned imbeciles at the Museum of Modern Art in Moscow (Morozov Gallery) who placed statistics on the rise of the French bourgeoisie alongside the Renoirs and Gaugins. These figures certainly cast a certain indispensable light on French art of the era, but the unique light that this art casts on the figures remains entirely unexplained. 1. The ideological (and psychological) superstructures have become so complex, so weighty, so rich in the more than two thousand years of continuous Western civilization, that they have acquired considerable involuntary creative or destructive autonomy in relation to the economy; to a large extent they live on themselves (a striking example: religion in Russia). (Other examples, nationalities and their traditions.) 2. Psychology highlights the fact that although man obeys social determinism, he bears within him mental burdens accumulated since his origin. (All in all, civilizations are recent.) 3. Certain of these burdens, whose power is incommensurable, predate humanity, date back to the animal state. 4. A correct vision of history must take into account the psychology of societies and individuals, even in the analysis of specific events. In daily life we must take into account the characteristics and mentality of groups, of masses, of personalities, and each of us of our own personality, which is difficult but not impossible, and in any case necessary.

Lenin's will predicted the split between Trotsky and Stalin and is, in this regard, an excellent anticipatory document. A while ago I asked Fritz Fränkel, after having related the scene of the break between Trotsky and Stalin at the Central Committee in 1927, a scene during which an outburst by Trotsky mortally offended Stalin,[5] if these two men, who believed themselves to be divided only by disinterested political concepts (and the ambitions connected to them: the feeling of a mission to be fulfilled) wouldn't have done well, before going to meetings of the Central Committee, to consult a good psychologist. "They would certainly have benefited from it," he responded. "They would have controlled and understood themselves better." This would perhaps not have changed the fight, but it would have taken it to a higher level through an increase in self-awareness.

Men are psychological beings. Impossible to act with them or on them without taking this fact into account—in the most serious sense of the word. Socialist schematicism strived to understand only productive man at a time when capitalist development was pulling along and grinding up, in different ways, both bosses and employees, failing to take their souls into account, and when scientific technique, producing machines, had not yet produced psychological analysis. "No psychology!" I heard this phrase in Russia thousands of times. It meant, We're fighting, we're working, efficiency first, material objectivity! And it was an outgrowth of the most narrow-minded industrial pragmatism. It reached its lowest point when the prosecutor Vishinsky pronounced it at the Moscow Trials—and Trotsky was called upon a short time later to defend psychology. What is striking is that the Russian Revo-

---

5. In the argument over Stalin's support of Chiang Kai-shek, who massacred the revolutionary workers of Shanghai, Trotsky called Stalin the "gravedigger of revolution."

lution was ended by a psychological drama. All of contemporary history gravitates around this drama and the Nazi phenomenon, which is both economic and psychological.

The present totalitarian times are those of psychology disdained and subordinated to the organization—economic in the first instance— of the state. Just as the impoverished science of the Middle Ages was conceived as the "servant of theology," psychology, reduced to a few violent and rudimentary practical applications by thought control, is conceived of as a servant of the state as the organizer of production. These are regressive times despite their technical progress, since they affirm the primacy of the organization over the human. Just as political economy was the revolutionary science of the capitalist era, psychology will perhaps be the revolutionary science of totalitarian times. Socialism can no longer ignore it without degrading itself and reducing itself to a kind of sterility.

HITLER MAINTAINS THE KOLKHOZES

Why hasn't the mass-circulation press published this significant news? We learn in an article by Maurice Hindus* in *The New Republic* that a decision by Hitler maintains the regime of kolkhozes in the occupied territories and that the magazine *Das Reich* published an article on August 17 proposing various improvements to the internal statutes of the kolkhozes. Maurice Hindus sees in this fact an homage rendered by Hitler to the collectivization of agriculture. The Soviet peasant would rather do without such homages and has showed this by spilling his blood in abundance. But one is surprised that Maurice Hindus hasn't realized something that seems to us to be a blinding truth: if Hitler is keeping the kolkhozes it is because he finds in them a nearly perfect apparatus for the exploitation of the peasant; it is that he realizes he couldn't do better in exploiting the labor of the people of the land. The conqueror is rendering homage not to the socialist principle, but rather to the perfecting of tyranny. We wrote in our book on the war in Russia that the invader, far from seeking to reestablish a monarchy or capitalism in Russia, would most probably seek to take control of the bureaucratic machine in order to use it to exploit the Russian people, and that with time he will certainly find accomplices among the young Stalinist bureaucrats. These facts provide us with our first confirmation, a strong one.

Is there any need to stress that the socialist principle of agricultural cooperation and large-scale collective rural exploitation have nothing to do with kolkhozes imposed by terror to allow the totalitarian state to mercilessly exploit the farmers? Remember that for several years the kolkhozes delivered veritable starvation rations to their members. And that in 1936 the Soviet academician Strumilin,* demonstrating that Russian peasants were finally enjoying real well-being, estimated the consumption of cereals per capita that year—a good one—at 261.6 kilos. But Lenin indicates in one of his first works as an economist that in 1892, in the government of Saratov, the annual per capita consumption of cereals reached 419.3 kilos (plus 13.3 kilos of lard—lard not being at all mentioned in the article by the academician Strumilin, who speaks of 4.07 kilos of milk and dairy products per capita annually).

These reflections on subjects that ceaselessly preoccupy me were brought into sharper focus in relation to the conflict that painfully separates me from certain comrades, militants of value who are far more dominated by deep-rooted feelings—of which they are not aware, sometimes have no idea of—than by objective convictions. Our socialist emigration lives on an elementary socialism, summarily Marxist, that hasn't been brought up to date for twenty years and which ignores the transformations of both the economy and psychology. Most continue to see nothing but the too-facile alternative socialism-capitalism and think only in terms of an impoverished historical materialism. In addition: distrust of and hostility to any new assertions; an inferiority complex in regard to intellectuals; resentment-disappointment in regard to all that issues from the Russian Revolution; the petty ambitions of defeated leaders, all the more bitter because they affect devoted men; and finally, the bad mental habits of political scheming inculcated by the life of destroyed parties. G. exclaimed at a meeting, "Our epoch has no further need of a Marx!" (I responded: "May it please God for us to find several.") A small, aggressive woman, at another meeting where I had spoken of the emigration's potential role, shouted derisively: "But where are the Lenins?" Gironella writes me: "Individuals are never indispensable." I observe that the fact of having a lengthy past as a militant and intellectual is a handicap for me. People have a tendency to reproach me for it; the past, the work accomplished, and present tasks displease, bother, offend. All of this is part of psychology of defeat among men lacking the means to know and observe themselves, who don't even know that they should try to know and observe themselves.

THE LOSER'S TRADE

February 19, 1944—The loser's trade is one of the most thankless professions: people, average or weak, feel defeat—their own and that of others—as a stain. Their own embitters them and, in embittering them, diminishes them. That of others—even when it is also their own—stirs up low instincts, and people feel the urge to give a kick in the ass to the annoying loser who continues to resist. S., talking with me about the correctness of certain of Trotsky's ideas, observed: "Yes, but even so he lost, and that totally discredited him." An unavowed discredit, which is the worst kind; one to which you wouldn't dare admit without blushing, and for which you seek reasons that aren't the real ones. Rare are those who simply say: For my part, I'm on the side of the strongest. People prefer to not even say this to themselves and to justify the disaffection felt for the vanquished by circumstantial arguments. Yet trial by power or success doesn't testify in favor of intelligence, nor in favor of justice, nor in favor of moral values (nor is it completely separate from them; power and success, in history's good moments, can be and are connected to real values, but the latter are more the values of peace than of war, more creative than destructive). The extreme inconsistency of this mediocre Nietzscheanism, this "morality of strength and immediate success," is that it is strictly opportunistic. Struggles go on: power and success change places, reverses and victories alternate for the same cause.

In contrast with banality is the attitude of great characters who fight on, reckoning on changes in destiny: defeated in external reality but not defeated in their souls. When I was fourteen, reading Houssaye,[6] I was swept away by Blücher, who, defeated at Ligny on June 15 [1815], trampled by a horse on the battlefield, stands up, begins the pursuit of the victor, meets up with him on June 18 at Waterloo, and defeats him. At the time Blücher was around seventy years old and had always been defeated by Napoleon. Other examples: Hugo prophesizing in exile for twenty years. The Russian revolutionaries between 1870 and 1917. These positive examples don't apply to the situation of today's European revolutionaries, whose defeat is far more profound in far more uncertain circumstances. Blücher had behind him the organized German nation, the enthusiastic youth, and the Kingdom of Prussia. Hugo was supported by the liberal spirit of the times, which ensured him immense popularity and an excellent material situation. The Russians, for fifty years, benefited from the sympathy of the Western world; they felt they were being carried along by history's current, their ideology was intact and progressive, and despite persecution their momentum grew. Today, for the socialists, even though historical developments largely confirm their ideas, the difficulties are infinitely greater. 1. Totalitarianism inflicts total defeat, annihilation, and via thought control aims at preventing the rebirth of ideas and the formation of characters (and totalitarianism is latent even in antitotalitarian states). 2. Socialist thought is no longer up to date, it has nearly lost its scientific mythology, and its major updating will only be possible with the liberation of vast movements of opinion. 3. Reformism and Stalinism have long been carrying out a reverse selection of intelligence and character, seconded by reactionary repression. 4. Since the Russian Revolution, the bourgeoisie's defensism has dragged along the European intelligentsia, only capable of living off the bourgeoisie. 5. Problems no longer have the same beautiful simplicity of the past. It was easy to live on antinomies like *socialism or capitalism*. We are now in the midst of a total transformation of the world, in a shifting chaos, surrounded by falsifications, complex facts, uncertain ideas, transitory interests, and violence. How

6. Probably Arsène Houssaye, prolific writer and administrator at the Comédie Française.

to find one's place? Nothing obscures consciousness more than interests of the moment, when they are involved in deadly struggles.

MICHOACÁN-PÁTZCUARO

February 20–27, 1944—Trip with Laurette in the Michoacán. Burned steppes, the earth rust red, yellow, arid, this vast country without villages, its ravines, its waterless slopes abandoned to the sun. One wonders what the cows graze on in this desert solitude. Adobe cottages between a few barbed magueys, sumptuously decorative because, with their severely rigorous forms, they proclaim vegetal energy, give an impression of sobriety and tragic solitude. Stations: Medieval beggars at the windows, their copper faces furrowed, virile, fierce. These are the brothers of our Russian beggars, and they constantly remind me of figures painted by Breughel. The sun scorches the earth, man, destitution, the will to live. Upon entering Michoacán the landscape changes, turns green: wide valleys, radiant fields: it does one's eyes good. I feel how close and necessary plant life is to us.

Saw Pátzcuaro again. The city is neglected, a little old, Hispano-Indian town, Spanish in its stones, Tarasco in its people. Odd to often see gray or blue eyes there.

Market day, bright colors, poverty. Tarascos climb the road there from neighboring villages bearing their humble merchandise, often only a few long, transparent fish the shade of soft horn. The women carry their children on their backs, wound in blue shawls. The wide-awake child who never seems to cry: there are dozens or hundreds of them, silent, already serious, as if resigned. Meat is sold—lamb, I think, dried in the sun in thick, flat dark leaves, which don't look too bad. The beggars wander about, old, infirm, beneath broad filthy hats and dusty serapes. Great calm. On one side of the plaza a handsome closed-up house painted red-pink with bourgeois curtains and a balcony. Behind a second-floor window a well-to-do man in European attire smokes as he gazes on the swarm in the plaza. He reigns. An ordinary-looking sixteenth-century *ayuntamiento*; three barred windows on the second floor, from which men in sombreros also gaze out onto the plaza as they converse. They are prisoners in the jail. I am told that some are serving sentences of several years, some of them for having eloped with their fiancée instead of asking her parents and then concluding the affair commercially by negotiating a dowry. On the side streets, lined with gaily colored low houses and large awnings, pass a type of conveyance I recognize: the *arba* of the Caucasus: two squat oxen with wide horns, a cart with two high wheels. A peasant drives it, just like his unknown brothers of Ossetia and Mingrelia, virtually the same wide-brimmed hat, a barbed whip in his hand. In a peacefully radiant street that climbs towards a baroque church the color of terra cotta, the young beggar crouching in the doorway, either an idiot or mad, rises as we approach, extending a pink and brown hand that's a horrible sight, scaled with hardened filth. His face is as motionless as a mask with brown lifeless eyes that see and understand.

The Hotel Principal has three cantinas side by side: El Sol de Oro, El Edén, Ternura. A bus painted faded lilac, banged up from collisions, the bodywork dented with missing patches, is named El Bolchevique. "An Old Bolshevik," says Laurette, "the last one, all worn out and covered in scars but still running, huffing and puffing, over the roads of Mexico..." —A woven basket on sale with this motto: "*Feo, pero me quieres.*"[7] In the center of the plaza, beneath magnificent trees, the bronze statue of Gertrudis Bocanegra,[8] a strong woman, body straining, full of virile energy. Gertrudis Bocanegra was tortured here for having fought for independence. Her breasts were torn off. O'Gorman placed her in his fresco in the library, dressed in white, her open breast bleeding like a fountain. Satisfaction at seeing that spacious library again— few books, few readers, many busy children, an elderly teacher advising them. The edifice is that of a church, the stunning fresco displaying its powerful imagery in its depths. This fresco continues the tradition of codices, which recount the annals in images. I leave it to others to say that this imagery isn't art because it expresses neither the metaphysics nor psychoanalysis of deluxe reviews and art galleries. In bright blue, in red, in fire, it sings a terrible and legendary story for children large

7. Ugly, but you love me.
8. Heroine of Mexican independence, executed by the Spanish on October 11, 1817.

and small with simple symbols that are easily touching; it is elementary and bright, it speaks to simple people and it speaks to me. And it would speak to you as well if you weren't so full of yourself, so distant from simple folk, so distant from the harshness of real life, which is neither literature nor beautiful editions. About this fresco O'Gorman told me: "I'm happy to have painted at Pátzcuaro because art must penetrate the pueblos. I start with the idea that the Indios need it more than the big financial centers." He's right. The former seminary of Don Vasco de Quiroga has become a museum, a museum without treasures, well maintained. A few Tarasco sculptures, a *Chac Mool*[9] found in the region that reveals the Maya influence. I admire plates resting on the three perfect breasts of a woman. Figurines of the dead, some painted red. On a patio full of flowers, the dwellings of fishermen have been reconstructed with beautiful sculpted wood. Inside, lace of colored paper, nets.

We cross the city on carnival day. A neighborhood crossroads. The streets tumble in gentle slopes towards the countryside. Triangular *plazuela*, a fountain, pruned-back trees with nothing remaining but gray, scarred trunks. Festival (small crowd, neighbors). A group of musicians; maskers act out comical corridas. A big devil half-hidden under a white cardboard bull carried on his shoulders and which charges the grotesque toreros with its little goat horns. Some of the toreros are dressed as women, wearing the long, red and black pleated skirts typical of the region. An admirably muscled young man, dressed up this way and coiffed by a large straw hat, does a dance with a machete. He strikes the pavement with his steel. This group goes from door to door bearing the homage of its comic dance, executed with verve and gravity and—given the heat—amazing energy. Total indifference of the dancers and spectators to our presence. In the heart of the city another group of dancers, this one striking because of its extraordinary bandit costumes. Several characters in rags and fedoras with wide, sharply snapped brims, one wearing a mask with a large black beard and Cyrano nose, the other a devil's mask like those primitives carve in wood. The first is wearing pants of torn fur, and the devil, who is

9. A type of pre-Columbian sculpture.

smaller, an old homespun overcoat. Those dressed like women on the other hand are wearing pink and white masks like tiny Breton maids with astonished eyebrows and content and blissful smiles. They act out their corrida while waving their whips and machetes: it's a ball of idiotic hoodlums and innocents. The music grinds, the cardboard bull waddles, attacks... They are so denatured that I am relieved to see one of them take off his white girl's mask, worn beneath a kind of yellow straw boater, to cool himself off. They will carry on like this for hours. Neither noise nor shouts nor laughter at this festival: it's the accomplishment of a rite in which what we call joy seems to be lacking. Not the least gaiety in the European sense of the word. Unleashed force, rhythmic, visionary, a kind of moderated frenzy. Joy and gaiety: I don't know if these words can be applied to the Indio. He is always calm, ruled by a passive energy, controlled, taciturn, violent, and his internal rhythm is slow, never agitated. He loves song, music that sounds like a litany or a cantilena, dances with ritualized steps that doubtless induce a kind of trance. No one laughs and we don't feel like laughing.

Standing before these Indians I can never forget that they only entered into contact with European civilization five centuries ago and that all they knew of it at the start was cruelty, and that they still only know the implacable aspects of colonial capitalist penetration. At the time of Cortés's arrival they were men of polished stone organized by a barbaric, patriarchal, and bloodthirsty civilization. Perhaps the gaiety, the cheerful forms of joie de vivre that we know are acquisitions requiring a culture several millennia older, with centuries of well-being and security. Or of wealth and free adventure. The French peasants described by La Bruyère probably didn't laugh very much either.

LAKE PÁTZCUARO—GIRAUDOUX

February 20–27, 1944—Lake Pátzcuaro offers a boundless landscape: opalescent, pearly, silky-gray, silver, shimmering... The impotence of words. When I write I'm often hindered, almost paralyzed by the irremediable gap between the sensation, the vision, and the words at our disposal. At bottom, description based on images is nothing but a petty game of more or less clever comparisons and parallels. The lake is "like a lightly moving mirror"; that's true, but why must I relate it to a mirror, to that little, useful household item which in reality it in no way resembles? The trick of the Surrealists and aesthetes to seek an unexpected comparison—"The plumes of voices burst from the burning bush of lips" (Benjamin Péret)—is excellent because it is perhaps spontaneous, but I doubt it's possible to produce many spontaneous (or elaborated) images of this quality without concentrating the mind on this production, a concentration that can only harm thought in general, observation, and other concerns. Rather than inventing unusual or simply new images, I prefer to consider things simply, describe them with ordinary words and pursue my problems. And I don't think there is a middle way. Aside from two or three books that are extraordinary successes, *Bella* and *Suzanne et la Pacifique*, Giraudoux lost himself in his sprays of sparkles, yet he projected an encyclopedic culture and constant concern for the intelligence into the taut poem of his prose. But I wasn't able to continue reading one of his latest novels, so poor was the plot, so blandly fashionable and bourgeois (Tolstoy would have disdained this jeu d'esprit, the Giraudoux style). I thought of Giraudoux because he has just died in Paris, stifled and bitter, yet working away relentlessly. About sixty. I'd found him (one day at the offices of Grasset) so young, so tall, with a strongly handsome face and a sharp and discreet gaze. He didn't suspect that he incarnated what was most diamonded in predisaster French literature. "Diamonded" isn't an adjective meant to shock here, but a mot juste: the diamond is hard, irreducible, sparkling, of high crystalline quality, but it's not alive.

Our boat, rowed by a young man with slanted eyes and a straight nose, who washes only rarely but is handsome all the same, is crossing the radiant, silk-gray lake. Above the opalescent hills in the distance shines the enormous plume of clouds from the volcano, apparently motionless, and spreading out in a mane of slightly leaden white clouds. In the evening, as the sunset embroiders the edges of the eruption in flames, one can see the trail of ash extending out over the horizon. We are approaching a green, rocky isle. Fishermen's nets, huts, a path climbing to the summit between blocks of fallen lava, little fields of maize, cactus bushes. Why do we feel such joy climbing up where the horizon stands out more clearly, expands? It is too disinterested to contain the least element of will to power (I thought of a vague feeling of world domination). It is rather the pleasure of escape, of community with earthly spaces (for every contemplation implies identification with the thing contemplated). We are happy to see the lakeshore emerging green under the limitless sun and sky. Lizards and snakes slithering through the dry grass are making a quiet sound of metallic friction. At the summit of the island, a square white house. At our approach a flock of dark children, whom we visibly amuse, pour out of it. These little Tarascos are healthy, tanned; half of them are truly beautiful boys and girls, with wide, bony, full faces, rounded brows, velvety brown eyes, firm gazes, white teeth. They differ little from the Mediterranean race. Three classes of eight children each in the same cool, open-air room. The teacher, an India who is probably in her seventies, pleasant and dignified, explains that she teaches Spanish and arithmetic; they already know Tarasco. The handwriting of the ten-year-old kids is good, she works wonders, this old woman in her fishing village. What wealth of unrecognized talents do the millions of Indio children of these lands possess? And the little money needed has not yet been found to bring together a hundred of them in a good high school that would reveal them to themselves. The nightclubs of Mexico City waste more every month than would be needed for this undertaking.

Another day the lake grew angry and, under a pure sky and bright sunshine, we had gusting winds and serious whitecaps. Laurette was charmed, I was nervous. It would be idiotic to drown in this enchantment.

PARICUTÍN

February 20–27, 1944—Between Pátzcuaro and Uruapan the countryside turns into a huge mountainous garden, slashed with dry streambeds. A lake appears in the hollow of the green mountains: blue enamel, not a single sail, but a tiny village lying on its shore, its church . . . (Near Ajuno.) The three provincial plazas of Uruapan, enlivened by beautiful trees, a naive monument to Zapata, the marketplace, the shops, everything coated in ash: the pink village is soiled. An oasis, Cupatitzio Park, the "Enchanted Waters" where the waters flow in all directions, spurting from the rocks in a thousand springs, leaping in cascades amid the tropical foliage—coffee trees—darkened by the rain of ash.

A car to Paricutín with a couple from Guadalajara, the man, an energetic gray face, perhaps a former sailor, the woman Spanish, flabby and white, conjugal as if she had just stepped out of bed. She calls him *papacito*. A region of the sky is losing the light, becoming oppressive and gray, as if strong rains ruled there, but the clouds are opaque and purplish. Ashes. For a journey of several hours we enter a landscape of gray desolation, creamy, a country of whiteness spread over the land, a spectral land. Ashes cover the plains, the crops, the roads, the woods, as far as the eye can see like a snowfall, colorless yet somber. A murdered land, vegetation dying or dead. Fallen trees, trees cut down, not a bird, not an insect; it is pallid and could just as well be the Siberian tundra, but deathly. Laurette thinks of a battlefield where the artillery has left nothing living. And it was in fact a battle between the subterranean fire and the living earth, the vanquished earth. Kilometers and kilometers like this, then the massive and shifting column of smoke filled with sand and ashes rises, flaring, its spirals slowing moving and melding. They move like entrails. It rains sand and ash, we progress through a white and mineral fog.

San Juan Parangaricutiro has become increasingly destitute, death is making progress there. The wide streets of the lovely village are disappearing beneath the ash, the fences are collapsing, the resistance of the barbed nopals is giving way, most of the houses are abandoned, the ash weighs on the roofs, the gardens are dead ... The rare children in serapes, horribly filthy and taciturn. On the church square the stores are closed, no more electricity, *tiendas* standing in the wind under the mineral rain sell food and drink to the last guides. The grayness, the filthiness of everything, even faces, even eyes, even gazes that seem weighted with black ash. The church, one of whose bell towers is unfinished, looks like it's been mutilated in a bombardment. On the square a stone cross weeps in silence. At the end of a street the black and visceral eruption invades the sky, dominating the site.

We start out on foot to climb the final slope towards the crater.

Atmospheric currents guide the monstrous plume of aerial lava towards the countryside we just left; we are climbing through the ever-stronger mineral rain. At sunset we cross a devastated, limitless plain, the entire horizon white and finely shaded, very beautiful; we are entering the murdered woods, we are sinking into the soft ash, the night is falling, the rain coming down harder; it is crackling on my hat. Laurette shelters her eyes with a handkerchief. At the *campamento*, after twilight, we have the feeling of a monstrous, inexorable burial. The nearby conical crater sinks into the night and the sandy mist it exhales. White smoke crawls on the left, and glimmerings of an incandescent red emerge from the massive dark eruption. They battle the smoke, grow pale, and vanish. The volcano exhales: we have been walking under its rhythmic respiration of terrestrial breaths, like cannonades. In the few huts the Indios leaning against the wooden counters where beer and coffee are served have crushed and deformed silhouettes. Smoky lamps pierce the shadows. The mules stand out fantastically against the night. Even so, one or two stars pierce the sky. This isn't a vision of cosmic power, of the beginning of the world, like the one I had the first time. It's a vision of monstrous suffocation, of the end of the world. It is said that Paricutín is dying, though some days its energy bursts forth anew in magnificent flames.

A railroad worker tells us how good business was here, the *cervecerías* set up beneath the splendid crater, the dances in the great red glow, the festive atmosphere of San Juan while most of the population was fleeing, the local authorities thinking of charging a toll on all the cars.

SIEVA
March 2, 1944—Ran into little Sieva [Volkov],* Leon Trotsky's grandson, on the bus. He bears an astonishing resemblance to his grandfather in photos from his youth, though the Jewish type is less pronounced. Sieva is entering adolescence; he must be seventeen. A bony face, harsh, severe, sad, glasses. "Do you still speak Russian?" "No, I've completely forgotten it." "But you must learn it!" "For what purpose? From sentimental attachment? No way." (This said violently.) I answer that before much time has passed Russia will change greatly; that we must

remain faithful to her and sustain great hopes for her. I sense that he doesn't believe this, that my words are meaningless for him. He is living in the tomb of Coyoacán with Natalia, seeing only a few mediocre sectarians incapable of understanding him. This is already living through his second uprooting. His mother, Zina Lvovna, committed suicide in Berlin; his father vanished into the prisons; he was wounded during Siqueiros's attack on Trotsky in May 1940; he saw his grandfather killed and knew the assassin as a "comrade."

We talk about David Alfaro Siqueiros, whose crime has gone unpunished, who has just returned to Mexico City and is enjoying success in high society. "Yes, Natalia is going to do something, the legal proceedings aren't going to stop, but none of this will serve any purpose," Sieva says. His has an expression of discouraged hardness.

I was forgetting: he saw his uncle Liova [Sedov] die a suspicious death and two tiny parties argue odiously over his corpse. Liova's companion, Jeanne Martin des Pallières, attached to the adventurer Molinier, hysterical, horribly ravaged by pain, wanted to keep the boy with her. It took a sort of kidnapping to take him from her and bring him to Mexico, which is what Marguerite Rosmer did. I was on the family council established before a notary to turn Sieva's guardianship over to the Rosmers. A justice of the peace or notary, I'm not sure which, in a room in a district town hall, a bizarre character received us, got our signatures, mumbled something in front of a clerk straight out of a play by Courteline, false collar of yellow celluloid and old-fashioned pince-nez. As for the magistrate, he was straight out of Molière. He could barely see, had to put his face right up to stamped paper to decipher a single word; he had a huge wart on his thin and gray nose, and if he didn't stutter, he might as well have. He was skinny, solemn, and stupid.

PAINTERS
March 5, 1944—María Izquierdo, at Michael Fraenkel's. She has aged greatly. Maturity on the downward slope, sorrow. Rather corpulent, a wide, mongoloid face, aquiline nose, slanted eyes, the flat planes of a North American Indian, of—to put it simply—a redskin, but she has a sallow, greenish tint this evening. In her youth she was a horseback

rider in the circus and learned to paint without knowing how to draw. Her drawings remain naive, spontaneously clumsy, but her eye is alert: it senses well, it senses better than it sees. Her feeling for color is acute as well. She uses few nuances, her colors are strong, warm and somber. Her themes: horses, the harsh Mexican mountains (backgrounds), schematic portraits, flat but intense and alive (she doesn't know how to express volume). The result is primitive modern, with vitality. Completely foreign, thank God, to the affectations of so-called advanced painting. María Izquierdo is body and soul within lived reality, loves and understands only this reality, without theories and psychological refinements. I notice her features are drawn. I had met her two weeks ago with her husband, Raúl Uribe* at the Iván Denegri show, both of them smiling, surrounded by a large crowd. Uribe: totally round: round head with a wide round smile on a short, round torso: he seems to roll as he walks. A painter as well (Chilean), but anemic, drawing and coloring unsubstantial, children, reduced to being no more than images of images. He seemed devoted to María. The day after the Iván Denegri opening Uribe disappeared, leaving everything, paintings, clothing, everything. She searched for him in the hospitals, the prisons, and then learned that, upon leaving the Chilean embassy in Manzanillo, he boarded or was put aboard a ship headed for Valparaíso. She received a letter from Guatemala in which he assured her of his affection. "I don't understand a thing. It's a political affair. For nine years he's been attached to a political coterie." That's not true.

David Alfaro Siqueiros, a founder of the Mexican CP and of *El Machete*,[10] colonel in the Spanish Republican Army during the Civil War (with no particular distinction), painter of frescoes, good artist, GPU agent, organizer of the May 24, 1940 attack on Trotsky (the murder of Sheldon Harte), freed on bail in 1941, left for Chile with the assistance of Pablo Neruda (renowned poet, consul general of Chile, Communist-GPU), has returned to Mexico City, despite having jumped bail. Protests in the newspapers. A magistrate declares that there's a

---

10. *El Machete*, magazine founded in 1924 by Xavier Guerrero, Diego Rivera, and Siqueiros, it began as the organ of the union of revolutionary sculptors and engravers and in 1925 became the organ of the Mexican Communist Party.

warrant for Siqueiros's arrest but that he (the magistrate) can't force the police to arrest him. Interesting fresco and portrait painter and landscape artist. Through intensity he achieves a primitive depth in the portraits I've seen; dark, violent tones, hot lively eyes, burning without spiritual fire. An adventurer straight out of the Italian Renaissance, born to manipulate plots, knives, pistols, paintbrushes. Rumor has it that a bloody incident involving a woman forced him to leave Havana.

LUCHA LIBRE—THE PRESTIGE OF FORCE—FAITH

March 14, 1944—Herbert Lenhoff gives us his impressions of a no-holds-barred wrestling match at the Coliseo. Perhaps ten thousand people around the ring: a mass, the masses. In the ring beautiful American girls enthusiastically attack each other. More brutality than at the bullfights, says H. L. The crowd goes into a trance when it cheers the victor. They'd shout insults at the loser if it were possible to insult and applaud at the same time ... H. L. frequents these spectacles and analyzes the public's reaction. The fighters are divided into two categories: the *científicos*, the skillful—but the word is more beautiful—and the *rudos*, the brutes. The brute is greeted with boos, general disapproval. But when he wins, mad ovations. This crowd knows it should honor honesty and skill and condemn brutality, force without art. Above all, though, what counts for it is triumphant force, victory. Conflict between instinct and conscious upbringing.

I observe that it's a banal and primordial conflict. Whole regimes, which individual conscience, enlightened conscience, disapproves of, earn praise or acceptation by appealing to instinct, through the seduction of force. The blindness and cowardice of certain intellectuals, even when they aren't personally interested or threatened, can be explained in this way. Among them, also, the primordial respect for triumphant force; obliterated intelligence tends to confuse it with life itself.

COLISEO, *LUCHA LIBRE*

March 17, 1944—The arena, poorly illuminated by a diffuse and hazy light, is a structure of reinforced concrete; bleachers up to the ceiling to a height of seven stories. It can hold several thousand people and fills up with the common folk, including many young girls with their lovers. The expensive seats: a few American tourists. The Coca-Cola sellers, in dirty white jackets, circulate. They look like hoodlums. Whistles, foot-stomping in the balcony. The ring is covered with netting to protect the fighters from projectiles.

The violent lighting blazes. A handsome young athlete with a European look, thin, built like a figure out of Michelangelo, is facing a stocky, heavy, thickset half-breed who has hardly any neck, a fat, wide, massive head, pale complexion, a mop of black hair, fleshy features, and a devious look. The first, Joe Silva, is the lightweight champion, the second, Adolfo Bonales, a violent and cruel brute (this is more or less how the program explains it). Everything is allowed in the fight except, obviously, blows to the private parts and poking out the eyes. They pull each other's hair, imprison each other's heads between their legs, suddenly box, and knock each other down with quick kicks to the chin. The most effective hold consists in grabbing the adversary's arm and twisting it or trying to break his wrist while immobilizing him with your legs. Bodies violently tied and untied, one lifts the other as high as he can, throws him down on the ring, and tries to knock him out when he gets up…There are moments when it's beautiful, and moments when it's disgustingly bestial. The athlete is an artist, skillful, the brute takes the blows admirably, rolls out of the ring, hangs into the ropes, sways beneath the *swings*,[11] resumes his cruel hammering. He obstinately seeks his adversary's face with his fingers in order to twist his nose, hurt his eyes, tear his mouth, cause him pain, make him bleed…The referee intervenes, he goes right back to it again. He emerges victorious from the bout, but he's booed and the loser applauded. When the brute leaves the ring they throw orange peels and lighted cigarettes in his face. "You, Franze!"[12] The wife of a psychoanalyst?" "Yeah, so? What a bastard!" The brute saddened me. I found it beautiful that he so clearly bore on his face the mark of what he is, but

11. In English in the original.
12. Franziska (Franze) Neumann, Fritz Fränkel's wife.

I felt no anger towards him. I wanted to shake the athlete's hand, I clapped for him.

There are no trainers to give first aid.

In another bout a Yaqui Indio the head of a warrior, a colossus with a powerful torso on long, lithe legs loses, disfigured by the twisting of his nose.

Admirable contest between Bobby Bonales and Dientes Hernández, a tall, calm, Mediterranean, small-time hood, and a slender, yellow Indio with the flat face of a coolie, smooth bodied, who dances with great agility on his bare feet. Both of them fraternal, polite, and dignified, clearly respecting each other, they're a delight to watch, showing that what makes a bout beautiful is its moral quality. The Indio is more skillful, as supple as a cat; the Mediterranean heavier, stronger, and, when he hits, he hits harder. For the final pass they seek and flee each other, fearing the final effort, in awe of each other. They seem to have an equal chance of winning. Suddenly knocked down by several direct blows, the Indio is left lying in the ring...

A colossus in a gray shirt, hideously masked in gray. The mask covers his whole head, with three horizontal openings edged in red. No opening for the nose. The Beast of children's (and adults') illustrated books. Gray Shadow, known for his "cruel brutality," is booed as he enters. He parades around while they throw peanut shells at him. Against him Carlos Lopez, "Tarzan," the "world champion," smaller but with the broad shoulders of a slaughterhouse worker, vulgar moustache, low forehead, the determined air of a bouncer who tosses annoying customers out of dives. Bitter combat in which pain plays the essential role. Tarzan dominates Gray Mask for a long spell, trying to render his arm useless and almost succeeding. Five or six times he picks him up, throws him down flat, and twists his arm. He strikes him with the side of his hand as if with the back of an axe. As the man lies gasping on the mat, the Mask, in a frenzy, comes down on his back with both feet, finally finishing him off with a horrific kick in the private parts that makes him howl. Shouts: "*Descalifíquelo!*"[13] The referee

13. "Disqualify him!"

awards victory to the defeated man. Joyful stamping of feet. The Mask leaves, protected by the police; a young woman slaps him. Laughter and applause, clamors. The disqualified fighter will return to the ring next week. They also hate him because he's American.

Circus sketch for the low end: four little women in black and white tights (Americans and an "extremely aggressive European") engage in a frantic catfight, tearing each other's hair while the referee, a redheaded Jewess in pants, bustles about. Ugly, low, no *sex appeal*[14] (for me). Joy, shouts, big laughs in the haze of the crowd: "*mátala!*"[15] A thin blonde with floating hair the color of wheat, a sharp profile, a wide mouth, the pink face of a shameless whore, small breasts, goes wild, biting her friend's foot ... It's all a show, but done with enthusiasm. Analyze the sentiments this excites. The profession of a streetwalker looks noble and natural—in contrast.

Outside, hysterical lighting and dark corners. "Hotel." Butcher's stalls, steaming tripe, girls with their hair let down in the swarming cafés. An evening of joy for these people. The newspapers announce that the Germans are still holding out in the pulverized ruins of Cassino and that the irresistible Russian advance continues ... What reigns over the world is massacre.

ON LITERARY CREATION
March 25, 1944—Wrote a short essay, flawed but dense and exhaustive, "The Writer's Message," defining the need to write in this way: "First, to grasp, imprint, understand, interpret, and re-create life; by exteriorization to liberate the confused forces one feels fermenting within oneself and by which the individual dives into the collective subconscious. In the work itself this is expressed as Witness and Message...." Perhaps the deepest source is in the feeling that marvelous life is inexorably passing, fleeing and eluding us and the desire to grab it as it goes. It was this despairing sentiment that, when I was around sixteen, impelled me to note the precious moment, led me to discover that

14. In English in the original.
15. "Kill her!"

existence (human, divine) *is memory.* Later, with the enrichment of the personality, one discovers one's limits, the poverty and chains of the Self. One discovers that one has but one life, a personality that is forever circumscribed but which contains many possible destinies and is not unique in the sense that, through countless roots, affinities, and communications (most of them inexpressible in rational terms) it is mingled with other human existences, the earth, beings, the All. Writing then becomes a search for polypersonality, a way of living several destinies, of penetrating the Other, of communing with him. All the characters in a novel, even the trees of a forest, even the heavens are integrated into the life of the author, since they spring from him. The writer becomes conscious of the world he brings to life, he is its consciousness and in this way he escapes the ordinary limits of the Self, which is both intoxicating and enriching in lucidity. (There are doubtless other types of writers, individualists, who seek only self-affirmation and can view the world only through themselves.)

I noted also that the work of art "is an act of lucid will and trance," which concerns only works that spring from the depths and not those deliberately constructed, though in the latter case there is also a gushing forth, but subordinated to the external finality and hence *feeble*, since it *can* be subordinated. There is a kind of suffering and a relief in writing. Amazing that no one has yet written the analytic novel of literary creation: too many psychological censors and repressions oppose it.

I am currently writing a novel that takes place in France during and in the immediate aftermath of the defeat.[16] I am frequently drowning in it, stopped in my tracks by darkness. I often don't know what my people are doing, where they're going: they're wrapped in fog, I feel tired, I don't feel like going on—I doubt it's worth the trouble. Then the impulse—aided by the will to work—arises on its own. According to the plan of the book—a hazy plan that's not panning out—I should carry on with certain developments involving N. I feel the urge, which I am unable to analyze, to pick up instead with Z, but I don't know;

16. *Les Derniers temps* (*Last Days*). All the characters mentioned here are from the novel.

in any case, I don't know either visually or precisely what it is he's doing, although I know the line he is following and sometimes the epilogue
he is heading for. Occupied these days with Félicien Mûrier, I suddenly
felt the need to return to Karel Tcherniak. I knew, without being sure,
that his fate was leading him to suicide. For several days I was tormented
by the presence within me of Karel Tcherniak, especially while falling
asleep, and probably as I slept. He prevented me from seeing the other
characters. I finally found a key phrase, insignificant and empty in
appearance, "Tcherniak opened the window," and I knew that the
solution was ready within me, that all that was left was to write, but I
didn't know what this solution was. It would have been impossible for
me to recount it in advance. I set myself to writing and in a few hours
this section was done, perfectly polished. K. T. opens a window with
difficulty, he fears this resumption of daily life. He sees Véronique in
the courtyard. Véronique emerged the very moment the window opens:
I hadn't consciously thought of her the minute before. K. T. as well
wasn't thinking of suicide on that day, but he is going to throw himself
into the sea without a thought, obeying a decision taken and matured
preconsciously, and detonated by the Véronique event. I wondered
what association of ideas inside me connected these themes, these
moments of life, to the action of opening a window. All I could find
was a beautiful verse by Pasternak: "Opening the window is opening
your veins," but I also feel that opening the window is a great joy in
many cases. (K. T.'s internal life followed its own course, K. T. isn't me,
though there is some of me in him; that is, I understand him and view
him from within, through identification.)

Spoke of this with Herbert Lenhoff. He says: "We've only begun
to decipher the mind. . . . The mind is infinitely mysterious." Me: "It's
barely half a century since we discovered it! Nervous center, organ, seat
of nervous life and thought, the mind was discovered earlier, in the
seventeenth century. Time was needed to go from the study of the
organ—which until now taught us little about the psyche—to the study
in depth of the psyche. This was the true discovery of the soul, of a soul
infinitely richer, more mysterious, more disconcerting than that of
mystical intuition—of a real soul.

GPU

March 21, 1944—I learn from a Catalan Communist expelled from the party that in 1940 in Moscow (he was there) it was known that the ambassador to Spain, Rosenberg,* as well as Mikhail Koltsov were alive, deported or imprisoned in Siberia.

X., arriving from New York, confidentially assures me that the name of the GPU agent who assassinated Walter Krivitsky in a Washington hotel (winter 1940–1941) is known, as well as all the details of the affair. Nevertheless, the "suicide" version remains quasi-official.

According to Willi Schlamm* a "Moscow Trial" was supposed to take place in Prague in 1937–1938 against Trotskyists and socialists; it had been agreed upon by the highest-placed personalities of the country upon Stalin's request. Its purpose was to prove that the Trotskyists are agents of Hitler, etc., by forging documents, etc. Confirmed by cross-checking the facts: the Grylewicz affair, I. Reiss's notes: Stalin several times called Yezhov, the head of the GPU, to ask him: "How is the Grylewicz affair proceeding?" (Reported to Reiss by the head of the GPU's foreign service, Slutsky,* who mysteriously died shortly afterwards.) The failure in Prague probably played a role in Yezhov's downfall.

The Mensheviks, the intelligence services of New York, and W. H. Chamberlin estimate that the population in the concentration camps of the USSR is somewhere between eight and twenty million.

GPU-COMINTERN

April 4, 1944—Conversation with Julián. A new slanderous note containing false information against us was published a few days ago by *Excélsior* (accusing us of fomenting troubles, of organizing an international party, of carrying out anti-Allied activity, etc.). These articles obviously emanate from the Stalinist embassy, they are orchestrated and pursue the same goal as the dispatches from the TASS correspondents in Moscow. The object of the reports is to alert the American and English censors and to prepare a file so stuffed with insanities that it will be impossible to figure things out. The upcoming congress of the CP has placed on its agenda: "The struggle against synarchism and Trotskyism." There must be a firm directive from Moscow with the aim of preparing something or other.

What? Let us recall the groundwork for the crimes against the POUM in Spain in 1936–1937. First a campaign of this kind, then diplomatic pressure, and finally the appearance of *forged documents* to prepare a trial. Rather than direct and compromising attacks, which the public would immediately see through, we should instead expect a police raid provoked by forged documents and perpetrated through functionaries who have, if possible, been bought off.

Stalin has opened the conflict with the United States and England (Poland, Yugoslavia, Italy, China, Finland…) and fears above all: 1. Militants who know and easily penetrate his policies; 2. The intransigent socialists over whom he has no control and who, as a result of the course of events, are capable of rallying the milieus that escape the control of the CP, which he is reorganizing, liquidating, and compromising. He is probably organizing the campaign against us personally and will stop at nothing in order to liquidate us. His final goal: assassination.

Numerous factors are working against him, in the first place his own foreign policy. We must waste no time and prepare our defense.

Openly form a defense committee. Assure ourselves of the assistance of one or two lawyers. Inform the press, our friends in the United States and England, and the local authorities of everything being plotted against us, keep an eye on publications, take note of everything. Prepare temporary refuges for exceptional situations. Locate funds…(?)

A month ago Eric Jungmann,* Ludwig Renn, and Paul Merker* of Free Germany[17] issued fantastic denunciations against us (Nazi agents, etc.) and the German socialists (Walter Oettinghuas, Thyssen). The GPU has no confidence in the Spaniards, not to be counted on, and prefers to use Germans, Hungarians, and people from the Balkans, over whom it has more control.

---

17. A movement of German exiles allied to the Communists and publishing in the USSR a review, *Freie Deutschland*.

JACKSON—GPU

April 17, 1944—One of the leaders of the CP of San Salvador [*sic*], currently living in Cuernavaca, author of a pamphlet published here, recently said about me that the CP keeps an eye on all my movements, is well informed, is "keeping me close"; that for the moment they don't envisage a physical attack on me but that they count on "obtaining my expulsion from the country."

I've been promised the name of this gentleman.

Some Spaniards think they recognized Jackson-Mornard-X? He's a Spaniard named Mercadé or Mercader* or Mercadet,[18] who participated in the Civil War as a member of the CP, was wounded in the arm, and is the son of a fanatical militant. One of his brothers was killed, his mother[19] is said to be in Moscow. Verifying the information: J. shouted a few seconds after having struck Trotsky: "My mother is in their power!" Mercadé was seen by B. [Josep Bartolí]* with a wound on his arm from an exploding shell; Jackson in fact has a scar on his arm, which he attributes to an accident while on maneuvers in France or Belgium. Finally, several people who know M. are in Mexico and it seems obvious that J. fears being recognized. He appears at all the court sessions with dark glasses and holds his face in his hands.

The writer A. S. P. is certain he recognizes him by his photo.

THE LIFE OF AN INDIO

April 18, 1944—Vlady, back from Zacapú, tells me that he was drawing an old Indio, a beggar, more than eighty years old, who was happy to talk to him, with great dignity, humility, and full lucidity. Shriveled, in rags, flea bitten, a *calavera* with lively, sad eyes under a broad hat . . . He remembered as a child having seen the French troops passing: "Handsome men with beards and moustaches and red pants. The general asked me the way. I answered: 'May your Lordship excuse me, but Don Benito (Juárez) forbids us to assist the French, so don't be

---

18. It was only in 1950 that fingerprints would confirm that his real name was Ramón Mercader.
19. Caridad del Rio Hernández.*

angry with me.' And the general said to me: 'Go, my boy.' In the year '15 or '16 of this century the Villistas arrived at the village in the Michoacán. They were bandits. They captured me and hanged me. I wasn't yet dead, being badly hanged, when an old woman set to attacking them: 'He's a father, an honest man, and a Christian.' A horseman then said, 'If I succeed in cutting the rope with my bullet he'll remain alive." The horseman fired and cut the rope. I lost consciousness (*me desmayé*)."

He has fond memories of the Carranzistas. Don Venustiano Carranza's troops occupied the region. They knew that this peasant had 200 pesos (around $40). Soldiers demanded he turn it over. He refused, showing them his children. They hit him and took him to headquarters. There he requested to appear before the general. The general told him that the citizens should support the army, but he refused to hand over his 200 pesos, telling them how poor he was. "Who hit you in the face?" the general asked. "Your soldiers, your Lordship." "My soldiers aren't bandits." "Whether they are or aren't, they're the ones who hit me, your Lordship." The general lined up his soldiers and asked the peasant to pick out those who beat him. He recognized three of them, and the general himself shot them in the head in front of the entire troop. "They fell at my feet and I pitied them. Three men dead for 200 pesos that they hadn't even managed to take from me."

Vlady paid him one peso for each session of posing (one day). After three days, the old man said to him: "I won't come to pose anymore. With the three pesos you paid me, Señor, I'll be able to take the bus and return to my village and die like a Christian." "It is far away, your village?" "Eight kilometers." Vlady offered him a fourth peso, which the old man gently refused: "I can't take it, since I didn't earn it." Vlady put it in the man's pocket.

"What dignity and wisdom among these old Indios!"

I answer: "Like among our old muzhiks."

KAFKA

April 25, 1944—Read *The Trial* by Franz Kafka, which he wrote in 1920 in Bohemia at the time of Central Europe's democratic euphoria. The book unfolds like a waking dream, a true waking dream, with a visionary sincerity acute and intelligent. It's not at all like the productions of the Surrealists, who seem to be telling you: "Watch out, we're going to release a dream in your face," and who in fact fabricate a dream in exactly the same way the Symbolist poets fabricated alexandrines. The drama reaches the heights of tragedy through the banality—confining and grandiose—of a vision that sustains itself without faltering until the final page, a vision of a perfect man struggling blindly against a formidable social machine, about which we do not know to what extent it exists objectively and to what extent it is the product of his inner complicity. The trial is absurd, the mechanism of justice turning in a void, always with reasons, as conscious and aberrant as an immense paranoia that embraces the social world. In the end, two gentlemen in bourgeois attire lead off the bank employee K., lucid and resigned, drive him outside the city limits, exchange courtesies over a knife—after you, Sir, not at all, after you—and cut his throat in the name of an impenetrable justice. This could be the visionary satire of an era yet to come. Kafka seems to have foretold totalitarian machinery, its perfect crushing of man, its throat-cuttings, and in this sense his novel is that of a visionary prophet.

The Cheka existed at the time he was writing, but it was far from having that meaning; it was even of a different essence by virtue of the revolutionary negation of the old forms of justice. And Kafka's drama unfolds on the ground of bourgeois life at its most banal.

ON HUMOR: CANTINFLAS

April 29, 1944—Cantinflas in *El Gendarme Desconocido*. Two years ago he seemed low and vulgar to me, since I didn't know Mexico. The salt of popular humor is the soil and one can only enjoy it by familiarizing oneself with the soil. Reduced to a universal common denominator, vulgarity that mocks itself is unbearable. The soil restores its slightly tragic charm, that of the human struggling with itself. The buffoonery of the bird with clipped wings who tries to fly. There is no such thing as Mexican humor, at least in the cities and in the press. The semicolonial structure is only capable of giving birth to revolutionary satire, and this has no practitioners in the privileged population of cities.

Cantinflas had been a circus clown. He stylizes himself—rather poorly—as a character vaguely inspired by the early Chaplin: jacket too short and pants falling down so that his belly is exposed down to his groin. It's quite unpleasant and often pointless. Facile stylization in order to provoke belly laughs from a childish audience. He'd do well to drop this. His manner of speaking is a perfect stylization of that of the streets, and even of the pseudointellectuals. The basis of it all is incoherence. But the power of the character comes from the fact that he is vigorous, healthy, aided by luck, which he constantly spontaneously elicits. He only ever wins by luck, without understanding, and is imperturbably bewildered. But though what he says is so incoherent as to be absurd, is it also internally coherent, instinctively so, with an innate wisdom. He seems to teach that poor devils live by chance, rolling and bouncing like balls, from stream to stream, from brawl to brawl, at times giving rise to a feeling of superiority in "the educated" (who are buffoons and profoundly limp). He has something of the urchin, of the joyous madman, of the village idiot and Père Ubu, without being aware of it, joyously, with the natural assurance of the synthetic poor devil to whom everything happens and who doesn't care, since it would serve no purpose. The only trait he owes the Mexican revolutions is a certain sense of dignity. He doesn't have an inferiority complex, he's not one of the humiliated, like the comic characters in Chekhov. He doesn't feel inferior to the overdecorated police chiefs, the bureaucrats of the ministries, or famous toreros. He seems forever to be repeating to them: Come on now, we're all men!

His language and gestures and intelligent bewilderment remind me of the characters of Zoshchenko,* but inferior. Early Soviet humor was, at bottom, sharply sarcastic and verbal. It used the amorphic syntax and neologisms of the period, showing the citizen struggling with the stammering speech of powerful and pretentious idiots in petty, pitiful situations. It underlined the intrusion of a new language, unintelligible to those who spoke it, into old, overwhelming, and stupid problems, along with the contrast between grand ideas and the enduring and overwhelming former customs. It was a bitter realism tinged with the counterrevolutionary spirit, to the extent that the implacable satire of a cruel and partially failed revolution can be called counterrevolutionary. In addition, Zoshchenko, who had grown up on powerful Russian literature, often touched on the greatest themes: "Socialism will be when violets grow from the asphalt. . . ." The story of the police dog brought to the courtyard of a building where a fur coat was stolen, and when the dog approaches the people in order to sniff them, they all loudly confess their larcenies. This leads to so general a confession that when the animal returns to his master, the militiaman also cries: "I confess, Citizens!" He had been stealing half his dog's pittance. (This was written around 1930.) The story of the fire in the small town. The firemen see that the shop on fire belongs to the Nepman, Tite, and the fireman turn around, for the Nepman is a kind of public enemy. But the fire doesn't upset Tite, since he's "insured," and the state will pay for the damage. Cantinflas's volubility and his obvious good sense through his persistent stumbling also recalls the Good Soldier Schweik, whose luck he shares. But Schweik is never incoherent: on the contrary, he's rigorously logical to the point of the absurd, as well as conscientious. He's the poor devil in a highly cultivated society who contains in a diffused state an enormous amount of benevolence and day-to-day intelligence.

The lowest humor I can recall, with the least significance, is recent Marseillais humor. Marius is an obese gentleman, a sweaty bon vivant, who laughs at dirty jokes, good wine, and broad farces, but for whom no problems exist in any form. The well-dressed, well-fed poor devil who's not even aware he's a poor devil.

The only healthy and living character created by the Mexican cinema is Cantinflas, an unwitting clown, destroyer of conventions, unimaginably lucky, infinitely agreeable. (He no longer makes satirical films, wasting himself on parodies, *The Three Musketeers*, *Romeo and Juliet*: there's no danger in them of social thought.) What should be placed in parallel to this is that the American cinema, notably in the great films of Capra (*Mr. Deeds Goes to Town* and *You Can't Take It with You*) gravitates around the theme of innocent and well-meaning madness. The healthy man, who escapes being totally obliterated by convention and the fatal mechanisms of daily life, looks to be a madman. Or the ordinary man when he opens for himself a breakthrough to the human appears to be a kind of madman. Which implies that life's norm is a kind of powerfully organized madness.

TOLTEC RUINS OF TULA (HIDALGO)

April 30–May 1, 1944—A small town, poor, colorful marketplace, in the center a feudal gray stone church, tall and crenellated, surrounded by a white wall; also crenellated. The adjacent convent is in ruins; a peaceful patio. *Ayuntamiento* painted dark green with white highlights; small belfry, clock. Neglect, heat.

A green valley, like the valley of the Seine or the Marne, but we cross over the *rio* on a suspension bridge made of a few wobbly planks placed on cables, above which run two thin cables—the handrails. We climb a chalky hill spiked with tall cactus. It's the Cerro del Tesoro. A few years ago people from the city came here hunting Toltec treasure and found beautiful sculpted stones. A municipal president had the stones laid out along the streets. Then the Americans came and bought them from him. Only one is left, which couldn't be sold because to buy it they'd have had to destroy a house.

The ruins on the summit are vast. Only one huge pyramid with at least six terraces has been cleared; another was discovered under a nearby tumulus. Tula is supposed to have been the city of the Toltecs prior to the year 1000, contemporary with Teotihuacan, which already existed for a thousand years, and posterior by five hundred years to the ancient Maya empire of Yucatan and the Zapotec civilization of Monte Albán, Oaxaca. The period of Tula's splendor was somewhere between the years 1000 and 1200. Whatever the case, the relationship between these cities is as striking as would be that of European cities of Romanesque and Gothic architecture judged by their ruins. The man-God seated and leaning slightly back, with a rectangular altar on his chest, the *Chac Mool*, is present here, as in Chichen Itza. The one here, sculpted in gray granite, is more than half-destroyed: all that is left are the hands and the altar. It seems that a long time ago a French archaeologist excavated here using dynamite. The great pyramid is well reconstructed, rectangular, resembling a fortress. But an enormous breach has opened in one of its flanks and it's here that was found, buried perhaps during the time of the Aztec invasion, the magnificent statues that they think formed columns supporting a temple on the highest terrace (the carved wood roofs probably didn't resist time). These are great, unique works whose equivalent can only be found in the tropical regions of Veracruz or Tabasco, where there are perfectly crafted, enormous monolithic human heads lying in a circle in the brush. The Toltec builders erected the human effigy dressed in ceremonial attire, sculpted in three monoliths with a diameter of almost one meter and a height greater than that. I admire its simple but lively stylization, feet in sandals painted red and yellow, knees whose curve is gentle and powerful, sober attire. But the perfection of the faces is striking. Its abstract grandeur is intriguing. Is this a hieratic human face, reduced to the elementary symbolism of its features, or of a divinized type which isn't of the builders' race? They have large, regular faces, the cheekbones aren't accentuated, and wide open, well-proportioned horizontal eyes, an aquiline, rather thin nose, and a small mouth with barely prominent lips. It could be the schematic portrait of an aristocratic European or a Mongol (closer resemblance, though, to the European). The appear to me to have a diameter of sixty or seventy centimeters. They contrast with the obvious realism of the bas relief portraits of chiefs on other sections of the square columns.

A terrace cemented with a vegetal and mineral cement, very well preserved in places; running around its base a ring of bas reliefs painted red, yellow, and blue, endlessly reproducing the same motif of a man seen in profile making an offering. The colors are bright, the art mediocre. Square holes on the terrace mark the placement of the columns, all of it well proportioned. Elsewhere the ocelot, wearing a collar, his tongue hanging out, muscular (sixty centimeters long, thirty high), is reproduced as an ornamental motif; and the eagle in profile. Note the use of the Greek motif, as at Mitla. (A ceremonial courtyard lateral to the pyramid.) On one of the faces of the pyramid they've dug out the foundations of habitations, finding much broken pottery. Wide drainage pipes, open and cemented on the inside.

These builders of the year 1000 were accomplished architects and engineers. It is obvious that in order to complete their great works, for example the mounting of massive columns made of several blocks, they had ingenious machinery of wood and rope at their disposal (like the builders of Christian cathedrals during the same era). The sections of the columns were adjusted by a kind of axle penetrating a round cavity in such a way that the earthquakes couldn't disturb the balance of the blocks.

Bas reliefs representing a snake holding a skull in its open mouth.

The sculpted *calavera*, in great numbers, can be found at the foot of the Pyramid of the Sun of Tenayuca and elsewhere. The Mexican *calavera* unites two symbolisms, those of pre-Columbian civilization and that of Christian death.

Strange coincidence in the names: Teotihuacan, in Aztec City of Gods, and Theo, God.

In Tarasco country, the station of Tarascon.

Tula—and in Russia, Tula.

HUMAN NATURE

June 1, 1944—Talk by Dr. H. V. at Fritz Fränkel's: "Six Portraits of Capitalists." H. V., with good, discrete diction and the air of a timid and amusing seminarian, describes men he knows, a sugar king, an extremely wealthy adventurer, and a wildly successful neurotic artist. He describes their character by highlighting their hidden motives, wonders "what will become of them under a socialist regime," explains that their true nature cannot change, that it constitutes a fact prior to social formation, and that in every noncapitalist society there will be men of this type. Michael Fraenkel grows comically indignant: "But they're total idiots, living only for money!" It's not so simple. F. F. reckons that human character is a primordial given, connected to the biopsychological constitution, either invariable or immutable. I have many things to say in response, and respond briefly.

To summarize, the Freudian psychology that reaches this conclusion (F. F.) harks back to the theory of innate ideas. To what extent are human instincts invariable? The difference between man and the higher mammals is derived from the modification of instincts as a result of the intervention of the intelligence (and sociability which is inseparable from it). Instincts are therefore modifiable. (Consider as well the example of the higher domestic animals, like the horse and the dog.) The millennia of social life have acted on man to such an extent that it is difficult to distinguish between the social and biological aspects of his formation. The social superego creates "new instincts." The depth of the social imprint—variable and fated to vary enormously—often seems decisive in the formation of man. This is what gives characters their form. The physical type has modified going from ancestral man to historical man to modern man: think of the skull of the Neanderthal, the prognathism of the troglodyte, of his villosity. Is it possible to doubt that their neurocerebral modifications were even greater? On the contrary, one must recognize the amazing stability of the historic human type over several thousand years. The most ancient Hittite, Egyptian, Babylonian, and Etruscan sculptures show *today's* man, and Roman senators have the heads of the bourgeois of our time: one encounters Socrates in every intellectual circle. All in all, history is short. Psychological variability is infinitely more variable than the variability in physical types, the psychological substance being what is most flexible and ductile. A recent example: blacks of central Africa transported like cattle as slaves to the United States during the eighteenth century today produce *businessmen*[20] and intellectuals in many cases little or not at all different from whites formed by one or two thousand years of civilization. Once again the extreme importance of the social imprint. Within European civilization we can observe changes in man's character, quite profound ones, that put in question the essential instinct, the libido: Hindu and Christian asceticism, Protestant sexual morality. Love as we know it, with the modern concept (or rather concepts) of the couple is a late fruit of Christian civilization, born of the Middle Ages. The understanding of the relations between men and women was profoundly different in antiquity, and *much poorer*, women being closer to servitude. The law of an eye for an eye, common to all primitive communities, and which still survives in the form of the Corsican, Georgian, and Far West vendetta, is on the road to extinction in private life and even in collective psychology. The spirit of vengeance is practically outmoded.

20. In English in the original

Rational intelligence and the scientific spirit obtained their first major victories only in the nineteenth century, and it must be said that they are still in question; but not by the power of instincts and characters, but through the crises and ruptures of the social organization, which Renan defined as "those Gothic edifices." In any case, they have profoundly modified the deep nature of modern man. Freud should be classified among the "saints" of modern society. Man's attitude in the face of death, which touches on the fundamental fear, is in the process of changing. The help of the "great mystical illusion" is often superfluous. (Recall the noble oeuvre of Marie-Jean Guyau and the optimism of Metchnikov.)[21] We are in the process of realizing the conquest of serenity (cf. Joffe's revolutionary testament as well). If religion is an immense collective neurosis, aren't we headed towards a relative cure? We can follow the formation and decline of bourgeois individualism from the Renaissance to the contemporary revolutions. Yet Social Darwinism was considered to be determined by "natural laws." The Russian Revolution demonstrates that the (capitalist) spirit of property can be easily overcome.

A development in consciousness as surprising and creative as the appearance of consciousness itself in the animal chain has occurred. This development is only at its beginnings and we cannot predict its consequences, its breadth, or its end result. At present it only really concerns minorities within the higher civilizations. Depth psychology is a recent discovery (and it has already noted important variations: neuroses connected to mysticism and witchcraft have almost disappeared; the neuroses studied by Freud are those of yesterday: the society of today, in the midst of transformation, reveals others connected to the great ideologies of the world in crisis, Bolshevism, Nazism, the Leader Cult). Practical psychology, psychotechnique, is only at its beginnings, but it is quite probable that it will transform education.

21. The philosopher Jean-Marie Guyau (1854–1888), author, among other books, of *Outline of a Morality without Obligation or Sanction*, who particularly influenced Serge during his anarchist years, and the Russian biologist Ilya Metchnikov (1845–1916).

Pavlov's biopsychology is only at its beginnings: impossible to foresee its future (its influence).

The social environment of this historical moment, a moment that may last for a half century, with its unleashing of barbarism, is enormously unfavorable to the study of these questions, and doesn't even allow them to be properly posed. Yet we are its prisoners: *inner captivity*, an essential notion. We should mistrust our lack of imagination.

MÉDÉRIC-CUERNAVACA

June 10–12, 1944—As I was leaving for Cuernavaca with Laurette and Jeannine I read that one of the leaders of the French Resistance, Jean "Médéric" Védy, arriving in Paris from Algiers, poisoned himself as he was being arrested by agents of the Gestapo. I speak of this with Laurette. Without saying so we both immediately thought of Gemähling. (Error: Jean G. survived.)

In Cuernavaca one morning: "The landing has begun." Before our eyes the image of the plains and beaches of Normandy.

Rather than ideas there are feelings, but deeply rooted ones: how unjust it is to be in these semitropical gardens while ... —that an inevitability presides over these events: not a place in Europe, not a hamlet will be spared. The fire will pass everywhere, will ravage everything. It will travel around the world. It broke out in Seville and Barcelona, it rebounded to Warsaw, Helsinki, Paris, Singapore, and Guadalcanal. It must pass everywhere.

It's easy to say to yourself that you should have no remorse for being momentarily spared; that it's mad to wish, even subconsciously, unconsciously, for everyone's participation in the catastrophe, for that would also mean a total catastrophe. And that viewing it as an ancient tragedy, governed by an unknown, blind, and pitiless divinity, is more a reflection of an almost desperate fear than of an active intelligence.

At night, more distinctly than during the day, the garden full of mango, lemon, orange, and banana trees and flowering oleanders produces a symphony of rustling, whispering, whistling, buzzing, and vibrations. The concert of the myriad insects has a metallic tone that

makes me think of a phosphorescent steel blue. Day and night I'm inclined to linger there without thought, without dreams, as if allowing
myself to be absorbed by this multitudinous, powerful, and rudimentary
life. Not a speck of matter, not a fragment of space that doesn't vibrate
and live, earth cultivated by plants and insects; air traversed by wings,
many of which are invisible; plants populated by insects. Hummingbirds
hovering in front of flowers; butterflies larger than them tracing disordered spirals; a column of tiny ants transporting rice; purple-collared
lizards eyeing me attentively, dinosaurs in miniature; a fat, black ta-
rantula with a velvet corselet and jaws as big as his body seeks his way,
drunk on light. I tried to work outside one evening under an electric
bulb. The attacking insects drove me away, covering my writing. Stupid
cockchafers colliding in flight into my glasses; spiders descending from
the foliage; huge moths blinded by the electricity.

    Cuernavaca in the evening is a small, sad city calmed and enchanted
by the presence of tall, magnificent trees. Not far from the marketplace
there are *cantinas-baile*, dance halls, announced outside by a few colored
lamps. The interior is bare, you would think it was a barn, with a
counter and a *sinfonola*.[22] The people around the counter look like
filthy ruffians who haven't slept in days. A flock of girls between fifteen
and nineteen line up on benches along the wall when the *sinfonola*
ceases its racket for two minutes (and no more). A herd of slovenly,
sweaty men, coming here from the garage or the workshop without
having bothered to wash their hands, look them over. Just beyond them
the broad hats, serapes, bare feet, tanned faces of the Indios of the
mountains, passing through and contemplating the pleasures of the
city. In the foreground, in front of the counter, a functionary in a jacket
and tie, totally drunk, staggers, stoops, and vomits on the floor. No
one pays attention to him. Beyond the swinging doors that give onto
the street, a short, wrinkled, and coppered policeman dressed in blue
stands watching, his eyes gloomy and shiny. The girls are slumped over,
vulgar, petite; a light-skinned blonde clashes with the rest of them. Two
stand out from the group, one dressed in white silk, Hispano-Indian,
with a squirrel snout, big, dark eyes, sharp cheekbones, a big mouth

22. Jukebox.

and teeth that shine from her provocative mouth. She dances freneti-
cally, laughing (everyone, incidentally, lets loose). The other has a heavy,
well-proportioned head, plebian and sharp, with serious eyes, and a
motionless, almost distant, expression. They're paid twenty *centavos* a
dance. In the crushing heat they shimmy for hours on end in the arms
of the coolies. In this monotonous frenzy, little if any laughter, no visible joy, a flat seriousness, the resignation of taciturn and exhausted
semidrunkenness. But in the ephemeral couple—the length of a song—
the man in his filthy shirt and sandals is correct if not amiable, sometimes
ceremonious, never crass. The girl is indifferent and when the occasion
arises kindly. No eroticism, nothing dirty. Those couples who love each
with a pure love, with tenderness and jealousy; those who limit themselves to fornicating do it bestially, without complications or debauch.
Existence in the three tonalities of animality, poverty, and seriousness.

THE WAR

June 20, 1944—I summarize various conversations about the war.

I express to Fritz Fränkel my concerns on the subject of rocket missiles. F. F.: Nothing decisive about them. The antidote will inevitably
be found in a few weeks. An increase in suffering, nothing more. Also
a significant event on the technical plane, a step towards automatic
war in which the intelligence will fight naked, in the form of machines.

We agree in thinking that the Germans have lost the war. El Alamein was the turning point; not a single success since then. The land-
ings in Normandy attest to an immense superiority, productive of
daring on one side and on the other to real inferiority.

Max Diamant: All that remains is to find the German Badoglio.

Me: Possible, but this seems to me improbable. We must never
forget that we do not know how single-party totalitarian states die.
I'm inclined to think that the Nazi apparatus, with its formidable
technical centralization made up of several hundred thousand men
who know that they can expect no pardon, will offer a lengthy, desperate, intelligent, and terroristic resistance. It can't take decisive account
of the mood of the masses when this mood is against it. In the last
bombed-out cities the last Nazis will put down through terror the first

resistance fueled by popular rage and will get themselves killed. No Badoglio likely under these conditions, at least not until there's been a terrible housecleaning. By resisting inch by inch it's possible that they could hold out another two or three years . . .

H.L doesn't think it can go on that long. We should expect a violent apoplexy. From here on in anything can happen. (Me: Agreed.) They'll seek to camouflage themselves en masse; a minority will be killed, the majority will betray, adapt, and constitute *underground*[23] movements . . . Also possible that they will deliberately play the card of revolutionary chaos.

FRITZ FRÄNKEL

June 21–22, 1944—I add these pages long afterwards; I recoiled before the pain of writing them, and I only do so out of duty, because I know all too well the fragility of memory and what an iniquitous and impoverishing oblivion covers over the dead. Fränkel deserved to endure among us, for us, but he wrote nothing, or almost nothing these last few years. He had dedicated the better part of his activity, outside of psychoanalysis, to the German CP and the International Brigades of Spain, and, since the Moscow Trials and the end of Republican Spain he became out of conscience an enemy of the totalitarian CP. Rejected by his former friends, abandoned even by Regler—for petty, unfathomable reasons—he had seen all that great past activity transformed into lies and dust. He was profoundly discouraged, attached by a few threads to ideas: socialism, science, psychology. Lately, while bearing up under an extremely hard struggle to survive and acclimatize himself here, he had taken to drink. He had experimented with drugs all his life without ever being subjugated by them, moved by curiosity about their psychic effects and the singularly benevolent need to understand man, the neurotic, the addict. When he drank he became affectionate, sentimental, his eyes grew moist and he was joyful, as if he wanted to reassure everyone: "Don't worry, *hombrecito*!" Now that his image has become clearer to me I can better see the essential motive forces of his

23. In English in the original.

life: active curiosity (the desire to know and live that knowledge); a simple, sincere, comprehensive love of man (he thought this emotional factor indispensable to conscious life and he saw in it the true foundation of revolutionary ideologies, when they are what they aspire to be). Twenty years and more of psychoanalysis had made of him an extraordinary being through his ability to understand and his total benevolence, in depth and in practice. Yet he exercised an untroubled severity towards offence or the betrayal of things of importance. Upright but never moralizing, never judgmental, infinitely indulgent yet clear in his judgments whenever he had to be. We were talking about a bad erotic painting by V. B. and he said: "It's human and the artist does well to express himself. This provides him with relief, but it's not art." He also said that one shouldn't try to cure neurotics, even disagreeable ones, when they draw their abilities and even their reason for living from the very neurosis. His curiosity: in Spain during the bombing he would come out of the ambulance shelter to see it, "the desire to see predominated over the instinct of self-preservation by a long shot." I never asked him a difficult or intimate question without receiving a clear answer, always extremely kind and irrefutably well thought out. I owe a lot to his example of intelligent equilibrium in fragility and to his intellectual wealth, which the malicious and the imbeciles failed to recognize because of his look of an amused, sad, and unstable bohemian.

Over the course of our discussions about Marxism he helped me understand the anticipatory and creative role of intelligence, the freedom that is part of the intelligence, the complexity of the problem of superstructures, and that the work of a Freud is equal to Marx's, with new discoveries about man which can no longer be ignored in any circumstance. (Our discussions of the role of personality and personal psychology at the outset of the Trotsky-Stalin conflict. Our work on the religious problem, which it is no longer possible to treat according to the materialist simplism which, since Voltaire, has been a kind of blindness. Our discussions on the psychological roots of Nazism, Blood, Race, the Father and the emotional roots of totalitarianism.) I always had the impression that he had it in him to produce important and lasting works, I even proposed one day to write for him, taking his dictation, his memoirs as a clinician who had sounded the depths of so many extraordinary cases, like that of the virile man who wanted to be a woman and a mother... He nodded his head and gently refused, for I had touched on his secret discouragement, which transpired onto the surface of his being. I think there were only two of us who learned many things from him and who did not underestimate him during these past few years: Herbert Lenhoff and me. It's strange that outside his patients he could be so thoroughly underestimated by the emigration and at times subject to so much rumormongering. But perhaps this is the lot of the psychologist who, however disarmed he may be, understands too many things at first glance: people are angry with him for having seen through the dark secrets around which their mediocre or vacillating personalities turn.

How light he was on the earth! This must have made a few malicious people laugh, with a laugh that he alone could have correctly analyzed. Thin and frail in appearance, not tall and capable of seeming small, he bore on his emaciated neck the head of a scholar such as Gustave Doré might have imagined to illustrate Jules Verne or a novel about the year 2000. His brow predominated, large and bumpy, mostly bald at the top, encircled by a flame of gray hair with large tufts at the temples. His eyes were watery gray, full of vivacity, sometimes very sad and even gloomy, but most often cheerful and sparkling. The lower part of his face was receding, with the mouth and chin of an old man (fifty-two years old.) This impression faded as soon as he grew animated. One day when I entered a café with him a waitress asked if I hadn't come with "Señor Einstein?" "But of course," I said, "*Como no*!" He walked with a light, dancing, lively, and swift step. Usually dressed in ill-assorted gray or beige, bareheaded, a white shirt, his tie crooked—and this did him harm with his clientele. I never knew another man whose seriousness and value were clothed with such carelessness, one that approached material deficiency.

He loved good food, bridge, alcohol, women, travel, the struggle, ideas, and knowledge. At his house two days before his death we played a Russian soldiers' card game that I'd just taught him, a childish game in which the aim is to naively and innocently cheat as much as possible: he quickly became expert, joyously laughing at the tricks he played on me.

We spoke of the anniversary of the death of the Rühles a year ago, which falls on June 24, and the idea of commemorating it. He didn't see what we could do in the void in which we find ourselves. And two days later, June 21, as he was finishing showering and shaving, singing all the while, he fell over backwards in the bathroom. He cried out, Franze and Chiki picked him up, and he asked for camphor, realizing what had happened. There was none, they ran to get some and a few minutes later he died without regaining consciousness. We had been worried about him for several months: he suffered from pain in his lungs and cancer was feared; the doctors had discussed this possibility. But after a stay in Acapulco, where he had gone swimming and relaxed, that seemed to have passed. Perhaps he suspected something and, although nonbeliever, had started reading the Gospels in the evening. We projected a study that I had proposed to him on the psychology of the militant. He had just finished correcting some notes on racism.

I enter the room where he is no more: all that's left of him is the body laid out under a sheet. The large forehead remains, the hardness of the skull, the eyes are closed and the eyelids wrinkled. A wine-colored stain invades his neck, his coloring has gone green in just a few hours, his mouth is twisted, dead, pitiful. There's something childish and tragically old in that beautiful dead face. Chiki stands sobbing near the window and I tense up all over. The odor of death in the house, the wake, the people, the flowers, the candles, Vlady, who does a horrific sketch of the deformed head as it disappears. H. L. refused a photo of this sketch: "It's a betrayal of the man." Death is a betrayal of the living man. Finished, Fritz. Adieu.

With Franze we decided on a Jewish burial because he felt himself a Jew and didn't want to sever himself from the community. Rites were of little importance to him and to us. A cemetery illuminated by the sun, a low house where the body is washed while biblical prayers are said. An old gravedigger wearing a fedora digs the grave, seeming to struggle with the earth with his last strength. A conventional doctor asks us to show tact in our speeches; he fears attacks on Stalinism. We tell him to get lost. The Jews keep on their hats or berets, a few atheist Christians are bareheaded. The coffin is lowered into the grave. Franze's face panicked and teary. Speeches. Julián, brief and good, an official but truthful revolutionary salute. H. L. very moved, stammering, but reading thoughtful, just, essential words. I, who speak of two wars, of revolutions defeated, and his tenacity in understanding man: too much weight for one human life. I also said: "No one who was close to him escaped his influence; each of us became a little bit better." "Don't believe it," H. L. said to me later. "You have no idea of how much hostility towards him there was." It was hard for me to speak, I didn't want to surrender to the emotion that took me to the brink of a kind of panic, but I felt myself borne along by a kind of fierce determination. Some found me to be a poseur and dramatic. But I'm happy to have said one more time that we will continue along the same road. I don't feel separated from the dead.

The cemetery personnel was made up of old Jews, tiny and wrinkled, unshaven, as miserable as in a Ukrainian village . . . I was one the last to leave; the gravediggers came over to me and spoke to me sympathetically in Russian; I was grateful to them for it. It was suggested that a subscription be opened to put up a tombstone, but Franze said no. No tombstone for you, Fritz; nothing but the earth and you. — Laurette didn't come.

I recall Fritz's emotion at the meeting we held to commemorate the dissolution—the death; or, more precisely, the slow murder—of the Comintern, to which, like me, he had given his youth. The Ibero-Mexican Center, an unswept room in a restaurant. There were about twenty of us. The nasty mugs of the M.s, yawning and picking their teeth, and Fritz, upset, red, reading his notes. And myself, on edge, meditating on so many dead and so much wasted hope and energy.

I know little about his long life. Military doctor in the German army during World War I. Spartacist from the first days with Karl and Rosa. Refused to join the Central Committee of the German Communist Party. Under Nazism sheltered the Central Committee several times. Arrested, a cellar in the Alexanderplatz—he didn't like to speak of it. The escape from Germany, assisted by paid-off functionaries. Emigration to Paris, journey to the Balearics, work for the party. Organization of the medical service of the International Brigades in Spain. The revelation of the Moscow Trial, the crisis of conscience. Marseille, the American Committee, the *Winnipeg* intercepted by the

JUNE 1944 · 421

English before Martinique, the (excellent) internment in Trinidad, poverty, friendships, and work in Mexico City. At the end a nearly good situation. A son, who has a delicate and gently energetic face at age twelve, who remained in Germany. Books published in Germany and lost. Had been a student of Saussure.

TUKHACHEVSKY

June 27, 1944—Reading an article on von Brauchitsch's disgrace in *Novy Journal*[24] of New York (B. Nikolaevski) I find this revelation: during the summer of '34 emissaries from the leading circles of the Reichswehr had discussions in Prague with the exiled Social-Democratic leaders (Otto Wels), seeking an accord against Hitler. The Reichswehr's collaboration with the USSR, established at Rapallo, was continuing. (I recall having told G.[eorges] Luciani of *Le Temps* a year earlier in Moscow that along with, I think, most of the militants of the Opposition, and Leon Trotsky first of all, I was for the immediate cessation of this collaboration.) Stalin certainly directed it himself, and it seemed infinitely probable that Nazi totalitarianism would crush the old cadres of the army and become a mortal enemy of the USSR. Later, Stalin made use of the contacts he had ordered or deliberately allowed to continue in order to liquidate Tukhachevsky and the other Red generals. —The idea occurs to me that, just as the leaders of the Reichswehr wanted a change of regime in the Third Reich, the Tukhachevskys wanted one in Russia and found themselves forced to approve when the extermination of the revolutionary generation—theirs—began in 1936. The formers must have been dreaming of an authoritarian democracy in Germany, the latters of a different authoritarian democracy in the USSR, and the two regimes would have supported each other. None of this would be inconsistent with the sole reliable facts published on the Tukhachevsky affair, in Erich Wollenberg's* *History of the Red Army* (London, 1938).

In any case, a hypothesis worth of examination.

24. Actually *Novy Mir* was a Russian-language émigré newspaper printed in New York. General von Brauchitsch was the German general who failed to take Moscow in 1941.

THE WAR: PERSPECTIVES AND TURNING POINT

July 28, 1944—A sad evening yesterday at Franze Fränkel's and Herbert Lenhoff's. Fritz Fränkel's absence weighed on me and expressed itself in an oppressive lowering of spirits. —With B. P., H. V., and Herbert Lenhoff we made a general survey.

Enormous events these past few days: military conspiracy against Hitler in Germany, bomb, bloody purge of the army leadership in the middle of combat. Surprising Russian advance in Poland: the Vistula crossed?

B. P. asserts that the war will end this year: the war against Hitler. H. L. thinks the eastern front has collapsed and that it's irreparable.

Me: That Nazism has disastrously lost the war is certain. Yet it is difficult to admit that it is powerless on the eastern front, in total contrast with the fight it is putting up in France. In my eyes the most probable hypothesis appears to be the following: Hitler's "intuition" provoked a new disaster in Vitebsk, after which an extremely dangerous general retreat began (note the difficulty of preventing a general retreat, executed as a result of a lost war, from turning into a general rout) a retreat of a strategic and, even more, of a political character. What character? That of transforming the war of aggression against Russia into a war of national defense and aggravating the Polish-Stalinist conflict among the Allies. What's more, who knows to what extent the Nazi leadership is still master of the general staff. The latter may well have the ulterior motive of capitulating—not without conditions—to Stalin (whose promises and "conditions" cost little because they don't commit him to anything), permitting the establishment in Konigsberg or elsewhere of a "democratic government" formed by the German committee in Moscow, playing the card of submission to Russia (submission-collaboration). Stalin would promise the leadership of the army, the bureaucracy, and the German technical apparatus that he'll leave them the ruling positions in the new "democratic" system, saving for himself the task of softening them up and purging them at will with the support of the popular movements he will inspire. Stalinist hegemony over Central Europe and thus the continent.

On the German side they may reason as follows: "Thanks to our high culture, our technical ability, our industrial concentration, and the weakening of the USSR, in five or ten years we will be, in reality, the most influential party within a combined Russo-Germanic power dominant over Eurasia."

Otto Rühle conjectured that before succumbing the Nazi Party would perhaps not hesitate to adopt "revolutionary" measures by decapitating the grande bourgeoisie in order to give the war's final convulsion an explosive social character.

With H. L. I examine the social condition of the war in Russia. We end up in agreement on the following facts: the 1939 pact was popular in Germany among all strata of the population, answering to a general hope for close collaboration with Russia. —The aggression against the USSR in 1941 was extremely unpopular. —It is certainly recognized today as a suicidal mistake. —The disaster and the winters have rendered this war, whose illegitimacy was profoundly recognized, more unpopular still. —The disasters increased the prestige of Stalin and Russian organization while they lowered the prestige of Hitler and Nazism. —In contrast with the Nazi yoke, the Russian totalitarian system, about which the average German has possibly many illusions, may become tempting. A fatalistic feeling: "Since the return of capitalism is impossible and the continuation of the Third Reich as well, this is the road we must go down."

All of this seems to open a huge conflict between Russian totalitarianism and the Anglo-Saxon world. In an era of violent social transformation Stalin has the advantage of still appealing, to a certain extent, to the revolutionary spirit and of pushing in the direction of a controlled and planned economy, that is, an ineluctable evolution. He will maintain this advantage as long as controlled and planned economies of a democratic type have not been established, and he will be all the more powerful because the reactionaries, by opposing socialist tendencies, will play into his hands. He will retreat before nothing to prevent the formation of socialist-leaning democracies that he won't be able to control and which will constitute a mortal threat to his absolutism. (He won't even hesitate to employ their slogans...)

About the end of the war, against B. P. and H. L., who believe it probable in 1944, I maintain that the hypothesis of a long, fierce resistance by the Nazis is the more likely and could prolong the combat until at least 1945. My thesis remains that the masters of the totalitarian apparatus, having burned their boats, expect mercy from no one and will continue to defend themselves among the ruins, amid hatred and devastation, through terror.

I also maintain that Stalinist power is in reality weaker than it appears due to the exhaustion of at least half the country, the maturing of new social forces, the economic and psychological interdependence of the totalitarian regimes, and the exhaustion of the old party... But it's the very gravity of the situation that forced the regime to pursue an offensive policy: there is no salvation for it outside hegemony over all, or a portion, of Central Europe.

H. L.: As long as these turning points have not been crossed, the return of socialist refugees to Europe will be impossible and we'll have no clear or optimistic perspective. In the uncertain and troubled situation that is commencing we will find GPU assassins or more or less camouflaged Stalinist concentration camps wherever we go. The technique of the Moscow Trials—slander, falsifications, and physical liquidation—will be widely applied as a form of conquest and to camouflage the crushing of all opposition.

COMINTERN: DR. STEPANOV (LEBEDEV)

August 5, 1944—Conversation with José B. about ancient Spanish affairs. Ercoli (Palmiro Togliatti, today Communist minster in Rome) was secretary of the Bureau for Latin Countries from 1929 to 1930 and went often to Spain, even during the Civil War (Albacete). During the Civil War the Spanish CP was run by Ercoli, Codovilla* (Argentine), and Dr. Stepanov.* The latter was in Spain at the time of Nin's kidnapping (but it's possible the kidnapping was the work of an autonomous secret service).

I knew Dr. Stepanov, Bulgarian, who must be about fifty today, if he hasn't perished... Medium height, pale complexion, massive face, a bit gorilla but not without beauty, broad forehead and an intense, dark gaze. Spoke French perfectly. Under the name Dr. Lebedev he was one of the first agents of the Communist International in France, along with Abramovich* (Zaleski) in 1920–1921. Physician, discreet, hardworking, extremely serious, a man of confidential missions quietly accomplished.

In 1927, when the Left Opposition, the Zinoviev-Trotsky bloc, formed its international affairs commission Radek, Fritz Wolf,* Kharitonov* (for Zinoviev), Nin, Stepanov, and Victor Serge (perhaps others as well, like Pauline Preobrazhensky) were members. Stepanov, belonging to the Left Opposition, had been authorized to maintain a rigorously conformist attitude; that is, to remain completely clandestine. I saw him in great secrecy in his room on (I think) the second floor of the Hotel Lux (we spoke of the attitude to assume towards Souvarine, Monatte, and others, and he wasn't at all sectarian). He never revealed himself to be an Oppositionist, and increasingly "adapted himself" until the point of total treason. In 1937 he was seen in Paris.

Fritz Wolf was among the first executed (I didn't know him). Kharitonov perished, along with his wife, with the Zinoviev tendency. In 1938 I learned that Pauline, feigning madness since Preobrazhensky's summary execution, lived in an asylum thanks to the complicity of certain doctors.

Abramovich (ex-Zaleski) stood out during the July days of 1917 selling party papers on the street, earning him a beating by the Cossacks. I met him in late 1921 in Tallinn, where he was embassy secretary in charge of liaison with the Communist International, then at the Vienna legation (1924), where he fulfilled the same functions. A typical Jewish worker, with curly hair and a little, wrinkled face. Disordered and cordial, of great personal honesty. Probably between fifty and fifty-five, but has certainly perished because of Zinoviev's confidence in him and his thorough knowledge of the Comintern's activities in its early days.

DARK TIMES

August 9, 1944—Read today:

A dispatch from Istanbul saying that a Turkish ship transporting 296 Jewish refugees was sunk on the Black Sea; a half-dozen people were saved.

Another dispatch on the water shortage and famine in Florence, an open city around which fighting is going on.

Notes on London's nightmare, bombed by rocket missiles. It's an absurd massacre and people have become accustomed to living under it.

An article by Léon Dennen on the extermination of Hungary's Jews—hundreds of thousands of Jews—by means of asphyxiation cars in a camp in Upper Silesia. The Nazi army brings with it *Judenvernichtung Abteil* [extermination cars for Jews] that function like efficient offices.

The report by an American journalist on the collective suicide of the Japanese population of the island of Saipan, occupied by the Americans. People witnessed an officer decapitating his last soldiers and then, saber in hand, throwing himself on a tank; young girls brush their hair and wash themselves before jumping into the sea; families perform their ablutions and then drown themselves to the last member... (The Americans nevertheless tried to reassure the civilian population and succeeded in interning a portion of it.) Laurette says that Japanese suicide is related to a deep-seated psychology, essentially different from that of the white man, "a psychology," she says, "that goes deep into physiology"; that is, to the sources of instinct—this seems to me correct.)

An official report of the execution by hanging of eight German generals rightly or wrongly implicated in the recent "plot" against the Führer. (I know how plots of this kind are manufactured.)

Scientific reports from America on the famine in China and the variety of deaths by starvation.

Saw, almost without emotion, photos showing the ruins of ancient churches in Russia and Italy; prostitutes in Cherbourg with their heads shaved; French collaborationists hunted down on the streets and begging for mercy on their knees.

We've reached the level of the dark times of the early Middle Ages. Need to reflect on this. Extreme difficulty of reflecting on this.

DEATH OF NADEZHDA ALLILUYEVA (1932)

August 10, 1944—A journalist in Stalin's service, who signs himself "G. W. Herald," published an article on Svetlana [Alliluyeva*] Stalin

which I read in *Todo* (issue of August 10). He writes that Nadia Alliluyeva* had become an "expert in poisons and antidotes" and tasted
the food served to Stalin—and that Stalin found this natural! Also
that although her death was officially attributed to appendicitis "it was
whispered in Moscow that in reality she died after having drunk a glass
of wine meant for Stalin."

I was in Moscow when N. A. committed suicide. At the Hotel
Metropole I frequented the Kolberg-Goguas (Julie Nikolaevna, my
relative, and her husband, Callistrate G., an old Georgian Menshevik
who had once been the Marxist leader of a group which the young
Stalin had been a member of). At their home I sometimes met old
Alliluyev,* an alert old man with a white beard trimmed to a point. In
this circle I learned the details of N. A.'s end; that she had had nervous
breakdowns and suffered from the famine, the terror, the unpopularity, and the cult of Stalin. N. A. shot herself with a pistol, in the chest
I think. First aid was given her by Kamenev's daughter-in-law (daughter?), the doctor on call at the Kremlin, who was arrested two days
later for having spoken in private of this drama. She was quickly released,
but I have no doubt that she later disappeared. Stalin's cooking was
done by people who were absolutely devoted: the insane idea of poisoning occurred to no one and it would have been greeted as the most
perverse imagining. I don't recall having heard of arrests among the
personnel of the Kremlin. It was said that a cook in Stalin's service was
arrested a short time previously for having, from an excess of zeal,
compared Stalin to a great emperor (while drinking to his health).

And now, twelve years later, the propaganda service launches the
semiofficial version of a poisoning! It thus admits that the official communiqué lied. The Florentine mentality created during the period of the
Moscow Trials is still being deliberately cultivated. (The deaths of Gorky,
of his son, and of Kuibyshev* were also retrospectively transformed into
"crimes" with an extraordinary—and stupid—psychological perversity.)

SAINT-EXUPÉRY

August 10, 1944—Today's *Time* magazine, twelve lines: "Missing in
action, Count Antoine de Saint-Exupéry, 1944, best-selling French

aviator-novelist . . . on a reconnaissance flight over Europe. . . ." I'd just learned of the death and torture of Max Jacob at the prison in Drancy a week after his arrest last year.

Twelve lines, two book titles, best-sellers, for Saint-Ex. It's true that one can still hope that the amazing luck he had in his accidents may have saved him yet again and that he's only been taken prisoner. But the calculus of probabilities is against him.

It always seemed to me that a mist floated about him, perhaps a protective mist for the hidden man. The face of an average Frenchman, a naive or veiled gaze, he had several destinies at which he failed as much as he succeeded. He was an excellent aviator until the day he became aware of the risk and grandeur of visions. He then became a good writer, limited but magnificent (*Night Flight*). The writer became aware of human and social problems, and the novelist lost in the deal. He wanted to understand things in depth and remedy them; he elaborated theories, sought social formulas, nearly drowned in his artless investigations and discoveries. I thought he would no longer be able to simply construct a good novel. He touched on politics, hemmed in by his bourgeois, aristocratic, etc. family milieu and by well-paid journalism; was a sympathizer of the Croix de Feu[25] and was passionate about the Spanish Civil War. He ended by allowing himself to be carried along by the waters of Vichy and only drew away from the French legation in Washington when Vichy's game was lost. But I continue to believe that he was always tortured by this inner struggle, groping about, penetrated with the hypertrophied conscience of a period of decadence.

One evening at a café with red leather seats on the place de l'École Militaire we discussed the Spanish revolution, production, and Marxism. Pencil in hand, he set out to demonstrate on paper napkins that the sum of human labor indispensable for collective life didn't vary with the advent of machines because the construction of the machines themselves absorbed the labor apparently liberated by chain production. This caused me to suddenly see in him a kind of discoverer of perpetual motion, a technician crushed by technology, just as the so-

25. Right-wing veterans' organization of the interwar period.

cialite was dominated by high society and money, and the sexual being by an exaggerated appetite.

Evenings at his home on the terrace on the place Vauban during the Paris World's Fair: fireworks over the Eiffel Tower, vast clouds over Paris, Consuelo in a Persian robe. His amazing card tricks on the large, pine table... It was beyond imagining. But I saw in his library fat books on card tricks, probably closely studied. His love for mystification, a counterweight to a serious view of life. Last encounter at Léon Werth's,* the night of the invasion of Belgium. He felt that all was lost, drowning in depression. (We didn't know the news yet.)

DEATH AND THE INTELLECT

August 30, 1944—While finishing the work on Fritz Fränkel's manuscripts with Herbert Lenhoff, I remarked that what is most tragic about death, what is most unacceptable for the intellect, is the complete disappearance of a spiritual grandeur, made up of experience, intellectual elaboration, knowledge, and understanding, in large part incommunicable. The means of transmitting the achievements of a fine mind are almost derisory in comparison with the value and profundity of that achievement. One must continuously start afresh, reinvent: how much of the essential is lost! We wonder if the belief in the immortality of the soul, so tenacious in educated societies, is not called upon to provide psychological compensation for the devastating feeling of this destiny. —Life has its continuity, its new beginnings, and the intellect, which is its most precious fruit, ends in annihilation, whatever its treasures... Perhaps this is also one of the sources of civilization: a colossal social effort aimed at making up for this obliteration. The individual seeks to ensure his durability by his works, by the influence of his activity (accomplishing of a mission, pursuit of glory, the need to fix the moment, to express, to teach for the writer and the reformer; the need to "integrate oneself into history").

H. L. considers that the theory of "the destructive or death drive" (*Totentrieb*) to be one of the two fundamental bases of Freudian psychology (libido, *Totentrieb*), even though Freud only formulated it at the end of his life and without having the time to delve further into it.

Freud himself worked until his death: his resistance to aging and death reveal his struggle with fear and the creativity he was able to draw from it.

... It was in Leningrad, at the Marie Hospital in 1928, as I lay dying (I really was and I knew it), that I made the resolution to write and, if possible, things that would stand the test of time; in any case, things that deserved to last at least for a while. My previous activity seemed to me to have been futile and insufficient. The impulse I then received— more precisely, which was born in me—was so vigorous that it has remained with me until this day, in the most trying circumstances and without it having been seriously tainted by considerations of interest, pride, or vanity.

THE JEWS

September 1, 1944—Jean Malaquais takes us home in his car after two meetings in a row (Spanish socialists, Prieto, Rivet, then the editorial board of *Mundo*). I'm tired, it's rainy, one would think it was an autumn night in Paris, which here has great charm. J. M., a Jew, doesn't want to be one, sometimes denies he is one, or says he's half-Jewish, profoundly tormented by a racial inferiority complex grafted onto a more general inferiority complex that renders him bitter, acerbic, aggressive, and mocking... Conversation about the Jews. I say that they constitute a superior variety of civilized man: more active, with a dynamic spirituality that is often very powerful. Powerfully materialistic as well in materialistic societies. "It's not by chance that the same ethnic group produced Christ, Maimonides, and Spinoza, and in our times Marx, Trotsky, Freud, and Einstein, incomparable men who have upended our way of viewing the world."

J. M.: "Let's not talk about Christ, please, his historicity being unproven."

I go along with him, though it would be easy to demonstrate that the Christian myth, even without Christ's historicity, is the work of the Jewish people and is a continuation of the tradition of the prophets.

J. M.: "And let's drop Maimonides, whom we know so little about."

But he seeks in vain great contemporary figures comparable to those I named. He briefly hangs on to Louis Pasteur, and when I said in passing, "That's a fact," he goes after the word "fact," that there are no objective facts, that everything is a personal assertion, debatable subjectivism, etc. He won't accept any other measuring stick for reality than himself and in support of this says there is no other. I feel like telling him: My poor friend, what pitiful weakness is revealed by your philosophical aggressiveness so devoid of wisdom. I hold myself back; it would do nothing but vex him.

I returned to this subject this morning with Laurette. Laurette observes that the Jews constitute the sole people whose cultural continuity goes back four thousand years (the reign of King David, about 1000 B.C.). The most ancient people, the most profoundly cultivated, the one most profoundly accustomed to thought. This, in fact, is an observation of immense importance. All the great peoples of white civilization today emerged from barbarism only in the first centuries of the Middle Ages. The Greeks, Egyptians, and Latins were engulfed by the barbarian invasions and disappeared as thinking collectivities; the Jews alone demonstrated the extraordinary endurance that allowed them to survive while constantly developing, beneficiaries of and contributors to all civilizations. Role of historical chance in this adventure; dangerous privilege of dispersion; spiritual factor (the most advanced, the most philosophical religion of the ancient world). Laurette outlines other striking ideas: that the hatred of the Jew was the hatred of the oldest people, the Father-People. (Jesus's revolt against the narrow Judaic law, revolt of the Son against the Old Father; Jesus forever preoccupied with the Father-Son relationship, matter for Freudian analysis.) (Jesus creator of the new concept of the Father, the Christian revolution, expansion of renewed Judaism, the beginning of the advent of the white man, his universalization.)

For obvious social reasons the Jews of Eastern and Central Europe have, for the last half century, demonstrated exceptional intellectual dynamism (their role in the United States). The Nazi extermination of this rich and fertile human mass diminishes Europe's vigor and influence.

THE DIFFICULTY OF WRITING—RUSSIAN WRITERS

September 10, 1944—Herbert Lenhoff, seeing me at work on the novel, asked me if I feel in full possession of my powers.

No. Never was I so far from this feeling. The novel on the Moscow Trials was painful for me to write, but I had the sensation with it of giving everything I have to give. And that of a duty fulfilled, of fidelity. Unpublishable until when? *Les Derniers temps* will be a sincere and probably satisfying novel, but nothing more, except on a few pages where the comprehension of man elevates it a little. Terribly difficult to create in a void, without the least support, without any atmosphere. If I could truly allow myself to let go, shake off the weight of the external and internal censors (the latter a reflection of the former), the book would be a hundred times more worthwhile and I'd feel a hundred times better, but psychologically this is a quasi-impossibility. To write only for the desk drawer, past age fifty, facing an unknown future, not to mention the hypothesis that the tyrannies will last longer than I have left to live, what would be the result? A rather rich projection against a background of despair; and I prefer practical compromise with the social censors than a deliberate dive into despair. And again: remain reasonable: things can and must change enough before long for me to be able to breathe more freely. Compromise is after all an act of confidence, of a confidence mutilated and hardened, but still alive. I've come to wonder if my name alone won't be an obstacle to the publication of the novel.

Strange to observe that in this free country of the Americas I'm writing the same way the Russians wrote around 1930, as the last spiritual freedom was dying there. Pilnyak, Fedin, Tynyanov,* Kaverin, and even the facile Lavrenev[26] talked to me the same way I talk to myself when I'm alone. Lydia Seifulina took to drink and became neurasthenic; Pasternak expected to go to prison... Osip Emilievich Mandelstam, an authentic poet, read us in private an inspired tale in Giraudoux's style, impressions of the Caucasus mixed with allusions to freedom of the imagination, which no power can ever wipe out (no

26. This Soviet writer became a renowned screenwriter, Lydia Seifulina, who is mentioned in the next sentence.

power except the censor and the political police). As he ended his reading his thin irregular face with its worried eyes, was exalted: "Do you think it's publishable?" Zoshchenko raised his yellow, reticent, regular face to say: "It doesn't seem so scandalous to me." I had the painful impression of the sneaky, roundabout rebellion of a fearful child, seeking subtle ways of saying things without seeming to. A short time later Mandelstam stupidly attempted to commit suicide by throwing himself out of too low a window. And he "had problems." One evening, at my house, he was strained and embarrassed. "It's that you're a Marxist," he admitted. When I showed him a volume of photos of Paris by night, the strain between us quickly evaporated before these images. "Thanks to these photos I feel confident again...."

IDEOLOGICAL DISPUTES

September 13, 1944—Second meeting of the Commission of Independent Socialist Groups for the study of the proposed political document drafted by Marceau Pivert, Gironella, and Wilebaldo Solano.*[27] It's a sort of "Communist Manifesto," very rudimentary, recycling all the old phrases of the genre. I strongly criticize it, thinking that texts of this kind can do nothing but discredit the handful of men who take responsibility for them. I'm listened to with interest and suppressed hostility. I say that today we no longer improvise documents of this kind; that every term, every idea must be revised in the face of new realities and launched in the middle of a hurricane. A confused and rather painful discussion. In passing I say that the Parti Socialiste Ouvrier-Paysan completely melted away at the beginning of the war. Marceau Pivert, visibly upset, affirms that "it exists and is a force," saying he's better informed than I, he who left France before the war... I point out that it's false to write that in a bourgeois democracy the working class has only its chains to lose, and that it enjoys—in Europe enjoyed—real well-being and real freedoms. M. P. speaks of the malnutrition of the masses in France before the war! I say that the nature of the state is changing and that it is no longer "the armed band of one

27. It's not certain that Solano was indeed in Mexico at this time.

class for the domination of another," according to Engels, except under the totalitarian regimes. The modern state is also the organization of communication, schools, public hygiene, etc. Indignation on the part of M. P., Gironella, and Jean Malaquais. For a moment, I feel they're going to accuse me of breaking faith!

I point out unintelligent naivetés like "the total organization of the world"; of comical incoherencies like the affirmation of the "complete sovereignty" of all the peoples of the colonies, the rejection of "every notion of tutelage over them," and the proposal of providing them "economic, moral, and armed assistance" (!!!). No one says anything much in response, but I see that I am offending feelings that can find expression only in this impoverished phraseology. (My thesis: that the emancipation of the peoples of the colonies can be the result only of close collaboration with the socially reorganized industrial countries— the metropoles on march towards greater justice and humanism... Coldly received without debate.) Narcís Molins i Fàbregas* says that "we want to act" and not only "engage in academic discussions, even interesting ones." What action if not that of typewriters and ideas: aren't correct viewpoints also acts in a certain sense? Finally, J. M. reproaches me for not talking about the "proletariat and the dictatorship of the proletariat!" (Has he ever spoken of them himself? That's another story.) At one point in the dispute I felt exactly as if I was in a cell of the Russian CP in 1927 when we were refuting the already bloody stupidities of the clamor for "socialism in one country" and denouncing the ongoing Thermidor. We argued as follows, I said: "I'm saying this is a white saucer; I didn't say it was a blue saucer, I didn't say it was a black pitcher, I said it's a white saucer!" During that time Bukharin recommended writing everything down and not entrusting the paper to your opponent! The psychological phenomenon of the politburo repeats itself to infinity. (At bottom: idealists hemmed in by the sclerosis of doctrines and circumstances, and dominated by their convictions and their emotional attachments; in short, by fanaticism. Under such conditions the person who disturbs the inner security of the others is a hateful heretic.) Molins i Fàbregas, Gorkin, and Pivert reproach me for calling into question convictions that they for their part don't question, hence their feeling of superiority.

The heart of the debate, independent of the poor quality of the proposed text:

Their extremely optimistic and schematic conviction that the Russian Revolution will soon be repeated in Europe. "The workers will occupy the factories (Pivert), they'll take power (Gironella), etc." Then the European revolution will form a socialist federation...New cadres will be formed everywhere; the underground resistance movements are already demonstrating the power of the masses...The Spaniards think they'll be in Spain in six months at the head of a great movement. M. P.: "The PSOP fights on!" and takes out a press clipping attesting that in an underground leaflet our friends in Lyon advocated "the formation of a Red Army" in France, which is the height of absurdity: in their powerlessness, and at the risk of their lives, they play into the hands of the reactionaries and the Stalinists.

My theses: that this war is profoundly different from that of 1914–1918, of which it is the continuation, and that it entails elements of international civil war. (Strong protests by M. P.)—That the economic structure of the world has changed, traditional capitalism making way for a planned and controlled economy, thus collectivist in tendency, which could be that of monopolies and totalitarian parties—or of democracies of a new type, if the latter succeed in being born. (Strong protest by M. P.)—That the defeats of European socialism cannot be imputed solely to the failures of leaders, though this counts, but are rather explained by the decadence of the working class and of socialism as a result of modern technology (chronic unemployment, declassing of the unemployed, immense increases in the productive capacity of machinery with less need for workers; increased influence of technicians). (M. P. rejects these views as a whole without attempting to refute them, and to speak of a weakening of the working classes as a class seems to them all to be a sacrilege. What can I do about this if it's the truth? A good Old Bolshevik, one of those who expelled and arrested us before himself being executed, would answer me: There is no truth that can prevail over the interests of the party.) —That we are well and truly being carried along by the current of an immense revolution, but that there will not be a repetition of the Russian Revolution unless as secondary episodes. That socialism must renounce the ideas of worker dictatorship and hegemony and become the representative of the large numbers of people in whom a socialist-leaning consciousness is germinating, one obscure and without a doctrinal terminology. —That in the immediate coming period the essential thing would be the obtaining the reestablishment of traditional democratic freedoms, which are the precondition for the rebirth of the workers' and the socialist movements. That we must try to emerge from the void we currently inhabit, seek the support and sympathy of the democratic masses wherever they are, make ourselves understood by them, and bring our ideas up to date. —That Stalinism, which molded and nourished the armed resistance movements in France, Yugoslavia, Greece, and elsewhere, constitutes the worst danger, a mortal danger which we would be mad to aspire to fight on our own. —That the years to come will be years of confused struggles in which the socialist movement cannot but be reborn. —That it must seek influence on the terrain of democracy, in the Constituents and everywhere, and accept many compromises with intransigence of spirit. —That if the socialist left muddles along in extremism without influence, with a language barely intelligible to people, and an out-of-date ideology dating from 1920, the Stalinists will manufacture a false socialism, flexible and unscrupulous, that could very well carry it off.

Whatever I might say, agreement is impossible and discussion difficult and sterile. Those possessed of inner flexibility will change beneath the cudgel blows of events; the rest will vegetate in tiny groups on the margins of life (which offers many satisfactions), or will be crushed.

COMMUNIST MENTALITY

September 14, 1944—Two days ago, after some conversations with wealthy young Communists, sons of a banker, Laurette told me that no argument makes any difference to them. In the first place because in reality they take nothing seriously, and then because, lacking in critical spirit, knowledge, and attachment to values, they have an answer to everything. "But the USSR is a totalitarian country!" "If that's the case it was a necessary evolution. What's more, Bernard Shaw writes that he saw loudspeakers on the streets of Moscow that broadcast criticism of Stalin (*sic*)." "But they executed all the founders of the USSR!" "Therefore, they had broken faith." "But how can you accept that all of the best and strongest men broke faith?" "Everyone knows that revolutions devour revolutionaries." "But there are enormous concentration camps for the wives and children of the executed." "I don't believe that at all." (And Laurette doesn't dare argue in depth.) "But thought control has killed all of intellectual life!" "I maintain that current Russian literature and poetry are the most beautiful in the world, look at Wanda Wasilewska,* and ambassador Umansky assured me of this."

This morning I met a young Stalinist lawyer, member until yesterday of the CP, since yesterday of the "Socialist Youth," founded by the CP. Conversation in the same tone. "Russian totalitarianism is an indispensable phase of social transformation.... And anyway, what party would I switch to? All of them are retrograde and corrupt.... The CP has it faults, but it represents a progressive state." I invite him to distinguish between *progress* and *bloody regression*. He admits he's ill informed and evades the issue.

Since the end of 1941 not a single book has been published in this country that simply tells the truth about the internal regime in the USSR. The last to appear were those of Jan Valtin* and mine on the Hitlerite aggression, nearly impossible to find today. On the other hand, pro-Stalinist literature floods the bookstores. No translations of the few books published on this subject in the United States.

A young doctor asks me if I consider Germany defeated, and when I answer in the affirmative—it's only a matter of time—puts on a dismayed expression. He says: "I hope for a victory of the Germans and the Russians, they're the greatest people on earth. They must end up coming to an agreement." Very *anti-gringo*.

P. M. spoke to me of communism's influence in Haiti. A backward mentality (the common people) or a superficially cultivated one (intellectual aristocracy of a tropical and primitive country) adapts itself to this confused idealism. Great accomplishments in social justice, anti-imperialism, cult of the leader, abdication of free inquiry, destructive instincts diverted towards terror and the repression of conspiracies.

ACAPULCO

Mid-September 1944—Acapulco with Dr. Gustavo Peter,[28] his son, and Jeannine. The trip, ten hours, about 450 kilometers, passes through a magnificent succession of landscapes, but is tiring: several times we exceed the altitude of Mexico City and several times we reach low and hot zones. I love discovering sites in this half of the world that I'm beginning to know, that I'll never finish knowing. The stone cliffs before Taxco, with water streaming over them and clouds clinging to them, remind me of the valley of the Loue, the Jura. Near Iguala tropics, sugarcane, the weight of incandescence, monotony. The Rio Balsas runs through low, intensely green brush. Its waters are brown and a boiling yellow. Thatch huts on the banks; the naked children, piglets, hens, lizards, insects, snakes, and scorpions living together. Further along, towards the Rio Papagayo, rises a marvelous, uninhabited Switzerland, light green with valleys, summits, waterfalls, and woods, all of it bathed in a vegetal aquatic blue. The solitude is total. Tierra Colorada, a large town on red earth (like in Adjaristan), abundance of fruits.

We enter Acapulco at nightfall. The pavement ends and the city is nothing but pitted, flooded roads and streets where the ruts disintegrate into deep mud. Darkness pierced with neon signs. Dampness, odors of decomposing vegetable matter. Polynesian silhouettes harshly illuminated by our headlights while we splatter them with fresh mud. The darkness poeticizes them, but in reality there are many young people, the girls more delicate than the boys but of a more obvious animality, with less strength. It's a tumbledown and do-nothing country. The people drag out an easy life in the heat, the humidity, and the filth, rocking in hammocks, listening to the radio or the guitar, lazily exploiting the tourists. Nothing either picturesque or well tended or organized. Filthy little marketplace, stifling and ugly *zócalo*, insignificant church. There are pleasant-enough alleys, peaceful and hot. Jewish and Syrian merchants. A luxury hotel in front of the port looks gray, seedy, uselessly insolent, defeated by indifference. There's no potable water or electricity; no fish on the shore of this opulent and nourishing ocean: people eat only canned goods. Fat Indio (and vaguely Negroid)

28. Founder of the Mexican Radiology Society.

fishermen offer me a boat ride that will bring them in more than a night of fishing. *Gracias*. The children muse naked under the banana leaves. In the port a convoy from the United States: a few massive, dark gray ships dozing on the treacherous water. All in all, an unlivable city. Two luxury hotels are being built on the heights where the rate will be 100 piasters a day, the monthly wage of an employee. The city is building a new cemetery. It needs it. The walls of the old one, which opens onto the road, have collapsed in spots under the rain and coffins are laid bare. Facing it, the noble power of the coconut trees. The villas are on the hills; the road is only for cars; torrid, no shade, no shoulder.

Meditated on the fact that this was Fritz Fränkel's final landscape, which gives it an undefinable tinge.

The sites are those of a vast country where man takes up little space, where one might think nature is inhuman. The ocean is desertlike and fearsome, swarming with life, marine insects, sharks: all of it danger-ous, the enemy. The sun consumes and numbs thought. The vegetation, though lacking the grandiosity of the *selva*, is victorious, oppressive, and deceptive, full of insects and snakes. These past few days the "breeze" is an energetic wind that fiercely rips the leaves from the banana trees, pursues you into your room, and provokes a fatigue similar to that of combat. The humidity attacks books and fabrics; when one lies down one has the vague feeling of beginning to disintegrate ... The tropics.

And what an extraordinarily electric night we had. The lightning lit up the inlet, the capes, the foam assaulting the rocks, and the ocean's horizon without let up. The lightning was silent, flashing in the warmth beneath the low clouds, seeming to explode at the zenith, but not a bolt could be seen. One followed another every second without our being able, in the intervals of total night, to count to two. We felt like we were bathed in the lightning, and it would stay like this for days.

On the beach the waves are high and violent. At Pie de la Cuesta one sees them arriving, rolling heavily, carrying along admirably green water and explosions of foam. Impression of an absolute power, elemen-tal and consequently unintelligible.

A primitive village, Pie de Cuesta, between the placid laguna and the vast beach attacked by the waves. In the past the laguna contained many alligators, which are here called *cocodrillos* ... An old India explains that now one can swim without fear, there are no more of them, perhaps further along, but not here . . . The landscape of the laguna is mild, blue hills in the distance, but the heat weighs on you. The village is made up of wide-open thatch huts built under the coconut trees. There are hammocks in front of the huts. Dozing children and adults sway in them. People live on nothing by apparently doing nearly nothing: fruits, coconuts, fish, a few centavos collected from the tourists. A businessman is building a hotel.

In front of Dr. Gustavo Peter's home there's a beautiful tree with large leaves of a damp, fresh green. The smooth, gray trunk is barbed with sharp thorns, wide at the base and very hard. The tree is venomous, its sap burns the flesh. Neither insects nor birds touch it; it grows in silence and peace. Two winged ants are resting on a leaf: they are dead. With a decoction from a few leaves Gabino exterminated the rats. Gabino tells us that the Indios in the area fear the tree and threaten to cut it down. They call it *el árbol de San Ignacio*—probably in honor of Loyola. They knew the Jesuits.

Gabino, thirty years old, athletic and handsome, with a moustache and velvety eyes in a kind, fleshy face. He comes and goes noiselessly, barefoot, neatly dressed. During the day he carries a pen and mechanical pencil in his shirt pocket, and in the evening a big revolver at his waist. Unhappily married, he's alone. It seems he beats women. I see him patiently recopying poems from a magazine. Above his bed the *Virgen morena* and pinup *girls*[29] cut out of an American magazine, tastefully assembled in a frame. He originated the montage.

He tells me that the solitude of this isolated village is driving him mad, *loco*, and that he wants to go to Mexico City, to become a good carpenter. He speaks of the corruption of the city in moral terms and explains to me that he doesn't drink. Very difficult to have him do anything in a fixed amount of time. He vanishes with a "*Si, señor, en seguida,*"[30] and the next day nothing has been begun . . . I saw him one day in the copse, strolling, naked to waist, a machete in his hand: he's handsome.

29. In English in the original.
30. "Yes sir, right away."

Pelicans flying over the sea. I love their ragged wings with large, hard feathers, their enormous beaks, their greedy way of grazing the waves, on the hunt. They make me think of prehistoric birds. At the edge of the road, large numbers of butterflies, enormous, red and black, yellow, the color of light lace. Brilliant green lizards. The rocks bathed by the waves are covered with sea urchins and crabs, the latter looking black but in reality dark mother-of-pearl, fantastically agile. The children catch large golden spiders, their bodies round and their long legs striped white and yellow.

One evening as we were dining Jeannine glimpsed the *alacrán*. This is a magnificent gray scorpion ten centimeters long. I just read that the scorpion long preceded the mammals: it's a survivor of the earth's youth. Cut in two it continues to frantically seek its way. The two halves run in all directions, aggressive. The claws bite whatever is offered them. Barely has it been killed than minuscule ants rush to devour it. Other ants, large ones, transport scraps of fruit all day long on the staircase. Each carries a load heavier than itself. At night the fireflies float over the foliage and enter the terrace.

Beach. Jeannine drank a lot of water, nearly suffocated. No sign of panic a moment later. She loves rolling for hours in the waves. The two boys, Felix and Frank, thirteen and fifteen years old, pay her lots of attention, but their ceaseless flirting takes the form of combat: teasing, pouting, chasing each other with water pistols, jokes. At less than ten years of age she is much more a "little woman" than they are young men.

Dr. Gustavo Peter brought along books on physics, geology, and astronomy, and we speak endlessly, in bits and snatches, in the wind in front of the ocean. He draws up a tableau of the electronic construction of simple bodies.

I wasn't able to do any work at all. An inhuman, dissolving atmosphere of enchantment. But all at once, sketched the outline of a big novel embracing very different men and the crisis of an entire generation, the other prewar period, the interwar period, the revolutions, philosophy, something extremely composite and stretching toward both the irrevocable past and the unknown future. There were moments when I missed Laurette, it seems to me that it's only together that we see or live well, but how difficult this is to accomplish! I childishly make plans.

INTRANSIGENCE, INTOLERANCE, CONFLICTS

October 2, 1944—I'm in conflict with many comrades, with the most active who, it is true, are also the least educated, with the exception of Marceau Pivert. Their fidelity to formulas I consider out of date, and from which I think socialism will die if it doesn't succeed in renewing itself, makes them hostile to me. To such a point that in debates they cease to understand me, not wanting to understand me, feeling in some way offended and wanting to fight more than to reflect. For me, this is a very old and very discouraging experience. The best-disposed men, professing in principle respect for free thought, the critical spirit, and objective analysis, in reality don't know how to tolerate ideas different from their own. Whoever "thinks differently," according to Rosa Luxemburg's phrase ("freedom is freedom for those who think differently") immediately is taken for an enemy. Or at least a heretic whose heresy contains a large dose of betrayal. In this feeling, which I can see is extremely strong in a dozen refugees who esteem each other and should be friends, intolerance in all its forms is in germ, with its inquisitions, etc. Offended faith, faith threatened by anxiety, is unforgiving. In Russia the bureaucracy was able to mobilize these emotional aggregates against us. New theses were identified with treason and the most solid, the most determined among us weren't exempt from a profound suffering, generating doubt and indecision. "Better to err with the party than to be right against it!" I heard this repeated many times.

The essential problem: you have to choose sides, there's always a truth to be sought, to find, to defend, an imperative truth that binds. There is neither action nor thought of any value without intransigence. Intransigence is firmness, is *being*. How to reconcile this with respect for the person who is different, with thought that is different? Nietzsche was right to consider the "possession of the truth" to be connected to the will to dominate. Scientific truth, it's true, is of another quality, a latecomer that appeared in the nineteenth century, and is experimental, subject to disinterested discipline, but as yet it only penetrates convictions (which are of an emotional nature) to a small degree. And it is precisely socialism, which had scientific aspirations, that lost its scientific spirit by allowing itself to be outstripped by discoveries and investigations and by totally committing itself to social struggles that, especially in Russia, turned it into a faith, and then a regime, thus doubly intolerant. (Seeds of totalitarianism within it: Erwin Wolf telling me in Brussels: "But Marxism is totalitarian, it embraces all of life and aims at its total transformation...." And, rejecting my advice, went to get himself murdered in Spain.)

I glimpse a solution. Combative intransigence controlled by a rigor as objective as possible and by an absolute rule of respect for others, respect even for the enemy... (The totalitarians render respect for the enemy difficult if not impossible.)

PAINTING, DR. ATL

October 7, 1944—Contrasts: in the vestibule of Bellas Artes an American woman named Robinson is exhibiting portraits so anemic that one turns away from them with relief. One enters a large room and Atl's landscapes sparkle, the presence of earth and man. These are large canvases revealing expansive Mexican sites, horizons curved as if one seized the sphericalness of the globe; hard nopals somewhere in the foreground spiked with humble primitive energy, smashed rocks. One feels that geological catastrophes are present and have by no means ended, the blue crests in the background are fractures in the planet and the clouds roll their power above it all... "You have the cosmic sense," I said to old Atl, "and you extract Nietzschean poems from it...." A feeling of a proud solitude (sometimes ingenuous, as in the portraits where the artist paints himself, modeling his own face like a rock so that the skull melds into a snow-covered peak)—a feeling for life that achieved plenitude before World War I, at a time when great hopes were not yet mutilated and when man felt he was the dominator and conscience of the world (Whitman, Verhaeren, Nietzsche, Reclus).

> (Robert Browning, "Parting at Morning"
> Round the cape at a sudden came the sea,
> And the sun looked over the mountain's rim:
> And straight was a path of gold for him,
> And the need of a world of men for me.)

Old Atl himself was seated in an armchair, wearing a threadbare tweed suit, his hands leaning on a cane. The hard bowl of his skull sits atop a shrunken face, thin and pale, his eyes, blue marbles, bulge—These eyes didn't recognize me, I had to remind him of our conversations on the volcano, and then the memory pierced his inner haze. He told me that he wants to exhibit his drawings and paintings of Paricutín and that he's in a hurry. "Yes, yes, my painting is sometimes very good, I said something with it!" He added in a confidential tone: "Of course, it's not all perfect, there's some junk." Me: "All the same, thanks to your canvases you put a part of your life to good use." He, with a determined air: "Exactly, exactly!" How much the old man resembles a child! (This is perhaps only true of old men who have a certain grandeur: there's no grandeur without innocence.) He no longer has the joyful vigor that I saw on the slopes of Paricutín, the liveliness of spirit of our nocturnal talk beneath the explosions and flames of the crater…I sense that his life is nearing its end. Humiliated by a bad leg that makes walking difficult.

Then met Michael Fraenkel and, speaking of Atl, he told me that he was a faithless, lawless adventurer, a paid agent of the Nazis, a hysterical anti-Semite, after having been a brave revolutionary, an intelligent and unscrupulous archaeologist, and an amoral swindler. All of which is true. He demonstrated a fervent vitality amid social chaos, instability, and the fundamental irresponsibility of nearly everyone. It's appropriate to compare Atl to a character of the Renaissance like Benvenuto Cellini, who killed people with ease, who fought off poison so vigorously, and who, ill, saw death seated at the foot of his bed, felt death's hold on his members, and resisted him. And who must have been neither easy to deal with nor scrupulous in financial matters.

As I was leaving the Atl exhibit I saw in the upper gallery a large fresco that had just been begun and which looked bad to me. I learn that it is by the assassin Alfaro Siqueiros, a great painter, Trotsky's assassin, the GPU's henchman, etc. He is under criminal charges and here he is executing an order from some authority or another. And in town he runs with high society.

MALAQUAIS

October 17, 1944—Break with Jean Malaquais, inexplicably stupid and violent. An incident at a meeting, his wife's insults, his incredibly insulting letter. Herbert Lenhoff, reading the document, says: "It's a remarkable example of the rationalization of a subconscious impulse.... He wrote this while in a strange state and one could conclude that he hates you because he loves you."

For a long time I've felt this attitude towards me, and Laurette sometimes perceived it more clearly than I. At bottom: inferiority complex, great vitality, aggressiveness, from which jealousy, envy, a touchiness containing a grain of persecution mania. In short, the temperament of a neurotic (incurable, says Herbert Lenhoff, and Fritz Fränkel thought so as well). His invariable tendency to see what is most base in people and things. [...][31] With this, a certain lucidity, a constant and sometimes fruitful effort to rise above himself, to construct a different, a better personality. We were often moved by this. The strange vision he has of me through himself.

The difficulty of understanding people other than through yourself and through a self-image with which you are not very happy, which you sculpt and repress. The danger of an inferiority complex and lack of imagination. The former terrorist in power feels he's surrounded with "terrorists" who plot his death since they tell him they don't agree with him.

Disquiet and difficulty of reacting to J. M.'s aggression. The insults give rise in me to a violent reaction which I have trouble controlling.

PERMANENT WAR

October 24, 1944—Conversation with Herbert Lenhoff about permanent war. Leon Trotsky correctly predicted that we risked entering a period of uninterrupted, permanent war if humanity doesn't succeed in the short term in a social (and psychological) reorganization, whose means, in truth, appear to be minimal. The answer of a Chinese peasant

31. Illegible passage.

questioned by an American journalist: "When do you think the war will end?" "*Never.*" We see today that the war of 1914–1918 (which was prolonged in Russia until 1921–1922) began to pose the problems of the organization of the world, economic and otherwise, of which no one, or almost no one, was aware at the time. (The Russian and German revolutions were relatively conscious of this: the totalitarian development of the Russian Revolution shows that this was only imperfectly the case. Their political consciousness was clear for the time, but unclear concerning historical development.) The end of the war against Nazism approaches, but we can clearly see the oncoming conflict between the "Soviet" economy and the other systems. No solution visible for Asian questions. To believe in complete victories would be puerile. Concerning the social reconstruction of Europe, the balance of power, the racial-colonial questions, no real solutions can be foreseen, nor even any ideological proposals capable of animating the masses in great numbers. Christianity will remain important, but lacking in social dynamism and a creative faculty. It will only be able to resist, adapt, survive, console, and sometimes guide the perplexed. Liberalism still maintains a hold on precious spirits through the sanity of humanist judgment, but the end of private enterprise reduces it to a secondary factor. Conservatism is a hardening, an egoistic blindness whose lack of a sense of reality is sometimes stupefying—it is catastrophic, the proof being Nazi-fascism, its monstrous bastard. Socialism is no longer up to date, rendered outmoded by the sciences, technology, and the obscured class struggle. True, it's possible that it can be made current, since what is essential about it remains infinitely more valid than the other ideologies. It seems destined to dilute itself throughout the whole of society and social consciousness. As I wrote in 1937, Marxism has so thoroughly entered modern consciousness (several of its main principles) that it can no longer be distinguished within it as a separate doctrine capable of giving rise to enthusiasm. The fundamental articles of the socialist program will be applied by almost anyone, sometimes by antisocialists (which is quite dangerous): nationalizations, federations, minimum social security. Scientific education is not yet up to replacing the religious education of the past in providing man with a thorough and morally imperative vision of the universe and fate. War brings in its wake the emancipation of women and the destruction of the traditions that dominated sexuality, without giving birth to a new security and a new ethics. The masses will obviously cling to national feeling—the expanded family, the expanded tribe, community of character.

H. L. responds that this is a form of solidarity and that with a bit of rational spirit it achieves wider solidarities possessing a deep foundation in the soul and material necessity. He agrees that we are on the threshold of a long period of confused struggles. He says that the questions of psychology and education will increasingly occupy the front stage for those who opt for historical optimism, for we must increasingly try to act directly, as directly as possible, on man's mentality. And we are taking possession of forms of knowledge that permit the development of appropriate techniques.

MECHANICS AND LIFE

October 26, 1944—At Dr. Gustavo Peter's home in Lomas, evening. It's cold out; we're on the terrace, from which the lights of Mexico City can be seen. We are waiting for clearings in the cloudy sky so we can direct the telescope at the half moon. When we succeed, the sight is magnificent. It's like a Sahara seeded with craters. At the border of light and darkness, an immense crater stands out against the outline of high mountains suspended in space above a dark hole. The delicate head of G. P. comes and goes between the light of the room and the cold night of the terrace. I find he resembles, probably more than physically, Bergson, whom I heard at the Sorbonne in 1909 or 1910. Bergson appeared in a frock coat, frail, with the neck of a bird posed on the hard ground, a balding oval head, a pale pink complexion, a thin nose and mouth. I was in the back of the amphitheater and from there he seemed as disincarnated as a man could be, fragile, as if reduced to the minimum amount of flesh required to support a mind. He also had delicate and white hands. Women in fancy hats listened to him from the front row. G. P. has the same bald skull, the same oval face, though a little bit redder, the same slightly hooked thin nose, and a blue-gray gaze that lays bare a contemplative and piercing intelligence. I know that he's someone who worries about the why of life, the why of death, the human problems that the disintegration of religion has left in suspense. For an hour we browse together through several treatises on astronomy, physics, and biology, notably that of Spemann published by Yale University, and that of Uexküll. (Uexküll is a Junker, and I just read in a Russian communiqué that fighting is going on in Uexküll). U. is probably no more than a modern vitalist, he endeavors to demonstrate that life is essentially a matter of accordance (*fügung*) between function and necessity, consequently invention, creation, and finality pursued and achieved. All of this was contained in the determinist term of "adaptation," which has never been closely examined. Spemann, less philosophical in the ancient (metaphysical) sense of the term, carries out laboratory investigations. He notably began by analyzing Driesch's experiment. A triton egg cut in two produced two complete tritons. It was thus impossible to localize in the chromosomes distributed in a certain architecture the "data" of the being to be reproduced; it's the entire substance of the egg that contains the capacity for reproduction (and for compensation if a portion is cut off). Spemann presents his prudent conclusion only in the last lines of the book, formulated with timidity and without insistence, which is that the entire unfurling of life seems to be made up of complex phenomena escaping mechanical (and consequently strictly spatial) definitions, analogous to those that take place in the nerve cell (sensitivity, memory, thought.) The old materialist schools would be outraged by this, yet it is quite obvious that however mysterious nature may be, thought is the product of life, is consubstantial with life, and there's nothing particularly bold in maintaining that it is life itself succeeding in discovering and knowing itself. (I realize that the term "consubstantiality" is nothing but an explanatory truism.)

We discuss it: It was Descartes, I think, who was the first in philosophy to apply mechanics to the intelligence of the living being, to man first of all. Since then all the science of the era of the explosion and development of machinery followed this trend. Just as Darwin discovered natural selection (greatly exaggerating its importance) in the period of exploding capitalist competition, involuntarily applying to the evolution of species a horrific and in his case only latent "Social Darwinism," so all of scientific knowledge is strongly marked by social ideology. Industrial capitalist society evolved rapidly, progressed in the blink of an eye (increase in the means of production and well-being); from this: *evolution* and *biological progress*. (Human society being nothing but a fragment of nature—this is not entirely false, but it was simplistic.) Bergson observed that intelligence was formed in *Homo faber*—Man the Maker, how just this term is!—by the manipulation of solids. In fact, Euclidian geometry, Newtonian mechanics, and modern science, up to today, for today we are at a turning point... (The manipulation of electrical and atomic energy is no longer that of solids, of brute matter.) The marvels of mechanization implicitly admit that life is the result of a mechanism infinitely more complex and necessary than machines, but of the same nature. But this is obviously not so. *Homo faber* cannot escape the concept that there is a *mechanism* in the living cell, in the thinking cell (if, that is, thought could be localized in given cells, which is not proven), but the time has come to recognize that it is a mechanism so profoundly different from that which our hands are able to construct that it deserves another name. Qualitatively different, it should be understood in a completely different way. There is arrangement and creative organization with means profoundly different from those that control human labor and the creation of machines. Above all, there is a power of synthesis, emergence, and creation of the immaterial (which is in no way unreal, but on the contrary an essential form of the real: thought) totally inexplicable according to the rules of the mechanistic science of yesterday. I write the word "immaterial" with difficulty, having to shake off in order to use it the weighty rigor of antiobscurantist thinking (the infantile spiritualist explanations of postreligion).

Uexküll, Driesch, and Spemann are Germans... Returning from Dr. Gustavo Peter's I find in an issue of *Free Europe* an article by Lord Vansittart on the overall responsibility of the German people in the current calamity. Lord V. obviously has no idea what a totalitarian machine is and how totally it imprisons men. He has no idea that once

established *in any place in the world* this machinery would produce
the same effects. There is an immense lack of imagination and understanding at the heart of his theory. He breathes British liberalism and
his mind doesn't escape it for a single second. The refutation of his
philosophy of war is of a nearly comic childishness. What would a
Hindu Vansittart write about the English? A Polish V. on the Russians?
An Ethiopian V. on the Italians? What will the V.s of tomorrow write
of the Russians, given that Stalinist totalitarianism will assume the
terrible historical succession of Nazi totalitarianism? It must be noted
that this easy refutation doesn't close the question of national psychology: it exists.

JEANNINE THE REALIST

October 2, 1944—Jeannine, while eating supper, notices the painting
by V. Brauner: a large, symmetrical flower whose stem is the talon of
a bird of prey grasping a tree trunk. At the center of the flower a crystal contains light and color…Jeannine: "Papa, why do people paint
things that don't exist? There's no flower like that, with a bird's claw
and a crystal. It's not real. Why paint what's not real?"

"But perhaps there are flowers that are like that."

"No, I'm sure there aren't. You're telling fibs."

"Maybe we see them in dreams."

"Ah…but dreams aren't real."

"In any case, it's very beautiful."

"Yes, but it's not real."

I have long been surprised by her concrete and positive mind-set.
About a story, she always asks: "Is it real? Did it really happen?" No
real interest in fairy tales and the marvelous, which Lunacharsky and
many others asserted correspond to a child's needs. The influence of
Laurette, who reads her tales by Anderson and who loves the marvelous,
has had no impact on her. In this sense she is different from Vlady,
whose imagination freely runs wild (and past twenty continues along
the levels of distorted reality). In this sense, she takes after me, my
scrupulous concreteness, without my ever having taught her anything.
(This was also my father's mind-set, who considered himself scientific

in all things.) But aren't children infinitely more realistic and interested in reality than grown-ups, who need escape into the marvelous, the mystical, the surreal, and the unreal—or that other fantastic reality of the inner world?

DUPLICITY

November 3, 1944—We invented many things in Russia, many disastrous things, and it wasn't our fault. The State's total stranglehold over man originated with us, our misfortune. Around 1928–1930 a new word appeared in party life, *dvourouchnicthestvo*, of which the French *duplicité* is a weak translation. We laughed at the Old Bolshevik (with an average hero's life) who, over the course of three days, made a public declaration in favor of the Opposition, retracted it in front of the Control Commission (Yaroslavky having come during the night, pulled him out of bed, subjected him to an interrogation) and the following day, recovered from his nocturnal fears, retracted his retraction ... Later, he doubtless retracted his assertion that he was an Oppositionist again, and this probably did not prevent him from winding up in prison or being executed seven or eight years later for a various reasons ... We knew epidemics of duplicity: it was even a political tendency, that of Zinoviev and Kamenev: the retraction with mental reservations in order to win time, to serve the party, and to be there (instead of in prison) for history's next turn. Along with a handful of Trotskyists, I condemned this disintegrating moral gymnastics and advocated the Don Quixotism of resistance in broad daylight, and we were told we were pursuing a politically suicidal tactic, which appeared to be the case. The malady spread to all of Europe and a large part of Asia. How many people serve or collaborate with totalitarian regimes despite themselves, finding inner salvation only in mental reservation: sometimes hateful, sometimes despairing, most often (simply?) cowardly.

French newspapers: it seems impossible to make sense of them. A large number of acknowledged collaborationists rendered service in secret to the Resistance ... All of France lived under a regime of duplicity. The naked and disarmed man living under the machinery of the state has only this pitiful and degrading flight. One can only expect heroic rebellion from a tiny minority driven by exceptional personal qualities and material circumstances.

MAX JACOB, BENJAMIN CRÉMIEUX, AND OTHER
DEAD MEN

November 5, 1944—Benjamin Crémieux* has been murdered by the Nazis. I barely knew him, his vacillating and complacent attitude towards Russian totalitarianism not having allowed us to frequent each other. Under the regime of the Molotov-Ribbentrop Pact he "saw things clearly," with bitterness, and we met each other in the corridors of the Quai d'Orsay. He, in an officer's uniform, a rabbinical beard and glasses, very bourgeois-ly and nobly the Jewish intellectual, with an astute mind. Without much force, he was intelligent and cultivated, truly attached to the values that were being threatened. They seized him, humiliated him, insulted him, and killed him. He must have suffered enormously, like so many others, and no one will ever know. A newspaper devotes eight lines to him in the same issue that Brillat-Savarin gets several columns and idiotic chitchat fills whole. Everything in its place.

An enormous indifference greets the announcement of deaths. Giraudoux is dead; Max Jacob was tortured and murdered; Saint-Exupéry disappeared, no reaction, no moved or moving note, no real interest among people who know the works and the men, nothing, or almost nothing, in the press. And when something is published it's so stupid and pitiful that it would be better not to publish anything. Obviously there are too many deaths and they can no longer be counted. Books and ideas are henceforth worth so little that there's no need to even speak of them. I recall the indifference that greeted the announcement of Sneevliet's death. Are there more than three or four of us who truly remember Otto Rühle, Alice, and Fritz Fränkel? I'd like to believe that someone whom no one thinks of has maintained a heart-stricken memory of them. It's possible. Decline in value of man and a decline in the quality of people's character. I'm surprised that people don't fight harder against this general degradation. It's possible to have a strong reaction and to remain alive in a more dignified manner. The devastating current is strong, but people surrender to it too much. Always the problem of cowardice and courage.

I recall with gratitude a letter from Duhamel that I received in Leningrad in 1931 or 1932. I'd written him to announce the death of Maximilian Alexandrovich Voloshin,* whom he had known since their shared youth. He answered: "I passed a night meditating on that life and that death...."

Death of old Maillol in an auto accident on a road in the Pyrenees. Suspicious.[32]

SPEECH BY PRIETO

November 11, 1944—Prieto at home, in the bright and pleasant comfort with which he has surrounded himself. Corpulent, he seems enormous: soft, pink, thick featured, tiny eyes between thick pink eyelids. He leans back in an armchair, swinging his leg, dressed in a suit of soft fabric. Speaks with clarity, intelligent and well thought out. He probably works little, but everything is in his active head. The Junta de Liberación lacks money and material means while the Communist Party and Negrín possess unlimited amounts of them. De Gaulle has agreed to the transfer of the Junta to French territory, but there are others who are opposed... He doesn't write out his speech for this evening, scarcely a few notes. It will be taken down in shorthand. He thinks as he speaks and speaks at the tribune after having composed a mental speech. The mind of an orator, like Jaurès.

Between 1,500 and 2,000 people in the ramshackle offices of the Pablo Iglesias Center, Calle de Tacuba 15, the former offices of the Israelite Central Committee. A few very pretty women, simple, friendly young men, who will applaud enthusiastically. A majority of middle-aged or elderly men with the look of old militants or worn-out intellectuals. Met a founder of the Spanish CP and some deputies. Prieto is a great orator, extremely skillful. An architecturally perfect speech with laugh lines from time to time, vehemence unleashed at the right

32. Several rumors—false ones, it seems—circulated about the death of the sculptor, said to have been assassinated because of his collaborationism.

moment, and simple arguments reduced to a persuasive schema: he seems to be expressing only what is obvious. He begins by reading the names of thirty-four Socialist deputies to the Cortés (out of ninety-nine) executed by Franco, of Besteiro, dead in prison, of Caballero, imprisoned in Germany, of others dead in exile. Not a single one of them compromised his conscience! A good preamble, to precede his denunciation of the CP's jesuitry, its appeals to the right, its usurpations, its appeal to the absolutist *requetés* who have the blood of 25,000 workers massacred in Navarre on their hands.

In reality a civil war speech. The combat has opened between the totalitarian CP and socialist democracy, in Spain as in Poland.

Statement of facts. That the events of 1917–1918 can't be repeated at the end of this war. The former opposition between socialist revolution and capitalist reaction has been replaced by civil war between Stalinist totalitarianism and democratic socialism. Conservatism and neofascism benefit from this tragedy. Those who still think in the theoretical terms of 1917–1918 (not to mention those of 1871!) place themselves on the plane of disastrous illusion.

THE EXTERMINATION OF THE JEWS

November 12, 1944—Read *The Black Book of Polish Jewry*[33]—horrific. Repeated a hundred times with technically organized variants of sadism and bestiality, the same tale of violence, insults, and finally of rationalized extermination in purpose-built factories. Counting Russian Jews, this must add up to three million murdered—at least: an entire people. This is beyond imagining: one's lucidity is shaken. Difficult to think clearly.

Absolute mystery surrounds the extermination camps: asphyxiation wagons, asphyxiation chambers, etc. Probably all the personnel selected for these horrible tasks are then killed themselves: either the agents become dangerous half madmen or the system plans in advance for the disappearance of such witnesses. Nevertheless, propaganda, both printed and illustrated, broadly reveals the humiliation of the victims. News-

33. Published in New York in 1943.

paper photos: stooped old rabbis, guarded by young brutes, digging in the earth. This is a necessary psychological preparation for the crime. It's certain that the Nazis found thousands of zealous agents, wide-ranging complicity. Does this sully the German people with responsibility? It is impossible that people, reacting instinctively, should not believe this: this reaction is legitimate because natural. But the reality?

In reality the system appealed to destructive instincts, to sadism, to the castration complex in choosing a few thousand brutes ready to do anything. It's not difficult to find one hundred thousand out of sixty-five million inhabitants, and these hundred thousand are largely sufficient for all tasks. In addition, the totalitarian machinery (inconceivable for anyone who has not experienced it) offers the average man—neither good nor bad, more or less sociable, more or less molded by one or two thousand years of civilization—no choice. Sent to Poland in uniform, posted not far from an extermination factory, the average man can only resist through suicide, the suicide of revolt, or mental reservations (which is manifested by a neurotic, sometimes explosive, passivity). H. L. observes that escape can also be sought in an exalted acceptance, in fanatical consent, implying the sacrifice of the best of oneself in a willed blindness. (Imagine Lord Vansittart in a totalitarian uniform and designated by his chiefs to participate in a *Judenvernichtung* brigade.)

The attitude of the Jews themselves, among whom social consciousness is particularly strong. In the ghettos and the camps, auxiliary service was and is carried out by the Jews themselves, chosen from among the healthiest, who are exterminated after a certain amount of labor. They know this but they gain a few days or weeks of hellish delay. There are those who, having accepted the "work," later ask to be executed—and an SS shoots them in the head. In the meanwhile, they are allowed to eat the food brought by the herds who are asphyxiated, electrocuted, or machine-gunned. The last meal matters to the famished and condemned human animal. The well fed and the noncondemned are not allowed to censure in cases such as these.

November 12, 1944—Until now this crime, unique in the annals of man, has given rise only to insignificant reactions, even among the

Jews. It is rather poorly known and it has been little spoken of, as if it was surrounded by a vast complicity. Political and psychological reasons? The anti-Semitism latent everywhere in the backward and reactionary world? Yes, but also the (healthy) repression[34] of monstrous and dangerous images and thoughts. The divulging of such a crime brings with it involuntary contagions whose consequences are unforeseeable. The sole wise attitude to adopt would be, if possible, to destroy even its memory. That the truth about man today cannot always be spoken; that a part of him must be annihilated in order to save that man.

The extermination was organized by ministries and prepared by a Scientific Institute for the Study of the Jewish Problem (Dr. Alfred Rosenberg). Here I feel lost. I cannot conceive the mentality of the functionaries who knew its inner workings: this mixture of rational mind, inhuman psychosis, total cowardice, professionalism, and ferocity... The Nazis have marched against the current of all of human evolution, which was advancing from bestiality to humanism. In this sense they have created something new and begun the destruction of the gains of thousands of years of history. The consequences are impossible to predict. It's certain that the elementary Marxists who see in this war nothing but "imperialism" demonstrate a pitiful blindness that shields them from the knowledge of facts. The imperialisms play their part in this, but anti-Semitism is a psychological and social phenomenon of another type, infinitely more serious than all the other psychological phenomena unleashed by the war, giving Nazi neoimperialism a particular quality by taking instincts back to the point they were at during the wars of tribal extermination.

Regression. At fifteen I read Victor Hugo's *The Last Day of a Condemned Man*. The abolition of the death penalty in France had been proposed; the execution of the madman Soleilland, who'd raped and strangled a little girl, became a worldwide event. Socialist congresses spoke out for the abolition of the death penalty. There is no Victor Hugo today to write *The Last Day of a Million Men*... No civilized man is certain he won't be either murdered or executed or killed by a rocket-propelled bomb.

34. In the Freudian sense.

POPO

Sunday, November 19, 1944—A good road, climbing gently, takes us
just below the snow line. The rarified air is impregnated with light; the
weather is cool. Pine and fir woods, calm, transparency. Feeling of
space, of lightness, skimming on the surface of the earth. I feel peacefully luminous. It seems to me that the others must feel the same as
me. Way high up is Cortés's crossroads, "where the first horse of the
conquistadors passed." The Veracruz road passed between Ixtaccíhuatl
and Popocatépetl. From this crossroads the horizons of a virgin planet
can be seen, the snow slopes of Ixta, sheer and gentle; the more massive
and rounded slopes of Popo; the green woods downhill, the plains
below resembling the sea; piles of horizontal clouds, and above their
vapors a bluish peak, the Malinche, and further away the sparkling
peak of the Orizaba ... The road is made of rust-colored volcanic ash,
which becomes pale gray as we climb higher. We walk with short steps
in an intoxicated breathlessness: you want to run, perhaps to dance.
You feel a lightness of soul, as if the transparency of the world and the
cold whiteness of the snow purified it, cooled it, freed it—and your
chest weakening, your heart vacillating. (A beautiful place to die.) And
while we were enjoying ourselves there someone did die, a mountain
climber who fell into a crevice an hour from here ... Some young men
talk about it. (Three hours later we met up with the ambulance that
came to get him—from Mexico City since there's no first aid post in
Amecameca.) We don't reach the snow line—shortness of breath. The
real climb would take another four hard hours after special training.
Laurette and Jeannine descend the slopes, barefooted in the radiant
ash. Moedano, the youngest of our group, suddenly lies down on the
side of the road, his heart beating and taken with dizziness. He has a
good *mestizo* face with Negroid blood; big, kind eyes, an air of strength.
We admire a rock that hangs over the road, which is gray but from up
close shows itself covered with high-altitude flowers of bright and
delicate colors, a dim, muted vegetal light. "Looks like the bottom of
the sea," says Laurette. Dr. Gustavo Peter attaches his ideas about the
universe onto everything: heredity, the structure of matter, and human
research. We speak of these things endlessly, in fits and starts, breathing in the mountain and the exalting fatigue: there is laughter in his

eyes. From behind the flowered rock there emerges the silhouette of a young man with an angular face and longish hair, and I think it's Vlady: no encounter would be surprising here. He's a Hungarian *globetrotter*,[35] smiling, his arms full of kaleidoscopically colored plants, who proudly shows us his cane, upon which he's nailed the emblems of all the cities of Europe: Istanbul, Sofia, Vienna, Genoa, Barcelona, and the Eiffel Tower. He speaks good French. "I'm traveling across the world on foot." It's a goal in life, a goal of innocent egoism. I wish him to be able to redo the tour of a Europe at peace. "Oh, no! I'm too old: I'm already thirty."

Afterwards the magnificent site of Amecameca, perhaps the one I love most in Mexico, along with Pátzcuaro. The plaza is festive. We see a wedding straight out of 1830 go past, the bride in a white dress and orange blossoms (pink-cheeked peasant girl), the groom awkward, as is appropriate. Solemn little boys, prettily dressed, hold the white train; a fairy-tale girl-child carries a cushion on which there's something I can't make out. The rings? The key to the nuptial chamber, an amulet of the Dark Virgin? The little girl walks in front of the newlyweds, a crown of gold paper on her head. The groomsmen wear the uniform of a military academy, the bridesmaids are in pink silk dresses. This cortege advances through the crowd in the marketplace, the bright patterns, the sun, the colors, towards the church, beyond which rise the snows of Ixtaccíhuatl and the blue mountain capped with moving clouds. Alongside the church a school with comically Gothic windows is painted light blue. Near us, incredible buses fill up with Indios, their baskets, their turkeys, their grub, their kids. You wonder if the moment will come when these vehicles will no longer be able to take on board even one more passenger in a sombrero, but in fact, that moment never comes. Young girls are returning back from mass, probably the daughters of the town's caciques, wealthy and smiling. One of them is of a rare beauty (but perhaps it's simply the enchantment of the plaza and the nearby mountain): pure Spaniard, straight nose, large, laughing mouth, dressed tastefully: sober mantilla, jacket of grayish white, short skirt, black fishnet stockings on squat, muscular legs. She erases the

35. In English in the original.

image of a perhaps leprous beggar. The gleam of the oranges and pepper in the market; light gild of braids and ropes.

From Sacromonte the landscape opens out with a plenitude I'd never before seen in it. With each station of the cross, the two white volcanoes emerge more powerful above the foliage. The church of Fray Martín de Valencia is a jewel of colors, old pink. We walk over ancient graves and all around the lands appear, a valley leading towards a horizon of countless hills, the city in light and gray, the peaks white, enormous, looming, streaming with light. We see them turn gold then be extinguished in a pale fire. At the side entrance of the church an excellent bronze statue of Fray Martín has been placed, a simple silhouette, thin and grave. The candles are lit in front of the chancel, we're between the horizon and the altar. Again saw the uppermost chapel and the attractive, dilapidated cemetery, still full of dried flowers left on the Day of the Dead. On the walls of the chapel and many graves, the multiplied sign of the hand. I thought of the Arab hand of fate.

Good translation of Ixtaccíhuatl, the *Mujer dormida*: Sleeping Beauty.

AMERICAN INTELLECTUALS IN THE FACE OF THE STALINIST USSR

The New Republic has just published, on November 17, a special issue dedicated to "Russia Today," which may be considered striking evidence of a double failure, intellectual and moral. Lack of courage in the presence of facts that, in order to be understood and mastered, demand courage; lack of scientific spirit, refusal to see clearly, to distinguish between the true and the false, flight into omission and circumstantial interpretation. Let us look a little closer, without going into too much detail.

Mme. Vera Micheles Dean* sees in the Moscow Trials "an explosion of xenophobia." This deliberately ignores the social causes of the massacre of the revolutionary generation and, what is more, the friendly and almost enthusiastic attitude of the Russian people towards foreigners. This lady considers that "anti-German" sentiment played a decisive role in the Stalinist purges: this completely ignores reality and the documentation published on this subject, and it forgets that, as chronology attests, the massacres laid the groundwork for Stalin's collaboration with Hitler.

M. Max Werner* speaks of the Red Army without mentioning its 30,000 to 40,000 men executed of 1937–1938; without indicating that it is an army decapitated by the destruction of its command structure. But he estimates that its reserves possibly reach 20,000,000 to 25,000,000 men (!!!), this in an adult population no greater than 90,000,000!

M. Roger N. Baldwin* speaks of a "democracy in production" that supposedly exists in the USSR, any other kind being lacking. And this is radically false, as is amply proved by the number of workers and technicians sent to the concentration camps. At "production meetings," the only speaking that occurs is one-way official intervention.

M. A. Yugov deals with the collectivization of agriculture without indicating that it was the cause of the great famine of 1931–1934 (which he doesn't mention) and the disappearance, according to official statistics, of 5,000,000 peasant families between 1929 and 1935. (Exact figures: number of farming households on June 1, 1929: 25,830,000; on July 1, 1935: 20,903,100.) M. Yugov also writes that "the living standard of the Soviet worker over the last few years was unquestionably higher than it was before World War I." But M. Yugov can't possibly be ignorant of the studies of Professor Prokopovich* on real salaries in the USSR, studies based on official data and whose conclusions run in the opposite direction. Real wages for most workers in the USSR were from 15 to 30 percent lower than what they were in 1913 and 1926–1927. M. Yugov speaks of the "improvement in living conditions in the countryside," where we so often heard people speak of how they miss the good old days, the time when it was possible to buy sugar and tea, and even shoes! It's true that we were there in 1936. But here is testimony from early 1941 which we find in the magazine of M. Yugov himself, *The New Road*, a Russian Social-Democratic organ published in New York, its May 6, 1941, issue: "As for consumption, the level in the Soviet countryside is extremely low. There are provinces where salt is almost a luxury, tea a rarity, needles—and even more so, scissors—exist only in dreams.... In entire cities a watch, a pen, a simple notebook constitute an unheard of luxury, obtained with difficulty by the privileged." M. Yugov writes in the same issue of *The New Road* that "the state of the Soviet economy is catastrophic."

M. Yarmolinsky* deals with Soviet literature without saying that

Soviet literature is controlled in its least details by the totalitarian state; without mentioning the periodic purges of libraries and the pulping of millions of books and the entire works of the best minds of the revolution; without mentioning the names of Bukharin, Kamenev, Voronsky,* Riazanov, Tarasov-Rodyonov,* Galina Serebryakova,* Lelevich,* and Gorbachev, all of whom disappeared along with their entire works; without mentioning the disappearance of the theatrical director Meyerhold; without indicating that Pilniak (disappeared, but named in the article) was one of the true founders of young Soviet literature.

M. John Hazard* speaks of legality without mentioning the extra-legal disappearance of the jurists Pachoukanis* and Chelenov and the people's commissars for justice Krylenko and Antonov-Ovseyenko. If ministers vanish at night into the shadows what legality do the poor people have a right to? John N. Hazard never wonders about this.

M. Maurice Hindus notes that the Russian people are attached to Stalin since Stalin is still in power in the fifth month of war. We will allow ourselves to remind this author that Nicolas II's unpopularity was clearly demonstrated on certain days in March 1917, but that was after three years of war during which the Russian armies showed the same valor as today with less disastrous results.

We can't too strongly recommend to lovers of intellectual curiosities that they put aside this issue of the *New Republic* and open it in a short while, let's say a year. That will be extremely interesting...

P.S.—Another word about Roger Baldwin's article, where he writes that foreign books and newspapers are available to the Russian public. This is utterly and totally false. Letters, newspapers, and books are all filtered by the GPU. Not a single foreign socialist publication enters the USSR; not a book that displeases the censors; and Soviet citizens are frightened of corresponding with foreign countries.

SOCIALIST PROBLEMS

November 25, 1944—Many socialists continue to pose problems in strictly traditional, if not routine terms. The schemas they have in mind are those of 1917–1918, and even of 1871! As if events were going to repeat themselves. (They could reproduce themselves fragmentarily, but the entire context being different the big picture will be profoundly different.) The extraordinary power of tradition, attaining a kind of blindness; also take into account the painful difficulty of mastering a new situation, full of pitfalls and disappointments; the spirit of objective investigation retreats and gives up rather than advancing towards discoveries it is not certain of being able to master and which, it foresees, may put in question the former foundations of its faith.

But the error thus committed risks being catastrophic. The publications of the English International Labour Party[36] present the problem from this obsolete viewpoint: reaction and revolution are confronting each other in Europe. Two adversaries are present, and this is certainly false: there are three: conservatism, socialism, and Stalinist totalitarianism, engaged in a fight to the death. Conservatism, weakened on the continent by the fascisms it gave birth to and which are dying, has much real and potential support in the democratic nations, and it will go as far as forms of neototalitarianism, if it can. Stalinist totalitarianism is on the offensive everywhere, probably because it feels so threatened by its internal weaknesses and by an international situation so critical that all it can do is exploit as far as it can its rivals' indecision and lack of comprehension. It plays both the revolutionary and the conservative cards: "Conservatives: I am order, hierarchical society, and social peace, and I know how to gun down troublemakers! Workers, peasants, intellectuals: I am the red star, the legend of Lenin, the nationalization of industries, agrarian reform, and security against unemployment! Businessmen:[37] I am profitable deals. Literati: I am huge print runs!" It talks this double language with a certain cynical sincerity because reality justifies it. The Russian totalitarian system is revolutionary in relation to traditional capitalism and reactionary in relation to liberal humanism and socialist aspirations. But what can aspirations do, even the most justified, even the most necessary—and I think they are—against well-organized state machinery? Between these two tendencies, that of socialism (and of American and European mass democracy), though firmly rooted and capable of (weakly) mo-

36. Serge is clearly referring to the Independent Labour Party.
37. In English in the original.

bilizing greater numbers, is nearly disarmed due to its lack of institutions it controls and of clear ideas. The tiny minority that represents its clear ideas has few material means or support. In truth, it can only fully manifest itself in the United States, and even there it is extremely weak. A situation of immense European civil war is being created with three unequal parties committed one against another in such a way that each of the three parties *must* aim at neutralizing one of the two others or at seeking an alliance. If socialism doesn't vigorously maintain its democratic and libertarian (in the etymological and not anarchist sense of the word) physiognomy it will be torn apart and crushed. Its worst enemy, the most destructive one at this moment, is the totalitarianism of postrevolutionary Russia, Bolshevism transformed into absolute totalitarianism of a type analogous to that of reactionary totalitarianisms. The sole natural allies of socialism are among the democratic masses of the countries where bourgeois democracy lives on with traditions predating big capitalism, England and the United States. The movement that followed World War I cannot be reproduced under such conditions, except to bring about results immediately worse than those of the revolutionary victory in Russia and the defeat of European socialism. In any case, there are neither large parties nor cadres nor an ideology capable of reproducing them. This results in a confused and dangerous situation. I'm inclined to think that Europe's fate can only be decided when Stalinist totalitarianism has been limited or destroyed in the new conflicts that it necessarily begins. (That it capitulates; that it is transformed or abolished by wished-for and quite probable internal shakeups; that it creates a state of heightened conflict with its rivals/allies of today.)—(Or that it victoriously imposes its hegemony over most of Europe and Asia, which will herald a Third World War.)

In the meanwhile, the socialist left contents itself with illusions and involuntary demagogy, its eyes blindfolded by grand principles. The comrades I see here dream of a little Comintern of their own; dream of being carried along by the waves of the masses. They remain isolated and the most clear-sighted see no alternative to the blackest pessimism while affecting a "Marxist" optimism.

Dialogue with Narcís Molins i Fàbregas:

Me: If the socialist left, which, with all its weaknesses, is the most idealistic element of socialism, isolates itself into a tiny sect it will end up exterminated by the totalitarian Communists. Its only salvation and its only chance to be useful are in rallying along with the old (moderate) socialist movements and the democratic masses. There it would be a beneficial leavening and would find natural defenses.

Narcís Molins: Do you think so? As soon as we opened our mouths in a socialist party the old opportunists and the Stalinized would gag us or throw us out. And the socialist parties, of which we would be members, would calmly allow us to be assassinated by the Stalinists.

I can't deny that this is possible—in the near future—but I think it's not certain, and that healthier reactions are also possible if not probable among the democratic masses, educated by so many experiences. In any case, I don't see what else we can try.

N. M.: We might as well be killed without abdicating anything we believe in, while clearly posing the questions.

I don't answer him that the questions have precisely not been well or clearly posed. A suicidal tactic can be a good one only in completely hopeless situations, and deep down I'm the less pessimistic of the two of us.

This conversation reminds me of what Bukharin said to Kamenev about Stalin in 1928: "If we follow him he'll drag the country into the abyss and we'll perish, and the revolution will perish along with him. If we denounce him he'll accuse us of treason and we'll perish." Bukharin and Kamenev chose to follow while denouncing, to denounce while following, to acclaim—obligatorily—while grumbling, and suffered ten years of psychological torture before perishing, as they predicted. We were right against them in adopting the intransigent attitude they called political suicide, but which was also forging ahead regardless, the most courageous and perhaps the most rational one on battlefields. (This is currently Stalin's attitude in international politics.)

Dwight Macdonald, in *Politics*, interpreting a correct observation (that in France and elsewhere social consciousness had made perhaps immense progress) thinks that the Communist movement can outflank its totalitarian leaders and fulfill a healthy function. I answer that he is seriously in error and that "the Communist apparatus controls perfectly and mercilessly all the movements it influences.... This ap-

paratus, with its functional, police, and psychological mechanisms, is an enormous new fact in history whose deadly importance has not yet been measured. You live in too free a country to imagine this...."
"I fear that we'll soon see arising in various countries Communist-totalitarian condottieri of the Mao Zedong and Tito type, cynical and *convinced*, who'll be 'revolutionaries' and counterrevolutionaries, or both at once, according to the orders they receive, and capable of turning about face from one day to the next."

SHORTNESS OF BREATH OR DEPRESSION

December 3, 1944—Michael Fraenkel is small and frail. An intelligent and delicate face, glasses, a lively gaze easily tinged with humor, the lower part of his face pointy. He writes, writes endlessly, having given up on finding a wide audience, and having almost given up on everything. "Why?" I asked him. Because I can't do otherwise, because I can't not write. (The touch of bitter humor is clear in his answer.) He's preparing a journal: sad visions of Mexico (he can't bear the spectacle of poverty and the lack of civilization amid the most beautiful but barren landscapes, and the intellectual void), reflections on books, encounters, and ideas. It is good work, for a man who is worried and short of breath. The labor of a stubborn man who hasn't found the tonic to lift his spirits. What keeps M. F. standing is his indomitable Jewish disquiet, which is never completely hopeless and which, despite it all, finds its resolution in activity. In Coyoacán he was once taken for Trotsky: he tells the story with pleasure, and there really is something of Trotsky about him, in the forehead larger than the rest of the head, the shock of gray hair, the glasses imperiously sharpening his gaze. This is where the fleeting superficial resemblance ends. We spoke quite intimately this evening. (Customarily his Saturdays, given over to chance visitors, are amusing or not, like encounters on the metro.) He shows me a page of his journal on the poet who must—who ought to—come and overcome death, decadence, despair, with a new human affirmation of unlimited power. "From a sociological point of view," he says, "I know this is crazy." "It's not as crazy as all that," I say. "It's simply contrary to the rules of ordinary determinism. But in exceptional dangers ordinary determinism is no longer the absolute rule. Instinct sometimes finds completely unforeseeable, miraculous solutions. In this case I don't give the word 'miracle' a mystical significance; it is simply something that defies prediction and comprehension through success, through the energy of unexpected effort. All you are doing is repeating the Nietzschean assertion that 'man must be overcome,' the wretched and distraught man of today's chaos. He will be; a poet may emerge as a precursor, perhaps there are already among us many unknown precursors who *will overcome.*"

Spoke of the incredible difficulty of working: shortness of breath. We realize that we have this in common. I think that the altitude of Mexico City diminishes me greatly by causing endless crises of breathlessness. (On the altitude: Dr. Gustavo Peter says that the medical doses of X-rays in use in Europe aren't valid here: dangerous, given the different dosage of oxygen in the organism. Another person explains to me that cats' lives are a third shorter here than in Europe.) M. F. shares this opinion, but he insists on the lack of an intellectual environment: the vast, sad city of *business*[38] and Indian poverty, the real inexistence of ideas, Europe's silence. We recall the unimaginable tonic the streets of Paris were for us. We're on a diet of shortness of breath in a desert.

ON THE END OF THE NOVEL

December 4, 1944... a regime of shortness of breath in a desert at an altitude of 2,400 meters in the tropics.

Henri Michaux, *La Cordillère des Andes*:

"Everyone here smokes the opium of high altitudes, low voice, little steps, little breath.

"... In order to enter this city we had to pay the face tax."

The tax on the human face, molded by the soul, is a heavy one to pay: it disfigures you.

I'm at the end of *Last Days* and I'm feeling an extraordinary difficulty in finishing this book. It's not just the physical breathlessness and the lack of a favorable environment. It's more that for me a novel must have

---

38. In English in the original.

an inner justification, internal to its characters and its atmosphere, and that in reality all the people I have attempted to bring to life seem to me condemned men walking through a fog. They need a solution, I need a solution for them—*and there isn't one*. History can only impose its solutions by walking over their dead bodies.

December 5, 1944—Arsenic and Old Lace, American film by Capra, acceptable. The play ran for hundreds of performances in New York. The leitmotiv of the American cinema at its best: that madness or manias are man's only escape in today's world, the great sources of laughter and the feeling of plenitude. In this instance it's a case of an amused plenitude at the spectacle of a gently tragic and macabre madness. Everyone is mad, believes himself mad, and even the sane are inclined to imitate the mad, so persuasive are the latter. (In order for a happy ending to be possible a little blonde star and an intelligently normal policeman are the exception.) A hereditarily insane family, become thoroughly bourgeois, in Brooklyn. Two old maids, pious and kindly sisters, overflowing with goodness, poison the old bachelors they invite over with a cocktail of wine, cyanide, strychnine, and arsenic, then solemnly chant the psalms for the dead and have their nephew bury "these nice men" in the cellar—their nephew, who thinks he's President Teddy Roosevelt and that he's digging the Panama Canal and burying the victims of yellow fever... "We're doing a work of charity—*of mercy*,"[39] the old ladies innocently say. It's a question of sparing aging men a too-painful end of life. Another nephew is a criminal madman who's escaped from an asylum in the grand (pure kitsch) tradition of the cinema. Everything is goofy, the corpses move between a large crate and the cellar, Teddy Roosevelt charges up the staircase with so much brio that the doctor come to commit him is tempted to imitate him; a policeman is a gentle, frantic maniac who thinks himself a playwright and, intervening in the middle of a crime, thinks he's participating in a rehearsal and exclaims: "You stole my plot!" Continuous whirl of madness in the middle of banality. I leave

39. In English in the original.

the film feeling oppressed and disappointed. This is what they come up with to amuse and relax the crowds that go to the movies? The world is crazy, sinister, and joyful, but even so everything works out for the beautiful blonde and her fiancé; they'll benefit from a normal grace, for a while in any case. In reality, this black humor is caricatural and false; the social satire it contains veers in the direction of a puerile nastiness. Nothing is thoroughly thought through and reflection is the least concern of the authors, for whom nothing exists but effects and theatrical business (nothing: not truth, not duty, not conscience, not—and here I plunge into the ridiculous—the love of man); nothing in them of the inner elevation that is the grandeur of a Chekhov or a Claudel, absolutely nothing.

In times that were also dark, but not as completely dark as ours, Leonid Andreyev created his theater of fright in the aftermath of a war lost by Russia and a revolution defeated by the hangmen and the anti-Semites. He was full of philosophical romanticism, he posed the question of fate, and he was the equal of the Greek tragedians in the quality of his disquiet; he was filled with torment and conscience. It is significant that we don't have an Andreyev but that we do have this theater and this cinema (O'Neill is in the Andreyev vein: he dates back fifteen or twenty years.)

DR. S. B.
December 8, 1944—Shortness of breath, nearly constant slight physical anxiety in the upper part of my chest, heart palpitations, and burdensome bouts of exhaustion. Visited Dr. S. B. He notes an elevated arterial pressure, a lack of "potential" on the EKG whose waves sometimes point down instead of pointing up. "What does this mean?" "A shortage of electric potential. . . . We need to keep an eye on your fatigue. We'll do another EKG in six months." "Explain it to me." "Impossible. It would take an hour's lecture." The doctor admits that he almost never knows precisely what the matter is. It goes without saying that he often can't say what he thinks or suspects; he seeks, guesses, senses, trusts in nature, says reasonable and comforting things as far as he can,

and moves on to the next patient. The situation of the Roman augurs, whose useful function was noted by Freud.

Me: Can the feeling of oppression be partially caused by nerves?

S. B.: Yes.

And we spoke of current events, of the times. He, suddenly extremely serious, abandoning the pleasant expression he has for the patient: "The end of the war looks increasingly bleak. No one imagined that. What have we lived for?"

Dr. Gustavo Peter recounts the case of a patient, a scientist, suffering from facial eczema, on whom he applied ten rounds of radiation in a case when normally three suffice. The scientist was desperate. And he came back—cured. G. P. had difficulty getting him to say what he'd done. Finally he confessed: "I'm a believer. I knelt before the Virgin of Guadalupe and she answered my prayers." G. P. comments: "That's obviously as effective as my radiation. Nevertheless, I'm going to verify that it wasn't the effect of the tenth session."

POLAND, GREECE, ETC.

December 10, 1944—Conversation with a Polish socialist. He thinks that at present Poland is lost. No one can prevent Stalin from occupying it and having "order reign" in his fashion. No one seriously wants to fight with him over this prize, so difficult to administer. Historically, this new tragedy doesn't seem like it can go on for a long time, but the immediate future is dark. "Since dignity and hope are all that is left to save, we're partisans of absolute intransigence." I answer that when dealing with totalitarians this is the sole attitude that is not only worthy, but useful. In resistance one must be as absolute as they are in order to make them feel that this is a game that requires their total commitment: that is, they must run every risk.

Two "end of war" perspectives after the defeat of Nazism, both equally somber: either war against Stalinist totalitarianism to prevent it establishing its hegemony over the European continent, Iran, and most of China, or (temporary) consent to this hegemony...

The Pole: I think that the democratic powers will do all they can to avoid an open and armed conflict during which Stalin will have a nonnegligible number of allies in their ranks. We'll see diplomatic conflicts, economic pressure, shady deals, bloody proxy wars in the center and east of Europe—civil war—and this will result in an unstable situation without real peace or war, a state of European chaos where the powers will measure each other for a long time....What do you think of Stalin's attitude?

Me: That he's extremely aware of this situation and that he alone knows his own weakness and his own strength, principally made of the ideological (social) weakness of his partner-enemies....That he will speak reassuring words, sign treaties, use all imaginable camouflages and invent new ones, will seek and accept deals but will never keep his word, will never really commit himself, and will do whatever he pleases; that is, whatever is in keeping with the needs and possibilities of his own situation. Power relations are all that exist for him, and he knows how to judge them boldly. This is what remains of the psychology of the "revolutionary materialist" in him.

At the moment we are speaking the Greek Communists are fighting other Greeks and the British on the streets of Athens. This is not independent of oversight. The newspapers write that "Stalin is giving the English a free hand." A double game. I was correct in writing to Dwight Macdonald two weeks ago that we should expect to see a repetition of the Warsaw tragedy on the social plane. False communes will rise up here and there under orders, serving designs they are themselves unaware of in order to exploit the old revolutionary romanticism, which has learned nothing.

THE COCLÉ CULTURE

December 12, 1944—Excellent chapter in *Old Civilizations of the New World* by A. Hyatt Verrill.[40] This author discovered in the late 1920s, on the plains of Panama in the region of Coclé, fifteen to twenty kilometers from the foot of the extinct volcano Guacamayo (Pacific coast), a vast buried city where digs revealed vestiges of a remarkable

40. The book was published in 1942.

high culture, the work of a completely unknown ancient American race that totally vanished, no one knows when. He surmises that this center of civilization was a small and that it was annihilated by the eruptions of Guacamayo and earthquakes: "The Pompeii of America." Otherwise there is no explanation for such a total disappearance or for the breaking of monolithic basalt columns whose fragments have been found, often turned upside down, as if from explosions. The earth exploded. For anyone who has seen the lava desert of Saint-Pierre in Martinique, this is a totally plausible explanation.

Other evidence reveals an ancient culture that developed over many centuries. Large temple of an intelligently conceived architecture, many colonnades, monolithic columns sculpted (how? with what instruments?) carried from a quarry located some distance away. Richly designed and stylized pottery of extraordinary colors; extreme variety of forms; no green (probably taboo). Vestiges of human sacrifice. Many graves. Realistic statuettes, all forms of fauna reproduced, with prehistoric or symbolic animals: the pterodactyl or flying lizard, the plumed serpent, the elephant bearing a load (attesting either to relations with Asia or the domestication of mammoths). Cult of the sun. According to Hyatt Verrill this culture belongs to the heliolithic cycle; various traits in common with the other cultures of the Americas, along with perfectly original traits. A peaceful people, hunters, fishermen, farmers working with wood, rope, clay, stone, with complicated hairdos but no clothing. The human type would have been different from that of other American races: "Neither the bulbous and heavy nose in the form of a beak of the Mayas and Aztecs, nor the aquiline one of the Incas and pre-Incas, nor the slanted eyes of the Mongols. The nose is extraordinarily straight or slightly aquiline with narrow nostrils. The eyes wide and straight, the lips thick and full, weak chins, wide eyes. It's not known if these men's pigmentation was light or dark, but they wore their hair long, combed or twisted ... and ornate hairdos" (p. 90). Hyatt Verrill reproduces a Maya figurine with a face of this type, and I am reminded of the basalt statues of Tula (Hidalgo), whose delicacy of features is Eurasian. Hyatt Verrill indicated the coincidence between the Nahua legend of the volcanic eruption that destroyed Tollan and the destruction of Coclé.

I'm amazed that this discovery has not yet been integrated into the research into American prehistory. Coclé isn't mentioned in Paul Rivet's *Les Origines de l'homme américain* or the histories of ancient Mexico I know. The pottery is truly splendid; stylization of the human face and birds, linear ornamentation, all of it perfect.

OUTLOOK FOR SOCIALISM—WAR OF REGIMES

December 19, 1944—The Nazis are unleashing a powerful counteroffensive on the Belgian border: not exhausted, as I was maintaining: the totalitarian machine possesses formidable resources, even in its death throes. In Greece ELAS-EAM,[41] Stalino-Communist influenced, is fighting other Greeks and the British. The newspapers are discussing the amputation or the more-or-less total sacrifice of Poland.

This war involves all the causes of past wars, but it is more—and this is perhaps the most important element—a war of regimes; more precisely, of technological regimes. (Decisive role of German technology in the victories of the early days and the effectiveness of the final resistance; role of technology and political planning over the long run in the USSR's victorious resistance; the technological supremacy of the Americans as soon as they planned their war economy.)

From the beginning the war was complex, dominated by multiple factors, a chess game with several players: Nazi totalitarianism, Russian totalitarianism, the conservative capitalist democracies, as well as factors pushed to the background but capable of moving to the foreground, and in any case important: the popular masses inspired by vaguely socialist aspirations and the colonial masses aspiring to independence. In reality, five players around the bloodstained chessboard.

It's obvious today that the defeat of Nazism will not be the real end of the war begun by the Nazis with the clear assistance of the USSR. The question of regimes will ineluctably be posed for Europe and less

41. ELAS, the Popular Army of National Liberation, was the armed wing of the National Liberation Front, EAM. When the Germans retreated from Greece in October 1944 ELAS controlled a third of the country's territory, at which point civil war broke out between British-backed forces and ELAS-EAM.

ineluctably elsewhere. Either the United States and England accept (temporarily) Stalinist hegemony over Central Europe, in fact over the European continent in varying degrees and as far as the Chinese interior, or the United States and England oppose it. In the first case no popular revolutions, except for those that totalitarian communism inspires and leads; the arms race continues; and the countries take a breather with the Third World War in view; or in the second case Stalinism compromises—without keeping its word—truly retreats in order to obtain a truce, and an unstable situation is established, presenting European socialist movements with real opportunities; or Stalinism refuses to compromise (being too weak and too threatened to carry out anything but a risky and offensive policy), the conflict is revived, and the socialist movements can only be manipulated by both sides.

I'm inclined to conclude that there will not be a possibility for the development of vast socialist movements in Europe and consequently for the establishment of nontotalitarian (democratic) regimes with regulated economies until the question of Stalinism is settled by its retreat or defeat, or by events that might occur in Russia itself.

Trotsky thought that the salvation of the Russian Revolution would come from the revolutionary transformation of Western Europe, whose contagion the Russian totalitarian apparatus would not be able to resist. Leon Trotsky was mistaken concerning the present for having not known the full power of the totalitarian state (Hilferding saw much more clearly on this point). This power is such that the USSR is capable of dominating, channeling, and crushing the revolutionary movements of Western Europe, Asia, and to a certain extent Latin America. It can nip in the bud those that stand in its way and can effectively support, foment, and arm the others. L. T.'s thesis can become true again only if the totalitarian Russian state, internally exhausted by its prodigious efforts, weakens.

It must also be considered that in the era of grand planned technology no mass means has any serious chance of imposing itself if it doesn't in its turn have this technology at its disposal, beginning with the means of propaganda, information, and organization. Conquering these means through insurrectionary methods only seems possible in ruined countries, on the condition that foreign forces abstain from intervening. The heroic acts of the Red Army of Leon Trotsky in 1918–1922, carried out in a country that didn't have aviation, cannot be reproduced anywhere (perhaps in the Chinese interior, but not for long). A popular revolution lacking in aviation would inevitably be defeated. Due to Stalin's power the development of socialist-leaning movements is checked or dominated; due to modern technology the old insurrectionary methods lose at least three-fourths of their effectiveness. They maintain a strictly local effectiveness, unless supported from without by one or several states.

Socialism was able to grow only under bourgeois democracy (of which it was in large part the creator). If from recklessness, lack of educated and courageous cadres, or various forms of corruption it hitches itself to "revolutionary" Stalinism (to the extent that a planned economy is revolutionary in relation to traditional capitalism—and this is a feeble extent, given the evolution of all of capitalism towards planning, management: collectivization), it will abdicate and succumb, inevitably being crushed and dishonored. Its sole chance for survival and for victory in the face of Stalinist totalitarianism is in intransigence, by sustaining a doctrine of democracy and humanism (excluding state-directed thought); and, in the face of capitalist conservatism, in the struggle for the reestablishment of traditional democratic freedoms, which have become revolutionary. Almost everywhere in Europe universal suffrage would result in socialist-leaning regimes able to bring about immense changes *without civil war*. (What Lenin hoped for in 1917—that Soviet power would allow for social transformation by avoiding civil war—is true today of universal suffrage and traditional democratic freedoms. Marx's and Lenin's concern to avoid civil wars as much as possible. The catastrophic inconveniences of the latter: state of siege, terror—depreciation of human life—the concentration of power, the abolition of freedom, the military organization of the state, even the 1918 Russian Commune-State, the sacrifice of the best and reverse selection leading to the establishment of totalitarianism...) The intention of most Spaniards to avoid civil war after Franco's fall is very healthy.

But the utopianism of Marceau Pivert, who counts on the explosions of the revolutionary masses to save Europe both from "capitalist imperialism" and Stalinism, is childish and naively dangerous. Ideology of the "spontaneity of the masses" which underestimates modern industry and mass psychology—an ideology forty years behind the times. The English Labourites and the International Labour Party[42] seem to be unwittingly cultivating it since they consider the movements organized by the CP of Yugoslavia (Tito), Greece (ELAS), of France and Belgium (FFI, the Resistance) as the early symptoms of an authentic European revolution that it is in no way a question of, *on this terrain and at this moment.*

42. Again, should be read as the Independent Labour Party.

1945

December 24, 1944–January 2, 1945—Laurette met me in Guadalajara on the 24th. She came into the hotel room around 10:30, tanned, with her air of a young lady big-girl-child, her arms full of pottery, a lovely red necklace with silver fish around her neck, full of joyous tales to tell. Having just traveled a whole day in one bus after another, all of them late and packed, carrying crockery, pottery, and cumbersome nothings. So full of impressions that even before taking off her coat and washing her hands she described everything, giving me portraits. My anxiety waiting all day for her dissipated and was replaced by a calm happiness. —Guadalajara, holiday eve, gloomy.

Ajijic, the narrow room, the lake, the mountains on the other shore. Laurette, Franze, Jeannine, the two bassets climb the mountain. Laurette feels good.

New Year's Eve. Visited Ernesto Butterlin* and Sylvia Scheuber.* A woman writer from America and a bitter lady are there. The author asks me what I'm writing. "A novel that takes place during fall of France." The author: "But that's a subject that risks being of no interest to the public very soon," etc. She's a woman who travels and writes about her travels for publications widely distributed in Kentucky and Tennessee, I imagine. Glowing with total incomprehension and acid self-satisfaction. Ernesto Butterlin puts me in mind of Pilnyak. He creates fervently, often with the auto-body lacquer paint, Surrealist or abstract paintings in scrambled lines and exuberant, sometimes decorative colors. He wants to make money in New York, become someone; this method worries him and he sincerely loves art and he's full of repressions and poses. Tall, blond, pince-nez, the placid face of a good

German. Sylvia Scheuber is a tiny American of Russian-Jewish origin with an irregular face and too big a forehead, worried and frustrated. Her husband has been fighting somewhere on the Pacific islands for a long time. She fears bad news and suffers from her solitude. She draws well, like a studious schoolgirl who leafs through old albums, knows her watercolors, and appreciates Persian miniatures. Since frustration and worry dominate her, the result is paintings in the style of a melancholic young girl, naive, delicate, and falsely naive, with a remarkable symbolic use of cats, birds, and eyes ... In a magnificent psychological painting depicting herself with her husband that constitutes a complete confession, she painted an eye on the chain mail of the warrior. She doesn't know that in dreams the eye often symbolizes sex.

NOTES ON ABSTRACT ART

Ajijic, January 12, 1945—Abstract art exploded on the scene in the wake of World War I in an era of new progress in technology, industrial rationalization, and the first case of economic planning (Russia). This situates it. —Its sources: 1. The machine; 2. Scientific abstraction (connected to technology); 3. The spirit of destruction. That *it is a destructive art.*

I. Consider the new human environment created by the development of mechanization. Spengler's beautiful pages on the modern city and the major alienation of man it creates. "Men only know each other experientially as the objects of an opaque process ... between the sudden shock and sudden forgetting they are no longer capable of feeling the continuous sense of time...." (summarized by T. W. Adorno, *Studies in Philosophy and Social Science*, New York, 1941). Man in the city of machines, leading a mechanized and disoriented life, rationalized by technology, feels disaffected from nature, a rancor towards nature and his own nature. He tends to compensate for this obscure and powerful sentiment by giving himself the feeling of superiority of the *ideal robot* and the *abstract vision* of this robot. (Stupid naiveté of Superman, of American manufacture.) Anatole France's intuition at the end of *Penguin Island*: the gigantic city and the man who dreams of blowing up the terrestrial globe. In *The Bride Stripped Bare by Her Bachelors,*

Even by Duchamp note the poor (childish) imitation of the drawing of a machine. Mondrian's oeuvre, which limits itself to combining black lines on a white background, with occasionally a rectangle in one of the six basic colors. Nothing but squares, numerous variations on the theme of prison bars. Compare the empty dryness of Mondrian with the prison bars in Raphael's vision, *The Deliverance of Saint Peter.* Mondrian touches on the basic issue: disappearance of art. (Kandinsky doesn't entirely belong to abstract art: concrete density of his visions and Impressionist character of his painting.)

II. Abstraction is one of the great discoveries of intelligence. Human genius discriminates between the orange and the color of the orange. From concrete reality it passes to the general idea of color, the quality of the color. Seduction and fecundity of the process. (The *realism* of the Middle Ages.) Power of higher mathematics in the modern world. Penetration of the methods of scientific-technological thought into all of cerebral life, even as far as sensibility. Its effects: enriching of the intellect by an increase in the number of available *signs*; economy of symbolic thought; destruction or disintegration of the former concrete notions; decline (bitter) of the love of reality (concrete, the only kind). (Observe in this regard that Surrealism, proceeding from psychological surreality, is in contradiction with abstract art, but that it rejoins it because of the psychological importance of the abstract.)

Civilizations prior to mechanization did not go beyond hieratism and symbolism—did not arrive at the destruction of being by abstraction. Inner captivity of man in the time of the machine.

III. That the substitution of the sign for the object (for being), ceasing to be a facile convention, becomes a destruction of the object (the being), or a retraction. In separating the color from the orange I disincarnate the color, which doesn't exist outside the orange and I begin the destruction of the orange. By inventing a fanciful geometry and perspective of the human face Picasso destroys it. Gordon Onslow Ford's expression: "He discovered several ways of destroying the human form...." (Gordon at the Picasso exhibit. Compare these words to Gordon Onslow Ford's painting *The Marriage*, reproduced in *Dyn*, no. 6; reminiscence of Duchamp, *The Bride* ...)—That abstraction is a loss of contact with reality. A domination of the intellect by signs:

vision and understanding are no longer anything but a play of signs. And this entails an abdication of the intelligence, since it renounces immediate, intuitive, and carnal contact with things and beings. To be reestablished: the full notion of living intelligence, inseparable from the complete man and hence complete, concrete nature.

IV. What is thus lost: the emotional relationship between the artist and the real, the love of nature and being. The Sistine frescoes express Michelangelo's love for the human body. Visionary mentality of Benvenuto Cellini: he sees Death and the angels, not the signs or symbols. He's a fanatic of the real.

V. Dual influence of snobbishness and sincere nihilism (despair) in the relative success of abstract art. Influence of technical art: photography, which discourages drawing and painting (wrongly, by rendering the problem too arduous). Facileness and clichés of abstraction. Slippery slope of least effort. What do Picasso's "portraits" of Dora Maar express? In contrast, the enormous expressive power of Manet's *Clemenceau* in the Louvre and certain of David's portraits. Reduction of the work to elementary ornamentalism: in Russia, Puni;[1] in the West, Joan Miró.

THE GUADALAJARA MUSEUM

January 16, 1945—This is a truly strange place that immediately made me want to spend a long time dreaming there, or to locate a story or a slightly delirious meditation there. It would have to be written in the style of Hoffmann or Kafka. The old, rectangular building of yellow-gray stone, impregnated with a kind of sleepy light, is a few steps from the cathedral and the commercial center. Its windows contemplate an amusing little square with a kiosk, fruit sellers and refreshment huts, palm trees and lawns ... Along the side, hackney cabs with one or two horses are lined up.

It was originally a convent dating from the early eighteenth century. The portal opens onto an attractive patio filled with golden vegetation, climbing, flamboyant, suspended in baskets, bursting from the earth

---

1. Ivan Albertovich Puni (1892–1956): Russian painter and graphic artist who actively furthered the early (prewar) development of the Russian avant-garde.

in an eruption of gigantic leaves.... It's also cluttered with a variety of objects: enormous old baptismal fonts of massive stone eaten away by time; fragments of statues resembling petrified beasts; sarcophagi. Under the arcades, in the coolness of the shade, a plaster statue of Prince Napoleon; elsewhere, dusty ceremonial carriages, their paint peeling. One is black, its leather upholstery sunken—spacious with solid springs—very comfortable. Attributed, I think, to Marshal Bazaine.[2] The fountain in the middle reigns over a blue and white stone floor. Jeannine and I are the only visitors. The sun, the flowers, the foliage, the shade, and the arcades are for us alone, and the paleontology exhibit with its windows covered with an ophthalmic film is closed to us alone.

Large staircase of uneven, worn stones. The rooms on the second floor sleep beneath oblivion's spell. It is enchanting to halt there at the grilled windows and contemplate the colorful lyricism, the sluggishness of life in the sun of the *plazoleta*. The cool rooms turn around the patio. There are some, full of an apparently orderly bric-a-brac, banally fantastic, where odd, rare, precious, useless, laughable objects proliferate and mingle in unpredictable series, and the masterpiece of a minor art fades away in the clutter and filth, while cheap antiquities shine forth—it's like the immense shop of a half-mad secondhand dealer in a Mediterranean port. You have to keep moving, flee, too many things assault you: they'll make you laugh and your laugh will quickly become a worried grimace. Each one, seen up close, especially in this secondhand shop atmosphere, is still in contact with a dramatic life, as if it had just been stolen, brought here by a barefoot child, or pulled out of a jumble after the pillaging of a hacienda.

Old Mexican banknotes of all regimes alongside bronze coins from all the countries of the world, from China to El Salvador, miniatures: ladies and saints and generals, marquetry, drawings of feathered birds, jewel boxes, Madonnas, mandolins, a plaster religious knickknack of Saint Sulpice, red and blue glass balls, a portrait of a young Garibaldi ... I filled a notebook, I was seized with a greed to store everything, everything seemed to me mad and alive, I imagined the hands that opened

2. French officer who participated in the Mexican expedition of 1861–1867.

the snuff box, the tales of deals and crimes and bestiality plotted around the banknotes, the life of the homely woman with the beautiful white breasts painted by the miniaturist, the use of the stilettos and water clocks that were probably placed not far from the bed, the canes, the fans of mother of pearl, of feather, of watercolor, of gilded paper—not a single one of which isn't Mallarméan:

(Vertigo! see how space
Shimmers in one vast kiss)[3]

But these designed rather for fanning away cadaverous breath. I thought of a Mexican Proust. Would one be possible? At first glance totally impossible. Proust describes a world that's like an overheated greenhouse; here we're in the open in the tropics, the earth burns and trembles. Proust analyzes beings who are refined and complex in the fashion of a certain Paris, for whom the adventure of living is social, sentimental, psychological, and conventional, filled with the charm of fine dining, petits fours pleasantly offered in a salon, loves as learnedly futile as the chatter . . . Here instincts prevail over psychology, of whose existence only professors are aware. The arid mountain is close to the city, the knife is hidden beneath the hand, anger beneath laughter. Here elemental passion kills without complication, faith causes delirium and ensures forgiveness, envy is a flame, love is a violence that relieves, and death isn't bourgeois: it is near and dark with the laughing teeth of the *calaveras*, it revives the memory of Dürer's danse macabre, and not that of a luxurious catafalque with plumed horses taking a beautiful coffin to Père Lachaise . . . Everything is torrid, brutal, vehement, simple—but simple like the life of carnal flesh, swollen with blood, which are nothing but meat and mystery: *nothing is cerebral.*

Let us pass by the chessboards and rosaries and stop in front of the products of ill-disciplined, foolishly naive dreams. Under glass, in a box, the reconstitution of a Walter Scott fjord, castle, willow, boat of shells, a surrealistic realistic object, the obsession of an old sailor or what? Numbers 665 and 666 two little paintings, naively erotic, portraits of the same reclining woman displaying her breasts and her milky back

3. Mallarmé: "Another Fan of Mademoiselle Mallarmé," translated by Henry Michael Weinfield.

nothing more, but the gaze is secret, the breasts live ... Harquebuses, sabers, pistols, crucifixes, the crucifix completes the arsenal. The delectable freedom of crime when one has repentance and forgiveness at one's disposal. Prayer becomes the complement to killing. Another Chinese chessboard, of ivory; an old decorative scale made of bronze; old porcelains. Through the window a cupola in the process of being demolished, but no one is working at it, it's destroying itself on its own from one earthquake to the next; and the angular yellow tower of the cathedral.

The accoutrements of Indian sorcerers interest me, recalling those of Siberian and Central Asian shamans: they're almost the same. Hand drums of blackened lambskin. The sound of the drum set the rhythm (still sets the rhythm) of incantations all over the world.

Leather garments in long, floating strips, flat sombreros decorated with colored feathers lying flat along the edges and upright at the top ... They've reconstructed, rather grotesquely, the costumes of pre-Cortés warriors and their weapons, clubs encrusted with carved stones. Our peasants in the Urals made the same ones during the revolution, but they planted bolts and nails in them. Obsidian arrows, shells, not-very-precious stones, herbariums showing mummies of flowers, fetuses in jars, stuffed snakes, butterflies, crickets of the fields carefully pinned, skeletons of tiny mammals, crocodiles. This could be the accouterment of a sorcerer, but the scientific sorcerer—not as scientific as all that, alas—is the conservator. Let's not speak ill of him; he must be very much the scientist, perhaps without knowing it, for having numbered this cow's hoof and that incredible flayed lambskin, brought together these two-headed animals with glass eyes that could become hallucinatory if their concrete dullness didn't exclude the imagination. Nothing's more ordinary than the two-headed calf, you see. What's suspicious is that, frozen on his thin folded legs he hurls himself towards the brown mummies ... *prohibido tocar los objetos*—it's forbidden to touch the objects. Obviously one would like to handle the little mummy warmed over in the oven, standing distortedly, the scalp dry and oily, the sex organ covered with a colorless rag—to touch the organ of a mummy, the mummy of a murderer! What a temptation! "The work of Dr. Macias Gutiérrez, assisted by Professor Narciso Cervera." It's the body of "a man condemned to death who died at the hospital of Belem." "By this German process *siendo inyectado* ("was injected," embalmed) *Señor Arzobispo Don Pedro López Parda* (Archbishop Don ...). They experimented on the murderer in order to embalm the prelate, a wise thing to do. Skulls snicker in a box of *galletas jalisciences.* Jaliscan cookies, whose symbol is a white swastika on a green background.

Certainly delicious, these cookies.

And here is the panel of faith through torture or torture through faith: hair shirts, ropes, whips, rosary beads, clothing of scratchy cloth displayed on the white wall, the black ropes like monstrous, hairy spider legs; a two-meter-long rosary chain is encrusted with marbles of orange wood and glass beads. I can't correctly identify the smallest instruments of religious torture, the hemp ropes are evil-looking, the iron coats of mail are spiked: it's sinisterly discreet. There's a mat of woven iron with a thousand points to lie on. Are a thousand thick needles enough against rebellious flesh torn by desire? The mummy of *Jesús Roma y Vivar, superiora del Colegio de San Diego* with hands folded over a collapsed body, its viscosity all dried out. The black lips are thin, the tongue a point of charred, black parchment. In the coffin they have placed a leather strap with metal spikes over her fleshless feet. In order to be nearly a saint and perhaps to better punish the wicked of her flock, Doña Jesús wore this cruel belt against her flesh. Did she need to combat the incubi who, according to the texts of the Holy Inquisition, rode on the backs of the devil-possessed doubly and endlessly, night and day?

The large fishing nets are restful ... Señor Sexto Reynoso, a painter, exhibits (his business card in the corner of the frame) an 1890 bathing woman with an open parasol ... Pharmaceutical jars, faded toys, furniture good for burning... Drawings by a decent animal painter, secondhand clothes, velvets, satins, lace, embroideries—dust, death of fabric: all unsalable. An edible Virgin of *chicle, "epoca actual."* Tiny objects in blown glass, palm trees in green glass, *epoca actual*; photos of industrialization, factory chimneys, powerful pipes—and the play of shadow on bare breasts—there is sin in all these pipes. I admire the samples of tropical woods in mellow, animal colors with their poetic names: *Cuerno de Venado*—deer horn; *Cortropico, Culebro*—garter snake; *Palo de oro*—golden stick; *Granadillo, Rosa morada*—pink violet; *verdecillo*, the guayacán is almost black. One would love to have a writing desk in *culebra* to loosen up one's writing; a bed of *rosa morena* for repose mixed with remorse; a smoking room of *tampiziron* mahogany—but not that poisoned flycatcher curtain woven by the prisoners of the Penitenciaría in 1902, nor that old blood-red trunk.

In the picture gallery the canvases are piled up with no order or classification under catacomb-like lighting. It would be disturbing if it weren't so mediocre and, even more, so abandoned that almost nothing there still has any meaning; the collection makes you think of the uselessness, the futility, the death of art, of the oblivion that descends on it: it has gone out of fashion, it no longer vibrates, it is emptied of life. And yet, a man worked on each of these things, gazed at it, contemplated it, reconstructed a fragment of the meaning of the reality he lived—and all of this could have been painted by mummies, and burned along with them for reasons of hygiene. But would the Madonna of San Sisto, before which we stood with ardor at the Dresden gallery, the Madonna with such unforgettable eyes, which perhaps foretold the destruction of Dresden, clash with this collection of exhausted paintings? I believe in its influence, but I wonder if abandonment and promiscuity aren't mortal dissolvents of artworks as of men? And perhaps Raphael's Madonna would invisibly fade away here, resigned to disappear with this abandoned crowd, resigned to giving rise neither to emotion, nor consent, nor that undefinable form of joy that is communion with a creative work. A work of art, whatever its human density, requires a certain exaltation in order to live. I enter this morass, where academic nudes and a frightful *Christ Bleeding for Humanity*, conceived by an imbecile, feebly vegetate, and I find surprising, deeply felt small landscapes by Joaquin Clausell,[4] someone who truly loved foliage and water. An imitation of Dr. Atl by Dr. Atl himself beneath a volcanic sky erects the rudiments of sharply broken mountains. Drawings by José Clemente Orozco cry out: a multitude of deformed pygmies rush beneath the banners of the revolution; American tourists contemplate an Indio dance they're paying for, and the dancers are little underfed monsters, bizarrely dressed, incapable of the least frenzy...

4. Mexican Impressionist (1866–1935).

Another pencil drawing by Orozco is a sketch of the motif of one of his grand, offensive frescoes: the reclining, spread-eagle whore, over whom the entire city of armed brutes will pass. I lean forward to look at these drawings tacked to the wall beneath a good old cavalry charge signed Chartier, 1908. And since the gaze is one of the most difficult things to master (the gaze, one of the sources, the instruments of thought) I see pell-mell the heap and the work, the sketch, the failure, the ruin of the work. Lifeless portraits surround the bear balancing a glass ball on his snout. A bargirl in a green sweater with a red heart on it, painted with fervor, recalls both Picasso's *Buveurs d'Absinthe* (which is in a gallery in Moscow and perhaps has a different title), Beardsley's aestheticism, and the humanitarian dissoluteness of the beginning of our century, when Tolstoy published *Resurrection* ...

Stark naturalist drawing then became an admirable means of expression and protest: it broke out in France (under Zola's influence?), and took over Germany, Russia, the world. It's quite well represented here by pencil drawings brought over from Paris at the time of the Mexican Revolution. Hoodlums and proletarians in the style of Steinlen, Grandjouan, Naudin; girls and bohemians in the style of Toulouse-Lautrec. Verlaine, naturally sitting at a table in front of a little glass, vaguely drunk; Marianne in a Phrygian cap, selling herself on the streets, arrested by the cops ... All this still has a certain vitality. The pencil can do much. Humbler than the brush it perhaps fails less often, in the same way that a letter from the past is more alive than a mediocre, dated novel whose conventions vanish in three hundred mite-eaten pages. What lasts is what is direct, concise, truthful.

It is pointless, indeed impoverishing, to interrogate the sober portraits of unknowns by unknowns (for canvases and drawings bear only their inventory number: neither titles nor artists' names: look for the signature yourself, if there is one: a potter's field of art). The name adds an element of reverie or of association of ideas to the most banal face. Your gaze awakens and it seems to you that its heat is in the eyes of the hypocritical demoiselle, brunette and pale, with her lips sealed, daughter of a *hacendado* of Jalisco whose name is Inés de la Vega y Balboa: you detect in this name the slow unfurling of a snake. *Vega* means "prairie," the Balboas were conquistadors, the only Spanish word similar to their name is *balbuceo*, stammering—the stammering conquistadors...The portrait of an intellectual by Diego Rivera decomposes and recomposes the face and the profile on the same plane. Rivera carried out these experiments well before Picasso—though he was already pillaging Picasso—and the result was interesting and boring work. No one else in these former dormitories, which make me feel like I'm underground.

And we pass into a vast auction hall where only maniacs would bid up the derisory prices on the old canopy bed, or the miter with fake stones, or the black uniform of a general of the wars of independence, or the rusted armor of a traitor...An Indian family in heavy white clothing meditates before the panel of the Assassin; the quiet whispering of the little girls is nothing but a lisping sound. Here is the black waistcoat of the Great Personage, General Ramón Corona, pierced by the dagger of "Primitive Ron" in Mazatlán in 1889. Here is the photo of Primitive: a handsome young man, either white or a light-skinned mestizo, barefoot, in white rags, clean, also stabbed, his blood streaming. He's standing, calm, half-smiling, showing the perfect wound he bears in his breast like a martyr. Here, under ice, the arm of Primitive Ron, embalmed and dried but decomposing, the arm that killed: the muscles, tendons, veins, and nerves are blackish filaments, like maleficent roots. Here are pleasant family photos from the past, General Ramón Corona surrounded by his family in their ignorance of the future; and the stocky, concentrated face of Benito Juárez, and Napoleon I's farewell at Fontainebleau—and a suction pump, an 1880 model typewriter, officers' vests, secondhand sacerdotal clothing for the *Threepenny Opera*. The Indian family is interested in ornamented saddles... In a corner a bathtub of white stone, flecked with grit, and near it, sitting on the tiles, the official bust, which was gilded and is sadly degilding, of President Francisco I. Madero, another assassination victim. We flee the catacomb to the side, wallpapered with portraits from the vice-regal period: too many bishops and monks either in ceremonial attire or ostentatiously humble float motionless in a chocolate haze...

The patio of deliverance glows with a charming light. A cypress sends up its dark, svelte foliage among the gently exploded leaves of the banana trees. I was told that the curator of this museum, who has dedicated his life to it, is an extremely erudite old man, full of amiable curiosity about everything that has lived. "Man and beings pass," he would explain to you. "Collections, sepulchers, and remains endure. Only remains endure." I think I recognize him in the joyful old man with the fleshy nose of a Maya sacrifice, dressed in the garb of the host in a flophouse who is speaking, in the green somnolence of sun-drenched plants, to a majestic horseman come down from the mountain, booted and spurred, his big revolver sitting on his hip in a holster of hand-embossed leather, his short white jacket embroidered in yellow and green, the green eagle devouring the yellow snake,[5] the broad black sombrero covered with silver arabesques—potbellied, peaceful, joyful …

The weather is torrid. One was tempted to let go and play that game of fabricated dreams invented by the Surrealist writers: Gradually, in a slow, rhythmic dance, the broad leaves of the banana trees changed into green horses hitched to Marshal Bazaine's carriage. The mummy of the Superior of the College of San Diego gracefully descended the staircase, her bones jingling like tiny bells of dry wood. Wrapped around her shoulders, she wore hairy black ropes made of the long legs of poisonous spiders. She was eyeless. The mummy of the assassin who died at Belem Hospital followed her, limping along, and she fanned herself with a mother-of-pearl fan. A two-headed dog-lamb skipped at her heels. All three of them got nobly into the carriage that passed, as if aerial, over the fountain, the blue tiles, the plants, the sarcophagi, the large founts, and exited through the main portal. The plaster bust of Prince Napoleon gave out a soft cry of fright. The green and yellow macaw with red epaulettes, perched in its cage, shouted *Bueno*! *Bueno*! in a guttural voice. "But that is strictly forbidden," exclaimed the old curator, dumbstruck, as he removed his cap, purchased at the Paris World's Fair of 1889. "The National Office of Sepulchers will never tolerate this!" The Horseman of the Mountain, his large black hat illuminated with silver, smiled magically. "I'll fix everything up, my friend," he said effusively, and from his holster he drew his beautiful blue revolver, whose carved hand grip twice depicted the copper Virgin

5. A reference to the symbol of Mexico, borrowed from the Aztecs and which appears on the Mexican flag: an eagle devouring a snake.

and the Angels. The Red Army marched in the ruins of liberated Warsaw…

THE DEATH OF KONSTANTIN UMANSKY

January 27, 1945—According to the Mexican press the investigation into the plane crash that took the lives of Soviet ambassador Umansky, his wife, and his closest associates leads them to believe that the plane flew into some wires as it was taking off. The plane, carefully checked over, had been the object of special surveillance.[6] *Excélsior* headlines: "Umansky had the premonition of a tragic death." (This is perfectly understandable for reasons we'll lay out.) The same newspaper speaks of "fate or a concrete cause destined to remain mysterious." Diego Rivera, whose delirious imagination we all know, alludes to "hidden forces that have just carried off a victory against the revolution."

In Mexico City the emotion is extraordinarily strong and isn't only journalistic: it's sincere. It can be seen clearly that the ambassador of the USSR had become the sole truly popular foreign diplomat, was the recipient of general sympathy, and had much influence. The case seems to me to be unprecedented. This amazing popularity must be attributed to Russia's shining reputation in the world at the moment and to a powerful propaganda that meets no counterweight, as well as to his personal qualities of flexibility, skill, and intelligence. Few people know that the so-called Soviet regime is totalitarian. And among those who are aware of this, many admire it for just this reason.

A few days before dying Umansky had finally succeeded in meeting the president of the Spanish Cortés and the Junta de Liberación, Diego Martínez Barrio, with whom he had dined at the home of the Colombian ambassador. On the eve of his departure for Costa Rica he participated in a commemoration of the "liberation of Warsaw" at the

---

6. Umansky was traveling in a Mexican Army plane loaned by the minster of war, General Lázaro Cárdenas. The plane crashed shortly after takeoff, and the causes of the tragedy remain unknown. Serge wrote in a letter to Isaac Don Levine on February 21, 1945, that Umansky's death was "highly suspicious."

Sans Souci restaurant with the representative of the Lublin Commit-
tee[7] in Mexico City, Jadwiga Ramonska (Stanyo), former secretary of
M. Grabski* (the Elder). This woman has formed a group of Polish
Communists here which is seeking official recognition in the name of
Lublin. The group has about fifteen members of Polish extraction and
many supporters.

The painter Diego Rivera, who was Trotsky's "friend" and host and
who belonged to the Fourth International and the editorial committee
of the Trotskyist organ *Clave*, now become the personal friend of one
of Trotsky's assassins, has published a strange panegyric to Umansky,
whose role, he says "would become gigantic in world history." No one
takes seriously the publicity statements of Diego Rivera whom, moreover, Umansky prudently refused to entertain. But buffoonish inven-
tions, when mixed with tragedy, merit our attention for a moment. If
we are to believe Diego Rivera, Umansky distinguished himself at the
age of eleven during the taking of the Winter Palace, which is supposed
to have led to his being adopted by Lenin "as a personal disciple, like a
son," nicknamed in Moscow "the child prodigy of the Revolution." This
legend was widespread in Mexico City. It is superfluous to add that it
doesn't contain a syllable of truth or likelihood, as the rich documentation published on the October insurrection and Lenin attests.

We knew Konstantin Umansky in Moscow during the years 1927–
1932, when he was a subaltern functionary at the Commissariat of
Foreign Affairs. Personally, I only really met him once, at the home of
our common friend, the remarkable Russian writer Boris Pilniak.
Umansky was then beginning a career as a censor at the press service
and the writer was beginning to be persecuted. The author of *The
Naked Year*, *Ivan and Maria*, and *The Volga Flows into the Caspian
Sea*; one of the founders of the vigorous Soviet literature, Pilniak was
to disappear a few years later, imprisoned in some harrowing jail or

7. The Polish Committee of National Liberation, largely Communist, was formed
on July 23, 1944, and acted as the provisional government of the country from August 1 to December 31, 1944.

executed.[8] In the meanwhile the young "Communist" functionary, with a gift for languages, remarkably elegant, and always "following the line," would outlive many other compromising relations—while receiving promotions.

Konstantin Umansky's true career began at the beginning of the persecution of the revolutionary generation, and he attained high diplomatic positions at the very moment when almost all the diplomats of the revolutionary period perished. Deputy director and then director of the press service of the Ministry of Foreign Affairs, the young functionary had the absolute confidence of the police at the very moment that Lenin's diplomats were being executed or vanishing into the darkness: Krestinsky (Berlin), Yurenyev (Tehran, Rome, Berlin), Karakhan* (Beijing, Ankara), Bogomolov (Nanking), Antonov-Ovseyenko (Prague), Davtian (Warsaw), Bersadian (Budapest), Yakubovich (Oslo), Rosenberg (Madrid), Ustinov (Talinn), Asmus (Helsinki), Sokolnikov (London, Paris), Rakovsky (Paris), Stomonyakov* (Berlin). During the same period the high functionaries of the Commissariat of Foreign Affairs were executed without trial, men like Stern and Baron Steiger,* about whom Joseph E. Davies speaks so emotionally in *Mission to Moscow*. Of course, this enumeration is quite inadequate. In any case, it will be agreed that one needs truly particular qualities to outlive so many chiefs and colleagues, and that, this accomplished, rising through the ranks becomes simple—and the fateful forebodings are explicable by normal psychology.

It's also true that a career made under these conditions ensures a tempering of the personality and makes the intelligence considerably more flexible. The man thus had great practical qualities. In Washington he was able to execute the policies of the Ribbentrop-Molotov Pact and later in Mexico City the exact opposite policy, with the same skill in both cases. It won't be easy to replace him.

The Mexican press is demonstrating perfect calm and tact. The Communist and pro-Communist and more generally pro-Russian milieux have been inexpressibly touched. Elsewhere people recall the

8. Condemned in 1938 for "counterrevolutionary activities" after a fifteen-minute trial, he was executed.

assassination of Trotsky. A fascist-leaning paper, *El Hombre Libre*, alludes to these and other rumors—while moderately refuting them. This paper is of little importance in Mexico City, but one sees it everywhere in the other states. In my eyes *it is certain* that sooner or later the horrible plane crash could be exploited *against anyone at all* if history makes it useful to return to the insane methods of the Moscow Trials.

January 30, 1945—Raya Umansky had consulted physicians about her nervous state and had spoken to them of her anxiety attacks, mentioning the executions of many friends and acquaintances in Moscow and the nightmare atmosphere in which the Umanskys lived. She really was full of forebodings, probably objective ones.

THE CASE OF JACQUES DORIOT

February 23, 1945—Newspapers: Jacques Doriot has just been killed in Germany. He was driving on a highway during a dive bomber attack. He was expected to take control of what was left of the Vichy government for the final exploitation of the French interned in Germany.

In 1922, in a small office of the *Rote Fahne* in Berlin, Julius Alpári* introduced me to a stocky young man in glasses, with reddish skin, an energetic mouth, and a modest tone...I saw him several times and never paid much attention to him. He passed for an excellent militant of the Communist Youth with the gift of gab and nerve. He admired the Russian Revolution, probably very sincerely, and the fact that he was traveling illegally while sleeping in good hotels and conspiring with the Bolsheviks clearly elevated him in his own eyes. The only impression he left on me was of modesty and firmness. A young man on whom you could rely. Zinoviev liked him, as well as Piatnitsky and Mickevičius-Kapsukas, the organizers of underground activity...He came out of the factories (metalworker). It was the era of the struggle against parliamentary corruption and the old reformism. Jacques Doriot engaged in antimilitarist activity in the occupied Ruhr, was sent to prison, left prison a deputy, was popular and considered a leader of the French CP. In 1924–1925, when the first slanders hit Trotsky, the greatest figure of the revolution after the death of Lenin, J. D. grew indignant, ready to speak out for the "New Course" that could have checked the precipitous degeneration of Bolshevism. When the defeated opposition surrendered, J. D. adapted and became one of the right-hand men of Zinoviev, whose star was rising. The militant was conquered by the apparatus, for the administrative apparatus of the International made and unmade leaders, gave or refused the possibility of serving the revolution and being at the head of a great idealistic party. J. D. entered the Politburo and the secret service. This was the usual road followed by the most committed militants: the accepted risks lead to the secret service, from which you never escape and which obliges you to lead a demoralizing existence. J. D. had an adventurist spirit and personality; it was not without resistance that he applied directives he knew to be absurd or commanded by interests other than those of the Party and the International. Conflicts. In February–May 1934, in the aftermath of the riot of February 6 outside the Palais Bourbon, he broke with the sectarian directives and proposed a united front to the socialists, who the day before had been denounced as social-fascists. He refused to go to Moscow to account for his actions, knowing he could very well disappear there. As deputy and mayor of Saint-Denis he had a fief, a section of the party bound to him by local interests and real admiration. For a few (short) months you could believe that the French working masses of the left were finally going to have a capable leader who would unify them. This was the opinion of Marcel Martinet* as well as my own, with reservations, for I wondered what could the mind-set be of a militant-leader who since 1927 had drunk down all the lies and unfailingly served the secret services?

In reality, Doriot was no longer anything but an adventurer trained in the manipulation of a few social forces. He rejected the career offered him by the revolutionary left, knowing full well that without considerable financial support a new movement could not be born and that a new left-socialist movement would not find such support. He could have gone over to the Socialist Party, but it was a party with bourgeois mores, lacking in dynamism, which he disdained and in which he could only vegetate. His whole education was based on the antisocialist mentality of the Comintern. Returning to the Comintern was impossible since he had lost the confidence of the bureaus: they would tolerate him only in order to make him submit and destroy him. The situation of an unemployed condottiere. J. D. parleyed with influential capitalists who made him an offer...This too flowed from his education. He'd often heard it said that fascism's victory was inevitable, that fascism alone could liquidate social democracy, and that in the short term communism would be the successor and liquidator of fascism. This ideological schema had become quasi-official backstage at the Comintern ever since the failure of the German revolution in 1923. J. D. bet his stake on the card of combative capitalism. He didn't sell himself all at once; he wavered, protected refugees expelled from the Comintern (Ruth Fischer and Maslov), but went over to a "national" policy (*L'Émancipation nationale*[9]). The incredible rancor he had built up against the leaders in Moscow and their secret back offices during the years of dissension, decadence, and reaction transformed him into an anti-Communist. He was never a socialist humanist; a harsh and manipulative Marxism had rendered him cynical. The deeply inculcated notion of history reaching its conclusion, which condemned the parliamentary Third Republic and would lead to planned economies, prepared him for total adherence to fascism. This adherence occurred during the Spanish events: informed of what was going on behind the scenes, immediately seeing that the Republic was doomed, he denounced the Spanish revolution as a Moscow enterprise and passed openly to the right. What is amazing is that over the course of this evolution he brought with him a strong ex-Communist nucleus from Saint-Denis, so ready were the militants to pass from communism to fascism, which seemed to them more powerful, certain of victory and healthier because of its national character. (Notice here the disenchantment provoked by the disaster of Bolshevik internationalism.) A common, totalitarian mentality was created, with variants capable of mixing together and succeeding each other.

J. D. worked with the National Employer's Confederation and probably engaged in talks with Nazi secret agents. The politician accustomed to working with secret services returned to them and met

9. Weekly paper of Doriot's Parti Populaire Français, it was founded in 1936 and continued to be published in the southern zone during the war.

with success. In 1940 he put forward his candidacy as the successor of Pétain, and for Saint Philippe (Pétain's) Day also had Saint Jacques celebrated. He called for the creation of revolutionary committees (of his party, the PPF) to carry out the "national revolution." His contempt for the bourgeoisie put him on the same footing as certain authentic Nazis. His hatred of Stalinism was that of a renegade, but it was also the turning upside down of a sullied and disappointed youthful idealism. His knowledge of the internal weaknesses of the USSR predisposed him to the role of ideologue of the war against the USSR, and he traveled the Russian front to encourage French volunteers in German uniforms... He was also an uncultured man who was exalted by the function of leader and a materialist who counted only on naked force.

Killed at forty-seven.

ALEXEI TOLSTOY

February 24, 1945—Deaths follow one after another, and how many of them! It's a time of death. This morning the announcement of the death of Alexei Nikolaevich Tolstoy, a minuscule note in microscopic characters in *El Popular*. Orders will arrive and there will be beautiful articles.

It was in 1923, in Berlin, Tauentzienstrasse, an airy neighborhood with lovely green grass under the tram rails: I see coming towards me on the sidewalk our handsome Sergei Zorin* of the dark days of Petrograd, tall, blond, a Viking look. With him a thickset gentleman with a massive head and chin, not a warrior, this one, but a thoughtful bourgeois with tiny brown eyes, cross-eyed, I think, behind crooked pince-nez: Alexei Tolstoy. At the time he was "rallying" to the revolution and negotiating a return to Moscow. "How self-interested he is!" Z. exclaimed. "He's got to have his complete works published by Gosizdat and his future royalties laid out to the last kopek." The three of us were seated in a small café when Zorin evoked the Chudin Affair,[10] which he still felt great sadness about: "We executed the best brother,

10. Chudin was executed under orders from Dzerzhinsky to set an example. See *Memoirs*, p. 95.

a man of 1905. He wasn't guilty but there was nothing else that could be done." (It was this discussion that crystallized in my mind the idea for one of the dramas of *Conquered City*.)

I began to know Alexei Tolstoy better in Leningrad from 1926, first at the sumptuous dinners of the historian Chtchegolev,* which were attended by Anna Akhmatova,* thin, delicate, white as a porcelain statuette, tremendously resistant and very mannered (her gesture of a long hand on a shoulder) and beautiful sad gray-green eyes; Karl Radek and Larissa Reisner,* amazon and intellectual, an extraordinary human success ... All are dead now, even little Pavel Pavlovich with his baby face of a young functionary from a comedy by Gogol. Tolstoy and Chtchegolev made millions of rubles putting on melodramas about Rasputin and the empress. They enjoyed life and believed in a moderate, liberal, and peasant counterrevolution. They called themselves "sympathizers" of the CP—worried, cynical, and inoffensive sympathizers. "My office boy at the editorial offices of *Byloe*[11] (the Past), having come in drunk," recounted Chtchegolev, "admitted to me that he was an informer for the Cheka. I said to him, 'I'll keep you on, my friend, that pleases me; now I know what's what.'" Chtchegolev detested Trotsky. I recall that he went into a kind of hysteria in front of me when speaking of "that little journalist, correspondent for the reactionary newspapers of Kiev," and that we had an altercation, calmed by Pilnyak. (Trotsky had already fallen from power, of course.) Alexei Tolstoy, on the contrary, only ever spoke of Trotsky with respect and admiration.

A. T. felt his situation insecure and sometimes wrote magnificent pages, for example a story about a Civil War fighter disoriented by the NEP. He spoke a magnificent Russian. He had a rather proud and reserved manner, but quickly grew warm, moved, and moving. I often went with Liuba and Vlady to his home in Dietskoye Selo. His wife was a Russian beauty like those painted by Kostodiev, plump with light eyes. Their interior was traditional, a small white house, a garden and birch trees, Paul I furniture, collections, miniatures, old books, landscapes, great well-being, simple and luxurious. A. T. invited us to hear the first

11. A journal published in London and later Paris from 1900 until 1913 by the Socialist-Revolutionary historian Vladimir Lvovich Burtsev.

chapters of his *Peter the Great*. He was greatly influenced by the sixteenth-century peasant economist Pososhkov, who died in the Peter-and-Paul Prison. He conceived his novel as a work of opposition that would be a cry about the sufferings and strength of the peasant people. He said: "What we're living through is the return to the revolutionary and autocratic barbarism of Peter the Great." (This was during agrarian collectivization when it seemed probable that Stalin would fall because of the famine and that the Rykov, Tomsky,* Bukharin "right," which A. T. was friendly with, would carry the day with a program of pacification of the countryside.) A. T. read in a deep and mellow voice, full of emotion. His first identification of Stalin with Peter the Great was that of a discreet pamphleteer, for the historical novel was an evasion for him. (All writers of the first rank seek this evasion: Tynyanov with Griboyedov and Pushkin, Kaverin with *Lieutenant Kije*,[12] others with Pugachev or Catherine the Great and even Toussaint-Louverture . . .)

When I became too compromising a figure our meetings naturally grew increasingly rare. Tolstoy verged on disgrace, but Boris Andrei-evich Pilnyak, who was unquestionably the first of the young writers, the leader (with Vsevolod Ivanov) of Soviet literature, plunged into disgrace and persecution, was fished out by Stalin, then semiboycotted again, controlled by Yezhov, (the future successor of Yagoda at the Interior, the future executed man). Gorky[13] returned from Italy but I didn't see him again, his secretary Kryuchkov (of the GPU) closed the door on me (K. was executed along with Yagoda). Gorky was in any case unrecognizable, ascetic and skeleton-like, I met him on the street and was struck at seeing the dead man beneath the living one. He wrote official articles, truly abominable, justifying the secret trials in the name of culture, proclaiming that "the enemy who doesn't surrender, we exterminate him," and in private he made bitter sallies, hardened himself against a scornful and violent bitterness, and sometimes exploded, entering into conflict with Stalin. All his old friends, like Julie and Ekaterina Pavlovna Piechkova,* broke with him because he allowed

12. Which is actually by Yuri Tynyanov.
13. Gorky, a childhood connection of Serge's mother from Nizhny Novgorod, was among the first people Serge went to see when he arrived in Russia in 1919.

his former collaborators at *Novaya Zhizn*,[14] Ginzburg and Sukhanov, whose probity he knew, to be arrested and because he refused to make the least objection to the execution of the technicians: he'd become the opposite of himself... It was in this atmosphere that, at a meeting of forty writers that Stalin attended at Gorky's house, Pasternak and Alexei Tolstoy had the courage to complain about censorship. Stalin rebuffed the secretary general of the Proletarian Writers, Leopold Averbakh, who had immediately called their statements counterrevolutionary, and gave Tolstoy a lift in his car... (Averbakh, nephew of Yagoda, was executed in 1937 or 1938.) And so the personal friendship of A. T. and Stalin was born in an outburst of frankness and courage that was perhaps stimulated by vodka. Stalin was liberal and affectionate, as he occasionally sought to be, and granted a passport for travel abroad to Alexei Nicolaivich's son. A. T. was seduced. Stalin was flattered at being likened to Peter the Great; all that was left was to humanize the reforming czar, and the order to do so was given. At that same period people began to speak ill of the grand (Marxist) history of Russia by Pokrovsky, until then considered a fundamental work, but which contained a horrific portrait of Czar Peter. (Pokrovsky would die in isolation, disavowed by the schools, in time to escape a worse end.) A. T. rewrote his *Peter the Great*, not without inner conflict, and adapted a stage play out of it which Stalin went to see, beaming with contentment.

In the heart of the famine, on a winter night, A. T. once gave a lordly feast at Detskoe Selo with buffets that all of Leningrad talked about: violin orchestras, troikas to take the guests on rides in the snow... We said: *Pir vo vremya tchoumy*, "a feast in time of plague."

A. T. was a thoroughbred writer, loving and understanding the human problem, a good psychologist and connoisseur of mores, adoring his craft, possessor of an irreproachable language: everything needed to make a great writer had there not been despotism and the cowardice imposed by despotism. He required a great deal of money and favor. He feared disgrace, censorship, and the repression which his émigré, bourgeois, and aristocratic past designated him for more than many others. He had the zeal of a convert, but he must have suffered greatly, for he

14. Menshevik newspaper founded by Gorky.

was intelligent, liberal, and rather kind. (I don't think he ever personally harmed anyone.) He probably found an inner justification for his conduct in his love for Russia, a love embracing the inevitable suffering of the chosen and martyred people, and in his expectation of a new Russian grandeur, which he could only truly conceive of in terms of empire.

The Ralliers group of 1923, Smenovekhovtsy (the Change in Orientation), of which he'd been a member, was decimated—and more than decimated—by the terror starting in 1929–1930. A member of the Union of Soviet Writers, A. T. saw his friend Boris Pilnyak, and Tarasov-Rodyonov, and Galina Serebryakova, and the theatrical producer Meyerhold and Babel and so many others disappear. He saw executed the great Bolsheviks who had admitted him among them while they were in power and whom he'd admired. He knew the totalitarian tragedy to its depths. He never raised the least protest and he explicitly approved—as was required—all the crimes. It's true that he described at length the executions of the *streltsi* (archers) within the Kremlin walls, during which Czar Peter forced the boyars and his favorites to kill with their own hands, as he did himself, and in so doing establishing the bonds of an open and shared complicity. He died at sixty-two, a millionaire in the country of the greatest poverty, weighted down with honors, having obstinately swallowed back his dark sorrow.

(I once flipped through a strange historical novel on the Civil War written under orders by A. T. in 1935, during the time when the recent past was being violently falsified. In it you saw Lenin being inspired by Stalin, they were winning the revolutionary war, and Trotsky wasn't mentioned.)

MURDERS WITHIN THE SPANISH EMIGRATION IN FRANCE

March 21, 1945—M. Vicente Lombardo Toledano, president of the Workers Confederation of Latin America (CTAL),[15] speaking before

---

15. The CTAL was created in September 1938 by Lombardo Toledano, succeeding the Latin American Confederation of Unions, founded in 1929 by the Red International of Trade Unions.

a large assembly gathered in Mexico City on the initiative of organizations of Communist refugees (FOARE)[16] to protest against Franco's terrorist regime, has declared:

"The regime of Francisco Franco is at war with the USSR and the USSR, even on its own, must solve this problem." "The moment will come when the USSR will act ... And neither England nor the United States will sacrifice world peace to maintain a bandit at the head of a country. Franco's hours are numbered." (*Excélsior*, March 21).

M. Lombardo Toledano is one the most authoritative spokesmen, not, to be sure, of the Soviet government, but of the Communist workers' organizations, camouflaged or not, who receive their inspiration from afar. He could be disavowed tomorrow, he could even disavow himself, but in the circumstances it seems he is responding, in conformity with his information and instructions, to the question often whispered by pro-Communist Spanish refugees: "So why doesn't the USSR declare war on Franco?" Let us recognize that this is a good question: the Spanish Blue Division (División Azul)[17] left thousands of dead in Russia and several thousand prisoners, between ten thousand and fourteen thousand, I've been told, whose international status is not at all clear. If they were deemed belligerents, there is a war on; if they were adventurers they fall under martial law. What should be remembered in all this is that the cause of the CP has been lost in the eyes of the Spanish people and emigration, as was again attested by the failure of Dr. Negrín's negotiations with the leaders of the Republican emigration in France; this lost cause could become a won cause tomorrow if a decision by Stalin provokes Franco's fall. From that moment on, in the three great Latin countries of the western Mediterranean, the political prestige of the CP would become tremendous.

Solidaridad Obrera, the organ of the Spanish syndicalists in Mexico (CNT), published precisely on the day when the Communists protested, rightly, against the Francoist atrocities, a terrible document entitled: "Communist-Style Unity: The Crimes of the Spanish National

---

16. Federation of Organizations for the Support of Spanish Republicans.
17. A unit of Spanish fascist volunteers who served under Wehrmacht command on the eastern front between 1941 and 1943.

Union (UNE) in France." The UNE is the Communist organization established in Toulouse at the time of the liberation in order to support the claim to power of the "Supreme Junta," invented by the CP in collaboration with some elements of the old Spanish right. The UNE never achieved hegemony in the Republican emigration in France. The great majority of this emigration has spoken out in favor of a Republic without a hidden Communist dictatorship, without secret prisons, without the assassination of antitotalitarian militants...The two big working-class organizations in Spain, the General Union of Workers (Socialist unions), UNT, and the CNT, thousands or tens of thousands of whose militants are refugees in France, have just sent a document to the provisional government of the French Republic asking it to put an end to Communist terrorism within the Spanish emigration. Let us sum up here a few of the quoted facts: In the Gironde on August 24, under the signature of an unknown "Ramon," an Allied Committee of Liberation (CP...) decreed the mobilization of all Spaniards between eighteen and forty-five. In "the region of Toulouse" on August 26 a "national leader" (!?) of the Spanish Forces Françaises de l'Intérieur (FFI) ordered the dismissal of all formations not belonging to the UNE; that is, who refuse to receive their orders from the CP. In Tarbes the intervention of the Americans prevented the demobilization of Battalion Bidon V. In the Lot-et-Garonne the same conflicts, and provisioning is cut off to fighters who refuse to submit to the UNE.

And here is a brief list of crimes:

Augustín Vidiella, arrested by the Gestapo in Poitiers in April 1944, interrogated by an officer of the UNE, refused to join that organization and remains in prison. Romero González Díaz, volunteer in the Eighth Brigade, was invited to join the UNE under threat of death but he managed to hide. Near Monséjour (Ariège) a Spanish couple (Republican refugees) was executed by the UNE. In Decazeville (Aveyron), Rodríguez, arrested by the UNE was found murdered in the woods. A certain Trujillo met the same fate. José Mana, alias Martín, communication agent and a trusted figure of the maquis of the Lot, was executed; Francisco Rodríguez Barroso, captain of the maquis forces of Ille-sur-Têt, was arrested and disappeared. Pedro Calzada and "various other" maquisards were illegally detained in a secret UNE prison in Bourrassol.

The Spanish Democratic Alliance's committee in the Department of Ariège, formed by the CNT and the UGT, denounced the following crimes: The refugee Roy, having refused to join the troops of the UNE, his wife, his father-in-law, his two daughters, and the refugees Gracia, García, and Soler, who were found in the house, were murdered on July 15. Roy, not being present, escaped. Miguel Guijarro, a well-known militant, arrested in Toulouse, was brought to the Hotel Litthe, occupied by the forces of the UNE, interrogated by Lieutenant Ervera, who demanded the names of the UNE's opponents—that is to say of the intransigent socialists and syndicalists—was taken to a deserted spot and executed at point-blank range by Lieutenant Ervera. He survived and is being treated at the hospital in Toulouse. He denounced Ervera as the assassin of the leader of the Resistance in the Ariège, Antonio Giro.

The militants of the CNT and the UGT who addressed this complaint to the French government offer to prove that their joint organization represents "90 percent of the Spanish refugees" and have no need to prove the passion with which they participated in the Resistance and France's war of liberation.

THE NAKED CORPSE

May 1, 1945—It's a beautiful, hot Mexico City evening, an evening of vegetal life. The Italian grocer who's serving me cheese looks at me from the side of his round eye like a frightened bird. I'm seeing him for the first time and I feel like he's judging me. "Did you see this?" he says." "This" is a newspaper headline: "Mussolini Shot." I read the news, surprised that Nemesis finally struck where she should strike, blindly, justly. The Duce, his mistress, and fifteen members of the final fascist government, shot. I lived so many years endlessly learning the deaths of upright and decent men who wanted nothing but a better, more noble future, that the punishment of executioners astounds me, like something I could no longer believe in. Yet I believe in it, and I even remember having once written about fascism: "We know how parades end!" A journalist describes fifteen corpses lined up in a warehouse;

he lists the names of ministers, members of the Grand Council, police chiefs. Among the names of the men of the last team of the *fascio* I recognize one. The naked corpse briefly appeared before me on the grocer's counter. Had he kept his beautiful, long, two-pointed beard, now white? Had he remained boney, as he was when I knew him, with a lively and laughing look in his eyes, a combative optimist in his diction and voice? The Italian newspapers call him the Arch-traitor. Pitiful naked corpse of the Arch-traitor! Is there a highest degree in treason? Theology recognized archangels, celestially greater than the angels, purer, closer to God ... I try to reason by analogy in order to better understand. In the treason of modern man is there an exceptional quintessence that touched my comrade of days gone by? The naked corpse demands a semantics.

We participated together in 1921 in great revolutionary festivals in Petrograd. Nicola Bombacci* belonged to one of the first delegations sent to the Russian Revolution by the Italian Socialist Party. Joyful, well spoken, fraternal, with a direct intelligence that was a stranger to intellectualism. It seemed that he only asked to be allowed to be guided by greater men, to believe what his eyes saw, to give himself good-naturedly to the future. He inspired that confidence that goes out immediately to plebeian natures whose stock of energy we guess to be intact; they bear within them unadulterated good and evil, a capacity for contact with harsh reality that more nuanced spirits sometimes are so well able to justify, even where there's nothing left to justify. A cool white night descended on the vast Neva, where the battleships of the Red Fleet were flag-bedecked. On the steps of the grand staircase of the stock exchange two thousand performers played the symbolic drama of the "final" world war and the advent of the Communes. Jaurès fell. Chorales rose, crowds of red flags sprung forward for generosity's final assault on the horizon. Nicola Bombacci's eyes were lit up with ecstasy.

He became one of the Communists of the early times; that is, the times of famine, of White and Red Terrors colliding head-on, of the uncertainty of living, of workers' insurrections defeated in the West, of tiny, flea-bitten armies in rags crossing the forests of Siberia and emerging from the sea at Perekop. Not a one of us doubted at the time that in ten years we would all either be hanged, shot, or prisoners or living in a world where there were free countries governed by reason and fairness offering the earth the example of an effective idealism. The Italian doubted this less than any other. He would smilingly cast aside the criticisms and worried hypotheses that a few others and I were already pondering, measuring the internal threat of dictatorship. "Oh, it'll all work out," he'd say. "It's nothing but birth pangs." This image was commonly accepted as a good answer. Man is born in suffering, for greatness—you're right, comrade!

I saw him on several occasions in Central Europe years later.[18] The Italian revolution aborted, the *fascio*, itself revolutionary (and more so than the old parties!) took power. I recall a conversation we had in Grünwald at the home of a mutual friend who, condemned to death, was hiding in cozy comfort. The hairless character who watered the flowers in the neighboring garden was one of the leaders of the Black Reichswehr, a proximity funnier than it was dangerous. There was nothing to be done about it but shrug. We engaged in a little practical psychology. Bombacci had once been a teacher in a small Italian town at the same time as another party comrade full of eloquent dynamism, Benito Mussolini. He analyzed the personality of the man who had become the Renegade, the Traitor, the Persecutor, the Dictator (Archtraitor never occurred to us . . .). He spoke of his disappointments, of his ambition, of the Allied financing of left-wing interventionism during the war, of the need for action that had led the young and the demobilized fighters to the *fascio*. Someone asked:

"But really. Since you knew the threat Mussolini represented, why didn't you kill him before his victory?"

Fingers in his beard and a crooked smile, Nicola Bombacci answered:

"Because everyone who could effectively fight him had gone over to his side."

Released from Soviet prisons, I returned to the West more than ten years later. Comrades I'd just left behind were being executed in the cellars. I made inquiries about faces from the past. The leader of the

18. In another version of this passage Serge wrote: "I saw him again in Berlin in 1923 or 1924, émigré. The first gray threads showed in his beard." "Pages de journal (1945–1947)" in *Les Temps modernes*, no. 45, July 1949.

Italian CP, my friend Gramsci, died in prison. I asked about Bombacci, in whom I had faith. "That scum!" they answered me. "He wangled permission to publish a paper in Italy that still dares call itself working class. He's playing the game of an admiring opposition." And we engaged in another quarter hour of practical psychology. The bitter bread of emigration, the defeats, the dissensions, the corruption of the International, the stifling of ideas, the rise of totalitarianism in the very land of the revolution without the flags being changed (very important, flags, for simple people). Among some Italians, particularly among the ex-Marxists and the ex-syndicalists, two visions became apparent: that with the liberal democracies exhausted and socialism weakened, the corporatist regimes were going to impose their new formulas; and that through this narrow gate would pass collectivism, the precondition for a socialism different from that desired by the nineteenth century, less humanistic and consequently corresponding better to man's basic nature. Mussolini, draining the Pontine swamps, improving the lot of the peasantry, constructing the *Impero*, respected by the good conservative bourgeois, implied that he was working for a socialist future. His prestige was that of daily victories. The antifascist émigrés looked like mad romantics or bitter old politicians. (The pejorative interpretation of men's conduct is that of intellectual weakness grafted onto the unthinking cult of force.)[19]

The assassination of Giacomo Matteotti and the massacre of the Rosselli brothers* were nothing but details, the cost of doing business. The former comrade swallowed these disgusting pills, and I think I know how. "Small crimes and even great crimes don't count, my dear sir! What counts is the magnitude of the intention and the accomplishments." I still often hear this reasoning in regard to another tyranny. It provides excellent excuses for stifling that mysterious and bothersome

19. In the earlier version quoted in the footnote above, Serge wrote: "Later, disappointed by the stifling attitude of the Comintern and probably not being able to adapt to exile [Nicola Bombacci] allowed himself to be offered by Mussolini the return to the country with the possibility of organizing a legal and loyal socialist-leaning opposition that in the end came to nothing. Mussolini had the skill of presenting himself to old militants as if he remained a kind of socialist despite it all and preparing a succession in accordance with his half-secret wishes."

thing called conscience. Once you accept there is only one drawback: that of stripping, stiffening, hardening, and freezing your soul, which becomes like a naked corpse.

The unforgiveable error is that of granting that the judgment pronounced by force is always valid and definitive. A historical event entails a correct judgment only if it goes in the direction of human fulfillment, if it defends and aggrandizes man. Without this, victories are nothing but mediocre or disastrous accidents. Where, it is true, to find true criteria in confused epochs? I don't think that thirty volumes of dialectic are required. The occasions to understand have not gone lacking in the past thirty years and they demand less from the intelligence than from simple courage. In the depths of defeat what is left to us is nonconsent to the inhuman; the refusal to close our eyes; the refusal to lose hope in ourselves and so in everything. Once we let go of this last rope we fall into the domain of putrefaction. And so here I discover the profound meaning of the word "arch-traitor," forged by the demagogy of hatred: he who in betraying great causes betrayed what was living in himself. Obviously, those who are less alive have less to betray.

And then came fascism's catastrophe, in germ for a quarter of a century in the prideful and inflated accomplishments of the *Impero*, like a cancer in a healthy-seeming body. There was the rise of just and of iniquitous fury around the hunted-down dignitaries, who at the end betrayed the blindness of their banal accomplices, since they were defeated. In Lombardy the world shrank to the dimensions of a hell with no exit. The most charming of landscapes repeated: No forgiveness! Guilty of despotism, of the war and the disaster, on top of the individual recantations, after having sold their souls to the demons of stupidity, vanity, wealth, and power—not to mention lust. Nothing was left to the former revolutionary who, I imagine, was perhaps enlightened about a few major errors, but a final hardening for one last paltry chance of salvation. I'm told he was one of the most active organizers of the fascist republic of northern Italy,[20] an antirepublican

20. The Italian Social Republic, also called the Republic of Saló, was founded September 23, 1943, in the center and north of Italy, in the area controlled by the Germans.

republic of a fascism in which fear replaced eloquence. He was thus one of the executioners of the men who defended the hopes of his youth.

In the midst of historical catastrophe, most men choose neither their role nor their death. To see clearly from time to time—this is without question a tremendous privilege; to feel strong enough to uphold those authentic values that are more durable than empires, even totalitarian ones—this is to be among the chosen. . . . But at least have that faith that, in our time, has so often marched men in the prime of life before the firing squad, but has also marched them down roads that are free of absurdity, unlike those beings without a compass, betrayed by their own betrayals.

ROMAIN ROLLAND

Erongarícuaro, May 4, 1945—I'd gladly write a "lived essay" on "The End of the Comrades," and among the comrades I would also make room for Romain Rolland, who died just a few weeks ago while writing *Péguy* and affirming to Aragon his fidelity to the CP. The old man at death's door still managed to write a last letter to Maurice Thorez, to that totalitarian bureaucrat with neither conscience nor scruples.

I knew him rather well, indirectly, through Jacques Mesnil, who had been his friend for at least twenty years and only broke with him—after annoying him with his unfailing probity—when Romain Rolland definitively went over to the party of the executioners. Like everyone in the World War I generation I had seen in him a "great conscience." For me *Jean-Christophe* was a revelation of the nobility of life, and the author of *Jean-Christophe* had known how to put himself "above the fray" during the European catastrophe—to remain completely human. On the ship that was transporting us, hostages just out of concentration camps, to Petrograd,[21] I saw R. R.'s books in the hands of young officers on their way back from the front, and we looked each other more easily in the eye. I knew that these books had earned R. R. a kind of persecution that, being feeble and frail, he bore up under, suffering from it, and he related that experience in *Clérambault*. The

---

21. Serge was exchanged in 1919 for French officers held in Russian prisons.

Bolsheviks with whom I spoke about him refused to see in him anything other than a troubled, weak, and well-intentioned intellectual. This was also Gorky's opinion, but Gorky expressed this judgment with infinite sympathy. Later, in 1922–1924, R. R. published articles on Gandhi and revolutionary violence in *Clarté* that irritated me all the more because they contained the most correct, the most prophetic opinions about the suffocating nature of dictatorship, while at the same time underestimating the terrible reality of a spontaneous revolution that survived only through ceaseless miracles of implacable energy. I once answered him in *Inprekorr*[22] that we were "the party of free men." I believed this, I saw this, I felt this, I wanted this like so many others, and none of us could possibly have known where we were headed, and this was probably in no way fatal. R. R. was unhappy with this somewhat harsh response, and he must have recalled it when in turn I was persecuted and he was asked to intervene on my behalf. He answered in substance that he had limited sympathy for persecuted persecutors. Nevertheless, he intervened on behalf of Francesco Ghezzi, imprisoned in Suzdal, and moderately for me. He showed his age (in 1929–1930), married late in life to a woman ("Princess" Kudacheva) who had worked in Moscow under the direction of Heinz Kogan, whose life I'd saved in 1919. He hung on to faith in the declining Russian Revolution, publicly consenting to all the repression, the strangling of all thought. He allowed Panaït Istrati* to be slandered, which was a total abdication of his clear-sighted personality, and what remained of a "great conscience" was reduced to demagogic and deceptive renown…
When I was deported to Orenburg we began a correspondence on the subject of the manuscript of *Les Hommes perdus*, which he offered to receive in order to send it to my publishers, which the GPU stole from him and stole from me twice without his raising the least protest. His letters were affectionate. He went to see Stalin in 1935 and asked that he put an end to the "Victor Serge Affair"; that I either be tried or be freed. Stalin said he wasn't aware of anything and promised my freedom

22. *Internationale Pressekorrespondenz* was a Comintern magazine that appeared between 1921 and 1939. It was published in eight languages, and Serge wrote for its French edition, *La Correspondance internationale*.

if it was at all possible...It was above all to this intervention that I owe my life, it seems to me. R. R. had been embraced by Bukharin upon arrival and amiably accompanied by Yagoda...He knew the regime quite well and I knew that his adherence to it filled him with anxiety, doubts, and scruples that he had to overcome daily. During the second trial of the Old Bolsheviks Pyatakov, Muralov, Serebryakov, and Boguslavsky I wrote to him denouncing the fraud, predicting the bloodshed, (harshly) begging him to intervene in time. I received no response and he did nothing, sadly slapped by my letter. He had previously allowed it to be publicized that along with other intellectuals of notoriety he approved the massacres in Leningrad that followed Kirov's assassination, and he had remained silent about the trial and execution of the Thirteen (Zinoviev, Kamenev, Smirnov).

Perhaps he knew his own impotence, but why did he refuse to at least liberate his conscience? At age seventy the author of *Jean-Christophe* allowed himself to be covered with the blood spilled by a tyranny of which he was a faithful adulator. For me this was something incomprehensible and demoralizing, and Jacques Mesnil found but one response: "He's old"—old himself, Jacques Mesnil, alone and wounded, but of an absolute uprightness. I was even more struck that such, identically such viewed from without, was the attitude of Gorky, whom I'd known as a fierce defender of the victims of the Civil War. There is thus an aging of the strongest personalities, of the most elevated, of the most humanely lucid, and neither their works nor their experience saves them from decline through stiffening, through hardening when, at the end of their lives, they hang on to the illusion of serving, despite it all, a great cause.

And I learned in 1938 that R. R., racked with remorse, kept a private journal intended to be published long after his death, in which he noted his scruples, his doubts, and the drama of his fidelity to communism. That he feared keeping this journal in his home and placed it in friendly hands. In twenty or fifty years these pages will say that his intelligence and his conscience were not dead, but rather put on the back burner.[23]

23. Romain Rolland's widow, Marie Kudachev, was a GPU agent and refused to publish these writings.

Posthumous escape. (We'll perhaps also learn something of Gorky's crises, of the reproaches he addressed to Stalin, of the repressed rage that exhausted the last of his strength.)

LENIN'S HEIR?[24]

Late May 1945—The controversy raised by James Burnham[25] cannot, I think, reach an objective conclusion without a simple reminder of the historical facts (it being accepted that ideologies are also historical facts) and without our attempting to consider for a moment the problem from the Russian point of view, quite different in the circumstances from the point of view of the American intelligentsia. Having for seventeen years been a witness and participant in the events in Russia, I believe it is my duty to make some small contribution to this debate.

James Burnham maintains that Stalin isn't the "remarkable mediocrity" whose portrait Trotsky painted. That he's a "great captain," a personage great in his crimes and his victories and who "during these war years . . . never lost the political initiative."[26] Finally, that Stalin is the legitimate heir of Bolshevism: "If anyone betrayed Bolshevism, it was not Stalin but Trotsky."[27] James Burnham recognizes the extreme mediocrity of Stalin's intellectual productions, both writings and speeches.

The "Boss" (in Russian *Vojd*, in German *Führer*) of an immense totalitarian state, planned and policed, has at his disposal such powerful machinery that he acquires a colossal dimension from it in the eyes of the outside world, even if he's nothing but an ordinary man destined to become the artisan of the most enormous catastrophes: see Hitler. The pilot of a Superfortress doesn't require extraordinary qualities to become the instrument of massive strategic destruction. Stalin's inhumanity immediately eliminates the concept of moral grandeur. The vicissitudes of a policy that twice placed the USSR a hair's breadth

24. In English in the original.
25. The author of *The Managerial Revolution* published a text titled "Lenin's Heir" in the winter 1945 issue of *Partisan Review*. The most often quoted passage was: "Under Stalin the communist revolution has been, not betrayed, but fulfilled."
26. In English in the original.
27. In English in the original.

from destruction hardly seem compatible with the concept of intellectual grandeur. The cost of these policies is so high that they tend to exclude from the Boss's means the rational thought of our times.

Stalin assumed power in 1927 and absolute power around 1932. The only initiatives he took were those of agricultural collectivization and of terror against technicians, workers, and the opposition within the party. The results of this were the horrific famine of 1931–1934, and a population loss of around twenty million. In 1932–1934, at the moment when Germany entered into crisis, Stalin's initiative in Central Europe resulted in the antisocialist tactic of the Third International and the bloc with the Nazis in Prussia against Otto Braun's government: in short, an initiative that favored the rise of Nazism. From that date Stalin *lost the initiative*, which passed over to Hitler. The USSR offered such a spectacle of poverty and terror that its influence over a demoralized Germany was reduced to almost nothing, and this factor facilitated the Nazi seizure of power. Stalin, while maintaining secret military collaboration with the Reichswehr, tagged along behind the League of Nations that he had denounced just the day before as a pitiful capitalist-imperialist anti-Soviet assembly. In 1936 Hitler and Mussolini took the initiative in Spain with the Franco plot. Stalin hesitated for two months before committing himself in this civil war—and when he did so it was too late: the Russian intervention did not prevent the disaster.

We have serious reasons to believe that from spring 1939 Stalin sought an agreement with the Third Reich through secret negotiations. We know that the Ribbentrop-Molotov Pact was concluded at least two weeks before being published (see Dino Grandi[28] in *Life*, February 26, 1944). From the time of the Spanish Civil War Stalin was outmaneuvered by his mortal enemy, Hitler, to whom he gave a hand in beginning the European war in the hope of turning it away from the borders of the USSR. He sought to countermaneuver, but it was on a secondary level, in Finland and the Baltic countries. A few days before the Nazi aggression against the USSR Stalin was so ridiculous as to accommodatingly recognize the phantom pro-Nazi government of

28. This Fascist politician, several times a minister under Mussolini, was one of the artisans of his fall on July 25, 1943.

Iraq! The invasion took him by surprise and immediately turned into a catastrophe. No one can contest that he showed courage during this crisis (let it be noted that none of his biographers disputes his courage and firmness). If he took on all responsibilities at this moment it was because they already weighed on his shoulders, whether he wanted them or not, and the existence of the regime was in danger. It is nonetheless true that without Anglo-American assistance (and without the divergence of political viewpoints in the Wehrmacht) Moscow would have fallen at that moment and no one can imagine what the condition of Russia would have been. Late 1941, during the battle of Moscow (won by Zhukov), Stalin envisaged a peace by capitulation (see on this subject B. Nikolaevski's study in the New York Russian review *The Socialist Courier*. This author prudently quotes a text from the US ambassador in Moscow.). Stalin finally inclined before Anglo-American firmness. He thus appears to us, in the course of the first phase of the world war, to have been successively maneuvered by the two coalitions facing each other, reduced to follow first one and then the other. And many things remain in the shadows! The same observation concerning his policy towards Japan. I know few episodes as grotesquely significant in this regard as the scene related by John Scott in *Duel for Europe*, where we see the "Brilliant Leader," the "Leader of the World's Workers" seek the embrace of Count Matsuoka before the journalists and diplomats assembled at the Moscow station . . .

So much for the statesman "who never lost the political initiative . . ."[29]

It is permissible to use the word "treason" when a man does, against his brothers, his party, and his people, the opposite of what he promises. The Bolshevism of 1917–1927 wanted a socialist regime founded on the democracy of labor and international solidarity. Lenin and Trotsky's companions believed in this, they never stopped believing it even while making their most dreadful mistakes. The Republic of the Soviets defined itself as a "Commune-State," "dictatorship against the expropriated possessing classes and the broadest workers' democracy," etc. The documents are so numerous that I'll be forgiven if I quote none of them. It is perhaps justified to nevertheless recall Lenin's final speeches

29. In English in the original.

and articles, in which is manifested his terrible fear of the bureaucratization of the regime. Neither the doctrine nor the intentions of the Bolshevik party aimed at establishing a totalitarian police state with the vastest concentration camps in the world. The Bolshevik party saw in the perils it confronted the excuse for its Jacobin methods. I think it is undeniable that its Jacobinism contained the seed of Stalinist totalitarianism, *but Bolshevism also contained other seeds, other possibilities of evolution.* The proof is in the struggles, the initiatives, and the final sacrifice of its various oppositions. I dare to assert that anyone who predicted before 1927 what Stalinism was to make of the Revolution would have been considered a contemptible and dangerous madman. (In order to be fair I add that the Mensheviks, the Socialist-Revolutionaries, the anarchists, and some opposition Communists, like Sapronov* and Vladimir Smirnov* demonstrated a clairvoyance in this regard that must be recognized today as admirable and which served only to render them unpopular, since they went against the general sentiment and the sincerity of the party.) It is too-little-known a fact that in 1925–1926 (I don't have the exact date at hand) the Left Opposition, of which Trotsky was only one of the leaders, examined the possibility of seizing power by a coup de force whose success seemed probable. It had great support in the army and the political police, but it preferred to appeal to party opinion in order to avoid having to resort in governing to military and police methods it condemned in principle. (Trotsky later published his reasons in the Russian edition of the *Opposition Bulletin.*)

It is appropriate to remind James Burnham that in order to establish the totalitarian regime Stalin had to proceed to the systematic massacre of the Old Party and the revolutionary generation molded during the Civil War. In this regard one should flip through Joseph E. Davies's ambiguous book *Mission to Moscow.* From one page to another, like a leitmotiv, notes like this reappear: "The terror is here a horrifying fact"[30] (April 1, 1938). The rupture between Bolshevism and Stalinism is bloody, attested to by figures that are, in fact, horrifying. More than 1,500 members of Soviet governments perished in two years; all the superior

30. In English in the original.

officers of the Red Army were executed or sent to forced labor; the purges extended to more than 30,000 officers out of a total of 90,000 (and this on the eve of a world war!). The official statistics of the party show that in 1936–1939 463,000 Communists were expelled, that is to say mostly sent to concentration camps, and the most energetic minority to firing squads. With the result that the fascist reviews of Rome praised Stalin as the exterminator of the Bolsheviks. Lenin's "heir," according to Burnham, had to inflict this treatment on Lenin's party in order to collect his inheritance! It is evident from this that the great majority of the revolutionary generation refused him this inheritance and that rising Stalinism was in absolute contradiction with the aspirations and ideas of that generation. I wonder how a commentator as qualified as James Burnham can be ignorant of a historic fact of such importance.

From the Russian point of view the "greatness" of Marshal Stalin is certainly not such as it may appear in the wartime American press. No genius is required to brutally and unscrupulously profit by circumstances as favorable as the collapse of the Nazi Empire, the powerlessness of a Poland bled white, and the weakness of the Balkan countries. In Russia Stalin remains, for those who know history, the fratricidal Old Bolshevik whom Lenin recommended be removed from power and with whom he broke before dying. For those who survived the purges he remains the exterminator of their generation; for the adult population he remains the principle person responsible for the agricultural collectivization and famine of 1930–1934; the man who allowed himself to be tricked by Hitler and who was unable to prevent an invasion comparable in its scope and ravages only to the Mongol invasions of the twelfth century. He also remains the symbol of a system of terrorist repression aimed at all citizens without exception. The great military victory he carried off with Anglo-American assistance at an unimaginable price in blood, misery, and terror leaves the USSR as ruined, if not more so, than Germany. All the information we have shows that the living standard of the Soviet population (except in the furthest regions, where the lack of communication protects them from the state) is presently lower than the part of Germany occupied by the Anglo-Americans. The victory obtained under these conditions doesn't bedazzle the citizens who must pay its cost. And the Stalin experiment isn't over; it is even being continued in such worrisome conditions for the USSR and the world that intellectuals concerned with understanding the march of history cannot be too prudent in their predictions.

"*Stalin is communism*,"[31] James Burnham concludes. Words change their meaning and this is perhaps nothing but a quibble over language. The Communist movement is in fact identified today with Stalin and his totalitarian system. It would be completely futile to go on trying to impose on the world a conceptual distinction that is a matter of pedantry, however correct it may be. It is nonetheless true that the humanist doctrine of Karl Marx, which brought the word "communism" back to a place of honor, has only a distant—and often contradictory —relationship to Stalinism.

JUSTIFICATIONS FOR DUPLICITY

July 5, 1945—We had been talking passionately about the leaders of the Polish emigration, who had just agreed to participate in the government fabricated in Moscow. Someone said: "They're traitors and imbeciles!"—I defended them. They are men hemmed in between self-abdication and heroism. (That among the group there are traitors and arrivistes capable of turning traitor doesn't interest me: only the others count.) They are playing an apparently hopeless game, destined to be duped, dishonored, and rejected when they're no longer needed— or destroyed. They know this. History is also made up of the unforeseen, and you must always, from duty, try your last chance, even if it's the only one. Peoples cannot emigrate and there is the duty to share their lot, whatever it may be, in order to try to save them or preserve the future. Emigration is only necessary when the struggle has become completely impossible and paralysis a form of annihilation, or when combat from without offers more chances of success and is combined with internal activity.

When I make this argument they reproach me for justifying dubious, self-interested, base accommodations and the double game that

---

31. In English in the original.

covers them. All this exists like a gangrene. But the fact remains that peoples can't escape defeats; that apparent submission is sometimes the final means of resistance; that terroristic despotism leaves room only for duplicity, the ultimate defense through hypocrisy, deception, mental reservations, and secret heroism. Russia having been the first complete totalitarian state, all Russians know this, consciously or not. I was of the party of those who repudiated duplicity, and I still prefer this, my whole personality sustaining me in this. But I don't for all that have the right to underestimate the facts. What a stunning intuition in these lines by André Salmon,[32] written in *Prikaz* in 1918 apropos of the Russian Revolution, which began without traitors or assassins:

> Traitors are saints
> And the purest hearts are those of assassins.

The hero in the time of duplicity betrays Treason, and this is more bitter, harsh, and perilous than denouncing it from exile. The hero of fidelity proclaims himself a "traitor" out of devotion to a party that demands this confession before executing him. Some of his fratricides, unaware of what is behind the scenes, believe these confessions with a pure heart and respond to them by assassination. It's the eighth circle of hell, the psychological circle. It proves that all man's previously acquired greatness is now threatened.

STATE-DIRECTED LITERATURE: FEDIN AND GORKY
July 11, 1945—My youth comes back to me reading Konstantin Fedin's *Gorky Among Us*, published in Moscow in 1943. It is remarkably well written. Gorky is alive, natural; Blok too, and even Zamyatin, presented in a few lines. I knew Gorky well at that period; the tragic inner richness of that endangered, polar Petrograd was mine. I can follow Fedin's memoirs (1919–1921) step by step. I only knew Fedin himself a few years later, when I reviewed his books *Cities and Years* and *The Brothers*. I

32. (1881–1969) Russian-speaking French poet, novelist, art critic and early defender of Picasso and the Cubists.

saw in him a young Russian Romain Rolland, concerned with human problems in an inhuman era, rich with a barely whispered yet very profound protest against everything that stifled man; incapable of understanding revolutionaries who know and feel all this but from necessity carry out the work of surgeons . . .

Fedin told me Gorky's saying: "The party commissar is the policeman, the censor, and the archbishop all in one: he collars you, crosses out your writings, and still wants to sink his paws into your soul." Fedin had a long, handsome face, a wide forehead, thin lips, penetrating gray eyes, an air of unassuming discretion—and great self-confidence. (Married, two children.)

He must have suffered incredibly, and if one day a free Russian literature becomes possible no one will be better than he to tell of that suffocation of the Terror. He survived, even becoming a master craftsman of that special literature, flexible and docile, that accumulates enormous silences and manifests the minimum amount of complacency indispensable in order to exist, and which still occasionally succeeds in producing valid works. Thus, this *Gorky*. The reader, foreigner or Russian but young and uninformed, will finish reading it enriched and even enthusiastic. He'll have seen a truly great man from up close; he'll have been initiated into a powerful form of the love of man and of the art that seems, at bottom, to be a form of the love of man.

Yet, if one were to judge this book with an objective severity, what indignation! Lies—of omission and silence—are infinitely greater in number in it than truth. Everything is truncated. To everything I have just noted, not an allusion. To the grumbling and at times vehement bitterness of Gorky, to his constant struggle against terror and the abuse of authority, a struggle that made him ill, not a single allusion. That Gorky spent more time appealing to the Cheka to save intellectuals and other victims than with writers, you would never guess. That he had confidence in Lenin because his intercessions with him were usually crowned with success, you would never guess. (One day I brought a message from Zinoviev to G. in his apartment on Kronversky Prospekt—Zinoviev who was censoring an article of Gorky's. He received me in a rage: "These Bolsheviks, you don't know them! So many crimes and stupidities! Tell Z. that I've had enough!" etc.—I had to soften the violence of the message and in any case G. gave in, and the censored article passed.)

The lies of omission sometimes reach the point of enormity. A beautiful and truthful portrait of Alexander Blok, but "he (A. B.) never says that he was reduced to silence." Alexander Blok is depicted as someone who went over to the regime. He was a revolutionary, a stubborn though discreet protestor. He never hid the fact that he was being smothered. Connected with the Left Socialist-Revolutionary Party, destroyed and persecuted, he remained friends with Ivanov-Razumnik* and Andrei Biely. He was imprisoned and a touching essay on A. B. in a Cheka cell was published. He died largely from sadness and privation, along with an onset of scurvy. Konstantin Fedin describes Blok's funeral; I was there. He doesn't say that it was a double demonstration of mourning and silent protest. In the first row were friends: not far from Lyubov Mendeleyeva-Blok* marched Anna [Akhmatova] Gumilev with her enormous brown eyes in the face of an emaciated child, the widow of the great poet Nikolai Stepanovich Gumilev,* who'd just been executed. C. F. is silent about Gumilev, silent about that execution that shattered Petrograd, silent about Ivanov-Razumnik, one of the leaders of Russian thought, because I. R. disappeared in 1933. What abominable silences!

A few lines on the defense of Petrograd, but not a single allusion to Trotsky, who saved lost Petrograd. A scene at the Second Congress of the Comintern at the Tauride Palace where Lenin spoke is well described, but not a word about the friends who surrounded L., of an affectionate circle that never left his side during the day: Zinoviev, Bakayev, Yevdokimov—all three of them executed. It is strictly forbidden to mention the executed! I'm worried at not seeing the name of Vsevolod Mikhailovich Eichenbaum [Voline]* and reassured at finding that of Nicolai Nikitin,* who has vanished from literature. Could this be an act of courage? (N. N. is only named in passing.) G.'s remarks on Lenin are faithfully reported, but not his remarks on Trotsky, whom he admired without loving and whom he often criticized. In general, I recognize G.'s language and the themes he often spoke to me about: "No phosphorous for the brain"; the mysterious, contradictory, elemental power of the *muzhik*; the drama of the city devoured by the country;

the mission of intellectuals; Russian incompetence; Russian anarchy; the beginning of new times. One word is lacking here, "planetary," which G. readily employed: "planetary transformation," and an essential motif, the *bezobrazia*, the abominations that G. collected and denounced with a tireless bitterness.

K. F. visited G. while the cannon were thundering over Kronstadt. This resulted in a reticent page on which G.'s anxiety may be glimpsed. I saw him several times during those days and I ran into him at the Cheka, Gorokhovaya 2, he was intervening on behalf of prisoners; he was gray and taciturn. I spoke with him about the case of Raphael Abramovich and Fyodor Dan,* both arrested, and whom the president of the Cheka, Semyonov, a little, narrow-minded redhead, wanted to put before the firing squad. Zinoviev would perhaps have allowed him to do so. G. promised me to intervene with Lenin and this was probably the salvation of the two threatened men. Not a single allusion in K. F. to the Terror, yet Petrograd lived the terror more than it did famine and literature! Is it prohibited to speak today of "the Red Terror"?

I recognize what G. had to say about the tortures the Siberian peasants inflicted on their prisoners, most often Communists (G. had been informed by Vsevolod Ivanov.) One day I asked G. the source of this difficult-to-invent tradition of refined tortures. "From *The Golden Legend*,"[33] he answered.

Yet another enormous omission, to cover a crime of state: Boris Pilnyak isn't mentioned.

And Fedin writes: "Art consists in expressing, as well as possible, feelings; and the most lucid feeling—which is to say that of the truth—is the one which can be expressed with the greatest perfection."

He accurately depicts Gorky's attitude towards the writer's mission, an attitude that G. passionately inculcated in the young. Literature is a vocation, a way of serving the people that involves the entire personality forever and demands probity and conscientious artisanship. G. liked to call himself an artisan (*masterovoy*). This was the central idea of several great lines of Russian writers. Literature contributes to elevat-

33. Medieval book of the lives of the saints (c. 1265) replete with hair-raising descriptions of their martyrdoms.

ing unthinking man to consciousness; its mission is to tell men the truth about man.

I one day asked Yuri Tynyanov (whom K. F. said "very much resembled Pushkin" and who also resembled a rabbi born old) why, with so profound a spirit of opposition, writers showed themselves to be so little combative. "Because," he told me, "each of them thinks he has something important to do, and so they are afraid to risk themselves, preferring to humiliate themselves and play for time." I admire Fedin for having drunk down so much humiliation, having known so many hideous things without having lost faith in himself—the sentiment of his own dignity—and the will to create. And for knowing how to adapt in this way, with cynicism and sadness, to write a short book that is nonetheless lively, touching, human, and precious in many ways, like a crystal from the Urals set in mud.

An edition of twenty-five thousand copies, so very well paid.

WORRIES ABOUT LARGO CABALLERO

July 13, 1945—After much hesitation the Spanish refugee socialists in Mexico City and a few Mexican socialists have just posed in the press the worrisome question of the fate of Largo Caballero. Let us recall the facts. Shortly after the capitulation of Nazism, dispatches from Russian sources announced that the leader of the Spanish Socialist Party had been liberated by the Red Army after having been found ill in a concentration camp in Germany or Poland. Later, Largo Caballero's arrival in Switzerland was announced, with such precision that the organization of the Spanish Socialist Party in France delegated Trifon Gómez to greet him at the border. Two months then passed without any direct news of Largo Caballero, and also without his returning to France, where his party, friends, and daughter awaited him. No one knew where he was, in what condition, and why he was unable to correspond with anyone.

Últimas Noticias, an evening daily in Mexico City, published on July 6: "It is feared that something happened to Largo Caballero in Russia.... His friends in France, and his daughter in Mexico City, despite numerous interventions, have been unable to establish contact with him. Russian functionaries limit themselves to responding that he is in a hospital." *La Noche*, taking up this theme, recalled the disappearance in Russia of the Mexican student Evelio Vadillo.[34] On July 10 *El Universal*, a big-circulation daily, published: "Lost in Russia... Largo Caballero, the old, renowned socialist who was president of the Council of Ministers of the Spanish Republic betrayed by Franco in 1936, has been lost in the vast territory of the USSR." *El Universal* stressed that Largo Caballero's daughter, residing in Mexico City, was able to obtain from the Soviet embassy only the confirmation of her father's "liberation"; she has no idea where he is, has received nothing from him, and can't send him anything... These articles in the Mexican press have received as unsatisfying a response as possible in the form of a telegram from Paris given in *La Prensa Gráfica* which simply says: "Paris July 11. Today's issue of *Le Populaire* says that Carmen Largo Caballero has just learned that her father is in good health in Moscow." Let's keep this good news in mind, which raises several questions:

Why ten weeks of silence and contradictory false rumors?

Why can't Largo Caballero correspond with his daughters, refugees in Mexico City and Paris, with his friends, with his party?

Is he "in good health in Moscow" of his own free will while the Republican emigration awaits him in France?

The great Spanish socialist remains the only antifascist statesman surviving Nazi persecution and liberated by an Allied army not able to rejoin his political and personal friends or to reestablish the free, simple, and easy communication to which he has a right.

NATALIA—THE TOMB OF COYOACÁN

July 21, 1945—Two visits to Natalia, whom I hadn't seen in some time. Once again the impression of crushing sadness I'd brought home from my last visits here, which led me to call Trotsky's house "the Tomb of Coyoacán." Natalia is the guardian of the Tomb, the tireless and reso-

---

34. The story of this Mexican Communist, who was incarcerated in the USSR for having either written or shouted "Long Live Trotsky!" inspired a character in José Revueltas's novel about purges in the Mexican Communist Party, *Los Errores*.

lute mourner of at least one hundred thousand admirable dead. Leaving the sidewalk, I'm on the bank of a muddy *río* the length of an abandoned cemetery. Tall trees here and there resist the drought and the burning sun. Old stone bridge, heavy vaulted arch. Calle Vienna is wide, incandescent, sparsely inhabited. On a low house a cardboard sign whose red letters dance: "All kinds of animals castrated here." The Old Man's house has remained the same fortress with gray walls topped by gun-ports, with an iron gate (but at the time of Siqueiros's attack neither those gun-port nor that gate existed...). The garden is lush with vegetation: cactus and palm trees encircling a small monument of gray concrete: a stele bearing the hammer and sickle, a flagpole... The rabbit cages the Old Man kept himself busy with are empty and abandoned. Sun, sun on all this, flights of butterflies sparkling in the calm; silence. Natalia has only slightly aged. I don't know how old she is, around sixty perhaps,[35] but her hair is completely white; she's tiny, wearing a black and white India cotton dress, she hugs a light black shawl around her shoulders. Her hands are strong, still vigorous. Her square face with its harshly carved chin. Her blue-gray eyes readily cloud up with tears; her voice is unsteady. We haven't seen each other for more than a year because of my dispute with the Trotskyist party, she welcomes me affectionately—and we won't speak again of those stupid incidents. It's so strange to be the only two survivors of so great a historic catastrophe. It's so mad and poignant and devastating that both us of, I think, have the same sensation of a struggle against an immense tomb. In the room with its bookshelves I see only books from the past, books that were destroyed, whose authors were destroyed, books of a generation that stirred the world. Preobrazhensky's *Modern Economy, How the Revolution Armed Itself* by L.D. and recent magazines, *Novy Mir*,[36] *Oktiabr* (October), which, under these faithful titles, betray everything...We speak of current Soviet literature, which produces apologies for the worst czars, like Ivan the Terrible and

35. In fact, sixty-three.
36. *Novy Mir*—New World—was a literary magazine published in Moscow since 1925 and was originally the symbol of the Soviet literary renaissance. It later became an official voice of Soviet literature, hewing to the party line.

Nicolas II's generals: the total rejection of revolutionary ideology and complete domestication of the writer. Then we speak of known faces, the faces of the dead, the executed, of those disappeared in jails… Natalia tells me that Walter Held's sorry end has finally been cleared up. He was a young German (named Epe*), a naturalized Norwegian, who was one of the Old Man's secretaries in Norway (along with Erwin Wolf, murdered in Barcelona). He committed the madly imprudent act of leaving for the United States via Russia and disappeared during the course of the journey with his wife and child. It's known that in Kuibyshev he shared a cell with Henryk Ehrlich and probably ended up executed like Ehrlich, in a cellar. Epe-Held had demonstrated the falsity of Pyatakov's confessions by investigating, with the Norwegian authorities, the planes that landed in Oslo at the time. (And Pyatakov had only confessed to this supposed airplane trip in order to himself denounce the imposture of the trial.) In two hours a hundred faces of the martyred rose up between us. I leave carrying with me a crushing solitude, but I didn't feel crushed by it. This solitude gives birth in me to a hardening stronger than everything.

Tomb. The ideas of the Revolution are dead. The hammer and sickle have become emblems of despotism and murder. The victories of the Civil War are dead, the heroism of the revolution is covered in lies. The intellectual works are destroyed—unknown to the world. The Old Man was killed in the next room. The press is closed to us. Publishers place our books under lock and key. An American scientific institute prohibits Natalia's access to L. D.'s archives, entrusted to the care of a university.[37] For years no direct news has reached us from Russia. N. doesn't know what's become of L. D.'s grandchildren, who were with Alexandra Lvovna Bronstein and Maria Lvovna Sokolovskaya. Alexandra Lvovna Bronstein and Maria Lvovna Sokolovskaya were deported in 1934, A. L. B. wrote she was in a small, glacial village—completely alone. Natalia thinks she must have died there quite quickly from lack of medical care.[38] We speak of agents provocateurs and assassins: they

37. Harvard University.
38. A. L. Sokolovskaya (1873–1938), Trotsky's first wife, died in the gulag of Kolyma. Maria Lvovna was her sister.

survive. The Old Man's assassin is doing well at the Penitenciaría, buys paintings, pursues his studies, dresses with care. The two Sobolevich brothers ("Lithuanians": Sobolevicius) were in Paris until the fall of Paris, it seems. ("Roman Well" and the "Senine" who visited me in Moscow in 1932 in order to betray me.)

DEATHS IN FRANCE
July 29, 1945—One laboriously carries out an accounting of the survivors, the disappeared, and the dead. Every letter brings its package of dark news. Out of the circle we formed in Marseille in 1941 I learn of the death of some of the best, all of them well-known militants whose memory deserves to be preserved. Here are a few names: Charles Wolff,* member of the Socialist Party, former editor of *La Lumière*,[39] music critic, colleague on the American Relief Committee, tortured and executed by the Gestapo[40] (his mother and sister committed suicide or were murdered in Alsace during the invasion). —Itkine,* actor, Trotskyist, member of a Resistance organization, tortured and executed. He was the organizer of the Croque-fruit cooperative, which found work for many hunted comrades. —Dr. Yves de Boton,* left-socialist militant, a young man of rare clear-sightedness, executed. These three were Jews. —Jean Salducci, a Marseille teacher, one of the leaders of the École Émancipée movement, who was remarkable for his intransigence and honesty, died in Dachau. Salducci had refused to emigrate, though well known. Also dead in a concentration camp the revolutionary teacher Rollo* (École Émancipée). —Also dead in a concentration camp Georges Lapierre,* CGT militant, one of the socialist leaders of the Union of Education Workers. —Executed, the French-language Belgian writer Augustin Habaru* (*Monde, La Lumière*), militant of the far left who for fifteen months was one of the most remarkable men in the maquis. —The poet Marcel Martinet is dead—a natural death! He was the author of *Temps maudits* (Accursed Times), which in

39. Founded by Georges Boris, it published 683 issues between May 14, 1927, and June 7, 1940. It had twenty-five thousand subscribers.
40. In fact, he was killed by the Milice.

1918–1920 resonated greatly. Collaborator at *La Révolution prolétari-enne*[41] he remained one of the firmest ideologues of antitotalitarian socialism, which of course earned him a nearly total boycott. The great quality of his poetic oeuvre prepared a place for him in the first rank of French letters, but his political courage barred him from it (*La Maison à l'abri* [The Sheltered House], novel; *Une Feuille de hêtre* [A Beech Leaf], poems).

VOLINE

October 29, 1945—Voline (Eichenbaum) died of typhus in France a few weeks ago. He was one of the most remarkable figures of Russian anarchism, a man of absolute probity and exceptional rigor of thought, full of talent, perpetual youth, and combativeness. He was just past sixty. He played a role of real importance in the Russian Revolution. In 1905 he was one of the actual founders of the first soviet in Petersburg. Later a refugee in the United States and Canada, he continued his life of a theoretician and militant, penetrated with Kropotkinian idealism. Returned to Petrograd in 1917, he participated in all the revolutionary struggles, briefly directed a syndicalist organ, *Golos Truda* (*The Voice of Labor*),[42] whose influence rivaled that of Bolshevik newspapers. From 1917 he considered that the dictatorship of the proletariat would necessarily result in a regime of terror destined to paralyze the democratic forces. From 1918 he was in the Ukraine with Nestor Makhno as the intellectual organizer of the vast movement of "rebellious peasants," which Lenin and Trotsky considered granting local autonomy (this just and generous solution would have spared the Soviet regime many internal calamities), but which Bolshevik centralization ended by

41. Founded in 1925 by syndicalists who had broken with the PCF, including Pierre Monatte, Alfred Rosmer, and Robert Louzon. It was an active participant in the campaign to free Serge when he was imprisoned in the USSR, and he wrote for it often after his release.
42. Before 1914 the organ of the Union of Russian Workers of the United States and Canada, it transferred to Petrograd and became the organ of the Union for Anarcho-Syndicalist Propaganda from 1917 to 1918 before being closed down by the Bolsheviks in 1919.

mercilessly smashing. Voline had split with Makhno before this bloody epilogue. He saw too well the defects and weaknesses of the libertarian movement of the peasantry, which he would have liked to cleanse and provide with a more intelligent leadership. Suffering from typhus, arrested by the Ukrainian Cheka, which wanted to execute him immediately, we had great difficulty in saving him, finally having Lenin intervene personally. In prison he was offered the post of commissar for public education in the Ukraine, which he refused. Thanks to the intervention of Emma Goldman and Alexander Berkman he was freed and sent into exile in 1921. He would live in Berlin and then Paris the hard life of the implacably intransigent intellectual militant; that is, unpopular among his own libertarian comrades. I saw him again in Marseille in 1940–1941 working as a ticket seller in a small movie theater, living on nothing, finishing the writing of his *History of the Civil War in Ukraine*. Though Jewish, he refused to cross the Atlantic, hoping to participate in European events, about which he maintained a romantic optimism. Thin, rather short, a mobile face terminating in a short, white beard, determined gestures, lively speech, brusque repartee, he put me in mind of the old rebel Blanqui. We were rarely in agreement, but for more than twenty years we were able to maintain cordial and trusting relations. Was his precious manuscript saved?[43] I don't know. One must hope that the future will render justice to this intrepidly idealistic revolutionary who was always, in prison, in the poverty of exile, as on the battlefield and in editorial offices, a man of real moral grandeur.

43. The manuscript in question is probably *The Unknown Revolution*, which was published by "the Friends of Voline" in 1947 and reissued many times since, including most recently in Russia, thanks to the Victor Serge Foundation. English translation, http://www.ditext.com/voline/unknown.html.

1946

PRIETO

February 7, 1946—Yesterday evening a soiree at B.'s. Former banker to the Spanish court, his handsome, trembly head of a fifty-plus Victor Hugo, the overworked, worldly, and friendly smile of his wife. Their children, three little centaurs with cleated shoes, make rather annoying noise trotting around the apartment. Don Indalecio, in the corner of the divan, less massive since he lost weight, his heavy pink face full of self-assurance and at moments showing a sudden disarmed weakness. The vast, bare room. Spoke of the monarchy becoming a possibility again in Spain, where there was a majority neither for the king nor the Republic; of Largo Caballero, who is dying, operated at age seventy-six on one of his kidneys and one of his feet ("But physically he's extraordinary solid," says Prieto); of the Republic's mistakes before the military uprising. I express my amazement that the plot was allowed to mature. Prieto grows animated. "We knew everything, the plot was hatched in broad daylight. In my articles published in Bilbao I warned of it tirelessly. General Goded, commander of the Baleares, sent the Marquis de ... (I don't recall the name) to London, Paris, and Madrid to warn of it; he was only halfway involved in the plot. No one listened to his messenger. Azaña didn't want to believe. The military sacrificed Goded by sending him to Barcelona, to defeat and execution." —"Caballero's responsibility is enormous. He allowed himself to be called the Spanish Lenin in pro-Communist propaganda; the party was nearly split; young people on the left, like Santiago Carillo, assassinated those of the right.... Largo Caballero is now said to be prepared to accept posts in the Opposition, if not to govern under a restoration. He's returned to his true nature, that of a moderate...."

The conversation changes direction and suddenly I. P. says: "I don't attend burials. Old comrades are dying one by one, and I accompany them to the cemetery. It sometimes seems to me that all that's left to me is the wish to die."

He's going to undergo another operation on his bad eye. "You know, I don't know anything about theory, after forty-six years of practical militancy.... This would be the moment to read and to learn, but this damn eye problem...."

When we leave E. B. takes his arm and guides him down Avenida Michoacán. I. P. in his large overcoat, his shoulders hunched, wearing an old light-gray fedora with a short brim, suddenly resembles a fat, sad child who walks like a penguin.

In a noisy café near here, made deafening by a *sinfonola*, we spoke calmly of death the other evening, Helmuth L. and I; of death and of these times.

BENJAMIN FONDANE

March 4, 1946—A letter from France informs me of the death of Benjamin Fondane at the Auschwitz concentration camp. He was a genuine poet of the prewar period, a Romanian Jew by origin, cosmopolitan by education (he'd lived in Argentina), thoroughly integrated into French culture. His poetry was clearly a prolongation of the post-Apollinarian currents, but with a combative character. His interests carried him from poetry to philosophy, and he was one of the first, in young literary nonacademic circles, to introduce the ideas of Kierkegaard. In a strange book (*Rimbaud le voyou*) he put forth a new analysis of Rimbaud's personality. Isolated, withdrawn, living outside of literary circles, he seemed not in the least interested in success... Today he must have been between forty and forty-eight.[1] Poet and essayist of anguish, Benjamin Fondane met his end in the gas chamber, taking the measure of the greatest anguish of the present time.

1. Born in 1898, he died in 1944 at the age of forty-six.

ALBERT GOLDMAN

March 14, 1946—Albert Goldman.* Slender, graying, beautiful gray eyes behind glasses, meditative and active, a type I hadn't seen for a long time: the revolutionary intellectual, more Russian-Jewish than American. Even though he's in Cannon's party[2] he thinks that almost everything must be revised, and that we should seek a fraternity that goes beyond the limits of small groups. He accepts that many of Leon Trotsky's predictions have been proved wrong.

Me: The greatest error in Marxist thinking in the Russian Revolution was not seeing that we were building a totalitarian state. Despite a few remarkable theoretical perceptions we were all surprised by the new facts. This was the source of L. T.'s greatest error. He thought that the European revolution would free the Russian Revolution from totalitarianism. It's the opposite that occurred: Russian totalitarianism, stronger, stifled a European revolution that couldn't even begin to build a serious resistance.

A. G. makes no objection.

He says that the English Labourites have posed the question of [Rudolf] Hess. To attempt to use the Nuremberg Trial to elucidate Vyshinsky's falsifications at the Moscow Trials: the so-called Hess-Trotsky plot.[3] Cannon and Goldman thought the Russian prosecutors capable of bargaining with Hess in order to get a false confession from him—I respond that the falsifications would be even more poorly fabricated now than in 1936–1938 and easier to pick apart. —But it's obvious that we have no press and no way of putting the question before public opinion. In Nuremberg the Russians will avoid interrogating Hess on this point, and the other prosecutors will fear upsetting the Russians and playing into the hands of the revolutionaries. The old Vyshinsky falsifications will be covered up, but everything possible must be done in order to one day have the right to expose this general complicity.

---

2. James Cannon, leader of the Trotskyist Socialist Workers Party.
3. Pyatakov, the main defendant at the second Moscow Trial (January 1937) claimed that Trotsky spoke to him of his contacts with Nazi leaders, notably Rudolf Hess.

A.G., without having studied the affair, thinks that Krivitsky probably committed suicide. (I was informed that the names of his GPU assassins are known . . .) As for Carlo Tresca, he thinks the assassination was carried out by an Italian gang.

John Dewey was ready to sign a public letter concerning Hess's interrogation. Suzanne La Follette* is against this: "We have demonstrated the falsity of Vyshinky's accusations against Trotsky and there's no reason to go back over this."

THE ROSMERS—NATALIA—MANDELSTAM'S END

March 26, 1946—At Natalia's, Marguerite and Alfred Rosmer. They seem strangely unchanged over the past twenty-five years that I've known them, wherever we meet, from one end to the other of the planet. He, his thin smile, the Gothic and harmonious sculpture of his face; she, short and squat, a massive head and neck. It is during our conversation that I become aware of her worn state and her hardening, of the fixity of her deliberate stare, such that at times it appears obsessive. There is bitterness in her voice, a tense expression as she speaks of the demoralization among the small groups, everywhere. They're returning to France with no illusions. But that's where they have to be. "America and Americans are fine, but we've had enough. . . ." Homesickness. He has vague hopes that things may get going, but no, it won't be tomorrow.

Natalia doesn't look at all well. She has shrunk further: how long can this go on? In black, she has the body of a little girl, a face growing taut, the tendons of her neck poignant to see. Life is leaving her. I look at her and I'm afraid for her, fear without fear, and I wish she could still experience joy, just one, one warming, radiant joy, and I think it is completely impossible. She shows me John Dewey's letter saying that it would be superfluous to interrogate Hess, to try to have him interrogated about Vyshinsky's falsifications in 1937. It would only result in a discussion between a madman and dishonest prosecutors (the Russians), and the dishonest press would even turn the madman's denials upside down. Dewey also thinks that since most of the Nazi files have fallen into the hands of the Allies it will one day be easy to refute the impostures of the Moscow Trials from the simple fact that they don't contain the least allusion to the alleged plot.

Natalia tells me about Osip Emilievich Mandelstam's end according to Boris Nikolaevski's articles. He wrote a comical quatrain about the Leader and read it in front of five people... Arrest. Stalin himself took the affair in hand, the "affair" of one of Russia's greatest, most authentic poets. He had Mandelstam brought to him... I imagine Ossip Emilievich, this frail man, this timid man, this hypersensitive scrupulous man, lyrical and a rebellious without daring to admit it, standing before the Grandest Inquisitor... He must have trembled to his bones and perhaps suddenly grew fearless. He was sent to prison. He begged in vain to be deported. He threw himself from a third-story window and broke both legs. Remained in prison in Yelets and died there or was removed from it to disappear forever... When the prison of Yelets was evacuated in 1941 he was no longer there, and no one knows what had become of him.[4] That's all.

During my time, in 1932, he lived in a small room in Herzen House in Moscow and, had already, harassed by vexations and terrorized, thrown himself from too low a window, without consequences. Short, an elongated face, brown eyes, a worried glance. How he loved Paris! His blue-eyed wife seemed apathetic and treated him like an overgrown child. There was something in him of a refined, intellectualized, Russian Hérédia, of Mallarmé, of Giraudoux, and Russian Symbolism. (Acmeism, from the word *akme*, meaning "supreme," founded in 1912 by Gumilev—shot. Expressing not symbols of the real but the real in its immediate purity.) "Foreign to our era," wrote *The Soviet Encyclopedia*. —Certainly true. Shortly before my arrest, he read to us in a fearful and warm voice his impressions of the Caucasus, Mount Ararat, a lake, which made me think of *Suzanne et le Pacifique*. Zoshchenko, Tynyanov, Nikitin and others were there. Within that embroidered prose, hidden praise for the incoercible imagination, which is freedom... He then cast an anxious gaze on us and asked: "Do you think this is publishable?" It seemed to me that the prose was too beautiful, disclos-

4. It's now been established that he died in a transit camp in Kolyma of hunger and cold.

ing and hiding too subtle a rebellion, to touch or frighten the censors....
He died of it. (Born in 1891.)

(Kaverin was there, and perhaps Słonimski.)

March 27, 1946—Hélène Gaubert, who knew Pyatakov, Yudin, Gurevich, and Ilya Yonov in Moscow in 1931. She learned a few years ago that Yonov was executed, like the others. "He had only capitulated out of cowardice, in the hope of saving his skin." It's not as simple as that, but at bottom it's true.

DIEGO RIVERA, LARGO CABALLERO

Spring 1946—The Mexican painter Diego Rivera has just officially requested, in a letter sent to the newspapers, membership in the CP. Diego Rivera, at whose house Trotsky stayed when he arrived in Mexico, was member for a certain time of the Fourth International and editor of its newspaper *Clave*, and he hurled denunciations at secret agents of the GPU. During the war he adopted the attitude of a *fellow traveler*[5] and particularly distinguished himself by publishing an imaginary biography of Ambassador Umansky. At the same time that he joined the CP he has made declarations in support of the expansionist policy of the USSR against "Anglo-American imperialism." He compares the Iran affair[6] to the problem of the "underground oil deposits on the Mexico-Texas border, deposits that the US is forbidding Mexico to exploit," and points out the sincerely democratic character of Soviet policy in Iran. He signs posters along with the painter Alfaro Siqueiros, who in 1949 led the first assassination attempt on Trotsky, was arrested, freed on parole, and fled to Chile. Upon his return to Mexico in 1944 Alfaro Siqueiros was mentioned in the press as being subject to an arrest warrant. The wide-circulation dailies demanded his arrest and then wrote that the proceedings were halted, the file having been stolen from the Palace of Justice. David Alfaro Siqueiros,

5. In English in the original.
6. The dispute between Iran, the United States, Great Britain, and the USSR over the exploitation of oil resources at the end of the war.

one of the founders of the CP, editor of the Communist organ *El Machete* in 1924, lieutenant-colonel in the Spanish Army during the Civil War, was expelled from the CP after having led the May 1940 attack on Trotsky. The obvious object of this strictly formal expulsion was to shield the CP from responsibility for the crime, which cost the life of the young American intellectual Sheldon Harte. Alfaro Siqueiros is now publicly requesting his reintegration into the CP, to which he has never ceased being faithful.

Friends who knew Largo Caballero in Paris during the final phase of his life have finally given us a detailed account of his captivity in Poland. During the Wehrmacht's collapse Largo Caballero was evacuated with other internees and had to make a long, exhausting march. The old man, debilitated, collapsed, and, seeing an SS man bending over him with a revolver in his hand, thought the end had come. He never knew why he wasn't killed at that moment. He returned to the concentration camp and awaited the liberators. Upon the arrival of the Polish-Russian troops he made himself known and was at first treated well. He was afterwards completely isolated and for many weeks, despite his protests, it was impossible for him to establish contact with his friends in Paris. He was closely guarded, miserably housed, ill, and deprived of medical care. The Spanish Communist Uribes* came from Moscow to propose political negotiations, which Largo Caballero refused to engage in, not being able to consult his party. In the meanwhile the appeals of the Spanish SP and the protests in the foreign press made his situation known. He was put on a plane and sent to Paris without money or documents. Contrary to what the correspondents of the American press agencies wrote, Largo Caballero was never treated "in a rest home near Moscow."

DO WE EXIST?—"ETERNAL VALUES"

April 6, 1946—Conversation of these past few days. With Jacqueline Onslow Ford about what we are. Is it possible to have a correct idea of oneself? —Nothing is more ironic than "Know thyself." Nothing more serious either. But whatever our drive and capacity for objectivity, of ourselves we have only an idea, an egoistic image filled with attachment to the unique being, the Self, which is identical to instinct itself, to life. A kind of artistic, subjective creation necessarily occupies more, infinitely more place than objectivity, impossible in the deepest sense of the word. All we know of ourselves is a kind of waking dream, finely worked by the will, enlightened by consciousness—but a dream all the same.

The Other sees me only through himself, even more poorly. Strange, the unimaginable deformations of our personalities in the eyes and intelligence of others. They are distorting mirrors. They caricature and diminish, most often lowering and degrading, misinterpreting the smallest act. A function of egoism, lack of imagination, the need to attribute to others the natural baseness that we have so much trouble repressing in ourselves. And so there exist only two kinds of moving images of a personality: the one it has of itself and the one that others have of it ... Two series of phantoms, more or less substantial, silhouetted against a more or less radiant fog. On the essential role of the imagination in the understanding of others, which is also creation (the value, in this sense, of the work of novelists). Without imagination the other is never anything but a diminished caricature of ourselves. Rule: Never believe that my fellow man is really like me. The key to the imagination: Admit that the other is profoundly different.

Oscar Wilde saw to what extent lack of imagination diminishes and paralyzes us; he wrote magnificently on this subject.

Jerry G. just asked me some difficult questions. His head of a wild, strong young man; Russo-Judeo-American. Abruptly: Do you believe in eternal values? I'm taken aback. I don't like the pomposity of these words. —No more eternal than we, but that asks the question instead of answering it ... That the eternal isn't absolute. I answer: for example, the truth; but what is true is the search for the truth, not the finding. The truth is a horizon and we march toward this horizon on shifting ground wearing shoes more or less good, on feet more or less alert, with a mind more or less clear—conditioned by all this—and the horizon retreats before us, changes, and we change as we walk ... It would nonetheless be absurd to deny the horizon, our march, the change, and the eternal value of all this ...

DEATH

Morelia, May 16, 1946—Yesterday evening, on a dark street in this
little Spanish city, cool and spacious in the evening, I was suddenly
seized by one of those vertigos that have become very frequent for some
time and debilitate me distressingly. My heart starts to beat strongly
and unevenly, a psychological anxiety [makes itself felt][7] in the upper
chest, more to the left it seems to me, and when it's really bad I feel
such a buzzing vertigo mounting to my head that I fear falling, that
remaining upright is becoming impossible. I sometimes succeed in
overcoming it by force of will, but more often I have to lie down and
wait for the dizziness to pass. It's not painful, it's perhaps something
worse than pain. Exhaustion of the heart? The altitude? A touch of
nerves; that is, a nervous reaction to a nearly constant state of worry
(immediate material errands of little importance against a vast background)? All this at once? Becker doesn't say anything, but even if it
were extremely serious, what could he say? I naturally thought of angina
pectoris, which would signify a not-too-distant death. But I don't think
this is the case, as the attacks seem to me too frequent and too directly
connected to fatigue and nerves.

In the alley in Morelia it suddenly appears to me that I could die
this way, suddenly, almost without suffering, and that in any case I
must henceforth live confronting this simple eventuality. A few steps
away a policeman was wooing a graceful young girl. The alley was [...],[8]
in dark blue. I decided to walk by force of will as far as the main street
and hail a cab there. My heart and the vertigo forced me to sit in a
doorway while an abominable drunken Indio stumbled past. He was
mumbling something, called me "doctor," was dressed in reddish clothes.
By chance a car passed and the driver agreed to drop me off at the Hotel
Roma. The idea of the proximity of death, appearing more clearly than
in other recent similar circumstances, causes me no fright, no fear, and
isn't even a real hindrance in my daily activities. The hindrance is
physical and great: I am afraid of wandering at random, not knowing

7. Certain words of this handwritten entry are illegible and the French editor attempted to complete them when he could. The added words are noted in brackets.
8. Word illegible.

whether the dizziness will appear unexpectedly. I feel myself to be in a state of readiness, ready to leave, to disappear *simply*. Not without effort, I tried to attain and thought I had attained this state of calm readiness at the internal prison of the GPU in Moscow in 1933, when I envisioned my execution. Today I think that at the time I believed I had attained it more than I attained it in truth, and I succeeded in achieving a calm more apparent, more superficial than profound.

Now, whether from the wearing down of life or from a more assured serenity (with its deep-down dose of despair), my readiness is more sure. Enough, in any case, that I do not feel any obsessive anxiety and have not lost the taste for anything I love: those close to me, life, ideas, and work.

That bad spell in Morelia caused me to draw up this internal balance sheet.

If death is imminent, revolt is useless; I must remain calm and continue life as if all of it lay ahead of me. The reasonable attitude of the lucid old man loving life, knowing how marvelous it is, even if a large part of him is [...]⁹ and he is nearly certain to soon depart. The surprise, the idea of a dark surprise leaves me dismayed and frustrated.

I was, I am firmly on the road to a long and full life. Still too many things to do, to know, to understand. This thirst seems to me to be as just and as pressing as a duty: a duty par excellence, that of fulfilling being.

A *sensual* attachment to life, even in its details, its dailiness, a ceaseless curiosity about the earth and ideas.

The wish to see better days, or at least the beginning of better days.

The frustration at being interrupted in the middle of my activity, with a matured mind, a personality filled with detritus but somewhat purified. The disagreeableness of not holding out until some form of victory in the long combat. (This is not the same as the notion of success, which is much more external. By victory I rather mean doing, accomplishing—succeeding in doing and accomplishing despite defeat, which is a social reality determined by factors that evade laborious consciousness.)

9. Word illegible.

The pain of "abandoning" my loved ones, Laurette, Jeannine, Vlady, a few friends (very few), even more strangers on the periphery. But Vlady is adult enough to hold out on his own. Laurette presents me with a problem, with her mix of detachment, attachment to me, and an eager and troubled instinctive vitality.

All our ideas about death are ideas of the living. To think of death is an act of life, an act of faith in life. Nothing exists but life. To nevertheless say that death doesn't exist is a pure verbal dodging of the negation of life that presents itself to us as a merciless, a revolting reality. If I feel calm in the face of this reality it is because I am more attached to life than to myself. I don't think I am all that attached to myself: I would very much like to be different from what I am, and I'm aware both of my significance (of what it could yet become, which I don't renounce) and my insignificance. It would be very difficult for me to clarify this and I'll do it, I'll try to do it one day [...].[10] Dying before one's time is a defeat, a privation, a frustration because it leaves things unfinished. It's as if a painting—a good work, maybe even a masterpiece— was destroyed by chance before being completed and contemplated. A moment comes when the death instinct must become strong enough to almost prevail: everything has been done, life is completed, strength exhausted, time exhausted. In this sense the only concrete death of man is that of an old man who lived much and worked and sees himself replaced. The painting has fulfilled its mission, it is no longer tragic (or it is less so) that the flames devour it. What is truly pathetic about human death is that there are men whose missions should never finish, never—apparently—being completed, as long as lucidity (a luminous soul) remains to them.

The thought of death puts the philosophical problem before us, hence leading to an eagerness to achieve even more awareness, even where we touch on the impossible. I'm too little attached to the contingent and deficient in myself to feel the least temptation towards personal immortality; too attached to the real to conceive of myself separated from it and to find in that illusion the shadow of a consolation—of a consolation I have no need of as long as I am upright or

10. Illegible passage.

lying down, the thinking Self. If I were bedridden and knew myself to be doomed I would perhaps not disdain consolations—earthly, real, those of the moment. Nor do I share the quite common belief in death that survives beneath the customary religious illusions. The only cert-itude that the conscious living person can have is that of life, of life that continues, creates, re-creates, seems to end and in reality begins anew. The conscious living person lacks objectivity by applying this certainty to himself: this means reducing duration to the present moment, life to one of those countless witnesses. Countless, minuscule, and fleeting. I have the absolute sentiment of the universality and eternity of life, while knowing the imperfection of these nonabsolute terms. If all the while measuring what is irreparable and definitive in the extinction of a spark powerful in its capacity of contemplation and influence: the Self.

BILL FETT

May 18, 1946—Tall, thin, broad shouldered, the youthful face of a young man not yet finished with adolescence; thin, sharp features, glasses that look like they're rimmed with zinc. Smiling and with a cheerful gaze, but beneath it a sadness. He lives in a small Indian house where Gordon Onslow Ford has placed some remarkable old medieval-looking Spanish furniture. From the courtyard immediate contact with the vast lake, chaotic rocks, tufted trees. Twilight, what is in the dark looks distorted; the flat water is calm. Lined up on the bookcase (philosophy, *War and Peace* by Leo Tolstoy[11]) a collection of the shoes of a wanderer of the roads, worn out and dusty...William Fett sleeps on a mat covered in old clothes. The next room has a good bed in it. His sweet little Mexican woman isn't there: I imagine something happened between them. W. F. is ceaselessly biting his fingernails. He tells me that when he worked in Mexico City for the engraver Leopoldo Méndez* he asked [him] for my address and met with an inexplicably hostile reaction. "But he's a Trotskyist." And from that point he was treated icily and his plates were eliminated from the exhibit. —He

11. In English in the original.

shows us, Gordon and me, a canvas he just painted that we find expressive ("*exciting*,"[12] says Gordon), and which is unquestionably good. "Abstract" painting; I see it as substantially psychological, the falsely abstract construction expresses the soul. —It's about one meter high by forty centimeters. Good, strong colors, intense, vibrant, strong contrasts. Is fond of intense and dark watery greens, uses light greens well in the middle, simulating ribbons or flowers—or supple spatial forms— bright carmine. The attraction of the vegetal, the earthy, and of rock. —Bill says that he posed himself problems of volume and space... Nevertheless, I can distinctly make out the line of the neck and back of a seated woman-child with a little-girl profile. The young woman with her face turned away (in light, watery green) appears against a rocky background in dark blue-green that forms a powerful masculine profile, hard, brittle, egoistic, opaque... I don't know if the artist sees this as I do; it could be a subconscious success. The problems of space and volume offer a language to his deeper emotional concerns. I suddenly notice at the bottom of the canvas, beneath the female form, a kind of dark, almost black phallus, quite dreadful. The bright colors of the middle of the canvas perhaps outline a shredded fish, perhaps a corsage of flowers. —I don't say anything about what I see, except to Gordon. —How much unwilling confession in automatic painting that calls itself abstract (precisely, perhaps, to avoid confession?).

During the dinner at Onslow Ford's, in the spacious, dimly lit country dining room, William Fett, just back from the United States, speaks with fear and discouragement of the expectation of World War III and the atomic bomb. —I took away a remarkable watercolor, intense in expression and color, which he very kindly gave me.

ANDRÉ BRETON

Erongarícuaro, May 21, 1946—Drought. Torrid heat. The beautiful lake seems about to fade away, the shore recedes, becomes marshy. The distance dissolves into light smoke. (Woods are burning on the hills.) Like the earth and the rocks, all of being desires rain. It's an organic

12. In English in the original.

and universal thirst. Laurette writes me that there was an earthquake in Mexico City; that a brutal heat wave is passing through. In Chilpancingo, the capital of Guerrero, there's a water shortage, the people go great distances to find it, to the rare springs in the mountains, to isolated wells; epidemics are expected.

I read André Breton's *Surrealism and Painting*, an extraordinarily finely worked poem to painting but one whose poetry at every moment is bound to perceptiveness, to knowledge, to a kind of penetrating and illuminating depth that proceeds by irregular lightning bolts or layers of light. There's nothing spontaneous or automatic about the writing; each page is thought out, worked over at length and with the care of a mystical engraver. It's also an incessant illumination. There's the best and the worst; lyrical obscurantism whose ideas are nothing but a facade, false diamonds (it's true that false diamonds can also be as beautiful—to the eye, but not to mind—as real ones), and real, pure diamonds. Overall it's charming, dense, bizarre, and revealingly intelligent.

I noted in passing a well-balanced page on the periodic conflict between academism and abstraction (or novation, apropos of Enrico Donati[13]), considered as "two perhaps complementary forms of human temptation in the matter of expression." From paradoxical, extremist judgments aimed at causing scandal, André Breton has gone over to balanced judgments that render justice to great achievements. —The Gongorism of the style, the patient effort to make and exploit the find, like a cameo in the middle of a diadem, are forgiven for the *internal richness* of those very finds.

On Matta*: "In my eyes the pearl is spoiled by its market value.... Matta is the man who best holds the star in place, which is doubtless the best road for reaching the ultimate secret: the governing of fire." (p. 145)

On Wilfredo Lam: "Lam, the star of the vine on his brow and all he touches aflame with fireflies." (p. 183)

On Tanguy: "Yves behind the gate of his blue eyes." (p. 177)

Apropos of Max Ernst, the "commandments":

13. Italian Surrealist painter (1909–2008) who settled in the United States in 1943.

1. Don't think yourself inside a carcass, but on the surface of an egg.
2. Wander and the wings of the augur will be affixed to your sides.
3. Put your desire out of reach and you will ceaselessly re-create it.
4. Beauty will be convulsive or it will not be at all.[14]
5. Deprive yourself. Revelation is the daughter of refusal.
6. Whatever happens, never doubt.
7. Love is always before you. Love!

Apropos of Ernst, a final image, remarkably appropriate: "The male horse observes the seahorse with tenderness and terror."

André barely glimpsed Mexico; he only understood one aspect of it through his poetic prism, and his custom of showering praise led him to write regarding Frida Kahlo de Rivera: "The art of Frida Kahlo de Rivera is a ribbon around a bomb." It could only be around a bomb emptied of its explosives and placed on a shelf in a studio. André's style is truly baroque and sometimes even *Churrigueresque*.

A great poet, a truly great poet, all that was lacking in him was a direct means of expression, sufficient faith, and sufficient firmness in faith to shake off the gilded dust of "literature," of that "the rest, which is literature" and to proclaim something essential and, of course, quite old in the world, like all essential things. His real greatness should make us put aside the disappointing and annoying pettiness with which he is covered "like a butterfly of iridescent moiré" (his own style!) or "like the marvelous undersea tortoise with a somberly protective carapace." (Idem.) Jacqueline [Onslow Ford] tells me that his time as an exile in New York was the darkest moment of his life, a time of persecution, "everyone was against him." Doubtless because he is too great: therefore his case falls under the rule by virtue of which people find an easy way to assert themselves in negating and (if possible) destroying those men who incarnate values. —André's defects must have very much assisted the attacks he left himself open to, a thousand times for one and often deservedly so, in the event people underestimate what matters about him.

14. The last line of Breton's *Nadja*.

Desire to write to him despite his hostile and stupid attitude towards me.

Reread bits of *Arcane 17*. A very beautiful prose poem that is also a manifesto, an inadequate manifesto, weak and even puerile, all pose, evasion, excuses, and a return to a profoundly ordinary conformism. (Attempt to hide all this beneath a form now [...],[15] now brilliant.) Astounding passages on landscapes, on a woman. "Neither God nor master." This is the challenge. Praise of Victor Hugo, through a quote from Auguste Viatte, a visionary Catholic writer, allows the challenge to pass. (André Breton was hurtful towards me because I contributed to *Esprit*...[16]) One idea: salvation through women, borrowed from the Saint-Simonians and the cranks of the nineteenth century, unsustainable. No allusions to Trotskyism, to the opposition to Russian totalitarianism, prudence to the point of resignation. His conclusion: "...this light can only know three roads, poetry, liberty, and love." Mention of "eternal youth" and "the human heart." All of this leads to the flat bourgeois philosophy of the early nineteenth century, Royer-Collard, and "the Beautiful, the Good, the Self"; a better turn of phrase, incidentally. André Breton was inspired by that nineteenth century, greatly inferior to that of Marx, Darwin, Taine, Renan, Wundt, Chamberlin (the astronomer), reconciling cranks and professors... His ideas are no longer "convulsive," they are respectable. The challenges of "Surrealism in service to the revolution" should be understood as youthful errors. (An explicit page about this.) (I imagine the unease that the poet feels at remembering the praise he wrongheadedly lavished on revolutionary defeatism by wishing France a Brest-Litovsk peace, as if Lenin and Trotsky signed it on principle and not with their teeth clenched, on the verge of despair.) This manifesto, despite the beautiful song that elevates it, is a defeat. If André Breton stands by it upon returning to France he's defeated in advance.

The color illustrations by Matta are dull watercolors, childishly

15. Word illegible.
16. Left Catholic review edited by the Belgian novelist and former Communist militant Emmanuel Mounier, who (unlike Breton) fought for Serge's release from the Gulag in 1935.

erotic, lacking in any charm. No talent in them. —Nothing to do with the text. It seems Breton doesn't like them but that an American woman paid $1,000 to have the book illustrated by Matta. The poorly made fake pearl is even further depreciated by its market value.

Surrealism and Painting—His self-interested, deceptive, toadying, etc. side, in reality touching on the denial of affirmed values. Descent into the tatty: the praise of Diego Rivera, whose self-betrayals André Breton must be aware of; his silence concerning Trotsky (when speaking of Diego); finally, the fat lie that André Breton allows the prefacer to write: that in Martinique he was "sent" to a concentration camp. An expression with two meanings: "brought," yes, but he never set foot in it, not even to visit the sick Lam.[17]

COMMENTARY ON THE PORTRAIT OF SAINT ANTHONY BY LEONORA CARRINGTON[18]

May 23, 1946—Anthony saw himself in a cool vault as if within a dark crystal that would have been barely less grand than a world by the measure of a few temptations. The multiple inner facets of the crystal offered neither high nor low, which was in no way a hindrance, but on the contrary of an intoxicating convenience. Anthony moved within it with a light spider's step over surfaces of polished rock that at times looked to him like mirrors, at others like surfaces of palms lacking in

17. The final paragraph added in blue ink.
18. Leonora Carrington participated in a competition for the painting of a Saint Anthony that would appear in Albert Lewin's 1947 film *The Private Affairs of Bel-Ami*. Also competing were Max Ernst, who won, and Salvador Dalí. On June 14, 1956, Serge wrote Carrington a short letter, enclosing his "commentary": "Dear Leonora, One of the greatest merits of any artist, it seems to me, is not to know just what he's up to. The true artist is a Voice from who knows where. The only people capable of properly understanding him are: 1. The Dealer (when he's doing a good business); 2. The Art Critic, whether obtuse or sympathetic, though in any case as a professional he has no obligation to understand; 3. The Observer, unknown and unknowable; 4. The Admirer, friendly and a bit of a poet, and when it comes to you, that's me. Utterly. So I figure that no other exegesis will surpass in accuracy, depth, meaningfulness, philosophicality, transcendentality, etc. this commentary of mine, here transcribed in legible form, on your portrait of Saint Anthony. *Heartly Yours*."

vegetal substance, which didn't worry him, for every worry emanates from the aridity of real and vanquished substances. Yet he recalled the flesh, the sole substance worthy of admiration, he thought (because his thought, too naively radiant, was ignorant of the substance of thought) and he desired its feel, its matteness, the thirst-quenching coolness, its depths, where there are so many fountains and fires. Anthony was thirsty. A door opened in one of the walls, in the one whose veins moved like smoke. Except, that couldn't be a door due to the lack of architecture, of an exit, of an entrance, of a lock, a rent, a jailer, a rampart, a prohibition. What is not a door is a beginning or an end, death or life, survival and sure death all at once. This made Anthony feel the contentment of a child at his mother's breast. He glimpsed a subway tunnel that grew wider as it grew longer until it became more vast than anything imaginable by a poor hermit lacking in imagination, though corrupted by good will. At that moment he invented His Portrait, unknowingly, since he breathed such a weighty innocence that the worst sins roamed peacefully there without his knowing. And the Sin of the Portrait, if he'd been able to grasp the shadow of a shadow disappearing from a consciousness, would have instantly plunged him into the abyss where similarities seek each other in vain, succeeding only in rubbing against each other only to mistake each other. Several of his faces formed constellations in his beard: did they resemble each other? His torment was that of fearing they were the same, but fortunately they detached themselves from him, moved away, headed towards the space beyond day and night, towards the depths of the subway tunnel, towards deliverance via the Gare Saint-Lazare or the Manhattan subway, the lawns of Hyde Park or the Calle Pimental, *quien sabe*? Anthony recognized himself in a Chinese landscape that was as refreshing as a spring. Upon which, he momentarily fell asleep, freed of the worst of sins, the Sin of Sanctity.

Erongarícuaro, May 24, 1946—Our long conversations with the Onslow Fords. We wonder on the basis of what central ideas a movement or program of study, combat, and artistic creativity could be formed. We comment on the fate of Surrealism. Gordon full of aspirations for collective efforts that would have social goals and repercussions.

Working in solitude weighs on him. He dreams of setting up in the United States, far from cities, in Washington State and of founding something.[19] He seeks to define the basic principles of a possible starting point. —*Freedom* to be redefined: investigation, struggle, innovation. —*Reconciliation* (of man with himself; on the plane of the work and of life with all those among yesterday's enemies who were victims more than enemies, even if they were above all victims of a faith). —*Intransigence and tolerance*, symmetrical, concordant values whose equilibrium is vital precisely because it's difficult to accomplish. —*Optimism in action*, called on to prevail over conscious fear. *Internal equilibrium of man*, to be sought and achieved, which implies social justice (a new equilibrium). —Assuming a firm attitude towards money and power. The lived, living affirmation of disinterestedness; the rejection of authority, but not in the way of the old anarchism. Consider power (for example, money) as a necessary technical means to which essential values should not be subordinated.

Gordon is worried about the problem of collaboration: With whom, with what reactionary and conservative institutions, to what extent? In my eyes the defect of these ideas is that of being too rational. It seems to be lacking an arbitrary but creative emotional element—a myth.

Erongarícuaro, May 25, 1946—Drought. The level of the lake has dropped and continues to drop. The flat shoreline has extended by 100 meters. Further out the earth shows through the water. The site is veiled with a light, white, bluish, leaden smoke, mauve in the evening. A large forest has been burning for several days on the mountain to our left. The blaze goes on for kilometers, in the evening tracing a long line of glowing embers. Waiting for the rain is the constant, abiding topic of conversation, just as hungry men speak constantly of food. The direction of the wind is scrutinized, the white clouds examined. The earth has been altered, the fields of maize are yellow, the stones pallid. We

---

19. In 1957 the Onslow Fords acquired a large tract of land in the mountains near Inverness, California, which would soon become a kind of commune. The Bishop Pine Preserve still attracts artists, ecologists, and New Agers.

share the earth's thirst. It's possible that there is much electricity in the air, which causes us to feel fatigue. I seldom leave the large, cool house: a few steps under the harsh sun would be a difficult trial. The light, with its greenish reverberations, is merciless, blinding, persecuting. The land belongs (rented, since it's communal) to the Onslow Fords, "as far as the lake." But the banks having expanded, a peasant has come and put up a stone wall in front of the house in order to create a garden. He is now asking fifty-five piasters for his labor, which no one had any need of. "Tell him to go to the devil" "That wouldn't be wise. He's useful, but he's a known murderer, horribly evil. He looks educated, Spanish, delicate.... We'll give him twenty piasters."

Last year the drought was going on and on, and a grand procession took place on the square. It rained: the priest had chosen the right moment. During the Easter holidays a cross covered with offerings, bread, flowers, ribbons, and colored paper is paraded around. The children, dressed as French legionnaires, do a machete dance in the four corners of the churchyard. Fireworks, two orchestras. One with fifes and drums, very old, very good, the other of noisy brass.

This is the time of weddings. Ten young girls have been kidnapped. They spend several nights in the mountains with the fiancé, then they return and the wedding takes place or the fiancé has to pay an indemnity (very rare). I saw one on of the kidnapped ones in a doorway, an ordinary young girl in a little flowered dress, rather Spanish. Jacqueline asked her if she was happy to be getting married; she laughed in confusion, bringing her hand to her face. —No pretty girls, it seems, or only by exception. The square plaza, a round fountain in the middle (dried up, people patiently scoop up some ladles of water). There should be water in abundance, for there are three good springs on the mountaintops, two of which are unused. Fifteen thousand pesos' worth of good piping is needed. Collections have been taken up and taxes levied several times without the needed sum being reached; no one knows what became of the money. A bank loan? It requires 12 percent interest annually, in reality more. The village is full of wealthy people, four or five groceries on the square, two of them well stocked. They hide their money. Water is transported through wooden pipes and is stolen along the way. The villages in the hills have it in abundance, stolen. It has to be fought for, and there have sometimes been fights, with several dead. Old Indios, sitting on concrete benches in the square resemble *zopilotes*[20] at rest. Black faces, wrinkled and hooked, silence. They're dressed in dirty white with dark serapes. Torpor on the trees, the violet bougain-villea, the nopals, which are all shriveled up and spiny. A few stands where they sell three potatoes, a mango, the servings of the poor. Alcoholism destroys the families. The drought killed fishing: they have to go too far out, five kilometers, to find fish ... The patient making of nets is a meticulous task: in two weeks they earn twenty pesos.

Jacqueline says that she knows the Indios. "You can't talk to them, since they have no ideas.... Childish beliefs, more superstitions than actual beliefs.... The bat is an old rat, dead and resuscitated.... Rain causes rabbits to abort...." A heavy torpor weighs on the resigned human being.

WILD DUCK HUNTING

May 25, 1946—In December, after the rains, flocks of wild ducks descend on the lake. The Indios organize grand hunts. An immense fan of pirogues pushes the flocks into a bay, then tightens. The flocks pass over their pursuers, but that's when they fire, with dangerous old rifles with a short range, but more often they hurl javelins. The javelin is made of bamboo and is four meters long; it's hurled by means of a wooden apparatus that's held in the fist and which it slides along. Swinging the fist is a way of aiming it, remarkably skillful. The range of the weapon varies between forty and eighty meters; it's mysteriously accurate. Children train in its use at a young age. The hunters in their pirogues sing in Tarasco. Gordon has seen the lake covered with thousands of canoes; it's a great, barbarian spectacle, an exalting festival. Most of the hunters come back with a dozen ducks. During the "combat" the rifle fire crackled in all directions; the javelins cut through the air, whistling; the birds whirled about; and the pirogues spun around with shouting... Tumult on the silky water, in the golden vibration of the sun.

20. Nahuatl word meaning "buzzard."

SHELDON HARTE

June 10, 1946—Fanny Yanovich told me a few days ago that in May 1940, on the day of the attack on Leon Trotsky by Siqueiros and others she had been working for many hours taking his dictation. The Old Man was feeling tired at the end of the afternoon and told her that despite aspirin he had too bad a headache to continue. F. Y. stayed on until it grew dark, copying the document about the Fourth International that the Old Man was writing. Sheldon Harte asked her several times, insistently, when she thought she'd be leaving. He was visibly nervous. In retrospect, F. Y. thought that he was afraid she would stay, knowing that the attack was going to occur. When he took her home by car they passed a suspicious-looking vehicle that S. H. showed no sign of worrying about. F. Y. is convinced that S. H. was an agent of the attackers.[21]

After the attack and S. H.'s disappearance she voiced her suspicions to L. T., who listened to her attentively but in the end shook his head several times in denial and said: "Don't keep on. That's completely impossible." She thinks that L. T. didn't want to admit that an agent provocateur was able to slip into his house with the assistance of the American Trotskyist party.

F. Y. believes she knows that Jackson was in contact with Siqueiros (which is confirmed by the fact that Jackson one day gave "his address" as that of an office occupied by Siqueiros). She thinks they were seen together by agents at the Villa des Acacias. (Otto Rühle lived in the same complex in Coyoacán and had noted the regular gatherings in the neighboring villa. —He spoke to me of this.)

TO BE DEVELOPED: SCIENTIFIC SOCIALISM

July 1, 1946—Read the idealist criticisms of Marxism by Dwight Macdonald and others.[22] In general, they confirm this truism of the dullest Marxist propaganda: that intellectuals follow only power and success,

21. In her declaration to the head of the detachment charged with Trotsky's protection, "Fanny Yanovich remains convinced that Sheldon Harte . . . was an instrument of the GPU."

22. Serge is probably referring to a series of articles that appeared in *Politics* magazine.

resist the shock of defeat weakly, and are easily demoralized...To be developed:

1. That Marxism taught (teaches) *conscious* participation (well-informed, objective scientific consciousness and moral consciousness spurring and nourishing the will) in history in the making. Man not the object of history but the subject. Making history. Is another attitude possible without man's renouncing himself? Consider the risks of this, the lack of objective knowledge, the motives of the will, the weakness of the individual in society.

2. That the socialist movement, first, then later the Russian Revolution (incompletely) succeeded in healing the oppressed and exploited masses (and the intelligentsia that rallied to these masses) of an age-old inferiority complex of the perpetually defeated...In this sense the fertile role of the socialist movement is inestimable. That socialism modified the modern notion of man and his rights. (Internationalism broke the circle of the humanism of the white man.)

JACKSON

July 3, 1946—Young and amiable, Manuel Zamorano Hernández, who came to interview me for the Chilean socialist press, related to me his visit to the Mexico City Penitenciaría where he met Jackson-Mornard. Manuel Zamorano Hernández visited the prison accompanied by the secretary of the administration, Fara (or Farra), and a well-dressed bespectacled gentleman who spoke in the familiar form to the functionary, and whom he at first took for a functionary himself. And when he asked to see Trotsky's assassin, the gentleman said: "*Su servidor*..." Jackson-Mornard even accompanied them to the women's prison, where a detainee came up to him, explained her needs, and received twenty pesos from him; J. M. had a well-filled wallet, and Dr. Esther Chapa displayed the greatest sympathy for him. J. M.'s condition in the prison is an extremely privileged one: he circulates freely, exerts great influence, and enjoys real comfort. The visitor's impression was that J. M. could escape whenever he wished. The administration says that he "makes himself very useful through his cultural work among the prisoners."

J. M. gives the impression of a vigorous man of enormous sangfroid, filled with the sentiment of his own importance, guarded, and cynical.

He spoke willingly of his crime, even though he knew he was in the presence of a socialist. Maintains 1. That he is an officer on the Belgian general staff; 2. That he committed the murder during an argument, having been insulted and offended by Leon Trotsky; 3. That L. T. had proposed that he go to China to form a Trotskyist military group and that he'd refused; 4. That he had the pickax on him because, having broken the handle during an excursion, he planned to have it repaired upon leaving L. T.'s home. (These are new versions, contradictory to his declarations at the preliminary investigation.) He lies with ease, not fearing contradicting himself.

Beneath his exterior of calm and cynicism a high degree of tension is visible in him. The visitor says: "Certainly a neurotic who controls himself very well."

In the administrative offices there was a stock of issues of *Cultura Soviética*, propaganda circulating in the prison.

He added:

Bartolí and Augustín Puértolas[23] believed they recognized in J. a certain Mercader (or Mercadet), a Catalan Communist. Mercader's mother was in Russia; he has a scar on his arm (Jackson as well, it seems). A policeman of Catalan origin is said to have affirmed that shortly after the arrest, in his confusion, Jackson reportedly spoke Catalan (indirect testimony, doubtful).[24]

Dr. Quiroz Cuarón[25] says that J. spoke Spanish poorly and learned

23. According to Gorkin, this Catalan photographer was the first person to identify Mercader.

24. Serge essentially repeats here the April 17, 1944, entry.

25. Considered the father of Mexican criminology, he studied Mercader's case and later went to Barcelona to corroborate his identity.

it during the preliminary investigation. "We observed his progress." Dr. Q. thinks that J. may be from the Balkans. I say: Perhaps from the Caucasus or the Middle East, going by his appearance. Possible. This is also the opinion of Marguerite and Alfred Rosmer. Dr. Q. thinks that J. probably knows Russian. During a "lie detector" test, he was shown a message in Russian of a kind that would move him (his mother). The detector registered strong emotion.

NATALIA—KOKA—KRAVCHENKO

July 6, 1946—Visited Natalia this morning. The big, empty garden. A young American woman with eyes a bit too attentive opened the steel gate to me. Natalia is lying in her room, which has metal doors and a large metal shutter on the window and which is as white, bare, dim, and sad as a convent cell. N. lying on the low bed, tiny, her head wrapped in a gray shawl, looks like a sick, exhausted nun whose determined chin and alert gaze will never yield. Her coloring is ashen, her skin faded. She has aged greatly in a few weeks. Suddenly, as I was speaking to her, I feared for her life. Within arm's reach, on the night table, a small black revolver. Jeannine shows interest in it. "Is it real?" "It is, my little one," N. says with her weak laugh and a touched smile, nearly in tears. "She'll grow up to be a beautiful girl," she says, and she insists that Jeannine take a banana from the dining room. The weather is gray, sad.

Natalia is not suffering from anything serious. Becker is treating her, and she perhaps requires a routine operation, which she speaks to me about. What gnaws at her in reality is an immense bereavement, infinitely greater than that of Lev Davidovich, which only finished her off. It is grief for an era and an uncountable crowd. And since I'm probably the only person to truly share this with her, our discussions are precious to us, but I nevertheless avoid touching on the numberless dead. Despite us, they rise up: the tomb of a generation is always present. This time it's because I spoke of Margarita Aliger,[26] "Tvoya Pobieba," and we recalled Osip Emilievich Mandelstam, who died in prison.

26. This poet, translator, and journalist (1915–1922) was extremely popular in the Soviet Union.

And then apropos of Olga Davidovna Kameneva, sister of L.T., who was Kamenev's wife. (I had glimpses of her in the old days; tall, with a virile face, she bore a striking resemblance to L.T. Briefly headed VOKS.[27]) Natalia says: "At the beginning of the war she may still have been in that hellish camp for the wives and children of the executed that was forty versts from Moscow and where the material and moral misery was hellish.... Did you know Koka, Rakovsky's daughter? She was also sent to that hell. Her, a child!"[28]

I met Koka with Panaït Istrati two or three times in 1927. She may have been seventeen (Rakovsky's wife's daughter by her first marriage, I think). Extraordinarily delicate and pretty, the statuette of a young girl with a porcelain face so white it seemed transparent, with a wide forehead and sparkling gray eyes. She showed no interest in politics. At an early age made a love match with Iosif Utkin,* a good poet. It didn't last. Utkin, submitting to official orders, wasted his talent and fell into the second rank. He died at the front, of an illness, I think. Koka's agony was a gratuitous crime, the most absurd of state crimes, committed because she was the adoptive daughter of the great Rakovsky, whose probity and years of torture she was aware of. "To think that purity should be treason!" I leave, with the image of the tortured Koka before my eyes.

We spoke, in total agreement, about Victor Kravchenko's book, *I Chose Freedom*, a best-seller in New York. Kravchenko relates the persecutions of the technicians, his colleagues, which he witnessed and against which he supposedly—he claims—protested. He lies: protest was impossible, even inconceivable. If he himself escaped proscription it's because he was in reality an accomplice of the political police. The proof of this is that years later he obtained a mission to America. He appears to have been nothing but a frightened and self-interested conformist who "chose freedom" quite late, when the choice posed no risk, probably when he was invited to return. The only voices that speak

27. All-Union Society for Cultural Relations with Foreign Countries, an international organization created in the USSR.

28. Olga Davidovna Kameneva was executed along with Rakovsky and 160 other prisoners in July 1941.

the truth about the USSR, who can speak it today, are those of men of that stripe. Naturally in his book there's not the least defense of socialism. He's gone over to the other side, that's all, and is rewriting his biography.

LUNGDAHL'S SUICIDE

September 9, 1946—Yesterday evening Franze informed us that three or four weeks ago Lungdahl threw himself from a fourth-story window in Cuernavaca. F. is very much tempted by suicide, which she considers her natural solution, and it seemed to me that she reported this news to us with a secret satisfaction, although she liked Lungdahl and saw in him an intelligent and good man who was touching because of his internal struggles ... He lived in a cheap pension on a pretty street near the cathedral, one of those streets that leave in me an image of pink and blue flowers because the stones of the churches are pink, because flowers overflow everywhere, because there are wide flowered patios and a very peaceful garden full of colors, light, and lush, vegetal peace ... But Lungdahl, who had been wealthy until his divorce two years ago, had nothing there but a wretched little bachelor room and lived on little, working for a small local newspaper, a rag, humiliated on Sundays by not being recognized by friends from the time when his affairs were going well. For them he was a "failure," a true failure in accordance with good Russian novels, and for complex reasons—but at bottom because he was worth much more than the "successes."

Swedish, a businessman, he'd made money and had an opulent but unhappy marriage. He then took to drinking periodically, to such an extent that he lost all contact with reality, which was clearly what he was aiming for. Fritz treated him sympathetically, but people must be cured of all of life, and that is beyond the power of even the most affectionate psychoanalysis. This unhappily married businessman (who made his wife, an entirely lucid bourgeois, very unhappy) knew whole pages of Shakespeare by heart, Roman history through and through, and was interested in socialism and ethics ... I met him for the last time last year in Cuernavaca. He seemed to have been liberated, told me he'd stopped drinking, that he was happy with his poor life with its idiotic activity for a small newspaper, where he listed the cocktail parties in English and wrote one or two articles a week in which, in reticent terms, so as not to frighten those imbecilic tourists, he managed to pose the great problems. He was wearing sandals and a brown shirt, very corpulent, a heavy and fleshy face, his blue-gray eyes giving off an even light. Our meeting was more than friendly, at that instant we entered into perfect communion in the small Italian restaurant where we went to have lunch over Chianti, on the edge of the sunny square with its tall trees...We talked about everything, in depth, I mean about the problem of living and this catastrophic world. Lungdahl told me that he had reached spiritualist conclusions; that he'd gone from Lenin to Tolstoy. He was happy with my responses, interviewed me for *El Informador*, wanted to publish an article in it on Vlady's fresco. (The owner forbade its being shown, photographed, or even spoken of. "They attack me enough," he said, "for being a millionaire." He was a gentleman who speculated in wholesale sugar, etc., a "success.") The anxiety brought on by thinking and solitude killed Lungdahl in that luxurious little town of the crude dollar. He must have relapsed into alcoholism and made the final decision.

PIERRE CHIRIAEV—TELEPATHY, PREMONITIONS, ETC.

October 7, 1946—William Seabrook, *Witchcraft*,[29] a book of personal experiments carried out in Africa, France, and the United States by a basically and healthily lucid mind. The tales of black magic in Africa are those I sometimes heard in Russia and which I could research here. William Seabrook thinks that by means of magic (the classic doll stabbed with a pin) one can kill someone who believes himself in danger and believes in the danger. Autosuggestion and suggestion. He thinks that one can also kill someone who doesn't believe in magic and even (consciously) ridicules it, for he can be subconsciously sensitive to the "evil spell."

I recall that Jacques Sadoul* came to see me one day in Petrograd (in 1922, I think). His mistress, Moussia's mother, had just died. She

---

29. *Witchcraft: Its Power in the World Today,* published in 1940.

had let herself die, and in her papers Jacques Sadoul had found a note indicating the date she had assigned for her own death. He was very much affected and felt himself responsible, having abandoned her; I had no doubts about the sincerity of his tale.

It seems to me that memory supplies numerous examples of telepathy, forebodings that were borne out, premonitions. I never made much of them; that is, they seemed completely natural to me. To me it seems that the whole of life, our communications with each other and with the world at large, is woven from an infinite number of visible, invisible, and partly visible threads. Intelligence, reason, speech discern the visible threads, but only those, and they are entangled with all the others. In the most basic human interactions, speech is the most formal and obvious vehicle of a more complex understanding that is in fact based on the interlocutor's intimations and intuitions, on expression (where does that begin and end?), intonation, lighting, setting, and, along with these, imponderables we can only begin to guess at. Neither trust nor love would be possible if we didn't continually go beyond the limited sense of words, of gestures, and indeed all our other outward forms of expression. Nothing matters more than that glimpse into the inner world of the other, which is the sister to our own introspection, and how are we to distinguish what part of that consists of clear perception and what of an intuition that almost beggars definition? The true novelist possesses a multiple personality that allows him to make use of such communions.

It's quite astonishing to note that no one has yet seriously studied the regular phenomena of *nervous or mental contagion*. The contagion within a narrow circle of an ill humor, happiness, eroticism, and of intelligence as well. Contagion of neuroses, of superstitions, of beliefs, of propaganda of whatever kind . . . The presence within a group of a profoundly neurotic person provokes an instantaneous malaise in me analogous to what I felt when I saw, when I sensed, that Liuba was on her way to one of her crises. One feels oneself, one *is* more intelligent when one or two clearly intelligent people are in the room. (This can provoke admiration, give rise to a slightly exalted well-being—or provoke irritation, annoyance, anger, a pitiful rebellion, according to the characters and circumstances. Observed on many occasions.)

Laboratory experiments involving telepathy, employing controlled scientific procedures (guessing at cards), result in a higher percentage of correct guesses than the laws of probability would predict. These experiments having been done "cold," outside the excitement of active life, should, it seems, be inferior to the spontaneous play of our spirit. (Rhine's tests.)[30] John Mulholland verified them with two hundred thousand cards drawn in parallel series by machines of the International Business Machines Co., and he obtained surprising results. Rare series appeared in greater numbers than less-rare series, contrary to probability. But this too should be included in the probabilities of a series infinitely greater than that of two hundred thousand. A competition between the machine and the brain established in this way is neither honest nor *real*; and the fact that a person guessing the cards would have a higher percentage of success than that predicted by the laws of probability remains—*at the very least*—troubling.

It's the idea of *success* that offers a key here. William Seabrook asks, like everyone: You had a clear presentiment of the accident your aunt Virginia had; but how many presentiments have you had that weren't verified? The worried—of which I am one—know that the number of these presentiments, more precisely, of these vague hints of presentiments, is incalculable. The question is poorly asked. It's not the failure of presentiments and premonitions that need to be explained but rather the success. The simple juxtaposition of numbers means nothing. Let's put aside the facile psychological analysis of the great number of errors. Everything in life, in living creation, is a unique success opposed to great numbers of failed possibilities. I don't know how many spermatozoids seek to penetrate the ovum to form a sole human being. Only one succeeds, the others are wasted possibles. Austrian musical culture of the nineteenth century produced only one Beethoven out of how many ambitious artists full of unexpressed symphonies? *Success* is *reality*. Jeans[31] somewhere says that life is probably the rarest of the rare

---

30. The "observer effect" is an argument of the supporters of the paranormal based on Joseph Rhine's postulate to explain the poor results of his research when analyzed by his colleagues: the presence of a skeptical observer causes the phenomena to vanish.
31. Likely the English scientist and idealist thinker James Hopwood Jeans (1877–1946).

successes, if not unique, in the universe. (I don't think that this is true, but I admit that it's rigorously well thought out.)

Memories. I must have been about fifteen. I was living in Ixelles, rue Goffart 66. A boy of my age, Alphonse?, whom I rarely encountered and didn't like, probably because a few years before we'd had a fight and I'd given him a kick in the privates that had caused him to writhe in pain. I still felt towards him a remorse mixed with antipathy that was doubtless cause of the antipathy. One evening I felt very sad and wrote a poem filled with anguish and sent letters to my mother and Vera [Frolova], asking after their health. A few days later I learned that Alphonse had hanged himself that evening from his door handle.

I'd known Pierre Chiriarev in Paris in 1909. He lived near Parc Monceau with Margot and Tilly. All three of them Russian students, he a secondary member of a Socialist-Revolutionary terrorist group. The soirees at their house were peaceful and stimulating: tea, chartreuse, Maeterlinck, Blok, good poems and ideas. I've still have a strong impression of this. In Russia, in around 1929, I saw in a display window a novel by Pierre Chiriaev. I recalled that he wanted to become a writer, I had no doubt that this was the same person, but we didn't have any mutual acquaintances. Illegality came and with it solitude. I really wanted to meet him. For a long time I wanted to write to him but never did so. In 1932, I think, I went one day, as I often did, to have lunch at the Union of Writers, Herzen House. Going down the stairs that led to the basement I thought of Chiriaev and recall having said to myself: "It's not worth it to write to him, we'll surely meet up without that." I was eating when a stranger called me: "Victor!" and introduced himself: Chiriaev. He was tall, rather thin, a long, craggy, pale face, strong, worried eyes. I thought I recognized him but obviously I couldn't have after more than twenty years. Our harmony was immediately perfect. I visited him in his tiny poor student's room not far from Butyrka Prison (passing in front of it I had correct but in no way mysterious forebodings). He'd fought in the Civil War in the Volga region, remained independent of the party, and felt deeply the tragedy of the postrevolutionary years. Soon afterwards I was arrested, we saw each other only one other time after the day of the premonition. I don't know if he's still alive (he must be slightly older than sixty), but I still feel a kind of trusting friendship for him, as if I were certain that if we were one day to meet again we would completely understand each other. This, it's true, is probably nothing but the reflection of an adolescent friendship.

COINCIDENCE: DR. VERDARO

October 8, 1946—I hadn't had any news of Dr. Verdaro* since 1939, when he was in Brussels. Three days ago Helmut showed me a treatise on meteorology and I started to talk to him about Verdaro because, having demonstrated in Moscow in 1928 as an Oppositionist, they didn't know what to do with him (in the Red Army) and made him a meteorologist.

This morning I received a card from him. (From Switzerland.)

For years he had not been as alive in my spirit as he has been these past few days.

THE TWO POSTWARS (THE IDEA OF REVOLUTION)— THE SPONTANEITY OF THE MASSES

October 14, 1946—Very useful discussion with Helmut on these subjects. It's generally thought that the end of the world war of 1914–1918 provoked grand, unprecedented events, the appearance of new forces in history (Bolshevism, the Russian Revolution). This opinion expresses only the force of the psychological shock that was felt. In reality the continuity in historical development was striking; there were events of a new type that created a new social environment, but they were the result and the continuation of an evolution previously begun. The distant origins of the Russian Revolution dated to 1825,[32] and 1917 only completed victoriously what began in 1905: since the time of their appearance, all the Russian revolutionary parties were part of the European socialist movement.

In the aftermath of the Second World War what movements are able to continue? Since 1920 socialism has gone from defeat to defeat;

32. Year of the Decembrist uprising of liberal officers.

Communist totalitarianism has been stabilized as counterrevolution in relation to the socialist movement and, on the economic plane, as the advent of a rigorously collectivist planned economy.

It requires an idealistic naiveté completely lacking in scientific spirit to imagine that these facts, exacerbated by the bloodletting, destruction, and privations of wartime, could produce a socialist revolution. It is evident that they would probably bring about a large expansion of Stalinism and of social disturbances of an obscure character, both progressive and regressive. The end to be pursued was, is, the reconstruction of vast movements capable of becoming salutary forces *after* a period of recuperation; and in order to do this, check totalitarian communism.

Pannekoek,* whose article I just read in *Politics*, still bases his hope on the "spontaneity of the masses" in an era when technology 1. Imposes large bureaucratic organizations (unions embracing hundreds of thousands of members); 2. Imposes more and more state planning, in clear or hidden forms, and; 3. Brings forces into play against the spontaneity of the masses that are literally colossal (press, organizations, and finally repression). But the real problem is much deeper. The "spontaneity of the masses" is their deliberate initiative, made up of countless individual initiatives. It can only be the result of long education, not in school, to be sure, but social, through struggle, through mores, through democracy. (To be considered in analyzing the Russian Revolution, the enormous amount of latent and effective democracy that was distributed across the dying ancien régime; the existence of clandestine and legal parties; an intelligentsia nourished by the most advanced liberalism in Europe; constant contact with European socialism.) The spontaneity of the laboring masses of Europe—which showed itself to be rather insufficient in 1918–1920—was the result of a good century of social struggles and more than a half century of socialist education within the bourgeois democracies, starting with the republican and working-class movements of 1830 (the Lyonnaise insurrection and British Chartism), which were animated by the breath of the French Revolution and the founding of the First International. And it was mainly the result of individual initiative under a flourishing capitalist regime—of Social Darwinism.

In our days, on the contrary, the new fact in the socialist movement since the founding of the Communist International was the growing importance of the tendency towards authoritarian and powerfully disciplined organization (and in this sense the Comintern was precisely in the line of social development towards planned, authoritarian collectivism; that is, totalitarianism ...). On different social foundations fascism and Nazism participated in the same tendency toward the regimentation of the masses. While capitalism and socialism always appealed to individual initiative and compensated it, here with social success, there through the formation of movements that improved the condition of the worker and conferred dignity on him (and according to the circumstances allowed the militant to attain recognized historical grandeur or the elevated situation of leader), the totalitarian movements taught obedience compensated by (quite relative!) security and positions in the hierarchy, and this for over twenty years.

PENAL SERVITUDE IN THE USSR

November 12, 1946—Victor Kravchenko, member of the purchasing commission of the Soviet government in Moscow, requested asylum in the United States on April 4, 1944. Technician, captain, high functionary of the RSFSR, member of the CP. *I Chose Freedom* (published in 1946 by Scribner of New York, 496 pp.), testifies to a truth that is striking and verified by comparing numerous accounts.

K. estimates that in 1942 the penal labor organized by the NKVD formed a "labor reserve" of about twenty million. In his function as director of industrial enterprises in the Urals and the Moscow area, K. had the occasion to employ this labor and visit the camps. The camps he saw (notably at Pervouralsk) were made up of barracks surrounded by barbed wire, were watched over by machine gun towers, and held two to three thousand prisoners. Indescribable misery and dilapidation of a camp for women delivered over to cold, hunger, and forced labor. Categories: common criminals and prostitutes in the minority; "enemies of the people" in a great majority. At the beginning of the war there was a general rounding up of suspects across the entire country. Countless executions, in the camps as well, but compensated for by masses of new internees. K. writes: "The USSR's war industries were based above all on slave labor" (p. 404). During the Hitlerite invasion, when it was impossible to evacuate this prison labor, it was frequently exterminated, since their loyalty obviously couldn't be counted on. This was the case in Minsk, Smolensk, Kiev, Kharkov, Dnipropetrovsk, and Zaporedje. Near Nalchik, in the northern Caucasus (Autonomous Republic of Kabardino-Balkaria) a molybdenum factory employed several hundred men and women belonging to the NKVD penal labor force; Commissar Anokhov had them machine-gunned upon the approach of the Nazis. Anokhov later became the president of the Council of People's Commissars of Kabardino-Balkaria. Industries fought over this low-cost labor force for which no labor code existed. Molotov, Stalin, and Beria made use of it. It was placed under the supervision of General Nedosekin of the NKVD's special forces. —A high functionary of the political police said to K.: "We haven't yet completed our plan for arrests" (p. 406). In the region of Podolsk K. inspected an underground munitions factory managed by the NKVD and hidden in the forest. A region completely isolated from the world. Unhealthy work, high mortality rate. "Early in the morning, under the icy rain, I saw a column of women pass . . . in ranks of ten. . . . They looked like walking corpses. . . . There were young women among them . . . all fantastically attired . . . some of them wearing galoshes, others in rags; some dressed like peasants, others wearing astrakhan coats reduced to rags. . . . I saw the remains of nice clothing come from abroad."

Concerning the *mobilization of the labor of adolescents*, decreed in October 1940 and which, that year, furnished more than eighty thousand adolescents (from fourteen to seventeen), torn from their families and subjected to a regime of barracks apprenticeship, then sent to factories, K. testifies that this system continued to develop and that he employed many teams of young people in the factories. Nikolai Chvernik,* then president of the Union of Soviet Trade Unions, member of the Politburo, was placed at the head of that institution. The distribution of adolescent laborers was entrusted to Maskatov.

Other sources. From a letter from Brunswick, Germany, dated July 17, 1946: in that city, in early July 1946, several thousand children from twelve to sixteen years of age who were rounded up (principally in Brandenburg, as they were playing on the streets), were sent to an unknown destination for two years, without regard to family, the children of Communists as well as the children of Nazis. (*Neue Züricher Zeitung*, August 8, 1946). Similar events in Saxony noted by Ruth Fischer, New York.

Commentary. Prison labor is, by its very condition, far lower than slavery or serfdom. Constantly renewed, not protected by any laws, employed in secret, it constitutes a veritable category of pariahs. (The owner of slaves or serfs had an interest in the preservation of his property; the NKVD isn't concerned with this, except in the case of technicians, scientists, and skilled workers.) *Totalitarianism thus establishes a category of labor heretofore unknown in history.*[33] Given its numerical importance, this penal labor exerts pressure on the wages of the working class, which it devalues. It demoralizes the wage earners exposed to shifting from one category to the other. (The law commands that workers guilty of being late to work by twenty minutes three times be judged by tribunals and renders them liable to imprisonment; the law anticipates analogous sanctions for directors and technicians who attempt to evade this legislation.)

Condition of the working class. Internal passports, established during agricultural collectivization (1930) were not enough to prevent superexploited workers from moving in the search for less intolerable living conditions. On January 15, 1939, the labor passbook was decreed. Breaches of discipline, rewards, etc., are inscribed in it. A worker can't be hired without a passbook in good order mentioning the authorization for departure from the previous enterprise, which is particularly difficult to obtain. *Industrial serfdom.*

Eight hundred thousand workers in the Urals, Siberia, and the Far East last summer received raises of 20 percent in order to compensate for the harsh climate and lack of comfort. An indication of the transfer of large-scale industries to the Nordic regions.

---

33. The Nazis were doing the same thing at the same time in Poland. However, this may not have been known to Serge in 1946: Jewish labor under SS control "loaned" to IG Farben with facilities at Auschwitz-III-Monowitz (to cite just one example).

Rationing. Aside from general rations, recognized as totally insufficient, the following cards exist:

A: High-level state personnel, artists, writers, fully sufficient rations;

B: My categories, lower rations, but still sufficient;

NR: Granted scientific workers;

R4: Similar to that of workers in arduous industries, accorded particularly to teachers.

Material conditions. From a letter from the north of Russia: large numbers of abandoned, homeless children. Terrible housing crisis (the norm of one family per room seems idealistic). Food: potatoes and low-quality bread. Travel authorization needed to take a train. (Communicated by R. Fischer. *The Russian State Party*, no. 7, September 1945, New York.)

Expansion of the totalitarian economy. Ruth Fischer (same bulletin). A plebiscite was held in Saxony on June 30, 1946, for or against the expropriation of Nazi property. Of 3,459,658 votes there were 2,683,401 for "yes." This concerns almost the entire industry of the country. The Sowjetische Industrie AG was founded with 51 percent of its shares belonging to the USSR and 49 percent to Saxony. It employs four hundred thousand German workers and takes in two hundred companies (Zeiss optics in Jena; synthetic gas in Leuna; the Krupp steelworks in Magdeburg; IG Farben—chemical industry; steel, coal, concrete, potassium). The Junkers-Dessau war industries, Reinsdorf explosives near Wittenberg, Daimler-Benz cars in Marienfeld Buna near Halle working at full speed. Production exported to the East.

A physicians' congress met in Vienna in May 1946 on the initiative of the Soviet command. The attendees were invited to visit a Soviet hospital train. The train started up. The attendees never returned. (R. Fischer, same bulletin.)

Espionage in Canada was the subject of an official report of 733 pages published by the Canadian government in Ottawa on June 27, 1946. —Nine individuals were questioned and charged in 1943. Five could not be identified. Three Soviet citizens were directly implicated but not charged. Among them the correspondent for the Soviet news agency, Jveinov. The service was directed by the military attaché, Colonel Zabotin, who disposed of a personnel of fourteen officers and employees covered by diplomatic immunity but named in the report. Among them: Lieutenant Colonel Motinov; Majors Rogov, Sokolov, and Romanov; Captain Galkin and the code employee Igor Guzenko. The latter, invited to return to Russia, requested Canada's protection and turned a large number of secret documents over to the authorities. That same day Soviet functionaries burgled his apartment and had a violent run-in with the Canadian police. The espionage service that was uncovered was only one of several parallel services about which the investigation has insufficient information, the most important one being directed by the NKVD. Colonel Zabatin regularly left Canada and embarked on a Soviet vessel in New York, which left port without fulfilling departure formalities. According to the captured documents, the ambassador was not connected to these activities.

Gussanov, second secretary at the embassy, directed the secret political service. His authority was equal to that of the ambassador. Organizer of the party cell. Former subordinate of Malenkov, who is one of Stalin's closest collaborators. Malenkov is (was?) the head of the foreign section of the Central Committee. Jveinov's work (TASS) was supervised by Dekanozov, deputy people's commissar of foreign affairs. Colonel Zabotin's service was led by the (unidentified) "director" in Moscow, who received detailed reports on every meeting, every intervention, and controlled every bonus, no initiative being left to the managing agents. Z.'s activities had ramifications in New York and Geneva, where there was a group of secret agents. Recruitment and work in Canada was directed by the leaders of the Canadian CP, reorganized under the name Labour-Progressive Party, Parti Progressiste du Travail,[34] Fred Rose, deputy for the riding of Cartier (Montreal) in the national parliament; and Sam Carr, "national party organizer."[35] Both are longtime Soviet agents (since 1924, it is believed); Carr is in flight. Both of Russian origin, naturalized. Though the Comintern

34. Actually, Parti Ouvrier Progressiste.
35. Fred Rose (Rosenberg) (1907–1983) was the only Communist deputy elected in Canada. He spent six years in prison for espionage and died in exile in Poland. Sam Carr (Schmil Kogan) (1906–1989) was a Communist militant born in Ukraine who was active in the Canadian party from his arrival in 1924. The Guzenko Affair cast light on his role as a recruiter of Soviet spies.

was dissolved on June 10, 1943, dossiers held by Zabotin refer to Comintern files dated 1945–1946. These files contain detailed notes about all the agents and foreign militants or sympathizers who are regularly referred to.

The psychological investigations of the espionage service are important. The investigations covered armaments, the manufacture of munitions, and the atomic industry. The CP and the Soviet Secret Service chose their informants among those scientists, technicians, and employees of the war industries who sympathized with communism. Sympathizers weren't asked to join the party, even the party camouflaged as "Labour-Progressive"; it was preferred that they be able to say honestly that they were not affiliated with the CP. Nor were they offered money, so as not to scare them off: they were asked to discreetly serve the cause of the USSR, of peace, and a new world. It was only when they were engaged in the "work" that they were offered compensation for their costs and occasional bonuses. The physicist Raymond Boyer, from the wealthy bourgeoisie, became a spy out of sympathy for the USSR.[36] Emma Woikina, a typist, Russian-Canadian from a poor family, and having known poverty herself, declared that she wanted to become a Soviet citizen because in the USSR "the poor have a chance," and she thought that she had very little information for the USSR. The report underlines the importance of para-Communist organizations, called "fronts," in the secret recruitment for the espionage services.

During the period when the affair was front-page news, the *New Leader* of New York ran a story that the American authorities had their eyes on two to three thousand individuals in the United States who might be—if it was decided to cast a net—involved in analogous affairs. *Time* said something similar.

These facts are cause for reflection about the extent of services of this kind in Europe.

Disappearance of the academician Vavilov. It's been confirmed that

36. Raymond Boyer, a chemist and professor at McGill University, had worked since 1939 on explosives and various other matters relating to the atom bomb and sent his results to the Soviets.

the biologist-botanist Nikolai Vavilov was arrested in 1943 and died shortly thereafter in unknown conditions. Vavilov, born in 1887, member of the Academy of Science, was one of the most illustrious Russian scientists. For many years was director of the Institute of Applied Botanics and New Farming. He was in particular charged with studying—and accomplishing!—the extension of the cultivation of cereals into the arctic regions ... No one will be surprised that he failed and fell under the accusation of "sabotage."

DOMESTICATED WRITERS, HUNTED WRITERS

December 2, 1946—One may well be aware that under totalitarianism literature exists in a state of subjugation, controlled by a police that disappears writers at will; nevertheless, one remains stunned and humiliated by some of its productions. I just read in *Novy Mir* (Moscow, number 6, 1946) the last part of Vsevolod Ivanov's novel *The Conquest of Berlin*. In it Stalin's soldiers lavish stores of bounty on the German population. For anyone who knows the story of organized rapes and pillaging, this is already too much. We learn that all the fallen fighters carried on them, along with cherished letters from their villages, Stalin's picture. We witness the surrender of Berlin, and that's when we are suddenly struck by the enormity of the political lie. The scene is meticulously described, without any mention of the presence of Allied generals. All in all, it looks to the reader that Zhukov won the war. If "the Allies" are mentioned two or three times in the entire book, it's only in passing. We are in the presence of a falsification of history that in its impudence goes beyond the most impudent falsifications of yesterday. The final chapter is that of Stalin's apotheosis on Red Square. Stalin climbs the steps of Lenin's mausoleum "with a slow and pensive step, the step of a thinker and sage, of a warrior certain of each step." He gazes on the parade of troops and "each of them saw in his face the love, the inexhaustible love he bore for his people," while the marshal shouts the "free and clear '*Hurrah*!' The immortal '*Hurrah*' to the great Stalin."

Even the style poorly supports so much flat servility, for it's hard to see what an "immortal '*Hurrah*'" might be. And given Zhukov's disgrace, the whole novel is revealed as completely out of date. We can bet that the reviews will be unfavorable.

The saddest part of all is that the author of this mediocre fabrication, the writer so enslaved that he loses even a shadow of professional honesty and a shadow of his great talent, Vsevolod Ivanov, was generally considered one of the most gifted and profound of Russian writers between 1920 and 1930. The author of *Azure Sands*, *The Child*, and *The Sanctuary of Sanctuaries* showed himself to be a powerful analyst of the most hidden contradictions of the human soul. Police-state totalitarianism, which murdered so many of his colleagues and friends, allowed him to live, but he only breathes in the uniform of the perfectly domesticated writer, well paid, it is true, but who only has enough awareness to weigh his fear.

As I was finishing this book, a moving letter informed me of the fate of some Ukrainian "proletarian" writers who enjoyed great renown: Mykola Khvylovy, the best known of them, committed suicide in 1933 ... Arkady Lyubchenko died while being tortured by the Gestapo. The last intellectuals of this movement, interned in a DP camp in Germany, live in fear, hoping to one day become free men in service to freedom...[37]

37. On April 26, 1947, the *New Leader* published an article by Serge, "Ukrainian Writers in the Displaced Persons Camps."

1947

CITIZEN VYSHINSKY

1947—In 1933 I was occupying a rather comfortable cell at the Lubyanka Prison in the center of Moscow. I didn't know what I was accused of, but I knew that I could be executed as had been many of my neighbors on the corridor. I was alone and held in secret. Nothing surprised me, since I belonged to the Opposition, which was demanding a little bit of democracy... One evening a tall, handsome, blond fellow entered my solitude, introducing himself to me as the chief of staff of the Secretariat of the Council of People's Commissars for ten years under Alexei Rykov, Lenin's successor. This forty-year-old veteran revolutionary, an Oppositionist as well, was expecting torture and death, for he thought that the prosecution was trying, through him, to get at Rykov, the former president of the council. We immediately became friends. He told me that at that very moment the prosecutor of the Supreme Tribunal, Vyshinsky, was conducting a strange trial against British engineers. "What a paradox," said my cellmate, Nesterov. "During the revolution Vyshinsky, a counterrevolutionary, organized supply provisioning strikes against the Soviets in the Ukraine. And the party sent me there to combat him! Now I'm in a cell, and he is pronouncing closing arguments in the name of the Soviet regime! I won't be able to count on his kindness." My friend Nesterov was subsequently tortured and shot; Vyshinsky continued his brilliant career. He is continuing it today, condemning the United States and Great Britain.[1]

Andrei Yanuaryevich Vyshinsky (now sixty-four years old) was an unknown throughout the course of the Russian Revolution, even

---

1. After the war Vyshinsky was the Soviet representative to the UN.

though he belonged to the revolutionary generation in his way. Of bourgeois origin, he studied law while an activist in the moderate, Menshevik, tendency of Russian social democracy. His biography, written since his ascent to power, attributes to him a certain activity in the "combat groups" in the Caucasus during the period of the first Russian Revolution (1905). At the time he did one year in prison; he was wounded by reactionaries. He knew the young Stalin in the Caucasus and even detested him as a member of an enemy tendency. In 1917, when the hurricane of revolutions broke out, it appears that Vyshinsky didn't participate in any important events but remained a moderate Social-Democrat, an enemy of Bolshevism. In 1918 Stalin, whom almost no one knew, was accused by his socialist adversaries of having participated in acts of banditry in the Caucasus and particularly of an "expropriation of funds" committed on a ship in Baku in 1905 or 1906.[2] Even though the facts were not in doubt and it was a question of a revolutionary act, Stalin considered himself defamed and sued his enemies before a tribunal. Vyshinsky abstained from testifying, but Russian Social-Democrats relate that he confirmed to them Stalin's participation in the Baku "expropriation."

In 1920 Bolshevism triumphed. Vyshinsky stopped fighting it and even joined the party. The revolution is generous to those who rally to it. Vyshinsky, received into the Communist Party, taught criminal law at the University of Moscow. He was named prosecutor of the Supreme Tribunal. He published pamphlets and books that went unnoticed. In his *Course on Criminal Procedure* he rightly maintained that the confessions of a defendant, when not corroborated by persuasive evidence or testimony, are insufficient for conviction. It was only in 1928 that the name Vyshinsky suddenly appeared on the front page of the newspapers. As president of the Supreme Tribunal he ran the trial of fifty-three mining engineers from the Shakhty (Donetsk) mines, accused of sabotage in collaboration with the French and Polish general staffs. Five executions followed. When studying this trial one gains the conviction that it responded more to political ends than a concern for justice.

2. Actually 1907.

Vyshinsky's method consisted in placing on a single defendants' bench a few guilty men and many innocents. The innocent would confess under pain of death and out of patriotism, as well as to save their families. And thus would the disorganization of the mining industry, due to the wretched conditions of the workers and the fatally authoritarian management of the Politburo, be explained to the public. This was in the wake of Stalin's seizure of power; the totalitarian regime was substituting itself for the revolutionary regime and it needed scapegoats.

From that year on, Citizen Prosecutor Vyshinsky participated in the preparation of all the trials of this type, even those that didn't take place (because the defendants were not accommodating or demonstrated astonishing courage by accusing in their turn, in which case they disappeared into the shadows). During the period of the implementation of the First Five-Year Plan, Soviet industry entered a period of extraordinary waste. There was a shortage of every variety of manufactured article. The forced collectivization of agriculture resulted in the destruction of livestock and the worst famine Russia had ever known. Technicians warned the government in vain that it was committing errors and crimes against the nation and that the famine would cause millions of victims. They were arrested, often tortured, thousands were condemned without trial, and certain selected ones were given propaganda trials in order to demonstrate to the poor Russian people that the famine was organized by agents of France and England. Those scholars and intellectuals of quality who refused these ignoble comedies, like the old Socialist Bazarov, like the great agronomists Makarov and [Nikolai] Kondratiev, vanished forever, without anything ever being known about their terrible fate ... An immense nightmare spread across the USSR. Sad jokes like these were spread: "How's your son, Citizeness?" "Alas, he's an engineer." "Sorry, I didn't know." "I mean, he's also in prison." The terror descended on the technicians, the intellectuals, the oppositional Communists sickened by the regime. Citizen Prosecutor Vyshinsky became one of the most influential personalities in Moscow. Another piece of black humor: "What can swallow anything but has no guts? —By Jove, the Citizen Prosecutor!"

And then came the hellish years 1936–1938. For nearly six years before, the entire Left Opposition, which was the first to rise up and denounce bureaucratic totalitarianism, had been in prison. But there remained in the Communist Party, even in power in secondary posts, many old Marxists, companions of Lenin, heroes of the Civil War, educated Marxists, socialist humanists, faithful to the ideals of the Revolution. This was not what they had wanted! Infinitely more capable than Stalin's coterie, they knew that the Soviet Republic could set the world a different example and give its citizens a little more bread and nights without fear. They protested, they denounced the Stalinist regime. Did they conspire? They would have had the right to do so, but the political police was so ubiquitous that everyone was watched over day and night. I lived through those times. I wasn't anyone of the first rank, yet in the very apartment where I was living three informers for the secret police were watching me; the surveillance office opened my letters. I was arrested from time to time. Try to organize a plot under these conditions! On the other hand, it's true that hatred of Stalin grew to be commonplace among party cadres. And then the Moscow Trials began, first prepared by the secret police of the GPU, then by the indefatigable prosecutor Vyshinsky. Almost all of the revolutionaries of 1917–1923 passed through them: the founders of the Soviet republic, Lenin's companions, the oldest friends of Stalin himself were executed in the thousands, the overwhelming majority without a public trial, in the darkness, some of them after three trials during which one could hear Vyshinsky hurl accusations for hours.

Prosecutor Vyshinsky showed a great talent for the handling of impostures, of the most outrageous lies, and of criminal phantasmagoria, with a cynicism defying common sense. Never was material evidence produced; never was a verifiable fact verified; never was an idea presented in its true light; never was an absurdity or an obvious falsification abandoned. The Old Bolsheviks were accused of having conspired with England, Japan, the Nazi Third Reich, the Socialist International! One of them confesses to having taken a plane to Norway during the winter of 1935 to see Trotsky. The Norwegian authorities attest to the fact that not a single plane arrived in Oslo during that time. The defendant is executed! Denials and proofs rained down from

Paris and London, from everywhere. The prosecutor ignored them. His stature as a counterfeiter took on monumental proportions. He executed the orders he received, and for him insult replaced proof. He invented a style of insult the likes of which had never been heard in a courtroom: "I demand that these mad dogs be executed!" The mad dogs were the greatest men of the Revolution . . . They die. A detailed analysis of the forgeries was done, notably in the United States, under the leadership of the most respected of American philosophers, John Dewey, but today there is more: the archives of Nazism are in the hands of the victors, and it's proved that the Citizen Prosecutor lied from the first to the last of lines of his texts.

Sometimes, during these trials, Citizen Prosecutor Vyshinsky almost lost his head, literally, in the face of the sudden resistance of an accommodating but desperate defendant. The prosecutor was able to remain calm and suddenly demonstrate great prudence. Thus when the former head of the GPU and the people's commissar for the interior, Yagoda, answered three times that he preferred not to say why he had lied at the secret preliminary investigation. "Allow me, Citizen Prosecutor, to not answer that question." It was important, that question, but Vyshinsky, his brow certainly covered in a cold sweat, allowed the defendant to not answer.

During this trial Vyshinsky collaborated closely with two of Stalin's henchmen, the heads of the political police, Yagoda and Yezhov, both of them executed, one after the other, because they knew too much and perhaps because they'd gone mad. Vyshinsky peacefully survived them: calmer, more cynical and less informed; offering perhaps greater guarantees of unscrupulous servility.

In conclusion, let us stress an essential trait of this excellent orator. He never pronounced a single word that wasn't dictated, word for word, by Stalin's secretariat. Vyshinsky is nothing but a robot in whose throat the Politburo plays its records, be it a matter of executing Old Bolsheviks or denouncing the Americans. This robot feels that his existence is tied to the most inhuman regime the world has ever known, for if the regime were to waver, change, or fall, the robot prosecutor knows full well that no forgiveness would be possible for him. The horror his mere name inspires is such that, recognized on the street, he would be immediately hanged from the nearest lamppost. He can have no doubt about this. He will continue to serve to the bitter end. Physically, he's a short, corpulent gentleman with white hair, good manners, very calm, with the face of a mediocre intellectual and an extremely cold, blue gaze…"A kindly little old man," said an American sailor who had recently observed him during an ocean crossing.

FIESTA IN ERONGARÍCUARO

February 2, 1947—Sunday morning, walking through the marketplace with Elisabeth Onslow Ford and Jeannine (large hat…). Out of an alley that leads to the mountains arrives a group of at least twenty dancers. Indian violinists, a clarinet player, two bassists. Very dark-skinned, in serapes and work shirts. Several dances on the plaza. It's the *día del Candelero*, the raising of Baby Jesus. (Victoria explains it to me.)

The dancers are chic, most in new suits of good material. Some are *braceros* who have worked in the United States, the others rented their clothing. Masked as whites, very blond, smiling, bearded men. These pink, flesh-colored masks, with their moustaches and golden beards, are well made with a variety of expressions and a uniformity of color. The blond-gold man is quite stupid, slightly drunk, he has a kindly-erotic expression. He's wearing a sumptuous hat overloaded with multicolored flowers and ribbons, from which fall plumes of ribbon, multicolored ribbons of paper and cellophane. The dancer has a cane, usually decorated with red, white, pink, green, etc. paper flowers. Several wear gloves, one put on sunglasses over his mask. Several have light yellow shoes. Clearly wearing their Sunday best. Two female dancers (played by vigorous lads). Dull red dresses (like those of the Kurds in Tiflis), cinched at the (thick) waist with a rebozo.[3] Masks of white women in hats, smiling stupidly, extremely realistic. —During the dance all these masks take on expressions due to the personality of the dancer. Their erotic smile may come from the fact that they have

3. Shawl.

fleshy eyelids half-lowered over immobile blue eyes: the hidden slit through which the dancer looks out is above the eyelids. Women: white stockings of the region. Two demons in shirtsleeves have black hardwood masks to good effect. *The devil leads the dance.* He's an agile lad who moves rapidly without seeming to. He's wearing a kind of cap, from the rear of which two thin horns decorated with pinkish flowers rise up. A beautiful, jutting black muzzle in the form of a boar's snout. White fangs protrude from his mouth, his tiny tongue of purple cloth darts in and out. On his black brow four hard little red horns, pointed symmetrically in two directions. Black tights with silver highlights over a red shirt. Officer's sword hanging from an Indian belt. White trunks, black stockings. He's quite decorative, the devil.

The music is a captivating, even lulling chant, repeated endlessly. The musicians play correctly, serious, unsmiling. —Few people seem to be having fun or to be discreetly enjoying themselves. Apathy (mixed with seriousness?). —The dancers stand in two facing lines, humming along, marking the rhythm of the chant with their flowered canes, which have tiny bells on them. Then a few of them start up a minuet among the others. —They begin again on various places around the plaza. Sun, calm, mountain, a wooly black pig wanders around, another strays into the legs of the dancers, a black dog who does the same seems confused. —The spectacle is rather beautiful without any real gaiety.

TARASCOS

People. Lots of very wide faces with prominent cheekbones. Eyes of generally so dark a brown that you can't make out the pupils. Few pretty girls. Young mothers thick-waisted, the child calm, whiter, on her back in a rebozo, a clean little foot sticking out.... The women wear their hair in two braids parted in the middle of the low forehead and more or less gathered at the back of the neck. Every one of the women: blue rebozo with ash gray stripes. Barefoot. The men often wearing *guaraches*.[4] Good, white teeth. They chew sugarcane, eat cooked, amber-colored calabash and palm roots, also amber. Living on the lake and

4. Sandals.

on the shores of the lake, the Tarascos rarely wash. All of their flesh is encrusted with old dust. Their feet are covered with a veritable carapace of filth. Rarely a clean face. Group of young girls chatting and laughing, just a bit: one or two pleasant Asiatic faces. A near-black, muscular little girl, thin, wearing a flowered dress, has the delicate features of a European. —Eyes generally large, nostrils thick, features heavy and regular. An Indio speaks to me, proudly tells me that he has been to Washington and worked in Montana. His well-formed hands haven't been washed in months, crusted in earth. A nice smile.

Poor marketplace: green peppers, small tomatoes, wretched bananas, green beans, onions, potatoes, resinous firewood.

Q. asserts that the people of Janitzio, rather wealthy, are very clean (as far as I remember, this is true). Those of the green island, Jarcuaro, less tidy. The dirty ones are those from the mountain, lacking in water.

In the afternoon, the dancers came to our mill and they performed their mystery. For it is a total mystery. Elizabeth held the plate, on which was lying a tiny Baby Jesus doll surrounded by paper flowers (and the money we'd put there). The *viejitos*,[5] forming two rows, hunched over, shaking their flowered canes and tiny bells and sometimes doing a dance step in place (imitating the stumbling step of an old man), two of them approached the Baby Jesus and clumsily declaimed a verse. I made out that the Child King had just freed man from sin. Then the chorus again took up the litany and it continued. At the end they mingled together in a confused dance, but several of them, standing in place, executed an agile cross step (tracing something analogous to old Cossack dances). They danced hunched over—old people—giving out little cries—a meowed ya-oo! The black masks were perhaps not demons but rather black slaves.

Odd that they all simulated blond Spaniards. Even the devil (in his tights and sword)—this Christian mystery being for them a mystery of white men and a white god.

It was colorful, touching, in reality very sad, almost tragic. G. and J. observed it and Jeannine had a concentrated expression on her face. At the end all the young men of the village shook our hands with their

5. Little old men.

strong, black workingmen's hands, clean for the festival, inclining their smiling white false faces and golden beards.

The sun began to set on the neighboring hills; the sky was rosy. The dance hall was pearly, shell colored.

A tale told by G.: A spring festival in Pátzcuaro. The looms, decorated ceremonially, are at work on the square. A group of bearded hunters arrives from the mountain, firing their rifles, sometimes loaded, in all directions. They're carrying a dead doe covered in orchids.

"Dance of the Capitalist": During the fiesta a character in a top hat, frock coat, boots, and the mask of a worried Spaniard, circulates around the square carrying his little attaché case, foreign to joy, to everything, nervous, grotesque, and in a hurry. He's the ridiculous man—the White Man—who thinks only of his money. And he makes you think of the devil.

"JACKSON," OR THE PRIVILEGED ASSASSIN

March 21, 1947—Mr. Louis Budenz's revelations bring nothing new to those who have closely studied the assassination of Leon Trotsky and who know the Comintern. But for the general public they're important, and from the point of view of the judicial investigation they constitute proof. In this regard I'd like to highlight a few little-known facts concerning the assassin, alias "Jackson," alias "Mornard," alias "Vandendreschd," and whose true identity has not yet been established, though there are reasons to believe him Russian and knowing Russian.

It was with a Canadian passport in the name of Frank Jackson that the assassin arrived in Mexico, and this passport was that of naturalized Yugoslav Canadian, a fighter in the Civil War, killed in Spain. And we know from Walter Krivitsky's book (*I Was Stalin's Agent*) that the secret service confiscated the passports of combatants of the International Brigades. The official account of the Soviet espionage affair in Canada, published in Ottawa in 1946, relates that a spy stationed in the United States used a passport of this kind.

Another fact. Throughout the trial and even today, in the Mexico City prison, "Jackson" had and has at his disposal considerable sums from an unknown source.

In November 1941, when I'd just arrived in Mexico City, I was informed with precision by a person worthy of confidence and able to testify that "Jackson's" escape was being prepared, set in principle for early December. Concordant information from other sources reached Trotsky's widow. The Mexican authorities, warned, took precautions. "Jackson," in the meanwhile, knowing that escape meant his disappearance, played for time, and this was what actually caused the project to fail. From the information I obtained it appears that in 1941 an emissary had arrived in Havana from Russia bearing a large sum of money, around $20,000, in order to organize the assassin's escape and disappearance. This emissary had conferred in Cuba with an influential member of the Cuban Communist Party, who was described to me as having a revolutionary past, being an intellectual of quality, perhaps of foreign origin, and officially in disagreement with the leadership of the Cuban CP. I didn't manage to establish the identity of this person, who at the time was in Mexico City, busy with the purchase of cars, the forming of a team, in easy communication with "Jackson," and in addition provided with considerable funds... A short time after the failure of this enterprise the Spanish CP in Mexico published in its organ *Nuestra Bandera*, under the signature of the Catalan Communist Joan Comorera (October 10, 1942), a merciless declaration of war against me and a few other antitotalitarian socialist refugees. On January 3–5, 1942, the plenum of the Mexican CP publicly adopted a similar declaration. The campaign of insults and slander, accompanied by assassination threats against my friends and me, reached an extreme violence. The organ of the Mexican CP, the *Voz de México*, even published a drawing showing Trotsky's skull bearing the name of socialist refugees who deserve the same fate. This campaign was supported by all the Communist organizations, German, American (the *Daily Worker*), perfectly orchestrated. Implicitly but very clearly, all the Communist organizations justified Trotsky's assassination.

On the eve of being tried by a Mexican court "Jackson" made statements to the broad-circulation Mexican weekly *Así* containing praise of Stalin.

The *New Leader* published in March or April 1946 reports on the new preparations for "Jackson's" escape and disappearance. *Time* repeated the *New Leader*'s report in these terms: "Jackson had committed an assassin's no. 1 crime: he had failed to escape. Said the *New Leader*: the Mexican police have discovered that the NKVD is now trying to liquidate Jackson: the operation is in the charge of a little-publicized US woman Communist who lives in Manhattan's Greenwich Village"[6] (*Time*, April 29, 1946).

In the Mexico City prison La Penitenciaría, "Jackson" enjoys, thanks to the constant protection of influential friends, an exceptional situation. Strange incidents result from this. Last year, when a photographer from the daily *Excélsior* took a picture of the assassin, a Communist functionary immediately grabbed his camera and demanded the destruction of the photo. Last March 8 the Mexico City newspapers wrote that a group of prisoners had just sent the president of the republic and other authorities a complaint about the bullying and ill treatment that the non-Communist prisoners are subjected to by the Communists, a woman functionary who is their patron, and the influential "Jackson."

One last thing. The true identity of the Russo-Communist secret service agent "Jackson" is not the only mystery surrounding him. His crime was preceded in May 1940 by a first attack on Trotsky under the leadership of a well-known Mexican Communist. In the course of that nocturnal attack a young American who was part of Trotsky's entourage, Robert Sheldon Harte, was kidnapped and murdered. His corpse was found. Sheldon Harte was the guard at the gate of the house and he was allowed to open the door only upon the request of a known voice; for example, at the call of "Jackson," whom he knew well. Does "Jackson" have an ironclad alibi for the night of May 24–25? Or is he one of Sheldon Harte's assassins? The question remains open. Between the attack of May 25, 1940, and Leon Trotsky's assassination, "Jackson" made one or two trips to the United States. Whom did he go to see to get his instructions? How did he spend his time in the United States?

Little by little a more complete light is being cast on the crime of Coyoacán. Do not the new facts fallen into the public domain justify

6. In English in the original.

a new investigation? In a civilized world the crimes of a totalitarian police cannot forever remain privileged crimes.

CRIMES ON TOP OF CRIMES

May 1947—Will we one day manage to exhaust the list of the crimes of Stalinist totalitarianism? It takes as long as ten years for sinister news to pass through the Iron Curtain. The news I just received is abominable. There are no words to describe it—like so many crimes, besides. The Russian (Menshevik) *Socialist Courier* published two photos on its front page. Two noble faces that are part of the history of the Russian Revolution and socialism. And a devastating note signed by the veterans of the two moderate parties of the revolution, the Socialist-Revolutionary Party and the Social-Democratic Party. They have just learned in the United States of the assassination ten years ago by Stalin's executioners of Mikhail Isaakovich Liber* (Goldman) and Avram Rafaelovich Gots.

These two socialists had been enemies of Bolshevism. They had fought against Lenin and Trotsky, Liber, a Menshevik, by agitating, Gots with weapons, from 1917 until 1921 or 1922. But never did anyone in Russia ever doubt their passion, their sincerity, and later the trustworthiness of their reconciliation with a victorious revolution to which, while reserving their right to think in silence, they had offered their abilities. Liber, since 1922 if my memory serves me, worked in the Soviet economy. The former leader of the Socialist-Revolutionary Party, Avram Gots, after being deported, I think in 1926, continued to work in the economic and financial services of the state. When I was banished from the USSR in early 1936, Gots, in a city on the Volga, had earned the general esteem of his former enemies.

We now learn from an escapee from Stalin's prisons that in 1937 these two old socialists underwent—in the worst conditions—a long incarceration in Alma-Ata (Turkestan). The overcrowding in the prisons was such that isolation didn't exist: there were some ten thousand prisoners in the jails of Alma-Ata. Liber and Gots were tortured. At the end of their physical and moral strength, they finally signed all the "confessions" they were asked for. They didn't hide this from their companions in suffering. They said they had thought only of saving their families, who were also imprisoned, and whose fate is unknown. While awaiting death they fully regained control of themselves. The European socialist who knew them at the time relates that they were dauntless, masters of themselves, faithful to their confidence in the future of the Russian people, faithful to their convictions. They were put before the firing squad without a trial in November 1937. And even though they belonged to the history of the Russian Revolution, the Stalinist regime managed to hide this crime for ten years! However sullied with crimes it may be, it was still ashamed of this one.

This regime of torturers and assassins, master of the most extensive concentration camps in the universe, possesses an all-encompassing strategy of crime and infamy. Absolute secrecy constitutes the first precept. Another fact of this kind must be recalled here. When the two leaders of the Jewish proletariat of Poland, Henryk Ehrlich and Victor Alter, were executed in Russia—after having been invited by Stalin to form a worldwide committee to defend the Jews—the Stalinist government allowed liberals and socialists to multiply their endeavors on behalf of the two corpses for nearly two years. The American Federation of Labor, Einstein, Eleanor Roosevelt, and the Polish government continued to request the liberation of the two members of the International Socialist Committee buried no one knows where. It was only in early 1943 that Ambassador Litvinov informed the American Federation of Labor that "considered Soviet citizens" Henryk Ehrlich and Victor Alter had been executed. The official message attempted to sully their image by accusing them of "espionage and treason." This crime contributed greatly to the enlightening of the American working class.

To the names of Old Bolsheviks, to the names of Trotsky and Andrés Nin, to the names Henryk Ehrlich and Victor Alter, let us now add the names of Avram Gots and Mikhail Liber. Crimes are piling up in an endless series. The piles of severed heads that Tamerlane had set up when he ordered the depopulating of a country would look pitiful compared to the pyramid of severed heads that the "Brilliant Leader" is building higher and higher every day. Bolsheviks, Mensheviks,

Socialist-Revolutionaries, syndicalists, anarchists, Jewish Bundists, the famous and the unknown, all the skulls gather there, reconciled. Whoever thought socialism since the beginning of this century; whoever in Russia passionately hoped for a grand liberation of men, brought there his poor head, his noble head, his burning consciousness or his hesitations, his doubts or his faith . . . If there remained in this ossuary the shadow of the shadow of socialism, socialism would be forever dishonored.

MICHOACÁN, JALISCO, PARICUTÍN

July 2–14, 1947—On the road with Clifford Forster,[7] Joe Anzaro, and Carmen de la Vega. Several times on the heights, we enter the clouds, we see them shred above the wooded sites.

Sweet enchantment of Morelia in the evening. Plazas, the dark pink of the cathedral, alleys, old Spanish buildings, young girls behind high, illuminated windows. We visit a library near the Hotel Roma. The ages of the spirit are superimposed there. It's a spacious desanctified church. Busts of sages and philosophers have been placed along the length of a circular gallery beneath the vault. A bookshelf stands against a bad fresco showing an Indio brandishing a hammer and sickle. We discover large numbers of old books from the eighteenth century, the complete works of Condillac, and treatises in Latin. The little old librarian, dark and simian, in ragged clothes, speaks lovingly of the precious manuscripts in the cabinets in the gallery. The large door opens onto a blue and vaguely pink street. Brown kids in rags enter and ask us for coins. Morelia breathes the spirit of live and let live, the noble past, youth. Students, male and female, populate the benches beneath the tall trees. They study a great deal without getting very far. More sexuality than brains. During the day the plaza is roasting hot, the pink and yellow street torrid. Sweets, fruit pastries under the arcades. "Here was Matamoros," on a half-erased slab at the entrance to the Hotel Virrey de

7. American lawyer, member of the ACLU, he was a regular correspondent of Serge's.

Mendoza. At the other end of the square a sober monument to others shot in the wars of independence.

The museum, former residence of an aristocratic family, its series of peaceful rooms, its old furniture, the cool, trellised windows opening onto a sunny exterior. *Licenciado* Antonio Arriaga,* an athletic young man, enthusiast for the antiquities of Michoacán, guides us through the room of Tarasco culture. Figurines of the dead (five to eight centimeters tall), striking and sometimes grotesque resemblances, terra cotta, painted. Sexualized. Men holding their members. A matron with a sagging belly, a big nose, a widely sly mouth, naked, with sumptuous necklaces and an ornate hairdo looks exactly like the madam of a brothel. The artisans who made these figurines were extraordinarily gifted portraitists: a few strokes and you get the whole personality. —Lip rings of finely worked obsidian, a few golden jewels, all of it marked by delicacy, detail, patience, and a kind of inner equilibrium. —In the courtyard two old carriages, one belonging to a wealthy *hacendado* who ended in front of a firing squad in the time of Maximilian.

Pátzcuaro. The workshop of the lacquer workers. An old abandoned convent with many courtyards. A poor family lives alone there. From the watchtower the vastness, lake, mountains, sky... Quiroga and Tzintzuntzan beneath a driving rain that animates, creates, and dissipates phantom landscapes.

Uruapan, a filthy city, strangely neglected, inhospitable, where the tourist is the prey. *Posada tarasca.*[8] Encounter with two demobilized Americans. One is a handsome young lad, marked for a diplomatic career, speaks bad French, refuses to express any opinions—already! I say to him: "You're right; opinions are dangerous, don't trust them. Even if you don't have any, this beautiful world will one day grab you by the seat of the pants and toss you back into war, the shit, and the rest..." It took him a moment to understand.

The beautiful park with a thousand springs, the *arroyo*, the coffee trees, the mighty banana trees, the festival of water spouts.

At a Syrian bookseller's, with *The Lovers' Secretary* and the *Key to*

8. Tarasco inn.

Dreams, along with Zweig and Bourget, books by my dear old friend Panaït Istrati make me dream of him.

After Zamora begin the mountainous steppes like the Tauride plateau, but spiked here and there with enormous candlestick cacti, dark in the flaming sun.

Paricutín. A good two hours by car to the volcano along a road through the undergrowth that I have already taken on twice, long ago. I saw these woods burned, these trees without a single green leaf, dunes of black and rust-colored ash covering the entire countryside. Beneath the ash the killed woods were sinister, an immense calm reigned, there wasn't a single bird ... Life has marvelously returned, the foliage explodes, green triumphs over the ashes: it is a total rebirth, no more the totally dead fields of devastation Laurette compared to battlefields. In the clearings the waves of ash are spotted by countless bushes bearing white flowers. Suddenly, on our left, a vast landscape of limitless sadness: the low cone of the volcano, gray beneath the pale sky, smoking a little. Around it the embankments and fields are white as snow, for it has hailed. Sulfurous fumaroles rise all round. There's an enormous motionless explosion of smoke and vapor, colossal, nebulous, alongside the volcano itself, with its delicate outline. Up to there the undulations of the plain are of gray, but light ash, with white-flowered bushes.

It's no longer possible to go to San Juan. The spacious valley that separated the village from the volcano and the pueblo itself were engulfed by the floes of lava. The floes descend and then, pushed along by their own weight, climb the hills: they seem to go wherever they want to go, obscurely, irresistibly ... Here we are on a hill, near a rudimentary *campamento* where I encounter the most taciturn Indios in the world. (They come from a strange village of stone, shacks of adobe and black planks, infinitely gloomy, which we passed through. Girls with long hair and a mournful gaze, their faces soiled with ash, watched us without the least discernible expression.) The church of San Juan appears 1,500 meters away, its belfry emerging from the lava field amid the desolation. The lava stopped here, forming a rampart at least six meters high. But no word could explain what it is. It's a vastness of mad chaos where forms of all kinds jut out and tear each other apart, frozen in gray black—all the formless forms, defying imagination, life, geom-

etry. Nothing there resembles anything else, a pure chaos whose formation seems not to have obeyed any intelligible law. I contemplate it,
struck by this direct contact with the cosmically unimaginable. The
lava is hard and friable, heavy and light, another chaos of notions.
Incandescent, it came up to the shrubs and bushes, half of which it
devoured, while the other half lives on in intense green. On a hill of
ash a half-burned maguey, a half-burned palm tree, alive. Beyond the
lava field, which looks limitless, the wide low cone of the volcano is
smoking a little, the fumaroles spurting forth; there's the enormous,
quasi-immobile explosion of the low side crater. The cloud moves about
slowly. The sky seems low, gray, but penetrated with a diffuse light. My
friends have gone on muleback to the source of the lava. On his return,
Joe, transported: "You can barely believe what you see... It's unimaginable." He's right. My heart is giving me trouble, I wander the
plateau, contemplating. Indios are playing cards in scattered groups.
Americans return out of breath from a climbing path that runs over
the lava. People count for little in this primordial desert of the beginning or the end of the world. A fat gentleman with a ruddy head like
a toad's amicably hails me from his car, and we smoke together for a
moment—and I realize he's a madman, a real madman, lost, fearful,
eyes bulging. He suddenly starts in reciting Latin verses to me, a text
from Quixote. He tells me he's a professor at an American university,
then looks at me with fright, steps back. I sense that he thinks I'm
going to leap at his throat. He's wearing a woolen jacket with white
and blue stripes, which makes him look like a fat sailor or a jailbird.

THE ISLAND

The island[9] is small, sheer, rocky, of volcanic formation. Basalts. Alleys
of primitive staircases. Everyone there runs around barefoot. Seven
kilometers from Pátzcuaro. Under cloudy skies we cross the lake. Swells
and waves, the motorboat is roughly knocked about, the spray soaks
us. Wind. Then the sun, enchanting and harsh.

A few cows, lots of pigs and piglets, fowl, much decorative vegetation,

9. The isle of Janitzio on Lake Pátzcuaro.

a cascade of flowers, the site is one of pure grace, very beautiful, the vastness of the neighboring lake and its blue, green, red hills in the distance wherever you look. Dilapidated houses. It feels abandoned. No wood to maintain or reconstruct them; it's become too expensive. No running water or electricity. There's a nonfunctioning electric power plant. It's damaged and repairs would be too costly. A thousand inhabitants, Tarascos, fishermen. Large nets stretched out everywhere in the morning sun. Around three o'clock they go fishing. The island is an autarchy, tiny and poor. No crops, not even any vegetables: scattered lemon and fig trees. The people live exclusively on the products of their fishing. A very handsome and intelligent lad tells us that a fisherman earns about thirty pesos (six dollars!) a month. A few of them are able to fish the *lobina negra*[10] with their javelins, and they earn a few dozen pesos a day for three or four months, but the trout seek out deep waters, move away, it doesn't last. (It must also be hunted in clear water and aquatic plants abound.)

Daily life is nothing but work, peaceful, without agitation or noise, with serenity, even with good humor and gaiety. Peralte says: "The Tarascos are Indios who know how to laugh." It's true: they laugh among themselves. The big and little girls who fetch water from the lake, dressed exactly like adult women, walk gracefully, a vase on their shoulders, laughing as they take the goat paths—showing off their beautiful teeth. Often charming Asiatic faces, rather broad, prominent cheekbones, wide-open straight brown eyes, a mischievous glance. Black or dark brown hair, abundant, which they take good care of, washed, braided, then gathered in pigtails falling to their waist. Heavy skirts with multiple pleats cinched at the waist. Small red jumpers striped with black or brightly colored checks. Green, pink, violet blouses (and sometimes dresses) always of bright or light colors. Silver earrings, necklaces of colored glass, silver or often coral. The girls and young women walk with a balanced step, all the movement in the hips, the upper body remaining straight, leaning a little forward. Faces brown, tending towards lemony yellow among the young, burned and black

10. Bass or trout.

among the old. Tchitché-Ivé, eighty years old, serves us, vigorous, alert, active, bony, the sculptured features of an old European peasant.

The boys wear shirts often reduced to a web of shreds, revealing their bronzed flesh, their (dirty) white underwear reaching their ankles, like many of the men. —Sombreros, serapes; women and young girls dark blue rebozos with black stripes; the child rolled inside against their breast. The children do housework from age two or three. The women crush the maize by hand, cook, nurse, carry water, clean. "Their life is slavery," the young fisherman tells us.

In houses open to the cool, but decorated with pottery and painted dishware, (G. G. enchanted by the religious images), people live as in huts. Squatting female figures grinding maize. Mother, in the doorway, combing her daughter's long hair—serious, almost pretty—not without hunting for nits... Two little girls on the threshold embroidering attentively, not even turning their heads as I pass. One has a sweet, Asiatic profile, her hair spread over her neck and back. Squatting old men weaving or repairing the nets, a labor that never ends. Four russet piglets, small and still thriving, play at fighting, charging at each other. A litter of funny little white piglets with big, black spots suckling an enormous sow.

Broken windowpanes, wobbly staircases. Laughing children half-heartedly fighting each other. Some of them, under the age of ten, in white rags, almost naked; the others, older than ten, in sombreros and serapes.

Economy. The island exports fish to Pátzcuaro and the villages on the coast. Sometimes pork, a small amount of fowl. It imports firewood, precious (and now very expensive), candles, gas, string for nets, cloth... Naturally it imports much less than it needs. No hunger, but poor and primitive conditions, ceaseless labor without any possible improvement.

Young people find work on the outside, as far away as the United States, and bring back a little money. Not a single foreigner lives in Janitzio. Father P. himself is four-fifths Yaqui Indian with, it is said, Tarasca blood. But he's of the type of a corpulent "redskin" of the Far West.

The only well-constructed houses on the island, white with tile roofs, are the schools, the creation of General Lázaro Cárdenas. Janitzio: tiered houses, most with balconies/terraces facing the lake, where people work. The gestures of the old men tirelessly "sewing" the nets. Neat, crowded interiors; darkness, primitive humility.

Morality: neither murder nor theft nor adultery; brawls between drunken men, but no vendettas.

P. tells us about a recent wedding. (He is *the* popular man, the doctor, the obstetrician, the godfather, the spokesman, etc.) 1. The *novio* carries off the *novia*[11] in his canoe and takes her to his parents. Age: 15 to 17, sometimes younger. 2. The kidnapper's parents offer gifts to the young girl's parents, asking for forgiveness. This is a rite more than anything. The date of the nuptials is set. 3. Party. Canoes and pirogues with fishing nets decorated with flowers, fabric, and bright-colored papers. Crossing of the lake, wedding at the church of Pátzcuaro. 4. Triumphant return, recrossing of the lake in decorated canoes, the largest one bearing the newlyweds. The parents, in their finest attire. Others follow: musicians, guitars, songs and fireworks, rockets. The sun takes part in the festivities. 5. Rites. The courtyard. The first day the bride must grind the maize and prepare the ingredients for all the dough, a task that takes twenty-four hours: she demonstrates that she will know how to feed husband and children. The second day, processions from house to house. At the end of one ceremony the groom kisses his parents' feet. Familial submission. Dances, song, fireworks, some get drunk. The third day the newlyweds separately receive the advice of the elderly relatives and finally spend the night together, on a *petate* or plank bed.

Few fiestas: weddings, religious festivals, the great festival of the dead on November 2.

July 11, 1947—Young people from the village came to the terrace of the villa to sing with us in Tarasco and Spanish. Carmen de la Vega sang for them as well, accompanying herself on the guitar. Little conventional cabaret expressiveness, but it pleases. Dances. Warm atmosphere. A

11. Fiancé and fiancée.

half dozen Indios with broad hats, completely motionless, huddled in the shadow, respond along with us. Electric torches and candles burn behind the windows, giving off a little light. In the alleys below us, beneath the flowered shrubbery, in the darkness, glow two red points, cigarettes: the young people listen, motionless.

THE ASSASSIN AND HIS WIFE (J.)

August 4, 1947—The prison of Lecumberri (La Penitenciaría) has the classic look of all those built at the end of the last century. It reminds me of Saint-Gilles prison in Brussels and the one in Liège. A wide, two-story yellow-gray facade; walls and guard towers, crenellations. In front of it a wide, abandoned square, lots of trees. People idling. Slovenly guards, sitting on chairs, reading newspaper at the side entrances. A central carriage entrance; after passing through an antechamber one immediately enters the office of the director. It's four steps from the sidewalk. Relaxed surveillance.

The office is spacious, untidy. Doors and walls dirty. A sofa, a desk.

A young woman is already there when I am brought in. I saw her arrive when I was on the street. Medium height, plump and muscular, a neat waist. Dressed showily, elegantly, in her own way. The elegance of the wives of noncoms. Bright green suit of light silk, beautiful green, transparent high-heeled shoes, sunglasses with green frames, slanted Chinese-style. But it was overcast at 9:00 in the morning. The glasses are a precaution, but against whom or what? She is no longer wearing them; she's reading a newspaper. Between thirty and thirty-five, has lived a lot. Not in the least Mexican-looking. (Because of her full cheeks and light skin she puts me in mind of an ordinary Russian woman.) Dark auburn hair. Square face, delicate, straight nose, wide at the base. Flat planes, the lower half of her face vulgar, revealing a hard life. Her eyes are long, narrow, the pupils coffee colored, very dark. Her eyebrows dyed. Heavily made up. Strong, manicured hands with short fingers, the nails discreetly polished their natural color. —Roquelia Mendoza Buen-Abad,* Mexican. The name indicates Syrian origins, Abad. All of this is perhaps false.

Jackson Mornard enters with a rapid step. He's shocked when he sees me, but instantly regains his self-control. Tall, well built, vigorous, supple, even athletic. Thick necked, athletic, a strong, well-formed head. A man with animal vigor. Glasses, a fleeting gaze, sometimes hard and revealing. His features are sharp, fleshy, vigorous. All in all a handsome man, a strong nose, a mouth both thin and fleshy, bold. A strong chin, dimpled, jutting, and round. A square, elongated face. Thick hair, slightly curly, dark brown. Very well dressed: coffee-colored leather jacket (suede?); expensive. Under it a silk sport short, fashionable, khaki. Khaki gabardine slacks with a sharp crease; yellow shoes, good soles. Assurance and physical well-being in his bearing.

I try to figure out his type. Not Jewish. Or Russian. Or Belgian, French, or a common Spaniard. I'm confused and proceed by process of elimination, in vain. I think of the types I don't know well: Balkan, Turk, Caucasian, Arab, Syrian. Finally, the Syrian, Arab, and Turk seem to me the most appropriate: they are also found in the Caucasus. No precise clues.

It seems to me they are visibly struck and embarrassed by my presence, even though I pretend to be busy with a file in front of me. There are moments when their concern is visible. She plays at cheerfulness, puts her hand on his knee. They hold hands affectionately. Nevertheless, several times they look at me as if looking in front of them randomly. Does he know my photos?

Viewed head-on, his face expresses permanent nervousness and tension, insufficiently dominated by a constant effort of will. The creases around his jaw give him an evil look. Once, we stared at each other for a long moment. He has slit eyes beneath a massive brow. The pupils coffee colored, almost black. His gaze is terrible with concentration, darkness, nightmare and defensive attack. The gaze of a hunted but strong man. It's said of him that he's proud, sure of himself, scornful. I view him as hunted, evil, dangerous.

I observe that the woman has *the same gaze* but in more neutral tones. Her entire face bespeaks tension, self-control, aggressive defensiveness. Why? She is not at all some little Mexican employee with a crush on a prisoner; she is a strong woman who is consciously fulfilling a difficult mission. A dangerous woman. I think that this very evening she'll transmit her report giving a detailed description of me. Vis-à-vis Jackson she is perhaps sincerely playing her role. Observing her caresses I nevertheless thought of professionals, whose tired, made-up face, rosy coloring, and painted mouth, wide and mobile, she has. Almost pretty when she smiles. Common.

It seems she was accompanying her sister who was visiting a prisoner named Crispi. That is how she met J., and they fell for each other. All of this could have been arranged, her identity could be fake. In any case, she has the complete confidence of the secret apparatus. For years Jackson received his meals from his defense attorney, Medellín Ostos; now he receives them from his "wife." Roquelia lives (Puente Alvarado II—?) with her mother or mother-in-law, Madame Crispi, who does the cooking; a teenage girl delivers the meals. R. says that J. is extremely distracted, "to such a point that he doesn't see the salt on the table." This is understandable. She's dressed well beyond the means of a petty employee, changes her clothes often, always wears sunglasses (when arriving) whose frames are the color of her attire. This is how I recognized her. Well paid. Recently worked at the Distrito Federal (where the Stalinist A. C. is an important functionary, our Communist defamer in *Popular* in 1941). A short time ago, since the change in J.'s regime, she was assigned to work at the union of functionaries, probably controlled by the Communists (etc., etc.). It should be noted that the secretary of the prison, José Fara (pro-Communist), is also of Syrian origin.

He: a strong brute with practical intelligence. Nothing of an intellectual. Thick. Opaque. The type of a noncom in the secret service. He lives in a nightmare, knowing that the service will protect him up until the moment they impose on him his escape and "disappearance," or until the moment it has him killed in prison in order to suppress this embarrassing witness. His only possible salvation would be total treason, but to attempt this under poor conditions would be suicide. He could request conditional release in three years. Depending on the political situation. Can an unidentified prisoner, secret agent of a totalitarian power, be granted conditional release? Release with the assistance of the secret service would mean his "disappearance." He knows and endlessly weighs this. I'm told he is afraid of two prisoners housed in the same security unit with him: the influential "Diablo" Huitron, who commanded a whole series of crimes, and Pancho Pistolas,[12] a killer-for-hire. He knows that if they decide to kill him, the secret service must remain outside of all suspicion.

In 1939–1940 poor Sylvia Agelov was nothing but an instrument for him. He now knows that Roquelia is probably nothing but an instrument in relation to him.

LOMBARDO TOLEDANO FOUNDS A PARTY

October 7, 1947—Until now four parties existed in Mexico: The Institutional Revolutionary Party (PRI), the governmental party founded by the men of the revolution; National Action (AN), the party of the Catholic bourgeoisie, a largely minority party; the Catholic-Indian Synarchist Movement, quite widespread in the countryside, capable of becoming formidable; and the Communist Party, numerically insignificant but relatively strong through its influences and infiltrations, and also because there is no Socialist Party. It is thought that the CP has several thousand members, ten thousand according to the most optimistic observers. Yet it benefits from two factors: the traditional antipathy of the average Mexican towards American capitalism and the prestige of the USSR among intellectuals. It must be noted in this regard that not a single one of the sensational books that over the last few years have revealed the truth about Stalinism has yet been translated in Mexico or Latin America. A few years ago the CP founded a "Socialist League," but this little political masquerade had no impact, having fooled no one.

A few months ago, upon his return from Europe, M. Vicente Lombardo Toledano, president of the Workers' Confederation of Latin America (CTAL) and member of the International Trade Union Federation, shared with the public his enthusiasm for the "new democracy" of Tito and announced the upcoming founding of a large party of the left (?!), the Mexican People's Party (PP). Mr. Lombardo Toledano, whom the newspapers ironically call "the continental leader," is known

12. The name as well of a Disney cartoon character.

above all known for his fidelity to the "general line" of the USSR, a fidelity he has maintained without fail for a good fifteen years, through his approval of the Moscow Trials and the Hitler-Stalin Pact, the campaigns against Trotsky and in support of Trotsky's aggressors, the attacks against antitotalitarian socialist refugees, and the ceaseless apologies for Soviet policies during and after the war, in all circumstance and without exception! For this reason most Mexican newspapers think that the inspiration for the founding of the Partido Popular came to him from afar and on high. They observe that the PP is an application of the popular front tactic successfully applied by the CPs in the Balkan countries and elsewhere.

At first the new party of *fellow travelers*[13] was not taken seriously. The influence of the CP and of Mr. Lombardo Toledano rests largely on good relations in governmental circles organized by the PRI, and it was obvious that an attempt to draw the elements of a new political formation from the PRI would compromise and even risk destroying this influence. But decisions taken had to be applied, it seems. Mr. Lombardo Toledano and his friends went to work. A new review, *Política*, was published, without anyone noticing. A branch of the Mexico City Worker's University, led by the president of the CTAL, was inaugurated in Tampico, the center of the oil industry. Finally, a grand ideological banquet took place in one of the classiest restaurants of Mexico City, the Sans Souci, where it is said the wines are excellent but where the average Mexican can't afford the smallest sandwich. It would have been the perfect place for the gathering of an "un"-popular party...The PP then announced the election of its national executive committee. Lombardo Toledano is naturally its president. The best-known Communist and pro-Communist intellectuals are naturally members. (Messrs. Narciso Bassols,* José Mancisidor, Víctor Manuel Villaseñor,* and...the ex-Trotskyist Diego Rivera!), as well as a few personalities considered to be of the "center right." A recruitment and agitation campaign began across the country, disposing of considerable means.

A new party should, it would seem, have a new program...The

13. In English in the original.

cleverness of the PP is in not having one. Obviously, the aim is to preserve the best possible relations with the authorities and feeding its members with clichés that provoke no disagreements. So what then is its real object? The PP declared itself a friend of the PRI, a supporter of the economic and spiritual development of Mexico (without indicating its methods of choice), prepared to "tenaciously defend the independence and sovereignty of the Mexican nation" (against whom?). It launched an appeal to women. The effect of its declarations is that of hollow phraseology of the same kind we've known in many other countries. Only in Mexico this initiative comes perhaps too late. The international situation is too clear, the United States–USSR conflict too well defined, the internal problems too serious for political maneuvers in the fog to succeed.

Recently, there have been strong reactions against the PP. The PRI expelled two senators from its ranks, Elizondo and Palacios, and a deputy, Vidal Díaz Muñoz, who joined Toledano's party. The Confederation of Mexican Workers (CTM), weakened by a recent split and led by Senator Fernando Amilpa, known until now as a friend of Lombardo Toledano, after some hesitation took a stand against the PP and removed three secretaries from his national committee because of their work for the PP. As a result, the president of the CTAL has no working-class organization behind him; the CTM, over which he had decisive influence since its foundation, is escaping him and condemning his political maneuvers. As head of the CTAL and the International Trade Union Federation, Lombardo Toledano now represents only himself and a few Communist friends. What is more, the fight is not yet over within the CTM, but if the PP organizes indiscipline and local splits within it this will provoke, within an already anemic trade union movement, the most painful crisis, without attaining any real profit for itself. Already General Abelardo Rodríguez, former president of the republic, is categorically denouncing the PP as "divisionist and subordinated to foreign dictators."

An interesting parallel could be drawn between the agitation maintained by [Henry A.] Wallace in the United States and that of Lombardo Toledano in Mexico. But the latter has neither the personality nor the audience of the former. His new political enterprise seems doomed to rapid failure, unless the PP is content to vegetate modestly in the CP's wake, which its name predestines it for. PP (pronounced "Pepe" in Spanish) is a nickname for Joseph, and Stalin is sometimes called "Tío Pepe," Uncle Joe...[14]

MODIGLIANI

November 1947—Giuseppe Emanuele Modigliani* died in early October in Rome at the age of seventy-nine. An Italian Jew, he had been, since his youth, a member of the working-class and socialist movement of Italy and Europe, and he became one of its most illustrious and noble figures. A moderate socialist, more humanist in truth than reformist, he'd known the times of optimism and those of distress, confronting them with the same intellectual firmness. Internationalist during World War I, admirer of the Russian Revolution, then enemy of the Comintern, intransigent antitotalitarian, he had, in Italy itself, fought relentlessly against fascism. When his friend Matteoti was assassinated by Mussolini's accomplices, Modigliani made himself the widow's lawyer, the accuser of the dictator, the first intrepid defender of a great memory. He was soon forced to emigrate and continued his combat overseas. He lived mainly in France. He was one of the few socialist leaders to contribute to the impartial investigation of the Moscow Trials and concluded it was a sham. France's collapse in 1940 forced him onto the road, but he refused to emigrate to America. He did not have doubt in the cause of the democracies or in the imminent fall of fascism and, though threatened with being turned over to Mussolini's Italy by Vichy, felt that his place was in France. We have reason to think that at the last minute, when the Nazis were marching on the Mediterranean, an American committee facilitated his escape to Switzerland. He later returned to Rome in order to fight the pro-Communist tendency in the Socialist Party, led by Nenni. Soon illness, more exactly the natural exhaustion of a noble vigor, overcame him.

There was in him a truly natural nobility, made of serenity, intellectual elevation, devotion to the cause of a European renaissance, and

14. In English in the original.

also of simplicity. We have no doubt but that his exemplary name will remain among most worthy in the history of socialism.

The Italian-Jewish family of Modigliani is thus twice illustrious. Giuseppe Emanuele Modigliani was the brother of the painter of the same name, who is rightly considered one of the founders of the modern tendencies in art.

GLOSSARY OF NAMES

Abbiate, Roland (François Rossi, Dr. Benoit, and Vladimir Pravdin) (1905–1970)—GPU agent active in Paris during the 1930s, he was the main assassin of Ignace Reiss, killed near Lausanne September 3, 1937. After World War II he was a TASS journalist and Soviet diplomat in the United States.

Abramov, Fedor Fedorovich (1871–1963)—Czarist officer, he fought in World War I and in the White Army during the Civil War. After the kidnapping of the White general Yevgeny Miller he was president of the Paris-based Russian Military Union. He collaborated with the Nazis during World War II.

Abramovich, Alexandre (Zaleski and Albrecht) (1888–1972)—Close to Lenin during the latter's Swiss exile, he was one of the first Comintern delegates to Western Europe. He survived the purges.

Abramovich, Raphael (Adolf Rein) (1880–1963)—Russian socialist member of the Jewish Bund. An internationalist, anti-Zionist, and leader of the left Mensheviks, he briefly collaborated with the Bolsheviks after the October Revolution but left the country in 1920 for Berlin and later New York. He was the father of Mark Rein, assassinated by the GPU in Spain in 1937. Abramovich was the editor of the *Socialist Courier* (*Sotsialisticheskii vestnik*).

Abrams, Jacob (1885–1953)—Of Russian origin, member of a Jewish anarchist group in New York, he was a victim of repression for his opposition to US entry in World War I. Expelled to the USSR in 1921, he joined the Golos Truda (Voice of Labor) group. Expelled from the Soviet Union in 1923, he settled in Mexico in 1926, where he died. Was a member of the exile group Tierra y Libertad and wrote for the review *Mundo*.

Adamov, Arthur (1908–1970)—Russian-born French writer close to the Surrealists who was arrested for his opposition to Vichy.

Adler, Friedrich (1879–1960)—Son of the leader of the Austrian Social-Democratic Workers' Party, Victor Adler, he killed the Austrian prime minister in 1916. Amnestied in 1918, he participated in the worker and soldier council in Vienna. General secretary of the Socialist International from 1923, he resigned from the group in protest against its inaction in the face of fascism.

Agabekov, Grigori Sergeyevich (1896–1938)—Member of the Cheka from 1920, later chief of the eastern section of the GPU, he lived in Kabul, Tehran, and Istanbul. He was one of the first Soviet agents to defect.

Agelov, Sylvia (1910–1995)—American Trotskyist, member of the Socialist Workers Party. In 1938 she traveled to Paris to participate in the founding conference of the Fourth International, and during a meeting orchestrated by the GPU was seduced by Ramón Mercader, Trotsky's future assassin. In January 1940 Agelov joined Trotsky's secretariat in Mexico City, and thanks to her Mercader was able to infiltrate the bunker at Coyoacán. She had nothing to do with the plot.

Agranov, Yakov Saulovich (1893–1938)—Member of the Cheka from 1919, he became Yagoda's deputy in 1933 and his principal assistant in the organization of the great purges. Expelled from the party for his "systematic opposition to socialist legality" he was arrested July 20, 1937, and executed as an "enemy of the people" in August 1938.

Akhmatova, Anna (1889–1966)—Russian poet, one of the principal figures of Acmeism. Her third husband, Nikolai Punin, was detained in 1938 and disappeared after the war. In his writings on literature Serge particularly commented on her romantic verse.

Akulov, Ivan Alexievich (1888–1937)—Vice president of the GPU and attorney general of the USSR between 1933 and 1935. He presided over the first trial of Kamenev and Zinoviev (January 1935) but refused to condemn them for the assassination of Kirov (1934). Executed after being accused of Trotskyism.

Albornoz, Álvaro de (1879–1954)—Politician and writer, several times minister during the second Spanish Republic (1931–1939). Named ambassador to

Paris in July 1936, he lived in exile in Mexico and was head of the Spanish government-in-exile from 1947 to 1951.

Alcón Selma, Marcos (1902–1997)—Catalan anarchist, president of the union of entertainers, he played an important role in the cinema. Exiled to Mexico in 1940, he contributed to the magazines *Regeneración* and *Tierra y Libertad* and was a member of the CNT and the Mexican Anarchist Federation.

Alliluyev, Sergei Yakovlevich (1866–1945)—Railroad worker and Old Bolshevik, he was Stalin's father-in-law. Published his memoirs of the Georgian revolutionary movement in 1946.

Alliluyeva, Nadezhda (Nadya) (1901–1932)—Stalin's second wife and mother of **Svetlana** (1926–2011), she was found dead after an argument with her husband. The official cause of death was peritonitis, but strong suspicions of suicide have dogged her death. Two doctors who refused to sign her death certificate were executed in 1938 at the Trial of the Twenty-One.

Alonso Rodríguez, Elfidio (1905–2001)—Writer and politician from the Canary Islands, he was deputy of the Republican Union in 1936. Editor of the daily *ABC* after the fascist uprising, he went into exile in Mexico, where he continued to work as a journalist.

Alpári, Gyula (1882–1944)—Hungarian Communist, he worked for the Comintern in Germany in the 1920s. Accused of Trotskyism, he managed to escape Stalinist repression and went into exile in France. Arrested by the Gestapo in 1940, he was killed in Sachsenhausen.

Alter, Victor (1890–1943)—Jewish socialist militant, he was exiled to Siberia under the czar and then moved to Great Britain. From 1918 he was in Poland, where he headed the Bund. Arrested in September 1939 in Soviet-occupied Poland, he was released after the German invasion and then arrested again, along with his Bundist comrade Henryk Ehrlich, on Stalin's orders. Both were sentenced to death on December 23, 1941, and executed February 17, 1943.

Álvarez del Vayo, Julio (1891–1975)—Militant of the Spanish Socialist Workers' Party (PSOE), he was a member of the Largo Caballero and Negrín cabinets during the Civil War. Exiled to Mexico after the war, he moved to the left and was expelled from the PSOE, and founded the Revolutionary Anti-fascist and Patriotic Front.

Andreyev, Leonid (1871–1919)—Journalist, photographer, and writer, he supported the February Revolution but opposed the Bolsheviks. Emigrated to Finland, where he died.

Annenkov, Boris (1889–1927)—Military commander of the White Army's Cossacks in Siberia and Kazakhstan, known for his brutality, he formed the Partisan division in 1918 that expelled the Soviets from Siberia. Defeated in 1920, he fled to China. He returned to the USSR in 1926, where he was tried and executed for atrocities during the Civil War.

Antonov-Ovseyenko, Vladimir (1884–1938)—Menshevik militant, he participated in the 1905 revolution in Saint Petersburg. Went into exile in Paris and returned to Russia in 1917, where he led the taking of the Winter Palace. Charged with the repression of Kronstadt (1921) and the peasants of Tambov (1920–1922), he joined the Left Opposition in 1923 and was named to various diplomatic posts. Having gone over to Stalin in 1928, he was named consul in Barcelona in 1936–1937 and participated in the repression of the POUM and the anarchists. Recalled to the USSR in September 1937, where he was arrested and executed.

Araquistáin Quevedo, Luis (1886–1959)—Member of the PSOE since his youth, he became one of its main thinkers. During the Civil War he was ambassador to Germany and France before joining the Republican Army. During his short exile in Mexico he, like Serge, wrote for *Hoy*, criticizing the Communists. He later lived out his exile in Great Britain and Switzerland.

Arenal, Angélica (?–?) and **Luis** (1909–1985)—Angélica was the wife and biographer of Siqueiros; her brother Luis was a painter and sculptor. Both Communists, they were implicated in the assassination attempt on Trotsky of May 24, 1940, led by Siqueiros.

Arquer, Jordi (1907–1981)—Catalan Communist, between 1927 and 1935 he assisted in the creation of the Marxist Study Circle, the Catalan Communist Party, the Worker-Peasant Bloc, and the POUM. After their defeat he went into exile in Mexico, where, along with other members of the POUM, he joined the Socialism and Freedom group.

Arriaga Ochoa, Antonio (1911–1974)—An enthusiastic young man whom Serge met in 1947, became an expert in Mexican history and director of the National History Museum of Chapultepec.

Atl, Dr. (Gerardo Murillo) (1875–1964)—Mexican-born artist who studied in Europe. A seminal national painter and writer, precursor, with Diego Rivera, of the Mexican Muralist movement, teacher of Orozco and Siqueiros in the early 1900s. Long fascinated by volcanoes, in 1950 he published a book on the birth of Parícutin. A longtime, if eccentric, socialist, he veered into anti-Semitism in his later years. Serge was more interested in the man, his art, and his geological thought than in his political incorrectness.

Audry, Colette (1906–1990)—Militant of the Revolutionary Left faction of the French Section of the Workers' International (SFIO) and then of Marceau Pivert's PSOP, she edited a pro-POUM newspaper during the Spanish Civil War. Active in the Resistance in the Grenoble region.

Averbakh, Leopold Leonidovich (1903–1938)—Editor in chief of the literary review *Young Guard*, he was leader of the Russian Association of Proletarian Writers. Brother-in-law and collaborator of NKVD chief Yagoda, Averbakh was arrested and executed along with him in 1938.

Ávila Camacho, Manuel (1897–1955)—President of Mexico from 1940 to 1946. Despite being supported by the left, his administration took a right turn. General Maximino Ávila Camacho was his brother.

Azcárate, Manuel (1916–1998)—Leader of the Unified Socialist Youth and later of the Spanish Communist Party.

Azef, Yevno (1869–1918)—Founder of the Socialist-Revolutionary Party and organizer of the execution of Minister Plehve in July 1904, this agent of the Okhrana, the czar's political police, was unmasked in 1908.

Bakayev, Ivan (1887–1936)—President of the Petrograd Cheka during the Civil War, close to Zinoviev, member of the Soviet executive and the party's control commission, he was expelled and later accepted back into the party. Arrested in 1935 after the Kirov assassination, he was condemned and executed the following year.

Baldwin, Roger (1884–1981)—Founder of the American Civil Liberties Union.

Barga, Corpus (Andrés García de Barga y Gómez de la Serna) (1887–1975)—Spanish journalist and writer, left Republican, he opposed Primo de Rivera's dictatorship. Went into exile in Peru after the Civil War.

Barmine, Alexander (1899–1987)—Soviet soldier and diplomat, his first wife was a relative of Serge's. After participating in the Civil War in the Red Army he was assigned to Persia, Paris, Milan, and Athens. He broke with the regime in 1937 and in 1939 published *Twenty Years in the Service of the USSR*, translated (and according to Serge's son, Vlady, partly written) by Serge. In 1940 Barmine migrated to the United States and served in the army during World War II. He collaborated with the State Department and the CIA during the 1950s.

Bartolí, Josep (1910–1995)—Catalan illustrator, member of the POUM. After being interned in a camp in France, he managed to reach Mexico in 1943, where he worked as an illustrator for *Mundo* and was a friend of Frida Kahlo's. Later moved to the United States.

Basch, Victor (1863–1944)—Hungarian Jew brought to France as a small child. He studied at the Sorbonne and became a university professor at Rennes, where he was a friend of the socialist Jean Jaurès and played an active part in the Dreyfus Affair. He was later president of the French League for the Rights of Man (1926–1944) and was prominent in the Popular Front. In 1918 Basch intervened to have Serge released from the camp of Précigné. Assassinated by the Milice Française on January 10, 1944.

Bassols, Narciso (1897–1959)—Mexican politician and founder in 1929 of the National Revolutionary Party, precursor to the Institutional Revolutionary Party (PRI). Several times minister and ambassador, notably to the League of Nations, where he took a pro-Soviet line. He resigned when President Cárdenas granted Trotsky exile. Back in Mexico, he was accused of facilitating the entrance of Soviet agents into Mexico.

Basteitch (or Basti), **Pavel** (?–?)—Serbian nationalist converted to communism. Returned to occupied Yugoslavia in 1940, where he was murdered in a concentration camp.

Bazarov, Vladimir Alexandrovich (1874–1939)—Marxist economist and philosopher, translator of *Capital*, he was one of the accused at the trial of the Mensheviks but refused to confess.

Bedny, Demyan (1883–1945)—Soviet writer and poet, immensely popular in the 1920s. A Bolshevik since 1912, he was expelled in 1938.

Beimler, Hans (1895–1936)—German Communist, deputy in the Reichstag, incarcerated in Dachau in 1933, he escaped and joined the International Brigades. Those close to him affirm that his death in Madrid was the work of the NKVD.

Beloborodov, Alexander Georgievich (1891–1938)—Bolshevik since 1905, in 1918 he signed the czar's execution order. Member of the Opposition during the 1920s, he was executed in 1938.

Bénédite, Daniel (D. Ungemach) (1912–1990)—Member of the Revolutionary Left tendency of the SFIO and later of the PSOP, from 1940 he was one of Varian Fry's main collaborators in Marseille and lived with Serge and André Breton at Villa Bel-Air. Until 1942 he continued Fry's work after the latter's departure and then participated in the Resistance.

Bergery, Gaston (1892–1974)—Lawyer and originally a member of the Radical Party, he founded an organization that was a precursor to the Popular Front. Elected a deputy in 1936, he supported the Munich Agreements out of pacifism and voted to grant all powers to Pétain in 1940. He was Vichy's ambassador to Moscow and Ankara.

Besteiro Fernández, Julián (1870–1940)—Spanish philosopher and politician, key figure in the PSOE and the UGT, he was president of the Cortés from 1931 to 1933. He called for a negotiated peace with Franco's forces at the beginning of the war, was then ambassador to Great Britain, and, after supporting the Casado junta, was executed by the fascists in 1939.

Blyukher, Vasily Konstantinovich (1889–1938)—Member of the Bolshevik Party in 1916, he became an officer during World War I. His many successes led to his being given command of the Fifty-First Section of the Red Army, which fought the counterrevolutionary Russians and the Czechs. Military adviser in China from 1924 to 1927 and promoted to marshal in 1934, he assumed command of the Red Army in the Far East. After presiding over the trial of the Red Army generals in 1938, he was himself then tried and executed.

Body, Marcel (1894–1984)—Drafted into military service in 1916, this typesetter volunteered to be part of the French military mission in Moscow in 1917. Gone over to the Bolsheviks, he worked as a translator for the Comintern and later alongside Alexandra Kollontai in the Soviet diplomatic service. Back in France, he was expelled from the PCF in 1922.

Bogdanov, Alexander (Alexander Malinovski) (1873–1928)—Philosopher and economist, he joined the Bolsheviks in 1903 and was a target of Lenin's attacks in his 1908 book *Materialism and Empirio-Criticism*. Expelled from the party in 1909, he was an early critic of Leninism.

Boguslavsky, Mikhail Solomonovich (1886–1937)—Printer, member of the Bund, he joined the Bolsheviks in 1907. A member of the United Opposition, he was deported in 1928 before renouncing political activity. Condemned at the second Moscow Trial and executed.

Bombacci, Nicola (1879–1945)—Syndicalist in the CGIL in 1911 and secretary of the Socialist Party from 1917 to 1919, he was arrested for defeatism during World War I. A member of the current favorable to the Soviet Union within the Italian Socialist Party, he represented Italy at the Comintern's Second Congress in 1920. Editor of the party journal *Il Comunista*, he saw affinities between the Bolshevik revolution and the fascist revolution, for which he was expelled in 1927, moving closer to the Fascist Party and finally joining it in 1934. He founded the review *La Verità*, which posited Italy as a "proletarian nation" forced to confront the existing imperialisms. One of the mainstays of Mussolini's Republic of Saló, he was executed along with the Duce.

Bosch, Evgenia Bogdanova (1879–1925)—Bolshevik since 1903, member of the left faction of the party, she held a military command in Ukraine during the Civil War and was later a functionary of the Ministry of the Interior. She committed suicide in January 1925.

Boton, Yves de (1907–1944)—Born in Haifa, this physician was a member of the SFIO and the "What Is to Be Done" group after having been a Trotskyist. Active in the Resistance, he was arrested in August 1944 and executed.

Bouché, Henri (?–1970)—Former student of the philosopher Alain, this specialist in aeronautic matters was a member of the pacifist tendency of the Comité de Vigilance des Intellectuels Antifascistes (CVIA).

Bourtsev, Vladimir Lvovich (1862–1944)—Journalist close to the Socialist-Revolutionaries, he was famous for his campaigns against the police agent Yevno Azef.

Brandel, Kuno (1907–1983)—German syndicalist, journalist, and antifascist militant.

Brandler, Heinrich (1881–1967)—Member of the SPD from 1901, he was a key figure in the Spartacist group, president of the Workers and Soldiers Council of Chemnitz, then copresident of the KPD in 1921. Sentenced to prison after the failure of the "March action," he fled to the USSR, afterward returning to Germany as president of the KPD. Scapegoat for the failure of the insurrection of October 1923, he was relieved of his functions in the KPD the following year and became a central figure of the "right opposition" in the Comintern. Founder of an opposition Communist party in 1929, he went into exile in France in 1933 and obtained a visa for Cuba in 1940.

Brauner, Victor (1903–1966)—Surrealist painter of Jewish-Romanian origin, in 1941 he was with Serge, Breton, and Péret at Villa Bel-Air. He was unable to leave France, though, and in Mexico City Serge, Pivert, and Gorkin organized an exhibit of his works at Gustav Regler's home to support him.

Bredow, Ferdinand von (1884–1934)—German general who was an important figure under the Weimar Republic. Assassinated by the SS.

Breitscheid, Rudolf (1874–1944)—Economist and journalist, he was a member of the German SPD. He emigrated to Switzerland in 1933, then to Paris. Handed over to the Gestapo in 1941, he was deported to Buchenwald and died in an Allied bombing.

Bronstein, Zinaida (or Zina) **Lvovna** (1901–1933)—Eldest daughter of Trotsky, editor at age eighteen of the organ of the Communist Youth of Petrograd, she participated in the struggles of the Left Opposition. Authorized to leave the USSR in 1931 with her son Sieva Volkov, she committed suicide in Berlin.

Bubnov, Andrei Sergeievich (1888–1938)—Member of the Bolsheviks since 1903, he was arrested in 1916 and deported to Siberia. Having become a member of the Moscow Revolutionary Committee in 1917, the following year he joined the left faction of the Bolsheviks. Gone over to Stalin in 1924, he was named head of political control of the Red Army and people's commissar for education (1929–1937). Arrested in 1937, he was executed the following year.

Burnham, James (1905–1987)—Early member of the Trotskyist movement, this Columbia University professor engaged in a polemic with Trotsky on the nature of the USSR and published his most important work, *The Managerial Revolution*, in 1941.

Butterlin, Ernest (1917–1964)—German painter who settled in Ajijic (Jalisco) during the 1930s, where he lived until his death.

Cachin, Marcel (1869–1958)—Longtime member of the leadership of the French Communist Party.

Calas, Nikos (N. Kalamaris) (1907–1988)—Poet of Greek origin, he moved to Paris in 1937. Close to André Breton, he moved to the United States in 1940, where he helped popularize Surrealism.

Caleffi, Giovanna (1897–1962)—Italian anarchist journalist and militant and companion of Camillo Berneri, who was murdered by the Stalinists in Barcelona in 1937. A refugee in France, she was detained in 1940, deported to Germany, and handed over to the Italians. She lived an underground life after her release, reorganizing the anarchist movement.

Calligaris, Luigi (1894–1937?)—Italian Communist worker, he did underground work against fascism and was under house arrest in Trieste. He managed to flee to France and then the USSR, where he worked in a factory in Moscow with other Italians. After Kirov's assassination he was arrested as a spy, denounced in the Italian Communist press, and died in deportation to Siberia.

Cannon, James P. (1890–1974)—Founder and leader of the American Trotskyist Socialist Workers Party.

Cárdenas del Río, Lázaro (1895–1970)—Career officer and president of Mexico from 1934 to 1940. A central figure of postrevolutionary Mexico, his time in office was marked by the nationalization of oil, the promotion of "socialist education," the support of the Spanish Republic, and agrarian reform. Trotsky and Serge owed him their Mexican visas.

Cardona Rosell, Mariano (1900–?)—Anarchist economist and militant. He died in Mexico sometime in the 1970s.

Carrington, Leonora (1917–2011)—Mexican artist of British origin, novelist, and Surrealist painter.

Chabion, Mikhail (?–?)—Russian history professor arrested in 1938.

Challaye, Félicien (1875–1967)—Professor of philosophy, journalist, writer, anticolonialist militant, pacifist, and Dreyfusard, he was a member of the Central Committee of the League for the Rights of Man and president of the International League of Fighters for Peace. During the war he wrote for socialist-leaning collaborationist newspapers, was tried for collaborationism and acquitted in 1946, and continued to be active in pacifist groups.

Chamberlin, William Henry (1897–1969)—American journalist and historian, he was at first sympathetic to the Russian Revolution but became a harsh critic of communism after a long stay as correspondent in the USSR, where he witnessed the famine in Ukraine (1932–1933).

Chardon, Pierre (Maurice Charron) (1892–1919)—Individualist anarchist, he was demobilized in 1914 for health reasons and opposed those anarchists who supported the defense of democratic France. From 1916 he was the main collaborator of Emile Armand on the review *Par-delà la Mêlée* and later, after Armand's arrest, *La Mêlée*. Serge wrote for both of these under the name Le Rétif.

Chernov, Viktor (1873–1952)—Socialist-Revolutionary who served in Kerensky's government, he went into exile in the United States after the Bolshevik victory.

Chevalier, Paul (Leo Valiani) (1909–1999)—Italian antifascist and Communist. He lived in exile in France before going to fight in Spain. In Mexico he broke with the CP and joined the Socialism and Freedom circle. He returned to Italy in 1943 and participated in the Giustizie e Libertà resistance movement.

Chtchegolev, Pavel Elisseievich (1877–1931)—Russian historian, along with Serge and others he founded the first Museum of the Revolution.

Chvernik, Nikolai (1888–1970)—Bolshevik since 1905, he became a docile apparatchik who climbed the ranks to become president of the Supreme Presidium of the Supreme Soviet of the USSR (that is, titular head of state), from 1946 to 1953.

Ciliga, Anton (Ante) (1898–1992)—Croatian born, he was a militant in the Yugoslavian Communist Party and became a member of its Central Committee. In 1925 he moved to Moscow, where he taught history and joined the Trotskyist Opposition. He was arrested in 1930 and deported; thanks to the Italian citizenship he had obtained though his wife, he was able to leave the USSR for France in 1935. Imprisoned during the war, he later moved to Rome.

Codovilla, Victorio (1894–1970)—Italian-born immigrant to Argentina, he joined the Argentine CP in 1924 and was its leader until the 1960s. Head of the Latin American Bureau of the Comintern, he carried out various missions in Spain between 1932 and 1938.

Comorera i Soler, Joan (1894–1958)—Stalinist Communist and secretary of the Unified Socialist Party of Catalonia (PSUC), he played an important role as member of the Generalitat in the persecution of the POUM and the members of the CNT-FAI. In exile in Mexico he was one of the partisans of the campaign against antitotalitarian socialists. He returned to Spain clandestinely in 1950, was captured in 1954, and spent the rest of his life in prison.

Companys i Jover, Lluís (1882–1940)—President of the Generalitat, he was handed over to the Francoists by the Gestapo and executed.

Cordero Amador, Raul (1896–1989)—Costa Rican pedagogue who migrated to Mexico in 1921 and founded the Mexican Academy of Education.

Crémieux, Benjamin (1888–1944)—Member of the editorial committee of Gallimard publishers and one of the leading literary critics between the two world wars, he was a particular bête noire of the French right. Member of the Combat resistance group, he was arrested in 1943 and died in Buchenwald.

Dan, Fyodor (Fedor Ilyich Gurvich) (1871–1947)—Social-Democrat and opponent of the Bolsheviks, he was a member of the small group of opposition deputies in the Russian Constituent Assembly. He was arrested in 1921 and sent into exile.

Dean, Vera Micheles (1903–1972)—American political scientist.

Deborin, Abram Moiseyevich (1881–1963)—Steelworker turned philosophy student, he was an early supporter of Lenin but in 1907 went over to the Mensheviks, though he joined the Soviet Communist Party in 1920. Member of the Soviet Academy of Sciences; his ideas were dismissed as suffering from "Menshevik idealism."

Debs, Eugene (1855–1926)—Railroad worker and union leader, America's greatest socialist.

Denegri, Ramón (1887–1955)—Participant in the Mexican Revolution, he was a follower of President Lázaro Cárdenas and was several times a Mexican ambassador, including to Spain in 1936. He was a close friend of Serge during his Mexican exile.

Dewey, John (1859–1952)—Pragmatist philosopher, he presided over the International Investigative Committee into the Moscow Trials and, at the request of Dwight and Nancy Macdonald, wrote a letter to American authorities requesting a visa for Serge in 1941.

Diamant, Max (1908–1992)—German socialist who lived in exile after 1933 and was a representative of the Emergency Rescue Committee in Mexico.

Dimitrijević, Dragutin (1876–1917)—Colonel in the Serbian Army and leader of the Black Hand, a secret organization. Was one of the people responsible for the attack on Franz Ferdinand in Sarajevo.

Doriot, Jacques (1898–1945)—Former Communist leader who went over to fascism and was leader of France's most important fascist party, the Parti Populaire Français.

Drobnis, Yakov Naumovich (1890–1937)—Bolshevik from 1906, he was one of the leaders in Ukraine during the revolution. Supporter of the Left Opposition, he rallied to the government in 1929 and was executed in 1937.

Duby, Gertrude (1901–1993)—Swiss-born Communist, journalist, photographer, and ethnologist. Member of the KPD and the Comintern, she left Europe for Mexico in 1939 and settled in Veracruz, where she supported Spanish Communist refugees. She later lived in Chiapas and married the Danish ethnologist Franz Blom, dedicating her life to the *lacandona* forest.

Ducomet, Pierre-Louis (1902–?)—French communist, he participated in GPU activities and was arrested and interrogated during the investigation into Ignace Reiss's assassination.

Dumbadze, Lado (?–1936)—One of the principal Communist leaders in Georgia, he was president of the Tiflis Soviet at the end of the Civil War. Member of the Left Opposition, he was deported in 1928 and died as a result of inadequate medical care.

Duret, Jean (François Korla) (1900–1971)—Of Polish origin, this history professor at the University of Moscow worked as a commercial representative of the USSR in Paris. Refusing to return to the Soviet Union, he was expelled from the CP. Active in the CGT.

Dzerzhinsky, Felix (1876–1926)—First head of the Cheka, greatly admired by Serge, who called him "a man of faith." Died of a heart attack after a stormy meeting of the Central Committee.

Eastman, Max (1883–1969)—Longtime left-wing writer, close to Trotskyism, he shifted to the right after the Moscow Trials. He helped Serge get a visa for Mexico.

Eberlein, Hugo (1887–1941)—Close to Rosa Luxemburg and member of the SPD from 1905, he was one of the organizers of the Spartacist group. Later a deputy to the Prussian Landtag, he worked for the Comintern, was arrested in Moscow in 1937, and was shot by a firing squad in 1941.

Efron, Sergei Yakovlevich (1893–1941)—White Army officer and husband of the poet Marina Tsvetaeva, he worked for the Soviet secret service in Paris in the hope of being allowed to return to Russia. Recruited by the GPU, compromised in the Reiss assassination, he managed to reach the USSR, where he was executed.

Ehrenburg, Ilya (1891–1967)—Russian journalist, he went into exile after the 1905 revolution and lived in Paris from 1908 to 1917. He returned to Russia and was one of the most important figures in Soviet journalism and propaganda.

Ehrlich, Henryk (1882–1942)—Bund leader and member of the executive committee of the Second International, he was arrested in the Soviet Zone. He was sentenced to death but his sentence was commuted to life imprisonment. Freed after the Nazi attack on the USSR, he was again arrested and executed soon thereafter. His execution, along with that of Victor Alter, was announced only in 1943.

Engler, Victor (1885–1935)—Glazier and later dockworker, after a period as a Communist he was close to the Communist oppositionists around *Révolution prolétarienne*, defending Serge at the 1933 CHTU Congress.

Epe, Heinz (Walter Held) (1910–1942)—Leader of the German section of the Left Opposition, he was sentenced to death by the Gestapo but took refuge in Norway, from which he tried to reach America with his wife and son. Passing through the USSR in order to do so, he and his family were arrested and executed.

Feuchtwanger, Franz (1908–1991)—Militant in the KPD, he went into exile in Mexico in 1940, and though never openly critical of Stalinism he was expelled from the Party and dedicated the rest of his life to the study of pre-Hispanic cultures.

Filonov, Pavel (1883–1941)—Avant-garde painter, he died during the siege of Leningrad.

Fimmen, Eduard Carl (Edo) (1881–1942)—Dutch unionist, general secretary of the International Transport Workers Federation from 1919 to 1942, he was the guiding spirit behind its antiracist, anticolonialist, antifascist, and internationalist stands.

Fischer, Ruth (née Elfriede Eisler) (1895–1961)—After studying in Vienna, she was active on the left wing of the KPD. Expelled in 1926, she attempted to bring together the Communist oppositionists in the Leninbund. She emigrated in 1933, first to Prague, then Paris, where she collaborated with Trotsky. She made it to Cuba in 1940 and later the United States.

Fourrier, Marcel (1895–1966)—Journalist at *L'Humanité* and *Clarté*, he was expelled from the PCF in 1928. After a time among Communist oppositionists, he joined the SFIO and after the merger of the Resistance newspaper *Franc-tireur*, which he edited, with *Libération*, he was editor in chief of the latter until his death.

Fraenkel, Michael (1896–1957)—American writer and philosopher, he emigrated to France in the 1920s. Upon his return to the United States he founded Carrefour Press. He went to Mexico in 1940 with his wife, Daphne Moschos Gillam (1900–1991), frequenting antitotalitarian socialist circles.

Francés, Esteban (1913–1976)—Catalan Surrealist painter who, after spending time in Paris, went to Mexico in 1940 and five years later settled in the United States.

Frank, Pierre (1905–1984)—A Communist from age fifteen, he took Trotsky's side in 1927 and two years later participated in the launch of the first French Trotskyist newspaper, *La Vérité*, and in 1930 the founding of the Ligue Communiste. A central figure of the Trotskyist movement until his death.

Fränkel, Fritz (1892–1944)—Physician, neurologist, and psychoanalyst, he was the author of important studies on cocaine and opiates. After World War I he collaborated with the Spartacists and was a founder of the KPD. Arrested by the Nazis in 1933, he escaped to France, where he was a friend of Arthur Koestler and Hannah Arendt. He abandoned his studies in 1936 in order to create the sanitary service of the International Brigades in Spain. He broke with the KPD in 1937, moved to France, and then in 1941 to Mexico, joining the Socialism and Liberty Group. In a letter Serge called him "my closest friend."

Frolova, Vera Vladimirovna (?–?)—Serge's older half sister, member of the Translator's Union of Leningrad, she was deported and her daughter committed suicide.

Frossard, Ludovic-Oscar (1889–1946)—Teacher and socialist militant, he was secretary of the SFIO in 1918 and supported adherence to the Comintern at the Tour Congress that founded the PCF. General secretary of the PCF, he resigned in 1923, rejoined the SFIO, and was minister several times.

Fry, Varian (1907–1967)—American journalist sent to Marseille in 1940 by the ERC in response to the outrage in the United States caused by the clause in the Franco-German armistice calling for the French to turn over refugees from the Reich, he founded the CAS, which saved and assisted thousands of people, including Serge.

Gaggi, Otello (1896–1945)—Italian worker and antifascist, he went into exile in the USSR in 1922. Arrested in 1934, he was deported to Siberia as a "Trotskyist counterrevolutionary." Serge requested assistance for him from PCI leader Palmiro Togliatti in 1944, without success.

Gemähling, Jean (1912–2003)—Paris-born chemist, he worked with Varian Fry and was later active in the Resistance.

Gershuni, Grigori (1870–1908)—One of the founders of the Socialist-Revolutionary Party, he was a member of its combat group and died in exile in Switzerland.

Ghezzi, Francesco (1893–1942)—Italian anarcho-syndicalist, he was a refugee in the USSR, where he worked in a factory. Arrested in 1929, he was the object of an international support campaign, which resulted in his release in 1931. He was rearrested in 1937 and died in the camp at Vorkuta.

Ginzburg, Yevgenia (1904–1977)—Russian writer and history professor, she was sentenced to ten years' imprisonment for Trotskyist activity and wrote of her experiences in *Within the Whirlwind*.

Gironella, Enrico (E. Adroher Pascual) (1908–1987)—POUM militant and commissar general for transport in the Generalitat in 1936, he was arrested in 1937 for his participation in the May events and sentenced to fifteen years' imprisonment. He escaped to France and reached Mexico in 1940, working with Serge in the Socialism and Freedom group and editing its review, *Mundo*. He returned to Europe in 1946 and Spain in 1947.

Gitton, Marcel (1903–1941)—Construction worker who climbed the ranks of the PCF, reaching the third-highest post. In November 1939 he left the party as a result of the Hitler-Stalin Pact. Accused by the PCF of being a police informant, he founded a collaborationist party and was executed by a Communist commando.

Goldman, Albert (A. Verblen) (1897–1960)—American Trotskyist lawyer, he was the defense attorney at the Dewey Commission.

Gorkin, Julián (1901–1986)—Spanish Communist journalist, he worked in Moscow for several years until joining the Left Opposition. One of the founders of the POUM, he was international secretary and editor of its newspaper, *La Batalla*. Arrested along with the leadership of the party, he was tried and sentenced. He was able to flee to France and then Mexico and was close to Serge and the other antitotalitarian socialists.

Gots, Avram Rafaelovich (1882–1940)—Revolutionary militant, veteran of 1905 and 1917, he was one of the twelve principal defendants in the trial of the Socialist-Revolutionaries in 1922.

Grabski, Stanislaw (1871–1949)—Polish nationalist politician. Imprisoned in the USSR, upon his release he joined the exile government in London.

Groman, Vladimir Gustatovich (1874–1932)—Menshevik who went over to the Bolshevik government, he was arrested in 1930 and sentenced to ten years in the trial of the Mensheviks.

Grylewicz, Anton (1885–1971)—German mechanic, he participated in the preparations for the failed insurrection of 1923. Member of the Opposition in Germany, he went over to Trotskyism. He went into exile in Prague in 1933, and in 1937 was victim of a plot by the Soviet secret services with the aim of organizing a Moscow Trial in Prague, but he was acquitted. He went into exile in Cuba, where he lived until 1955.

Guerrero, Xavier (1896–1974)—Mexican painter and Communist, he was one of the main figures of the muralist movement and founder of the Communist newspaper *El Machete*.

Guilbeaux, Henri (1885–1938)—French writer and journalist of anarchist-pacifist tendencies. Sentenced to death for contact with the enemy, he went to Moscow in 1919 and was correspondent for *L'Humanité*. He returned to France in 1932 and died in poverty.

Guiteras Holmes, Antonio (1906–1935)—Cuban revolutionary leader, engaged in the fight against the dictator Machado. After the fall of the latter he participated in the "hundred-day government" before being assassinated by Batista's henchmen.

Gumilev, Nikolai Stepanovich (1886–1921)—Husband of Anna Akhmatova and one of Russia's great poets, he was arrested by the Cheka and executed. Serge fought in vain to save his friend's life and reports in his memoirs that when he asked Dzerzhinsky "if it was possible to execute one of the two or three greatest poets of Russia, Dzerzhinsky answered: Can we make an exception for a poet?"

Habaru, Augustin (1898–1944)—Born in Belgium, named editor of the Belgian Communist Party newspaper in 1924. Henri Barbusse named him editor of the weekly magazine *Monde* four years later. He joined the French Resistance in 1940 and was executed in Savoy by the Germans.

Hansen, Joseph (1910–1979)—American Trotskyist and Trotsky's secretary from 1937 to 1940. One of the principal leaders of the SWP.

Hasenclever, Walter (1890–1940)—German poet and dramaturge, his work was banned by the Nazis and he went into exile in France. Incarcerated as an "enemy alien," he committed suicide at the concentration camp at Milles to avoid being handed over to the Gestapo.

Hasfeld, Marcel (1889–1984)—Founder of the Librairie du Travail publishing house, he published several books by Serge and about Serge's case.

Hazard, John N. (1909–1995)—Pioneer in the study of the USSR in the United States.

Heidenreich, Carl (1901–1965)—German painter, his pro-Communist positions earned him the ire of the Nazis. Fled to the United States with the assistance of Varian Fry.

Heijenoort, Jean van (1912–1986)—Born in France to Dutch parents, this mathematician was Trotsky's secretary from 1932 to 1939 and secretary of the Fourth International in New York during World War II. At the end of the war, as a result of disagreements with the International's leadership, he ceased all political activity.

Helfer (or Guelfer), **Georges** (?–?)—Member of the French military mission in Russia, he joined the French Communist Group in late 1918.

Herbart, Pierre (1903–1974)—French writer and associate of André Gide, he joined the PCF in 1932 and was named editor of *La Littérature internationale* in Moscow in 1935. He accompanied Gide on the trip that resulted in *Retour de l'URSS* and was involved in the polemic that followed its publication, breaking with the PCF.

Hernández Tomás, Jesús (1907–1971)—Founding member of the Spanish Communist Party, he was elected to the Central Committee in 1930 and sent to Moscow. From 1936 he edited the party paper, *Mundo Obrero*. Minister under the Republic, he fled to Moscow after its overthrow and lived there until his expulsion from the party.

Hidalgo y Plaza, Manuel (1878–1967)—Chilean worker, he was among the founders of the Socialist Workers Party in 1912. After becoming a Communist, he joined the Trotskyist movement. Chile's ambassador to Mexico from 1939 to 1943.

Hilferding, Rudolf (1877–1941)—Marxist economist and main theoretician of the German Social-Democratic Party during the Weimar period.

Hindus, Maurice (1891–1969)—American journalist and writer, contributor to *The Nation*. At the end of his life he adopted a critical position towards the Soviet government.

Hirsch, Werner (1899–1941)—Militant in the KPD, editor in chief of *Rote Fahne*, and close collaborator of Thaelmann, he was arrested by the Nazis, savagely tortured, and then freed. Called to Moscow from his Prague exile, he was arrested for "counterrevolutionary Trotskyist activities" and sentenced to ten years in prison in 1937. Died while in prison.

Hoelz, Max (1889–1933)—Tireless KPD militant, member of the KPD's combat forces, he spent many years in prison. Threatened by the Nazis, he fled to Moscow, where the NKVD attempted to implicate him in an antigovernment plot. He "drowned" during a "boating accident."

Holitscher, Arthur (1869–1941)—Budapest-born bank employee turned writer, he lived in Paris and Munich, where he became editor of the review *Simplicissimus*. His books were burned by the Nazis, and he left Germany for Paris and then Geneva, where he died in poverty.

Istrati, Panaït (1884–1935)—French-language Romanian writer, comrade, and friend of Serge, with whom he coauthored (along with Souvarine) a trilogy entitled *Toward the Other Flame*, extremely critical of the Soviet regime. Oppositionist, he was attacked by both the Stalinists and the fascists.

Itkine, Sylvain (1908–1944)—Actor and leader of workers' theater groups, he appeared in *La Grande illusion* and *Le Crime de M. Lange*, and directed *Ubu enchaîné* by Alfred Jarry. He met Serge in 1940 and remained in France, participating in the Resistance in Lyon. He was arrested August 1, 1944, and was killed shortly thereafter.

Ivanov-Razumnik (1878–1946)—Publisher, critic, and historian of Russian literature, he was close to the Left Socialist-Revolutionaries. Formed, along with Blok and Biely, the Scythians and the Free Philosophy Association, which Serge was a member of. Arrested many times between 1919 and 1939, he died after the war in a refugee camp in Germany.

Izquierdo, María (1902–1955)—One of Mexico's most important twentieth-century painters.

Jackson, Frank (actually Jacson)—*see Mercader, Ramón*.

Jager, Alida de (1890–1976)—German journalist active in socialist and union circles in Hamburg. Went into exile in Holland and then Mexico.

Jaquier, Maurice (1906–1976)—Communist and antimilitarist, he nevertheless joined the SFIO. He opposed Blum's policy of nonintervention in Spain and in 1938 he joined Pivert's PSOP. Fought in the Resistance, was briefly a member of the PCF after the war, and then was in the PSU until his death.

Joffe, Adolf Abramovich (1883–1927)—Militant since his adolescence, this Russian revolutionary and diplomat led the Soviet delegation at Brest-Litovsk. Shaken by the struggles within the Bolshevik Party and ill, he committed suicide on November 16, 1927.

Joffe, Maria Mikhailovna (1900–?)—Wife of Adolf Joffe, she was arrested after her husband's suicide, survived deportation, and ended her days in Israel.

Jouhaux, Léon (1879–1954)—Leader of French CGT union 1909–1947. Pro-war in 1914, anti-Bolshevik in 1919, with Communists in Popular Front in 1936. Pacifist in late thirties, then anti-Nazi (survived Buchenwald). Awarded the Nobel Peace Prize in 1951.

Julien, Charles-André (1891–1991)—History professor and socialist militant, he joined the PCF immediately after its foundation but left it in 1926. Dedicated the rest of his life to the fight against colonialism, particularly in the Maghreb.

Junco, Sandalio (?–1942)—Considered the father of Cuban Trotskyism, he became familiar with the Opposition thanks to contacts with Andrés Nin in the USSR. Expelled from the Cuban CP upon his return there.

Jungmann, Eric (1907–1986)—One of the most important functionaries of the German Communist exile community in Mexico. Editor in Mexico of *Freie Deutschland*.

Kaliaev, Ivan Platonovich (1877–1905)—Russian poet and member of the Socialist-Revolutionary Party, he was the assassin of Grand Duke Sergei Alexandrovich. Hanged.

Kantorowicz, Alfred (1899–1979)—Born in Berlin and renowned as a theater critic, he joined the KPD in 1931. Exiled to Paris in 1933, he worked with Willi Münzenberg for the Comintern. Officer in the International Brigades, he was interned in France, reached Marseille, and from there the United States. He returned to Germany in 1946.

Karakhan, Lev (1889–1937)—Armenian, member of the Bolshevik Party from 1917, member of the delegation at Brest-Litovsk, and ambassador to Poland, China, and Turkey, he was arrested and executed during the Great Purge.

Karpov, Nikolai Alexandrovich (1900–1937)—Bolshevik from 1919, commissar in the Red Army in 1919 and 1920, Serge participated in meetings of the Opposition of 1923 held in his home. Executed.

Kartashev, Anton (1875–1960)—Theologian and minister of religious affairs under Kerensky, he was arrested by the Bolsheviks in 1919, went into exile inland and in Paris, where he was active in the White Russian diaspora.

Keppler, Otto (1888–1957)—Finance secretary in Otto Braun's socialist government in Prussia until 1933, he fled the country for Mexico. In postwar Germany was the founder of the *Frankfurter Allgemeine Zeitung.*

Kharitonov, Moise Marcovich (1888–1938)—Bolshevik from 1905, exiled in Switzerland, he returned to Russia with Lenin. Opposed to Stalin from 1925, he was twice expelled from the party before disappearing in the purges.

Kibalchich, Jeannine (1935–2012)—Daughter of Victor Serge and Liuba Russakova, she was born in Leningrad while Serge and Vlady were in deportation. Serge saw her for the first time in April 1936. She lived in Mexico.

Kibalchich, Nikolai (1853–1881)—Distant relative of Serge and Narodnik militant, he was hanged as the bomb maker in the attack on Czar Alexander II.

Kibalchich, Vladimir (known as Vlady) (1920–2005)—Serge's son, born in Petrograd, he accompanied his father in his deportation to Orenburg and then exile. After their expulsion from the USSR he lived in Brussels (1936–1937), Paris (1937–1940), Marseille (1940–1941), and then Mexico. In the early 1950s Vlady would be the inspiration for a generation of Mexican painters who wanted to break with their elders (Rivera, Siqueiros) for their Stalinism and socialist realism.

Kingdon, Frank (1894–1972)—Former Methodist pastor, he was head of the New York branch of the anti-isolationist group the Committee to Defend America by Aiding the Allies.

Kippenberger, Hans (1898–1937)—Participated in the preparations for the Communist uprising of 1923, from 1926 he was head of the KPD's military apparatus. Exiled to Moscow after the Nazi seizure of power, he was accused of espionage and executed.

Kirdetsov, Grigori (1880–1938)—Journalist and translator, specialist in Italian literature, he worked at the Ministry of Freight Affairs, but was twice condemned and died in an internment camp.

Kisch, Egon Erwin (1885–1948)—Born and died in Prague, this Communist writer and journalist wrote in German. Member of the International Brigades, he lived afterwards in Paris and then Mexico, where he worked for the Stalinist review *Freie Deutschland*.

Klement, Rudolf (1910–1938)—German student, Trotsky's secretary in Turkey, and participant in the secretariat of the Fourth International. Leon Sedov's collaborator in Paris, he was kidnapped by the NKVD in July 1938 and his decapitated body found in the Seine.

Koltsov, Mikhail (M. Efimovich Fridland) (1898–1940)—Soviet journalist and writer, member of the Bolshevik Party from 1917, served in the Red Army. Editor of *Pravda* and its correspondent in Spain in 1936, he was arrested in 1938 and accused of "anti-Soviet activities" and executed two years later.

Kondratiev, Nikolai Dmitrievich (1892–1938)—Economist and theoretician of economic cycles, he was accused and found guilty in the trial of the "industrial party" and executed in the gulag.

Kondratiev, Vadim (1903–1939)—Fought in the Civil War with the Whites and was active in White circles in Paris in the 1920s. Worked for the NKVD, and his presence in Lausanne at the time of the Reiss assassination has been proved, even if he wasn't in on the actual killing. He escaped Swiss justice, fled to the USSR, and was murdered there.

Kostrzewa, Wera (Maria Koszutska) (1876–1938)—Polish militant, first in the Socialist Party, then the Communist Party, where she was on the Central Committee, she was called to the USSR in 1930, arrested in 1937, and executed the following year.

Kotziubinsky, Yuri Mikhailovic (1897–1937)—Bolshevik who participated in the taking of the Winter Palace, he escaped execution at the hands of the Whites during the Civil War but, after joining the Opposition, was executed after the second Moscow Trial.

Kreps, Mikhail Evseevich (1895–1937)—Ukrainian fighter in the Austrian Army, he went over to the Bolsheviks in 1919 and held important posts in publishing.

Krestinsky, Nikolai Ivanovich (1883–1938)—Bolshevik in 1903, he was secretary of the Central Committee (1919–1921), then ambassador to Germany (1921–1930). A repentant Oppositionist, he defended himself to the hilt at the Moscow Trial, but was executed nonetheless.

Krivitsky, Walter (Samuel Ginzburg) (1899–1941)—Of Polish origin and a childhood friend of Ignace Reiss, in 1937 this spy was at the head of Soviet intelligence in Western Europe when his friend was assassinated, which led to his defection and a rapprochement with Serge and Henk Sneevliet. Arrived in the United States in 1938, where he wrote *In Stalin's Secret Service*. He was either murdered or committed suicide in Washington in 1941.

Krupskaya, Nadezhda Konstantinovna (1885–1939)—Lenin's widow, close to the Oppositions of 1923–1927, member of the Central Committee from 1927. Opposed the executions.

Krylenko, Nikolai (1885–1938)—Bolshevik from 1904, he was in the front rank of the soldiers' councils during the Russian Revolution, named to the revolutionary tribunal in 1918, and attorney general of the USSR, enforcing many repressive laws during the 1920s and 1930s. Liquidated without trial in 1938.

Kuibyshev, Valerian (1888–1935)—Member of the Central Committee of the Communist Party from 1922 and the Politburo from 1927. Stalin's principal economic adviser, he died of a heart attack at the hand of his doctors on the orders of the NKVD.

Kutepov, Alexander (1882–1930)—White general, president of the General Union of Russian Fighters, he was kidnapped in Paris by the NKVD and died while being transported to Moscow.

Labin, Édouard (1910–1982)—Active in solidarity groups with the Spanish Republic, member of the PSOP, he lived in exile in Latin America during World War II.

La Follette, Suzanne (1893–1983)—American feminist and journalist, secretary of the Dewey Commission.

Lagardelle, Hubert (1874–1958)—An early ideologist of revolutionary syndicalism who helped to found the review *Le Mouvement socialiste*, he moved towards fascism between the two wars, was minister of labor under Vichy, and sentenced to life imprisonment after the Liberation.

Lapierre, Georges (1886–1945)—Teacher and union activist, he was a pacifist opposed to the Nazi-Soviet pact. Arrested for his Resistance activities, he died of typhus in Dachau.

Largo Caballero, Francisco (1869–1946)—Spanish socialist leader and briefly head of the Popular Front government in Spain in 1936, he was driven from office under Stalinist pressure. Living in exile in France, he was deported by the Nazis, liberated by the Red Army at war's end, and died in Paris.

Larrea, Juan (1895–1980)—Poet, essayist, archaeologist, and major figure of Spanish poetry, he went into exile in Mexico, where he founded the magazine *Cuadernos Americanos*, before immigrating to the United States.

Last, Jef (1898–1972)—Dutch writer and poet, he traveled to the USSR with Gide in 1936. Fought in Spain with the International Brigades.

Latzko, Andreas (1876–1943)—Hungarian-born former officer in the Austro-Hungarian Army; his writings were burned by the Nazis. He fled to New York, where he died in poverty.

Laurat, Lucien (Otto Maschl) (1898–1973)—Austrian Communist militant who worked as a translator at the Comintern, he taught classes at the CGT's educational institute, but during the Occupation contributed to socialist-leaning collaborationist newspapers.

Lazarevich, Nicolas (1895–1975)—Born in Belgium to Russian parents, this anarchist worker went to Russia to join the Red Army. Arrested in 1924 for having published syndicalist tracts, he was freed two years later, and in 1936 it was he who greeted Victor Serge upon the latter's arrival in Belgium.

Lecache, Bernard (1895–1968)—Writer and journalist, member of the PCF until 1923, he traveled to the USSR in 1927 and was on the board of the Friends of the Soviet Union. Founded the International League Against Anti-Semitism (later the International League Against Anti-Semitism and Racism—LICRA); he was interned in a camp in southern Algeria and freed after the Allied landing.

Lelevich, Grigory (Labori Kalmanson) (1901–1945)—Bolshevik Party member, he wrote frequently on the history of the Revolution and the party. Expelled from the party in 1928 and arrested in 1938.

Lenhoff, Herbert (?–?)—Doctor and psychoanalyst, he was one of Serge's closest friends in Mexico. After emigrating to New York in 1945 he had an extensive correspondence with Serge about the psychological aspects of totalitarianism and the future of Western culture, among other subjects.

Leval, Gaston (Pierre Piller) (1895–1978)—A draft dodger during World War I, this French anarchist went into exile in Spain, where he was active in the CNT, which sent him to the USSR in 1921, where he met Serge. After a lengthy stay in Argentina and then Spain, he returned to France in 1938. Arrested and imprisoned, he escaped and worked in soup kitchens organized by Pétain's government. He remained an anarchist militant until the end.

Liber, Mikhail Isaakovich (M. I. Goldman) (1880–1937)—Member of the Central Committee of the Bund, he was a member of the Petrograd Soviet in February 1917 but was hostile to the October Revolution. Arrested many times after 1923, he perhaps owed his longevity to his being Dzerzhinsky's brother-in-law. Arrested in March 1937 and shot later that year.

Lombardo Toledano, Vicente (1894–1968)—Influential Mexican intellectual and political figure, he was president of the Confederation of Latin American Workers (CTAL). Calling himself "the best friend of the USSR," he attacked antitotalitarian intellectuals. Founder of the Partido Popular in 1946.

Longuet, Jean (1876–1936)—Lawyer, son of the Communard Charles Longuet and Jenny Marx. Socialist militant. He was present at Jaurès's assassination. Editor of *L'Humanité*, he opposed the SFIO joining the Comintern.

López Mena, Héctor (1880–1957)—Mexican officer, in 1910 he joined Madero's revolutionary forces and was later a senator and governor of the state of Guerrero.

Lozovsky, Solomon Abramovich (1878–1952)—After participating in the 1905 revolution he went into exile in France from 1909 to 1917, where he was active in the CGT and the SFIO. Originally opposed to Lenin, he joined the Bolsheviks in 1919 and held several official posts, among others in the Ministry of Foreign Affairs. Member of the Jewish Antifascist Committee during World War II, he was a victim of the repression that struck the organization after the war and was executed on August 12, 1952.

Lukanov, Todor Stanchev (1876–1946)—Bulgarian Communist refugee in the USSR. Briefly arrested in 1929, he rejoined the Bulgarian Communists in 1946.

Lunacharsky, Anatoli (1875–1933)—Joined the Communists in 1903, he was the first people's commissar for public enlightenment after the revolution. Died suddenly under mysterious circumstances while in France.

Mabille, Pierre (1904–1952)—French doctor, philosopher, and anthropologist, friend of the Surrealists. Worked in a Haitian hospital while in exile during the war and created the Haitian Institute of Ethnology. While traveling in Mexico in 1943 he gave public lectures and wrote for *Cuadernos Americanos*. He returned to Europe in 1948.

Macdonald, Dwight (1906–1982)—Member of the editorial board of *Partisan Review* from 1938 to 1944, he was a friend of Orwell and of Serge, providing the latter with material assistance from 1940. Married to **Nancy Gardener Rodman** (1910–1996).

Magyar, Ludwig (1891–1937)—Hungarian Communist militant, he was a journalist for the TASS press agency, was delegated to Shanghai in 1928, and was in charge of activities in the Far East for the Comintern. Arrested and tortured in 1937, he admitted to being connected to Trotsky and was executed.

Maîtrejean, Rirette (Anna Estorges) (1887–1968)—Serge's first companion, they worked together at *L'Anarchie* and were both tried as a result of the Bonnot Affair in 1912. Rirette was acquitted and Serge found guilty and sentenced to five years. They went their separate ways after Serge's imprisonment, and she retired from political activity but contributed to various anarchist publications until the 1950s.

Makhno, Nestor (1888–1934)—Ukrainian peasant organizer and guerrilla; leader of insurgent anarchist Black Armies allied with the Reds during the Russian Civil War. From 1918–21 he helped establish an autonomous anarchist community of workers and peasants in Ukraine. Defeated, he settled in Paris in 1926, where he worked as a carpenter while remaining active in anarchist circles until his death from tuberculosis.

Malaquais, Jean (Vladimir Malacki) (1908–1998)—Born in Poland, this French-language writer arrived in France in 1930 and frequented far-left circles. In Spain he was in contact with the POUM militia, and upon his return to France met Serge and Ante Ciliga. Close to Gide, he won the Prix Renaudot in 1939 for *Les Javanais*. Fleeing the Nazis, he lived in Mexico from 1943, and while running in anti-Stalinist circles had a serious falling-out with Serge. He ultimately received a US visa.

Mancisidor, José (1894–1959)—Mexican writer and politician close to the Communists.

Marion, Paul (1899–1954)—Member of the PCF and writer for *L'Humanité*, he spent two years in the USSR from 1927, and after publicly expressing his dissatisfaction was expelled from the party. He later joined Doriot's fascist PPF and was an active collaborator. He was sentenced to ten years in prison for his activities during the war.

Martinet, Marcel (1887–1944)—Revolutionary and pacifist militant, he was part of the internationalist minority opposed to the *union sacrée* during World War I. Literary editor of *L'Humanité*, he was later part of the nucleus of *La Révolution prolétarienne*. Was active in the campaign to free Serge from his Soviet imprisonment.

Martínez Barrio, Diego (1883–1962)—Spanish politician, he founded the Republican Union Party in 1934, which was part of the Popular Front government. Several times president of the Cortés between 1936 and 1939, he was president of the Spanish republic-in-exile from 1945 until his death.

Martov, Julius (Yuri Ossipovich Tsederbaum) (1873–1923)—Founder along with Lenin of *Iskra* in 1923, he became the main Menshevik theoretician. Died in exile.

Maslov, Arkady (Isaak Chemerinsky) (1891–1941)—Born in Russia into a wealthy Jewish family, he studied in Germany where he met Ruth Fischer. They were both leaders of the KPD and were expelled in 1926. Later forced to emigrate, he was active in the international Left Opposition. Died suddenly (and for Fischer, suspiciously) in exile in Cuba.

Matta, Roberto (1911–2002)—Chilean painter, architect, philosopher, and poet, collaborator on André Breton's review *Minotaure*.

Maublanc, René (1891–1960)—Philosophy professor and Soviet sympathizer. Propagandist of Marxism in its Stalinist form, he ultimately joined the PCF and fought in the Resistance.

Maurín Juliá, Joaquín (1896–1973)—Originally a syndicalist militant, he was delegated to the Second Congress of the Comintern in 1921, where he and Serge became friends. In 1935 he became secretary general of the POUM and a year later Catalonian deputy. Arrested at the beginning of the Civil War, he was believed dead but in reality had been sentenced to thirty years' imprisonment. Freed in 1946, he emigrated to the United States.

Mazin, Vladimir (V. Ossipovich Lichtenstadt) (1882–1919)—Member of the left wing of the Socialist-Revolutionaries, he participated in the failed assassination attempt on Prime Minister Stolypin. Sentenced to life imprisonment, while in Shlisselburg prison he translated Stirner and Goethe. Freed in 1917, he joined the Bolsheviks in 1919, worked alongside Serge at the Comintern, and died in combat against the Whites. Serge named his son after Mazin.

Mdivani, Polikarp (Boudou) (1877–1937)—Georgian active in the Red Army, he played an important role in the invasion of Georgia. He opposed Georgia's entry into the Transcaucasian Socialist Federative Republic. Expelled from the party in 1936, he was executed without trial the following year along with his wife and two sons.

Medellín Ostos, Octavio (1892–1952)—Mexican lawyer and journalist close to the Stalinists, he was Mercader's defense attorney.

Mella, Julio Antonio (1903–1929)—Cofounder of the Cuban CP, exiled in Mexico, he was a key figure in the Communist movement in Latin America at the time of his assassination in Mexico City.

Mendeleyeva-Blok, Lyubov (1881–1939)—Actress and dance historian, daughter of the chemist Dmitry Mendeleyev, she married Alexander Blok in 1903.

Méndez, Leopoldo (1902–1969)—Famous communist engraver and president from 1937 until 1952 of the Taller de Gráfica Popular, an artist collective that supported popular struggles.

Méndez Aspe, Francisco (1901–?)—Spanish politician and economist, member of Izquierda Republicana, he was in charge of the transfer of 501 tons of gold from Madrid to Moscow.

Mendoza Buen-Abad, Roquelia (1922–1989)—Mexican woman and sometime nightclub singer who married Ramón Mercader in 1947 (or in 1960 according to other sources).

Ménil, Dominique (née Schlumberger) (1908–1997) and **Jean de** (1904–1973)—Wealthy heirs born in France, art collectors and patrons. During World War II they lived in the United States, from which they frequently traveled to Mexico.

Mera Sanz, Cipriano (1897–1975)—CNT militant, he led an anarcho-syndicalist column in the early days of the Civil War. A refugee in France, he was handed over to Franco in 1942, was liberated in 1946, and returned to France.

Mercader del Río, Ramón (Paul Mornard, Frank Jacson, and Van den Dreschd) (1913–1978)—Born in Barcelona, Trotsky's assassin was the son of Pau Mercader, an anti-Communist, and Caridad del Río, a fanatical Stalinist. Recruited for the NKVD by Naum Eitingon, his mother's lover, he was trained in the USSR and infiltrated Trotskyist circles through Sylvia Agelov. Caught at the scene of the crime on August 20, 1940, Mercader spent twenty years in prison, insisting he was Belgian. His identity was officially established in 1950, though Serge's notebooks show that the exiles had divined his true identity. Resided in Moscow upon his release from prison in 1960, receiving the award of Hero of the Soviet Union; in 1974 he moved to Cuba, where he spent the final years of his life as an adviser to the Ministry of the Interior.

Merker, Paul (1894–1969)—German Communist militant, member of the Prussian parliament from 1924 to 1932 and the Central Committee of the KPD from 1934 to 1946. Emigrated to Mexico, where he worked for the Alemania Libre movement.

Mesnil, Jacques (Jean-Jacques Dwelshauvers) (1872–1940)—Anarchist and later Communist journalist and art critic, born in Brussels, he was one of Serge's closest friends

Meyer, Hannes (1889–1954)—Swiss urbanist and architect. Director in Germany of the Bauhaus school, he worked in Moscow in the 1930s. He emigrated to Mexico in 1939 and exerted great influence over Mexican architecture.

Miglioli, Guido (1879–1954)—Italian syndicalist, he was forced to leave Italy in 1926, going to the USSR in the early 1930s. Turned over to Italian authorities by Vichy, he was liberated in 1945.

Miller, Yevgeny Karlovich (1867–1939)—Lieutenant general in the czarist army during World War I, he was condemned in absentia after the October Revolution. Commanding the White Army of the North, he was defeated in 1920 and settled in Paris, heading a czarist veterans' group. Kidnapped by the NKVD in 1937, he was tortured and executed in 1939.

Milyutin, Vladimir Pavlovich (1884–1937/8)—Menshevik from 1903, Bolshevik from 1910, he was commissar for agriculture after the revolution. Arrested in 1937 and "died in prison."

Minev, Stojan (Stepanov and Lebedev) (1893–1959)—Bulgarian-born Communist militant, he was Comintern emissary to various Western European nations, later working in Stalin's personal secretariat. After 1939 he returned to the USSR, where he worked for Georgi Dimitrov, the head of the Comintern.

Modigliani, Giuseppe Emanuele (1872–1947)—Born into a Jewish family in Livorno, brother of the painter Amadeo, a militant in the Socialist Party, he opposed World War I and participated in the Zimmerwald Conference. Participated in the Dewey Commission, questioning Serge and Leon Sedov. Returned to Italy in 1946 and was elected to the Constituent Assembly.

Modotti, Tina (1896–1942)—Italian-born photographer and Communist, she was close to Diego Rivera and Frida Kahlo in Mexico. She was the lover of the Cuban Communist Julio Antonio Mella at the time of his assassination, and later of Vittorio Vidali, who was perhaps responsible for the murder. Expelled from Mexico, she lived in Berlin and Moscow, and after a brief stay in France was in Spain during the Civil War as a reporter. She returned to Mexico in 1939 and died under mysterious circumstances in 1942.

Moix i Regàs, Josep (1898–1973)—Catalan Communist who went into exile in Mexico.

Molinier, Raymond (1904–1994)—Militant in the Young Communists in France, he was among the first to visit Trotsky in his Turkish exile in 1929. Expelled from the CPF upon his return, he was one of the founders of the Ligue Communiste in 1930. Throughout his life he was a key, and controversial, figure in the Trotskyist movement.

Molins i Fàbregas, Narcís (1901–1962)—Catalan journalist, writer, and Communist militant, close friend of Serge and even more of Vlady, he was a member of the executive committee of the POUM and editor of *La Batalla*. From his Parisian exile he worked with Serge doing POUM support work, and, after going into exile in Mexico, was a member of Socialism and Freedom.

Monatte, Pierre (1881–1960)—Key figure of revolutionary syndicalism in France, he was founder of two essential papers, *La Vie ouvrière* (1909) and *La Révolution prolétarienne*.

Morizet, André (1876–1942)—Socialist militant who joined the PCF in 1920, later leaving it for the SFIO. Mayor of Boulogne-Billancourt and senator, he remained in his city during the war, firmly opposing Vichy and the Germans.

Münzenberg, Willi (1889–1940)—Known as "the red millionaire," he was a member of the Spartakusbund and then the KPD. President of the Young

Communist International and later in Berlin charged with organizing an immense group of newspapers, publishing houses, and film production companies. Exiled to France in 1933, he worked tirelessly in support of the USSR and against Nazism. From 1936 he started to distance himself from the USSR and was expelled from the KPD in 1938 for protesting against the murder of German Communists in the Soviet Union. Interned by the French government in 1940, he managed to flee, and his body was found hanged in a forest, the cause—suicide or a disguised murder—never discovered.

Muralov, Nikolai I. (1877–1937)—Bolshevik from 1903, head of the Moscow insurrection in 1917, he was one of the main leaders of the Red Army. Member of the Left Opposition of 1923, he was deported five years later. Refusing to abjure Trotsky, he was arrested, and after his "confession" was executed following the second Moscow Trial.

Muste, A. J. (1885–1967)—An early American Trotskyist, he abandoned Trotskyism for pacifism.

Naville, Pierre (1904–1993)—Participant in the Surrealist movement, he joined the PCF in 1926, going to Moscow in 1927, where he met Trotsky and Serge. Denounced Trotsky's expulsion upon his return to France and was expelled from the PCF, becoming one of the leaders of French Trotskyism. Was leader of the independent left PSU from 1960 until 1969.

Nervo, Amado (1870–1919)—Mexican writer, poet, and diplomat.

Neumann, Heinz (1902–1937)—Member of the KPD from 1920, he was a Comintern envoy to China, where he was made to accept the responsibility for the Canton insurrection of 1927. Played a key role in the Stalinization of the KPD, and after defending the official party line against social fascism grew opposed to the Stalinist line. Sent to the USSR in 1932, he was arrested in April 1937 and executed in November.

Nicolaevsky, Boris Ivanovich (1887–1966)—Russian Social-Democrat, in charge of the Central Archives for the History of the Russian Revolutionary Movement, he was arrested along with other Menshevik leaders at the time of Kronstadt. Expelled to Berlin in 1922, later a refugee in Paris, he headed the Paris branch of the International Institute for Social History. In 1940 he moved to New York.

Nikitin, Nikolai (1895–1963)—Russian writer, member of the Serapion Brotherhood, he joined the Communist Party in 1932 and adopted socialist realism.

Nikolaenko, Dr. (?–?)—Tolstoyan anarchist and close friend of Serge's in-laws, the Russakovs. He was repatriated, along with Serge and the Russakovs, to Russia in the prisoner exchange of December 1918.

Nin, Andrés (Andreu) (1892–1937)—As secretary of the national committee of the CNT he participated in the Third Congress of the Comintern. He settled in Moscow, where he met his wife, Olga Tareeva (1900–1983). Close to Trotsky, member of the Left Opposition in the USSR, he returned to Spain and was a founder of the POUM in 1935. Trotsky broke with him for sectarian reasons, which Serge harshly criticized. Seized by the Soviet political police, he was tortured and killed.

Oettinghaus, Walter (1883–1950)—German syndicalist and socialist, he joined the KPD in 1931. A Communist deputy, he fled to France after the Reichstag fire. Critical of the Moscow Trials, he was expelled from the KPD. In 1940 he went into exile in Mexico and then the United States.

O'Gorman, Juan (1905–1982)—Mexican muralist and architect, his mural covers the walls of the library of Mexico City's University City campus and he was the architect of Rivera and Kahlo's Casa Estudio.

Onslow Ford, Gordon (1912–2003)—English Surrealist painter and sculptor, he moved to Paris in 1937 and New York in 1940, where he married Jacqueline Johnson. They both emigrated to Mexico in 1941 and were close friends with Serge there.

Orlov, Alexander (Leib Lazarevich Felbing) (1895–1973)—NKVD agent charged with liquidating Spanish revolutionaries, he was the man in charge of the destruction of the POUM and the killing of its leaders (among them, Nin). In 1938 he defected to the United States and wrote an account of his life in Stalin's service.

Ottwald, Ernst (1901–1943)—German poet, writer, and screenwriter. A nonconformist Communist, he went into exile in Moscow, where he was later arrested for espionage and deported.

Pachoukanis (or Pashukanis), **Yevgeny** (1891–1937)—Bolshevik from 1918, he was legal advisor to the People's Commissariat for Foreign Relations in the early 1920s. He left government service in 1924, when he published his General Theory of Law and Marxism, and was executed at the time of the Moscow Trials.

Panitsa, Todor (1879–1925)—Bulgarian revolutionary, he believed in the creation of a Balkan socialist federation. In 1907 he assassinated the leader of the right-wing faction of the nationalist group whose left-wing faction he belonged to. After World War I he developed ties with the Bolsheviks and was assassinated in Vienna.

Pannekoek, Anton (1873–1960)—Dutch astronomer and Communist, he was a central figure on the left of the Second International. A founder of the Dutch Communist Party, from 1921 he was active in the council communism movement.

Parijanine, Maurice (M. Donzel) (1885–1937)—Paris-born writer, before Serge he was Trotsky's principal translator into French.

Pascal, Pierre (1890–1983)—Member of the 1916 French military mission to Russia, two years later he participated in the formation of the French Communist Group in Moscow and worked at the Commissariat of Foreign Affairs and the Marx-Engels Institute. In 1921 he married Serge's sister-in-law and returned to France in 1933, where he was active in the campaign in support of Serge. From 1937 he taught at the École des Langues Orientales and was one of France's great Russian specialists.

Paz, Magdeleine (1889–1973)—Pacifist during World War I, she joined the PCF shortly after its founding. Expelled in 1925, she joined the SFIO and was at the heart of the campaign to free Serge. Member of the pacifist and anti-Stalinist minority in the League for the Rights of Man, she resigned from its central committee in protest against its inactivity during the Moscow Trials. Prefaced Serge's *16 fusillés à Moscou*. Abandoned all political activity after World War II.

Paz, Maurice (1896–1985)—Husband of Magdeleine, the lawyer who defended the French sailors who mutinied on the Black Sea, joined the PCF at its creation. Expelled in 1927, he launched the review *Contre le courant* and, like his wife, resigned from the League of the Rights of Man. Also like his wife, he abstained from all political activity after World War II.

Péret, Benjamin (1899–1959)—Poet and Surrealist, he joined the PCF in 1927 and then went over to the Opposition. Member of the Internationalist Workers party, he fought in Spain with an anarchist militia. Arrested in 1940, he managed to make it to Marseille, migrating from there to Mexico the same year, living there from 1942 to 1948.

Perkus, Hyman (?–?)—American anarchist, among those deported to Soviet Russia on the *Buford* as a result of the Palmer Red Raids of 1919.

Pestaña Nuñez, Ángel (1886–1937)—Spanish anarchist clockmaker, he was one of the main leaders of the CNT, which he represented at the Second Congress of the Comintern in 1920. Unlike Nin, he opposed entry into the Comintern. Part of the CNT's moderate wing, he was expelled in 1931 and founded the Syndicalist Party and was elected to the Cortès in 1936.

Petrovsky, Grigori (1877–1958)—Bolshevik from 1903 and member of the Russian delegation at Brest-Litovsk, he held high posts in the Communist Party, including membership in the Central Committee and the Politburo. Expelled from the party, he vanished from view but reappeared in 1940, abandoning all political activity thereafter.

Piechkova, Ekaterina Pavlovna (1885–1967)—Gorky's first wife, after the revolution she headed the Political Red Cross. She was the last person Serge saw before his departure from the USSR.

Pioch, Georges (1873–1953)—Beginning as an anarchist, he joined the SFIO in 1915 and founded the pacifist paper *Le Journal du peuple*. He joined the CF at its creation but was expelled in 1923. He returned to pacifist activity and during the occupation wrote for collaborationist papers.

Pitaud, Henri (1899–1991)—Socialist agricultural militant, publisher of *L'Émancipation Paysanne*, participated in the Resistance and settle in Paraguay after the war.

Pivert, Marceau (1895–1958)—Founder of the Revolutionary Left tendency in the SFIO and then the PSOP (1938); in charge of international relations for the latter, he was in the United States in 1939 when war broke out. Expelled along with other militants in April 1940, he went to Mexico and remained there until 1946.

Plevitskaya, Nadezhda Vasilievna (1882–1940)—Russian singer, she rallied to the Bolsheviks and sang for Red Army fighters. Captured by the White general Skoblin, who she married, she went into exile with him in Turkey and then France, where she became a Soviet agent.

Pokhitonov, Boris (1893–1963)—Bolshevik militant and emissary of the Comintern in France during the 1920s. Close to Alfred Rosmer and the Left Opposition.

Pokrovsky, Mikhail Nikolaevich (1868–1932)—Historian and precursor of the Marxist approach to history in the USSR. He played an important role in the reorganization of education after the revolution.

Polevoi, Mikhail Andreevich (?–?)—Left Oppositionist, member of the Moscow Trotskyist center, friend of Andrés Nin, he was arrested in Kursk in May 1931 and deported.

Pope, Generoso (1891–1950)—Pro-fascist Italian-American journalist, friends with most of the mafiosi involved in the assassination of Carlo Tresca but never questioned.

Posthumus, Nicolaas W. (1880–1960)—Dutch historian who, as a result of his belief in the importance of the collection, preservation, and publication of historical sources, was the founder of the International Institute for Social History in Amsterdam.

Poulaille, Henry (1896–1980)—Leading French writer of the proletarian school, friend of Serge from 1912 and one of his most ardent defenders in the 1930s.

Preobrazhensky, Yevgeny Alexeyevich (1886–1937)—Bolshevik of the first hour, architect of NEP, author with Bukharin of *The ABC of Communism*. Spokesman for the Left Opposition in 1923–1924, he fell into disgrace and was deported in 1928. Accepted back into the party, he once again went into opposition, was arrested in 1936, and was tortured and executed without trial in July 1937.

Prévost, Jean (1901–1944)—French writer and journalist, he was responsible for bringing Saint-Exupéry to the public's attention. Died while fighting in the Resistance.

Prieto, Indalecio (1883–1962)—Member of the PSOE from 1899, he was head of the party in Basque country during World War I. Opponent of the regime of Primo de Rivera, he was minister under the Republic. In 1939 he fled to Mexico and was head of the PSOE until his death.

Prokopovich, Sergei Nikolaievich (1871–1955)—Russian economist who was minister of supply under Kerensky. Forced into exile in 1922 after publishing damaging data on famine and poverty in the USSR.

Pyatakov, Georgy Leonidovich (1890–1937)—Bolshevik from 1910, he was close to Bukharin and the Left Communists in 1918. Expelled from the Party in 1927, he was nevertheless elected to the Central Committee from 1930 to 1934, but was sentenced to death at the second Moscow Trial after making outrageous confessions.

Quintana, Valente (1890–1968)—Security chief of Mexico City, he was in charge of the investigations of the murders of President Álvaro Obregón (1928) and Juan Antonio Mella (1929).

Radványi, László (Johann Lorenz Schmidt) (1900–1978)—Hungarian-born Marxist sociologist, he taught at the Marxist Workers' School in Berlin. Along with his wife, Anna Seghers, he fled Germany in 1933, first for France and then in 1940 to Mexico. There he taught at the Workers' University and the UNAM.

Rakovsky, Christian Georgeievich (1873–1941)—Romanian Socialist-Revolutionary, friend of Trotsky, he joined the Bolsheviks after the October Revolution. A founder of the Comintern and member of the Central Committee of the Communist Party, he was head of the Ukrainian Soviet government and ambassador to London and Paris. Deported in 1928, accepted back into the party, judged and condemned in 1937, he was deported again and executed by the NKVD in 1941.

Ramzin, Leonid K. (1887–1948)—Engineer and professor, he was one of the main defendants in the plot of the industrial party. Sentenced to death, he was amnestied and later received the Stalin Prize.

Rappoport, Charles (1865–1941)—Born in Vilnius, he was a member of Narodnaia Volia while a student and had to flee Russia for Switzerland, where he received his doctorate in 1897. In Paris he was a Dreyfusard and friend and follower of Jean Jaurès, later adopting the ideas of Jules Guesde. Correspondent for *Izvestia* in Paris during the 1920s and 1930s, member of the PCF from its founding, he resigned after the Bukharin trial in 1938.

Regler, Gustav (1898–1963)—World War I veteran, fighter for the Council Republic of Bavaria, he joined the KPD in the 1920s, working as a writer and journalist. Exiled after 1933, he fought in the International Brigades in Spain and was briefly interned in a French concentration camp. He broke with the KPD after the Hitler-Stalin Pact and in exile on Mexico wrote *La GPU prépara un nuevo crimen*, with Serge, Gorkin, and Pivert.

Reisner, Larissa Mikhailovna (1895–1926)—Russian writer and Bolshevik, she was commissar of the Fifth Army, fighting the Czechoslovak legions.

Reiss, Elsa (Elisabeth Poretskys) (?–?)—Wife of Ignace Reiss, she wrote an account of his assassination. She was critical and suspicious of Serge, whom she considered "irresponsible."

Reiss, Ignace (I. S. Poretsky) (1899–1937)—Communist of Polish origin, agent of the Red Army Intelligence Service, he warned Trotsky of an assassination threat and broke with Stalin in a letter to the Central Committee sent July 17, 1937. He was assassinated September 4, 1937, the eve of a meeting with Serge and Henk Sneevliet.

Rens, Jef (1905–1985)—Belgian syndicalist, he was part of the group that greeted Serge upon his arrival in Belgium and eased his insertion into Belgian society. Named chef de cabinet of the socialist prime minister Paul-Henri Spaak in 1938, he called for the abandonment of Belgian neutrality in the face of the Nazi threat. Member of the Belgian government-in-exile, while on a mission in Mexico he reconnected with Serge and organized the publication of *Last Days* in Montreal in 1946.

Riazanov, David Borisovich (D. B. Goldenbach) (1870–1938)—Russian intellectual who dedicated his life to the spread of Marx's writings. After several years in exile he returned to Russia in 1917 and founded the Marx-Engels Institute. Arrested in February 1931, he was sent to several camps, released, then rearrested in July 1937 for "conspiratorial activity," judged by the military tribunal of Saratov, and executed January 25, 1938.

Río Hernández, Caridad del (1893–1975)—Spanish Communist, mother of Ramón Mercader, she was the lover of NKVD agent Naum Eitingon and member of the network assigned the task of assassinating Trotsky. She was in Mexico City at the time of the crime and returned to the USSR in February 1941.

Rivet, Paul (1876–1958)—Professor at the National Museum of Natural History in Paris and director of the Musée de l'Homme and specialist in American Indian civilizations. Member of the SFIO, in October 1940 he laid the foundation for the famous Musée de l'Homme Resistance network. Threatened, he left France for Colombia. He moved to Mexico after de Gaulle named him cultural attaché for Latin America.

Roland Holst, Henriette (1869–1952)—Dutch writer and poet, close to the Marxist left, she collaborated with Pannekoek on his review *De Tribune*. Internationalist during World War I, she joined the Communists but left them in 1927. She defended Serge in 1937 and participated in the Resistance.

Rollo, Joseph (1891–1945)—Teacher and syndicalist, he headed the teacher's union within the CGTU. Expelled from the PCF in 1931, he was close to the SFIO afterwards. A Resistance fighter, he was captured and died at the Neuengamme concentration camp.

Rosenberg, Marcel (1896–1938)—Soviet representative at the League of Nations, he was named ambassador to Madrid in 1936. Recalled to Moscow at the request of the Spanish government, he perished in the purges.

Rosengoltz, Arkady Pavlovich (1889–1938)—Bolshevik from 1905, military collaborator of Trotsky's during the Civil War, he was member of the Central Committee from 1927. Arrested in 1937, he was condemned—along with Rykov, Bukharin, and Rakovsky—and executed.

Rosenthal, Gérard (1903–1992)—After participating in the Surrealist movement, he joined the PCF in 1927 before becoming one of the leaders of the Trotskyist movement in France from 1929 to 1939. Best known as Trotsky's lawyer.

Rosmer, Alfred (Alfred Griot) (1877–1964)—Proofreader by profession, he was an internationalist during World War I. Gone to Moscow in 1919, he was member of the Comintern's Executive Committee along with Souvarine and the Politburo of the PCF in 1923–1924. Expelled from the PCF, he was at the heart of the review *La Révolution prolétarienne*. He left the Ligue Communiste in 1930 and in 1936 participated in the committees investigating the Moscow Trials. Along with his companion Marguerite, he brought Trotsky's grandson to Mexico in 1939. Caught in North America at the outbreak of the war, they stayed in the United States until 1946. Rosmer worked for *La Révolution prolétarienne* until his death.

Rosmer, Marguerite (1879–1962)—Alfred Rosmer's wife, she was cofounder of the investigation committee for the Moscow Trials.

Rosselli, Carlo (1899–1937)—Italian historian and antifascist politician, he was sentenced to five years in prison in 1926. After his escape his book *Liberal Socialism* served as the founding document of the Giustizia e Libertà movement. After fighting in Spain he and his brother Nello (1900–1937) were assassinated by French fascists of the Cagoule.

Rous, Jean (1908–1985)—Lawyer, member of the SFIO and later the Ligue Communiste. One of the elders of French Trotskyism until the war, and the man upon whom Trotsky depended in France. Joined Pivert's PSOP in 1939 along with the minority of French Trotskyists. Participated in the Resistance in the South of France.

Rubin, Isaac (1886–1937)—Economist and close collaborator of Riazanov's, he was accused of sabotage and sentenced to deportation at the trial of the Mensheviks. Released in 1934, he was rearrested in 1937 and executed.

Rudzutaks, Jānis Ernestovich (1887–1938)—Steelworker and Bolshevik from 1905, he was imprisoned until 1917. A supporter of Stalin, he entered the Politburo in 1927 and was People's Commissar for Transport. Arrested and executed in 1937.

Rühle, Otto (1874–1943)—German Social-Democrat opposed to the national unity government at the beginning of World War I, founder of the KAPD in 1920 and favorable to council communism, he was one of that movement's most eminent spokesmen. He emigrated to Prague in 1933 and three years later to Mexico. Though standing by his councilist ideas, he was sympathetic to Trotsky and was a member of the Dewey Commission.

Rühle-Gerstel, Alice (1894–1943)—Wife of Otto Rühle, she was an Adlerian psychoanalyst, writer, and feminist.

Russakov (family)—**Alexander Russakov** (1874–1935) was an anarchist who lived a poverty-stricken existence in Russia, Hamburg, New York, Buenos Aires, Barcelona, and Marseille. With his wife, **Olga**, he had seven children, of whom **Liuba** (1898–1982), Serge's wife, was the eldest. Her sister **Eugénie** married Pierre Pascal. The family returned to Russia in 1919, and Serge met them on board the ship. **Alexander** played a role in the Kronstadt uprising, being part of a group of anarchists (along with Emma Goldman and Alexander Berkman) who attempted to mediate the dispute. The family's woes began with the persecution of Serge, and nearly the entire family knew a tragic end: Liuba went mad in the early 1930s and died in an asylum in Aix-en-Provence; Alexander died of a heart attack in 1935; the sisters **Olga** and **Esther** "disappeared"; and **Anita**, **Joseph**, and **Paul-Marcel** spent decades in the Gulags.

Sadoul, Jacques (1881–1956)—French Army captain sent to Russia in 1917, he went over to communism. In 1937 he published slanderous articles in *L'Humanité* about Serge.

Saint-Exupéry, Consuelo (1901–1979)—Born in El Salvador to a wealthy family, she met Antoine in Buenos Aires in 1930 and married him the following year.

Salvemini, Gaetano (1873–1957)—Italian historian and socialist militant, he was an early critic of totalitarianism in all its forms. In 1925 he went into exile in France and was one of the founders of Giustizia e Libertà. Later moved to the United States.

Sampaix, Lucien (1899–1941)—Worker and PCF militant, he became general secretary of *L'Humanité* in 1936. Arrested in December 1939 and then again in March 1941, he was executed with other hostages, among them Gabriel Péri.

Sánchez Añon, Mariano (1909–1941)—Spanish illegalist anarchist who went into Mexican exile in Chihuahua in 1939. In 1940 he murdered the owner of a finca and, hunted by the police, went to Mexico City, where he founded a direct action group that carried out several expropriations.

Sandomirsky, Herman Borisovich (1882–1938)—Former terrorist, he was director of the Balkan service of the Commissariat for Foreign Affairs and member of the writer's union. Deported and executed.

Sapronov, Timofei V. (1887–1937)—Bolshevik from 1911, member of several opposition groups within the party after October 1917, he was expelled in 1927, interned in 1932, and executed by order of Stalin in 1937.

Sats, Natalia (1903–1993)—World-famous director and head of the Moscow Children's Theater, she was arrested in 1937 and sentenced to five years' deportation in Siberia. She survived and returned to her theater work.

Savinkov, Boris (1879–1925)—Member of the combat groups of the Socialist-Revolutionaries, he lived in exile in Paris and returned to Russia in 1917. Secretary of war under Kerensky, he fought against the Bolsheviks. Exiled again, he plotted against the Bolsheviks and, falling into an NKVD trap, he returned to the USSR in 1925. Arrested, he committed suicide in prison.

Sazonov, Igor (1879–1910)—Socialist-Revolutionary, he assassinated Minister of the Interior Plehve in 1904. Arrested, he committed suicide while in prison.

Scheuber, Sylvia (S. Fein) (1919–)—American Surrealist painter, she lived in Ajijic for three years during World War II.

Schildbach, Gertrude (1894–?)—Communist militant and Ignace Reiss's assistant, she played a central role in his assassination. Found refuge in the USSR after the killing, before being arrested and deported.

Schlamm, William (Willi) (1904–1978)—Austrian Communist and journalist, was sympathetic to the Left Opposition before breaking with communism in 1928. He moved to the United States, where he worked for *Time*, *Life*, and *Fortune* magazines.

Schmierer, Paul (1905–1966)—Parisian doctor close to the POUM, he worked for an American aid group in Marseille and fought in the Resistance.

Schüssler, Otto (1905–1980)—Saxon born, he joined the KPD and rallied to the Left Opposition. Was Trotsky's secretary in Prinkipo, and rejoined him in Mexico. Remained in Mexico and active in the Fourth International under the name Julián Suárez.

Schwartzenberg, Pierre (Piotr) (1896–?)—White Russian émigré, he worked for the GPU in Paris, recruiting Renata Steiner, who was involved in the Reiss assassination. Disappeared in Spain during the Civil War.

Scott, John (1912–1976)—American steelworker who emigrated to the USSR out of conviction (writing a memoir of his experience in Magnitogorsk). Back in the United States, he worked for the OSS and probably spied for the Soviets.

Sedov, Leon (1906–1938)—Trotsky's third child and closest collaborator, one of the main leaders of the international Opposition. The debate about the cause of his death at a clinic remains open.

Sedova, Natalia (1882–1962)—Trotsky's second wife and a militant, she shared in all his battles. With Serge she wrote *The Life and Death of Leon Trotsky*, and she broke with the Fourth International in 1951, believing that capitalism had been restored in the USSR.

Seguí Rubinat, Salvador (1887–1923)—Housepainter, he participated in the Barcelona uprising of 1909. Opposed terrorism in the anarchist movement. Was a great influence and close friend of Serge's during his time in Barcelona in 1917. Assassinated by henchmen in the pay of the bosses in 1923.

Séjourné, Laurette (Laura Velentini) (1911–2003)—Of Italian origin, she was Serge's companion from 1937. She rejoined him in Mexico a year after his arrival there and became a noted ethnologist, carrying out digs in Teotihuacán and publishing several books on Mexico's native population.

Seligmann, Kurt (1900–1962)—Swiss Surrealist artist close to Breton who immigrated to the United States in 1939.

Selsam, Howard (1903–1970)—American philosopher, founder of the American Institute for Marxist Studies.

Semard, Pierre (1887–1942)—Railroad worker and syndicalist, he was secretary general of the PCF from 1924 to 1928 and held union positions thereafter. Arrested after the Hitler-Stalin Pact, he was executed as a hostage at the demand of the German authorities.

Serebryakov, Leonid (1888–1937)—Longtime Bolshevik, he was secretary of the Central Committee from 1920 to 1921. Member of the Left Opposition, he was expelled from the party, accepted back, and then executed after the second Moscow Trial.

Serebryakova, Galina Josifovna (1905–1980)—Novelist and wife of two Bolsheviks killed during the purges, Serebryakov and Sokolnikov. Held in a labor camp because of this from 1936 to 1956.

Serrati, Giacinto (1872–1926)—Italian socialist, hesitant about the twenty-one conditions for admission to the Comintern, he joined the Italian Communist Party in 1924.

Serre, Édouard (1896–1942)—Aviator and pioneer of crossings of the South Atlantic, he became technical director of Air France. As a member of the left of the SFIO, he organized arms deliveries to the Republicans.

Shachtman, Max (1904–1972)—Leader of American Trotskyism in the 1930s, he broke with Trotsky over the nature of the USSR. Founded several splinter parties afterwards, all the while remaining in contact with Natalia Sedova.

Sheldon Harte, Robert (1915–1940)—American Stalinist agent, he infiltrated Trotsky's personal guard in Mexico. Trotsky never accepted that he was an NKVD agent.

Shulgin, Vasily (1878–1976)—Born to Ukrainian nobility, this monarchist writer and journalist joined Wrangel's counterrevolutionary army and emigrated to Belgrade in 1920. Arrested by the Soviets in 1944, he remained in prison until 1956.

Siqueiros, David Alfaro (1896–1974)—One of the leading figures of the Mexican muralist movement, he fought in the Mexican Revolution with the constitutionalists and then with Carranza against Villa and Zapata. Member of the Communist Party, he was active in its cultural activities. He fought in Spain and, upon his return to Mexico, organized the first attempt on Trotsky's life. Sought by the police, he fled to Chile thanks to a visa obtained for him by Pablo Neruda.

Skoblin, Nikolai (1892–1938)—White Army general, in exile in France became involved with the NKVD and participated in the kidnappings of White generals Koutiepev (1930) and Miller (1937). Disappeared in Spain.

Slastchev-Krimsky, J. A. (1885–1929)—Brutal White general, he lived in Istanbul after the Civil War and negotiated his return to Russia to work for the Red Army. Amnestied by the Bolsheviks, he was murdered.

Slutsky, Abram Aronovich (1898–1938)—A member of the Cheka in 1919, then the GPU and then the foreign intelligence service of the NKVD, he was in charge of the hunt for Whites and Trotskyists and was involved in the theft of Trotsky's archives in Paris as well as Ignace Reiss's assassination. Died suddenly in his superior's office.

Smilga, Ivar Tenisovich (1892–1938)—Economist and Lenin's right-hand man in the Baltics, he was a signatory of the Opposition Platform of 1927. Expelled from the Central Committee in 1929, he was accepted back the following year. Expelled again in 1932, he was relegated to the Far East. He was arrested again in 1935 and executed three years later.

Smirnov, Ivan Nikitich (1881–1936)—Member of the RSDLP from 1899, Lenin called him "the conscience of the party." After occupying high functions in the military, he went over to the Opposition and was expelled in 1927. While in Siberian exile he rallied to Stalin but was arrested in 1933 and sentenced to five years' imprisonment. Tried again at the first Moscow Trial, he confessed and was executed.

Smirnov, Vladimir Mikhailovich (1887–1937)—Economist and Bolshevik from 1907, he was one of the leaders of the revolution in Moscow. Left communist, he opposed Trotsky's bureaucratization of the army and became a theoretician of a section of the left. Expelled from the party, he was sent to a prison camp and died there.

Sneevliet, Henk (1883–1942)—Dutch revolutionary. While living in Indonesia he laid the groundwork for the Communist Party there and was a Comintern delegate to China from 1921 to 1923. After breaking with Stalinism in 1927 he founded the Socialist-Revolutionary Workers Party of Holland. During the Spanish Civil War he went to Barcelona and worked with the POUM. During the occupation of Holland he set up a resistance network (the Marx-Lenin-Luxemburg Front), was captured by the Nazis, and executed.

Sobolevicius, Abram (Jack Soble) (1903–1967)—Born in Lithuania, he was a GPU agent trained to infiltrate the Trotskyist movement in France, where he played an important role, not being unmasked until after the war. His brother **Ruvin** (1899–1962) was also a GPU agent and became leader of the German section and member of the international secretariat of the Left Opposition. Denounced as a Stalinist agent in 1933, he settled in the United States, becoming a well-known psychiatrist under the name Robert Soblen. He committed suicide when he was unmasked.

Sokolnikov, Grigori (1888–1939)—Sorbonne-educated Russian economist, Bolshevik from 1905, he met Lenin in Paris in 1909 and returned to Russia with him. Active on several fronts during the Civil War, signatory of the Brest-Litovsk Treaty, he was people's commissar for finance during the NEP and then ambassador to London from 1929 to 1932. Sentenced to ten years at the second Moscow Trial, he was assassinated in prison by the NKVD.

Solano, Wilebaldo (1916–2010)—Leader of the POUM, he was arrested by Vichy while in French exile, was freed by the Resistance, and fought in a battalion of Spaniards and Catalans.

Solonevich, Ivan Lukianovich (1891–1953)—Extreme right-wing journalist before the revolution, he fled Russia in 1934, wrote an account of his flight, and in exile became a monarchist and member of conspiratorial circles.

Souvarine, Boris (B. Lifshitz) (1895–1984)—PCF delegate to the Comintern, the only Frenchman to be named to the secretariat of the Comintern, he became a strong, insightful, and effective critic of Stalinism and the degenerated Soviet Union.

Spiegelglass, Sergei Mikhailovich (1897–1941)—Militant Communist re-

cruited by the Cheka before becoming a high official in the GPU. Charged
with secret missions in Paris, he played a key role in the surveillance of Leon
Sedov and the murders of Ignace Reiss and Rudolf Klement. Arrested under
Beria's orders in 1938, under torture, he confessed and was executed.

Spinasse, Charles (1893–1979)—French socialist deputy and minster of the
economy under the Popular Front, he supported the policy of collaboration
and published a collaborationist newspaper.

Steiger, Boris Sergeyevich (1892–1937)—Soviet functionary and NKVD
agent. Arrested and executed.

Steiner, Renata (Renée S.) (1908–1986)—Swiss communist sympathizer, she
was an accomplice in the assassination of Ignace Reiss.

Stepanov—*see Minev, Stojan*

Stetsky, Alexei Ivanovich (1896–1938)—Bolshevik from 1911, political commissar in the Red Army, he was close to Bukharin but survived him by a few
months as Stalin's ideologue. Executed without trial.

Stomonyakov, Boris (1882–1941)—Bulgarian Communist, commercial attaché at the Soviet embassy in Berlin. He climbed the ranks of the Commissariat of Foreign Affairs and perished during the purges.

Strasser, Otto (1897–1974)—German political militant who traveled from
socialism to communism to Nazism, he attempted to form "national revolutionary" alternatives within and without the Nazi party. His party banned,
he fled Germany.

Strumilin, Stanislav Gustavovich (1877–1974)—Economist and sociologist
close to Lenin. Director of the USSR's statistical service, he was mothballed
for his critical positions.

Sukhanov, Nikolai (1882–1940)—Menshevik and economist, he moved closer
to Bolshevism at the time of the October Revolution. Opposed to collectivization, he was arrested in 1930, judged at the trial of the Mensheviks, exiled to
Siberia, arrested again in 1937 for espionage, and executed.

Sulimov, Daniil (1890–1937)—Bolshevik from 1905, he was president of the Council of People's Commissars for the Russian socialist republic from 1930 until his expulsion from the party in 1937. Arrested soon after this expulsion, he was then executed.

Tarasov-Rodyonov, Alexander (1888–1938)—Soviet writer. Executed as a Trotskyist.

Tasca, Angelo (André Leroux and Rossi) (1892–1960)—Italian Communist leader, expelled from the PCI, he left Moscow for Paris, collaborating on Henri Barbusse's newspaper *Monde* and then for the SFIO's newspaper *Le Populaire*. Remaining in France during World War II, he worked for Vichy's information service.

Tchaikovsky, Nikolai Vasilievich (1850–1926)—Member of the Tchaikovsky Circle, a literary and revolutionary society close to the Populists, he went into exile in the United States, founding a commune in Kansas. Returned to Russia in 1905, he was opposed to the Bolsheviks and headed a White government in Arkhangelsk. He fled to London and carried on his anticommunist activities.

Terracini, Umberto (1895–1983)—Founder with Gramsci and Togliatti of the newspaper *L'Ordine Nuovo*, he was a founding member of the PCI and edited its paper, *L'Unità*. Imprisoned by the fascist government from 1926 to 1943.

Téry, Simone (1897–1967)—French novelist and journalist, member of the PCF. Left France for Mexico in 1940, returning after the war.

Thalheimer, August (1884–1948)—Member of the caucus within the German Socialist Party that supported Rosa Luxemburg in 1914, mobilized in 1916, he participated in the workers and soldiers councils in Stuttgart. Member of the KPD, he was the theoretician of the right wing of the party; he then lived in the USSR from 1924 to 1928. Founder of the Opposition Communists in Germany, he went into exile in France, then Cuba, where he died.

Thüring, Babette (B. Gross) (1898–1990)—German journalist and sister of Margarete Buber-Neumann. She was the lover and collaborator of Willi Münzenberg. After his death she went into exile in Mexico.

Tittel, Hans (1894–1983)—German Communist militant, went into exile in France in 1933 and then to the United States.

Tomsky (Mikhail Pavlovich Efremov) (1880–1936)—Bolshevik from 1904, he was an ally of Bukharin and was named president of the Council of Soviets. Removed from office in 1930, he committed suicide in 1936 when he got word of his imminent arrest.

Toor, Frances (1890–1956)—American anthropologist and writer who settled in Mexico in 1924, she wrote on the folklore and culture of the Indians of Mexico.

Tresca, Carlo (1879–1943)—Italian anarchist who emigrated to the United States in 1904 and was active in the International Workers of the World. An active antifascist, he was assassinated on a street corner in Manhattan on January 11, 1943.

Trilisser, Meyer Abramovich (1883–1941)—A Bolshevik of the party's first days, exiled in Irkutsk, he participated in the revolution in that city in 1917. Joined the Cheka in 1920, was in charge of its foreign service from 1921 to 1926, a leader of the GPU, and on the executive of the Comintern. Involved in all the disappearances and assassinations of Soviet émigrés, he was arrested in 1938, sentenced in 1940, and executed the following year.

Tynyanov, Yuri (1894–1943)—Soviet novelist and literary theoretician; one of the founders of the Russian formalist school.

Uhse, Bodo (1904–1963)—German writer and journalist, first a member of the Nazi Party, he went over to the Communists. Fought in Spain and then went into exile in Mexico, participating in the group Alemania Libre. Returned to East Germany in 1948.

Umansky, Konstantin (1902–1945)—Soviet journalist, diplomat, and spy, he lived in Austria and Romania until hired by TASS in 1922. Soviet ambassador to Washington (and according to Krivitsky a spy) from 1939 to 1941, he was thought by Natalia Sedova to be a possible organizer of the assassination of Trotsky. Named ambassador to Mexico in 1943, he died in a plane accident there.

Unszlicht, Józef Stanislavovich (1879–1938)—Polish Communist, member of the Russian party from 1900, he joined the NKVD and fought against Trotsky. Disappeared during the purges.

Upstein, Fayna (1906–?)—Soviet Communist, member of the Opposition in 1927, deported to Orenburg in 1932.

Uribe Castillo, Raúl (1912–?)—Chilean diplomat and painter who lived in Mexico from 1937.

Uribes Moreno, José Antonio (1911–?)—Spanish Communist, after the Civil War he lived in Moscow, where he was a member of the foreign committee of the Central Committee of the Spanish Communist Party.

Uritsky, Semen Petrovich (1895–1938)—Bolshevik from 1912, he joined the Red Army in 1919 and led a Soviet military delegation to Germany in 1932. Intelligence chief of the Red Army from 1935 to 1937, he was victim of the repression.

Utkin, Iosif (1903–1944)—Soviet poet and journalist for *Komosomolskaia Pravda*, he died in an airplane crash returning from the front.

Vaillant-Couturier, Paul (1892–1937)—French Communist and journalist.

Valetski (or Walecki), **Henryk** (Maximilian Horwitz) (1877–1937)—Mathematician and physicist, he was a leader of the Polish communist movement and from 1921 was delegated to several countries, including the United States, by the Comintern. Member of its control commission, he was arrested and executed by the NKVD in June 1937.

Valtin, Jan (Richard Krebs) (1905–1951)—German seaman and Communist militant, he was an agent of the Comintern carrying out clandestine missions in ports around the world. Arrested by the Nazis, he played a double game before fleeing to the United States, hunted by both the Nazis and the Soviets. His memoir *Out of the Night* was a best-seller.

Varo, Remedios (1908–1963)—Spanish-born anarchist and Surrealist painter, wife of Benjamin Péret.

Vassilieva, Vera Yakovlevna (1900–1959)—Soviet Communist and feminist activist. Member of the Comintern executive from 1931 to 1938.

Velásquez Guerrero, Juan Luís (1903–1970)—Peruvian writer, poet, and diplomat. Expelled from France and Spain, he lived in Mexico from 1936 to 1944. He joined the Fourth International and was briefly Trotsky's secretary, and in 1941 Serge gave him the only interview published during his Mexican years.

Venturi, Lionello (1885–1961)—Italian art critic, he was one of the twelve university professors to refuse to swear loyalty to fascism in 1931. Active in antifascist circles in exile in Paris and New York.

Verdaro, Virgilio (Gatto Mammone) (1885–1960)—Italian Communist, he was close to Bordiga. After emigrating to the USSR in 1924, he formed a left faction and was expelled from the party. Left Russia in 1931 and lived in exile in France, Belgium, and Switzerland, remaining an important figure in left communism.

Vereecken, Georges (1896–1978)—Belgian Communist, expelled in 1927 for his support for the Opposition. Disagreed with Trotsky on several issues, including entry into the Socialist Party and over the POUM. He joined the Fourth International after World War II, leaving it in 1953.

Vidali, Vittorio (Eneas Sormenti and Carlos Contreras) (1900–1983)—Italian communist and Soviet secret service agent. Founded the Fifth Regiment in Spain and was an organizer of the International Brigades. Suspected of playing a role in many murders, including those of Nin, Julio Antonio Mella, Trotsky, and even his beloved Tina Modotti.

Vierny, Dina (D. Albinder) (1919–2009)—Bessarabian-born French Trotskyist, she helped antifascists cross over to Spain from occupied France in 1940.

Villaseñor, Eduardo (1896–1978)—Mexican economist, publisher, and writer.

Villaseñor, Víctor Manuel (1904–1981)—American-educated economist, he traveled to the USSR with Vicente Lombardo Toledano in 1935. Along with the latter founded the Workers University and the Partido Popular.

Vinogradskaya, Polina (1896–1978)—Russian Communist and member of the women's section of the Central Committee of the Soviet Communist Party.

Vlakhov, Dmitry (1878–1953)—Bulgarian Communist and Comintern functionary in the Balkans.

Vogeler Regler, Marie-Louise (1901–1943)—Painter and companion of Gustav Regler.

Voikov, Piotr Lazarevich (1888–1927)—Russian revolutionary implicated in the killing of the Romanovs, assassinated while Soviet ambassador to Warsaw.

Voline (Vsevolod Mikhailovich Eichenbaum) (1882–1945)—Central figure of Russian anarchism, he participated in Makhno's anarchist fight against the Bolsheviks. Later exiled to Germany and France, he called the Soviet state "red fascism." His best-known work about the Russian Revolution, *The Unknown Revolution*, was published posthumously in 1947.

Volkov, Vsevolod (Seva or Esteban) (1926–)—Trotsky's grandson by his mother, Zinaida, his father was the murdered Oppositionist Platon Ivanovich Volkov. Sieva was reunited with his grandfather in 1939 and was subject of a long legal battle over his custody.

Voloshin, Maximilian Alexandrovich (1877–1932)—Symbolist poet, translator, and painter.

Voronsky, Aleksandr Konstantinovich (1884–1937)—Bolshevik from 1905 and close to Trotsky, he was attacked from 1927 by the Association of Proletarian Writers. Member of the underground Left Opposition, he was arrested, eventually capitulated, and died in jail.

Vuyovich, Voya (1897–1936)—Yugoslavian Communist, leader of the Young Communist International, he was sent to Germany in 1922–1923, where he met Serge and joined the Left Opposition. Recalled to Moscow, he was expelled from the party along with Trotsky, sentenced to forced labor, and executed.

Wasilewska, Wanda (1905–1964)—Polish writer and Communist, she was one of the pioneers of the Polish United Workers Party, the postwar Communist Party.

Werner, Max (Alexander Schifrin) (1901–1953)—American political analyst.

Werth, Léon (1878–1955)—French anticlerical, antibourgeois, and anarchist writer. Friend of Saint-Exupéry, *The Little Prince* was dedicated to him.

Wolf, Erwin (1902–1937)—Born in the future Czechoslovakia, he lived in Germany and was a member of the KPD and the Left Opposition. Trotsky's secretary in Norway, he went to Spain, where he disappeared, almost certainly executed by the GPU.

Wolf, Fritz (1890–1937)—Russian revolutionary, Bolshevik from 1917. Connected to the Opposition, expelled in 1933, he was arrested and executed.

Wolfe, Bertram (1896–1977)—American author and art critic, he was involved in the founding of the Communist Party in the USA, later going over to Trotskyism and finally anticommunism. With his wife, **Ella Goldberg** (1897–2000), he met Diego Rivera, Frida Kahlo, and Trotsky during their Mexican stays.

Wolff, Charles (1905–1944)—A journalist in Paris and a member of the French group of proletarian writers. Member of the Resistance, he was arrested, tortured, and killed by the Milice.

Wollenberg, Erich (1892–1973)—German revolutionary, member of the KPD, he went into exile in the USSR, was persecuted for "counterrevolutionary activity" but managed to flee the Soviet Union and survive.

Wullens, Maurice (1894–1945)—Teacher, member of the École Emancipée and publisher of an anarchist paper, *Les Humbles*, which would eventually become a collaborationist paper. Active in the campaign to free Serge.

Yagoda, Genrikh Grigorevich (1896–1938)—Bolshevik since 1907, head of the NKVD between 1934 and 1936, he led the campaign against Zinoviev and Kamenev. He was arrested by his successor, Yezhov, and executed.

Yakovin, Grigori Iakovlevich (1896–1938)—Russian revolutionary, he was a member of the 1923 Opposition and the unified Opposition. As repression struck he was able to live illegally until captured, transferred to numerous prisons, and executed in 1938.

Yanovich, Fanny (?–?)—Trotsky's final secretary, she was present during the Siqueiros-led assassination attempt.

Yarmolinsky, Avrahm (1890–1975)—American writer, biographer, and Russian-language translator.

Yenukidze, Aveli Sofronovich (1877–1937)—Georgian on the staff of Iskra in 1901, he was arrested several times under the czar. After 1917 he occupied various posts, including head of the Bolshoi Theater. A childhood friend of Stalin's, he was nevertheless expelled from the party in 1935 and executed two years later.

Yeltsin, Boris Mikhailovich (?–1938)—Bolshevik from 1903, he was president of the Soviet of Ekaterinoslav and member of the Pan-Russian Executive of Soviets. One of the leaders of the Left Opposition, he was sent to Orenburg along with Serge and Vlady. Executed in 1938 along with his two sons.

Yevdokimov, Grigori E. (1884–1936)—Worker and sailor, Bolshevik from 1903, member of the Central Committee from 1919 to 1925 and secretary of the CC in 1926 and 1927, close to Zinoviev, he was expelled from the party, reaccepted, sentenced to ten years in prison, and ultimately executed.

Yezhov, Nikolai Ivanovich (1895–1940)—Bolshevik from 1917, member of the party's Central Committee from 1927. Assumed leadership of the NKVD in 1937 by orchestrating he elimination of his predecessor, Yagoda; he was the main executor of the Stalinist purges. Arrested in 1939, his execution was ordered the following year by Beria, his successor.

Yonov, Ilya Yonovich (1887–1942)—Poet and publisher, overseeing all publishing activities in Leningrad. Executed.

Zamora Padilla, Francisco (1890–1985)—Mexican economist of Nicaraguan origin, friend of Trotsky, and the only Mexican on the Dewey Commission.

Zapata Vela, Carlos (1906–1990)—Mexican deputy and organizer of the Mexican Committee to Aid Russia. Mexican ambassador to the USSR from 1967 to 1971.

Zetkin, Clara (C. Eissner) (1857–1933)—German socialist and feminist, friend of Rosa Luxemburg, KPD member of the Reichstag from 1920 to 1933 and the executive of the Comintern from 1921 until her death.

Zoshchenko, Mikhail (1895–1958)—Soviet writer and satirist, he fell into disgrace in the 1920s due to his opposition to the official cultural doctrine.

Zorin, Sergei (1890–1937)—Bolshevik exiled in the United States who returned to Russia in 1917 and was secretary of the Communist Party in Petrograd during Kronstadt. Member of Zinoviev's opposition group, he disappeared during the purges.

104
99
91
108 !
113
130
132
250 Stalin
251
256
278 the moral capital of the
revolution
417
446
505

OTHER NEW YORK REVIEW CLASSICS

For a complete list of titles, visit www.nyrb.com or write to:
Catalog Requests, NYRB, 435 Hudson Street, New York, NY 10014

* Also available as an electronic book.